Hyperthematics

SUNY series in American Philosophy and Cultural Thought

———————

Randall E. Auxier and John R. Shook, editors

Hyperthematics
The Logic of Value

MARC M. ANDERSON

Cover art: *Green and Blue at Play* courtesy of Marc M. Anderson

Published by State University of New York Press, Albany

© 2019 State University of New York

All rights reserved

No part of this book may be used or reproduced in any manner whatsoever without written permission. No part of this book may be stored in a retrieval system or transmitted in any form or by any means including electronic, electrostatic, magnetic tape, mechanical, photocopying, recording, or otherwise without the prior permission in writing of the publisher.

For information, contact State University of New York Press, Albany, NY
www.sunypress.edu

Library of Congress Cataloging-in-Publication Data

Names: Anderson, Marc M., author.
Title: Hyperthematics : the logic of value / Marc M. Anderson.
Description: Albany : State University of New York, 2019. | Series: SUNY series in American philosophy and cultural thought | Includes bibliographical references and index.
Identifiers: LCCN 2018040463 | ISBN 9781438475332 (hardcover) | ISBN 9781438475349 (pbk.) | ISBN 9781438475356 (ebook) Subjects: LCSH: Values.
Classification: LCC BD232 .A4825 2019 | DDC 121/.8—dc23
LC record available at https://lccn.loc.gov/2018040463

10 9 8 7 6 5 4 3 2 1

To Beijia and Merengel
my two loves who interpret me
and
To my Beloved Teacher Josiah Royce
separated now in time but not in Spirit

Contents

Acknowledgments ix

Foreword xi
    by Randall Auxier

Introduction 1

Part I
Mode of Expansive Exploration

Chapter 1   Beginnings and the Hyperthematic Structures of Game and Narrative   9

Chapter 2   Hyperthematic Structures of Dance and Music   53

Chapter 3   Hyperthematic Expansion of Light and Color   101

Chapter 4   The Hyperthematic Structure of Visual Arts   143

Part II
Mode of Expansive Reconstruction

Chapter 5   Hyperthematization of the Corporation   203

Chapter 6   Expansive Reconstruction of H5 to H15   255

Chapter 7   Expansive Reconstruction of the Hyperthemes of Light and Color   287

Chapter 8	Expansive Reconstruction of the Hyperthemes of the Visual Arts	341
Conclusion		391
Summary of the Hyperthemes		419
Appendix A	Aesthetic Taste for Hyperthematics and Hume's Notion of Taste	423
Appendix B	Devaluation and Symmetric Consequence	429
Appendix C	The Expansion of Currency	437
Appendix D	The Relation of Royce's System Sigma to Hyperthematics and the Origins of Dyadic Logic	445
Diagrams		459
Notes		465
References		483
Index of Proper Names		489
Index of Subjects		491

Acknowledgments

Two people in particular, both of whom I consider to be friend and mentor, have helped me in the creation of this work. Professor André Cloots of the Katholieke Universiteit Leuven, patiently and regularly read and offered suggestions to the first rough version. His constant support and encouragement, in response to my straying beyond the conventional bounds of research into the undiscovered country of creative construction, is the hallmark of a great teacher, and I thank him for the privilege of being his student. Professor Randall Auxier, whom I first met on a noisy train pushing through the Polish countryside, has been essential to the development of this work. He inhabits those regions where I am most at home philosophically. He was an explorer there before me and it was through his influence that I first came to realize that metaphysics was at the service of ethics in Royce's philosophy. Without his ongoing effort in a multitude of practical ways, I could not have completed this work. He has my profound thanks.

I would like to thank the editorial team at SUNY Press also, and Andrew Kenyon, Rafael Chaiken, Chelsea Miller, and Diane Ganeles particularly, along with the patient and insightful reviewers of this work.

Most of all, I would like to thank my family: my ever faithful wife, Beijia, for her optimism and unwearying care over the many years of finishing this, and my son, Merengel, who constantly reminded me as I wrote, that the spirit of philosophy is really best expressed in those words of little children: "can we play now Baba?"

Foreword

I first met Marc Anderson ten years ago on a train that would take us from Berlin to Opole, which is a charming city in southern Poland. There we would discuss the philosophy of Josiah Royce for a week with a group of distinguished philosophers from around Europe and North America. I was fortunate to meet Marc early in the trip and since it was a long ride, we had an opportunity to discuss quite thoroughly what he was working on. He was then a PhD student at Katholieke Universiteit Leuven (Louvain), in Belgium. By the end of the week I was aware that I would be in discussion with Marc for the rest of my career. The overlap of interests combined with differing talents and perspectives meant that I would be able to learn from Marc as from few others.

At that time Marc had been studying Royce's logic, as indeed I also do, and he had some interesting ideas about how to apply Royce's most mature logical ideas, which is called System Sigma. Marc explains this connection in what follows, but what he will not say is how unusual it is for someone studying pure logics to become so deeply absorbed in practical applications. In my first conversation with him, Marc gave me an image that I have never forgotten, and I now offer it to you. You have seen the beauty of birds flocking and fish schooling. You have surely wondered "How do they do that? Why don't they run into one another? What sort of communication is this?" Such is our common wonder at such a sight. Yet, have you ever paused to consider not just the visible forms and movement, but the logical and mathematical structure of what you are witnessing?

Process philosophers hold that this sort of order is abstracted from our experience. It is not that the logical order and mathematical order explains what we see; it is the other way around. What we see is what *is*, and what *is* explains whatever we learn from that starting place. It is not that we know the math or logic and then explain the flocking and schooling;

it is that the flocking and schooling occurs and from that we learn the math and the logic. But here is the catch. We haven't gotten very far with the forms of order implicit in flocking and schooling. The mathematical and logical order of living systems and ecological relations is enormously complex. We are only beginning to puzzle it out. But what is important is that as we discover the forms of living order, we begin to see that many social behaviors, both of humans and nonhuman animals, actually exhibit tremendous commonality and continuity with the logic and mathematics we are discerning in the activity of complex systems.

I visited with Marc again in 2011 when we met in Indianapolis at a gathering of the Midwest Pragmatism Study Group. In the three intervening years Marc had finished his dissertation project and returned to Canada. I read this work and followed closely his development of ideas from Whitehead and Royce. The historical work he undertook to give these two figures a close reading will, I am sure, eventually be published as a scholarly book. But the conversations in Indianapolis led us to collaborate in a study of the structures of intensive logics. We began looking at C. I. Lewis's *A Survey of Symbolic Logic* (1917). Lewis was Royce's star student studying symbolic logic, and this book was essentially his dissertation, reworked. We sought to connect Royce's System Sigma to its grounding in classical and intensive logics, for the sake of a more thorough understanding of his thinking. Royce left behind thousands of pages of scattered logical writings, beginning very early in his life (his undergraduate notebooks from Berkeley have the earliest existing records), and extending until his very last days. These unorganized piles of thinking may contain amazing breakthroughs, but our aim was to try to follow the thread of his thinking so that we could mine these materials for whatever they may contain. Lewis's dissertation and early papers represented a fine mind engaged with this work at the very end of Royce's life.

Our logic research group consisted of Marc, me, and about five other people, in the beginning. The membership rotated through another seven or eight people over the next six years, as graduate students left and advanced undergraduate students became graduate students elsewhere. Marc and I were the only members during the entire run, although Gary L. Herstein was there during most of that time. Marc was refining the manuscript for the present book during this time, and he was bouncing ideas off the group. I think it is fair to say that this group was crucial to the final form of the present book, but the reader may benefit from just a bit more of the background. This book is highly creative, unlike anything published before, and it may not be easy for readers to grasp what is happening or how to classify what is being learned. Is this logic? (Yes.) Is it aesthetics? (Yes.) Is it applied ethics? (Yes.) Is it normative ethics? (Yes.) Is it moral philosophy? (Yes.) Is it social philosophy? (Yes.) Is it epistemology? (Yes.) Is it metaphysics? (Yes.) Perhaps one begins to see the problem.

Enter the idea of a "hypertheme," which Anderson will explain from the outset. He had this idea on the basis of System Sigma, and before I met him. He was working with ideas from Whitehead and Royce's critique of Kant back in 2008. I suggested that he look at Lewis, which he did, but at that time he was unable to draw from Lewis's work much illumination for developing the idea of the hypertheme. Part of the motivation for starting the logic research group was to see what we could contribute to developing this rich (dare I say revolutionary?) idea. I am convinced, now as I was ten years ago, that Anderson has had an insight comparable with those of the greatest moments in the history of thought, a stroke of genius. The hypertheme, rightly understood and developed will, I believe, become the dominant and standard logic of the future. This volume is the first look at it to be published, but there is much more to do. Anderson has been using the theory in his other research—in military history, in the history of the origins of Canadian nationhood, and obviously in the history of philosophy. The applicability of the hypertheme to other fields is basically limitless. A number of these will be demonstrated in these pages.

The logic group did not get very far with the C. I. Lewis book before we discovered that he had not been able to grasp or to make much headway on the issue of intensive logics, which meant that he had really failed to understand System Sigma, which was nothing if not an intensive logic. We were convinced that the structures we were pursuing would have to be formalized intensively. What does that mean? Intensive order is non-monotonic, and nonlinear, and it carries forward its "history" as a feature of its kind of order. Meaning and reference are not separate until actively separated in an intensive logic. Oh, and I should mention that intensive logic is difficult. So we went back into the actual historical documents Lewis cited to see whether we could do any better. We could. Part of the difference is made by the fact that we can get access to materials Lewis could not.

Among these were the published writings of Frederic Castillon, the late eighteenth–early nineteenth-century logician, professor of mathematics and logic at the Berlin Military Academy who was a critic of Kant's logic and defended a version of the theory of judgment set out by Christian Wolff. Kant's theory of reflective judgment is a classic effort at developing and applying an intensive logic. Castillon claimed to have developed a logic that formalized intensively all of Aristotle's valid syllogistic forms. This was the sort of thing we were seeking. But after more than a year of work with Castillon's extant writings, we were unable to piece together the system he claimed to have created. Joining Royce's fragmentary writings to the tradition from which they emerged was still beyond our grasp at that point. But Castillon had some very provocative ideas about the relationship between thought and perception that ran well ahead of the genius of C. S. Peirce's "New List of Categories" (1867).

Among the ideas that emerged during this phase of our research was the realization that, very possibly, our human thought processes and our perceptual affordances are instances of the same kind of order as flocking birds and schooling fish. If that is true, as I am convinced it is, then the idea of the hypertheme may well enable us to formalize the order of thinking and perceiving as overlapping dynamic orders—if you imagine that a flock of birds in its airy medium (the order of thinking), and a school of fish in its watery medium (the heavier realm of physical perception), have enough spatiotemporal interpenetration to create common quantum disturbances, which in turn create a third order of hyperthematic eddies we name "consciousness," then you will begin to grasp the true breadth of this idea. Part of the reason to pay attention to the present book is that it begins with applications that range throughout human social life and which take more seriously than anyone before the idea that human social existence, and thus human culture, is the outcome of something like a genuine, concrete, and very real social mind. We may be less like bees and ants than like birds and fish, however, because the individuation that is our biological endowment comes from a centralized nervous system. To watch the humans as if from above, in a day's activities, is not as much to watch a hive or an insect colony as to watch a flock, or a school. We tear off into individuated activities, but when we school and flock for a major league baseball game or a soccer match, an outside observer might watch our gathering, processions to and from the stadium, and to give an obvious example, enactment of "the wave," with exactly the same fascination we feel in watching the fish or the birds.

In short, hyperthematics is an art, a science, and most importantly, a logic of forms of dynamic existence. The closer we get to a logic of dynamic activity, the closer we are to understanding the even more fascinating questions about a logic of possibility, unencumbered by the unempirical notions of "necessity" that have descended through the work of C. I. Lewis, and which have stunted the growth of logic since 1917. Philosophers of the twentieth century wrung their hands to try to relate actuality and possibility. The book you have in your hands (or on your screen) is the first of what will be many works in a new logic of dynamic change that will, in time, include a more articulate and useful logic of possibility. Our human prospects are more important to us than our mechanical needs. Hope is the ground of striving, not vice versa. Life is lured into its future, not driven by its past. If we were merely driven by the past, our values, moral, social, and religious, are inexplicable and vain. Fortunately, reality is not mechanical. If it were, we wouldn't be here. Philosophers and mathematicians owe the world a logic and a mathematics of change, of dynamic becoming. The fact that it is difficult to provide does not change our duty. The order of an ecosystem is non-mechanical, nonlinear, dynamic, and complex. Human society is more complex by many orders of magnitude, and yet, the second is somehow *in* the first. We must dig out the "in" and make its form explicit.

That is what you will learn to see by studying this book. As for our ongoing research, after a long period with the historical writings on the failure of everyone to develop a formalism for intensive logic that would join with Royce's System Sigma, we stumbled upon an unnoticed writing by Delton Thomas Howard called *Analytical Syllogistics* (1946), in which Howard had accomplished what Castillon claimed to have done. We spent almost two years working through every detail of Howard's system and have broken away from our flock to develop individual projects. But when the time comes, I am sure the flock will re-gather and migrate to the next piece of the journey for which we must have use of one another's minds.

In the meantime, as you read the remarkable pages that follow, bear in mind that the swirling thoughts you will have possess and exhibit an order, and that order is coming from the movement of your perceptual powers as your eyes convert light and text into an order that disturbs your active thinking, and which makes you conscious of some things and not others. The person sitting next to you will have a different conscious configuration even while reading the same passage from the same book. Do you not believe that your consciousness and your neighbor's are also interacting? If they are not, then how is it that you can discuss the book and compare and contrast what you noticed? You actually do manage to use one another's consciousness through the medium of language, but that works only because you were already swimming in the same water and flying in the same sky.

Randall Auxier
Carbondale, IL
August 2018

Introduction

This work attempts to re-envision experience as a fluid process of creation and destruction of value. It offers a way of looking at the world which is practical, in that it not only discloses areas in which there are unstable lacunae of value or unstable accumulations of low-level value, but also offers a method for solving such problems of value.

Like all philosophical offerings, this one has a lineage. That lineage can be traced to the ideas of Josiah Royce (1855-1916) and Alfred North Whitehead (1861-1947). These two great thinkers—I do not hesitate in upgrading this to *greatest*—with their pragmatic emphases on the world as an organic process of community subtly but definitely shaped by the *human* aspect of experience, have been my guiding stars. I have attempted to blend the vision of these two, if not in equal measure, then as seemed wise to me, in an interpretation that builds upon the best of both. A few words on that blending will serve to orient the reader.

From Royce the preeminent insight made use of is the assumption that the world is a community of interpretation, or as Royce put it in *The Problem of Christianity*: "The world is the interpretation of the problems which it presents."[1] The simplest way to explain this to the reader is to say that if we view our experience as presenting us with tasks, challenges, difficulties, and differences, then, following Royce, our most promising opening move in engaging that experience is to assume that *there is always an interpretation*, i.e., an experience between any two other diverse and so far problematic experiences, which, when once achieved through some action which appropriately engages experience, joins the diversity of experience—solves the problem if you like—in a way which creates *meaning* in the chain of experience. The diverse experiences thus meaningfully joined, or *interpreted* to one another, are then called *a community of interpretation*, and the world as a whole is one of these communities. The notion of a community used here is far broader than is usually understood, although it certainly includes everything that the usual and historic notion of a community—as, for example, of a village built through the cooperation of its inhabitants—includes.

The notion of interpretation used here meanwhile may be said to differ from the usual use of the word only in that it remembers what is generally forgotten in our usual uses of the term. As Royce illustrates the use of the term interpretation: the Egyptologist who translates an inscription into English requires both an inscription and an English reader for her translation, and she thereby becomes the interpreter *between* the inscription and the reader, i.e., the Egyptologist interprets the inscription *to* the reader, i.e., interprets a sign (the physical inscription) of one who has acted (the ancient writer) to another who is acting (the contemporary physical reader).[2] The simplified chain of interpretation is thus: ancient writer—inscription—Egyptologist—modern reader. The elements within the chain (inscription and Egyptologist) are thus *placed and placing themselves between*, or, *interpreting*, the outer elements (ancient writer and modern reader). The outer elements in turn are interpreting to further elements, e.g., the ancient writer's sources and the modern reader's friends. There are other interpreting elements moreover which can be emphasized or uncovered as necessary, some will be human, e.g., the publisher who interprets between the Egyptologist and the modern reader, and some will be human created objects, e.g., the glasses of the Egyptologist which help her read the ancient inscription, and some will be natural objects, e.g., the desert wind which has uncovered the ancient stela that holds the inscription.

Each element, human or otherwise, may be called an experience, i.e., it is the locus of a chain of experiences. The various interpretations interpret these experiences. The interpretations are practically speaking endless: the glasses were made by someone and thus interpret their maker to the Egyptologist, for example, and the publisher's secretary stands between the publisher and the Egyptologist, and so on. We thus have an expanding chain of interpreted experiences, joined to other chains of experience, which, woven together as a whole make up *the world to be experienced*, that world being a problem to solve wherever the interpretation between any two or more experiences is not yet complete and evident.

The foregoing illustrates partially the expanded sense of interpretation I am after here. The process of conscious reflection that an individual undertakes in order to interpret herself, illustrates it further. In the latter case, for example, the *present individual*, remembering something which their *past self* promised or undertook to do, and saying something like "this is what I promised or meant to do," goes on to address their *future self* in some such way as "therefore such and such is what I will do to fulfill my promise." In this way the individual, interprets her past self, *to* her future self, *through* her present. **I ask the reader to always bear in mind that whenever I speak of interpretation in what follows, the foregoing is the sense of interpretation which I have in mind.**

But again, this is no different from the usual sense of interpretation, except the usual use of the term forgets, or covertly assumes the former conditions. Thus, in Royce's sense and mine, if I say, as in common speech: "I interpret this old letter of mine to mean so and so," it means that I, as the present self, am interpreting the letter as a sign of my past self *to* my own future self. The usual use of interpretation simply fails to bring these assumptions out into the open, it likes to assume that "I am interpreting something" means something less than "I am interpreting something *to* something else." My suggestion throughout is that it never means less than the latter. This ongoing connecting of one's past and future experiences, through an interpretive effort in one's present, is a community of selfhood and gradually becomes a community of ethical selfhood, both to be discussed later. The self is thus a community of interpretation, as above, a "village built through the cooperation of its inhabitants," i.e., a community formed by interpretive contributions from, for example, "the curious child I was at 8; the brash young adult I was at 23; the man I will be next year, etc."

From Whitehead, meanwhile the preeminent insight made use of is the assumption that experience is preeminent, i.e., that we do not come upon the world as abstracted into objects which influence one another according to cause and effect in unit instants of time, but rather that the world is an organic community of processes of action, of fluid experiences, which are continually interacting with—interpreting—one another so as to create new processes.

To explain this in another way with a linguistic analogy, this view does something like favoring the verb over the noun. Thus, as Whitehead would say, our experience is that "something is happening," some event, and out of the interactions of such events, such processes, the world is continually created (and destroyed). So for example, *the experience of jogging* is preeminent, and from that experience a man in this body, in these running shoes, on this road, in this direction, during these hours, etc., may be abstracted.

Combining these positions—and they naturally combine themselves in the pragmatic action of living—we get a series of processes of experience which can act to interpret one another so as to form and reform into communities. Royce's chains of interpretation of experience and Whitehead's organic processes are taken—by the author—to be essentially the same, though viewed in subtly different ways. To use a visual analogy one may imagine the processes as threads woven into a piece of fabric if one likes, with the temporal aspect of the experience being the length of the woven threads. These processes of action are free, although their freedom, particularly for human processes, means far more than any abstraction from their "own" experience can indicate to them. Moreover, being free and having interest in acting, they act together to join experiences to one another meaningfully, to interpret experiences, or—ostensibly—to sunder experiences from one another. And the more of such experiences of meaning there are, or otherwise put, the greater the meaningful experience is, the more *valuable* it is, i.e., the *better* it is, to put it in the ethical terms most people are comfortable with. In this creation and destruction of meaningful experience is to be found value, on the basis of pragmatic action, and thus not absolutely—in the clear-cut "good and evil" sense—but always as a *tendency* which depends upon the freely selective engagement of experiences in diverse regions of experience of varying complexity.

From this beginning we have the foundation of a philosophical methodology, the material which that methodology will engage, and the initial pragmatic results of that engagement. When I speak in the coming chapters of tendencies of action which lead to expansions or constrictions of experience, these tendencies are expanding or constricting the threads of acting processes, the chains of interpreted experience.

The goal is always the pragmatic understanding of how we create and destroy value in the world through our various types of action, i.e., how can we bring these threads of acting processes together in harmonic ways so as to create new processes—to weave a thicker fabric, or braid a stronger "rope," of world process, to use yet another analogy—and how can we resolve the inharmonic clashes between processes which have left us, and continue to leave us, with regions of diminished value—regions of frayed or tattered fabric—i.e., regions of relatively meaningless experience (think of the destruction and chaos of a war zone as a more extreme example).

In order to do this the methodology itself must be flexible, it must be expandable, it must be applicable at all and every complexity of experience, if not immediately, then on the basis of future effort. Hyperthematics is logical but flexibly logical, which is to say that it assumes that logic is built upon possibility rather than necessity, and it is carried out as a logic which is deliberately held as close as possible to everyday experience, and not constricted down to formulaic technicalities.

It accepts the assumption of the interpretability of experience as such and plays with it with respect to certain regions of human experience which many—perhaps most—of us find problematic with regard to value. On the other hand, if that assumption is rejected, then we part company, at least for a time. Our parting company would be a matter of indifference, depending upon who is willing or not willing to accept the opening assumption. Except for one thing: the whole point of my effort is to present a worldview which, when adopted, can actually solve some of the great difficulties which we face according to our contemporary viewpoint. I aim to "sell the goods," by demonstrating their usefulness. I am confident that consistent application of Hyperthematics can solve a host of problems and that the results of such application will become apparent, so that eventually the logic will prove itself beyond any formalism. The idea of logic presented here, in good faith, is a pragmatic one then, with the adage: "try it, you might like it." For its best effect, it should be understood and applied from within each process of experience acting upon the world, *if* value is sought after. Hyperthematics is "the ways of creating value." The Hyperthematic tendencies are already at play in the world of our experience. Through them we have made the world what it now is without consciously knowing it. What I am offering is a framework, a series of flexible rules built upon an assumption, for recreating our world deliberately in a more valuable way. The only way of "proof" is to offer the framework, hope it gets applied somewhere, and then look to a corresponding increase in value to prove it.

Some of the greatest difficulties of our contemporary worldview cluster around what may be called the problem of quantity and quality, or again of objective and subjective, or of bad and good. Given our contemporary context, it seemed to me best to engage the problematic of the creation and destruction of value in the region of the actions of commercial corporations. In that region the difficulties are, if not most obviously, then very obviously, to be found. The history and the actions of the commercial corporation thus became the testing ground for the plausibility of the methodology and the opening assumption. An engagement with the actions and products of commercial corporations thus serves as a conceptual test of Hyperthematics. And yet in the course of that engagement, *any* avenue which seemed promising has been followed out, at least until the trail was marked out for future exploration. The problem of commercial corporations is only one of a great many contemporary problems. So, although it is the *main* problem addressed here, the main test case for Hyperthematics, I have not been shy to lay as much as I could of a groundwork for the solution of other problems of value in the world.

Whether I will have the opportunity to follow those other trails, or whether others will explore them, remains to be seen. Regardless, if you, reader, can get from any aspect of this work, a sense of how value is the result of ongoing action in the world, and if at whatever scale and complexity you can apply that sense practically in creating value in the world, in making it a better place, then my effort will be worthwhile.

Part I

Mode of Expansive Exploration

1

Beginnings and the Hyperthematic Structures of Game and Narrative

Working Definition of Hyperthematics

The traditional way of metaphysics is to ask: what is real? The traditional answer is that x is real. What x is has differed greatly among philosophers. For Plato it is ideas, for Hobbes matter, for Hume sensory experience, for Kant the unknown, for Schopenhauer will. The philosophers initiating all of these metaphysical endeavors have in common that they do not take us humans to have access to the real. The real is "over there," further on, to be attained, if indeed it can be attained. Whatever the real is, it, from its side, holds all the weight in the issue. It is the real which when attained decides the unreality of all else and its value will decide the value of all else. In this view, we humans are passive observers as metaphysicians, discoverers at best. Too bad for us.

It is a curious thing that very often philosophers take themselves to have the one true method, or interpretation, according to which we can arrive at the real. They value their own philosophical interpretations above that of others. Another curious thing is that often our philosophers do not claim for their method that it can attain the real—e.g., Francis Bradley—but they nonetheless insist that their method, their interpretation, has value above all others. The problem is that none of these philosophers have ever succeeded in convincing his peers that his way is the one holy way. Every philosopher, and especially the great philosophers, has a tendency to try his hand at a new and superior interpretation. And the result in every case is that every philosopher's interpretation is indeed superior, for himself. A second, less welcome result is that most philosophers, in their effort at an interpretation, tend to view the world as a specific problematic, as I noted above, which inevitably leaves out some or all of the problematic of his or her peers, in short, some aspect of experience.

It is based on these several observations that another starting point offers itself, the starting point of Royce, and, with somewhat different emphasis, Whitehead. This starting point holds that the experienced world is a problem in a general sense which is common to the efforts of all philosophers. But the solution of a problem in general is just solution itself. Hence, rather than begin from a view that says "there is a fixed reality *over there* which holds value and which can be attained from our 'non-real' point of view through just this one method of transformation, or philosophical interpretation," here we will say "one begins in the middle of reality, which being a fluid reality, or if you like a general problem, suggests further reality as being the *general solution* to that general problem." In short, the solution as such is the reality and if reality is that which holds value, then the value is in the solution.

Hence if the experienced world is a problem, then there ought to be a solution to it, i.e., a solution to it would be valuable. Hereby value arises from the creative process of interpreting the world, and reality is shot through with value but always and only through a process which originates from a given standpoint, or problematic, but which *nonetheless* recognizes that the specific solutions for the problematics engendered by the selective engagement of diverse regions of experience will only be available if *solution as such* is available, along with the consequences for metaphysics which that recognition entails. Under this viewpoint, every attempt to further define the solution, that is to say the path of the processes of transformation which leads between selected aspects of experience, will be a filling out of reality. On the other hand, every filling out of reality based on selected aspects of experience will further the solution.

I will define Hyperthematics as follows. *Hyperthematics is the attempt to contribute to the solution of the world problematic as such, by considering and creating metaphysical structures of action harmonization which promote meaningful interpretation and thus realize the world as a world of value.* Our experience of such structures is more fluid in proportion as the structures grow more valuable, i.e., as their capacity for interpretation expands.

The principle difference between Hyperthematics and other metaphysics is the emphasis on expansion through creative action as opposed to mere discovery or exploratory action. But it is not a hard-and-fast difference, merely a relative difference, one of proportion. The structures with which Hyperthematics deals are linked just as surely to present experience, but their links may be more complex and sometimes more difficult to see. At the same time Hyperthematics will be more adapted to this greater complexity, which is precisely why it has to be fluid, and thus will be able to deal with multiple processes of action. If it is helpful, Hyperthematics may be thought of as an alternative to analysis in philosophy. It seeks to expand rather than to reduce. It disregards for its purposes such conceptual rules as Occam's razor, whenever such rules run afoul of the need for fuller meaning of experience. The world is not primarily to be uncovered according to Hyperthematics, it is to be created, or realized through the play of interpretation, hence we can and should postulate freely, *though consistently*, for there is no necessity preeminent to the ought which engenders meaning.

I will suggest a new technical term for the structure which is sought in Hyperthematics: the *hypertheme*, defining it as: *a postulated principle of transformation according to which a hyperthematic structure of interpretation, as well as acting elements adopting it, can be consistently interpreted to the opening postulate of Hyperthematics.*

Having defined Hyperthematics I will now begin to lay its foundations. In what follows, there are two things that I hope to accomplish. In the first place, I want to provide a fluid scheme according to the order of complexity of harmonizing structures. If this can be done, then in principle any human activity, i.e., interpretive engagement of any particular experiential problematic, can be interpreted so as to find its place within the scheme, and can be more easily interpreted by reference to the scheme. This would give a basis for an ongoing practical application of Hyperthematics to any and all problems.

In the second place, by disclosing that scheme on the basis of carefully selected interpretive structures which span the contemporary range of complexity of hyperthematic structures, I want to disclose a set of principles of transformation, the hyperthemes, between various complexities of hyperthematic structure, but particularly a set of hyperthemes based on such structures which clearly promote harmonization of action. In other words I will deliberately select examples to be interpreted, from regions of human endeavor—active experience—which appear to promote harmonious action.

Methodological Considerations of Hyperthematics

My method will build upon Royce's method as practiced in his *Problem of Christianity*. The reader may look back to that work—particularly volume

2—if interested, although this is not necessary to understand what I am up to here. I will select a group of central themes, or organic regions of experience, which exemplify harmonizing structures. For Royce, Christianity was such a theme. I will interpret these themes to an opening postulate and its derivatives which I will freely make about the world. I will interpret aspects of the themes to other aspects within themselves, and I will interpret aspects of the themes to aspects of other themes. When it suits I will postulate further secondary themes beneath our central themes, and interpret these in turn to our central themes. I will usually postulate on a lower level of generality in order to attempt interpretation to a higher level. I will not be slavish, rigid, or exhaustive in the order of the method, but will rather follow up lines of interpretation which arise and seem promising. Everything is valuable in this sense. Nothing in the process of the method is wasted. The method is to be of minimum rigidity with regard to its particular actions and maximally fluid with regard to the order of application of those actions.

In principle, what will be developed could be developed in a skeleton form by strict deduction, based upon selections of postulates. Royce has provided the tools to do so in the selective logic of his System Sigma. But due to the complexity of the themes which we must approach to carry out our task, the effort required would be daunting. Nor would it be at all satisfying to proceed in this way in the beginning. To remove the flesh in order to study the abstracted bones would be a mistake. The bones are not preeminent to the living flesh of the active experiential process. If we palpate the flesh of the issue first, its bones will become evident underneath before long. In time, and given a community of skilled, artful, and visionary philosophical interpreters willing to engage in and unite both a technical and non-technical form of interpretation, an approach which makes use of the more technical aspect—as practice—will be possible and perhaps desirable. As it stands, the most fruitful approach for the moment is to lay out, by an interpretive disclosure of its working principles, the broadest practical outline of the system.

General Considerations of Hyperthematics

A few words about the postulatory character of the endeavor will be useful. The hyperthemes to be advanced are postulates. Their postulatory character follows from the opening postulate of hyperthematics and from derivative postulates following that postulate. If the opening postulate is accepted then the derivatives follow, and if the latter are accepted then the hyperthematic endeavor may proceed. The hyperthemes are never assumed to have stronger than suppositional validity. They can be thought of as the metaphysical cousins of a set of mathematical functions which depend on the initially accepted postulates. Nonetheless they are intimately related with experience as fact, in the guise of being generalized principles indicating how interpretations link together experience as concept and percept, as concept and concept, and as percept and percept, and in general organic experience. They are envisioned as *tools with which to understand and guide the flow of active experience*. Moreover, I am going to forego the unhelpful language of concept and percept as much as possible—although I will certainly slip back at times through mere force of habit—in order to speak of more and less *complex* regions of experience, i.e., interpretable signs of varying complexity. More complex experience is tending toward concept, whereas less complex experience is tending toward percept. The hyperthemes are disclosed from such examples of interpretational structures as will be seen shortly. The examples are postulated structures, which nonetheless intersect with fact. But in every case the facts with which they intersect are the facts that are verified for the writer of the work, and hypothesized as facts for the reader. The whole assumption behind this endeavor is that it is worthwhile because the writer supposes that you as a reader experience for yourself at least some of those facts which I experience. But I never verify your experience, which is precisely why it is—suppositionally—*your* experience.

The endeavor is thus tentative from the point of view of someone who insists on rejecting the opening assumption. It is no proof; rather *it is an attempt to give an expansively meaningful and accordingly pragmatic account of the world according to a particular opening postulate*. But the range of what constitutes proof is greatly reduced according to our opening postulate. The real world is a world of meaning and value first, rather than proof. In a sense, this is also a bypassing of epistemology. The very instituting of epistemology is a symptom of the embracing of the divide between idea and sense experience. There is no such divide. Hyperthematics is an attempt to move beyond the assumptions of epistemology and toward a base in action. The question *What can we know?* is replaced by the question *How can we act?* Here, metaphysics is an applied effort, i.e., an attempt at a general interpretational structure of the world according to an assumption that the world is a meaningful world, and thus an ethical world in which reality is a structure of created value. In the more rigorous sense of "applied" it is an attempt to create an interpretational structure which can bridge the regions of experience of specially selected problematics.

Despite the foregoing, I suppose that someone may object that nevertheless since this is merely a game of postulating, any postulate will be as good as another, e.g., we can postulate for any problematic that it can be interpreted according to the hypothesis that the moon is made of green cheese. To this I can only reply that in a sense this is so. But we are after meaning finally, and if such a supposition renders meaning to the objector, then she is welcome to hold to it as she can. This is the nature of Hyperthematics as a fluid metaphysics, it is non-dogmatic, we do not seek proofs but rather meanings; and interpretations can be expected to change, not least by expansion. On the other hand our supposed objector appears, according to our interpretation of her, to want to convey something meaningful to us. She values her objection. But just so, insofar as she does mean to convey something, she cannot be doing any less than sharing our view that meaning is possible, i.e., the world is interpretable relative to specific problems, that is to say particularly interpretable as well is generally so.

Thus, while I can accept the fanciful supposition of the green cheese moon as a caution—and this is truly all that she can have meant by her offering the objection—I cannot accept that there are not better and worse interpretations. If all interpretations are alike for all problems, then she has neither meant nor interpreted anything to us. Interpretation involves value because value arises according to the active standpoint of the interpreter. Hence, some interpretations will have greater value than others, depending on the broadness of the interpreter's vision. As Royce puts it so aptly: "The real world has a genuine relation to the various personalities that live in it. The truth is diversified by its relation to these personalities. Values do indeed alter with the point of view. The world as interpreted by me is a fact different from the world as interpreted by you; and these different interpretations have all of them their basis in the truth of things."[1] In this meaningful diversity lies the hope and promise of the world as a world of value.

Definitions

Nb. The definitions have mainly been arrived at through the course of the application of the method as need arose. They are more *results* than foundational moves. They are stated here for convenience and my suggestion to the reader is to skim over them and then look in again upon them as needed.

The reader who understands what is being suggested here in Hyperthematics will soon enough pass beyond the need for strict definitions.

Meaning—the awareness, as such, of experience in some relation to differing experience, which relation has come about through a creative interpretation; meaning always presents a solution to a problematic of experience; a simple example at a relatively quantitative complexity is the <u>awareness</u> of the range of natural numbers between one and nine

Value—the awareness of a process of interpretation as solving some problematic of experience through an ongoing accretion of interpretation; e.g., the <u>counting</u> of the natural numbers from one to ten; an experience "holds" and presents value as meaning

Interpretation—the active creation of experience in an attempt to generate meaning and value in order to solve a problematic of experience (see Introduction)

Feeling—the relative letting be of experience as a given-ness, i.e., as an abiding recurrence of sameness (see Conclusion for examples)

Knowing—the relative engagement of experience in creative interpretations which transform an abiding recurrence of feeling as sameness into new experience; e.g., the creative invention of a musical instrument transforms experience(s) of the world process as nature (felt natural sound, the felt tactility of wood, etc.), into a new experience, e.g., the experience of the sound of a harp string

Creativity—the active varying of interpretation to the available facets of experience(s) in a region of given complexity; its opposite is *Sameness*—a relative "letting be," in interpretations, of available facets of experience(s) in a region of given complexity

Complexity—the relative diversity of facets of an experience or region of experience which other experience or regions of experience are being interpreted to; experiences or problematics, of low complexity are relatively similar; those of high complexity are relatively diverse; spans a range from quantitative to qualitative, e.g., counting "1, 1, 1, 1, 1, 1, 1, 1, 1" engenders relatively quantitative or low value, while counting "1, 2, 3, 4, 5, 6, 7, 8, 9" engenders a higher value <u>relative</u> to the former act; its opposite is *Simplicity*—the relative lack of diversity of facets of an experience or region of experience which other experiences or regions of experience are being interpreted to

Hypertheme—a postulated principle of transformation according to which a hyperthematic structure of interpretation, as well as acting elements adopting it, can be consistently interpreted to the opening postulate of Hyperthematics

Hyperthematic Structure—a suppositional metaphysical action harmonizing structure, made up of a set of hyperthemes, which promotes meaningful interpretation engendering value, when accepted by acting transformable element processes

Anti-Hypertheme—a postulated principle of transformation according to which a hyperthematic structure of interpretation, as well as acting elements adopting it, cannot be consistently interpreted to the opening postulate of Hyperthematics; adoption of anti-hyperthemes gives rise to false communities which devaluate regions of the world process

Sectional Action—the interpretive relation of lines of action to one another across, or sectionally to, a time process which contains them both; (in the same orientational sense as synchronically); e.g., think of two hockey players passing the puck back and forth while both are skating toward the opponent's goal, interpreting one another in relatively the same time[2]

Parallel Action—the interpretive relation of lines of action to one another parallel to the time process; (in the same orientational sense as diachronically);* e.g., a member of a relay race team passing the baton on to the next in line, or, mailing a letter to oneself to receive tomorrow and thus interpreting from the past toward the future

Transformable Element—an interpreting actor, a process of experience embedded within the temporal process of the world (here I will call the actor an *acting* transformable element), e.g., a human dancer, writer, game player, etc.; and/or a representative of the interpreting actor (an extension or *extensive* transformable element), e.g., the human body, written word, chess piece; this is an expansion of the term *sign* in Royce's terminology; (when the context is clear I will sometimes simply use the term element)

Sectional Transformable Elements—those which promote interpretations to other elements in the time process sectional aspect

Parallel Transformable Elements—those which promote interpretations to other elements in the time process parallel aspect

Solution—an interpretation by acting transformable elements adopting a hyperthematic structure

---

*I avoid diachronic and synchronistic because their usual uses have non-interpretive connotations which I wish to avoid.

Problematic—a division within experience, a gap between differing experiences, which serves as a lure for interpretation and which may be engaged by actors adopting a particular hyperthematic structure

Local (or *localized or localizing*)—an assessment of interpretive value according to the complexity or simplicity that an initiating locus of interpretation intends or achieves; e.g., interpretation based upon human embodiment, properly speaking, tend to be only as complex as the ranges of the limbs allow, thus interpretation according to dance is a relatively localizing tendency

Degree of focus—the proportion of solution to problematic which a given hyperthematic structure engenders; a hyperthematic structure which emphasizes solution at the cost of problematic will tend toward localized harmonization of action; a hyperthematic structure which emphasizes problematic at the cost of solution will tend toward the propagation of itself as a method of engagement of experience according to its complexity as a leader structure

Elimination—an action which intends—and <u>ostensibly</u> succeeds—to remove a transformable element or elements, or a community of interpretation formed by such elements, within a hyperthematic structure; there are degrees of elimination ranging from annihilation of an element to ejection of an element; unless otherwise stated I will use elimination to mean killing in this work and exclusion to mean weaker forms of elimination, e.g., barring someone from a community

Constriction—an action which intends—and <u>ostensibly</u> succeeds—to remove a part of a transformable element or community of interpretation formed by such elements, within a hyperthematic structure; the part is an abstraction of lesser complexity relative to some selected defining abstraction of the process which is the element or community in question, e.g., removing a man's arm, or blocking its range of action, is a constriction relative to the embodied human process of the man; constriction is thus a lesser degree of elimination relative to a given range of complexity

Leader Structure—a hyperthematic structure whose transformable elements have a range and degree of complexity greater than some other selected structure. A hyperthematic structure may contain multiple leader structures. A hyperthematic structure may be the leader to multiple less complex hyperthematic structures.

Interpretive Freedom—the capacity for interpretive actions under a hyperthematic structure occasioned by the complexity of the transformable elements of that structure along with any constrictions at play in the region of experience guided by the structure

Interpretive Capacity (or *ethical capacity*)—the ability of an acting transformable element, particularly a human process to, engage ranges of complexity of experience in valuating interpretations, relative to other acting transformable elements, particularly human processes; interpretive capacity may be more or less destructive, seeking to destroy value according to various inconsistent assumptions adopted, usually to gain localized power in some aspect of experience

Saturation—the expansion, by a leader structure, of the interpretive freedom of elements acting under a given hyperthematic structure, to the point at which the transformable elements of the given structure lose the guidance of the structure in their processes of interpretation

Community of Interpretation—consistent engagement in interpretive action by the acting transformable elements guided by a hyperthematic structure

False Community (or *localized community*)—engagement in interpretive action by the acting transformable elements under a hyperthematic structure which is inconsistent with the hypertheme H; *localized* in the sense that the community creates an apparent "pocket" of value within and around the region of its action, but only by devaluating some other region of experience further beyond it in terms of complexity

Community of Selfhood—consistent engagement in interpretive action from the locus of the human body recognized as a process of action, to its future and past as a process; the community of selfhood is the default community of interpretation, our primary resource for learning to engage the world process in the creation of more complex communities

Constructive Action—an interpretive action by a member of a community under a hyperthematic structure, which is consistent with the hypertheme H and thus propagates or initiates the community in question

Destabilizing Action—an action by a member of a community under a hyperthematic structure, which is inconsistent with the hypertheme H, is destructive of interpretive process, and thus destabilizes the community in question

Reconstructive Action—an interpretive action by a member of a community under a hyperthematic structure, which is consistent with the hypertheme H, directed at the problematic resultant from a destabilizing action, and thereby reconstructs, heals, or stabilizes the community in question

Valuate (*valuation or valuating*)—to take interpretive action which, being consistent, creates value within some region of the world process

Devaluate (*devaluation or devaluating*)—to take action which constricts experience for interpretation in some region of the world process and destroys meaning and the possibility of value

Simplicity/Complexity Tendency—action either toward simplifying or toward complexifying—or engagement of the given range of simplicity to complexity offered by the world process—in the interpretation of diversities of experience

Sameness/Creativity Tendency—action either toward sameness or toward creativity—or engagement of the given range of sameness to creativity offered by the world process—in the interpretation of diversities of experience

Practice (or *Localized Practice*)—an aware action toward constriction of interpretation within some region of the world process, which understands that the constriction is undertaken <u>only for practice</u> (the practical) and continually looks for the gradual giving way of such constriction in favor of a more consistent growth of value, e.g., deliberately breaking down muscles in body-building in order to build them up more, or deliberately focusing (constricting interpretation) while teaching in order to later get across to students a broader concept (expanding interpretation)

The Hypertheme **H** and the Derivatives

We begin with the opening postulate, following Royce, which becomes our ultimate hypertheme, our overall assumption regarding the range of the world's interpretability:

H—*the world is the community of interpretation of the problem which it presents, or, the world is a hyperthematic structure of interpretation which contains three transformable elements: experience, different experience, postulated interpretation of the resulting problematic of experience (i.e., solution)*

Its practical correlate is: **HG** (Hypertheme of the Goal)—to create a community of interpretation, select a problematic, a goal, to engage.

From **H** we can postulate at least four additional principles in a negative formulation and their four correlates in a positive formulation:

H1'—*if H, then any <u>hyperthematic structure</u> which tends toward the elimination of the elements of its own, or other hyperthematic structures, is an unstable or inconsistent structure*

H2'—*if H, then any <u>element</u> acting under the guidance of a hyperthematic structure which tends toward elimination of the elements of its own or other hyperthematic structures, including itself, is an unstable or inconsistent element*

H3'—*if H, then any single element, or pair of elements cannot make up a community guided by a hyperthematic structure according to its own level of complexity, though it (they) can do so within a more complex hyperthematic structure than its (their) own*

> With regard to **H3'**, anything short of a single complete experience recurs to the hypertheme **H**, i.e., the world is a problem unless it is solved.

And now follows:

H4'—*if H3, then any <u>community</u> which eliminates other communities or elements of other communities, is inconsistent with H, since if H and H3, then these may be elements of communities under a more complex hyperthematic structure*

Nb. n general, in what follows, when I assert that a hyperthematic structure, or part of one, is *inconsistent*, this means that it contradicts the hypertheme **H** in some way which **H1'–H4'** (and **H1–H4** below) make obvious, i.e., *that it reduces the possibility and thus ability to interpret.* And what my whole endeavor is going to show is that what we usually view as *bad* or *worse* in the ethical sense is intimately tied up with the constriction of interpretation, while what we usually view as *good* or *better* in the ethical sense is intimately tied up with the expansion of interpretation. I am often going to favor the notions of *better* or *worse*, as being tendencies, over the notions of *good* and *bad*, because the former are more fluid and practical for describing the play of value.

A community is thus a number of elements consistently interpreting to one another according to some of the consistent assumptions (hyperthemes) which together make up the hyperthematic structure, i.e., the metaphysical structure which guides the action of interpretation of experience.

Further practical *positive* correlates of **H1'–H4'** are:

H1—*create hyperthematic structures which do not eliminate elements*

H2—*take all transformative means to guide the transformable elements acting under a hyperthematic structure out of eliminating other elements of the structure*
H3—*create communities of three or more elements under hyperthematic structures*
H4—*create communities which do not eliminate other structures, or communities or elements of other structures*

H1'–H4' and **H1–H4** are derived from **H**. The further hyperthemes which follow in this work are also derived from **H**. Nonetheless, all of these, insofar as formalizations of logic, need the process of experience to make any practical sense of them. Hence, in what follows, the hyperthemes above are expanded upon in musements[3] upon living experience, while further hyperthemes are also derived, but through that expansion.

Hyperthematic Expansion Compared to the Scientific Method

The hypertheme **H** has been postulated: *the world is the community of interpretation of the problem which it presents*. Every problem will take the general form of a gap to be bridged between regions of experience, i.e., experience and differing experience. The most general problem is thus postulated as solved, but every problem lesser than the world problem will admit of a multiplicity of solutions. Thus every hyperthematic structure which promotes sub-interpretations consistent with the initial hypertheme will be a harmonizing structure.

In searching for other hyperthemes the problem now becomes: where to begin the search? The only answer can be: wherever it seems best. Further hyperthemes will be uncovered by presenting harmonizing structures one after another and attempting to interpret them to our founding principle and derivatives. It may help to see the point of this by contrasting the method with the interpretive efforts of the natural sciences—which also use hyperthematic structures unknowingly—and seeing how the structures to be mused upon stand with regard to the usual view of science itself.

Let us take the field of paleoanthropology as an example of a current realm for interpretations. It engages a problematic. The problematic might be, for example, that of the difference between our morphology and the morphology evidenced in various ancient bones which appear to be human-like bones. The field of paleoanthropology has a "background hypothesis" relative to which it makes interpretations, e.g., perhaps it hypothesizes most generally that there is a transformation of body structures from the entity to whom the old bones belonged and our own body structures. Yet it also has a hyperthematic structure under which its acting elements—paleoanthropologists and their tools—make interpretations to one another and to future paleoanthropologists. This is "the way paleoanthropologists, and scientists more generally, go about their work." The hyperthematic structure of paleoanthropology has similarities to what will later be elaborated as the hyperthematic structure of narrative, e.g., part of what such scientists do is to fashion a lengthy story of the change of the human process in its objective aspect.

If you participate in the community of paleoanthropology you accept the communal goal of constructing a full and consistent account of the transformation of proto-human forms of life up to the form of say *Homo sapiens*. There are postulated elements, e.g., *Australopithecus afarensis*, which relate to other structures such as *Australopithecus africanus*. There are also gaps in the account. Natural scientists never rest content with mere gaps, so wherever these gaps occur they are bridged by what science calls hypotheses. But in the case in question there is that overall hypothesis which is *to bridge all gaps* which may come. That overarching hypothesis tells the paleoanthropologist that if humanity has come up from the earlier forms, then the various bits of empirical evidence which continue to be found will continue to slot into the overarching account. If bits arise which do not slot in, they will prove it to be a false account in need of modification: a false image of a greater empirical reality which is the true sum of the empirical bits of evidence. This approach differs from that of Hyperthematics.

Hypothetical structures as understood by science have the characteristic that they are tested or proven by postulated experience of lesser complexity than themselves, i.e., experience which offers less of a problematic. In other words, you feel vindicated in paleoanthropology with regard to your "background hypothesis," when you can get your hands on some bone or other which "proves" or "verifies" the hypothesis and when you fail to find bones which disprove the hypothesis. The more bones you can collect, the more your hypothesis seems likely. If the hypothesis were incorrect the bones in question would not be found, or those that were found would be very different from what has come to be expected.

The ancient bone held in our hands is an experience. It is hard, heavy, substantial, solid, right here, right now. It conforms to expectations. It is empirical. The more empirical it is, the better it is for the hypothesis. The more empirical it is, the fewer problems it offers to be solved. Conversely, the more problems it gives rise to, the less empirical it is. The average scientist does not want more problems beyond a certain small range. An extremely problematic bone is a bother for the hypothesis.[4] It doesn't fit the usual pattern perhaps. It's not the usual shape; it's not the usual weight or color; it has the characteristics of a bone found in another ancient camp site which is supposed to be a million years older, or maybe it has characteristics of bones found on a whole other continent. It has characteristics which lead to further questions, i.e., which lead the scientist—if she lets herself—to begin comparing it to another time period, a faraway place, and so on

This comparison of vastly diverse experiences becomes suddenly difficult and complex as a problem for interpretation. Complexity is increased by the sheer number of experiences—empirical evidences—which are going to be necessary to bridge the gap in order to save the overarching working hypothesis. Even if the vast new problem which a strange new bone gives rise to can be solved empirically, it is going to require a host of new discoveries of bones which differ only subtly and through which the endpoints of the new problem will eventually be linked. To look to the empirical to solve a problem then is to cultivate the urge toward low complexity, toward a series of experiences each of which does not vary greatly from other experiences. *Low complexity is just this relative invariance of diverse experiences.*

But scientists in their role as bone diggers very often come upon bits of experience of a higher complexity: the strange bone that they cannot make consistent with their hypothesis. Some brave soul in the wilds of the Gobi Desert comes upon a new type of hominid skull with some strange feature for example. Hereupon there is a type of scientist—the predominant type and the same who does the most digging—who strives to save the hypothesis above all. The hypothesis is holy and cannot be disturbed, says this type of scientist.[5] Such a scientist often acts analogously to someone, who, while searching in the box for certain pieces to complete a puzzle, comes upon a Lego brick: she says "how did *that* get in here?" and tosses it aside, certain that it has no place in the completed puzzle. If this were the only type, science would grind to a halt.

Another type of scientist sometimes engages such a problem however, a type which is in the minority. This scientist, rather than look steadfastly down at the bones to try and verify the hypothesis or convince his community to discard the offending bit to save the hypothesis from falsification, looks *up* toward the realm of the hypothesis and so also at the structure of interpretation of which it is the centerpiece. She looks far and wide, at other hypotheses and types of hypothesis, considers changing the structure of interpretation—the framework within which the field of science in question does its work—searches for analogies perhaps, consults other fields of science, other fields of study beyond scientific fields even, and through this process comes up with another overarching hypothesis altogether. When there is such an effort, new overarching hypotheses are presented and the interpretive structure of a field of science—"the way the scientists work together"—and perhaps the interpretive structure of the scientific endeavor as a whole, is changed or added to. Evolutionary theory is an example of such an effort.

But it takes a visionary, a creative scientist, to generate a great new hypothesis and to commence a field by building the structure of interpretation which will guide it. That is to say, it takes a scientist engaged in Hyperthematic endeavor in an unconscious and perhaps rudimentary way. Such a scientist sees that the strange bone—the out-of-place Lego brick—which provokes large and difficult questions relative to the usual empirically stable experiences in the field in question, is an opportunity to interpret a vast realm of further experiences, interpretation leading to expanded meaning and value.

The strange bone does this because it is a type of experience which connects with experience of a higher complexity. It is a relatively low complexity bit of experience which nonetheless bears relations to high complexity experience. Its new and strange characteristics, whatever they may be, evoke broad problems, making it a center for expansion of interpretation.

If the reader will recall what was said earlier about metaphysics, it should be evident that the bone-digger types cherish the metaphysics of an empirically based science, the holy hypothesis, as the true reality "over there" which must be preserved. They are metaphysical fundamentalists at heart, cousins of certain prominent strands of philosophy. For such scientists, the real "over there" is what experience here must conform to.

The strange bone discovered is a springboard from which to break free of the fixity of such an external metaphysics however. The world process presents such opportunities. But we need never wait on chance discoveries. The Theory of Evolution and natural selection, for example, is *not* empirical in tendency in its beginnings. *Darwin deliberately went in search of experiences which would create and expand his great hypothesis*, strange creatures in strange and foreign places—the Lego bricks of our puzzle analogy—creatures which would present the observer with a dilemma that only a vastly expanded and creative hypothesis could explain.[6]

If his hypothesis could not explain these creatures than it would indeed be in trouble, but an even broader hypothesis would then have been needed to account for them. On the other hand, if his hypothesis could account for these empirical curiosities of nature, these "severe tests" as Ayalla calls them, then the hypothesis would be broadened tremendously. Either way, *Darwin's deliberate choice of irregular bits of empirical evidence was calculated to stretch his hypothesis to the breaking point, to the point where great creativity and daring at the level of hypothesis as such, must come in play to fashion it.* For Darwin, putting forward the theory of evolution was a creation of the real. Deliberately observing vast diversity "here" in the process of experience, welcoming a large problem to be solved, he created a vast metaphysical structure "out there" in the more complex reaches of the process which would begin to solve it. He did the reverse of the usual.

Some readers will still have the urge to reply: "yes but Darwin was merely uncovering the way the world *really* is . . . we know now that he was right and the traditional views were wrong." If you can still utter this line, you miss the point entirely. There is no way the world *really* is, prior to our creation of it. To take this line is to divide experiences of lower complexity from experiences of higher complexity, and then to set up the latter as a static and untouchable framework to which the former must conform. You, who will reply as above, look back on Darwin's work from a point in the world process where he has succeeded creatively. But in order to succeed, he had to give up the very view that you hold to. Darwin had to create a new structure at a level of complexity of experience beyond the level we call "empirical." Having succeeded, the structure now guides the actions of a number of processes in our world, including scientists, but also social actors, and others.

The idea that evolutionary theory is a reality "out there," which scientists are confirming by finding and fitting in bits of experience, is an illusion. That illusion is caused by the passage from a creative period of the theory to a constrictive period; Darwin himself even fell prey to the illusion, later labeling himself, as Ayalla notes, a staunch upholder of inductivism, proceeding "on true Baconian principles."[7]

In a creative period the minds of those who can follow are stretched. The potential for new value is felt as a great interpretive freedom. Those who cannot follow at higher complexities begin to fill up this "expanse" of interpretive freedom with interpretation in quantity of low complexity experiences which are similar to one another—as a newly bought home slowly fills with the stuff of living. Eventually, because those who do this filling in are more numerous—commensurate with the tendency of interpretation as quantity—even those capable of creation at higher complexities of experience can be waylaid by the illusion that the reality is set "out there." It isn't.

The human tendency is always to fall back toward the constrictive tendency relative to interpretation. Filling in bits of similar experiences to solve a gap of interpretation in a problem of experience *is easier* than playing with more complex experience. The tendency is even useful—if properly understood. This constrictive urge toward verification by the empirical intends that a hypothesis be "solidified" as true. It supposes that there is a real, a true, experience, and that the hypothesis has—at last!—fortuitously or skillfully been hit upon as the true image of that experience, and finally that various bits of experience, gathered together according to the true image, will prove in the end to have been part of this one large "solid" experience "behind" the image. Here the lesser experience is simply a portion of the greater experience, the real assumed to be "out there," but is given preeminence to the hypothesis precisely because it (the lesser experience) is taken as a part of that eventual larger experience.

The assumption is that the underlying solidity of the world is uncovered. This is like a man blinding himself intentionally in order to better feel things without striving to see them in a hopelessly long dark night. Coming upon a large object in the dark he touches several bits of it and feels rubber, cold metal, etc. "I guess it's a car," he says, and continues moving about the object touching this and that to verify that his guess is still the best one. The latter is the best he can do for, in his world and crippled by his assumptions, the sun never will rise in the end, and he will have to make do with his many bits of touching. The urge to verification intends that a series of experiences which all are *forced* to accept—this is their nature as empirical—sum together into a larger whole which one is then supposed to be forced to accept in turn.

It is hopeless to try to refute such a view. Those who insist on such a view have enslaved themselves to the tendency of force in experience, a tendency which will be further elaborated upon in a later chapter. What we can do is to suggest that the creation of a new hypothesis such as the Theory of Evolution does not work this way.

The Theory of Evolution is an example of *a complex experience*, nonetheless joined to less complex experiences, for the world is a whole process of interpretation. The nearer reaches of the experience, the eyes of fruit flies and the beaks of finches, are its less complex elements. They are linked in interpretations to more complex elements: mathematical equations, statistical data, historical records of the explorations of Darwin and others, pictures and drawings of animals, the ocean voyages made to retrieve those pictures, dedicated museum exhibits, the history of animal breeding, and so on and on to the further reaches of a vast woven fabric of interpretations. The Theory of Evolution is experienced, as a complex experience, by anyone interested enough to begin and continue interpretations with its various elements in its *region of experience*—i.e., somewhere on the fabric. The interpretations of such people find their value in relation to the theory, in its role as a complex experience filled with unsolved gaps of interpretation of vast breadth which inspire and guide the interpreters, whether their active interpretations be relatively simple or relatively complex.

We never "verify" a more complex experience by a less complex experience in any way which is valuable. It is the process of experience of greater complexity which grants interpretive freedom to that of lesser complexity. The process of experience of greater complexity opens a region of potential value creation by which the process of experience of lesser complexity measures its interpretive efforts. For us, in this work, the "test" of any experience is whether it can be meaningful. Meaning, as assumed in this work, is the result of interpretation of experiences, the growth of the chain of interpretations, and the expansive tendency presented in meaning is value. It follows that any experience, of whatever complexity, can only be meaningful in interpretation to a greater complexity of experience. The experience of greater complexity, ultimately the notion of interpretation as creation of value suggested by **H**, is the measure, or standard, of the worth of a lower complexity experience.

Hypotheses are exploratory in the scientific sense; their use is meant to serve as a bridge between low complexity "empirical" experience and experience which is of a quantitatively higher complexity—i.e., between the "small empirical" and the "large empirical." The hypothesis (lit. placed under) in the sense espoused by the scientific majority, is viewed as subservient in the role it will play as a middleman between the empirically small and the empirically large, the hard final reality.

Hyperthemes are creative; their role is not subservient; their use is meant to create, or realize, experience as value by facilitating interpretation between low and high complexity experience, experience of which they remain part, and chiefly from lower to higher complexity. The hypertheme (lit. placed above) fulfills the role of a standard for active interpretation of experience by means of its continually expansive character.

Let the preferred method of science be characterized in a twofold manner as (1) the formulation of hypotheses followed by experimental verification—the hypothetico-deductive method, and (2) the inductive method of gathering empirical data to uncover a larger experience. Then in distinction the method of Hyperthematics can be characterized as the attempt to interpret the processes of experience within various regions of felt value to the formalized postulate of value in general.

Science searches for a mirror image of an external real world which will ultimately allow a manipulation of that external real world, *but only according to the dictates of that external real world*. Science, in its impoverished aspect, thus views the human as a slave to the external force of the world.

Hyperthematics views the human as a process capable of creating and re-creating its own world. Hyperthematics searches for principles of value creation and attempts to apply them. The formal "test" of the principles (hyperthemes) is their logical consistency with the ultimate postulate of interpretive value **H**, but their discovery and exposition come from an exploratory engagement of experience as a living process, made in constant relation to the ultimate postulate or its derivatives. The informal test of the principles is their application in creative action which creates value.[8]

Science aims to uncover the relations of diverse aspects of experience without judging—ostensibly—that experience as to value, and without attempting to modify that value. Ultimately this cannot be, because scientific activity—as will be suggested much later in this work—has an effect on the value of the world process and because felt value drives the interpretive action of scientists. Their activity has value for them, which accounts for the fact that purely inductive modes of science cannot be sustained.

Hyperthematics aims to conjoin or add whatever consistent hyperthemes it gains to the hyperthematic structures of any and all fields of human endeavor, particularly those which suffer from felt loss of value. It is creative in intent. It intends to create value.

The foregoing will have to serve as a preliminary elucidation of the difference between the received view of natural science, particularly relative to hypothesis, and Hyperthematics. In Hyperthematics I will present a method for the deliberate undertaking of what is sometimes achieved arbitrarily by the most creative of scientists. Rather than looking down primarily we are going to look up to test such structures as we select against higher structures, and to deliberately use the results to create new meaning structures of the kind that open new fields of interpretation, connect disciplines, and give overall meaning to the process of experience. In short Hyperthematics is predominantly expansive in character, according to the nature of its opening assumption.

Now, where can one look for examples of the type of structures in question? The answer is not hard to find, for the structures in question are all around us, though rarely if ever *deliberately* created all at once. Rather, they usually grow out of a sort of trial and error of activity which hits upon harmony because harmonious action is interesting, fun, meaningful, and valuable.

The Hyperthematic Structure of the Game

The first example that comes to mind is the game. Games are found in almost all human societies. Let us consider the game of chess as representative of a game and thus of the hyperthematic structures we are after. Chess in its usual variety is a two-player game. Each of the two players, as acting transformable elements within the game structure, alternately takes actions in response to the actions of the other, responding both sectionally to the present action of the opposing player and parallel to the larger time successive actions within the game structure as a whole. For example, there is said to be an opening game, a middle game, and an end game; and there is a strategy which covers the tone of the actions as a whole, as well as tactics, which are groups of actions directed toward limited aspects of the overall goal.

And the lines of action are unbroken. During the period when each player allows the other to move, not only is there an action of thoughtfully anticipating the opponent's move, but even if there were to be a complete passivity, i.e., no action, or waiting, then this also is an action precisely because we are within, or adopting, a guiding structure. In other words *remaining in the game* as we wait for the opponent's move is a more encompassing action in a process which includes moving one's pieces. The various transformable elements of the game, such as the pieces, are, in their turn, signs of lines of action which can be interpreted to the two main lines of action of the two players participating in the game. Thus there are interweaving strands of action of considerable complexity.

Now, to begin we ask: how does the game of chess, as a representative of game structure generally, stand in meaningful relation to our opening postulate, the hypertheme **H**? or again, how is this less complex hyperthematic structure assumed to be exemplified in chess to be interpreted to the more complex structure of our founding principle?

To begin with we are dealing with multiple elements, or signs. At the upper level the elements are the lines of action which are the processes of each player as engaged in the larger process of the game. These lines of action are to be harmonized ultimately. But the game itself is the interpretation of the actions of the players with respect to one another. It is a general triadic structure which is the community inclusive of the players. Within this general structure there are elements—the players with their past, present, and future as playing the game—which are yet further triadic or interpretive structures. Each player, insofar as she has the goal of playing chess, is herself an interpretation of her past to her future with regard to the process of playing chess. Moreover, the elements of the community of chess as a game in which our two players are engaged—e.g., the chess pieces representative of their specific actions—are themselves both signs from the past of the community of those engaged in the development of the game of chess and signs of the moves of each player according to their position on the board and relation to other pieces.

So far then the hyperthematic structure of the chess game is clearly consistent with the opening postulate which we assumed, and its actors have adopted that structure. To remind the reader, a "hyperthematic structure of x"—here the chess game—just means the hyperthemes as they manifest themselves as guiding a consistent community of experience within the world process. **H** at least is guiding the players of chess. Yet so far also, the elements indicate a complexity which we must approach subtly. In the sort of interpretive effort we are engaged in, one must forgo the urge to "go too deep," lest we become hopelessly entangled. A metaphysics which aims at applicability will satisfy itself with a fluid structure and here we are searching merely for the principles, or hyperthemes, being manifested in the fluid processes of experience. Renewing our interpretation then we ask: are the derivative hyperthemes also part of the hyperthematic structure?

Evidently they are. Recall the practical correlate **H2** of our hypertheme **H2'**: take all transformative means to guide the transformable elements acting under a hyperthematic structure out of eliminating other elements of the structure. Does the hyperthematic structure represented in the chess game abide by this? Indeed it does, and it does so on multiple levels.

In the first place, the players themselves as actors in the community of chess playing do not eliminate one another. They enter into the community according to the hyperthematic structure of the chess game, harmonize their actions in playing one another, and exit that structure. Their freedom to enter and exit is their own. The structure remains intact. Repeated active participation in it remains an option. A single game of chess holds its players to the completion of its goal as a sub-community and this in turn is a harmony of action which finds its place in the larger goal of the community of the game of chess as such, i.e., chess playing. The goal of the community of chess is to play chess, and every successful game between two players supports that goal.

In fact, however, there is another sense in which the elements are not eliminated. Here I am talking about the chess pieces as elements of the community, which are extensions of the elements that are the acting human players. During the chess game we say that one piece "takes another," or—when teaching children—"eats the other piece," or sometimes eliminates another, or again that the king is "in check" when he would be eliminated regardless of any move that can be made. Despite this, the elimination in question is precisely a sort of play elimination, or imaginary elimination, a hypothetical elimination which does not intend existential elimination. It is the kind of transformation of "real" elimination which sustains the hyperthematic structure under which the community of the chess game is possible. We can show that according to the following considerations.

First, we could change the terminology of the chess game. Rather than saying that the chess pieces "take," or "eliminate," or "eat," one another, we could say that they touch, or meet, or stop, one another. Such expressions would not change the nature of the chess game. The same moves would be carried out, the same result achieved. Is there a use of the original terminology which this fails to address? The pieces *are removed* from the chess board, someone may object. Perhaps this is the significance of the terms take or eliminate?

To this I must differ, and I must challenge our objector to show how the pieces are eliminated by being removed. Imagine a chess board whose squares are created large enough that they hold multiple chess pieces. Now imagine that as the game is played, each piece as it is taken, rather than being removed from the board is somehow marked, and because marked is thereafter allowed to remain where it is, but not to be used for any of the game actions specific to its type. In this case, the game will proceed as usual. The literal removal of the chess pieces will make no difference to the structure of interpretation of the game.

Still, replies our objector: if you have not literally removed the pieces from the chess board, nonetheless you have removed it from the game; you have removed it in its capacity of *acting* and is it not therefore eliminated from the game? Once more I must suggest otherwise. In our new scenario the piece remains on the board though it no longer moves. According to the hyperthematic structure of interpretation which is the chess game, it has lost its ability to be used in game actions specific to its type, but it has not lost its power to act in general. By not acting, specifically *by not acting within its substructure in a way which makes that substructure consistent with the hypertheme H, i.e., the general structure of interpretation, it is acting in the interest of the game structure.*

This willed inaction is no different than simply not moving a piece according to the usual rules, and what is happening, in effect, is something positive along the lines of: once you take such and such an action under certain conditions, I agree—in fact I agreed in advance—to willfully not engage in this other action with this particular piece. So you didn't eliminate my piece, rather *I will* to not move it, and so to harmonize my actions with yours. And that is why games work so well.

Thus we see that elimination is not essential to the hyperthematic structure of the game as exemplified in chess. The significance of the usual expression that one element or piece "takes another" in chess inevitably finds its way back to the structure of interpretation which the piece takes part in. This is the reason why we could propose such a transformation of the elements as we did above and the structure remains essentially unaffected. A little further thought can show us that countless transformations of the elements can be made which do not affect the overarching hyperthematic structure at all. Chess can be played with wooden pieces, or metal, or glass pieces; with boards of various sizes and shapes, with chess pieces of varying shape and color, without pieces at all but only symbols, with variants of rules, and with many other transformations

Now why is this? How can the structure support such a transformation of its elements? The answer is clear enough: its elements have *already* undergone transformation and they are the signs of that transformation. Moreover, they are now a type of signs, i.e., the type of signs which have undergone a transformative interpretation from being signs which eliminate elements of a community of interpretation to signs which do not eliminate elements of a community of interpretation. In effect they have been stabilized as signs worthy of harmony of action with respect to a community of interpretation.

But how have they been transformed? If you look at the history of chess you find that chess has military roots. Though we cannot know the details with any finality, it clearly began as a sort of representation of military units with their different capacities. From ancient India where the game originated it was passed on to Persia and then through the Arabic Empires to Western Europe. From "realistic"—we will have more to say about "realistic" later—pieces which literally represented the features of foot soldiers, cavalry, generals, and so forth, the pieces were gradually transformed into the signs that they now are.[9]

Military communities are comprised to a large degree of elements which eliminate other elements, and which therefore render their community inconsistent with our opening postulate and derivative postulates. I will muse further upon this later. For now what I want to get across is that chess is a living structure which signifies at least one possible transformation of such inconsistent elements. The original foot soldier, an acting element destructive of community because of his tendency to existentially eliminate acting elements of other communities, has become a foot soldier on the chess board, a pawn. In being transformed in this way the inconsistency of its action in the original military group, a false community, or "pseudo-community," is overcome. The sign of the acting transformable element which disrupts communities becomes part of a new structure, the game structure, which now promotes meaningful communities.

In the case of games, the goal is the playing of the game itself. The fun of games is the harmony of interpretation which they make possible, a harmony of interpretation especially suited to bringing human-acting transformable elements together in what we might call *small projects of community*. In other words, the game as a structure has arisen to make it simple to engage in action in a short-term yet meaningfully harmonious way, with a person whom you may have just met minutes ago, but whom nonetheless you must suppose to be a temporally extended individual, a process of experience, in order to play with.

So it is that often the depth of interpretation which lies behind the signs of a game enhances even further the ability of the game to draw actors into harmony. Its elements are the signs of our ability to approach our experience by means of interpretive structures which engage its richness without denying or eliminating some aspects of experience. A chess piece which "captures" another piece, for example, is drawing into the sign which it is, the various meetings and actions of the pieces which it has "captured" with regard to the past playing out of the game. If the bishop captures a rook it takes into itself something of the rook's overall effect on the game: the rook's horizontal and vertical freedom over the board are reinterpreted into an enhanced freedom for the capturing piece, as well as for other pieces. A chess piece can do this precisely because as a game piece it has been primed as a sign that gathers up other signs into itself for further interpretation rather than eliminating them.

This is a tendency not merely of games, but of all the accretion of meaning according to the time process whenever an interpretation has succeeded. The game of chess has an old and noble history. That history finds its way into the meaning of the community of the game through the elements of the game which display in this case not only the history of the community of the game of chess as such, but also the transformation of those military elements to which it is related historically. This is so for many games, and one often finds that new games and newly made games are less interesting for this reason. Chess even accretes the significance of its own history as a game: it is often thought of as one of the "classic" games.

It appears then that hyperthematic structures are prone to being made consistent with our opening hypertheme by accepting transformable elements which include in themselves prior interpretations that have moved them away from being elements given to elimination. Just as chess is rendered more interesting, more meaningful, because its rooks, kings, knights, and so forth are signs of the transformation of military elements into elements worthy of harmony of action, so, when selecting the elements with which to construct communities guided by hyperthematic structures we would do well to choose elements or signs—if there are any—which already have begun the transformation from elements inconsistent with harmony into elements that promote it.

If we now elaborate this as a hypertheme available to be included in a consistent hyperthematic structure—as it already is in the game structure—we get our first result, which I shall usually try to express so as to be compatible with the format: "in order to attain a better, that is a more harmonizing hyperthematic structure, or again, in order to increase value in experience, then do such and such with regard to experience. . . ."

I formulate it as:

H5—*Insofar as you can, populate the community guided by your hyperthematic structure with transformable elements which are signs of transformation away from eliminative elements that destabilize community toward elements that promote harmonious interpretation.*

Whenever I use the expression "insofar as you can . . ." in formulating hyperthemes, I mean insofar as is pragmatically consistent while bearing in mind both the ranges of complexity of experience and the suggestions of other hyperthemes. The reader will get a better sense of what I mean by this caution as the hyperthemes accumulate and are applied in later chapters.

Elements such as those encouraged by **H5** retain meaning fluidly. This means that hyperthematic structures are to gather up as much transformative history as possible into themselves, through those elements, as is relevant to their problematic. If with regard to a hyperthematic structure which engages a given problematic you have an old community, then happily, in whatever respect its elements are old, you may already have this. If you do not, then construct or reconstruct your structure with elements which promote this gathering up of transformative history, perhaps by finding elements that have undergone transformation so as to be more consistent with interpretation, and that thus lend interpretive depth to the community. If you cannot find them, then create them. Suggestions for such creation will be offered in the second part of this work.

So far we have found the game structure, represented by chess, to be consistently interpretable to the opening postulate, to the derivatives generally, and to **H2** more expansively. A further hypertheme at work within its structure has also been uncovered. Since the effort has just begun we do not yet have the resources to compare the game structure to other structures nearer to its level. Every new endeavor must begin humbly and we will add to our beginning slowly.

Before leaving the game structure, there is another aspect of it which we can address however. From the beginning, with the negatively formulated derivatives of the opening postulate, it has been obliquely suggested that there are types of actions that work against the postulate of interpretation toward meaning and value, which is **H**. There are actions which tend to damage communities of interpretation under hyperthematic structures. One type of action, which occurs in chess as well as most other games, is cheating.

In a sense it is not easy to cheat at chess in the more technical sense—i.e., leaving aside the cases of a stronger player secretly helping a weaker player to win. Nevertheless, if cheating occurs it can take several forms. Its most obvious form would be to take an action with a piece in a way which is not allowed for that piece, e.g., move the piece in a way in which it is not supposed to, move when it is not your turn, move with two or more pieces in a turn, rearrange the positions of the pieces, or substitute pieces for one another. Notice that these types of actions directly affect the hyperthematic structure which the chess game, as a game, is played under.

On the other hand, if someone sits down to play with you and halfway through the game she knocks over the board deliberately, refuses to move her pieces in a reasonable length of time, refuses to move them entirely, or continually moves carelessly or without regard to your moves, then we no longer call this cheating. Such actions appear to have no reference to the structure of the chess game particularly, or even of the broader structure of games. Whatever else they may be called—"being a jerk" comes to mind—they are not usually called cheating. Rather, they appear to us as rude or senseless, a refusal to take part in some communal activity generally. In these cases our reaction is usually: "why did you even bother sitting down to play if you didn't want to?"

Cheating actions however have reference to the community of interpretation which is guided by the hyperthematic structure of the game. Cheating is a form of action, a destabilizing action, which attacks and perhaps damages that structure and the community of interpretation it guides. The rules of the game as embedded in the ranges of transformation of the game elements and joined in by the acting players as a community, make up the structure within which and according to which one willingly interprets certain actions to those of another player. To agree to the structure and then willingly act against the structure is a terrible and potentially destabilizing act for the community. Notice the common phrase: "you broke the rules." We do not defy the rules of a game, or ignore them, or fail to abide by them. No, we break them if we cheat. The use of this expression is not accidental, for only such a structure—a triadic or polyadic structure—as the kind we are considering can be broken in the sense that its elements lose their meaningful relations to one another as a whole when one element is disturbed or eliminated. The cheater is a sort of traitor to her community, whose acts can be countered by other consistent members.

I suggested that cheating is relatively rare, perhaps, in chess in average play. Why? Because the structure itself defends against it. The game structure represented in the game of chess is inherently a stable structure because it promotes simple and definite actions on the part of the elements that form its communities of interpretation. This is part of the constructive action of games in general as structures whose primary goal to bring together elements and harmonize their actions: to "have fun together." There are simple actions available according to the structure, actions which are sub-goals relative to the main goal of the community. Players playing a game in good faith, by the rules, take part in similar simple actions which are initially constructive and sustaining of the chess community. We are offered to play, to take part, to enjoy the game. This aspect of the game—a characteristic of all games because their elements are at a certain range of complexity—is an initial stabilizing characteristic, an opportunity for small projects of community.

Nonetheless, when there is a cheater, the cheater may or may not repent, and he or she may be shunned, but the community which plays chess continues on. If the range of action which the game of chess facilitates were less compact and less simple, then the ability of the community to cope with the destabilizing action of the cheater would be proportionally reduced. If a chess game took years to play, or years to learn to play, then the difficulty of sustaining the chess community by its constructive action alone would quickly become insufficient.

The suggestion is that insofar as the structure is such as to simplify action undertaken in community with it, it will be a stabilizing structure, for it will be evident to any actor in the community that there is some action which can be undertaken to sustain the goal of the community. You move your pawn; she moves her bishop; not too complicated. This is not a restriction of complex actions; rather it is an offering of simple actions which may be interpreted to more complex actions. It is the creation of a smooth range for inspiring interpretations at varying capacities. You learn to play chess from its simple actions so that you may then go on to master more complex actions built upon those simple actions.

One can elaborate this as: **H6**—*Insofar as possible, given the problematic, select transformable elements of a community such that their ranges of transformation promote actions which are simple enough for any actors in the community to carry them out in interpretations which sustain the community.*

In other words, select the transformable elements appropriate to your problematic, for the community, by offering the possibility for action appropriate to the problem. If there were a hundred different pieces in chess or if their movement possibilities where far more complex than they are (for example if we said: the chess knight moves 2 squares and one perpendicular unless it passes the third row in which case it may move 3 squares and 3 perpendicular, unless it manages to reach the back row of the opponent in which case it is reduced to moving one square in any direction), then the potential for destabilizing actions would be increased manyfold.

Cheating, though reduced by this, certainly does happen sometimes. Where is the constructive response within chess, the reconstructive action, for such destabilizing action? For this we look to the special rules of chess. The touch move rule for example, i.e., if you touch a piece you must move it, is very old—from the Middle Ages at least—and was evidently created to combat many forms of cheating. It is this sort of special rule which is the fruit of the reconstructive action of some creative member of the community of chess.

Such rules are fewer than the rules of the game, because they are rules created in response to the destabilizing actions which have affected the game community, actions that the creative moment of the initial creative development of the community was meant to interpretively address. We may call such rules the rules of etiquette of the game. There always appear to be fewer of them for healthy communities because they are due to the reconstructive actions of members of the community. They are the result of the ongoing testing—as in "testing one's patience"—of the structure by those members of its communities who undertake destabilizing actions. Other games have etiquette rules as well and typically cheaters are also not quickly excluded, because the core of the game structure promotes interpretation in general and various actions of etiquette have been added on precisely so as to face the problem of cheaters without resorting to exclusion. So, for example in card games, say Hearts, someone shuffles and someone else cuts the deck, or in Hide and Seek, the counter must count out loud.

The historical origination of chess etiquette is in large part lost to us. Yet the growth of some very recent games is illustrative of the reconstructive response to the breaking of rules within communities guided by the game structure. Cheating most often involves a move which goes contrary to the whole spirit of the game, often making use of a loophole or omission, which is then responded to by some skilled and wise change of the rules. The relatively new game Magic the Gathering—whose popularity is challenging that of chess—illustrates the way in which the game community responds by the skillful formulation of new rules of game etiquette, equivalent to the touch move rule, which address specific attempts to abuse loopholes in the rules. Magic has given rise to dozens of such rules over its twenty-five-year history.

Can there be exclusions used by a consistent game community? Again, yes; but they arise through the adoption of inconsistent tendencies, the tendency to eliminate elements—here players—which runs contrary to **H1** for example. The inconsistent tendencies chip away at the interpretive community rather than building it. They can also arise in response to external attacks on the community, but to the extent that the community takes exclusionary action it is degrading as a community, for defense by exclusion is ultimately inconsistent and highlights the creative poverty of the hyperthematic structure of the community. If the game of bridge is in decline for example, it will do little good to ban collectible card games, or to ban anyone who plays other types of games from playing bridge. A consistent response is to creatively look to the rebuilding of the elements and structure of bridge, its rules, the cards it is played with, and so on.

Can there be games which are false communities? Certainly; but then the game should not be called a game in the first place. It only appears to be one. Such a community is still more extreme in its forms of exclusion. Whenever you have a "game" which prima facie forms its community partially through exclusion, you can be certain either that some core hypertheme behind the game is inconsistent to begin with, or that inconsistent hyperthemes have been tacked on over time.

We can illustrate this with a game whose core assumptions are based on exclusion: fox hunting, even though it is on the porous border between game and sport (and game and sport are cousins in complexity which blend together). It has been much easier historically to say of the "game" of fox hunting that "so and so can't play." "So and so" is excluded because he or she doesn't have a horse, or hounds, or money, or the right connections, etc. The elements of the "game" of fox hunting are anything but simple. They are not suitable for drawing any and all comers of varying capacities into the small projects of interpretive community, as a game like chess does, and hence are inconsistent with **H6**. Moreover, the center of the game, the fox, is going to be physically eliminated, inconsistent with **H** and its derivatives. The exclusionary tendencies are thus plain to see; and in this case, in one area of activity, we can also see that they are side-by-side with more obviously eliminatory tendencies.

I will put aside the consideration of reconstructive modifications of the transformable ranges of the game's acting elements for the time being, however, and take them up again later in other contexts. As will be seen, if the account is consistent, other structures will have their versions of these rules of etiquette, though they may be both more and less complex.

The Hyperthematic Structure of Narrative

The second example of a harmonizing structure of human activity that I will interpret to our ultimate principle is the hyperthematic structure of narrative. Already we are in a better position than when we interpreted the hyperthematic structure of the game in order to disclose its principles. Having those principles in hand, we can look to see whether they also find their place here in the hyperthematic structure of narrative. If the narrative structure has similarities with game structure, still there will be no simple reduction of one to the other. The two structures may use the same hyperthemes, since our suggestion, to be supported as we go, is that *every consistent hypertheme can be applied in any region of experience, with some creativity*; but they will use those hyperthemes at different levels of complexity and upon different elements. It will always be through a higher level of complexity, that of the ultimate postulate **H**, that one will be able to see meaningful contrast. Hence, my comparison of narrative to game must remain—through limitations of space as much as anything else—secondary to my comparison of narrative to the opening principle. It will be enough here to show that the hyperthemes of the hyperthematic structure guiding narrative are not inconsistent with those of the game structure, and that some mutual applications are evident.

The question to ask again to set up our problematic is: How is narrative to be interpreted to our founding hypertheme? How is the more specific structure of narrative to be transformed to the structure of interpretation as such, so that a meaningful linkage is evident?

To begin with, narrative too has its actors engaged as processes of action. Most prominently there is a narrator. The narrator interprets one region of experience to another region of experience across the gap of the problematic of the world process which interests her. On the other side of that gap is the "reader" or "one who is being narrated to,"* whose reading is another process of action, which, according to the hyperthematic structure of narrative, harmonizes with the process of action of the narrator.

To engage our problem here I will deliberately interpret narrative in the sense of *story* as often as I can. I do not consider at first whether the reader disagrees with the narrator. This may well be so, particularly when I move beyond considering narrative as story. In the sense in which I mean narrative here, *if* the narrator narrates and someone attends to her—e.g., reads or listens to her narration—*then* a community of interpretation according to the structure of narrative has been formed.

There are at least two diversities of experience, i.e., the narrator and the listener/reader, and the former is interpreted to the latter through a third, i.e., the narrative itself. Thus, the structure of narrative as a community of interpretation is consistent with hypertheme **H**. Does it also square with our derivative hyperthemes?

We see immediately that it fulfills **H3**, for the communities under the structure are indeed comprised of at least three elements. If a text is written, for example, then the interpretive linkage is narrator–text–reader. There will be further elements as well, both anterior to the narrator and posterior to the reader, and still others to be located between the narrator and text, and between text and reader; recall the examples given in the introduction.

---

*The one who is being narrated to may be a listener, a watcher, etc.

Does it also fulfill **H1**: create structures which do not eliminate signs? Is narrative a structure which uses **H1** to guide its acting elements? Narrative is such a structure. The narrator, e.g., a writer, writes the story and does so through the structure of narrative. That structure in no way prevents the narrator from engaging in it again. A writer may write many books and in doing so may consider a great diversity of problems. On the other side, the reader may read the books of that particular writer, may read many of her books, and may and often does read them over again. Meanwhile, the narrative community of interpretation will accept any and all acting elements to carry out interpretations under it. Just as the hyperthematic structure of the game, e.g., of chess, welcomes all players to play and replay, so the hyperthematic structure of narrative excludes no one from being a narrator, just as it excludes no one from being a listener.

Again, do elements under the structure accord with **H2**? Does the structure engender communities whose elements do not eliminate other elements? It does, and in ways which relate to our considerations of the game. To engage in the structure of narrative as a narrator or listener is to assume the completion of the process of interpretation and thus the integrity of the structure itself, just as to begin a game with someone is to assume the completion of the game.

Remember that I have taken narrative as something like story for the moment. Yet even on a level very far removed indeed from this, we could bring what we might call perverted examples of narrative into line with our account. If a warrior in battle, shouts "die!" to another warrior, then nonetheless, he is interpreting to the other through a very brief narrative and means to make good his interpretation before the elimination of his foe. The inconsistency here is not within the structure of narrative itself, though the narrative may be being used in an inconsistent or destabilizing way as I will show later.

It is doubtful even, whether in the history of the world, there has ever been very much narration such that the narrator engages in the community of narrative structure with the intent to signify to the *listener*, his or her instant elimination. Here I have in mind something such as: "while reading this you will be eliminated"—a more constricted cousin of the above warrior example. Even if there are such cases they assume such inclusion into the community of narrative structure as will complete the interpretation in question, in a meaning which gets across to the listener, whether the motive be revenge, domination, etc. In the old Bond movies, Blofeld or other villains always utter some variation of: "you are about to die Mr. Bond. . . ." But they never attempt the deed until Bond has well and truly savored the meaning of the words . . . and so they always miss their chance.

Indeed, reflect on the history of narrative and you will see that the whole thrust of narrative structure works rather more against this. For example, there are narratives which constitute *warnings* from the narrator to the listener. Such narratives postulate the hyperthematic structure of narrative not only because it will not eliminate an element of its own community, i.e., the listener, but because *it aims to prevent elimination of elements of yet further communities that the listener has interpretive connections to*. Here I have in mind such narratives as prophetic warnings urging reform, tragedies, fairy tales which issue moral lessons, and so forth.

Clearly, in this most general respect, narrative structure tends to prevent elimination of elements of its own community, but moreover—and here we have disclosed already a hypertheme which, though in no way specific to the hyperthematic structure of narrative, finds in that structure one of its greatest exemplars—it tends to stabilize other communities by inhibiting the elimination of their elements. We can elaborate it as: **H7**—*Construct communities such that they tend to engage the elements of other communities and prevent them from elimination.*

We must go further still however, for just as the game structure allowed transformation of its acting elements, so also the structure of narrative allows the transformation of elements. This consideration leads us immediately into rich interpretive territory.

The structure of narrative has evidently had a part in human attempts to interpret experience for as far back as we can see in our history. Writing dates to approximately the fourth millennium BC in the Mesopotamian region and possibly to the mid-sixth millennium BC in China. Certainly spoken narrative predates this considerably.

The elements making up the structure of harmonization of the narrative are fluid and transformable. A great variety of media, which are the signs of the transformation of those elements, show it. Narrative has used the spoken word, as when ancient man memorized his tales of the gods, passing them on through generations. Narrative has used the picture-word as in Egyptian hieroglyphics and perhaps Paleolithic cave paintings. It has used picture-signs in a more complex and yet still more fluid way in the Latin alphabet and the Chinese *hanzi*. Narrative has mixed the spoken word with music, as in opera and poetry, and has used purely musical elements, such as the tone poems of various composers. Narrative has used the moving image in film, mixed with all of the above.

Moreover, just as for games—perhaps more so—the elements of narrative retain a significance of meaning which carries the transformation that they have gone through from being signs less suitable to harmonized action to elements more suitable to harmonized action. Words for example, have an etymological history, and their history captures their meaning as the gradual adaptation to the use of a community of interpretation. If you take a word with any considerable etymological background, e.g., an English word, and you look at the variants in its background, e.g., old Norse variants, old German variants, etc., then you see how the word has come down to us as a sign of an element of narrative structure which has interpreted diverse cultures, i.e., regions of experience, to one another.

Consider a fairytale as a type of story. Originally such a story will no doubt have sprung from a certain experience. But very often—as in chess—it will have sprung from experience according to structures that did not abide by the hyperthemes which we have disclosed so far. Perhaps, for example, such structures *did not* prevent elimination of their own elements. Such structures may have been an apparent, or, as I have called it, a *false community*. In other words, either the elements, or the so-called community which they were in, failed to prevent the elimination of elements. Somebody died or was killed, or somebody lost his place in the community, or somebody was pushed out of the community, and so forth.

The tale of Hansel and Gretel for example, possibly far older than the incarnations we know it in, may be considered as a narrative which signifies some such instability of community. An element which tends toward exclusion—the bad stepmother—enters the community, i.e., the woodcutter's family. The children are excluded from their family. They begin the search for another community. They encounter yet another inconsistent element—the witch—who promises what is in fact, despite appearances, a false community, here a community that eats its members.

The children are excluded from their original community of the family, but faced with an even worse community they refocus themselves as communities of selfhood, interpreting their own pasts to their futures in various ways. Hansel thinks ahead in dropping pebbles in the tale's beginning and in showing the witch a bone instead of his finger; Gretel meanwhile acts alone to save her brother by anticipating the witch's intent in testing the oven. Both help one another on the basis of the memory of their original community of the family—they are siblings and owe one another help through that community. Eventually they kill the witch, the unstable element of the false community created when the witch took them in while promising to help them, but meaning to eat them. The children then return and rejoin their father, reconstituting the original consistent community.

The tale has variations but in the one I am considering we see that in the first instance the offending element—the stepmother—is arbitrarily removed by "fate," while in the second instance the offending element—the witch—is eliminated. The destabilizing effect of such offending elements and communities based upon them is thus highlighted. Exclusionary and eliminatory elements eventually perish—one way or another—as the tale warns us. They also damage consistent communities before perishing: the stepmother wrecks the original family for example. Moreover, they influence elements of consistent communities into adopting and applying tendencies which are ultimately inconsistent with value: the stepmother convinces the father to abandon the children against his better judgment; the witch ultimately teaches Gretel—incorrectly as later chapters will suggest—that the tendency to eliminate, here by killing the witch, is a consistent response to attacks upon one's community.

The narrator may even convey to a reflective reader aspects that are left directly unsaid, but which are felt in the strangeness of the tale. That "all anxiety was at an end, and they lived together in perfect happiness," as one version of the tale says, thickly glosses over the outcome that a more contemporary account of such an experience would present. One can imagine that the PTSD of a ten-year-old boy locked in a cage for weeks waiting to be eaten or a ten-year-old girl who had just shoved an adult into an oven and listened to her scream horribly while burning up, might last awhile, making the happiness not quite perfect and the anxiety all too present.

A great deal comes across then in such old tales as a warning regarding the effects of exclusionary and eliminatory tendencies. We can postulate that these exclusions and eliminations were part of some original experience of instability of community; historical research might enlighten us further. The point is, however, that the hyperthematic narrative structure has facilitated and provoked the transformation of the original elements into the tale we now have. The tale stands as a warning from narrator to listener, a warning that excluding elements fail the community and ultimately themselves: don't act like the father did, and don't act like the stepmother and the witch did. Fairy tales are not terribly subtle.

The narrative structure as a community of interpretation, including the listener and the narrator, has allowed the narrator to bring the original experience up to us as listeners. It has harmonized the original offense through reinterpreting it through a new structure with consistent and transformable elements, respectively, i.e., the narrator, listener, narrative structure, and the signifying words of the narrative (bad stepmother, faithful but fallible father, evil witch, siblings who support one another). The postulated original experience can now be part of a consistent community of interpretation. The story can be told and retold and listened to again and again. There can be transformation from witch, to hexe, to sorcière; there can be transformation of the story setting, from a German setting, to a French setting, to a Japanese setting; from a period in the Middle Ages, to one in the twenty-first century.

Narrative structure thus abides by the hyperthemes we have so far disclosed, and it does so very successfully. Here is a structure which has the potential to, and has, harmonized the actions of multiple actors across spaces, times, and tremendously different environments.

Consider the Bible. We cannot hope to grasp its significance in its full complexity, but in broad strokes we can say that those who developed the Bible developed it by dipping again and again into that pool of interpretation which is the hyperthematic structure of narrative. In one aspect, the experiences we postulate behind the Bible have been interpreted from narrator to narrator. The Bible is an artifact-sign of layers of narrative interpretation built upon earlier layers of narrative interpretation. Thus, someone originally narrates scattered experiences—experiences of those of the region inhabited by the Semitic peoples of the Middle East—into the narrative of a people, the Israelites; thus again, the prophets narrate this experience of the people back to their later selves as a people. But later prophets interpret earlier prophets again through the structure of narrative, and later still, Christian elements, i.e., acting narrators within Christianity, engage in yet further interpretation through the narrative structure.

In a second aspect however, with respect to the Bible, experience has been interpreted from narrator *qua* reader to a further reader. Some readers will never re-narrate the signs of the Bible. Some will. Each new reader has the potential through the structure to become a narrator in her own right.

The mother reads the book while the child listens. In doing so the mother becomes a narrator and later the child will grow to be a narrator. Every fresh reading is a new narration, which if it does not rewrite the text, nonetheless draws the unique experience of the reader into itself according to the structure of narrative. We tend not to read out loud and so we forget the effect even of our own reading capacities—not to mention life experience—on the interpretation of a text. If books were read out loud there would be as many new narratives as readers for the "same" text; indeed there are if we reflect a little. At the same time every listening, though it does not rewrite the text, nonetheless draws the unique experience of the listener into itself. The overall effect of this incredibly fluid structure is a rarely surpassed harmonizing of action which spreads out and unites the actors temporally well beyond the acting elements as embodied and embedded in the time process in the narrow sense.

Every time the Bible has been read there has been a new participation in the community of narrative structure between the process of action comprising its narration and the process of action of the reader. In the act of reading the Bible untold millions have *willingly* harmonized their action both with the narrators of its story and with other readers so as to participate in the hyperthematic community of narrative. *If you now pick up the Bible and read it you are engaging in a process of action which has its definite and harmonious relation with every other reader who has ever engaged in that process of action, not to mention the army of narrators who have produced the biblical story. It has this relation, not despite, but by virtue of the principles underlying the hyperthematic structure of narrative, which allow the transformation of the elements of its community of interpretation.*

Of course not every narrative is as successful as the Bible. Yet many narratives are just as successful, from the works of Plato to the *Bhagavad Gita*. This prompts us to ask why? Answering this question leads back to the structure of narrative. We can postulate that the relatively failed narrative has failed somehow to abide by our opening hypertheme **H** and its derivatives, or to principles more specific to narrative.

A narrative might be produced which fails to attract anyone to attend to it. What has happened? The narrator may have failed to bridge the gap between those diversities of experience which compose her problematic. Interpretation has then failed, or so far failed at least. We cannot assume permanent failure, for then, contrary to our hyperthematic assumptions, we would have a disjointed world, a problem without an answer, and no reality of value at all.

We can assume *local* failure however, i.e., the narrator has engaged a problematic without the proper resources to approach it. An example of this would be—ostensibly—a work that does not impart meaning at all.

Yet this is rare, for the structure of narrative is *such* a fluid structure and allows *such* a wealth of transformations, that *failure in narration is in some sense proportional to not engaging in the community of interpretation which is narrative*. For example, short of the book that is never written, every book seems to find *some* listener. Even bad books have their readers and in the very worst case the narrator often becomes his own future reader: "Oh god . . . did I write *that* . . . ?"

Then again, selecting a problematic, which has already found meaningful interpretations, can also lead to relative failure of a narrative. You can select the problematic of *Romeo and Juliet* and rewrite it, but you will be hard-pressed to better Shakespeare. Even in such a case, the narrator has failed to engage in the community of interpretation which is narrative. Perhaps he wrote a cheap knockoff merely to make a few bucks, which is a way of not really engaging in the community. Perhaps he simply failed to engage in the community as a reader, i.e., a listener, who, had he participated as a reader in the great community under narrative structure by reading broadly and deeply before he began his narration, would never have merely copied Shakespeare. The above are failures to engage in the community, though not yet deliberate destabilizing actions.

But just as the most general structure of interpretation has its potential to suffer destabilizing actions, and just as the hyperthematic structure of game can face such actions, so also the hyperthematic structure of narrative can face them. Such actions take an interesting form with regard to narrative, a form which is rarely acknowledged. If there is a book or narrative which is *not meant to be read by some*, then this is an elimination—more specifically an exclusion here—of elements from the community of narrative, an elimination inconsistent with our derivative hyperthemes. Such a narrative arises from an intent counter to the goal of the community of narrative.

In this case it may be that the narrator is an element of a false community that attempts to exclude other elements, and so through the inconsistent action within his false community, he acts in a destabilizing way toward the structure of narrative. He attacks the community of the structure of narrative. There are both mild forms of this and stronger forms. There is genre writing for example, the work of science fiction deliberately written only for the science fiction crowd, or the mystery novel only for the mystery novel crowd. Stronger forms would include the book of secrets, meant for "our cult alone"; the partisan political narrative meant for our political group alone; and—if we depart yet further from narrative as story—the top-secret report "for your eyes only." Moreover, such attempts at exclusion using the narrative structure, are by no means confined to written narrative. The gossip told behind someone's back, which they are not meant to hear, also exemplifies well enough the destabilizing action toward a community under the structure of narrative.

The community of narrative structure provides for initial constructive actions to support the community of narrative, akin to those in the game community under the game structure. There are simple and evident actions to be undertaken by any and all members of the community, consistent with **H6**. Write or tell the tale faithfully and in doing so you harmonize your actions with the community of narrative past, present, and future. Read or listen attentively and again you harmonize your actions with that community.

Moreover, there are other actions, often combined with the above type, which engage in interpretations within the community that have a particularly healing, or reconstructive character. Such reconstructive actions are called upon as interpretive responses to such narrative products as *Mein Kampf*, or Mao's *Little Red Book*, which are the extremes of the use and thus abuse of the structure of narrative for exclusionary or eliminative action. Members of the narrative community often make the most artful and creative advances under the narrative structure in response to abuses within and against the community of narrative interpretation. The literary career of Aleksandr Solzhenitsyn, for example, illustrates a reconstructive engagement of the many destabilizing actions which can threaten the community of narrative interpretation both from within—in written propaganda—and from without, in the manifold techniques of seizing and silencing narrative. Eventually, as Solzhenitsyn proved—and as Chinese activist Liu Xiaobo, near death even as I write this, will no doubt one day prove—all such attempts fail before a steady determination to use the interpretive expansion of narrative as its resource in order to heal devaluating acts.

If we have now some sense of why some narratives are unsuccessful, nonetheless we have not quite arrived at an answer to why narratives are successful. On the basis of the view of the world, which we accept if we accept the opening hypertheme, what is always at stake is interpretation itself, i.e., the world as a problematic. Success in our sense of harmonization of action will thus be a matter of bringing actors together into community to engage in a problematic. On the level of narrative structure proper, this must account for the enormous success of narrative. Our interpretive engagement with the world process results in signs of varying complexity which others take up. These signs give rise to further problematics of experience in turn.

Beginnings and the Hyperthematic Structures of Game and Narrative | 49

If, in this regard, the diversity of experience in those problematics that you present to those who are listening to you is *so* diverse as to be *practically* unbridgeable as a problem, than the value engendering play of interpretation falters and stops. If on the other hand you can introduce a problematic, not nakedly, but such that the resources for its possible solution come with it, then you draw further actors into a community. In other words, a successful hyperthematic structure introduces neither a problem without a degree of solution, nor a solution without a further interpretable problem, though the proportion between these may be stretched very far indeed. The structure of narrative does just this at its level of complexity. Someone narrates and in narrating presents a problematic together with the resources for further solution. Someone listens and in listening becomes both part of the solution and passes on a new problematic.

We can interpretively compare this at once with the game structure. Across the community guided by the game structure the result is, e.g., a chess game. Across the community guided by the narrative structure the result is, e.g., a book. In comparison with the book, the chess game as a problematic does not tend to increase the structured problematicity of the world beyond itself to a similarly high degree. One player plays with another player and with respect to the game they tend toward being equal elements.

The game structure is symmetrically tending. That is to say *nothing within the game structure itself*, no hypertheme, tends to promote the spread of the structure. Chess is indeed promoted, but it is promoted through another hyperthematic structure, e.g., narrative, in which we tell one another about this interesting game. Narrative, on the other hand, initiates an interpretive directionality that moves sectionally across the world process. It begins an expansive series in which someone narrates, someone listens and narrates in turn, and so on.

It would seem that narrative as a harmonizing structure is more successful than game if the definition of success is the number of actors acting together in community under the aegis of the structure. Narrative *lures* further actors, whereas game structure is merely *open* to further actors. If this is so, then another principle can be formulated, this time arrived at by considering two types of hyperthematic structures. The principal will be **H8**—*to create hyperthematic structures which engage further actors, insofar as possible make the sectional acting elements of those structures transformable rather than replaceable.* In other words, in chess, with respect to the game itself, any player is simply replaceable with another; whereas in a narration even though narrator can become listener and listener can become narrator, there is a directional transformation involved which initiates a new problematic in a new "dimension," or aspect.

Is this principle, offered to account for the great success of narrative, also consistent with the specific structures created by narrative? Apparently so; I offered as a tentative definition of the success of specific structures, that the narrative garners many listeners, or, e.g., a book such as the Bible is read widely—forms a community of interpretation—both sectionally and parallel to the time process. One can go further though. If we can postulate that a transformation between elements which offers further problematics is the key to success, then we can further postulate that this transformation is made possible by the fluidity or range of the transformable elements themselves of any given hyperthematic structure. In other words, still in terms of our chosen examples, words are going to be better than chess pieces at facilitating transformations, if for no other reason than that there are more types and more of them.

This may be easier to see if we first compare chess to checkers, a game community that is also guided by the hyperthematic structure of the game. Checkers has fewer sectional elements, or types of pieces that differ from one another than chess, in fact only two types—the regular piece and the queened piece—in comparison with the six types of chess. Consequently, checkers has fewer possible interpretations than chess, i.e., fewer possible harmonic interpretations as solutions to its problematic. Under the structure of narrative the equivalent of the game of checkers will be, e.g., a particular book under a particular genre of writing. Just as in games, a particular book will have both sectional and parallel transformable elements. And just as in games, some books will have fewer possible interpretations than others, e.g., a toddler's first book as compared to Plato's *Republic*.

The words of the book are its transformable elements, just as the chess pieces are the transformable elements of chess. Each word is a signifying locus which binds together, time process parallel interpretation, i.e., interpretation from the past into the future, with time process sectional interpretation, i.e., interpretation between experiences in a relatively same time. But the hyperthematic structure of narrative allows a vast wealth of these elements to be used in interpretations as compared to the hyperthematic structure of the game as exemplified in chess, and as compared to most games.[10]

But just so, the book that results from the structure of narrative invites proportionally richer and further interpretation than does the particular game, and this has nothing to do with the fact of the book as an object in the world. For the reality of the book in its fullness is the interpretive transformation from narrator to reader and nothing less than this. We can see this by noting that a book with blank pages would be no true book at all, although it would be a book-like object and we can see it even better by noting that a real object will result from the game structure of chess just as it will from written narration.

The famous "Game of the Century" played between Bobby Fisher and Donald Byrne on October 17, 1956, in New York City, for example, is the analog of a particular book in a particular genre. Relative to the game structure of chess, it is a great and famous game because it makes the most of the possibilities of transformation inherent in its game structure. Yet it cannot compete with a great literary work according to our definition of success. You can replay this famous game, just as you can re-read a book, i.e., a narrative, but to do so is to make a simple replacement with regard to the game structure of one set of players for another. Indeed, you can even replay the game by playing both sides. And you can reinterpret the game, but only if you step outside the game structure of chess. Insofar as the game's elements admit of sectional transformation, they are deliberately limited more or less to the six types of pieces of chess with their particular possibilities of movement. Insofar as the game's elements admit of parallel transformation, they signify, as we saw, a transformation parallel to the time process from military elements to elements capable of promoting harmonization of action. Thus the chess pieces are fluid, but not *so* fluid.

By contrast, the words with which we narrate books are incredibly fluid with regard to both their range of sectional and parallel transformations. Every use of words in a book presents a considerable further problematic, both as to how the words are interpreted to the multitude of other words in the book and how they are interpreted to their whole past process of transformation which constitutes their significance. The relative success of great works of narrative, such as the Bible, depends on combining the tremendous degree of fluidity of elements with as much structure as is possible under the aegis of narrative. This is to pass on both the hyperthematic structure, i.e., the interpretively consistent structure under which communities engage a problematic of a certain range of experiential complexity, with transformable elements admitting an appropriate degree of transformation, and to pass on some solution of the engaged problematic, i.e., a partial interpretation.

Or to put it another way: the chess game is passed on but not *qua* game, rather as something relatively fixed, whereas the narrative is passed on *qua* narrative with all that this implies in terms of further interpretive possibilities. The issue is one of degree, however. The first book of the toddler is far from the great work of narrative. Nonetheless, it leaves open the problematic to some degree, whereas the completed or solved chess game does so to a far lesser degree.

Thus, we can postulate another principle related to the previous one: **H9**—*in the creation of communities under hyperthematic structures, increasing the number or degree of transformable elements such that they pass on both structure and problematic, increases the growth of the structure at the expense of solution of the problematic; while decreasing the number or degree of transformable elements increases the chance of solution within the structure at the expense of its growth.*

Therefore, in order to increase value through expansion of interpretation, adopt the growth tendency whenever possible, but fall back on the solution tendency as needed. In other words, the game of chess will promote local harmony—getting people together to play together—better than a book; but the book will tend to spread the structure of narrative far and wide promoting a wider harmony at the expense of definiteness of solution.

That we can plausibly postulate this can be shown with one further consideration. If you don't like chess then you don't play it, but if you don't like a book you will often read and reinterpret it deliberately, i.e., criticize it. The book has influenced you despite yourself. Such is the interpretive success of the hyperthematic structure of narrative. Chess is a fluid structure that produces a *relatively* static harmonization of action as a result, whereas the narration of a book produces a semi-harmonized result that promotes further and thus more complex harmonization of action.

2

Hyperthematic Structures of Dance and Music

The Hyperthematic Structure of Dance

The sketching in of the hyperthemes of our Hyperthematic endeavor is well begun. A number of principles have been disclosed by interpreting structures which promote harmony of action to our opening hypertheme of the interpretability of the world as such. The principles are open to further musement, but so far a good indicator is that I have been able to link the principles of one type of structure to that of another, i.e., the principles are consistent with multiple structures, even if used to varying degrees in those structures.

I already noted the difference in emphasis with regard to the elements operating under the first two hyperthematic structures. You may already see how a game is somewhat like a very simple narrative being told by one player to another. You may also have a sense of how a narrative is somewhat like a highly complex game in which the moves of the players—narrator and reader—are respectively: moves of skillful interpretation which join problematic and solution under structure, and reinterpreting responses, which then issue yet further problematic and solution. The structure of narrative promotes harmony of action across time and space in a broad way. The game structure promotes harmony of action in a less broad way. Just as the hyperthematic structure of narrative will be more likely than the game structure to harmonize action between actors on opposite sides of the globe,[1] so it will be more likely that action is harmonized between narrator and reader across a time span of two millennia than that action is harmonized between two game players across a time span of two millennia, or even two years.

Already our structures present us with something of a hierarchy, wherein narrative is more broadly harmonizing than game structure. It might be useful then to consider a harmonizing structure that appears to be less broad than game structure. This suggests the next move in our expansive exploration: the interpretation of the hyperthematic structure of dance to the opening hypertheme. In terms of success in the spreading of harmonizing structure at the expense of solution, if game structure lies below narrative structure, then we can postulate that the hyperthematic structure of dance in turn lies still further below game structure.

Back to our usual question to set up our problematic: How is dance to be interpreted to the opening hypertheme? What is the meaningful linkage which allows the interpretive transformation between the structure of interpretation as such, postulated in **H**, and the more specific structure of dance? Secondarily, is the structure of dance consistent with the hyperthemes disclosed from the other structures?

Clearly dance is everywhere in and even beyond human culture, even more so than the structures we have considered already. A brief survey of what falls under the heading of dance will include solo dancing, dancing with a partner, dancing with multiple partners, dancing between multiple partners, dancing according to pure rhythm, dancing with music, dancing without music, dancing with nonhuman objects or extensions, dancing in and on media such as water or ice, dancing between humans and animals, dancing between animals, dancing between insects. And under all of these categories there appear to be forms and variants innumerable.

The pervasiveness of dance is somehow bound up with a more localized set of communities. Although dance is practiced throughout the world, forms of its practice appear to be locally initiated, and therefore all the more diverse because of this. Dance appears to spring up locally apart from the sectional transformations by which the structure of narrative, for example, propagates itself. There appear to be more forms of dance than forms of narrative. For the most part forms of dance appear to just spring up not merely within cultures, but in smaller aggregates of humans, as well as animals; think, for example, of how often people do a little Julie Andrews style twirl, or dance an impromptu jig, to express to others some momentary satisfaction.

Dance is one of the harmonizing structures of human action which brings people about as close together as is physically possible. Sex *can* bring closer physical togetherness than dance, but just as often, in some variations, it brings less physical togetherness than dance and less harmonization of action. Dance represents, therefore, an opportunity for considering how deeply—if at all—the harmonization of action is bound up or constricted by what we sometimes unreflectively take to make possible all our "real world" actions: the physicality of the body.

It seems that the hyperthematic structure of dance agrees with our founding hypertheme. Just as for game and narrative there are actors engaged in lines of action. If there is a dancer who interprets some region of experience to another dancer, then there is the community of interpretation—the dance—between them as the third. The diversities of experience which are interpreted through the dance are particularly physical regions of experience, i.e., a physical movement is initiated by a dancer, which interprets a physical experience across the gap of the problematic—a largely physical problematic of spatiality—to another dancer who initiates a further physical movement as a response and harmonizes her process of action with the first dancer. Shortly we will try to better interpret what we mean by physical.

Hence the structure of dance agrees with our opening postulate **H**. Does it also agree with our derivative hyperthemes? It contains three elements at least, initiating dancer, responding dancer, and the dance as community of interpretation, thus it is consistent with **H3**.

It is also consistent with **H1**, for, as a community of interpretation, it is a structure which does not eliminate signs. The dancer and a counterpart dancer, or dancers, are free to engage in the structure of the dance again and again. They are free to harmonize their actions in any one of the multiple solutions of the dance structure, i.e., genres of dance.

Is the hyperthematic structure of dance also consistent with **H2**? Does it guide its elements into actions other than eliminating one another? Like both game structure and narrative structure, it does. First, it assumes a completion of the process of interpretation. One dances *a dance*, which is *a type of dance*, often part of a larger substructure again called *a dance*—e.g., the high school graduation dance—and both are substructures within the hyperthematic structure of dance. Hence dance has its equivalent to the chess game, and the particular book, with regard to the structures we have already considered, and engaging in the structure of dance is to assume the completion of the process of interpretation which in turn assumes the integrity of the elements engaged in that interpretation. You do not eliminate your partner in a dance.

Are there not free dances someone will ask? Are there not types of dance in which a partner—if not eliminated outright—is nonetheless rendered largely irrelevant? Here one may have in mind forms of popular dancing. To this objection I reply that such examples as we can conjure up are both rare and recent developments in the history of dance. Moreover, they retain most of the structure of a community. People dancing disco, or other relatively free forms of dance with pop music, nonetheless dance *with other people*. Indeed, this is part of their appeal, i.e., they allow the largest groups of people to harmonize action according to an extremely localized problematic which is strongly biased toward the region of physical experience. Thus you can find crowds of thousands dancing—however vaguely—on New Year's Eve for example, but this would be impossible for other types of dance.

If I remember adolescence aright, it was a rare bird who stepped out to dance alone ahead of everyone else. This is a matter of courage in part, but more a matter of the lure of dance as a lure to interpret the body physically to *other people*. Dancing in its contemporary popular forms is: "let's dance!" On the other hand, insofar as such types of dancing become less and less structured, they lose their appeal, because the simplicity of solution which they offer to the problematic engaged by dance provides far less range for meaningful interpretations. In effect, we get bored of such substructures and when the group begins to melt away, and the community degrades toward the mere group, this feeling is increased all the more. The speed at which types of contemporary mass dance—such as disco—can arise and decline illustrates this.[2] Inevitably, when such types of mass dance recover from decline, if at all, it is on the basis of the building up of a history. Thus forty years from its speedy decline, disco may be undergoing a revival.

If even the mere lure of being within a group, regardless of interpreting one another, becomes irrelevant, then the dance has arguably become not dance but something else. Contemporary activities such as slam dancing or mosh dancing illustrate this. Departing ever further from what can be called dancing, they are influenced by many factors outside of the structure of dance, e.g., group drug use.

What about solo dancing? Does this make a community according to a single element in a way that would be inconsistent with our derivative hyperthemes? I suggest that it doesn't. The belly dancer, for example, is engaged not as one might think in an harmonizing of action with regard to their audience—for one may dance with no audience—but rather *in an interpretive harmonizing of action with their choreographed model*.

The use of choreography with regard to dance illustrates the depth of dance as an interpretive structure. The recorded use of choreography is some five hundred years old, and its unrecorded use may be as old as dance itself.

Choreography is a model of a process of action, which a dancer engages in, completes, and later in time interprets a further process of action to. In the absence of another dancer or dancers as partner, the solo dancer follows her choreographed model, interpreting her new action to her old action and trying to harmonize them as closely as possible. The dancer remains engaged in the community of interpretation of dance in the sense of a transformation of elements parallel to the time process. She is dancing with her past self and dancing for her future self. This is a community of selfhood like that of someone who promises to her future self to carry out some act, the person of our introduction who mails the letter to herself to receive tomorrow, and so forth. Here the elements of the community are the dancer's current and former self as engaging processes of action and the community of interpretation according to the hyperthematic structure of dance; while the value aspect of the interpretation is known most often under the name of *practicing*, which engages value as having "become better" or perhaps having "danced perfectly," on the basis of "having practiced" the model of action as it was run through alone or with a choreographer.

Recall the examples from our earlier structures. Chess also has its practice. It has its models, its famous games and classic openings in which the player interprets his actions in order to better himself. Narrative too has its models. For example, the old rule in writing is, if you want to write better according to a particular style, examine many and varied examples of books written in that style.

The point has been reached to suggest a further hypertheme: **H10**—*to enhance the meaning of the transformable elements within hyperthematic structures with regard to interpretations parallel to the time process, creatively postulate historic or futuristic interpretive models for the elements of your structure to interpret themselves to.*

In other words, if you have or can find historical processes of action which appear to be consistent as possible solutions with regard to your hyperthematic structure, then hold them up as models and interpret your current process of action to them. And if you cannot find such historical processes as models, then postulate them freely and once again interpret your current experience to them.

To give an example, if you are engaged in a hyperthematic structure dealing with the political realm of experience, then your model might be the great statesmen and stateswomen of the past. If none are consistent with your hyperthematic structure, then by creative postulation, correct their defects by all means. If Lincoln could have been a better statesmen had he done so and so, then hypothesize that he had done so and so, and then use this as your model. Or create a model from scratch by running a fictional actor through your structure to attain by interpretation a solution of your problematic, which will become your standard. In other words do a test run. Either way, having selected a model, you will have initiated a standard *for practice*, and you will be realizing the world as interpretive meaning, and particularly your own community of selfhood in relation to more complex communities within the world process.

Notice something further though. We already remarked—somewhat mysteriously perhaps in the context of the hyperthematic viewpoint thus far—that the hyperthematic structure of dance deals primarily with what we can call physical regions of experience. It seems at first that this is best described in terms of elements of the community of dance, the dancers, being literally "close" to one another. Yet the solo dancer has no partner to be "close to" in anything like the usual sense of what we mean by closeness, no "dancing cheek to cheek." Clearly the solo dancer is interpreting the problematic of an *extremely physical* region of experience, perhaps even more so than the dancing partners. Watch, for example, the ways in which Canadian dancer Margie Gillis interprets the ranges of action of embodiment, ways which are very much alone and yet very much physical in all obvious aspects.

What on earth do we mean then by "close"? The answer is suggested by the considerations which led me to advance **H10**. Not only solo dancers engage in choreography. Dancers in types of dance in which multiple dancers participate also use choreography. In both cases the dancers are engaged in processes of action that are interpreted to other processes of action. In both cases there is interpretation to choreographed models in the direction parallel to the time process, i.e., the past or future of the dancer. Yet in the case of a dance with multiple partners, there is a further sectional interpretation of one dancer to her partner, whereas in the case of the solo dancer there is no such sectional interpretation, or, if you count the audience, a minimal one, for the audience is usually outside the dance *qua dancing*, a suggestion which I will strengthen further on. And I suggested that the solo dancer can seem more physical than the dancing partners, skillful belly dancers almost seem to be dancing with themselves in the most sensual possible manner.

Now why should this be so? The explanation, given the foregoing, is that the solo dancer *is deliberately rejecting one of her axes of interpretation, specifically, the sectional one, across the time process*; and to reject or diminish one or both of the axes of interpretation is to reduce the possibilities of interpretation.

The solo dancer has one model as a dancer, if any, the model of the choreography. She has a standard with which she wills to harmonize her action. The success of her dance is measured, if it is measured, by how *closely* she follows her model. This then, is what we mean by "close."

Dancing partners have two models, the model of the choreography and the model of the partner. There is thus room for more complex interpretation. But insofar as there is more room for interpretation, there is proportionally less "closeness." As more dancers are added according to the type of dance, potential interpretations increase in proportion as "closeness" decreases. Yet the dance remains proportionally engaged in a problematic of the physical region of experience because the structure continues to promote closeness to the axis of interpretation parallel to the time process, i.e., the dance troupe follows its choreographed model created in the past and interprets it to the future.

If a group of dancers ignores the parallel axis, as in forms of popular dancing among large numbers of participants, then nonetheless the dancers retain one another as models and the dance is particularly physical in the alternate way. If, finally, a "dancer" has neither a parallel nor sectional model, then we have pure physicality, but arguably no longer dance. I have deliberately ignored the function of music so far, but will examine it shortly.

How closely you interpret your models depends on the complexity of your models. If your models are postulated interpretations that are narrow in one or both of their axes of interpretation, then you follow them all the more easily. The structure of dance always tends to use simple interpretations as its models, e.g., with respect to the parallel axis dance does not use choreographic models which take months, or even days, to perform; and with respect to the sectional axis the partner as a model is postulated as one or several rather than multitudes, and as in the same time.

As dance moves away from this simplicity it begins to move toward the use of other hyperthematic structures. Ballet, for example, is moving toward narrative because the model which is being interpreted to is a model of narrative. In that model, there may be a great many processes of action—usually human actors—a context of the world process—e.g., a selection of temporal history and of human or natural environments created within that history; there may be a context of interactions—both consistent and inconsistent—between processes at a level of complexity which narrative can readily engage successfully, but which dance cannot unless it moves toward narrative, e.g., a plot which presents to us revenge, faithfulness, perseverance through adversity, and so forth.

Other structures besides dance are consistent with these considerations as well. In terms of game structure, chess has its models, and the particular range and degree of its models determine our sense of its physicality. Chess is less physical than dance, but more physical than narrative. The range and degree of models, which we interpret to in narrative, may be said to be much wider than in both dance and chess. Sport would no doubt fall between game structure and dance structure if it were explored.

A further illustration of the above can be found with respect to animals. Humans dance, but so do animals. Among humanlike behaviors that we interpret animals as displaying without any human training, dance is one of the most preeminent. From seahorses to jumping spiders to blue-footed boobies and grebes, animals dance.[3] The above interpretation of dance with regard to its physicality can incorporate this. Clearly animals appear to interpret signs, but what is at issue is the complexity of those signs. Animals dance, but we do not view them, apart from very rare instances, as engaging in narrative. Yet if animals can engage in processes of action such as those we have considered above, then we can postulate that this is because they can engage in the interpretation of models on a very simple level, just as humans do when they engage in the hyperthematic structure of dance. We cannot follow this lead further here, but it is suggestive; it appears to be consistent with our current knowledge of animals, and it bears further exploration.

Moving in a Whiteheadian direction, a fluid interpretive definition of *increasing physicality* can now be postulated as: *a transformation from wider to narrower complexity of interpretation with respect to a postulated model*. Following on this, the converse is a fluid interpretive definition of *increasing mentality* as: *a transformation from narrower to wider complexity of interpretation with respect to a postulated model*.

The stage is thus set to elaborate another hypertheme: **H11**—*to move the range of your hyperthematic structure toward a more local and physical harmonization of action, simplify, and reduce (but do not eliminate) the models to be interpreted to, and do the reverse to move the range of your structure toward a more broad and mental harmonization of action; and, in order to engage in the experience of your problematic in the most efficient way, postulate a diverse range of models which can be interpreted to*. In other words, to create a hyperthematic structure which efficiently promotes the harmonizing of actions, you must be able to harmonize actions at the local and physical level as well as the broad and mental level. The more diverse your range of models is, the better your structure will be able to do so. There will be a trade-off between efficiency and complexity and every structure will only be able to engage a certain region of experience. But if you want to get the best range of solution for the particular region of experience, which is your problematic, then *at least diversify your models to engage fully with the range of that experience.*

Having suggested the above I also add the following. A model in the sense we use it here, is a community of signs within experience, holding meaning. Hence, the choreography model is a community of past memory, history, imagination, etc., linked to present experience.

If the model is more complex than our own community of our selfhood—e.g., as when the life of some great and inspiring person becomes a model for us—then we aspire to the model because in it is the promise of meaning and value.

I may aspire to someday dance as well as Fred Astaire for example. I can never simply *become* Fred Astaire though, for the very reasons which have just allowed us to redefine the physical and mental. To become Fred Astaire would be to physically become him ultimately, because the decreasing possibility of interpretation between myself—the aspiring dancer—and Fred, would eventually—ostensibly—arrive at no possibility of interpretation, i.e., no difference between my Fred model and myself. This loss of problematic and closing up of interpretive freedom *is* physicality viewed fluidly (as a tendency).

But this implies that our interpretations to other communities of selfhood (other lives) as models is always only pragmatic, as an expansion of our own processes in *practice* which, when consistent, understands that practice, or *copying*, must always give way to the creativity of interpretation that passes beyond those models which we delight to *learn* from, but cannot consistently stop at by being *the same as*. Further into the work you should get a fuller sense of what I am suggesting here with regard to sameness and copy, tendencies that I will return to again and again.

We have seen that narrative and game have their form of destabilizing action. Can there also be destabilizing action relative to the community of interpretation which is dance? There can be, though it is more difficult to interpret. It is more difficult to interpret because, as we saw, the structure of dance engages a particularly physical problematic of experience *just because it reduces and simplifies its models so that there is less to interpret*. With less to interpret, there is less opportunity for destabilizing action toward the community whose *goal* is the interpretation of the particular problematic in question.

Look at this from the aspect of rules. Chess has fewer rules than writing, while dance has fewer rules than chess. The latter may seem counterintuitive at first, but upon reflection it is not. First, if we asked which is easier to learn, clearly there are dances which are easier to learn than chess, our chosen example of games. Chess in turn is easier than writing. Or, to consider it in the order of learning: little children can dance simply and can imitate more complex dances with very little practice, older children learn chess and other games, and still older children—and sometimes not until adulthood—learn to write. But what is easiest to engage in, is easiest to refuse engagement in deliberately.

You might expect then that actions which destabilize dancing communities would take the form of some very simple and openly evident actions against those communities of interpretation. Not surprisingly this is exactly what we find in actions that are forbidden according to the etiquette of dancing.

The most damnable insult to another with regard to dance is to *refuse to dance* with them when asked. But note this, it is an insult precisely because you are at the dance, and then refuse. If you never went, there is no insult. Perhaps even worse is to refuse to dance with someone and then accept the offer of another for the same dance. If a gentleman can dance but refuses to do so, he is to refrain from coming to the ball, so the old rule goes. To deliberately dance badly would be so far beyond the pale as to need even an unwritten rule.

All of these are forms of action which are inconsistent with some one or other of our various hyperthemes, preeminently that elements are not to *eliminate* (here exclude) other elements of the community. The response to them meanwhile, has been—just as we noted briefly in chess—the very growth of etiquette.

Etiquette is a term that runs across human forms of activity harmonized under many and varied structures. Chess has its etiquette, as does sport, as does dance. Writing too has its etiquette. Etiquette at first appears to be just a set of rules. Yet if rules are standards, or models which actors interpret themselves to, then etiquette may be more than mere rules. Dancers, I suggested, interpret their models relative to the problematic engaged by the dance. If etiquette were *merely* rules, then it would be quite specific to and interwoven with the structure it arises under. This is not the case. You may for example dance very well, but be considerably lacking in the etiquette of dancing. Moreover there is etiquette for some areas of human action which is practically similar to the etiquette for other areas, although applied to different experience. Just as one does not refuse an offer to dance in dancing, one does not refuse an offer to face an opponent in fencing.

Etiquette is not a mere set of rules then. Yet it does postulate models for action, and its models for action, though suggesting positive action, are always presented on the basis of what one is *not* to do. I am to accept a fencing match, or a dance when offered. Why? Because it is inconsistent with the community of interpretation of fencing, or dance, to refuse. I can entertain the latter principle because by hypothesis, someone, somewhere, *has refused to do so*. If they have however, they have been a destabilizing influence upon the community of fencing or dancing.

Recalling what was suggested in the earlier chapter on chess, it should now become clear what etiquette is. Etiquette is not a mere set of rules, or models, which members of the communities in question postulated simply and constructively as rules, or standards, to interpret to. Rather, etiquette is a set of rules, or models, deliberately created with skill and wisdom in response to destabilizing acts within some community of interpretation.

We have mostly lost in the depths of historical time the original reconstructive acts performed with skill and wisdom by some wise member of any given community, which have come down to us as models to interpret our actions to. Yet certain it is that every lasting principle of etiquette has come from just such an act. I open my hand and shake hands with another and in doing so I interpret my action to the model of some long forgotten genius, who, having suffered the destabilization of his community through a weapon hidden in someone's clenched fist, henceforth determined to meet others with an open and honest hand.

Not surprisingly, we are often intuitively aware of the added significance which the "rules" of etiquette present. They are rules of a higher standard than the regular rules of any of our communal endeavors, precisely because of the creative skill and wisdom in their crafting. When we say such things as: "being a good sport, is more important than whether you win or lose," our intuition is correct, though our understanding of why this is so may be deficient.

We thus arrive unexpectedly at another hypertheme, one which has become clearer and more defined here through our ability now to interpret back to our earlier hyperthematic explorations: **H12**—*to create hyperthematic structures which engender greater stability and potential to interact with other hyperthematic structures, make every effort to include models which capture how* *reconstructive action has creatively responded to destabilizing actions within and against the community under the structure. Find such models if you can; creatively postulate them if you cannot.*

In other words, fill your hyperthematic structure with models of reconstructive action. If you have not got such models because your hyperthematic structure is striking out into relatively unexplored problematics of experience, then postulate them. Create an etiquette. Creative response to hypothetical destabilizing actions lying in wait for the community in the future is the wisdom we call foresight. Lay aside reconstructive models for a rainy day. In this way you strengthen your community by engaging it as a reconstructively stable community by means of the higher standard which is common to all communities, i.e., a capacity to heal and rebuild itself.

This hypertheme is complementary then to our hypertheme from the interpretation of game structure, which told us to include elements in the community that, as far as possible, retain the significance of their transformations from unstable elements to elements capable of harmonization of action. Whereas that earlier hypertheme bids us keep the element itself as being a sign of its transformation toward harmonizeability in a specific and historical sense, and therefore as being co-original with the foundation of the structure in question, our hypertheme here bids us seek out and create the element as being a sign of the creative skill of those members already engaged in the community under the structure.

In other words, the earlier hypertheme deals with the initial construction of the hyperthematic structure and the later deals with the internal, ongoing, and future testing of the hyperthematic structure. Whatever destabilizing actions arise will test the ability of the structure to heal itself, and the result—here exemplified in etiquette—will be a set of models of reconstructive acts undertaken to heal the damaged community.

It should be evident that there are hyperthemes which apply across the hyperthematic structures of diverse communities of interpretation. This raises the question: can hyperthematic structures borrow *simpliciter* from other hyperthematic structures?

I offered ballet as example of a type of dance under the dance structure, which clearly participates with the structure of narrative. So far and without further musement, this appears to be a rather happy and positive sort of borrowing. Other examples of borrowing are less happy. One which comes to mind while interpreting the dance structure is the military use of dance-like activity: military drill. In what follows I will interpret military communities to the opening hyperthemes and to dance to begin to illustrate some of the extremes of constrictive tendencies which deny interpretation.

The Military as an Eliminatory Community, Drill, and Leadership

According to the ultimate hypertheme **H** and its derivatives, the elements which make up a military community—remember I have already called it a false community, for reasons which will now become clearer—make up a structure which is inherently unstable according to the tendency of its elements to *eliminate other elements*. Those elements which concern us most here are other soldiers, although they may be any sign liable to destruction: civilians, buildings, ideas, cultural elements, social structures, etc.[4]

Now you may object that a military is not well characterized as a community which eliminates elements by killing some enemy. You may suggest that there are multiple elements in an army which do not kill, most prominently chaplains and medical personnel. Again you may insist there are other types of communities which—directly or indirectly—eliminate elements of another community and so cannot be characterized as military communities. Further, since there are such communities, military communities ought not to be singled out. There are street gangs for example, which kill rival gang members; there are slaughterhouse employees who kill animals; there are governments that deliberately or through incompetence allow their citizens to die from starvation and other governments that allow their police forces to kill their own citizens.

I agree with you on all of these counts, along with others which could be imagined. But I disagree that the fact that such personnel and such communities exist exempts military communities from being defined as false communities in the sense being elaborated in this work. On the contrary, such examples support the definition. Each of the communities mentioned *is* a false community for the same reason and to the same extent as a military community: they include some inconsistent principle or principles (anti-hyperthemes) which guide the elimination of elements of another community, or that community as a whole, no matter the nature of that other community. Yet they also include principles side-by-side with those inconsistent principles, which hold them together as a community. They must include such principles for the simple reason that without them they would destabilize and collapse as a community. Even among thieves, to use an idiom, there must be some degree of honor.

The variations of false communities then, are relative to the anti-hyperthemes and hyperthemes that they contain. Their strength as an eliminatory community is proportional to the former and their—misguided—value as communities is proportional to the latter. Thus a street gang is a disorganized cousin of a military community, although this also is relative. A mafia, for example, may be more organized than a common street gang, with hyperthemes which stabilize it as a localized community, but still far less organized than a military community. A military community may indeed have far more consistent principles in it than such "looser" communities, alongside of its inconsistent principles, principles which do create greater localized value. Moreover, it does not—presumably—have further anti-hyperthemes which promote the various constrictive or eliminative tendencies which we associate with the word crime, e.g., theft, smuggling, extortion, bribery, etc. Nonetheless, the relevant question is: can you pick out the military community according to its essential assumptions, those without which it would not be a military as usually understood? Can you distinguish it *from consistent communities* by pointing to the deliberate acts of killing undertaken by some of its members, and the guidance toward such acts which prevails in the community? The only answer to this can be in the affirmative.

Military communities exist ultimately for the elimination of an enemy and be the proportion of their member elements who engage in this elimination ever so small, nonetheless other more consistent elements such as medical personnel are primarily included in the community to support the eliminatory elements. This is the difference of the military, along with other false communities, from consistent communities such as we have begun exploring.

Dance, for example, does not have principles which guide any of the members of its community to eliminate members of other communities by killing; even exclusionary tendencies—weaker eliminatory tendencies—which arise through deliberate attacks upon the structure, are minimized by deliberately created principles of etiquette, as I have suggested. You may invoke the rules of war, the Geneva conventions, as having definite similarities to the etiquettes of dance. Again I grant this. But you cannot escape the fact that, in the military, side-by-side with those rules, lie deliberate principles for killing.

If you insist that a military could be transformed so as to be without eliminatory elements, then I salute your insight and agree, but then I am no longer willing to call it a *military* in the current and historical sense.[5] If you suggest that contemporary militaries are growing to be more defensive oriented, then—with definite doubts about Western militaries and deepest reservations about the greater part of non-Western militaries worldwide—I hope you are right and recommend such a creative transformation wholeheartedly. But I still maintain that the current primary training of militaries is to kill when the powers-that-be judge it necessary.

You may argue that the physical destruction of the enemy may not be necessary at times, and that, as Colonel J. F. C. Fuller argued, the destruction of the enemy's will, and his plan, and above all the organization of his army, take precedence over piecemeal killing.[6] Physical and mental experience is not so easily separated however, as I have begun and will continue to show in greater breadth in what follows, and the elimination of interpretation relative to more complex elements of a process tends inevitably to coincide with the elimination of simpler elements of that process. Even Fuller, despite his strenuous attempts to found the purpose of war on considerations other than killing, lapses all too easily back into "common sense": "Men who take on the nature of vermin must be exterminated. . . ."[7]

No amount of such considerations as offered above can paper over the following: a military community is one whose hyperthematic structure is at least partly built of principles which guide the act of killing. Now what does dancing have to do with the military?

It is difficult to know how dancing is related to military drill historically. Something like the following can be supposed however. I have already suggested that part of the lure of a game like chess is that its playing pieces retain the history of their relation to military elements in the realm of military activity, i.e., in the false community of the military. The transformable elements of a game retain the significance of their transformation from being predatory elements to being elements capable of harmonizing action. Turning aside now to focus on an example of such predatory elements, something interesting may be uncovered with regard to the interpretation here in question.

A community with a predominance of eliminatory elements faces a problem in terms of the playing out of the assumption **H**. The eliminatory elements of the community adopt an anti-hypertheme. The adopted anti-hypertheme promotes eliminations of some degree. The anti-hypertheme creates a "dead zone" for meaning in some region of experience, a region where interpretation, meaning, and thus value are refused. Each adopting element guided by the anti-hypertheme incorporates this lacuna of interpretation in some aspect of its process of experience, and multiple such adopting elements create greater lacunae.

Let the element in question be an infantry soldier in an army, for example. Let us say he is taught to kill when confronted with an enemy and ordered to do so. The anti-hypertheme will take some form such as: *when faced with an element recognizable as such and such, take such or such an action in order to deny the other element the continued interpretation of the experience of the world process* (i.e., his life). The type of action may be aim and pull the trigger, it may be thrust your bayonet like so, it may be pull the grenade pin and throw like this, etc. Whatever the action, its goal is to eliminate an element—the enemy—from the world process. Yet, according to our opening assumption, every such elimination of an interpretable element is a loss for potential value.

The tendency of the anti-hypertheme is thus inconsistent with the opening assumption **H**. **H** assumes that value is created through interpretation between elements. Removing those elements thus lessens the ability to interpret, lessens meaning, and lessens value. The eventual result of the tendency is the removal of sufficient elements to form an interpretation at all, i.e., the logical transformation from a polyad of elements, to a triad of elements, to a dyad of elements, and then to a monad element. Interpretation stops (locally) below the triad, but it begins to weaken at any time when the *tendency* toward elimination is put into play.

A soldier who was taught the anti-hypertheme is thus a locus for the weakening of interpretation. Whenever he kills he removes an interpretable element from the world process as a process of value, i.e., from the ultimate hyperthematic structure. The soldier does not even have to kill to *affect* the value in his region however. I have suggested that killing is near the extreme of the range of the tendency of elimination with regard to devaluation. In the other direction that range includes various degrees of suppression of the will of another, suppression of physical freedoms, suppression of ideas, etc. The adoption of the anti-hypertheme may open up the extreme of elimination as an engagement of experience, but by default, therefore, it also opens up all these lesser variants of elimination as acceptable modes of engaging experience. Thus a soldier may kill his enemy but he may stop at less than this and take that enemy prisoner—a lesser constriction of interpretive freedom, or even simply instill the psychological sense of constriction which arises when living under martial law.

The effect of an anti-hypertheme thus spills out beyond its intended range. In the history of warfare this has meant an uneasy assumption that the types of actions guided by the anti-hyperthemes could be successfully controlled, that the primary task of the soldier could be contained within set boundaries.

The soldier is to attack and kill an enemy but not his fellow soldiers; he is to attack an enemy but halt his attack when that enemy gives quarter; he is to attack an enemy soldier but not an enemy civilian. I call the assumption uneasy because the history of human warfare has continually shown its futility. No group of soldiers ever trained in killing, no fighting force ever yet invented, has been able to achieve the results demanded of the above assumption in any thorough way. Every seeming success has been merely the result of some consistent hyperthematic tendency—such as will be illustrated here in dance used as drill—put in play, and every such "success" merely "covers over" in a localized way, the devaluation caused by some anti-hypertheme.

For my limited purposes here, the most interesting aspect of the effect of the anti-hypertheme is its effect on the soldier's own community. One may be able to excuse the spillage of an anti-hypertheme relative to an enemy civilian—who is still an enemy in some sense. One may be able to excuse it relative to a surrendered enemy—still a former enemy after all. But how to explain it away relative to the elements of the soldier's own community—the soldiers on his own side? There's the rub. That an eliminatory anti-hypertheme, besides destabilizing other communities, destabilizes the very community which adopts it, is amply illustrated in any military you may please to name, ancient or modern, in one degree or another. Military communities are constantly "at war" within themselves and a few examples will suffice to show it.

Elzéar Blaze, who served as a Captain in Napoleon's Grande Armée, in Poland, Spain, and Germany gives detailed accounts of the culture of dueling which was a fact of army life at the time. Blaze speaks of dueling at the Military School of Fontainebleau resulting in deaths.[8] He speaks of duels between his friends over trifles:

> Two of our comrades suddenly quarreled and resolved to settle things immediately, sword in hand. We tried vainly to get them to be reasonable; they would listen to nothing . . . all was useless However I could see that the two champions were really no more anxious to fight than we two witnesses—that they were trying hard to appear angry, in continuing out of vanity a quarrel which they both regretted having started.[9]

Not anxious to fight then, *but guided by their adopted principles to fight*, in circumstances which would otherwise have been amenable to more meaningful solutions.

Blaze speaks of men who did personal favors for one another before their scheduled duel, and then, "they went gaily off to try to cut each others' throats."[10] He speaks of army men, such as one of his acquaintance named Hémère, for whom "the slightest smile, the least gesture could be misunderstood; he would demand satisfaction . . . because of his tendency to taunt and to get angry over trifles, he finally found someone who didn't joke. The poor devil was killed in a duel, the evening of the battle of Wagram."[11] He speaks finally of dueling as "that evil which is corroding our society," and goes so far as to propose methods to end the practice.[12]

You may respond that the instability of the military community is not to be singled out, as even Blaze speaks of a social evil, or that the military practices of two hundred years ago have no relevance to contemporary military experience. You would be wrong on both points. The military is indeed always part of a larger society, surrounded by other communities, but Napoleonic France was also a thoroughly militarized society. Moreover, the age one lives in seems to make little difference to the fundamental instability within the military community—beyond that of the tools by which that instability is expressed—as more recent events can illustrate.

Sometimes the internal instability is inspired by issues beyond the eliminatory principle of the military community, as in the case of the death of American private Barry Winchell, yet it culminates through action facilitated by the guidance of those principles.[13] Just as often it is inspired by some lesser degree of that principle, as in the "welcoming" of a newly promoted infantry sergeant by the unit's other NCOs, each lining up to strike their comrade as hard as possible, as recounted by U.S. Army Sgt. Maj. Ralph L. Phillips.[14] "Less enlightened" militaries such as that of South Korea illustrate more extreme versions of these internal failures to contain the eliminatory principle: death by beating after various forms of torture; the large-scale reprisal which sometimes accompanies similar incidents; and in general a systemic problem.[15]

The problem is not confined to the lower ranks of a military. Generals have fought on the physical level, as Blaze noted.[16] They have also fought one another on more complex levels, in keeping with the higher complexities of experience to which they apply the anti-hyperthemes of war. The struggle between two Canadian Generals of World War One, Sir Sam Hughes, and Sir Arthur Currie, a war of words, of publicity, and of high command level orders, show the heights that the use of the eliminatory tendency can reach internally in a military community.[17] Nor was it a middling fight between minor players. Hughes was the architect of Canadian mobilization and of the distinct Canadian army which entered World War One, while Currie is recognized as the most successful military leader Canada has ever produced.

If the foregoing shows the destabilization of the military community by its own adopted assumptions, one can safely assume that efforts have been made through history to address the problem. In their better judgment at least, men tend to take note of what they see around them, i.e., what works, in addressing problems. Hence, confronted with such a problem as I have outlined, military-minded men would have turned their thoughts upon community activities which did appear to promote the internal stability of communities. Phrased in the terms of this work, it would have been useful—necessary even—to any military endeavor, to borrow from, or parasitize from hyperthematic structures which promote consistent and stable communities of interpretation. One may postulate that this is just what military organizations over the ages have done in the guise of the military drill.

In organizing a military the goal is to combine a group of fighting individuals, soldiers, whose defining attribute is the willingness and ability to kill or eliminate other such individuals. But to effectively carry out their tasks those soldiers must be more or less able to overcome the sense that the enemy is part of some community to which they themselves also belong. Nonetheless, to carry out their tasks effectively, soldiers must also be able to work together precisely as a community with a goal.

For a soldier, an enemy is to be "not of my community" and ultimately—when dead—"not of any community"; but nonetheless, for that soldier also, "I am part of a community," and except for the former assumption: "my enemy might also be of that community." The constrictive principle is thus set against the expansive principle. The result, as illustrated above, is that any time someone else even remotely appears to be "not of my community" he becomes liable—through the inconsistent guiding principle—to being excluded in some degree and ultimately to being killed, so as to be "not of any community."

But communities, both consistent and inconsistent, are as numerous as you please, and spring up anywhere, including within militaries. The soldier, abiding by the anti-hypertheme, is thus constantly faced with "other communities than his own" *within* the military, in response to which the anti-hypertheme offers its dubious guidance. A fellow soldier might come to be "not of my community" in the smaller sense because of some trifle as looking at me the wrong way—as in the examples of Blaze—or he might come to be "not of my community" because of his different intelligence, strength, size, appearance or color, sex (in contemporary militaries), religion, or any of a host of other differences. He then becomes fair game for an engagement through some action guided by an anti-hypertheme.

The military thus requires a counter to contain its anti-hyperthemes. Not that they can be contained so as to generate any lasting value, as I will begin to show later. Nonetheless the attempt has been strenuously made throughout history. Given time, your soldiers will develop a shared history. They will take on aspects of community, following **HG**, just by having some goal set for them and achieving it, e.g., having gone through such and such a hardship of battle together, they develop an *esprit de corps* of the experienced military group. The goal will often be inconsistent—e.g., eliminate an enemy unit—but nonetheless will also have consistent goals embedded within it that are formative of a community of interpretation—e.g., "*move* together to some location over such and such terrain," or "*build* together a military camp in this spot," or simply *live* together. Yet in the beginning they have no shared history as such, based on the accomplishment of a goal. How then do you overcome this problem initially and make your soldiers into a community, when nonetheless as elements of that community they are to eliminate other elements similar to themselves, an injunction which if unchecked leads them even to eliminate their own fellows?

Among other things, *you make your soldiers dance together*. The interpretation of dance I have offered so far, as being a hyperthematic structure capable of forming strongly *locally* and *physically* biased communities of interpretation promoting harmonic action, makes it an ideal structure to borrow from when you want, as a military does, the elements of your group to have an extremely *localized* sense of community—"just our own guys." Hence the military borrows from dance.[18]

Yet military groups never quite make it to being communities. Their imbedded anti-hyperthemes make them inconsistent, false communities, until those anti-hyperthemes are given up. Sometimes they succeed in becoming true communities if they manage to transform their elements into consistent elements. Such, for example, are honor guards who have purely ceremonial duties and have given up killing an enemy. Such is any community like the Royal Canadian Legion in which former soldiers have made the transformation from elimination to creative interpretive acts of community service and charity.

While militaries hold to their inconsistent principles, they remain unstable internally however. Nevertheless, they strive mightily to internally mitigate the inconsistent principles of the acting elements which are their members. They do it through drill, through building up a shared history, and through other methods which illustrate what I will later call the tendency toward mere quantity, e.g., short haircuts and common uniforms. These methods tend to remove differences internal to the military group in question, the very differences from which simple communities could spring up within the military and cause the troubles under discussion.

The whole thrust of the attempt to contain the eliminatory principle is directed at making very simple physically biased communities, for, as suggested earlier, physicality is just a tendency toward simplicity of interpretation. The goal is not for soldiers to think much, to begin to broaden and complexify their interpretations—mental, but rather to train them to make very simple interpretations—physical, to make them together, and to make them on command. Drill borrowed from dance is an ideal tool for this. The soldier learns simple motions in tandem with his fellows, e.g., parade, where he is "dancing" with the members of his unit. He also learns other motions which are sometimes carried out alone, e.g., weapon drill, where he is "dancing solo" with himself according to a choreography given to him by his instructors.

You may object that not all militaries have used drill. This is so, but a review of military history suggests that the most successful armies have used drill, and by successful we mean the localized "success" of eliminating elements of other military communities. Examples include the armies of the Romans, the armies of the Mongols, and the armies of Europe during the wars of religion. All of these armies were horribly good at killing in systematic and efficient—drilled—ways. Familiarity with accounts of the wars of ancient times finds battles characterized as affairs in which the victory goes to the side which can sustain what in military terms is called cohesion. The barbarian armies of the classical era, for example the Gauls of Caesar's *Gallic Wars*, are typically characterized as a mad rabble which—all things being equal—melts apart when faced with the sustained cohesion of drilled military units.

Even though the dance itself is consistent with our prior disclosed principles because it helps stabilize other communities, nonetheless, in the end the military community cannot be helped, i.e., as long as, and insofar as, its goal and the goals of its elements remains eliminative. In drill, dance is thus being used to a bad end, so to speak. There is something valuable to be gained in this interpretation to our opening assumptions. If a parasitic false community can borrow from a stable community and do so to good effect, then a true community of interpretation can also do this. Notwithstanding that an inherently unstable community will fail eventually, it nonetheless gains whatever stability it does have from this type of borrowing from stable communities. If, then, for example, we have a stable community based upon a hyperthematic structure whose tendency is to propagate itself broadly at the expense of solution—of the type exemplified by narrative—it can benefit by borrowing from hyperthematic structures such as dance, which issue in interpretive communities whose focus is narrow, local, physical, and emphasizes solution at the expense of problematic.

We are ready to formulate this as a principal: **H13**—*in correcting hyperthematic structures, borrow from other stable structures, and in particular look to those hyperthematic structures guiding stable communities whose degree of focus complements the emphasis of the structure under correction.*

In other words, just as the military, in order to counteract its inherent local instability, borrows a locally stabilizing assumption from the community of dance, let your structure borrow from other stable communities according to its need. If your community is narrowly focused, then it will benefit by borrowing from a broadly focused community. Conversely, if your community is broadly focused, then it will benefit by borrowing from a narrowly focused community. In this way you find action to complement your problematic and fresh problems to engage with your well-defined local action structures. Sometimes your community will be stable already and then it will be enhanced by such borrowing. If your apparent community is actually deficient and unstable, then you may stabilize it so, and it may eventually transform into a new community thereby.

Before I end with dance I will interpret yet another method used by military communities to stabilize themselves, one which can be expanded out of my suggestions concerning dance and drill, and one which can lead us into a consideration of music, often but not always associated with dance, as a hyperthematic structure. Besides the foregoing, militaries attempt to manage inconsistent elements through a type of element which has certain unique characteristics: the officer. The tendencies of this method can be illustrated, in particular, by considering the relationship which officers of military communities share with enlisted soldiers.

First off, consider that relationship relative to drill. It is the rank and file primarily who engage in drill. Officers, as they rise to higher ranks, begin to *lead* the drill—as NCOs—and then increasingly to observe the drill at still higher levels, which is to say that they initiate the borrowing from the structure of dance, among others, but they participate in it less.

Officers are paradoxical creatures. On the one hand they are certainly susceptible to the spilling effect of the anti-hyperthemes used by militaries, as I already noted. The deep animosities that can arise between officers of units or of armies is well documented. If you read an unvarnished assessment of what Generals in an army deeply embroiled in war think of one another, such as J. L. Granatstein's candid interviews with the Generals of the Canadian army in the Second World War for example, while also forgetting the tendencies under discussion which are holding them together, you can wonder how any army has ever managed to keep together.[19] Occasionally they also resort to the extreme of elimination at the highest levels, as did Union General Jefferson C. Davis, who killed General William Nelson after a quarrel in 1862, although thankfully this seems rare today.

On the other hand, successful officers are often deeply engaged with communities beyond their own military community, sometimes even more than they are in the military community in its eliminatory sense. This may appear counterintuitive at first. Recall what I said above, however, regarding methods other than drill which have arisen to smooth over differences internal to military groups, short haircuts and common uniforms, for example.

Common uniforms and short haircuts are a recent innovation in the history of warfare. The modern standardization of uniforms began around the time of Cromwell and increased thereafter. Uniform short haircuts—and shaved faces—did not arrive *en masse* until World War One. The reason behind these changes had to do with the quantitative increase of soldiers in armies, from tens of thousands, to hundreds of thousands, then to millions. This increase engendered all the problems common to interpretation as sameness in quantity—to be explored further as this work progresses. The effects specific to armies were problems such as lice and hygiene, and the difficulty of supplying clothing for huge masses of men, thus initiating short hair and standard uniforms.

The increase of soldiers as quantity gave rise to another problem, however, this one related to officers. I suggested that officers are paradoxes. They fight one another as enlisted men do, being susceptible to the internal instability caused by the anti-hyperthemes. They fight the enemy as well. They die by the enemy. But on the other hand there is a definite sense that they are *not* like the enlisted men. This sense varies over time and over different officers of course, but it is always there. It has been a perennial observation—at times a distinction that both sides take pride in—that officers are not like enlisted soldiers. In this the enlisted man's intuition of his extremely limited communal role, and the officer's intuition of his much expanded communal role, appears to have been entirely correct.

James Davis, a soldier and later sergeant who served on active duty in Rwanda and Yugoslavia with the Canadian Airborne Regiment, describes the intense dislike felt by soldiers for the type of officer who didn't share the hardships of the enlisted men.[20] He also evokes the awareness of the gulf separating enlisted men from general officers and staff officers, even though that gulf could sometimes be bridged by a general officer. Of a chance meeting with General Lewis MacKenzie, who had asked his name, Davis writes: "I was well aware of the cloud of staff officers who were staring at me like I was some kind of bug, obviously upset that the General was bothering with an obvious nobody in the grand scheme of things."[21]

Sir Arthur Currie successfully led some of the largest and bloodiest battles of the First World War. He was meticulous in his planning and did everything to prevent the unnecessary deaths of his soldiers.[22] Despite this, he was admired by his men, but not liked.[23] Unlike General Haig, Currie did not sit a horse well, as Cook observes, and moral courage and brilliant planning notwithstanding, to his men "the Canadian Corps commander looked like a pudgy accountant."[24] The question came down to whether you had engaged physically in the fighting, and in the danger, or even, in Currie's case, *whether you looked like you had*; Currie had. If either case applied, then the officer was *not* like the enlisted men. As J. L. Granatstein notes, for Canadian officers of World War One who had returned home alive, whether you had had a "good" war or not, depended upon whether you had been up front in the fighting or, or in the rear, or in relative safety in England; and the public memory on these matters was both deep and long-lasting.[25]

Now it should be obvious that as an officer rises in the chain of leadership, his opportunity to be physically fighting up in the front lines, or even *to be* up in the front lines, diminishes. It is the increase in quantity of soldiers in an army that drives this trend. Accordingly, as the size of armies has steadily increased over the last few centuries, the sense of the distinctness of officers, particularly general officers from enlisted ranks, has grown stronger.

John Keegan traces the change in command style through history on the basis of the continually increasing size of armies.[26] An ancient commander like Alexander the Great could make personal interventions in a battle. As the size of armies increased, however, a point was reached at which the commander could no longer be *seen* at the front of the battle line by all of his men, let alone engage in physical heroics; the last general able to be seen by his whole army was Wellington at Waterloo.[27] More recent generals, e.g., Rommel and Montgomery, who temporarily reversed the trend away from "heroic" personal interventions in battles, have tended to be successful in variations of "forward control," but not on the scale necessary to win the wars they were in—only the battles. The numbers simply do not allow it.

General Eisenhower, who Montgomery derided as never having heard a shot fired in anger, and who MacArthur, on his off days, described as "the apotheosis of mediocrity,"[28] had problems of an inconceivable scale to manage during the Allied invasion of Europe. For Eisenhower, personal heroics must give way to the new kind of skills needed in an officer, skills apparently working against the eliminatory aspect of warfare. "No allied commander, in any of the theaters of war, was so eager to avoid casualties by scaling down the intensity of the campaigns, or avoiding them altogether, if the same ends could be secured by a political arrangement. Ike was always looking for political windows through which he could enter by agreement rather than the force of brutal military power."[29]

The officer then comes to differ from the enlisted man in the loss of his physical connection with battle. What then is his role? My suggestion is that his role, which is becoming increasingly prominent and obvious in modern militaries, is an expansive role. The history of warfare has blurred this, assuming that engaging in physical fighting—killing or the nearest thing to it—is the hallmark of command success. Yet the briefest reflection upon instances of personal heroism in officers shows this cannot be so.

All personal heroism in officers depends ultimately upon the officer's interpretation of some problem of experience, an interpretation which guides those who observe it—enlisted men—to interpret that or similar problems of experience themselves. This and nothing else is what it means to lead. If he leads, the officer leads by becoming a symbol or, in our terms, a sign—living and breathing—of an interpretation of a problem of experience.

Alexander fought in front of his men perhaps more than any other general ever has, but his primary role there was not to kill the enemy. *No amount of enemies killed by his own single hand could win his battles.* One man alone could not kill enough enemies to win even an ancient battle, no matter his courage. Thus, his elimination of a few enemy soldiers was secondary. His true role was symbolic. Alexander typically charged at the strongest point of the enemy's formation, a tactic which could mean nothing in terms of merely killing a handful of the enemy's low-ranking soldiers. Killing a few of the enemy could have been done on the flank of the enemy's position just as well as at the strongest point. Charging at the strongest point meant everything in terms of symbolism however, the symbolism which told his men that he thought himself greater than the greatest and strongest of the enemy army; and that they must act likewise.

General Brock's charge against American troops at Queenston Heights in the War of 1812 achieved far more in symbolism than it did in any actual physical elimination of the enemy. It was not because Brock killed anyone or even the fact of his death in the charge that inspired his men and later men. It was *the taking of action swiftly and without hesitation*. The interpretation was thus one relative to the temporal aspect of experience: "act now and continue to act," was the sign Brock gave to his men to guide them.

At the Battle of Arcole in 1796, the interpretation was predominantly one of space. Unable to drive his men over a narrow bridge across the Alpone River in the face of vicious fire from the Austrian enemy, Napoleon grabbed a flag and stood on a dike near—but not too near—the head of the bridge, while bullets whistled past him killing his staff. He killed no-one and did not die. By all accounts he did not even cross the bridge and was dragged down to safety by one of his staff who must have thought him mad. Yet he symbolized to his men *the taking of the space and the command of the space*. Indeed Vernet's painting *La Bataille du Pont d'Arcole* (1826), falsely shows him crossing the bridge leading his men. The *taking* of the space was a sign of *movement*. To his watching men it signified: "if Napoleon can walk forward and take this space, then we can go over that bridge." Such is interpretive guidance.

General MacArthur had perhaps the greatest awareness of the power of interpretive expansion of any general in history. He deliberately built it up during World War One, in dashing raids over no-man's-land into the German lines. He created himself as a legend larger than life. To see pictures of him later wading ashore at Leyte is to view the expansive aspect of the modern army officer, exemplifying the interpretation of experience in movement, through space, over time.

Officers, as expansive interpreters, always inspire men to expand their sense of: "what we can do," "where we can go," "what we will be able to accomplish," an expansion of interpretation into the larger processes around an enlisted soldier, which counteracts the anti-hyperthemes trained into him. The only value in the officer's act in all these cases is the value engendered by the expansion of interpretation under some hypertheme, even though it is wrongly applied to facilitate the use of the anti-hypertheme (elimination). Real leadership opposes killing, even though it is mistakenly used in the military to direct it. The tendencies are used together, but in terms of realized value *only the former creates whatever value there is*. No value arises from the anti-hypertheme, even though we can often—wrongly—think that it does. That the source of value we feel in an activity is often not where we first assume it to be is an issue I will address again in my later musings upon realism in video games.

If the above examples have shown that the expansive aspect is the other half that makes up the paradox, which is an officer, I must immediately add that this expansion is in no way limited to acts near or within battle. Contemporary opportunities for the latter are far rarer than interpretations by an officer which reach out to communities beyond the military community. The physical acts of heroics of commanders tend to become prominent in accounts of battle, simply because from the point of view of the enlisted man—he who the sign guides—trained as he is to function in the very localized and physical region of experience by methods such as the drill, the opening up of the possible interpretations of that experience near to him in terms of complexity will always be easiest and most accessible. When guided to think beyond himself, his first reaction will be to think beyond himself in physical terms. One of the most often heard expressions of tribute to a successful officer, is "I would have followed him anywhere." Its use, illustrating the physical sense of time and space being signified, remains as current today as it did a hundred years ago.[30]

Yet all of those tasks which made Currie appear as a "pudgy accountant," and Eisenhower as "just a chief clerk,"[31] increasingly make up the bulk of the activities subject to the expansive interpretations of the officer. Among the many tasks officers undertake in relation to some outside community one can note: interaction with enemy officers (this one very ancient), the writing of dispatches and reports, the formulation of battle plans, participation in the bureaucratic management of an army, teaching and training, and sitting on disciplinary committees that often enough relate to life outside the military community. Officers are constantly engaged in other communities than the military community, communities which are often consistent stable communities. Officers are the link between the military community and those communities, and they have been that link throughout history.

General Norman Schwarzkopf recounts in his autobiography his appointment as community commander in Mainz, Germany, on which his first day, "turned out to be a surprisingly big deal . . . a representative of the lord mayor of Mainz was present, along with the mayors of the city's eight neighborhoods and the county commissioner, plus a dozen other local officials."[32] Schwarzkopf describes this task as the most challenging part of his work in Germany, "Before long I was up to my neck in the administrative details of the child-care center, the enlisted men's clubs, the elementary school, and other services essential to the well-being of troops and families both on and off the base."[33]

Over the course of his career Schwarzkopf, among other things, had to: act as a spokesman for the army, act as a liaison with U.S. politicians and presidents and foreign leaders, learn other languages and other ways of expression with those languages such as the "courtly style of Arab conversations," learn to wear foreign clothing, interpret international law, and even organize a visit by the Pope.[34] Officers must constantly interpret communities external to the military, to a degree proportional to their rank, just as Schwarzkopf.

The foregoing has suggested that borrowing is useful among hyperthematic structures. But it has also suggested, in the guise of considering the role of officers as elements of a community which enter into liaison with other communities, that there might be hyperthematic structures which themselves have this character, as their *primary character* relative to other structures.

Considering harmonizing structures on a more complex level, one is led to suspect the hyperthematic structure of music as having such characteristics. Hence, having let be the relationship of music and dance so far, we are now ready to turn to a hyperthematic interpretation of music.

The Hyperthematic Structure of Music

Music appears to be a complex activity to interpret indeed. All the resources gained so far are available to interpret it however, which will help. By this time the method of my procedure should be familiar to the reader. As always I begin by asking: How can music be interpreted to the ultimate hypertheme? Which hypertheme or hyperthemes allow the transformation from the structure of music which is assumed to be a harmonizing structure, to the structure of interpretation opening out of **H**?

Clearly music has its processes of action in its performing musicians. Here we go beyond the direct case of musicians playing with one another to the broader case in which the musician, engaging some realm of experience, plays her music and interprets that realm of experience to a listener—who may be another musician—whose act of listening is harmonized with the act of the musician, through the third of the musical community of interpretation under the hyperthematic structure of music. Hence, music appears to be consistent with the opening principle.

Can we say that our derivatives are satisfied as well? We can, for in the first place with regard to **H3** we clearly have at least three elements: the musician, the listener, and the music, which make up the community of interpretation.

In the second place, the hyperthematic structure of music is consistent with **H1**, it does not eliminate its signs or elements. The musician can play many pieces of music, the listener can listen to many pieces of music, and multiple and recurrent interpretations are possible.

In the third place, **H2** is satisfied. The elements that participate in the communities of interpretation engendered by the hyperthematic structure of music do not eliminate one another. Just the opposite in fact. More than any other structure we have considered, the elements of the hyperthematic structure of music support one another and enhance one another. The question is: how do they enhance one another? If we can see this we can see how they support the elements of other communities as well.

One can approach an answer by considering where an acting element within the hyperthematic structure of music stands with regard to its model, i.e., how complex is its model and how closely does it follow it? First, with regard to the time process sectional aspect, the acting element or musician clearly has the most complex model we have yet seen from any of our hyperthematic structures. In a way which should now be evident from the other structures, but which I have not yet explicitly stated in this manner, musician and music are a process of action, which we call the elements of the hyperthematic structure, and from which sub-elements could be abstracted. The single note is thus an abstraction from the process of playing the music.*

The musician looks to her model, let us say a baroque era piece, e.g., one of Bach's pieces, composed some four centuries ago. There are notes that stand in an ordered relation to other notes. Notice, however, that the model does not promote exact reproduction of action on the part of the musician. A piece by Bach can be played on a violin, on a guitar, on a piano, etc. It can be played fast or slow, the composer's initial model can allow for considerable interpretive leeway.

We may contrast this with our other structures. The dancer strives for exactness of reproduction according to the model of a type of dance, it

---

*Those interested can refer to Whitehead's sense of abstraction.

breaks down as a type of dance or a specific dance piece much more easily than does a piece of music. The same degree of changes—if they could be brought about—which can be effected upon one of Bach's works, yet which keep the music as recognizably a piece of Bach's would destroy a dance as a particular type of dance. On the other hand, the game structure as exemplified in chess promotes exactness within small ranges such as a type of opening or middle game tactics; its range of transformation is greater than dance. The structure of narrative exemplified in a particular book promotes relative exactness according to one axis, i.e., that which in a book gives rise to the plot, while it leaves open a tremendous range in the other axis, i.e., that of the meaning of the words.

The structure of music has transformable elements whose range engenders models of action with a complexity greater than that of any of the foregoing structures. The notes have a range of pitch, they have a range of duration, they have a range of loudness, and depending on different instruments they have a range of tone color. The range of variations of stress upon them creates rhythm. Their relation to one another in terms of pitch creates melody, while their transversal relation to one another as chords is the basis of musical harmony. These are only some of the possible ranges of transformation that are available through musical elements.

Nor can it be said that all of this is due to the nature of sound itself. Sound as a medium is bound up with what we call music certainly, but we cannot go on to say that therefore music in the sense of a structure which allows harmonization of actions arises solely from the nature of sound. Increasingly, there is an experimentation with producing visual music for example, which uses the principles of music to varying degrees, but not the medium of sound.

Moreover, the endeavors of the composer belie the assertion that sound as a medium gives rise to music simpliciter, for the composer does not always simply sit at her piano tapping out notes until she hits upon a melody *through* the sound which comes forth. She hits upon melodies in the "mind," wherein there is no obvious vibration at those physical levels of complexity such as give rise to sound *as it manifests itself in the medium of air*, even though hyperthematic tendencies are at play, as our later chapter on light will suggest. Without being a composer, we can imagine music very well in general and often run through complex melodies in our minds without even humming.

Let us say rather that sound as a transformable technical entity is an abstraction from the active process of making music, with which it is convenient to make interpretations according to the range of complexity which the hyperthematic structure of music engages in its problematic. That problematic appears to be something like a problematic of moods or feelings—I will have more to say on feeling by the end of this work. Narrative can engage the problematic to some extent, but it has the tendency to turn to poetry, which is on the doorstep of music, in order to do so. Games can interpret this problematic less well, and dance (without accompanying music) even less.

If it seems counterintuitive that the elements of music have a greater range of transformation than the elements of narrative, consider that narrative as exemplified in a great work of literature generates multiple attempts to pin down a particular or canonical meaning. The Bible illustrates this, of course, but even laying aside this as due to special and external interests, Shakespeare's works, Plato's works, and so forth all illustrate this.

We humans are never quite comfortable with narrative which is crafted with such skill that its particular choices of signs, e.g., words, leave the range of the meaning of the words at its maximum. We rebel against the problematic, even as we recognize and revel in it. This causes us to fill reams of paper in essays with variations of topics such as "the true meaning of Shakespeare's *Macbeth*." We never really get *the* "true" or "real" meaning of such works of course, for the structure is such that it permits a range of meaning. The very attempt to pin down the meaning is made on the basis of recognizing that—relatively speaking—the meaning is less complex than that engendered by other structures, e.g., music. In other words, in narrative, there is some hope of pinning down a definitive meaning, relatively more so than in music.

Continuing on down through our hierarchy to the game structure, we find consistently that the attempt to find the true meanings of the range of the transformable elements of a game like chess is both highly welcomed and well underway. There are weighty tomes on chess which lay out thousands of moves and their consequences. Even now, there are computer programmers busily working on the complete solution, or meanings of the range of transformable elements of chess. Indeed, checkers has already been solved by computers acting as extensions of human effort.[35]

Nor does dance fail to link up with our interpretation in this regard. The transformable element in dance is the human body, with its limbs and its corresponding ranges of motion. If the dance is to remain something that we are ready to call dance, that is, if it is to keep the complexity and duration of the models to which it refers in the time process parallel aspect, within the scope of human embeddedness in the time process, then—to take the case of the solo dancer—the range of all possible meanings available under the structure of dance is intimately tied to the complete range of motion of which the human body is capable. If we add more dancers, nonetheless, they are limited according to the same considerations, for, as we noted, dancers in a troupe dance primarily in reference to the model, not to each other.

Of course, what we are willing to call dance may change. Someday two or more people may be said to dance with one another on opposite sides of the globe, or despite living in different eras. For the moment we do not call this dance, and if one did one would simply be taking the term used here for a hyperthematic structure that engages in a certain level of complexity and conferring it upon a structure which engages a more complex level. Dance would be evolved far beyond its current complexity—increasing its potential for value.[36] As it stands, dance is the outcome of harmonization of action according to the guidance of a structure that engages a range of complexity, which can be broadly defined as being *embodied*. But if this is its range, then in principle the "solution" of dance at that complexity could be worked out just as for checkers and chess.[37]

Returning to music, now it should be clear that the range of the transformable elements, and thus the complexity of the problematic which the hyperthematic structure of music engages, if consistent, ought to be the farthest away from this, at least with regard to those structures considered so far. If my account is plausible, the structure of music ought to engage regions of experience in its communities of interpretation which are, if not furthest away, then far away indeed from the type of embodied, *physical*, or localized complexity of experience that is engaged by dance.

The sheer range and types of range of the musical notes as transformable elements looms large in our initial intuition that the enhancement of the elements by one another is very strong in music. Any note, or part of music, can support another note precisely because it can stand in a transformable relation to it in *so many* different ways.

Of further interest is how this translates into a less abstract view when the musician and the listener are viewed as broader acting elements within the structure. Consider the case in which a musician playing for a listener produces a single note, e.g., with one pluck of a string. Is this music? Ordinarily not, for then any sound would be music. Insofar as it anticipates music the note demands further notes, further context. It gets that context according to some combination of the vast array of interpretive relations which its multiple ranges of transformation allow.

Yet if it is the element of the note in its possibilities which *allows* the context, nonetheless it is a musician as an acting process who *creates* the context. How does this creation of context by the musician as an element of the structure, enhance other elements? Take the simple case in which a single musician interprets a region of experience to a single listener. The musician plays a musical piece to her listener. The piece of music has a meaning as a whole, be it ever so simple. The musician must get this whole meaning across, sectionally across, to the listener.

Let the music be Beethoven's Sonata no. 17 for example, a piece of music whose meaning is often recognized as falling within a certain more or less generally evident range. Now whatever else may be the case, the musician must get *some* meaning of the sonata across to the listener; this is the only way in which it makes any sense to speak of the sonata as "The Tempest." The successions of single notes which the musician plays are always embedded in the context of the whole of the piece. If they were not so embedded they would be meaningless. The musician in such a case might make an interpretation in the act of producing sound, but we would not call it music. No, the musician must get across the whole and within the whole parts of the whole, yet not parts so simple as to be incapable of meaning. Thus, while we can divide up the sonata and speak of the meaning of its movements, as we approach simpler parts than this the possibility of meaning becomes proportionally thinner and we begin to talk of meaning in terms of music theory rather than music.

If the musician must get across the whole as meaningful, then can the listener accept any less? Clearly not. If the listener merely receives a series of single notes then interpretation has failed. Obviously the interpretation can fail, according to a lack of technical skill on the part of the musician. Somewhat less obviously, though nonetheless certainly, the interpretation can fail according to the listening skill of the listener. The listener must take part in the interpretation in a way that goes beyond the mere null action. Both the musician and the listener, if they are to take part in the community of interpretation under the hyperthematic structure of music, must engage a more complex level of experience. The experience of the single note is a less complex experience. The experience of the piece of music as a whole meaning is a more complex experience. It is the second of these that must be engaged in a willful action in order to participate in an interpretation under the hyperthematic structure of music.

When interpretation fails on the side of the listener it can be because the listener—analogously to the writer who has not widely read—has not engaged in the broader level of experience. Since this is willed act, then such an engagement cannot easily be forced even by the most skilled musician or composer. In short, there must be willed participation in the community of interpretation. Certainly the listener can listen merely for the pleasure of the sound itself, a listening on the sensuous plane, as Copland called it.[38] But while this is a large part of music, it cannot be the whole of music, insofar as it fails to engage in the interpretation. The sound of a bubbling brook can be pleasure to the ears, but except poetically we are not inclined to call it music. On the contrary, somehow it is the interpretive action of engaging more complex experience which adds to the pleasure of the sound. A nice illustration of this is the tuning of instruments before or between the parts of a concert. Even the anticipation of the broadening of experience to come gives the separate and jumbled notes heard an anticipatory aspect above that which they would otherwise get. Indeed, when a composer deliberately inserts a silent pause in a piece of music, the effect on the potential for subsequent interpretation can be tremendous. Here the pause is used as a very simple transformable element, a constriction of interpretation deliberately inserted to lure the listener to re-engage in the coming music in a willful move to interpret experience of higher complexity. Such a pause is *practice* for the listener. A pause so used is very different from a prolonged silence due to a ban on music, for example.

Beyond the merely bad musician, another way in which the interpretation can fail on the side of the musician can be illustrated in the case of the child music prodigy. There have been many young musical prodigies in more recent human history, and indeed, seemingly, a great number of them in very recent history. A regular observation regarding the musical prodigy, however, is that mere technical mastery can be considerably deficient in meaning. The composer Hector Berlioz remarked of the child prodigy Camille Saint-Saëns: "il sais tout, mais il manque d'inéxperience," presumably implying that his technical mastery far outweighed his ability to engage experience as a problematic which could be interpreted to express meaning; the music did not well lure the listener to interpret it.[39] But even though Saint-Saëns "never had a childhood," as Gounod put it,[40] so as to lack the benefit that the normal transition to adulthood would have given to his interpretations, this was corrected a good deal by his long life of perseverance. It is not always corrected and can often lead to great difficulties for such prodigies, particularly in recent times, as some have observed.[41]

Music demands engagement of a complex level of experience to gain meaning. As Copland put it,

My own belief is that all music has an expressive power, some more and some less, but that all music has a certain meaning behind the notes and that the meaning behind the notes constitutes, after all, what the piece is saying, what the piece is about. This whole problem can be stated quite simply by asking, 'is there a meaning to music?' My answer to that would be, 'Yes.' And 'Can you state in so many words what the meaning is?' My answer to that would be, 'No.' . . . [music may] express a state of meaning for which there exists no adequate word in any language.[42]

The meaning may and often does change for us with regard to a particular piece of music. It may differ for other people. Nonetheless, interpretation demands *some* meaning. Whatever the meaning may be which is engaged in a more complex experience, if it is offered with skill on the part of the musician and if it is accepted with skill on the part of the listener, then there is a community of interpretation between musician and listener through the third of the musical community of interpretation under the hyperthematic structure of music.

Another principle thus appears: **H14**—*as the range and degree of the transformable elements of a hyperthematic structure increase in complexity such that its models of action harmonization allow interpretations which pass on signs of meaning as a type, it tends to draw the elements of a community engaged in it away from the locus of attachment in the time process which marks the beginning of the range of its problematic of experience, toward a homogenous appraisal of that problematic. Such a structure will be called a <u>leader structure</u>.*

A leader structure opens up a wider vision before the acting elements of a given community under a given structure. Music, as a leader structure, promotes the transfer of meaning as such, relatively speaking, when it is engaged in order to interpret experience. A skilled and artful musician increases the ability of the listener to experience meaning as such; she expands the interpretive freedom of the listener. This only occurs to the extent that the listener willfully participates, for it is the will which engages experience as meaning.

Nothing is forced through the structure of music. A leader structure is a structure which offers meaning, but does not force particular meaning. It is alluring without being restrictive.* If the particularity of meaning is so

---

*To relate this to Whitehead's concept of the lure: God is the ultimate leader structure.

absent, that practically speaking nothing but meaning as a type is imparted, or signified, then we are listening to music in terms of what Copland called the sensuous plane. But even then this is not listening merely for the pleasure of the sound; it is a listening *to* meaning without a listening *for* a particular meaning. This is why music has always given us humans the sense of broad vistas and infinite and heavenly visions, most especially in successful music to which we listen for the first time.

This expansion of interpretive freedom is not restricted to music, or even to the influence of music as a structure. Any structured activity that is a new activity to us, e.g., a new hobby, presents itself according to an inexplicable newness, a newness which we engage in with what longtime practitioners of Zen meditation are apt to call "the mindfulness of the beginner."[43] This "newness" is the homogenous vision of the activities possible under the structure, a vision not yet reduced by being anchored in the time process by reason of our finitude. All things seem possible to the beginner because nothing has yet been attempted beyond the engagement of the structure as a structure capable of engendering interpretive meanings at some range. Even to the seasoned veteran of a particular structure this synoptic vision presents itself at times. The veteran chess player may sit down to a new game with a certain anticipation, a certain vision—which we sometimes express as the "thrill" of the activities we enjoy—of the fuller range of possibilities in what is to come.

This newness is conferred by the interpretive world as such, as the ultimate leader structure—the world is a problem to be solved—with regard to any new engagement in its problematic, and even to mere changes of engagement as such, as e.g., when the office bound worker's mental activity is enhanced by physical exercise. The latter would take the form of an expansion of interpretive freedom according to the very high level difference between taking an action as such, i.e., engaging in some interpretation, and not taking an action as such, i.e., waiting passively in the world. This is the continual "freshness"—imagine each new morning—in which the world presents itself to be interpreted in new ways. Music is not the world structure, but it is nonetheless a leader structure at a very complex level of experience, which explains why music can be combined with so many other activities.

In the foregoing interpretation of dance, we deliberately left out a consideration of music. The relationship of the structures of dance and music can be explored by reflecting upon an objection which may arise with regard to our interpretation of music as a leader structure, namely, in the combination of music and dance how can we be certain that it is music which is the leader structure and not dance? "The dancer," so one may assert, "may also have an audience which must therefore participate in dance in the same manner as the listener participates in music. Therefore dance and music are equivalent with regard to their ability to expand interpretive freedom." Yet a moment's reflection will show that not only is this not the case, but, on the contrary, the fact that it is not the case exemplifies what was already suggested.

Imagine first some ancient and relatively simple forms of dance. Then ask, in the case of the dancer or dancers having an audience: what it is that the members of the audience are participating in? In the case of a folk dance, a square dance say, it will seem at first that the audience participates in the dance. Imagine a case in which folk dancers dance within a circular area; then, as is often the case, there may be a crowd at the periphery clapping, stamping feet, etc.

But now notice something: if you can at once reflectively separate the clapping and stamping from the general atmosphere of the dance, then you see that it accompanies the music primarily and the dance only secondarily. If the music were to stop then so most likely would the peripheral activity; yet the dance could go on without the music though it might be more difficult, for reasons which will become clearer in a moment. On the other hand, without the dance, the clapping and stamping could go on also, but if so it would be precisely to produce in a crude way what was lacking by way of music, that is to say rhythm.

Rhythm supports the dance, but it has nothing to do in principle with the more physical aspect of the dance as a process of action which follows some model, e.g., the model of a square dance, for it can just as well be produced with the voice as with the tapping of feet. This is because rhythm is a form of music, but more importantly it is because rhythm is not addressed primarily to the particular interpretation being acted out with regard to a model under the hyperthematic structure of dance, rather, it is addressed to the interpretive freedom of the structure of dance as such.

If the folk dance lacked musicians, then this creating of rhythm by the onlookers would replace music. One may suppose that this is what happens in small villages that have perhaps only one or a few musicians; the onlookers engage the dance as creators of rhythm to enhance the relatively weak music of one or a few musicians. The musician may initiate the rhythms only to have the onlookers enhance it in strength. African music illustrates this very well, with its considerable emphasis on rhythm, often without highly specialized instruments.

Other kinds of dance however, such as ballet, or European-style ballroom dancing with orchestras, present a considerable difference. Here the rhythms may be more complex because the number and resources of the musicians permit them, and they also may be less complex because for the same reason other aspects of the music have taken on a far greater complexity than in the folk dance jig. Accordingly, we do not find the apparent participation of the onlooker, which is an enhancement of the music.

The audience, or onlookers, at a dance are participating in the music, but they are not participating in the dance unless they actually dance. The simple rhythms of the music are signs that expand the interpretive freedom of embodiment generally, which is closely allied to the structure of dance. The result of this is the urge to tap the fingers or toes, to sway, to clap, etc.

A further illustration of this is that a good case can be made between the complexity of a given type of music and the type of dance which develops in response to it. This implies that the music supports the dance rather than the reverse. A relatively complex type of music, e.g., Baroque music, gives rise to a relatively complex type of dance, i.e., the Baroque dance, which was a forerunner of classical ballet. A less complex type of music, e.g., rock 'n roll, gives rise to a proportionally less complex type of dance.

Musicians engaging themselves in interpretation under the hyperthematic structure of music have, relatively speaking, a tremendous range of complexity to play with, but every such engagement of a particular range of complexity has the ability to signify to a potential dancer a homogenous vision of his range of transformation as an embodied acting element. A certain complexity of music—e.g., classic rock 'n roll—will lure with an interpretive freedom as a range of possible action in which the will to interpret that interpretive freedom in various actions will make one wiggle and shake and twist, i.e., the music 'makes you want to' wiggle and shake and twist. Another complexity of music will lure toward interpretations, which take the form of wide and slow arcs with the limbs maximally extended, e.g., ballet. Yet other music such as punk rock will evoke simple repetitive and forceful motions. Or, as in jazz music with its relatively higher proportion of improvisation, it will promote a general "looseness of motion," which rests on the edge of being a dance, e.g., the flowing motions of the cabaret singer. And finally music may become so complex, as in some compositions by Charles Ives, that the expansion of interpretive freedom which it offers goes beyond the interpretive capacity of the acting transformable elements (we humans) engaged in the dance structure. With such music the vision is so complex that we do not know where to begin in action, and so very few people dance to it.

So music is the leader structure which supports dance. Yet, in principle, any hyperthematic structure can act as a leader structure with regard to a structure engaging a lower level of complexity. To understand how the structure of dance could act as a leader structure one would have to descend to an action harmonizing structure whose transformable elements are more restrictive than that of dance. This is not so very difficult to do. Thus, for example, if we were to assume that there is a hyperthematic structure under which walking becomes an interpretation of a problematic of experience—here with regard to the individual person as a community—then in principle the hyperthematic structure of dance which is more complex can act as a leader structure to the hyperthematic structure of walking. The transformable element will still be the human body, but it will be the body with regard to its range of actions restricted so that interpretations under the structure are all solutions to the experiential problematic of moving along one spatial axis in one direction, for example. In this case the supporting aspect of the dance structure can be illustrated by the grace and elegance with which seasoned dancers both walk and move in general. And indeed grace and elegance in movement has been intimately bound up with dancing as a social activity.[44]

All of this should go far to explain why dance is almost inevitably accompanied by music. If, at least in terms of the four structures already considered, music is furthest from dance in the complexity of experience it engages, then as a supporting or leading structure it is most likely to be "recruited" by the structure of dance because the structure of dance gets the most benefit from it, and—apart perhaps from the engagement of music with the listener as engaged willingly in nothing but listening—it is dance to which music can offer the most support.

Music of some kind seems to go with everything, but although it goes with everything it offers more to structures in proportion as their complexity is less than its own. A survey of music and its relation to the other structures already examined, ought to, and appears to, bear this out.

Music goes well with games. Chess in particular has a long relationship with music. Not only are many of its terms similar to musical terms, e.g., tempo and repertoire, but a number of highly regarded musicians have also been strong chess players. There is considerable agreement that listening to music—of certain relatively more complex genres—expands the chess player's overall vision of the game situation and her possibilities. The above appears to apply to many games. Sport, which could be viewed as occupying the middle ground somewhere between the dance and game structures, has also, particularly recently, been combined with music.

Consider that the ability to play music in a recorded form without having to engage live musicians is a fairly recent advance in human history. This accounts for the relatively more recent level of support by the music structure to activities which are not as far removed from it—and consequently less in need of its support—than is the structure of dance. The practical effort of making the music was bound to combine music first with the structures which needed it most.

Narrative appears at first to create an inconsistency in our account, for is not drama a form of narrative, and is it not the case that music has supported drama for long in human history? Ancient Greek dramatic productions had musical accompaniment for example. I admit this, but if you look more closely at what drama is you realize that there is a fine line which separates it from dance. In the case of ancient Greek drama that line is very fine indeed. The origins of ancient Greek drama lie in the dithyramb. The dithyramb, as a forerunner of Greek drama, appears to have been a form of dance accompanied by the singing of a chorus as well as simple wind instruments. Gradually this developed into what we are more familiar with as the tragedies and comedies of the classical Greek era.

Thus it appears to be the case that drama is an outgrowth of dance developed through the support of the structure of narrative and that narrative also can act as a leader structure with regard to the dance structure, but equally clearly, with regard to that support in the development of the Greek drama, narrative did not support the "pure" hyperthematic structure of dance, rather it supported the further development of a type of dance which had already found support from music. Music got there first.

From our perspective it will tend to look as if narrative precedes or at least co-originates with drama because the written word is our preeminent record of the issue. It may be, however, that it was dance already supported by music which was then engaged by the narrative form, first orally and then in writing. Further support of this assumption can be drawn from the history of the Chinese form of drama. Chinese opera even now retains a much closer relationship to its historic origins than does Western drama. The order in which the performers learn to perform Chinese opera appears to be one in which, among others, a series of very formalized and standard dancelike actions are learned in conjunction with music and only then strung together with the support of narrative structure.

One further illustration of the way this works can be found in the history of the early development of film. I do not have space here to consider it at length, e.g., to consider whether it is a hyperthematic structure in itself or merely a new medium which simplifies the support of other structures for one another, but what seems evident is that film as a new and rapidly developing sphere of human action has developed consistently with the above account. The earliest films, from about 1890, were short action sequences: two men boxing, a man engaged in athletic activity, people going about daily affairs, and very often someone dancing. All engaged the particularly localized and physical problematic, i.e., the less complex cousins of dancing if not dancing itself. These films were accompanied by music from almost the very beginning.

It took nearly a decade however—an eternity in terms of the development of film—before the first attempts at narrative film were made.[45] These attempts resulted in a gradual improvement in the ability of film actors to interpret narrative meaning. Nonetheless, during the first great era of film that followed, the era of the silent film, musical accompaniment long dominated as the preeminent support to the physical action of the film, so much so that film music became an industry in its own right. In the early 1930s, when the first major new technical advancement came in the form of recorded sound which accompanied films, the pattern repeated itself. "Recorded sound added new dimensions to all existing Hollywood genres, inaugurating many sub-genres in the process. It gave rise to only one completely new type, the feature-length musical."[46]

In hyperthematic terms then, the new advance in sound immediately put music to use in the birth of what is arguably that apotheosis of film culture as physicality—imagine Astaire and Rogers in *Top Hat*—which the new musicals were. Even by the late 1930s, by which time narrative had well begun to catch up, a film like *The Wizard of Oz*—winning an Academy Award for its music—could still be saturated with that physicality blending into dance in its more and less complex forms. Indeed, the near universal presence of musical accompaniment in the contemporary film industry indicates that film by its nature remains very much wedded to interpretation at physical complexities, although certain genres of film at least have slowly given way to an emphasis beyond physical complexity over the passing decades. Films that lack development beyond the origins of film as a medium, e.g., the typical contemporary action blockbuster, seem to regress by default to the point where predominantly physical action is supported by music.

If the foregoing appears to support the consistency of my suggestion that more complex structures have a greater tendency, as leader structures, to be drawn upon by less complex structures in proportion as those structures have a greater range of difference in their complexity with regard to the leader structure, and if it supports that suggestion with regard to drama as a form of narrative, then the strength of the suggestion is increased by considering the written word as narrative.

Hence, if one looks at last to the written word as the preeminent type of narrative, then it seems clear that books, though they might benefit to some degree by combination with music, are not evidently in demand of such support. If drama can be as complex as narrative, nonetheless it lies in the lower range of complexity which belongs to narrative as such. Its use of embodied action in human actors guarantees this. Books, on the other hand, occupy the upper range of complexity of narrative. Words as transformable elements open up incredible ranges of meaningful interpretation. Reading a skillfully crafted book often expands interpretive freedom both during and after reading it. Books as narrative are too close in complexity to music to need the support of music.

With this observation, however, another issue pops up. Books seem to support any and all human activities. Manuals of dance can be created, for example, compendiums of the moves and strategies of chess and other games, and books about music. How can it be that narrative can encompass music, which I suggested is a more complex structure? The answer, of course, is that it only appears to, but cannot ultimately. Books on music need further elements, elements which have a more complex range and degree of transformations, in order to be able to seemingly "encompass' music."Words as symbols are given the task of acting as musical elements in musical notation.

Musical notation does not expand the interpretive freedom of music. As an appeal to narrative it constricts the interpretive freedom of music. Yet writing down music in musical notation is perfectly consistent, if deliberately done as a mode of practice which later results in more complex musical interpretations. This is the application of the earlier **H13**, the consistent borrowing from one structure to help another. Here music borrows from narrative, a less complex structure. Through that borrowing it presents manageable problems to be interpreted, e.g., by beginning musicians. This aware practice aids the creative expansion of music. It helps the practicing musician solve problems at her capacity. Apart from this—it helps to be imaginative here—to write down music in musical notation is merely to bind or "crystallize" it onto the page. The only point of going backward in the restriction of practice can be to later go forward to greater creativity with more complex interpretations. Hence musical notation (as narrative) cannot capture the range of interpretation, which the structure of music engages in, or lead it. But it can help it consistently in the mode of practice.

It would take a still more complex structure, with a fuller and more transformable range of elements, to lead music. Mathematics may be such a hyperthematic structure. Mathematics can help and support music; music does not help or support mathematics as a leader structure, though again it might very well complement it in relation to practice according to **H13** and in the formation of models for guiding more localized possibilities of action according to the hypertheme **H11**. What would it be like for mathematicians to look to music in the mode of practice? Both mathematics and music make use of narrative symbols; they constrict to the page for practice. What it might mean for mathematicians to constrict to music for practice could perhaps only properly be addressed by mathematicians themselves. My suggestion—that of a non-mathematician—is that the mathematical interpretation of musical pieces, as problems to be interpreted in mathematical terms, would have an effect in terms of practice analogous to that of the practice, which the use of musical notation facilitates in going from music down to narrative.[47]

Mathematics is an example of a very complex leader structure. Besides its leading relation to music, it appears to be the leader structure to which all scientific hyperthematic structures, structures of a lower complexity than that of mathematics, look for support. Are there limits then to the supporting capabilities of a leader structure, according to its complexity? One may suppose that in the ongoing interpretation of the world's problematic, there is a tendency for less complex structures to be created earlier in the time process with respect to other structures in proportion as they are less complex than those structures. Thus dance ought to arise long before mathematics, long before music of any considerable complexity, somewhat less long before narrative (e.g., as spoken), and even less long before games (as simple structured play).

A considerable digression would be needed to show this, but the following highly suggestive point can at least be noted, particularly because it avoids consideration of human actions. Many animals appear to interpret experience through the structures of dance in its more complex range as we noted, and through structured play, which borders upon dance. On the other hand, the ubiquity of the animal use of narrative, music, and mathematics, seems to decline in the order given. Many animals appear to make simple signals to one another approximating "proto-speech," fewer animals—the songbirds and perhaps some crickets—make simple music, and mathematical ability appears to be exceedingly rare.

If the above holds good, then while it is plausible that in principle the hyperthematic structures furthest in complexity from a given structure should support that structure the most; nonetheless, on the one hand the structures furthest in complexity from a given structure will not support or influence that structure first if they are so complex as to be still *undeveloped*. Hence mathematics may be on a higher level than music, but if it is at such a level of complexity as to be relatively undeveloped, then it will not tend to act as a support structure to dance, for example, before other lower-level structures have acted in support, e.g., music.

On the other hand, if the structure is *too* complex relative to the complexity of a given structure of a lower complexity, its support will simply *saturate* the interpretive freedom of the lower structure. Thus mathematics may well support dance, but as I noted with regard to extremely complex music such as that of Ives, even music cannot support dance if it is too complex, i.e., there may be an expansion of meaning to the point where dance as a structure is overloaded. Even if mathematics could be used to make the dancer experience on the higher level the full possible range of the acting human body as a transformable element, undoubtedly this would be too much. The richness of action, which that guidance would bring, would simply make us freeze up with regard to any action, for the boundaries of interpretation of types of dance within the structure would dissolve in a moment of "what should I do now?" Adding the further consideration that it would take a tremendous skill both on the part of the mathematician and on the part of the dancer to engage in a supportive interpretation of such complexity, you begin to see why mathematics has hitherto not given much apparent support to dance.

Nonetheless, in principle mathematics *could* interpret the meaning of the complete range of transformation of one or many acting elements engaged in the structure of dance. Yet, while it could so interpret that range, there may be little use at present for it to do so. The sign of such an interpretation might take the form of the solution to checkers. The solution of checkers is only a solution, however, that has relevance according to an initial restricted selection of moves in the checker game.

The billions of moves and responses that are the solution of checkers would have an equivalent in terms of the solution of the dance structure. Yet the latter—the mathematical guidance toward a complete interpretation of dance—would quickly begin to lose its relevance as a support because the embeddedness in the time process, or localized character, or embodiedness, of the acting human elements within the dance structure, is so far removed from it in complexity as to be able to make use of only scraps of the solution. This once again is what I mean by the saturation of interpretive freedom, here akin to presenting the dancer with "all the motions possible for the human physical body in space and time."

Of course multiple dancers, as well as complexities of dance beyond anything we now know, could be created to take advantage of the mathematically supported expansion of the interpretive freedom of dance might take such forms as dances greatly extended with regard to a human lifetime—e.g., a dance which is performed over several years—or even extended to encompass several human lifetimes. All this is possible, even likely, but we are not there yet.[48]

In effect then, when hyperthematic leader structures expand the interpretive freedom of less complex structures, it is on the basis of each structure having, according to its complexity, a certain capacity for interpretation, i.e., a certain capacity for harmonizing interpretive action with regard to a particular problematic of experience. The leader structure helps the less complex structure operate at greater capacity. If it opens up the structure to its full capacity, then the structure may or may not be saturated. Generally the effect of opening up the capacity of interpretation of a structure is beneficial to the elements of the community: first, a greater capacity means that more elements can engage in interpretations under the structure, and second, the elements which so engage are less likely to repeat old interpretations.

A greater capacity for interpretation means more room for interpreting elements to maneuver; it means more creativity and less staleness of interpretation and consequently greater value. It means a stabilizing of the community of interpretation. This is nicely in evidence in the history of music.[49] The history of Western music is so far full of genres of music of various complexities, each of which lay claim to a certain range of the total capacity of music, and each of which is eagerly interpreted until it is "mined out" by a multitude of actors. Thus Baroque music's range of complexity was interpreted until it reached a high point and then began to repeat its old interpretations. At that point the interpretive freedom of music expanded, or perhaps was helped to expand, and gave rise to the Classical period of Western music, whence again the same thing occurred, and led to the Romantic period, and so forth.[50] If mathematics is a leader structure for music as I suggested, it would be interesting to explore whether the increasing complexity of music was driven at least in part by an increase in mathematical complexity. There does appear to be a nice parallel between mathematical and musical advances in the Western world. The advance of Eastern music, particularly Hindu music, may be open to similar speculations.

The moment has been reached to suggest another hypertheme which captures the foregoing: **H15**—*hyperthematic structures are best supported, i.e., their communities of interpretation are stabilized, by hyperthematic leader structures whose complexity is furthest from their own.* Although in principle any structure with a level of complexity higher than the structure in question could act as a leader structure, nonetheless, since there is a tradeoff between complexity and the time process situatedness of the acting element, then the leader structure, which will be able to give the best support, is that which is both well developed, and whose complexity is not so far removed as to saturate the interpretive freedom of the supported structure.

Choose the most complex leader structure you are able to while bearing in mind the pragmatic aspect of diverse ranges of complexity. If, for example, mathematics is too complex to support dance as it stands at the moment, still it may support narrative very nicely, though this also is something that is not yet far advanced, since narrative is further from mathematics than music.[51]

I have suggested that an attentive interpretive engagement on the part of both musicians and listeners is needed to form the community of interpretation engendered by the hyperthematic structure of music. Insofar as music is at such a level of complexity as to be a leader structure for many of the other hyperthematic structures which we humans engage in, then we might expect that destabilizing and reconstructive acts in music would not only be very complex, but would be, for music, more visibly bound up with the characteristic of being a leader structure than for lower structures. What then constitutes the destabilizing act for music and what constitutes reconstruction?

As for narrative, only in a more complex manner, one source of destabilization in music will be an engagement that attempts to eliminate other elements of the community, and now in the case of music it will manifest itself as an engagement which attempts to eliminate the elements of other communities to which it ought to be a support structure. Both of these will be exemplified in exclusionary tendencies.

In the first case, engagements in music that are eliminative of ranges of complexity, i.e., various types of minimalism, will, if carried through, destabilize the community of interpretation under the structure of music. As always, a distinction must be made here between selection of elements and elimination of elements. To concentrate upon a certain range of complexity within music—engage simpler problems—in order to better interpret later is consistent as practice. Yet if the above account is consistent, then the deliberate exclusion of complexity, *as such*, is destabilizing, a restriction of elements which chokes interpretive action for the community.

The second case will be exemplified in attempts to exclude and thus effectively eliminate acting elements—e.g., human elements—from the musical community of interpretation or from other communities. Such attempts often occur hand-in-hand with the attempt to eliminate ranges of complexity. Here something larger is also at stake. Exclusionary music, like exclusionary narrative, is a deliberate engagement in the hyperthematic structure of music—and the same occurs in art as we shall see later—so as to exclude elements of its own community, or elements of other communities. As narrative has its secret books just for our group, so music has its songs, chants, or other musical efforts, just for our group. In proportion, since music is more of a leader structure, this type of destabilization runs deeper than, for example, that toward communities under the hyperthematic structure of dance. A structure engaging a more complex experience does more harm, if misused, than one engaging a simpler experience.

Music in the service of an exclusionary nationalism can illustrate the above. The exclusionary uses to which music was put in Nazi Germany are an example: music for "our kind," or "our race." The music of early post-revolutionary China—songs such as the subtly titled "The People of the World Will Surely Be Victorious!" which was prominent during the Chinese Cultural Revolution—also illustrates the tendency. Such musical interpretations are made with an intent counter to the main characteristic of music as a leader structure that expands interpretive freedom for other communities.

Another case will be music whose intent is to expand the interpretive freedom, especially of the elements of another community, to the point of saturation, so that some acting element effectively loses the ability to interpret within that community. Marketing uses music in this way, e.g., jingles and more complex music used in television advertising, and ambient music used in big-box stores. Such music usually has the intent of expanding the interpretive freedom of an acting element engaged in interpretation within the community of what we might loosely call the community of traders, i.e., in which buyer and seller engage in interpretation.

The point is often to render the buyer incapable of interpretation within the trading community. Advertising music is meant to make you forget yourself as a buyer with limited means, with specific interests, and so forth; and to reduce your interpretive participation in that community under which you are a buyer to nothing more than the act of buying, i.e., the least selective act of interpretation possible in the region of interpretation in question. You can't afford this new car perhaps, and it may not be the best car for your needs, nonetheless "your possibilities are wide open, you are free! Go ahead buy it!" urges the music. The music, like that of the Pied Piper, tries to draw you out of other communities—e.g., the community of a family, sharing economic constraints—and practically eliminates you momentarily from participation in that community.

Leader structures can have considerable impact upon the stability of many communities when abused in this way, for there are always other communities linked to the affected communities. Mathematics, for example, as a leader structure, has for some time now been used to saturate interpretive freedom on a grand scale by presenting a dizzying show of economic figures and statistics, a chimaera of endless growth and borrowing capacity, along with the endless babble of Wall Street busily engaged in the nonsense of technical analysis of securities, all of these calculated to deaden real economic interpretations, leaving Western and global society with far greater devaluations than those prompted by the abuse of the hyperthematic structure of music.

The complexities of music suggest that the acts of healing reconstruction, which will meet such destabilizing actions, will themselves be highly complex acts. On the other hand, the use of recorded music, which has made such destabilizing actions as the commercial abuse of music more prevalent, is a very recent invention in human history. Accordingly, the fitting acts of reconstruction, which will meet those acts, are not yet very evident. But they will arise.

Music that takes the form of a constricting exclusionary nationalism in musical interpretation has already sometimes been met with the skill, wisdom, and creative artfulness of reconstructive action. The Fifth Symphony of Dmitri Shostakovich as a response to the Stalinist repression of the Russian musical community is perhaps illustrative of just such an act, as are the various efforts of Sergei Prokofiev.[52] Such responses may still fall short of all that we could dream of—as the ongoing debate over the deeper motives of Shostakovich and others indicates—but creative response *at all* in the face of severe constriction is always already a brave step in the right direction.

3

Hyperthematic Expansion of Light and Color

The last region of human experience that I will submit to the exploratory mode of Hyperthematics will be that of the visual arts. Before I do that, however, I am going to digress somewhat. I am going to undertake a hyperthematic musement upon light and color. Part of my motive is that color is central to the visual arts. Yet more than this it is intimately bound up with the aspect of the world process as physical, being the cousin of shape and density, and as we move into the region of the visual arts more properly so called, the effort put into this chapter will provide much to play with in the expansion of the visual arts, showing how the visual arts, although consistent as communities under a hyperthematic structure, are nonetheless limited by inconsistent tendencies that also give rise to the physical range of complexity of the world process in which human processes find themselves embodied. Insofar as I succeed, both the vision of the smooth range of complexity of experience to be engaged on the basis of the method and the results regarding the various consistent and inconsistent assumptions of hyperthematic structures will be made more plausible. Further hyperthemes will no doubt be uncovered to fill our "toolbox" with for later use.

There is no easy way to begin a musement upon light and color. As good a tack as any is to begin by asking the question: "what are colors, or better, what are colors in hyperthematic terms?" The opening hyperthematic assumptions hold that the world as value is a world in which diversity of experience is linked through interpretation. If that is plausible may it not be that we may engage color and consequently light as regions of experience to be deciphered according to those assumptions? In other words, taking light and color to be just so many diverse experiences, can we not interpret them according to the opening assumptions, as already done with the experiences in the regions of music, dance, and so forth?

If so, it suggests that the meaning of light and color is to be uncovered through a series of functional relations in our hyperthematic sense, which constrict or expand interpretation at some range of complexity of experience, according to inconsistency or consistency with hyperthemes akin to those already formulated. Furthermore, light and color also surely participate in the value and valuation of the world process according to the various constrictions or expansions of interpretation which both engage and create them within that process. In short, *light and its colors and the relations between them arise on the basis of a valuating or devaluating engagement of experience by means of restrictions or expansions of interpretation.* This is my opening suggestion.

Still, you may now insist: "what we have always wanted to know is why there are the colors that there are *at all*, and not merely why the colors have relations to one another or what those relations are. Why is there for example the experience that we call red?" This is the old problem of qualia and the answer to it depends on countenancing what you are asking for, in other words, what an answer would look like. Or again it depends upon the problem.

Color as a Creation of Interpretive Action

Well what could an answer look like? Its question is a why, as are so many of the questions in the world. Accordingly, it intends to be a meaningful answer. Thus it intends to be an interpretation. An interpretation of what though?

When we are at the seemingly simple level of color at all we feel that the experience is one which is not a problematic at all in the sense of a diversity of experience which can be bridged by an interpretation; or rather we feel that its only answer could come from a source "behind" experience so to speak. Yet such a feeling is misplaced, for the question demands its answer in the only terms it knows: as a solution to problems *at all*. It demands an answer of *meaning*. Demanding such, it is akin to the question: "why is there anything at all?" with the bare color experience substituting for the anything at all. And just so it will be solved in the same manner as I have suggested the problem of value can be solved, by changing the assumption through which it engages experience, so as to be consistent, and then working its way back from the dead end it has worked itself into. Let us try this route in hyperthematic terms.

There is color *at all*. Its *at all* character looks to an experience which would hold the color, any of the colors, say red, as interpreted to another experience. This other experience will be a not-red experience, and the interpretation between it and the experience of red will be the interpretation of one who *himself as a process brings about the experience of red out of an experience of not-red*.

Those so inclined will immediately object: "indeed but the line of your argument is still within the experience itself. Having got the experience through your world process as you call it, it merely gives the formula of the manipulation of experience which brings us back to the experience of red, rather than explaining why there is such an experience at all, or more directly where the source of the experience lies." And my reply will be: "your objection highlights the urge to slip back into the dead end line. Your question itself assumes that the answer to it will be found as an interpretation, not as an appeal to a source which is neither experience nor connected by meaningful interpretation to the experience of red. This is what you intend when you ask *why*, you intend *that there should be meaning*.

The appeal to a source, which is neither experience nor connected by meaningful interpretation to the experience of red, is the result of a mistaken assumption—or at least one that is not made in this work—i.e., that the world has unbridgeable disconnections. But according to the assumption **H** the tendency engendered by this assumption is a tendency of constriction. To get out of that trap we must, according to our opening assumption, countenance an expansion which looks not "inward" in constriction to the ultimate but independent source, rather we must look outward to an expansion with regard to experience. In short, the answer is going to come from pulling back, rather than digging deeper, so as to view the problem in the light of a greater experience.

And here is how it can be done with regard to the experience of color at all. The objection has insisted that: the interpretation of one who *himself as a process brings about the experience of red out of an experience of not-red* is not what is sought because this would be merely an understanding of how to bring about a color which is already given to experience, or, if you like an understanding merely of how to rearrange experience so as to present something which is already there. Well, this is a simple thing to do isn't it? We can make our objects red. We paint them or so create them that their surfaces are red. As is known to the scientifically inclined we do that through techniques that merely manipulate what we do understand, i.e., what we do hold before ourselves, as experience connected through interpretation. And our objector above is right in insisting that this is not what we are after in our question regarding "color *at all.*" We may make a surface of our object reflect redness, and we may make an object such that the red from other sources comes through it. But this is but a small part of what we seek when we seek to answer the question.

Yes, but we may also produce the red in a direct way. We may fashion a red light, for example, which converts white light to red, although this is clearly a variant upon the manipulation of object surfaces. Even better, we may directly manipulate the energies of what we call the electromagnetic spectrum so as to produce wavelengths of electromagnetic energy which are red to us.

Still, red feels like more than light energy to us—even our manipulation of the surface of objects hints at this—and the answer to the question of color at all does not feel answered by it. The meaning of color, e.g., red, *at all,* to those who ask the question, feels eerily like the sort of thing that could not be gained by us as we are presently. Even as this is admitted however, there is something in our musement which hints at an answer. We are expanding the scope of the presumed answer to the question by playing outward over the various ways in which we engage experience so as to bring about red. Hitherto digging to *find* an answer, we are now engaged in filling in toward *creating* our answer so to speak. Let us continue in this.

Indirect manipulation is not enough, no. Direct manipulation is but a little better. Let us try our method directly. To answer the question of "why red?" one would have to be able to create red, one would have to be able to behold meaningfully why it is created. Yet to create it, is so far, in the ways I have noted above, only to *recreate* it. This was admitted when we admitted that the manipulations noted above, simply and scientifically complex, direct and indirect, were not satisfying as answers to "why red at all."

Now with regard to the existence of red, I will assume that we are ready to admit that red exists, at least I, the author, am. Yet if it exists, then to recreate it is to gain its existence again in some region of experience where it was not. But this, in short, is to *copy* it. I have already suggested earlier in the expansion of the hyperthematic structure of dance, that copying is a tendency which—unless it is consistently viewed as merely local *practice*—diminishes value. This is because the tendency toward copying gives rise to symmetries between the original and the copy. The copy comes to "mirror" the original, in one sense or another. The more symmetric, the fewer facets of interpretation there are to interpret between in the diversities of experience, which are symmetrical to one another. But the tendency toward "less to interpret," engendered by symmetry, is inconsistent with the opening assumptions and begins to degrade value.

To create red then we are going to have to do more than just copy it. To create it we are going to have to engender new interpretations with respect to the existent fact, the experience of red. The issue before us now is: can this be done? It can be done. The tendency toward symmetry is a constrictive tendency. Very well, let us formulate a corrective which we will call the *Hypertheme of Creativity*, **HCr**—*in order to create experience, engage in interpretations which insofar as possible interpret a portion—an existent fact—of experience within the world process to a portion of experience within the world process which does not include the original portion within itself.*

In other words, develop threads of interpretation which begin, or have begun, or will end at your selected experience (e.g., red) and proceed as far as possible away from it without reinstating it as it existed at the beginning of your effort. Insofar as you do this, you are on the trail of the seemingly mysterious "source" which lies "behind" the existence of the color (e.g., red), *for the source as a carrier of meaning, cannot, under the opening assumptions of hyperthematics, lie outside of the whole process of the world as a ground of all realizable meaning.* Insofar as you do *not* do this, then eventually you find yourself reduced to the experience of "red *is* red," while digging in vain for the "source" of the fact.

Let us apply the hypertheme **HCr** now. In fact, our many endeavors do this already. The community of science does this already with colors, just as the community of painting does it. They do it in every *new* interpretation or series of interpretations that are *creative*. They fail and fall into inconsistency whenever they merely *copy*. To indicate where they might go further I will give several instances of actions which satisfy the tendency of **HCr**.

The **first** instance falls within the region of experience guided by the Hyperthematic Structure of Science and, though in this work I will not tackle that structure beyond more than suggestions, both **HCr** and the hyperthemes I will formulate presently are hyperthemes of the community of science in its consistent aspects. Keeping red as the example, the first instance then would arise when human actors interpretively expand from the region of an experience that includes red to a region of experience, which—ultimately—does not include red. Let us select the human body as the region for our example (although others are possible—such as changes of coloration in species, or of rocks, over long periods in nature).

The human body as the locus of a process can be interpreted with regard to the history of its development. Let us say one begins at the makeup of the contemporary human body (or alternatively of the human visual system), as known to the endeavors of science according to its branches: biological, psychological, physical, among others. We know that "red" arises within the region of its experience, at a certain complexity, as a result of what we call biological, physical, and psychological causes.

We now take action to interpret the contemporary account of seeing red in its various aspects backward through time by means of interpretations of the present situation (i.e., the signs at that range of interpretive complexity, which indicate the temporally nearer interpretations within the world process with respect to our bodies), to interpretations of our developmental history, i.e., the signs that are more complex. This of course is the usual work of consistent scientific action. Each new step further back is a creation of a unique interpretation. It is an interpretive link of our contemporary selves with regard to the selected aspect—the visual experience of the color red—of our physical bodies, qua physical bodies, to our historic biological selves. To both feel and know, i.e., to interpret at various ranges of complexity, how the earlier visual systems of our eyes differed from their current state in their biological, psychological, physical, etc., aspects, is to expand ourselves with respect to our being the loci of various facts of our experience.

"But," you may say, "even if your scientific action is a great success, you have still only given the *how*, but not the *why* of the matter." I reply: the action proceeds in its aspect of *how* only so far as we forget the intention which begins it. The intention, (or willed action to engage a problem as a problem) that begins it by putting into action the tendency **HCr**, which we decided to abide by above, is here put to the use of interpretively connecting my current physical body as an experience, to the stages of its own temporal development.* The meaning of every new and creative interpretation arrived at in the scientific pursuit which interprets my bodily development, is based upon this building of a community of myself with my older self, a community of selfhood, albeit here only at the level of physical bodily complexity. If you ignore this *intent*, you have a mere succession of

---

Intention will be defined as the willed action to engage a problem *as a problem to be solved through interpretation*. Intention always—though very often implicitly and unconsciously—adopts our foundational assumption **H**, engaging a particular region and problem of experience on the basis of accepting that *problems in the world are solvable through some interpretation so as to gain meaning*. But very often we forget this more or less in the act of solving the selected problem, so as to engender inconsistencies in the tendencies of action with which we engage the problem, e.g., when a scientist views the scientific effort as a *mere* fact-collecting endeavor, free of interpretation.

existent facts. You may ignore it, and when science is pursued without it, it is pursued to gain the mere *how*. When it is pursued deliberately (rather than merely locally) in this manner, it is inconsistent. It is tending toward a mere playing over the facts, even though it is never merely this because other tendencies in living life as a whole are at work beyond being a mere scientist. The test of which approach has come to the fore in a given case is an easy one. The *how* is always that which can be and is *copied by others*, whereas the *why* is a new and unique interpretation which, insofar as it is merely copied, degrades toward a meaningfully diminished technical how.

There is practice of course, as was noted in the chapter on dance. Consistent practice is always aware that it is only locally consistent however. It allows copying locally for the sake of an increase of value through later creation. Insofar as it is not consistently aware of this it tends toward mere rote learning. Insofar as we have a consistent scientific engagement of the problem of our contemporary physical visual systems to those of our remote ancestors, and insofar as we are making greater and greater strides in those newly creative interpretive connections between our current and past visual systems then we are gaining meaning and value. That meaning and value is the answer to the *why* of our visual systems (in this, the chosen case, it is the *why* with regard to seeing the color red).

I experience red with my current eyes. I engage in scientific interpretations of the historical physical signs available to me and push my interpretations further and further back in time to the development of the eyes of my earliest human ancestors. How did *Homo rhodesiensis* see red; how did *Homo ergaster*; how *Homo erectus*, and so on. Insofar as this gains meaning, it goes beyond mere facts. I see red. The facts indicate that *Homo erectus* saw red in the way that he saw it, as the scientists tell me. So far I am in the way of a mere *how* as a series of facts. But when I see red *in my way* and the facts indicate that *Erectus* saw red *in his way*—that is, he saw it in part *as a function of his biological visual system*, which differs from mine and yet has its functional relation to mine—and between those facts I make an interpretation that is backed by the awareness of *the very intent to interpret*, then his red gains its new and unique interpretation to my red and I am aware that the interpretation is *mine, and part of the ongoing community of my ethical self as a self of value.*

In other words, the existent fact of red for him is expanded with regard to its connection to mine. My red *is not* his red, and yet verily the latter now has its *meaningful interpretation* to my red, and this is just the tendency that our **HCr** advocated: that we interpret an experience *to* *a portion of experience within the world process which does not include the original portion within itself.*

Now this will appear suspect at first because we are un-used to viewing the matter in these terms. Yet it cannot be otherwise if the world is a world of value as I have suggested, for the tendency toward viewing aspects of experience as perennially unchanging—the tack of the older empiricists—results ultimately in a world where past experiences can have no interpretive relation to present and future experiences beyond a copied sameness distinguishable in an abstractly quantified temporality within the process of experience.[1] In other words, there are no sacred aspects of unchanging experience, no pegs upon which to hang the hats of those "mere visitors" which are the aspects of changing experience.

The experience, which we now call red, needs its ongoing reinterpretation as a creative development out of its own *distant sources* if it is to have value in a world of value. And if we go further with regard to the same example we will through enough interpretation reach a point where our human ancestor did not see red at all *as we see it*. As we tend toward that goal, interpreting ever anew in creative ways, each of us who does so gains an expanding and unique answer—according to these creative ways—to that mysterious *why* of the experience of red.

That then is the first example, with its portion of the answer to the why of red, i.e., the meaning of red as the *aware interpretation* of the developmental history of red with regard to the biological visual system of the human body. Each of us insofar as he undertakes this—and only some of us will do so very far[2]—will arrive at a unique meaning of red for himself with regard to the developmental aspect of the biological visual system. Those who consistently take these actions over a longer temporal span we call *the great scientists*, the value of whose uniquely meaningful lives as scientists are built upon such actions.

We have explored as our first instance of a use of **HCr** an example of an expansion from a region of experience which contains red to one which moves toward not-containing-red. For our **second** instance we will give an example of *an interpretive expansion from a region of experience which does not contain red to a region which does contain red*. Again, this will be an example informed by a hyperthematic exploration of a few of the contemporary results of science, this time with regard to the human visual system and the physics of light. The import of my suggestions with regard to the example will only arrive near the end of that exploration; indeed they will only make up a very small part of it.

Hyperthematic Expansion of Light and Color | 109

As is well known, according to the current view we humans, in our physical aspect as biological systems, view light as color within what we call the *visible spectrum* of light. Meanwhile, the light we understand as an energy travels in waves at certain frequencies. But other animals evidently see light from our visible spectrum as well, and moreover in many cases they *see* light beyond the bounds of our visible spectrum, which we can register by means of various instruments but cannot *see*, i.e., cannot experience as we experience light color from our visible spectrum through our unaided visual systems. They have their own visible spectrum in which they *see*. Certain snakes such as pythons and pit vipers are said to have evolved these abilities both independently of one another, and multiple times, over evolutionary history. Such animals will serve as the basis for asking the question around which the second example of the use of **HCr** will coalesce: *how can we explain these varying capacities to see light in hyperthematic terms?*

To begin it will be necessary to expand somewhat upon the nature of light as it is already understood and also upon space, for, as the reader will see, the question is intimately bound up with the issue of physical space. A very brief contemporary description of light will include some of the following points.

The visible spectrum of light is made up of light energy whose wavelength runs from approximately 700 nm to 400 nm. It is part of the electromagnetic spectrum of energy whose wavelengths, so far as we currently understand them for our use, run from many km to 0.1 Angstroms (an Angstrom being one ten-billionth of a meter). The wavelength meanwhile is the measure on our scale of distances between one (selected) point of the wave and the next repetition of that point. Light waves recur in a manner that is captured mathematically as the function of a sinusoidal wave, a function that captures the smooth oscillation of the action of the light energy. The action, which recurs in the sinusoidal wave, is in turn captured in its non-repetitive aspect by the sine function, which can be viewed as an action of movement around the edge of a circle viewed over time. When that action repeats, as it does for the light wave energy, the sine function action becomes the sinusoidal wave action.

Light waves, as an action repeating over time, have a wavelength as noted. But they also have a *frequency* of repetition. The frequency of repetition is the number of times the light wave repeats itself over a selected unit of time (or in our terms: with regard to an abstractively selected event of the world process). The frequency of the electromagnetic spectrum, as we currently understand it for our use, runs from less than 10^6 Hz, or cycles per second, to more than 10^{19} Hz. The light waves of the spectrum run from approximately 430 to 750 trillion Hz. So much will suffice for a brief description of certain aspects of light waves.

Now, let us turn the hyperthematic method upon the various aspects of the light wave to see how they fare with regard to the assumption **H**. **H** tells us broadly, through the various direct derivatives and the hyperthemes of the previous structures already explored, that constrictions of interpretation are inconsistent and lead to a diminishment of value while expansions of interpretation are consistent and lead to an increase of value. A question now arises: can nature be viewed hyperthematically at a very basic level—which I have called the physical level of complexity of experience within the world process—as being subject to the implications of the assumption **H**?

I leave aside for the moment—hoping to take it up in a later work—the issue of the broader character of the aspects of nature viewed according to our not knowing from whence the sources of nature's actions emanate. All I will do now is engage the character of nature—as exemplified here in the characteristics of the colors of light—with regard to that low-level physical group of facts regarding light, which include wave, wavelength, frequency, etc.

Interpretive Action and Value at Lower Physical Complexity

I will do so by first noting the implications of the suggestions that proceed from **H** about constriction and expansion with regard to physical *shape* as a result of actions at the physical level of complexity of experience. One could start anywhere in the region of shape, but the two-dimensional *line* will do well enough. How do lines stand with regard to **H** and its derivatives, i.e., can they be interpreted to **H**?

They can. A line is often described abstractively as a series of points. The repeated action of drawing a series of points forms a line. If the intention of the repetition is simple, the line is formed as a straight line. Let one be drawing upon paper with a pen. Let one be repeatedly touching the pen to paper, as when making a period. If one moves the pen slightly in one direction, say horizontally across the paper—in one plane as we say—the line (of points) grows in that plane as a straight line. In other words, we have expanded our interpretation with such an action. We have interpreted the initial action—and do so anew with each dip of the pen—to a new part of the paper. The line grows, straight, but also longer with each dip.

We have here initiated an expansion of interpretive complexity with regard to experience; we have added a facet of interpretation to the sign—the line on paper—that we are drawing. The line is more valuable than if we had not done so; the interpretive play of our action over it has created a meaning that is greater than if we had not. We have taken up our time in the world process to draw the line. If we had not done so, if we had dipped pen to paper repeatedly *without* moving in the horizontal, we would have what? A point. It would still have meaning and value *if* we interpreted it to the greater experience we are drawing it in. But the issue here is not this; the issue is where does the point stand with regard to the line? With regard to the line it has less value. Relative to the drawing of the line, it is tending toward *being a series of copies of an action with regard to the experience of the paper,* i.e., the point is tending toward a sameness with regard to its location on the paper. Its value suffers accordingly.

Let us go back to our line. The line has advanced from a sameness with regard to its location on the paper in one plane (say horizontal or side-to-side across the paper), but it has still that sameness with regard to the vertical plane of the paper (bottom to top). We continue drawing our line and the line is straight so far. But now we undertake another expansion, and as we continue horizontally we also begin to interpret the pen dipping at each moment to the vertical aspect of the paper as well as to the horizontal. The result is: a *curve.**

The meaning of the curve is greater than that of the straight line by the opening assumptions—for more facets of interpretation have gone into it to be present before us—and considerably greater than that of the point. As we transition to a curve the action that we have selected is one which has its interpretation to several facets of the experience of the paper, and thus the value of this ongoing interpretive process is accruing likewise, horizontally as well as vertically, as the solving—in the action of drawing—of the problem which the blank paper presents. The curve is more valuable than the straight line (hereafter I will simply use *line* and *linear* interchangeably for *straight line* and *curve* for *curving line*). It is the engagement of a more complex experience. It leaves for a new interpreter a more complex sign to guide further interpretation.

Let us say that in our drawing we attempt to add yet another aspect of experience. We have covered the horizontal aspect of the paper and the vertical aspect. We now take action to add a depth aspect to the paper, a

---

*See Diagram 1 in *Diagrams* section near the end of the volume.

third plane if you will. Now, if we are confined to paper and pen our success in this will go only so far, as everyone knows, and the effort often naturally moves toward so drawing on our paper that the effect—we much too lightly call it the *appearance*—of depth is created by making interpretive linkages now to the *human visual system* and to our *memories of experiences in the depth plane*. But nonetheless we get an expansion to another (or perhaps several) aspects of experience with regard to the paper, wherein the meaning is greater than the point, the line, and the curve. Again the meaning and value are increased. Yet we may do this easily enough so as to either build up the paper or, which is more likely, to pass beyond paper to a medium such as sculpture clay. When we go to such a medium the expansions and contractions of interpretation due to the tendencies of action are going to behave similarly.

The line becomes the flat plane; the curve becomes the curved surface. And what of the point? The point in our abstraction of experience as having three dimensions is tending toward constriction of interpretation—toward uninterpretability—just as it was in our abstraction of experience as having two dimensions.

Very well, if the reader has followed so far she will begin to see the import of our expansion, namely, that at a very simple physical level the world conforms to **H** and the derivatives. The physical world is abstracted from the world process of experience with regard to our actions. This was my suggestion. To carry out the expansion and show that it was plausible I chose briefly an action within the region of drawing, which is familiar enough to everyone, being a simple type of visual art. If we are engaged in drawing in the sense above, how do we stand with regard to our four hyperthematic derivatives (I will use the negative formulations here for convenience)?

H1' says: do not eliminate elements of experience. If we pass from drawing in two planes to drawing in one plane we eliminate the element of the second plane. If we pass from drawing in one plane, as in the above example, to—ostensibly—drawing in no planes, we eliminate a further element. The first constriction would be to go from curve to line, the second from line to point. We are losing facets of experience to interpret; we are losing meaning and losing value. In short, we are moving toward uninterpretability, toward denying **H**.

H2' says: An element is unstable if it eliminates from its own or another community under a hyperthematic structure. A human actor may be such an element. In this case if he is an artist or a draftsman he eliminates elements of the drawing of another within his community, or he eliminates elements of another community with his drawing (draws over something of another community, for example). Or the element need not be a human actor; it might be a solvent which dissolves ink, for example. Either way we are losing value.

H3' says: a single element or pair of elements cannot make up a community under a hyperthematic structure, though it may make up part of a larger community. In our drawing terms, neither a point alone, nor two points without interpretation, may make up a community. Yet the point or points may make up a community on another level of complexity, *the drawing of the artist.*

H4' says: a community cannot eliminate other communities, or elements of other communities. The community of art in the normal course of things does not.

The community of art is not yet the main interest here however. Rather, I have wandered into drawing as an engagement of experience with a very physical character in order to test the consistencies and inconsistencies of actions engendering the physical point, line, curve, etc., with respect to **H**. This will indeed serve as a base of an expansion on the visual arts, which is to come shortly. Before it does, however, there are several further things to note as implications and I am going to apply them to an expansion upon light color.

I have suggested that the tendencies to interpret *more* or *fewer* aspects of experience lead to shape in the physical world. If that suggestion is plausible, then, based on the opening assumptions, the following are implied. Linearity is better, i.e., more valuable, than pointedness. Curvature is better, more valuable, than linearity. The maximum of curvature is better than lesser curvatures. The perfectly circular is better than all other curvatures of two dimensions. Moreover, the three dimensional is better than the two dimensional, which in turn is better than the one dimensional. The plane surface is better than the point in three dimensions. The curved surface is better than the plane surface. The spherical surface is better than the three-dimensional surface of a lesser curvature. The sphere is better than the limited spherical surface. There are further interpretive aspects of experience, e.g., dimensions, whose shapes, if we could achieve them, are better, more valuable, still.

The reverse of the above is also implied, and it must not be forgotten that *tendencies are being dealt with*, so that our recognition of the tendencies in experience is always going to depend upon the complexity of our selected problematic, and so forth. Yet more is implied however, and some of it must be expanded upon. I have suggested already that tendencies toward symmetry are tendencies toward diminishment of value. A position has been reached to see briefly how this works itself out at the level of complexity of the physical world in terms of shapes.

If a shape—let it be two or three dimensional for our purposes—tends toward the loss of aspects of experience, then the ability to interpret it diminishes and its value diminishes accordingly. It is a worse shape, a relatively *bad* shape. If, for example, a shape tends toward a point, it is tending toward a loss of value in the manner suggested above. If it has *corners* they end in points which are regions of experience presenting a loss of value. The more curved it is and the fewer corners it has, all else aside, the better a shape it is, value wise.

This brings us to symmetry. For if a shape has corners, its corners tend toward symmetry. A corner of a square for example is formed of intersecting lines, but the lines can be mapped onto one another as a mirror image by bisecting the shape of the square through two of its corners. Whenever portions of a shape can be mapped onto other portions, most prominently in mirror-image symmetry there is a loss of interpretation. The mapped shapes, the sides or "hands" of the symmetry are nearly the *same. Insofar as they tend toward being the same, toward being equal, there is nothing to interpret between them*, beyond a simple much reduced aspect of experience as spatial quantity.

Curved lines—sticking to two dimensions here—can run together to form points as well; a teardrop shape exemplifies curvature which turns to a point of symmetry at one side of its shape, for example. Insofar as curved lines do this they move toward a dampening of curvature which approaches linearity and eventually pointedness, and my suggestion is that they are hyperthematically interpretable with regard to all the shapes we are aware of—particularly obviously at physical level complexity but no less present through the whole range of experience—as being *worse* than shapes which retain the fullest possible curvature.

You may now object that if we speak of symmetry, then curvature has its symmetry. "Is the circle not considered as the most symmetric of shapes?" you may ask, "for it can be divided in any way through its center so as to produce a perfect symmetry of its two halves."

I reply that yes indeed the circle is *considered* as such. I would even suggest that *at the range of their complexity of experience*, circles—and spheres if we cared to move to a three-dimensional spatiality—are the highest instances of interpretation and meaning. They are better than all other shapes which have closed edges or surfaces. *But they are not symmetric.* The objection forgets something. It forgets that the symmetry of a circle is only a symmetry *after special selection.* The circle (and sphere) can be divided symmetrically but *only when an actor deliberately makes an interpretive selective action with regard to a plane of division with regard to the circle.* The usual view smuggles this assumption in and hushes it up. It is made, however, and moreover the opening assumptions of Hyperthematics are built upon it: I assume that there is freedom of action, which selects problematics of experience and interprets between them. Circles are *hyperthematically asymmetric.*

The symmetries of *worse*—pointed and symmetric—shapes meanwhile are no less tied to this assumption, but those symmetries always manifest the selection as a region of experience which the beholder of the sign *has no choice in receiving* if she decides to countenance the shape at all and often even if she does not. This is easily exemplified in three dimensions: if I hand you a pointy object—a dagger for example—you cannot ignore the point, and all too often I do not mean for you to. It is that portion of the experience in what I gave you that is *relatively uninterpretable.* Such shapes manifesting *given symmetry* may be called *hyperthematically symmetric.*

A circle or a ball is very different from the latter. No symmetry is *given* in the sign which it is. If I hand you a ball, it is the handing on of the maximal range of interpretive possibility (within a certain range of complexity of physicality). This is why we tend to *play* with balls in our sports, and why in sports where the "ball" tends toward directed symmetry in some way—e.g., hockey, and particularly American football—the character of the game takes on a relatively more violent tone, i.e., inconsistent for value. In short: curvature, circles, spheres, etc., are tending toward an increase in value.

Moreover, this goes beyond shapes with closed edges or surfaces. Relative to the above, the *golden spiral* in mathematics can be defined in our hyperthematic terms as an action of interpretation at the physical level of complexity—in this case say an action of drawing—which, for every 90 degrees of its arc, reinstates, by means of the proportion of interpretation between the progress of its arc and its radius, the maximum curvature approximating a circle which it can, so as to grow indefinitely without turning into a pure circle. That proportion is phi. In other words, the golden spiral according to the proportion phi is the physical level extension of maximum curvature and thus interpretive expansion of experience according to (unconsciously) adopting a tendency toward greater interpretation which is consistent with **H**. The felt value, as beauty, of the golden spiral, golden ratio, etc., arises from just this.

Indeed, the above considerations regarding symmetry apply at experience of higher levels of complexity. "You get the point" we say to someone, and "he made an irrefutable point," and again "she wrote in point form." These uses of physical level devaluation at the narrative level of complexity are no accident and their import is the cousin of the suggestions given above. To adopt tendencies toward them, if the tendencies are not understood as localized practice is to adopt tendencies toward diminishing value.

They will apply in mathematics as well. Mathematics is going to have its beauties, some of which are going to come from the above considerations. I will be bold here and suggest that mathematical functions and the mathematical experience which is built upon them are going to be better or worse depending upon whether they abide by the valuating or devaluating tendencies shown above. The Weierstrass function, for example, is a relatively diminishing value, or bad, function. The mathematical structures built upon it will be "infected" with the inconsistency of its assumptions as well and in time the physical manifestations which the function describes will be discovered to be physicalities of diminished or diminishing value.

These suggestions aside, though indeed I cannot undertake it here, in a future work, *Hyperthematics of Conflict* that is already in progress, I am going to suggest through Hyperthematic expansion that the weapons of war and indeed the whole historical development of the weapons and the actions of conflict are in large—though not entire—part due to actors adopting inconsistent tendencies which attempt to produce symmetries—weapons—with which to destroy an enemy by diminishing his ability to interpret, even as they consistently attempt to produce curvatures—e.g., armor and shields—with which to defend themselves by expanding their own ability to interpret.

There is much more to be said about symmetry and shape but it would wander too far from the goal of this chapter. A future hyperthematic engagement will have to take them up.

Light as Vehicle for Maximal Interpretation at Physical Ranges of Complexity

Enough has been suggested, however, to take up where I left off with light color and expand it hyperthematically with respect to this digression upon spatial engagement. Before doing that I am going to offer two further hyperthemes as a formulation of the above however, which gain for practical use tendencies that have been slowly disclosing themselves since the beginning of this work.

The first can be formulated as **HCu**—*in order to increase value within regions of experience at the physical range of complexity, make every effort to create physical shapes which are curved and to avoid the creation of shapes which diminish curvature.* I will call it the Hypertheme of Curvature.

The second, which technically follows from **HCu**, but which it will be helpful to formulate on its own is **HAs**—*in order to increase value within regions of experience at the physical range of complexity make every effort to create hyperthematic asymmetry and to avoid forming physical shapes which are hyperthematically symmetric and which thus copy portions of themselves.* I will call this one the Hypertheme of Asymmetry.

These two will go a long way toward a satisfying expansion upon the visual arts, which I will undertake after having applied them to light color. I noted earlier that light travels in waves of a certain wavelength and frequency. For light, the wave shape is sinusoidal. I noted also that the sine function can be viewed as an action of movement around the edge of a circle. Light energy then, at its level of complexity within the experience process, abides by **HCu**. Whatever action within experience creates it—and for the moment I let this question be—is an action that is consistent, and consistent to the maximum extent within that range of physical complexity in which we see light. Light is then, in experience, in its physical complexity as a waveform, a good thing. Very few among us would disagree with this. Light itself is accounted both good and beautiful as a facet of experience relative to an absence of it.

We are after tendencies however and the tendencies of light as a function of certain changes in its shape are what are sought here. Electromagnetic energy (EMR) is visible light to us at a certain range of wavelengths. Hyperthematics suggests that as the wavelength of the light changes the interpretive freedom will change with regard to it.

There are waves (e.g., radio waves) whose curvature changes depending upon their wavelength. The wavelength of visible light does not appear to cause a change in its curvature however, nor does the wavelength of further electromagnetic energy change the curvature of light. And yet it ought to change, according to what we know of shapes in the experience of physical space. In order to hold to the sinusoidal shape, if the length of a wave is shortened, without a proportional decrease of amplitude, the wave ought to grow thinner; and if it is lengthened without a proportional increase of amplitude, the wave ought to grow fatter.

Now, if we attempt to interpret this to the hyperthematic considerations above, namely **HCu** and **HAs**, we would conclude that two things ought to happen with the light wave with regard to value. If—its amplitude remaining the same—the wavelength got longer and thus fatter, its curvatures would be attenuated. It would begin to collapse to a line. On the other hand, if—its amplitude remaining the same—the wavelength got shorter and thinner, its curvature would be attenuated as well and would be tending toward a series of pointed "spines." Either way, if the earlier suggestions are plausible, we are in trouble with regard to value.

But this is not yet the whole story for hyperthematically, the trouble, i.e., the tendency toward the diminishment of value, cannot be an equal diminishment. The point is worse than the line with regard to value. This follows from the previous suggestions regarding the aspects of interpretation in physical shape in our example of drawing. The point expands to a line; the line expands to a curve, etc.

Where this is reversed and the curve is constricted or collapses as a curve, it can collapse toward the line. But here in the case of our light wave—assuming a constancy of amplitude—it can also collapse toward multiple symmetric points. And each "point tendency" is going to be a region of relative uninterpretability and diminishing value. Well, this is what it ought to do, yes? And yet it doesn't. Light and indeed all electromagnetic energy appear to us to retain its sinusoidal waveform, with the curve which can be viewed as the motion around the circle. Why?

Continuing the attempt to interpret what we have so far to **H** and the derivatives as expanded with regard to physical shape will find us the answer. That is to say: the why of the answer lies there. The what of the answer, the technical aspect, is no doubt going to elude humanity yet awhile.

So far we have this. The light wave shape is sinusoidal. The sinusoidal waveform is a transformation from the motion around a circle through time. The circle, we suggested, was the manifestation of maximum interpretive value at physical complexity for an enclosed shape at two dimensions. The circle comes from the curve. The curve constricts to a line. The line constricts to a point.

If the sinusoidal light wave could change shape as a result of compression of its wavelength, it would change its shape in two ways, either flattening toward a line or compressing each curve toward a pointed spine. Both would be a loss of value, but the line would be less so than the curves tending toward spines. The line tendency is moving toward a lower level of interpretation relative to the sinusoidal curve yes, but at its level—if the curve were to reach a line—the line retains an aspect which we noted earlier with regard to the symmetry of circle and sphere, namely, the line can be viewed as symmetric unto itself if it is divided, but only if the division is the result of a deliberate selection made upon the line.

The selectability is poorer than for the circle, as indeed it should be, for the division point at which the line can be divided is given according to the boundaries of the line, and any effort to "hand over the symmetry to someone"—if it could be done as in our example above with the ball and the pointy object—is going to depend upon a selection with regard to the action of beginning and ending the creation of the line. Which is to say that, whereas the circle has no inbuilt symmetry, the line has an inbuilt symmetry, but the length of the line will have to be actively interpreted before that inbuilt symmetry is evident as the equal division of its length.

The spiny tendency of the light wave undergoing the tendency toward compression or shortening of its wavelength is going to have multiple inbuilt symmetries however. Each compressed wave will tend toward being a point and a point whose symmetry makes it relatively impossible to ignore if the compressed wave is to come across within experience at all. In other words, the spiny compressed sine wave of the reduced wavelength light has multiple inbuilt symmetries, which you cannot ignore and which are relatively un-interpretable. And this is a tendency of the wave as you compress it.

But again, it doesn't happen this way according to modern physics. Light waves do not change amplitude, and they retain their sinusoidal shape. Where then does the tendency toward the diminishment of interpretation and thus value manifest itself?

The hyperthematic answer is this.

The circle is the physical complexity level manifestation in two dimensions of the interpretive action most consistent with **H**. The sinusoidal light wave is a transformation of the circle over time in three dimensions. It is a higher physical complexity manifestation in three dimensions of the interpretive action most consistent with **H**. This action within experience has the characteristic that it can absorb physical level action which engages it. More specifically for our purposes here, it can absorb action which acts according to inconsistent tendencies.* It acts, if you will, defensively.

---

*And also consistent action as the sum of the sine waves.

I am going to define defense in a preliminary way as: the tendency of a region of experience to expand interpretation when engaged by a tendency of action which constricts interpretation. With that definition I am going to suggest that the spatial aspect of curvature of the light wave expands incoming action into avenues of interpretive freedom which cause that action to be interpreted—despite the contrary tendency of the incoming action.

Thus the light defends itself so to speak. But the tendency that engaged it must manifest "somewhere" if the world process is consistent with **H**. It manifests itself in a different type of experience which, as it comes across the loci of action which engaged it with inconsistent tendencies, causes those loci of action to expand their interpretation so as to learn from those inconsistent tendencies that they drew from their inconsistent assumptions. That is to say, it reinterprets the incoming inconsistent tendency so as to pass back to the loci of the inconsistent action the interpretive consequence with regard to the implementation of its inconsistent tendency of action.

The constriction of interpretation, which gives rise to the greater symmetry, the spiny points, is essentially a tendency of action which attempts to fashion such symmetries at various levels of complexity. Simply put, it is akin to the attempts of human actors to fashion pointy spiny shapes. Pointy spiny shapes are mostly meant to be uninterpretable insofar as possible, e.g., to stab with. The interpretive action tends toward being contained in the point region of such shapes, according to the intent of the initiator of the action which produces them.

In the case of the light wave, such actions as would tend to push the sinusoidal shape toward the point shapes are actions toward uninterpretability. But as the inconsistent action engages the defensive shape of the light wave, the light wave, maintaining its defensive structure, turns the action into a further interpretation of what was intended. This interpretation then manifests itself at the physical level of complexity in two forms.

The first is the frequency of the light wave. If the light wave did not maintain its sinusoidal shape as its wavelength was increased or compressed, it would remain at a steady frequency, but its curvature would begin to collapse to lines or to point shapes. Instead, the defense provided by the maximally interpretive shape which the light is, relative to its range of complexity, ensures the safety of its curvature. Nonetheless, if the incoming interpretive action is to have a consistent interpretive relation to the world process assumed in **H**, some aspect or aspects of experience besides the curvature must account for it. Frequency is one of those aspects.

Frequency increases as wavelength decreases, and it decreases as wavelength increases. But frequency in our hyperthematic terms is intimately related to symmetry. The compression of the wave would lead to the point shapes which are uninterpretably symmetric and which are more numerous, but it doesn't since the wave shape interprets it onward. Yet the numerical increase must out. And it does. It comes out in the frequency. As the wavelength decreases, the frequency increases, i.e., (the number of light waves within a temporal event of the world process increases). Yet since each wave is alike, there are more of them per event, i.e., abstractedly per unit time. In effect there are more copies of the wave per unit time. An increase in copies is a tendency toward uninterpretability however, and as the number of copies increase per temporal event, the uninterpretability increases.

Still, if **H** holds, the light wave must interpret the second aspect of its wavelength constriction, the point symmetries. This results in the second form of its interpretation which manifests itself at the physical level of complexity. Spiny point shapes, I suggested, are the containers—literally—within physical level experience, of inconsistent action which forms them. All the interpretive action is directed into the point, so that the point—as is usually intended—becomes uninterpretable: the scorpion's tail, the porcupine's quills, the murderer's dagger, and on and on.

The point tendency is thus a tendency of interpretive action in which action is gathered in an attempt to impart an interpretation to some region of experience. This tendency stems from the assumption that if all the interpretive action can be undertaken with respect to a region of experience, then no further interpretive action can be taken within that region. If I am the locus and initiator of such a tendency for example, then my intent is that, by taking every action that can be taken with regard to some region of experience, you as a further locus of experience will have nothing to interpret, i.e., you will have to accept my interpretations in the region, i.e., again I will give you <u>my own</u> interpretations and you will be unable to interpret them further.

Having reached this point we are ready for a new definition: the definition of power. We will define increasing power in hyperthematic terms as: a tendency of interpretive action in which interpretive action is directed so as to constrict interpretation in a region of experience in an effort to bring about or propagate that constricted interpretation as an uninterpretable given of experience. My suggestion is that both power and force in modern physics and "power over others" and "forcing others" in human social affairs stem from this assumption and tendency; they are simply cousins at different levels of complexity.

The second aspect of the wavelength constriction in the light wave thus manifests at physical complexity as power. When the defensive light wave engages inconsistent incoming action so as to expand its interpretation, the incoming action as a diminishment of value goes in the first place to the frequency of the wave, and in the second place into the power of the wave, i.e., in the photon aspect of the light wave. Thus, as the wavelength of light—and EMR—decreases, the frequency of the wave and its power increase.

Now if all of this is plausible it should manifest itself in the facts about light waves and EMR insofar as they are known. And it does. Light is the carrier of a huge aspect of interpretation within experience. If there is going to be interpretation within experience as **H** assumes, then there must be some aspect of experience at the physical level of complexity which can carry the maximum of interpretation with regard to the complexity of aspects of experience in the physical range. Light is that aspect. It must arise on the basis of the assumption of **H**.

Not only must it arise but it can only arise at a physical level as a spatial shape which retains the interpretability to be engageable. For this it must take on the physical shape in relation to the time process that has the maximum interpretability over the range at which it manifests. This is the circular motion stretched over time. If it did not thus maintain itself, maximal interpretability at its range of experience (the physical) would break down. Where interpretations are attempted with respect to light, which would break it down, it transforms them so that the breakdown occurs elsewhere.

Devaluations at Physical Ranges of Complexity from Light to Spatiality

All actions under inconsistent assumptions that tend toward constriction of the light waveform result in some version of the diminishment of value manifesting itself at the physical level of complexity of experience.

As the wavelength of EMR decreases, the frequency of the light wave increases. But electromagnetic radiation becomes more harmful, more destructive—to us, to nature in its nearer aspects, and more broadly to the physical structures of experience within the world process—as its frequency increases. Ultraviolet waves are more harmful to us than light waves, x-rays are more harmful still, and gamma rays are extremely harmful.

On the other hand, if the light wave is stretched, it would tend—if its amplitude did not remain steady by means of its defensive curvature—to a flattening, as I suggested. While this is a diminishment of value, my suggestion was that it is a lesser diminishment than that of the compressive action upon the light wave. This should bear out in the perceived value of the light (or EMR beyond the visible spectrum), and again it does.

Infrared is somewhat harmful to human and other biological systems, but not nearly as harmful as radiation whose frequency increases from the other end of the range of visible spectrum of light. The harm of infrared comes chiefly through our inability to see it and so to avoid it. As we pass infrared and move on toward increasing wavelength and decreasing frequency we get to microwaves. These again can harm but only through prolonged exposure, at unawares, by heating (which we put to local use in microwaves ovens). Passing further to radio waves, and still further into long radio waves, we are moving into ranges that do not evidently hurt us at all.

We are now in a position to take this behavior with regard to value at both ends of the visible light spectrum, as the basis of a hyperthematic explanation of light and color.

The visible spectrum of light is bounded upon one end of its range by ultraviolet and on the other end of its range by infrared. The luminous intensity of a light source depends upon the quantity of light that a light source allows through itself or produces. The luminosity function meanwhile shows how bright different colors are to us, and it drops to darkness on each side of the visible spectrum. But the luminous intensity is dependent upon the character of the object in trapping light. From the hyperthematic viewpoint all trapping of light is the result of a tendency of constriction of interpretation. Now we leave aside for now the "source" of the tendency in the process. The important point is that this constriction has a clear relation to the perception of luminous intensity by humans.

As the luminous intensity increases and decreases, i.e., as we tend toward expansion or constriction with regard to the experience object, e.g., in its shape or in the shape of its surface at microscopic scales, there is a predictable effect on the human perceiver in terms of value which makes itself felt as a psychological effect of the color at that intensity. Thus toward both ends—infrared and ultraviolet—of the function of luminous intensity, we are moving toward darkness, i.e., a relatively complete constriction of interpretation for the viewer, and the feelings generated in the viewer change accordingly. As we move toward darkness we get, for example, the feelings gathered around anxiety and fear. These feelings are the experience of the loss of value.

Darkness as well as blackness is caused by a more or less complete absorption of light, or by an absence of light. The surface of an object can be black to us if it absorbs light. My suggestion is that the absorption of light depends upon the shape of the surface understood in hyperthematic terms at certain levels of complexity and on the analogs of constrictive and expansive shaping of experience at other levels of complexity. As the surface of an object tends toward uninterpretability, it tends toward greater absorption. Whether you view this as the light wave engaging the surface or the surface engaging the light wave matters little; when we humans fashion surfaces we can be said to be fashioning them in ways that engage the light in the way of diminishing value.

In effect, we trap the light wave, which is an attempt at constricting it. The surface of a solar cell illustrates this. The absorptive capacity of solar cells are improved by the fashioning of multitudes of pyramidal surface structures, either upright or inverted.[3] As one would expect by musing further upon the implications of this, the absorptive ability of surfaces is increased even further by moving from the pyramids toward a dense forest of spiked shapes.[4] All efforts to trap the light wave give off force through the transformation by the defensive structure of the light wave, in the form of heat, according to the explanation given above. Perfect absorbers of light, so-called black bodies, give off thermal radiation proportional to the EMR waves absorbed and again, the usual models of such black bodies, e.g., an enclosed structure with a cavity to admit EMR, are simply constrictive traps for the light waves.

The trapping of light can be viewed then as an inconsistent action with respect to the aspect of experience, which is the light wave. If it is a local action taken with consistent global awareness with regard to **H**, it can be useful as we shall soon see with regard to painting. If, on the other hand, it is an action without such awareness, its tendency leads inevitably toward the diminishment of value. All darkness is thus the indicator of a diminishment of interpretive value somewhere in experience, despite that we do not know in many—or perhaps most—cases, the what and how of the source of the diminishment. In effect regions of experience such as cosmological black holes are extreme regions of devaluation. Whatever they are, the suggestion of Hyperthematics is that they are extremely bad.

I will return now to the earlier suggestion. Our usual understanding of light waves is an understanding based upon pushing aside certain features of the situation. We easily say of the proportion of EMR wavelength with regard to frequency that: "as the wavelength diminishes the frequency increases." But in hyperthematic terms we cannot say this consistently. Rather, as was the case of the symmetry of the circle, the EMR is subject to an interpretive action within experience, so that more consistently we may say "as an action of interpretation is taken with regard to the EMR (or light wave), which tends to constrict the wavelength, a portion of experience is transformed so as to manifest that action of constriction."

This will sound strange at first, but only at first. All of our science of EMR is the result of either a direct or an indirect manipulation of experience of EMR, so as to view the consequent tendencies of an initial tendency of active interpretation. You measure wavelength of light waves for example, how? Namely, by first harnessing them somehow, by selecting them so as to separate them somehow from their companions. You subject the light to certain actions, nearly always tendencies of constriction.

Light is given yes, but it is given in ways that we must reconstruct as to their being given, by that which we experience in terms of meaning as *nature*. We never get light as interpreted with respect to ourselves as a part of the process we call nature. Rather, we create that interpretation by engaging nature through the consistent aspects of our sciences. Every such *new* interpretation of how light does so and so as we subject it to so and so is an advance. These advances add up as the meaning of the why of nature, which we slowly build up as an accumulation of value embedded in our new and creative actions toward the existent experience of nature.

In the case of the light wave, what I am suggesting is that the similar hyperthematic considerations are in effect as with the selection which makes the symmetry of the circle. The light wave (EMR) shape is temporally circular; it is the experience of openness of interpretation according to its level of complexity. It suffers incursions into its openness of interpretation, which it transforms so as to manifest the manifold forms of diminishment of value within experience at its complexity. Some of these incursions we are already aware of as diminishments, e.g., the harm of X-rays or gamma rays; some we have yet to discover.

In these hyperthematic terms then we can explain the various constants that dot the field of this area of physics, such as Planck's constant, the speed of light constant, etc., as the mathematical level interpretations of *the proportion according to which one tendency of interpretive action toward the light-wave experience results in another tendency of action on the part of the light-wave experience so as to retain the maximal interpretiveness of the light-wave structure as a portion of the world process.*

Thus, all of these constants have their relation to the circle (and the sphere), and to forms such as the Golden Spiral, the latter of which, through their expansion of facets of interpretation—e.g., dimensions—carry maximal curvature beyond the ranges of complexity of circles and spheres, so as to appear unbounded relative to (i.e., within the context of) fewer facets of interpretation, but bounded relative to more facets of interpretation. I suggest that all of these constants could eventually be derived similarly to those forms as a function of outgoing transformative result versus incoming active engagement, or i.e., forms such as the Golden Spiral are simply less complex cousins of the abovementioned constants of physics, and all of these together manifest variations of the defensive function of maximal interpretation.

The so called "wave function collapse" should also be explicable in terms of the hyperthematic viewpoint. The wave at the quantum mechanical level of complexity of experience manifests its version of the defensive aspect of maximal interpretability, similar to the above. The effort of an observer to observe the wave is an effort toward the diminishment of value; it is the interpretively constrictive effort taken according to the assumption that the experience of the wave can be "fixed" objectively, i.e., as a sameness for all. The interpretive action thus leads—but only locally—to a physical state, which is the outcome of the constriction, but a physical state that can be engendered by *any constriction* operating in the world process, not merely human observation.

Finally, the curvature of space and its relation to the various characteristics of light, finds meaning in the hyperthematic expansion, for all efforts toward constriction of interpretation, say out of the range of three dimensions of complexity of interpretation toward line and point, can be seen as regressions of valuation of the world process. We cannot actually bring about those regressions of valuation, except locally, if the opening assumption **H** holds. Thus, for example, if we engage experience in repetitive action that copies itself, say we attempt to build a tower up into the sky in linear fashion, by stacking a series of identical bricks, which are no more than quantitatively different, then the world process itself in its manifestation as the region of nature, will tend to prevent us as our effort advances: the tower will begin to curve as it rises higher and higher. When we undertake consistent interpretive action to engage the higher complexities of the world process however, e.g., setting our so far crude spacecraft into the curving motion of orbit, the world process as nature begins to support us.

Viewed relative to these last two examples—the failure of linear action and the success of orbital action—gravity is just the "brake" that the valuative structure of the world process as nature puts on our inconsistent actions relative to the upper end of the range of physical complexity. If an action is taken to send an object "up" through a relatively inconsistent valuating interpretation, e.g., linear tending, it merely succeeds locally; beyond the locality it fails—it comes back "down." The opposite of this is our ability to invoke "gravity" by taking an action at physical complexity that re-institutes linear tending interpretation in some region of interpretation tending otherwise toward curvature, e.g., twirling a ball on the end of a line of string.

Movement and embodied relatedness of higher value—e.g., planetary orbits—at physical complexities of experience can only be gained and only manifest themselves through tendencies of expansion of interpretation. Space-time is not curved. *Successful interpretation is curved at the less complex levels of experience we call physical.* Eventually we will learn to interpret in still more valuable ways than curvature. Spatiality, as we now know it, is thus our construct in its tendency toward objectivity, a region of experience which is the outcome of our various consistent and inconsistent actions in engaging the experience of the world process.[5] I will not explore these issues further here. It would take us too far afield for this work. They will serve as suggestions for future expansion.

Gathering together the foregoing suggestions, the following hyperthematic vision of the wave nature in its relation to light can be presented. The sinusoidal wave is fundamental at current physical levels of experience, as that region of experience imparting a maximal interpretiveness to the future of the world process. And *the grades of physicality, qua physicality, which exist for us are the manifestations of freely selected inconsistent tendencies of interpretive action which give rise to diminishments of value.* The aspects of physicality—to hearken back to our earlier definition—are the "flavors" if you will of—ostensibly—interpretive actions which bring things to a sameness, as modes of being inconsistent with **H**.

Sometimes we are aware of our direct engagement in these actions and sometimes we are not yet aware, for the manifestations of the tendencies in nature have not yet been much corrected or creatively interpreted by us, so as to be meaningfully ours. In the signs of the evolution of plants, for example, the conifers with their spiked shape and spiked, light trapping, "needle" boughs, precede the deciduous trees with their relatively more curved and consistent leaves and rounded shape. Plants are thus evidently processes evolving toward higher value, just as we ourselves are. Remembering our example of the solar cells above, we can say that nature has here proceeded toward consistency. Why? That is ours to explore meaningfully as the interpretive construction of who we are in our relation to nature.

Light as the Leading Edge of our Interpretive Capacity

The means to answer the original question as to the nature of light color, as such, are now available to us however. Light waves propagate as waves of action because it is consistent with the world as a process of value (assumed by **H**), to do so. An ending would be a diminishment, e.g., it would have an end (a point) rather than a constantly newly interpreting action (the motion of the circle moving in the added interpretive aspect of temporality, a coil shape).

Again, why do we see red or green, etc., as colors of light? We see them due to actions of interpretation, which fix the wavelength to some definite length, an inconsistent tendency, or we see them as a result of actions, which add wavelengths together, a consistent tendency, of which the production of white light is the highest result.

If you ask further, why do we experience light as visible in the range of the spectrum it is in and not elsewhere, the answer must be that you *do* experience it elsewhere. The wave as infrared is heat. It is the "seeing" of heat, or again, it is the interpretation of heat, an interpretation that has a value depending upon the various tendencies at work engendering the experience. Every sense that has developed in our biological loci of embodiedness, is the sign of an interpretive action within experience—e.g., by our ancestors—whose meaning, discoverable anew in a creative interpretation, is attainable through a new interpretive action at a higher level capacity of interpretation.

Thus heat has its value as a part of the whole range of the physical level complexity of experience. Namely, heat as the experience of a creative interpretive action, with regard to say nature, feels good or bad to us depending upon our action, or good or bad to another depending on our action with regard to it and them. And heat, in its "natural" relation to EMR has its value with respect to light. In this sense *it is not as good as light*, as such, and as one of our senses it takes a lower place in our valuation than does light. This will follow for the qualities of the other senses no less, i.e., those experiences we gather under the headings of sound, touch, taste, smell, though I will not work out their valuations here.

What I am saying is that at each grade of complexity of our experience the abstractions which we call heat, light, or ultraviolet energy, etc., get their "sense"—and here my use of the word spans both its English uses—for us as a function of our ability to interpret them meaningfully. If we wanted to relate the various ranges of EMR experience to a selected portion of the range, e.g., the range which visible light occupies, then we could lay out that set of relations as: we *see* radio-waves as sound value, we *see* infrared as heat value, we *see* light wavelengths as color value, we *see* ultraviolet wavelengths as _____ value, we see X-rays as _____ value, and we see gamma rays as _____ value. In our age we *see* the last three as diminishment of value, i.e., we *see* them as harming us (literally as the feeling that they are harming us in the various ways that they do). So far as they harm us, we call them bad.

After that long digression we can finally return to our second example. I said that other animals see light from our visible spectrum, but that they also see light beyond the bounds of our visible spectrum. We asked the question: how we could explain these varying capacities to see light in hyperthematic terms? The path to that answer now lies open before us, and it begins in the suggestion that: eventually we will expand our capacity to interpret and, when we do, *visible light will become for us as infrared now is for us*, just as the descendants of animal processes such as the pit vipers, which now *see* heat, will undoubtedly come to forego heat as the leading edge of their interpretive capacity so as to take up the "seeing" of light according to a new more expansive capacity.

The pit viper is perhaps mostly in the dark now with regard to our visible light, just as we are with regard to ultraviolet light, just as almost certainly our far off ancestors were with regard to light. And we may creatively interpret ourselves as far back as we like, even to that time when our ancestors—e.g., the ancient thermophilic bacteria—had no sense of light at all. The experience of fire and its heat felt good to our ancestors, both hominid and earlier, in a way that is increasingly lost on us unless we creatively interpret it anew to ourselves in our current age, because we have passed beyond it to a new capacity of interpretation. This then is the second instance, which illustrates the sort of answer we can expect when we ask why an experience of red at all, an example of *an interpretive expansion from a region of experience that does not contain red to a region that does contain red.*

If these suggestions are plausible we can begin to build up the valuations of color in its "natural" state. As I proceed to this, remember that these valuations of color are the expressions of tendencies. Can absolute valuations be given? They can, but they would still only be absolute valuations on the basis of selections of problematics of experience. It will be much more helpful to view the issue, as I have all along in this work, as a matter of tendencies that are consistent or inconsistent with **H**. So that one can say, as we tend toward such and such with regard to light shape, we tend toward such and such with regard to value. The extremes of tendency will be easiest to pick out. The others will give hints of valuation, which could be expanded with some effort. Here the outline will suffice.

The Relative Value of the Colors

First we experience darkness, and black colors as *bad*. They feel bad to us. They give us the experience of a diminishment of interpretation, of devaluation. All things being equal—i.e., taking the interplay of valuating and devaluating tendencies at work in each case into account—all human societies have the recognition of this. Blackness usually represents mourning when mourning is focused upon loss; it represents power; it tends to represent corruption, rot, disease, and a host of other manifestations of diminishment of value in nature and otherwise. In effect it represents the many manifestations of a more extreme uninterpretability.

Human actors also deliberately bring about the constrictions of interpretation, which blackness represents, and use it to evoke the devaluation in others in some manner. So, for example, black clothing is usually deliberately chosen for its effect on the viewer: most often power over others, particularly sexuality as power, combined with mystery—think of Sargent's *Portrait of Madame X*. The judge in black robes is to be uninterpretable to us as well, a sign of the judge's power; the Jesuit in black similarly; the black belts of the martial arts as well. The parliaments of the Westminster system have the Usher of the Black Rod, a direct and deliberate linkage with power. The dark void—e.g., the dark basement to the child—is a place of fear, of mystery, etc.[6]

Yet darkness as an absence of light also has it variety. *Close* on the one side of the visible spectrum—the infrared side—it is a warm darkness or blackness, e.g., when confronted with warm charcoal. In other words, remembering the earlier suggestions, it is the variant of darkness that has the greater interpretability when compared to the darkness of the ultraviolet side of the visible spectrum. One may feel this interpretability easily enough. Enter the smoldering ruins of burnt out buildings for example—I have had such an experience—and attempt to interpret the experience. The experience is one of loss of value relative to color experience, and yet the darkness and blackness are interpretable experience in the way of heat. Because the heat *has* been interpretable, and more centrally interpretable according to the interpretive capacity of our ancestors, the experience of a burnt out building is one of loss of value, which may be described as "primal." This feeling is that of an uninterpretability with regard to light, which is still interpretable with regard to heat, a *heat-darkness*.

Or again—a favorite theme of fairy tales—take the dark night in the woods. Here the darkness is again uninterpretable, but now its interpretability has fallen below that of heat. The darkness is interpretable experience in the way of sound. There are clicks, creaks, cracks, hoots, etc. There are noises; it matters hardly at all *what* noises. That there is sound *at all* is part of the region of uninterpretability as such, and it is a lesser interpretability than the heat darkness, which is, if you like, more "primal" still in the way of experience. It is the *seeing* of the darkness, as what we might call an *aural-darkness*.

Beyond the aural-darkness one may come to the darkness of smell and taste, the *olfactory-darkness*, an uninterpretability below sound that nonetheless still presses us from the end of its range. This is the darkness of rankness and decay, of the taste of the damp and the earth.

That darkness is on its way to the cool darkness wherein the interpretability is failing beyond even sound and smell. It is failing with regard to the pressures of heat and sound and smell as tactile. This is a darkness of the cold, clammy, and silent, of the cool damp pit. It is the darkness of slimy limpid things of which only touch and texture remain, but of which even they are giving way, a darkness we might call *tactile-darkness*.

The reader will likely get the point. All of these darknesses as experience are losses of interpretability that manifest in the psychology of primal fear. They are darknesses of capacities of interpretation which we find diminished and endangered based on the experienced situation at hand. Being subjected to them is bad enough, but their diminishment of value is always experienced as a loss of what we had, a regression into "primality." Fear is generated more often than harm; in other words the loss of value of these lower darknesses manifests in us as what we call fear. We play with them sometimes—e.g., in film or narrative—in ways which we do not often play with the uninterpretability on the other side of the visible spectrum.

Yet there is the darkness of the other side of the visible spectrum as well, and its uninterpretability is more profound as a diminishment of aspects of interpretable experience. This side of darkness is the side of increasing uninterpretability as a darkness of harmfulness. The ultraviolet dark is harmful to us, the X-ray darkness more so and the gamma ray darkness still more so. Yet they are not darknesses of fear as the primal darkness, but more purely uninterpretable.

The difference is something like saying that the primal darkness is the darkness which a regression in our interpretive capacity would remove fear from because we would revert to the primal—become more animal-like—whereas the darkness on the ultraviolet side of the light spectrum is merely a darkness of harm, which simply devalues impersonally without the threat (the fear) of devaluing, relative to capacities we have gained, since we have never yet interpreted it. The former is fear wherein we are aware of the source of the loss of value. The latter is merely an empty impersonal harm ranging to deadliness. But words fail somewhat in this region which we have not yet interpreted at the physical level of complexity of embodiment and exemplification is difficult accordingly. Nonetheless, the sense of the empty darkness of space, of mere void, serves somewhat imperfectly to exemplify the lower range of this *harm-darkness*. The solar eclipse gives us this, somewhat, as a feeling of *extra darkness* than the usual with respect to our visible light.

The higher range, in the X-rays and beyond might be exemplified by experience of the radioactive area after a reactor core meltdown; Chernobyl for example. Here we may express the darkness as the feeling of harm which operates without regard to embodiment. Its diminishment of value engages experience equally, or better yet *indifferently* as one might say, and this in keeping with the nature of the inconsistent tendency that creates it—from our human view—as producing a greater sameness of shape with regard to the waves over a selection of time (the frequency). Its uninterpretable character goes beyond the loss of visible light even. It is "*a darkness which is darker than darkness itself*" in its uninterpretability. It is the darkness of uninterpretability that harms you at unawares *even in the light*, and in a way far beyond that of the eclipse.

Finally, the darkness of the black hole exemplifies the further deadly darkness, of our range, which is for us the *extreme of the darker than darkness itself* uninterpretability. Here interpretation fails utterly, *so it seems*, even though it cannot be so if **H** holds. This darkness has gone well beyond our ability to express its uninterpretability, science fiction notwithstanding. Whatever actions cause them, black holes are very bad, indeed utterly evil, in our human terms, as regions of experience in which devaluation is being undertaken.

On the ultraviolet side of darkness it is we humans who are very often initiating the harm, depending upon the inconsistency of the assumptions behind out actions, e.g., in our uses of X-rays. We have begun to go beyond this to the X-ray darkness and to the gamma ray darkness, but we are not far in this, and our capacity of interpretation is not expanded enough so that we mainly cause ourselves harm with our urges toward fixing and observing.

Darkness can be engaged with tendencies of expansion of interpretation as well. The soft, warm, and tranquil darkness of the bedroom at night has arisen from the actions of humanity away from the primal darknesses. Yet these are local efforts at consistency and even then the more consistent darkness can always revert back to the primal darkness, e.g., through the "bump in the night."

This is the darkness in hyperthematic outline then. What of the light as such? What of white? Since darkness is explicable in hyperthematic terms as a manifestation of a range of uninterpretability according to inconsistent tendencies engaging the wave, there ought to be a manifestation of the wave action as being undisturbed by such inconsistencies. That manifestation is white light and the color white.

If the wave is undisturbed it carries out its fullest interpretation according to its complexity. Its uninterpretability will be least, and the devaluation, or badness, or again harm, which it engenders in experience, will also be least within its range of complexity. We find this in the relative force it causes. In the range of visible light, the white light wave has the lowest need to transform the incoming inconsistent action upon its waves. Its energy output is lowest (or at least would be if it could be observed without engagement). Moreover, it is built and rebuilt (it reforms itself) by the harmonizing of actions of the lesser colors. It is said that before Newton's experiments with prisms, white light was considered the primary wavelength of light. In the hyperthematic view it is the manifestation of the maximal tendency toward consistent interpretation within its range; it manifests the greatest value. Forgotten in the old story, however, is that Newton *took an action*, which split the light, to discover its *more primary* components, an action which itself evokes the sense of primal already discussed.

In the terms suggested earlier, the force of the EM wave in the spectrum of visible light and its luminance should be different. White light has the highest luminance and is followed in this by color in the yellow-green range. If we recall the suggestion that the light wave has its maximal interpretive region, wherein it is most curved in a sustained way, then we can explain this hyperthematically by redefining luminance and force.

Luminance will be the manifestation in experience, the sign, of the consistency of engagement of the maximally interpretive region of experience of physical level complexity (i.e., white light). Luminance will vary in proportion as the light wave is engaged through consistent action. The less you disturb the light wave, the greater—up to the maximum of its range—will be its luminance. Thus, white light has the greatest luminance. Green-yellow light follows as being that part of the range of visible light at which the light is least constricted in engagement, i.e., that part where the action upon the wavelength is—in our age—such as to approximate a maximally interpretive curvature of the sinusoidal waveform. Either side of green-yellow the luminance lessens accordingly, but it lessens more gradually in the red direction as it should according to our suggestions. Luminance is highest where we freely accept the experience of the light at the physical level, i.e., where we allow the white light to simply *give itself most* according to its capacity of expansion of interpretation.

Energy, meanwhile, as a *power* that has been drawn out of the experiential process to be manipulated, slowed, etc., will be the manifestation, in experience, of the transformation of inconsistent action which engages the maximally interpretive region of experience of physical level complexity (i.e., the white light wave). It will be, if you like, a *disturbance in the process of experience* arising through tendencies of inconsistent action.

Energy will increase as the inconsistent action—an observation, etc.—to break* the interpretive defensiveness of the white light wave increases (i.e., becomes more uninterpretable). Thus, to break the light from white to blue will result in more energy than it will in the attempt to break the light from white to green-yellow. But the energy given off by the transformed action of the "breaking" is then attributed—in our problematic contemporary scientific view—*to* the blue light wave rather than to the breaking *action*, as it should be.

Human valuations of white light are a sign of these suggestions regarding white. White, all else being equal, has always meant goodness, innocence, purity—the white wedding dress and so forth.

What of light colors apart from black and white? Can we make sense of them hyperthematically? We can, with the foundation already laid down. I said that increasing physicality is interpretation to a model. The model here is our ancestral self in its locus of physicality. Color then is valued as a feeling of its goodness or badness with regard to that model.

Thus red is nearer to the heat darkness interpretive capacity of our ancestral physical selves. Accordingly, the value of red as a feeling to us is

---

*I am using the term *break* as the sign for the intent, even though, as I noted, the light (white light) defends itself and simply transforms the action into power/force without breaking.

hot and tends to associate itself with the sexual aspect of our embodied primality. Yellow is less so.

Blue meanwhile is actually hotter than red as a color directly connected with the abstraction of heat as used by physics, but as our interpretive capacity with regard to the electromagnetic wave has its leading edge not much further than blue (in violet), the blue is that much more uninterpretable. Its uninterpretability in those terms, namely with regard to the physicality of color as such, is further away from the ancestral heat experience that we have known, than is red. And thus it is that it will feel much cooler than red. If you doubt this, look at the colors of a natural fire. The natural wood fire—as in a fireplace—is predominantly black, red, orange, and yellow as a function of the stages of its heat, with occasional bits of blue. But the red holds first place in what we have called its "primal" feeling. The orange follows, the yellow is hotter but less interpretable. Sustained blue flame is a relatively strange and wondrous thing to us. The blue flame is the flame of the blowtorch. It is the sign of a practical engagement with experience that is expanding our physical level interpretive capacity.

Blue is more difficult to interpret, relatively more uninterpretable than the red. It presents us with a relative lack of interpretive value with regard to the model of the physical interpretive capacity of our ancestral selves at the physical level of complexity. In effect it holds just the right proportion between problematic and solution so as have the value of a "challenge" to our capacity to interpret. So it is that blue has always felt like the spiritual, i.e., our process of engaging regions of experience wherein the proportion of the problematic predominates, as a deliberate action toward interpretive expansion. It is a liberating color, an expansive color; it has been called a calm and cool color. It is all of these because problematic begins to predominate in it, offering us the best mix of interpretive challenge in proportion to the interpreted signs of our past process. She "went off into the blue" we say, or "off into the wild blue yonder." The blue sky has this expansiveness of uninterpretability just as the blue flame.

Between red and blue we have yellow and then green. Yellow is cheerful yes, but at the same time it holds more of problematic than does red. Where red is the color of the hot, yellow is the color of warmth, of pleasure, of happiness (in China, for example). It is the color of reason and wisdom, i.e., the color of interpretation gained already from out of the more primal (red).[7]

After yellow we would expect to get a color whose problematic is still greater than that of yellow, a color whose valuation depends upon a more definite leaving behind of the signs of the past process in a fairly *simple* way and stepping up to the challenge of new interpretations. And this is what we get in green, the color whose valuation tends toward growth, simple new interpretation (which newness as such is). The association with green in Islam was very strong. Islam begins in the desert and out of the desert where little grows, comes the new growth (of the religion) which would lead to paradise—literally at the time of Islam's beginning—the place of the garden. The association with fairies and their company is no less strong. In other words, a move toward spirituality, but of a simpler sort, a more primal-spirituality than that associated with blue.

When we go beyond blue to violet we have ratcheted up the challenge of interpretation in the other direction somewhat too far for our current human situation. Violet (and purple) has always been a color of heavy uninterpretability, even if less so than black. Violet is more uninterpretable than red even though it borders on black on its end of the spectrum. It is distant from the primal darknesses, and near the more harmful darknesses. Purple robes are the robes of power on emperors or kings. It is the color of the wealthy as well as kingly, the color of the difficult to attain—literally in the case of purple dye—in the history of man's technical prowess with color and also in nature. It has been used as a substitute for mourning in the Catholic Church, and as a sign of penitence and humility (humility before the bishop, archbishop, etc. who once again is the focus of power).

Despite all of this, not only will humans try everything in their freedom, so that inconsistent tendencies abound, which will, if viewed superficially, appear to throw our scheme of valuations out in local cases (someone somewhere sometime will use yellow for mourning, e.g., the Egyptians[8]), but moreover, all these colors will sometimes manifest as a result of inconsistent tendencies so as to manifest the color as a sign of devaluation with regard to the inconsistency.

Thus we can be green with envy, or green as to experience, or sickly green. We can be in a blue mood or feeling blue. We can be yellow bellied, as being cowardly or treacherous. In each case the valuation according to consistent tendencies in terms of problematic and solution of interpretation is working as the "scale" for the use of the color as a sign of devaluation through inconsistent tendencies, and the color manifests itself accordingly in human use of language and sometimes beyond.

Thus also, if we are feeling blue we are low spirited, whereas blue was valuated in consistent tendencies as the spiritual. If we are green with envy, we desire the experience of another as a simple—undeserved because uninterpreted—newness; if we are green as to experience (a greenhorn) we lack the experience of another as a simple newness (mere time will get it for us); and if we are sickly green we lack that simple newness as the growth of renewal which belongs to the healthy, i.e., we are regressing as to health. Finally, if we are yellow bellied, or, otherwise subjected to the color yellow as a sign of devaluation—of which there are many prominent instances in the history of religious persecution particularly—"then we are not merely "primaly bad" as when a dog has turned on one in sudden primal rage (a "red rage," or as "seeing red"). No, we are reputed to be "wisely and reasoningly" bad, which is essentially the meaning of treachery and cowardice.

Our valuation of color according to interpretive capacity then is dependent on tendencies engendered from both consistent and inconsistent assumptions, although it advances only on the basis of the former. It is also dependent on other factors such as the process of the locus of embodiment within the larger process of the self. We are born, grow, and age, and our use of color—though not our tendencies of consistent valuation of it—change accordingly. Babies and very young children appear to like colors toward the primal and then grow out of them.[9]

On the basis of the above I will now formulate what I will call the *Hypertheme of Color*, as **HCl**—*in order to increase value within regions of experience at the physical range of complexity, make every effort to interpret those regions by means of those colors which tend toward expansion of interpretation by way of their being manifestations of consistent action upon that sign of maximal interpretability at physical complexity which we call light.*

The order of value in the colors, suggested above, from lower to higher, is in general from darker/black toward lighter/white, and proceeds through the sequence red, yellow, green, blue, after which it begins to lower again in the uninterpretability of violet. And this will ground the application of **HCl**. Nonetheless, that does not mean to simply take the highest value and throw out the rest, to "paint everything white," so to speak. That would fall afoul of other suggestions of the hyperthematic view—such as the promotion of diversity in experience—and moreover it would forget the practical implications of our always being within and thus having to respond to the world process such as we have made it.

What it means, more subtly, is to expand our various uses of colors toward broader interpretation and manageable challenges of interpretation, to move away from the more uninterpretable and primarily interpreted colors and toward those nearer the white light. This is to begin to view and treat light fluidly as a sign of our success in engaging the world process creatively in its aspect of physical complexity as nature. It is to treat light in ways which show our willingness to engage nature as something continually growing out of our own value laden actions.

The Creative Evolution of Interpretive Capacity and Future Color

Having got some sense of a Hyperthematics of light and color, we are now in a position to make a fuller answer to: what is color as such? First, *the visible light spectrum of color is the region within the physical level complexity of experience wherein interpretations are being made around the leading edge of our interpretive capacity as processes insofar as those processes are manifested in that locus of physical complexity which is embodiment.*

This region of visible light color is preeminent to us, and we desire it over other modes of physical experiencing because it is at that leading edge of interpretive expansion of our interpretive capacities with regard to physical level complexity. The implication however is: *it will not always be so.* We will pass beyond it, as we have passed beyond warmth, for example, which at some past time was that region within which the leading edge of our interpretive capacity was situated. Warmth—the warm-cool tendency—has been light for us, has been favored as our "sight" at some point, our "sight" being another term that stands for the high point of our capacity to interpret at the physical level of complexity. Just so light color, which is now our high point, will be outgrown. It will fall back to being as warmth is to us now. We will then have a new high point of interpretive capacity within what to us is now still the harmful darkness beyond the upper visible spectrum. It will be a *post light color* "sight."

Each color as such takes its place as to meaning according to the current high point of interpretive capacity. If you ask why red *at all*, your answer will finally come through a creative new series of interpretations which join your experience of the ancestral warmth-darkness to your experience of warm-red in the current embodied locus of your process. In other words you will see—hold interpretation before you as meaning—what actions took you from warm darkness to red, and when you accomplish this—and not all of us will select this problematic to engage—you will be able to answer why red, because in effect you will have expanded your interpreted experience of yourself so far as to have interpreted your *self*—at the physical level of complexity—as having *created* red. No more is ever sought than this as to the why of red as such. We do not ask the why of what we have truly created, for the answer to it is always a part of our creating. We have created red. We are steadily filling in the answer as to why we have done so.

Within the region of the leading edge which is the visible light spectrum, a similar play of interpretation is even now taking place. From that play according to consistent tendencies of action, new experiences at the physical level of complexity will arise. We may call these *future colors* if we like, although they will differ in complexity from what we now call colors. These future colors will occupy the lower levels of that future region of the leading edge of interpretive capacity that will come to predominance over light color. We will *create* them through new interpretive actions as we have created our current colors, though our future selves will continually have to interpret them anew in order to answer the *why* of their creation.

After all of the foregoing you may respond: "if your suggestions are plausible, why do we not all agree on these values of colors? For surely one of us prefers, for example, wearing red or blue while another prefers wearing black, etc.?" This is so, but it does not render the account implausible. The musement is always upon *tendencies*. The valuations of the colors as aspects of physical level experience are about tendencies. Moreover we will all have varying capacities of interpretation.

What can I interpret, what is my interpretive capacity? That depends only in part upon the interpretations built up in the sign which is the locus of my physical body in its actions at a physical level of complexity. It depends upon my interpretive capacities at other levels of complexity of experience as well, e.g., at those levels explored earlier in this work. How colors are evaluated according to the hyperthematic view, and what colors we tend to engage and desire according to our interpretive capacities, which may vary considerably, may be very different. Interpretive capacity depends upon the assumptions—the hyperthemes—according to which each of us engage experience. These assumptions will often lead to engaging experience according to tendencies that are inconsistent, e.g., the use of black clothing to signify mystery and sexual power, mentioned earlier.

Hence, while we humans will *tend* to valuate the color according to the suggestions advanced above, our valuations can and will be overridden temporarily by the will to be inconsistent, which will lead to desires and choices of colors that manifest the inconsistency, akin to the ways in which we saw the various attacks upon interpretive communities under the various hyperthematic structures operating earlier. Here the attacks are directed at the interpretively expanding community of the self in its embodied aspect as a creation of meaning according to our continued interpretation of our current embodiedness to the embodiedness of our ancestors.

This will be shown more fully in the next chapter in our hyperthematizing of the visual arts. Meanwhile, it is easy enough to illustrate in other regions. The black Nazi SS uniforms were good examples of this. The intent of the Nazi military was to be a killing force, and more than a killing force, a force that would inspire fear and uninterpretable authority in those who faced or had dealings with it. The black uniforms were the height of this intent.

Other tendencies, which later came into play based on inconsistent assumptions employed according to other aspects of experience, later necessitated the change to dark grey and grey-green field uniforms. The Nazis had provoked war and, in the inconsistency of the killing intended in war, if I want my enemy to be unable to interpret my attack I clothe myself in a sameness of color with my environment insofar as I can: the later SS field-Gray. Modern camouflage military uniforms have gone even further. But while the intent toward force and authority went unchallenged, before the beginning of the war, the color manifested the intent all too well. The splashes of red in the black clothing, being closest to our heat-darkness added the "primal" valuation to it according to the lower limit of the visible color spectrum.

Night rallies added the blackness of night to the manufactured blackness of all else. The rallies added the search lights as the furthest and most interpretable color relative to the darkness, rendering the blackness still more uninterpretable. The firelight of the torches on the long red banners—the red of "the heated blood of Germany"—went a step further into the primal effect. The Nazis could feel very well what they were up to, in the depths of their devaluation—their badness. With regard to color the Nazis were engaging in inconsistent tendencies of action which did not creatively interpret our far ancestors, but rather attempted a sameness with regard to our ancestors with regard to the color experiences of the embodiedness of those ancestors. It was a reversion and constriction with regard to our understanding of our ethical selfhood in its aspect of our embodiedness.

It must be born in mind that the above suggestions are an attempt at the Hyperthematics of the *physical level of complexity*. This means that we can give a sense of the gradations of manifestations of experience according to the hyperthematic view in terms of tendencies and capacities of interpretation at the physical level of complexity. At that level, in the direction of expansion of interpretation, actions within the world process according to consistent tendencies of interpretation are building that which we abstract as the *world of the senses* at the physical level of complexity of experience. According to this we can define red, for example, as: *that manifestation, at the physical level of complexity, of consistent interpretive action according to four selected aspects of experience which is being subjected to inconsistent action in one of those aspects (constriction of wavelength), at physical complexity.* Thus, beginning with white light, which is the most consistent according to the selection of aspects being engaged, the white light is subjected to an inconsistent tendency of action acting against one or more of its aspects of interpretation—e.g., a prism acting against its wavelength—and gives way to red (among others). The why of red, its meaning, is ultimately the creative new interpretation of the interplay of *red creating actions* in the world process, as interpreted to our growing selves.

This *world of the senses* as a region within the world process is becoming more interpretively expansive as the world process advances, and so it is tending toward resisting inconsistent tendencies of action which manifest as lower level signs within the range of physical complexity. Light is not much bothered by manifestations of heat, or of sound, for example. It holds its own against them defensively, due to its interpretive perfection relative to the physical range of complexity. It is bothered more by inconsistent tendencies manifesting further away with regard to uninterpretability, e.g., by tactile experience (mass), and by inconsistent tendencies of action higher than its range, e.g., black holes.

The relation of light to the levels of complexities of experience which were mused upon in the earlier chapters is thus a relation of a range of complexity—the higher physical—to the range of lower levels of complexity found within the range of the physical, i.e., those portions of the ranges of the physical that are guided by the structures of dance, games, narrative, music.

The signs of the world of the senses are manifestations of lower complexities of action, which are put into interpretive play at higher levels of creativity. Thus, dance begins in using the tactile sense to create more complex signs; narrative begins in using the aural sense and moves to add the visual sense; music uses the aural sense. Some uses of the sense signs have hardly been explored by humanity. An *art of the olfactory*—cooking is a beginning—could be created for example, as could an *art of the thermic*.

Visual art, however, uses light and light color primarily in its efforts. Like all the earlier hyperthematic structures it thus builds upon a less complex range of experience in order to create that which passes beyond that lower complexity. Yet, while it builds upon the upper part of that range which we call physical—i.e., upon light, as compared to sound, smell, etc.—this will not necessarily place it higher in our hierarchy of hyperthematic structures than those communal endeavors, which build upon lower sections of the physical range, if their use of lower level signs is more creative.

I have not the space here to expand the lower part of the range, e.g., a Hyperthematics of sound or smell, but they could be accomplished readily enough; tones for example, will have a value relative to one another, a better and a worse, and according to the same considerations of interpretation at the physical range of complexity—wavelength, frequency, etc.—as was shown for light waves. Enough has been suggested however to move onward to a musement upon the Hyperthematic structure of the Visual Arts.

4

The Hyperthematic Structure of Visual Arts

Introduction

This will be the last region of harmonic human experience I will address in the *mode of expansive exploration* of Hyperthematics before passing to the *mode of expansive reconstruction* in the following chapters. We are entering interesting territory indeed now, for, the further we go the more the results of the earlier effort there are, both to support us and to be interpreted back to, a situation which cannot help but strengthen and highlight the fluid and practical aspects of Hyperthematics, even as it increases the difficulty of the endeavor in its complexity.

The visual arts are a region of experience whose breadth is extensive. They gather around the creation of loci of experience, which are primarily visual for the purpose of interpretation. These include painting, drawing, sculpture, photography, and architecture, among others that are less prominent. I will select painting to begin with in order to explore the first hyperthematic pathways of the visual arts, and then touch on other of the visual arts as seems helpful. The opening question, as usual: How can painting as a harmonizing structure be interpreted to the ultimate hypertheme? How can the structure of the visual arts, here to be represented mainly by painting, be interpreted back to the opening assumptions so as to gain us new consistent hyperthemes to be applied further on?

Well, painting can clearly be viewed from the standpoint of interpretive process that we have used all along. The threads of action of painting are, to begin with, the visual artist—the painter—creating her painting, and the viewer of the painting. As in music, the painter engages some region of experience, the *subject* of the painting as we often call it, and interprets it to the viewer. The act of viewing the painting harmonizes the viewer with the act of the painter through that community, which is the community of visual arts as painting. So far then visual arts are consistent with **H**.

Are the derivative principles satisfied? Indeed they are. **H1** tells us to create structures that do not eliminate elements. Visual art as practiced in painting does not eliminate elements either as acting transformable elements, or as extensions of them, or as any signs of the region. The goal of the painter is to get something across to the viewer through the community of painting and thus to join the region of experience selected as her subject to the region of experience of the viewer. This is not a structure of elimination but a structure of expansion of interpretation, wherein **H1** is satisfied.

H3 bids us to create at least three elements in a Hyperthematic structure. In painting as a visual art there needs to be a painter, a viewer, and a community of painting, and painting as visual art cannot achieve its goal without them. Many subjects are engageable, many viewers are to view them, and the painter needs her community of painting, as the developing techniques of painting, or, i.e., *the action of painting*. Is the latter the painting as an object? I will say no in hyperthematic terms, though I will have to go further to show why I say this and show how it depends, as always, on my notion of tendencies.

To be consistent with **H2** the transformable elements of the structure of visual arts as painting must guide toward interpretation, rather than eliminate, the elements of its own or other hyperthematic structures. The transformable elements of the structure of the visual arts do so. The painter does not eliminate the viewer, for the painting is for the viewer; it is for many viewers in the community. The viewer meanwhile is free to engage the painter in the community, or other artists, and does not attempt as a viewer in the community to eliminate those artists. The third, or *between* element, of the community of painting, welcomes new elements to participate: who—without the encroachments of other inconsistent communities—would think of saying "you are not allowed to paint!" and it welcomes new viewers to participate in the interpretive process of action that is the community of painting. **H2** is clearly satisfied.

Yet of all the actions of consistent communities that so far have been examined, painting is the most tenuous if it is misunderstood. I have said that the community of the game is in the game. The community of music is in the music. The community of narrative is in the narrative. The community of dance is in the dance. In other words, for all four the process of interpretive action is the community and without the interpretive action there is no community, no third element interpreting between the other elements.

The Hyperthematic Structure of Visual Arts | 145

You cannot easily make music stay still, or dance, or game, or even narrative (despite the object, which is the book, it is narrative in the act of reading and listening). Yet painting *seems*, without musement, to be different. Painting has an object after all: the physical painting. Is it an object though? The hyperthematic answer to this will be built upon the suggestions of the previous chapter. Let us begin by musing upon the actions of the elements guided by the structure of the visual arts and then pass on to the development of painting, all the while keeping our eye upon our earlier efforts.

The painter paints—or perhaps sketches and then paints—a physical form, with the arm and the hand let us say. If she uses a brush, the brush held in the hand is an extensive transformable element joined to the human body, which facilitates the action of painting in a more complex way than simply the human body alone does (as it might in finger painting for example). As the painter acts, she selects bodily movements of the arm and brush which rearrange and manifest the experience of the canvas and paint so as to bring about shape, say the curve of a human thigh, or the jagged peak of a distant mountain.

Thus, the painter is a process of action engaged in *painting*. The complexity of the process of action is akin to that of the dancer. If you gave the dancer a brush and arranged it so that the dancer's arm movement would occur near a canvas, then you would have a sort of painting by the dancer. The painter engaged in painting is interpreting to a model just as is the dancer. Questions arise: Where is the "other dancer" in terms of painting. Who is the painter "dancing" with? To answer we are going to have to expand on what was already mused upon in a way which will give more meaning to those tendencies, which give rise to objects.

Another way of asking the question is to ask: what is the model, or again what initial sign is the painter interpreting *from* and what later sign is she interpreting *to*? Let us lay out some options of the signs in the region of painting. There is a *subject*, which is painted. There is a *community of painting (which includes historical painters)*. There is a *painting*. There is the *painter*. There is a *viewer* who is interpreting the sign of the painting. If we try these against one another we can come up with some of the more evident communities of interpretation, which are being guided by the structure of the visual arts. I will set them out briefly—and not exhaustively[1]—in an order that can be more readily followed in further musement upon them. Remember, however, that they are only abstractly so set out, and that in the world process many of the communities of interpretation are working together in the community of the visual arts.

146 | Hyperthematics

The active present self of the painter is always interpreting her past self to her future self, and to other strands of the world process, which meet her own, thus:

1) There may be a subject interpreted through a painter to a painting (subject—painter—painting). (Between first and second there is community of ethical selfhood in many aspects, especially temporal.)

2) There may be a historic painter interpreted through a painter to a painting (past painter/technique—painter—painting). (Between first and second there is community of painting in guidance, between second and third there is community of self as ethically expanded through practice.)

3) There may be a subject interpreted through a painter to another painter (subject—painter—contemporaneous painter). (Between the second two is a painting as community of painting—somewhat unusual.)

4) There may be a subject interpreted through a painter to a viewer (subject—painter—viewer.) (Between the second two there is painting as community of painting—usual, but strength of community varies.)

Let us take the first case. Perhaps the painter is painting a scene of nature or of some human event, for example. The subject is that experience of nature or that experience of the human event; it is the model which the painter will interpret through her actions to the painting. The subject is always bound up with a selecting of experience by the painter, as the sign which is selected within experience: "I choose to paint this." As a relatively uninterpreted selection—with respect to the painter's interpretive action of painting—the model exists, and its existence points to a reality, which is perhaps not the painter's reality to any great extent but which is *felt* as interpretive value that might be more real for the painter, i.e., for the ongoingly created ethical self of the painter.

So the subject-model is interpreted by the painter, i.e., it is painted by her through her actions of painting technique, and as it is painted it becomes more real for the painter and for the world process; the painting of the subject is being realized in interpretation to the painting, with the value of the interpretation depending upon the tendencies of action of the painter.

Let the subject be a landscape of distant mountains and the painter be painting these mountains while viewing them from a distance. Then the view of the distant mountains *exists* for the painter, the painter *feels* the reality of the mountains as an interpretation beyond her existent view of them—as given to her by the process of nature—and finally the painter is putting brush to canvas to interpret anew the reality, which is not her own—insofar as it is merely felt—and creates a reality, which is her own as *known* (as having been created by her) in the act of interpretation that is the creation, and that she will pass on as a sign to another.

On the other hand, if the mountains as a subject were in the painter's memory simply, then they are *more real* as *felt*—with regard to the act of painting—than if she were facing the distant mountains, but they *exist* less for the painter. And they are more real still if their relation to the self of the painter as a remembering self is countenanced. In the latter case we have an interpretation, which the painter knows as her own, as a portion of the reality of her self—"I once visited the Rockies"—and which will be interpreted anew in the coming act of painting.

Here the felt pastness of the subject is its tendency to be a sameness as the sign that exists, i.e., to not be reinterpreted. The painter, who is interpreting the subject-sign to the painting, is a community of the selfhood accruing value as an interpreter in painting, i.e., the subject and painting are united in and by the community of selfhood of the painter. The painting, which is created, is a sign passed on to exist for others who will feel the real interpretations of the interpreting painter, a painting which will either bear the expansion of value or the diminishment of value relative to the painter's actions. So much for the first case.

In the second case we can expand upon the interpretive relationship brought about through the participation of the painter in the community of painting, which results in the painting as a sign of *technique of the painter*, regardless of subject. In this expansion can be placed what most often is countenanced as the valuation of painting as a developing art, namely, the sense of how one painter develops and surpasses the creativity of another. As in the first case the painter is selecting a subject from experience as the basis of an interpretation. The interpretation will be carried out through the actions of painting. But *between* the subject and the painter there are the painting techniques (be they stroke techniques, compositional techniques, material techniques, etc.) of the community of painting that are guiding the painter through the interpretation. Painting techniques are signs of the accrued wealth of value of the community of painting over time. The painter is participating in that community of painting technique.

This second case then is the interpretation of the painter to the painting through the community of painting technique, and it can be better understood if we muse upon the development of a painter. A painter begins perhaps through simple drawings and paintings. She practices, for example, by selecting a prior interpretation of a subject and by attempting to copy that interpretation. In this way she learns the actions of technique that have been created by another.

The creation of these techniques by others spans the history of painting. All who have participated in this history of painting so as to create new techniques have joined a community whose goal has been a harmonization of action toward interpretation at that level of complexity of experience, which is painting. The community is the repository of its accumulated techniques, and those techniques are a sign of the community.

A sign yes, and also a model for our painter to interpret to, and to interpret through (to her painting), so that when our painter interprets a subject, she is interpreting her aspect of technique to the model of the techniques of the painters of the history of her community. Let the painter be a relative novice painting a selected subject visible before her, e.g., a still life by a window. The still life will be interpreted in the various actions of brush technique which she carries out. She has begun to learn a certain brush technique. She uses it in her painting, but she has not mastered it yet. The technique she is aiming at is the technique of Delacroix for example. The technique of Delacroix *exists* then for her—e.g., she may be referring to it as visible in some copy of Delacroix's paintings sitting beside her—and moreover she *feels* the reality of Delacroix's techniques and his contribution as a painter to the development of the historical community of painting beyond the existing example, which she experiences, and finally she is practicing to achieve the felt reality of Delacroix, which is not her own, so as eventually to knowingly pass it on and create a reality that will be her own and that she will pass on to the future community of painting.

Here then the model being interpreted to preeminently is the community of painting as technique, which may be centered in a historic painter, a group of painters, etc. So far as she interprets her subject to it she is being guided by the community of technique (e.g., by that of Delacroix). On the other hand, she is also practicing in interpreting her chosen subject to her own painting through this community of technique. As we shall see, the echo of assumptions and their tendencies of action with regard to **H** spread out over time, so that a painter in history guides living painters consistently or inconsistently, from which they in turn take further actions consistent or inconsistent.

In the third case we suggested that the painter is interpreting to another contemporaneous painter. This case is most closely akin to that of dancing, but it does not manifest itself much in our age. If it did it would be something like two artists painting as if they were dancing together. It happens no doubt, but not so often. Nonetheless, let us say that there were two artists working on a canvas together. The earlier suggestions would still apply. Their subject would be felt, and it would be realized through the community of painting, but now we would have added *the interpretation to one another* as a feeling of what the other was up to, being realized by each artist through the ongoing interpretation of the past of the other painter to her future self. I paint something. You respond, interpreting and offering the sign I gave you back to me. I interpret your response anew to you, and so it goes. Such sectional interpretation in painting could lead to quite an expansion of value in art, and someday it may be more fully manifested. What is usually being done over an expanded temporal span between painters participating in the community of painting is interpretation parallel to the time process.

We come at last to the fourth case: that of the painter interpreting the chosen subject to the painting and from thence on to another viewer. In this case, there is between the painter and the viewer a community of painting whose consistency varies greatly depending upon the assumptions. Here the community of painting is partly signified in the painting, and being so signified there is at once potential for expansion of value and for diminishment of value. Much depends upon the painting as an *object*.

Yet there are also aspects of the interpretation to the viewer that depend on the viewer's condition as a community. The viewer is—so far—the end of the chain of interpretation, and thus the signs of the accrual or diminishment of value from subject selection, through technique as guidance and practice, and through objectification of the painting, are all coming through to the viewer. The viewer meanwhile is also the embodied locus of a community of ethical selfhood in her own right, which is freely acting and which may take various actions with regard to the community of painting. Her ability to interpret the painting with regard to the creation of further value will depend upon these factors, so that her valuation of the art and participation in the community will depend both on what signs are offered and the situation—hers—from which those signs are engaged.

When a painting is completed and other elements, human actors, view it, the viewing is an action on the part of the viewer and the action is a harmonization with the painting action of the painter. The subject has been selected by the painter, but it also must be chosen by the viewer as worthy of reinterpreting. Apart from that the action can be more toward the physical, e.g., as the viewer follows the curve of the painter's brush stroke, and it can be more toward the mental, e.g., as the viewer follows the event interpreted in the painting according to her own capacities. Moreover, the action is coming through the community of painting in the technique that the painter is using, as I suggested.

Let the selected subject of a painter be a historical event, e.g., Caesar crossing the Rubicon, which she has painted. Let's say that the painter has interpreted the event through the techniques of the community of painters, and she has mastered those techniques and passed beyond them to add her own creative new interpretation in the aspect of technique or composition, etc. The painting is now displayed and some viewer chooses to view it. As the viewer views the painting, the painting *exists* for the viewer. The viewer *feels* the reality of the community of painting in the technique of the painter, she *feels* the reality of the painter as participating and adding to the community, and she *feels* the reality of the subject.

Where is the model here? The model depends upon the viewer as a participant in the community, i.e., as a reinterpreter of the sign which is the painting. If the viewer exists for the painter—e.g., if the painter had interpreted the event for Caesar himself as viewer, a variety of portrait painting—then the existing viewer would be one of the models for the painter to interpret to. Here I am more interested in the other aspects of the viewer as model however. As the viewer views the painting the viewer is going to interpret it, but to whom? To her future self; she exists to herself as an embodiment of her process, but she interprets the painting to the future self, which she intends as interpretively broader than the current self, as that which will feel her effort and if it is worthy come to know in creativity. In effect she is *learning* about painting, *knowing* it at a very low level of creativity.

Futurity and pastness then may be regarded as an attitude toward signs for interpretation: either the signs are engaged as received (as the result of interpretation), in which case they are past, or they are engaged as passed on (as the initiation of interpretation), in which case they are future. When, from the viewpoint of the interpreter, signs are given *to* the interpreter, and accepted *qua given*, the action manifests itself to the interpreter as felt pastness. When they are given *to* the interpreter and transformed by the interpreter the action manifests itself as a known pastness. When, on the other hand, they are given *by* the interpreter *qua given*, the action manifests itself as felt futurity. And when they are given *by* the interpreter with intent toward transformation beyond mere giveness, the action manifests itself as known futurity.

With regard to our painter, besides her future self she may also have other models, e.g., friends, colleagues, fellow art lovers, to whom she will interpret. And she may now choose to participate more or less fully in the community of interpretation of art. She may learn to paint, and interpret the sign of the painting back to the original painter, or to the community of painting techniques and painters. She may engage the subject of the painting as a model and interpret to it, i.e., to it as a felt but not achieved expansion of interpretation with regard to her future self. In other words she may broaden her knowledge of the subject. Thus the strands of interpretation and the models to be interpreted to are multiple. The feelings with regard to the realities that the painting signify may not extend far for some viewers, but altogether they, as a situation of the viewer within the process, *lay the basis for whatever value the reinterpretation of the experience of the painting is going to gain for the viewer as an ethical self.*

These are the various cases in brief and clearly the community of the visual arts in painting can be viewed here as more than a triad of elements. The interpretation from subject to painter to painting community to viewer has at least four and likely more elements. And in the reinterpretation of the viewer insofar as directed back toward the community the interpretations can grow longer than this and very long indeed with respect to their participating elements. Thus the interpretation is often multiply directed. It is always at least an interpretation to the future self of the painter, it may be an interpretation to other painters, it may be an interpretation to other viewers given to greater or lesser interpretive participation in the community, just as I suggested for narrative, wherein the listener interprets the narrative work onward.

The most interesting questions here are always: what assumptions are guiding the actions of the actors in question, and are they giving rise to inconsistent or consistent tendencies of action in hyperthematic terms? Insofar as we can survey the issue hyperthematically while bearing this in mind, we will be able to see where the strands of value are greater and where less in the region of the problematic of painting. Some insights into the "whys" of valuation in painting as a visual art, and thus the beginning of an answer to "what tends to make good art," i.e., art with value, should also begin to appear. In the process further hyperthemes will be uncovered to put to use in the second part of this work.

A way to begin will be to hyperthematically muse upon the development of painting over its history. I cannot survey in any great depth the whole history of art, nor would want to from the hyperthematic viewpoint since the goal is to expand the larger tendencies interpretable to **H** and expand further the derivatives of **H**. Musements upon various periods of art and selected examples from those periods will have to do.*

I will show that there is both hyperthematic consistency as well as localized inconsistency in the tendencies pursued by the community of the visual arts under the Hyperthematic Structure of the visual arts and I will formulate those consistent tendencies not already uncovered, for later use. When I evaluate a sign in the visual arts—i.e., "presume" to suggest what is valuable art—as I will do, it must be remembered that the evaluation is always an evaluation in hyperthematic terms with regard to a selection from the experience region of visual art. Thus, when I suggest that a sign—usually a painting—in the visual arts is expanded or diminished in value, then it is so with respect to *some other sign* of the experience of visual art, usually here in painting.

I will take each creative new expansion of value by some artist or period of art as a high point of value—and with further musement it might well be discovered that the high point was reached earlier of course—and with respect to that high point, a later artist may further expand, or may diminish, the value of her art.

The Development of the Visual Arts in Painting

Paleolithic and Ancient Egyptian Art

Painting is a very old endeavor of humans, having its beginnings, according to our current facts at least, some tens of thousands of years ago in cave paintings such as we find in southern France. But I will begin with the

---

*For each of my selected examples I interpret the aspects of purpose/viewer; color; brightness; shape; symmetry; model of technique; model of subject; time span of painting; time span of subject; etc., but not always in that particular order and not exhaustively.

painting of the Egyptians, who were engaged in the art since the beginnings of their civilization, and jump back to interpret the Egyptian's painting to the much older paintings of the Upper Paleolithic.

The Egyptians were fond of painting scenes of everyday events directed at the purpose of telling the life tale of a person. They lavished their art upon tombs, palaces, and temples in particular. In their art the various duties of the subject, e.g., the one buried in the tomb, were put on display. Such paintings typically showed the subject of the painting—the man or woman who had died, the ruler, etc.—painted in a larger scale, at work in the most characteristic of his or her tasks, or at war, or proceeding through the afterlife. The larger scale portion of the painting is often surrounded by paintings on a smaller scale, of events of secondary importance, yet to which the subject was connected in some way or another.

The tomb paintings of the tomb of Nebamun, in the British Museum, give us an example of the tendencies of Egyptian painting. One of the more famous fragments is that of Nebamun at the hunt. The Egyptians often blended paintings with descriptions in the words of their hieroglyphs, and in this case the painting tells us that Nebamun was an official of some rank around 1350 BCE. A central fragment shows Nebamun in the afterlife hunting in a marsh. He strides forward on a reed boat, about to strike three birds he has caught in one hand with a weapon held in his other hand. Other birds of diverse types and colors scatter before him along with moths and a cat hunting for his own part. His wife, painted much smaller, observes quietly from the background, and his much smaller daughter sits upon the reed boat beneath him. The scene is filled with action, with color and shape.

After one has viewed the fragment and gotten accustomed to it, one of the things that occurs most strongly is that not only is the painting filled with these shapes and colors, but it is literally "filled" as such. There is practically no space left unfilled. The space that is taken up is still a flat plane of two dimensions however. Occasionally something is behind something. Thus Nebamun's daughter holds on to her father's leg with a bit of her arm hidden behind it, the tail feathers of a bird are behind Nebamun's outstretched arm, or the marsh reeds lie behind the beak of a bird and the prow of the reed boat.

Now in hyperthematic terms this is an expansion with regard to interpretation. The artist is attempting to go beyond the two dimensions of the plane and indicate the depth dimension of the subject. The artist succeeds somewhat and the suggestion of hyperthematics is that he gives the painting more value by doing so. To see where the value is added we may look back to the cave art of earlier humans. When the more ancient artist of the Upper Paleolithic came to the aspect of depth of the subject, which was an interpretive step beyond the two-dimensional profile of the plane, how did she paint it?

The answer is that sometimes she did not paint it. In the "Salon Noir" of the cave of Niaux in southwestern France, where the artist was painting some 8,000 years before the Egyptian artist of the Nebamun tomb, the issue of depth in the subject of the bison is left partially unresolved. Here the bison are drawn/painted in the same plane. The hoofs of one bison are painted into the back of another bison; the head of a bison overlaps the head of another bison. Or again in the caves of Pech Merle where the artist was perhaps painting some 15,000 to 20,000 years before the Egyptians, the legs and hind quarters of the dotted horses are painted though one another making it difficult to tell which horse lies in the foreground and which in the background, except that one horse has a slightly shaded hind quarter, which seems to put it in the background.

Whether these paintings were accomplished by one artist or were completed by a later artist who drew over the first effort of another, we cannot be certain. If the latter case, then the later artist evidently felt it perfectly okay to let the parts of one animal intermingle with the other. The bison and horses in these examples of Upper Paleolithic art thus share a *sameness of space* in the painting, a lack of diversity in this aspect, which is so far a constriction of interpretation, and a diminishment of value. Do *we* make the depth interpretation nonetheless when we view the painting? Very often we do, for we are accustomed to make it in paintings of our age, but the artist has not guided us to do so, and faced with the same drawing or painting in the work of a child we might be inclined to say gently: "yes, but something is not quite right in your drawing . . . should we see that part through this part?"

Has the Egyptian artist done better? Yes, for the Egyptian artist has recognized the diversity of spaces in the subject with regard to dimensionality and attempted to interpret this aspect of the subject in the tomb painting. An element of experience cannot occupy the *same* space as another element of experience at the physical level of complexity. This is the Egyptian painter's insight—though it may have come before the Egyptians of course—and an improvement upon the mentioned cave paintings,

Yet for the ancient Egyptian artist all the things that are behind something are related to one another on another plane, which we might call the secondary two dimensional plane lying behind the main plane, as if one had taken a flat stage backdrop and placed another more prominent stage backdrop before it. The relation between the several two-dimensional planes then is an expansion with regard to the depth of interpretation of "physical space" in the painting but it is not yet a *very* good one relatively speaking. In other words, you do not get much sense of an interpretation to be made between the plane of the foreground and the plane of the background. The planes are just there. At the worst the hidden part of the subject—e.g., the arm of the daughter—simply disappears for us in the foreground to be replaced by another foreground bit and then reappears again. Despite this, the ancient Egyptian painting has advanced in value with regard to *this aspect*. And it has other aspects that display further expansions of value in comparison with the Paleolithic paintings.

It has a far more valuable use of color for one. The cave paintings are very often in black or black and red, red-brown, or yellow. Paleolithic man had not been able to interpret other materials to use, and his paintings tend toward value accordingly, in this aspect. That is only one side of the matter however. My suggestion earlier was that red and the red side of black were tending toward the primal in terms of colors—toward a diminishment of value with respect to ground already interpreted for us humans. Upper Paleolithic man had that primality much closer to him than we ourselves do. We can imagine the torch-lit caves, the darkness and the red, orange, and yellow of the fire driving the darkness back as these ancient artists worked on their art. Their world was a world where the darkness was felt in its primal grades as an experience that they had expanded upon with the reds, oranges, and yellows of their mastery of the light in fire. Their art captured this primality of color in its expansion away from the—often charcoal based—black of the lower grade primality. The Paleolithic paintings begin in black outline, to be expansively filled—if filled—with the reds, oranges, and yellows. So it cannot be merely that the cave man could not find further colors. No. Rather, his comfort with the color she chose to actively interpret—including searching for and finding them among natural materials—are a sign of his capacity to interpret in terms of his being embodied at the physical level of complexity.

Ten thousand years later the Egyptians had interpreted many more materials and could interpret the color aspects of the subjects accordingly. They did so. We find the colors of the Nebamun paintings to be bright relative to the cave paintings, and to occupy a long step up in their use of the color spectrum of light. The Egyptian painters make good use of the light at its most expansive, as whiteness in the backdrop of the scenes. The use of black has fallen away, even in the outlining of shapes within the painting, to become of relatively minor importance. They have moved away from the use of deep red into the use of brighter and less primal reds, they have expanded the use of yellows. Most importantly, they have embraced the use of blue in the Nebamun painting.

All of these changes with regard to color use tend toward a greater value with respect to the aspect of color. The use of brighter colors, tending toward white is an expansion from darkness toward light, which has passed beyond the Paleolithic expansion from primal darkness to the lower primal colors. The use of blue is a move within the value of the colors toward that color wherein the proportion of problematic to solution in experience is in that workable zone wherein we feel our possibilities of expansion of interpretation as the challenge which experience in the world process offers us. Indeed, the ancient Egyptians probably had to work at the challenge of obtaining their blue color in ways far beyond what Paleolithic man had attempted.

Let us go further and muse upon the consistency of the artist's choices with regard to the subject of the painting. The painting shows Nebamun engaged in the action of hunting, with his wife and daughter standing by. The subject is: *Nebamun in his active living relations with the world process (nature, animals, and other humans near to him in terms of embodiment)*. It is not simply this Nebamun as past however. No, the artist is interpreting the subject to the subject's future through the painting. We know this from the use of the painting in a tomb, and from the accompanying words, but could we know it from the painting itself? We could, and first with regard to the choice of colors. We said that the white background is the sign of maximal expansion of interpretation. The subject is interpreted within the white background, a background of light as such. The subject is thus interpreted—through the white light—as having an aspect of unbroken-ness or, as we usually say, purity and innocence, i.e., *as having not been engaged by an inconsistent action*. Since the subject is Nebamun in his active living relations, the white signifies the continuance of those relations in the world process, which have not been broken by his—seeming—death. In other words Nebamun is carrying on into the world process with the relations to the world and his family.

How is he carrying on? The heavy use of blue of the painting gives us the answer to this. If blue is the color of the challenge of interpretation as a predominance of problematic over solution which is still workable, then the blue of the painting as selected to interpret the subject is an interpretation of the subject as bound up with that challenge. In other words Nebamun will have further challenges in the beyond of his process that are at least akin to the challenges of the current life he faces in his relations to nature, other humans, etc. There is a zest for life in the blue of the painting, which is akin to other choices made in the interpretation of the subject. Nebamun is in action, striding forward, his hand about to swing and strike the birds he has caught among others that scatter before him. The subject being interpreted as active is a tendency toward expansion of value with regard to the subject on the level of embodiment, and we, the viewers, are led by the painting to feel the action beyond even what is presented in the painting. The birds scattering give us the action with regard to nature.

On the other hand, the painting also has tendencies of diminishment of value in this aspect. Nebamun's wife stands inactive, a mere onlooker, and his daughter is diminished further still in her sitting inactivity, her dependency upon Nebamun evident in her grasping his leg. Moreover, mother and daughter are smaller than Nebamun in a way that is not the smallness of the proportion of the natural world, for with regard to the natural world—e.g., the birds, fish, river, etc.—Nebamun holds the usual proportions. Mother and daughter are deliberately diminished beyond the usual proportion as being *subordinate* to Nebamun, and subordination is a deliberate constriction in human life of other human actors. For the artist to interpret this into the painting as the physical aspect of the painted subjects is thus a diminishment of value.

A tendency of diminishment of interpretive value in experience at one level—here at the level of the complexity of the experience of human actors as related through embodiment—when interpreted into another level of experience—here the two dimensional level complexity of the experience of a painting—remains a diminishment of value. The subordination of Nebamun's wife and daughter to him, his control and dominance over them within the relation of the family, are transformed into a difference in size in the painting. Yet this interpretation, while *consistent in itself as being an interpretation through the community of art*, retains the inconsistency of the originally interpreted sign within it. Simply to capture the devaluation, the badness, in the sign is to bring it forward into the new sign, and the value of the painting diminishes accordingly. And not only this, but the badness can only be brought forward by an interpretation at another level whose tendency also manifests in a diminishment of value, i.e., here a shrinking of Nebamun's family in terms of the painting.

This may seem contentious, but I will expand upon it further shortly. In the meantime there is another issue, that of the viewer in this aspect. If my suggestion is correct that we as viewers can see the tendency of diminishment of value in the subject as interpreted into the painting by the artist, then this indicates two further things. First, that *we have an interpretive capacity as a viewer with regard to value*. If we have such a capacity then our ability to have the sign—here the sign of the painting—interpreted to us is going to depend upon that capacity. The capacity is then an aspect of our ethical selfhood in its broadness in holding consistent assumptions engendering consistent tendencies of action, or in its narrowness in holding inconsistent tendencies. Second, that *the artist has both an interpretive capacity as a viewer with regard to value and an interpretive capacity as an interpreter of value in a subject, which interpretively manifests itself in her paintings*.

Here the case seems very mild, but you will see later how far it goes. Let us say that Nebamun commissioned the tomb painting himself, as was seemingly not uncommon in ancient Egypt. Then the artist had Nebamun in mind at least as a viewer to which the painting was interpreted, e.g., if it was completed before Nebamun's death. If so, if Nebamun could interpret the tendency of diminishment of value in the painting, and if the painting was destined—though not exclusively—for his interpretation, then he sought out that tendency. He thus had the painter reinterpret an inconsistent tendency, which he had engaged in as the subject, and he had it reinterpreted into the painting, repeating it in another sign. Nebamun thus actively participated in the inconsistent tendency. He had his badness—in this aspect—portrayed in the artwork. The artist participated in this as well, as a *viewer* of the subject, insofar as he deliberately chose to interpret this aspect of Nebamun into the painting and as an *artist* insofar as his act of interpretation passed on the sign of Nebamun's badness, his dominance, in such a manner as the painting allowed, i.e., shrinking Nebamun's family in the painting.

You may object: "surely to merely view a painting of something bad does not make one bad?" My reply is that in the case of Nebamun this objection holds from one angle but not from another. I suggest that Nebamun—and ancient Egyptian, and in fact all societies in which one dominates others—is inconsistent[2] according to **H**, in the constriction, the deliberate elimination of certain paths of interpretation for some other, which is domination. Now if the constriction was actively encouraged—as I have guessed that it was if Nebamun commissioned the tomb—then the constriction was a deliberate engagement in the inconsistent tendency on his part as a viewer. In worse forms we would call this by its other names: *propaganda*, for example. If you survey ancient art, e.g., of the Assyrians, the Egyptian Pharaohs, etc., you see this tendency, which is mild in the Nebamun painting, become much stronger. The king in such art is very often a giant compared to others, e.g., soldiers. Domination is portrayed very easily as your underlings being much smaller than you are in the painting.

Yet even if it weren't so extreme, then perhaps it was accepted by other viewers, the society at large, comprised of those like Nebamun, and if so they, as viewers, would be tending toward active diminishment of value. The objection above would hold insofar as one merely happens across such a painting, or has it forced upon one, but in this case Nebamun was *not* "merely viewing" a painting if he commissioned it and saw it himself or if he commissioned it and meant others to see it. He was seeking to reinterpret the subject (himself) in some of its tendencies to his later self and to others. Insofar as he succeeded—through the artist—he actively promoted the inconsistent tendency into the future, albeit into another level of experience (the painting).

There is a difference then between merely viewing signs of inconsistent tendencies and actively seeking out such signs and *seeking them out to interpret in their sameness*, and my suggestion—to be expanded upon further—is that the reinterpretation of inconsistent tendencies is itself an inconsistent tendency, whether engendered by the artist or by the viewer, and that the act of interpreting the signs of inconsistent tendencies as a sameness, i.e., at other levels of experience, is itself an inconsistent tendency as the promotion of devaluation. In short, *insofar as the viewer or the artist actively wills the bad, they actively reinterpret the bad (the devaluation) in the subject, into their painting, and actively seek out the signs of the bad in painting respectively.*

The implication of this is that the interpretive capacity to interpret into objectification and also to evaluate painting—and art generally—are both dependent upon the broadness of the ethical selfhood of the artist and the viewer respectively, and that this aspect of the evaluation has a bearing on the ability of any one of us to evaluate a painting, even though the painting manifests clear tendencies of value according to many other aspects besides this one. To put not too fine a point on it, *insofar as one tends toward devaluation, one will actively engage paintings which manifest badness in some manner and one will be unable to evaluate paintings according to those aspects in which one holds to the inconsistent tendency which manifests as one's badness.* And on the other hand, *insofar as one tends toward goodness, one will actively engage painting which manifests goodness in some manner and one will be able to evaluate painting according to those aspects in which one has expanded one's ethical selfhood so as to manifest as goodness.* Ethical selfhood as a habitual choice to valuate or to devaluate experience accounts for taste. But value is always more than taste.*

If the foregoing is formulated as a hypertheme for practical application, we get what I will call the *Hypertheme of the Viewer*: **Hv**—*in order to build consistent communities, make every effort to expand the acting transformable element being interpreted to—e.g., the viewer—as an interpreter of the sign in its own right, by selecting and passing on aspects of action-experience in the interpretation which manifest consistent tendencies according to H. Insofar as you do this you will expand the ethical selfhood of the viewer.*

This does not mean something like producing the "Cheap Repository Tracts" of early nineteenth-century England. It means keep the viewer in mind as an ethical selfhood. The consistent goal according to **H** is to expand value.

If—keeping painting as the example—the chosen subject manifests inconsistent tendencies, then the interpretation of the subject may follow at least the following several courses. It may add further inconsistent tendencies to the subject, "magnify the badness" so to speak. In this case—you will see it at work throughout the development of painting—while the interpretation is sometimes *new* as an interpretation, a weak form of value, it is nonetheless also a further diminishment of value. The interpretation may work to reinterpret the badness as a sameness. In this case the badness is transferred to another level of experience, and the interpretation tends to fail as an interpretation at all insofar as the resulting sign is a sameness. The interpretation may interpret aspects of the subject selectively so as to abandon the badness. In painting this would be exemplified in the variants of the use of the "fig leaf" as an expurgation. This is a newness of interpretation which tends toward expansion of value, but it also leaves the badness in the original sign of the subject to influence the value of the world process, perhaps to tempt an acting transformable element toward one of the worse options above. Finally, the interpretation may interpret the good *and bad* aspects of the subject so as to offer in the new sign a response and potential response of some element of the world process to the badness (and a creative addition to the goodness), which transforms it and moves its aspects toward consistency. This last is the better option with regard to expanding value in the world.

Visual art as exemplified in painting abides by this as a whole, by passing on the sign of the subject *at all*, though as we see with the ancient

---

*See Appendix A.

Egyptians and other artists further on, it is open to local inconsistencies. The Hyperthematic Structure of visual arts is consistent and develops because the participants in its community always act to interpret to further viewers as interpreters even though some of those participants act locally in ways which work against the community to varying degrees.

Here one can also formulate the first of a variety of hyperthemes that relate to tendencies of action, which interpret so as to result in manifestation of objects to various degrees. Here the painting is the "object," and the act of painting objectifies to some degree at the physical level of complexity. It objectifies the more so as the artist transforms aspects of the subject into aspects of experience at the physical level of complexity whose reinterpretation by a viewer is meant to be at the sameness of complexity as the physical level.

Thus the Egyptian painter interprets the subordination of Nebamun's wife and daughter as a literal spatial smallness with respect to Nebamun. This literal smallness with regard to another is an interpretation whose complexity keeps us firmly in the realm of the physical, but since the painting insofar as an object is at the physical level, then we as viewer are not guided to move beyond physical complexities of interpretation by it, and so it also fails as an expansion of value with regard to the technique of painting, on top of the above failure.

The implications of this are: **HOe**—*in order to expand value in a community which creates or engages objects, make every effort to act so as to transform the chosen sign being interpreted into a sign whose aspects tend away, through expansion, from the relations common to the objectification inherent in the sign, e.g., the painting.* In other words, in terms of painting, if you cannot *yet* avoid making objects on some level, then at least move away from interpreting your subject according to the same tendencies that give the painting its objecthood. I will call this the *Hypertheme of Objective Expansion*. The failure to observe **HOe** manifests itself in various ways, which are often more evident than the successes in observing it, and in ancient Egyptian painting this is much the case.

E. H. Gombrich, in *The Story of Art*, his great work on the development of art, understood the efforts of the ancient Egyptians very well in this respect. The Egyptians, said Gombrich, had desired to preserve life as it was, so as to continue it in an afterlife.[3] So far, as I suggested above, this is hyperthematically consistent and the Egyptians succeeded in imbuing their interpretations of the subject as continuing, with the *colors* and *active living relations* to indicate the continuity. When they came to other aspects, however, they failed to be consistent, and they failed to be consistent according to **HOe**. Since the aim was continuity for the ancient Egyptians, "what mattered most was not prettiness but completeness. It was the artist's task to preserve everything as clearly and permanently as possible. So they did not set out to sketch nature as it appeared to them from any fortuitous angle . . . [but rather] everything had to be represented from its most characteristic angle."[4] Thus, as Gombrich notes, and as is well known, the eye of a human in ancient Egyptian paintings is always painted as it would look in its fullest aspect, from the front, even though it is "stamped" onto the profile view of the head; the foot likewise is always painted from the side (and the inside at that), and so forth, regardless of whether this distorts the usual view of the man taken as a whole, or results in an overall image of the subject, which can never be seen with regular vision.

How does this way of proceeding stand with regard to **HOe**? Well **HOe** says to act so as to manifest the sign, which the subject is interpreted into as an expansion that moves away from those tendencies, which result in the painting as an object. A painting such as the visual artist produced in the time of the ancient Egyptians is created by engaging a plane surface. Certainly there were paintings upon curved surfaces, but nonetheless the curved surface—such as in a decorated bowl—is for the most part treated as the plane surface, and when it is not, then we have gone beyond painting as such, into sculpture, etc. What the Egyptians were doing then, was *to take the world, and their subject, as a series of plane surfaces which they then reinterpreted as plane surfaces onto another plane surface*. Each time they prepared to interpret some aspect of their subject they thought back to what Gombrich calls "its most characteristic angle"; but its most characteristic angle is always that angle that will signify it in its two-dimensional planar aspect, an aspect which—apart from scale—will then be transferred *as is* onto the plane of their painting, a resultant part of whose objecthood in terms of the painting is made up by this very two-dimensional planar aspect. This tendency is inconsistent with **HOe**. It is a constriction of experience into the subject as a planar subject, a selection of aspects of physical level experience so as to reduce interpretation even at physical complexities, and the transfer very easily becomes a mere *replacement* rather than a *transformation*, and is thus also inconsistent with **H8**, which was formulated way back in the first chapter, but which is a guide for interpretive action in conjunction with **HOe**.

And when the Egyptians acted to indicate an inconsistency in the subject, a tendency which, as such, was itself an inconsistency, as with the aspect of subordination of the human relations of the Nebamun subject, they fell back again on the planar aspect of the painting; they invoked the tendency of shrinking in the planar aspect. *Shrinking in the planar aspect is another of the tendencies which turns a subject into a painting with regard to the objecthood of the painting* however; it is the *capturing*, the *constricting* of an event, according to the interpretive freedom of two dimensionality at physical complexity. We do this regularly now in modern photography, and photography, insofar as it is a mere capturing of events without giving thought to the above, suffers accordingly with regard to value.

Does this mean that painting is inconsistent? The answer is no, no more than dance is inconsistent because its signs are embodied, since the higher consistency of the community of painting in visual arts is to interpret to another through the sign of the art. Painting works through and despite the inconsistency of our embodiment, as an action among objects—i.e., regions of constricted interpretation—just as dancing does. Yet *an artistic interpretation which <u>deliberately</u> moves toward further constriction of interpretation by engaging in tendencies of technique that interpret the subject into the very constrictions, which are tolerated in the sign*—here the painting—*chosen as the medium of an embodied community, is locally diminishing the value of its community*. It is one thing to interpret through and despite embodiment, but another to deliberately turn that interpretation toward the latter. The result with regard to value is evident enough in the Egyptian art. The paintings are full, "crammed" full of the aspects of the subject, as I noted, because the relations of the subject to one another are reduced to planar relations—the "cardboard cut-out" effect.

Furthermore, because the Egyptian artists tended to interpret the aspects of their subject signs so as to issue in a mere replacement upon the painting, they very easily fell into yet another inconsistent tendency: that of *copying*. Why they did this can be disclosed by musing upon the issue of "the most characteristic angle" in the case of one of its more unusual variants. If "the most characteristic angle" of a foot is as viewed from the inside side, then how does one interpret a subject with say: a misshapen foot? For the Egyptian artist the answer was to interpret the foot of the subject again so as to be most recognizable as that aspect of the subject, which he wanted to get across to the viewer, here the deformation. Nonetheless, the deformed foot would tend to be unrecognizable as a foot if it were painted apart from its relationship to the body, whereas the normal foot would be still quite recognizable. The compromise, as in the club-footed man of the tomb of Baqt I, is to paint the foot *as if* it were alone—as a transfer of the two-dimensional "most characteristic angle" of the deformation to the two-dimensional surface of the painting—while nonetheless having it "together with" the rest of the body of the subject, in the planar aspect of the painting.[5] Consequently, even the diminished relationship noted above, of the painted figure in its planar aspect, to other painted figures in the painting, in their planar aspect, is secondary, and can be disregarded whenever the artist is able to render the most characteristic angle by a mere transfer from plane to plane. In brief, *the transfer as a copy is all that matters to him.*

Moreover, this is a further source of the crammed look of Egyptian paintings, because each shape in its planar aspect on the painting *is on its own* according to the adopted assumptions even though it is indeed "there" with other shapes. Having once transferred like this, it was easy to carry on the inconsistency and transfer again, and this time not from subject to painting, but from planar shapes—manifestations of tendencies of objecthood in the painting—to other regions of the planar aspect of the painting. The result is the frequency of copying in Egyptian painting. If you look at the Nebamun painting you see many birds. Yet each of the birds is either a single representation of his kind, or he is copied—here transferred in the plane—so as to signify many of his kind, e.g., Nebamun holds three blue birds. The plants in the marsh near Nebamun are even more deliberately copies. Another painting from the same tomb shows flutists, dancing girls, and guests at a feast. Many of the guests are copies of one another, the musicians likewise, though—which seems rare in Egyptian art—several are shown facing the viewer, but even these are copies of a more unusual selection of the "most characteristic angle." These assumptions allow another to take up the work easily, i.e., they allow an artist to simply be replaced by another artist, which no doubt happened regularly in Egyptian art. But again with regard to **H8** also, this replacement is inconsistent with **H**.

Having done all this, having engaged in local inconsistent tendencies, it is no surprise that the Egyptians looked to other tendencies to interpret what the assumptions behind their techniques would otherwise fail to interpret. They did this in part by expanding the sign of the visual arts so as to allow relations in the planar aspect native to the painting. If the failure to abide by **HOe** meant that transfers of the planar aspect of painting were the norm, and if the painting sign thus stood alone as a planar shape, and if the planar aspect of the subject could be diminished by shrinking so as to contribute to the objectivity of the painting, then the interpretive freedom of the region of experience that the Egyptian painter could work with would be constricted, "smothered."

Sooner or later he would tire of this constriction and expand his interpretation and, if he could not or would not expand in the foregoing aspects, he would take the only route left open to him. He would *expand in the objectified planar aspect of the painting*, i.e., he would give the planar shapes a new interpretive relation to one another in the planar aspect which carried them far beyond the planar aspect in complexity. Once he had made that assumption his diminishments of value in the painting in the objectifying tendencies of *replacement* and *copy*, were engaged in an expansion by acting upon their constricted manifestations according to this expansion. The result was the *hieroglyphs* of ancient Egyptian narrative, in which planar shapes began to be interpreted to one another in further highly complex relationships that brought them beyond their relations *qua elements of a plane surface*.

I will not follow this further here, but having reached the point at which visual art in painting connects with narrative there are two things to note. First, that painting as a Hyperthematic Structure appears to find its place in our hierarchy of structures as coming before narrative and thus after dance and games. Narrative, in its written aspect, appears to arise as a response to the objectifying constrictions of action undertaken in a plane surface. It is, if you like, a sort of *super visual art* whose originally pictorial elements have been interpreted to one another in creative ways that expansively overcame the constrictions of the planar surface and vastly expanded the interpretive freedom for interpretation available in older visual art forms.

The breadth of potential interpretations in narrative is far greater than that of visual art precisely because of the creative expansion which takes actions in the plane surface beyond the complexity *of a plane surface*. An Egyptian hieroglyph, a Chinese pictogram, a contemporary word, and even a letter in the Latin alphabet, are greater in interpretive capacity than a sample of visual art as visual art, not because they are interpreted more with regard to the objective aspect of the plane surface than the visual art, because they are not—and may be even less interpreted than visual art—but because creative moves have been made to interpret them to aspects of experience beyond that surface, namely: other words beyond the surface, aural experiences, and so forth.

We can even see how the zeal to break out of the constrictions of visual art led—inconsistently, if more than in a local sense for practice—to further constrictions in which the larger ranges of the experience of visual art, e.g., color, were abandoned in order to explore the interpretive capacity of narrative. The relations of text on a plane surface are now mostly unexpanded with regard to the aspect of color, i.e., we are mostly presented in books with black text on a white plane surface. This need not be so and we could creatively interpret the expansive engagement of the lower ranges of visual art even within the higher ranges of narrative, say for example in using colored text so as to open up the interpretation of those word images both through color *and* all of the relations available to words.[6]

Second, if my suggestion is correct, we get a better sense of how consistent and inconsistent tendencies stand to one another in the world process. Constrictions of interpretation caused by inconsistencies reach a point where they work against themselves. That is to say, they so constrict interpretive freedom that the transformable elements—sometimes human elements—which cause the constriction are "forced," or better, *redirected*, ultimately by their own actions, to engage in expansion in order to continue in the world process. That in the case of human acting transformable elements this happens through the creative engagement of members of the community responding to the blows against the structure of the community is hardly in doubt. The inventor or inventors of the hieroglyphs would have been such members. Yet this way is the way of the world process as defensive and as safeguarding of expanding interpretive value. It is not the only or the best way, but merely a guarantor that the world process of expansion of value continues. The better way, the more mature way, is the way of deliberately willed consistent expansion.

Before I move on from Egyptian art I have one more musement to make. Clearly ancient Egyptian art has its value-expanding tendencies as well as its value-diminishing tendencies. Is the ancient Egyptian painting better than that of the artist of the Upper Paleolithic? This can be answered hyperthematically, but it can only be answered consistently in the awareness that the evaluation is itself an interpretation between the two based on a selection of the interpreter—e.g., the acting human viewer of our current age—of aspects of experience of the art. The evaluation is thus also a more restricted case of the evaluation of any sign with respect to the world process, and in this way also a painting could be evaluated, although the evaluation might be still more complex.

The value or lack thereof will be *in* the sign of the painting, but the viewer must have the capacity of ethical selfhood to interpret it, and as a viewer she must be aware and selective of the aspects of experience which make up the evaluation. I say this because, when speaking of art such as that of the Paleolithic and ancient Egyptian, there is a very prominent aspect, the interpretation of which the artist has only a small hand in, but of which the greater world process and the viewer in particular, have a large hand in. This is the aspect of temporality as an ongoing interpretive relation to the world process: the *aging* of aspects of experience, e.g., objects.

The artist cannot age her paintings much, although she can address aging somewhat in the choice of the subject. It is the world process and the viewer that are the great interpreters with respect to aging. The complexity of the world process as interpreter is such that we have the barest grasp of it yet. In terms of art, or paintings, just as in terms of fossils and such, some things survive and endure, some do not. The viewer as a participant in the community of art has a heavy hand in this however. The continued reinterpretation of the sign which is a painting—or any other similar artifact of visual art—is a tendency of action which values such reinterpretation. If you save a piece of art from the ravages of time and circumstance for another interpreter-viewer, you expand the interpretation with regard to its sign.

In case of the valuation of Paleolithic and ancient Egyptian art this tendency of aging has great prominence. It acts as a stabilizing tendency, which allows the world process to have a history, rather than a mere leading edge of interpretive capacity. Thus in valuations of two such periods or pieces of art, the age of the painting is the sign of an accrual of value, which may outweigh other aspects. If this aspect is ignored in the valuation then the cave paintings of the Paleolithic may appear as mere child's drawings with more diminishment of value than expansion of value. However, when you recognize the aspect of aging in the thirty thousand years of the paintings, then the paintings, of diminished value in other aspects are known as signs of tremendous value.

The question is whether the viewer has the capacity to recognize this aspect, and sometimes he does not: ancient artifacts have and will continue to be destroyed by those without such a capacity. In the meantime, Paleolithic art will have more value than ancient Egyptian art *in this aspect of aging*, just as the latter will have more value than e.g., a work of the nineteenth century in this aspect. If you hold in abeyance the age aspect however—as I did above—then Egyptian art can be said to be of greater value than Paleolithic art.

Following these considerations, I will formulate two further hyperthemes. The first hypertheme addresses one of the great inconsistencies of action of which **HOe** is a variant relative to various levels of complexity, namely copying. I will call this the *Hypertheme of Diversity* and formulate it as: **Hd**—*in order to expand value in a community make every effort to act so as to transform through interpretation the chosen sign into a different sign,* which nonetheless remains interpretable to participants of the community, e.g., artists and viewers, by taking into account the interpretive capacity of the elements of the community.

In other words do not offer in the new sign mere copies in whole or in part of the old sign, *copying is a diminishment of value which constricts interpretation at all levels of experience.* Rather, take into account those who will interpret your painting, etc. Offer them in the new sign, insofar as possible, an expansion of interpretation relative to the old sign with a proportion of problematic versus solution which expands the interpreters as ethically interpreting selves. Mere copying is deadly to value. All our terms for such action—imitation, impersonation, conformist, fake, etc.—carry within themselves the reason in hyperthematic terms, namely that the old sign is recognized as having had value by receiving a creatively expanded interpretation, while the sign which is a copy of it has arisen through a greatly reduced interpretation and thus has little or no creative value of its own.

On the other hand, the new sign, which is *so* far away from the old sign as to be beyond even challenging the intended new interpreter of it, fails in expanding or even in engaging an interpreter, e.g., a viewer. Such an interpretation causes confusion by offering an interpretation spanning such a diversity that—though it will eventually be interpreted—it presents many interpreters a gap within experience which their current capacities have little hope of bridging. Others must be able to "get" what you are "saying" at some level, in your interpretation. In painting and other human activities there have always been those who have—deliberately and without acting so as to take into account the capacities of the viewer—offered interpretations of chosen signs with such diversity that they have confused the viewing interpreters. We say of these people such things as "he was a man born before his time" and so forth. To act in such a way creates a confusion in the world process and there are better ways to offer and expand value.

The second hypertheme will be: **Ha**—*in order to expand value in a community make every effort to act with regard to a chosen sign so as to encourage further interpretation of it by oneself and by other interpreters in expansions of the span of its interpretation as a process relative to the world process.* This is the *Hypertheme of Aging*.

In other words, with regard to a sign—including experience at greater and lesser degrees of objectification—"give it time" with regard to the ongoing interpretation of the world process; and within that process "give time" for acting transformable elements—e.g., other humans—to interpret it. The more you can do this, the more valuable your efforts will become, especially if the effort tended toward value in many aspects in the initial creation. A good thing gets better with age, a shabby thing gets better, and even a very bad thing—or event—gets better insofar as it bears the accumulation of corrective interpretations which have engaged it. The effort toward aging creates the *community of temporality*.

The failure to follow **Hd** and **Ha** is usually accompanied by the inconsistent tendency toward "newness," not as an expansion of value but as a diminishment of value. Here "newness" is achieved—ostensibly—when a subject is interpreted to a sign which is both uninterpretable to many interpreters by way of extreme diversity of the sign from the subject (contra **Hd**) and intended to be uninterpreted by both oneself and by others (contra **Ha**). What the sign then exhibits we often call "shock value." It stuns our interpretive capacity with deliberate diminishments of value, or with a problematic between subject and sign so broad as to confuse us, or finally, by action upon the resultant sign which discourages further interpretation as aging.[7] This is a "newness" which depends upon the tendency toward engaging a narrower capacity of interpretation in the viewer. Such mere newness indeed has its value. I will explore it more fully later as a variant of what I will call *weak quantitative value*, a mere newness, a next and a next, even when the next is a diminishment from the previous, a race to the bottom where nevertheless each stage of the race is a *new* low. I will suggest, but cannot follow it out here, that much of modern and postmodern art of the twentieth century has been driven by this tendency to mere newness, and manifested a devaluation in art accordingly. Such art, based upon the gradual elimination of aspects of experience both in the techniques and results of art, betrays itself whenever phrases like: "this is just the newest thing in art," are used of it.

Minoan and Ancient Greek Art

Paleolithic and ancient Egyptian paintings have helped me make a beginning. Where did artists go from there? The ancient Greeks figure prominently in any account of the human development of art. Examples of ancient Greek painting have not survived well, except for some reproductions in Roman art. We can get an idea of the tendencies which the Greeks followed by referring to their paintings upon pottery, their statues, and their architecture. We can get a still better sense by comparing them to their own immediate predecessors with regard to pottery painting.

The Minoan pottery begins by being painted with shapes, which are somewhat geometric but neither very symmetric nor prone to being copied. The pottery of the early Minoan period already manifests tendencies away from symmetry, copy, and generally diminishment of value in line and point, at the complexity of physical shape in two dimensions. And it gets better. By the time of the later Minoan styles of the Kamares ware and late Minoan pottery we have painting on the pottery that manifests many of the value expanding tendencies already suggested. The designs are fluid and connected, whorls and whirls, leafy shapes, a tendency away from symmetry in our hyperthematic sense, a tendency toward curvature and away from line and point, which takes the curves of nature in the plant world and in the fluid, the aspect of the underwater world, as its model. The paintings and frescoes such as we have—e.g., at Knossos—display similar tendencies with regard to shape and symmetry, namely a forgoing of them.

However, it was that the Minoan culture transitioned to that of the Ancient Greeks—my guess according to the hyperthematic view and upcoming suggestions is that the former were destroyed by the latter—it must be said that these aspects of value creation were either lost or unknown to the early Greeks in their art. To a large degree, the earlier ancient Greek art in pottery of the Proto-Geometric period and the Geometric period lacks curvature in its decoration. All is line and parallel line, corner, and point, rectangle and triangle, with occasional closed circles. Fluidity of interpretation is gone. Shapes are copied, and designs are symmetric. The tendencies, which come to dominance with the Greeks, are thus the tendencies toward the objective, and this bears out in their choices of subject.

The Minoans leave us the signs of their being a people tuned to the expansion of value in their interpretations of shape, but no less in their choice of subjects. The motifs of vine, leaf, and flower center around the plant, and few regions of experience better manifest the continuity of process than do plants in their constant growth, flourishing, decay, and renewal. The other favored motif of the Minoans, that of water and the creatures of the water, manifest this continuity and process no less.

My suggestion is that with the Greeks—especially in the beginning—their assumptions engendering tendencies toward objectivity are manifested in shapes inconsistent with continuity and expansion of process. If so, their choice of subjects ought to follow a similar path. In fact they do. The most prominent subject for the ancient Greek was *himself*. The Greeks very smoothly moved from the geometric inconsistencies in the painting of pottery to the manifestation of those inconsistencies in art whose aspects went beyond the two dimensions of painting.

Nonetheless, the Greeks did make an advance with regard to value. They began to make use of foreshortening in their painted figures. This foreshortening expanded upon what had been static for the ancient Egyptians for millennia. The value of foreshortening lies in interpreting from a sign (e.g., a human body) to a sign (a human body as painted) in a way in which the move to the resultant sign expands beyond the relations which make the painting an object (the tendency of the painting toward the two-dimensional planar in terms of physical complexity). Consistently, with **HOe** the ancient Greeks brought three dimensions of physical complexity into a sign (the painting) whose objectivity was in part due to its two dimensionality. This was a great achievement for value and we rightly laud it.

And yet even as they advanced in that respect they regressed in other respects. Their subject was preeminently themselves as I said, and not merely the *human*, but *the man of ancient Greece*. The man of ancient Greece is the subject, whether he is painted on pottery or more obviously is shaped in the many extant statues. There is thus a symmetry in the art of the Greeks, as if that art were the result of a mirror imaging of the Greeks' embodiment, as well as other aspects; and that symmetry is inconsistent with our **HAs**.[8]

The symmetry went beyond that of the Ancient Egyptians and the Minoans with respect to painting. Take, for example, the painting on the Athenian black figure amphora of Exekias, of *Ajax and Achilles* playing a game. There are many aspects of symmetry in it, from the shapes of the warriors to the positions of the shields and spears. The artist mitigated this by giving the warriors a symmetry wherein one has the left leg forward and the other the right leg forward, etc. He used curves, which are an expansion of value, but he then diminished his expansion by using them as curves parallel with the curves of the amphora, e.g., in the shield and the backs of the warriors. In composition of subject scenes, such as that of the west pediment of the Temple of Zeus at Olympia, the symmetry is very evident on larger scales, wherein the figures which fill in the triangle of the pediment are approximate locational symmetries with their counterparts at the corresponding level of the triangle on its other side. Architecturally speaking, even the Greek temples themselves tend strongly toward symmetry, more so than those of the ancient Egyptians. Greek temples are structures of lines and corners, triangles and rectangles, parallels and points.

The statues of the ancient Greeks are usually thought to have broken new ground in "realism," and I have suggested that their *paintings* did break new ground with respect to the introduction of a new dimension of physical experience into the two dimensions of painting. But when we speak of sculpture, the object is in three physical dimensions and the tendencies which result in its objecthood are those which interpret its area of experience in ways that reduce down to its three aspects at the level of physical experience. Thus, if the interpretation of a subject must abide by **HOe** in order to expand value in the object of the sculpture, then to do this it must, for example, impart to the sculpture aspects of the subject which manifest as bringing the object of the sculpture beyond its three dimensions. In other words, where the Greeks brought three dimensions into the two-dimensional object, which was the painting, they would have to bring four dimensions into a three-dimensional sculpted object. In this they failed. The Greek statues are interpretations of their subjects, which copy in the three dimensions of the statue object the three dimensions of the subject. Just as the Egyptians had taken "the most characteristic angle" of a subject as a planar experience and transferred it into the two dimensions of the painting surface, the Greeks took the "most characteristic angle" of a subject as a solid experience and transferred it into the three dimensions of the sculpture.

What is "the most characteristic angle" of the subject as a solid experience? When the subject is in the region of the human, it is the subject as *embodiment*, the human body. The human subject as thus embodied will give rise to various tendencies in the interpretation which support embodiment. The subject will tend toward being signified by that state and stage, which appear least in process for human embodied lifespans, and toward being least interpretable through *extensions* of the acting transformable element as embodiment, and finally toward being least interpretable as anything other than a body with its characteristic ranges of motion. Thus the most usual subject for the ancient Greeks was the *unblemished human male body*[9] in the stage of *early adulthood*, mostly or completely *nude*,[10] *standing* or posed in some manner which shows the "most characteristic angle" of the body *as a body*, the latter often being a pose of war or physical struggle because war and struggle are the concomitants of a focus on embodiment and its ranges of action as a symmetry when the assumptions behind that focus are carried on so as to engender symmetries of higher complexity, e.g., with multiple bodies.

These tendencies of the Greeks work themselves out into other aspects of their culture. When the subject of the art is the gods, the Greek god is once again interpreted as the Greek himself, as embodied, and as having the characteristics in action of the various diminishments of value related to an inconsistently engaged embodiment, e.g., struggle, war, sexuality as dominance, etc. All of this has meant "realism" for later reinterpretations of Greek art, but it is inconsistent with the realism of the hyperthematic view. I will return to this urge toward "realism" later.

A hyperthematic evaluation of the Greeks then is mixed with respect to the art of other cultures already viewed. They expanded value in painting relative to the ancient Egyptians, as interpreting a three-dimensional experience into a planar surface, but they constricted it with respect to choices of subject—choosing war and struggle over the Minoan's choice of play. The Greeks tended to diminish value in their use of shapes at physical complexity, choosing the line, point, and corner, over the fluid curve of the Minoans. If we pass to sculpture, as I have, then more serious diminishments, explicable in hyperthematic terms, are evident.

Han Chinese Art

I will now pass on to alight on an example of non-Western art, the painting of the ancient Chinese in the Han period. The *feiyi* or flying banner of the tomb of Lady Dai of Changsha, about 180 BCE, gives us a sample of early Han painting. The colors of the banner are a mixture of reds, blues, whites, and browns on a red-brown silk base and, although degradation over time must be allowed for, the overall effect of the colors tend toward the primal side of darkness. This is in keeping with the subject of the painting in the way that the Han artist understood that subject. Yet comparing it to the Nebamun painting with regard to **HCl**, it is evident that the chosen colors tend toward a diminishment of value in the work. The blue upon the base of white of the Nebamun painting as a challenging yet spiritual process of afterlife stands against the predominant dark reds and blacks, upon the red-brown background of the *feiyi*, which give us a sinking feeling of the uninterpretability of death. Even though the Lady Dai is signified as escaping the more unsavory aspects, the colors are chosen to play up those unsavory aspects.

The subject event meanwhile confirms the choice of color aspects of the subject in this case. The subject is the Lady Dai, of the tomb, in the event of her afterlife, wherein the afterlife itself is also depicted as the subject in its aspects of underworld, earth, and heaven. The subject selection is thus an expansion of value for the work, for the event is depicted as the process of *an active journey* with regard to death. This differs from the Nebamun painting. Whereas the Nebamun painting appears to be focused upon a time of happiness in the afterlife—the heaven aspect—the subject of the Han funeral banner includes the earthly aspect of death as well as the lower and more disturbing stages of the journey of the afterlife.

The Nebamun selection already mused upon is of course but one part of a larger painting, which might lead one to think that a broader choice of the Nebamun art would draw close to the Han art. But this would not bear out since even that part of the Han *feiyi*, which clearly shows the Lady Dai as being at the upper stage of the afterlife journey, interprets that part of the journey in colors not very different from the lower stages of the underworld, etc. The Lady Dai *will* escape to the sunlit uplands indeed, but she has not *yet* escaped. Whatever the afterlife was for the Han artist in his culture, it was "darker," figuratively speaking, than for the Egyptian artist, and this manifests in the colors. Thus from the Hyperthematic view this "darkness" is a diminishment of an aspect of the *subject* according to **Hv**, *if it remains uncorrected* by further interpretation in the art which will expand the ethical selfhood of the viewer with regard to death. The interpretation of this aspect is *meant to scare the viewer regarding death*, a tendency inconsistent with value. The lower stage of the death process in the Nebamun work—if we had one to view—would have been an interpretation of the subject which gave way to the "higher" or more valuable stage which we have mused upon. The *feiyi* painting lacks this correction: heaven is yet *beyond* the painting, the darker and lower aspects of the journey, the experience of diminished value, are all we—the viewer—get in the painting.

Again, the flying banner is only consistent with **HAs** in a mixed way. There are often two of some kind of animal or other symbol—e.g., two leopards—which have locational symmetry, that is to say, they face one another across the middle of the banner. But these locationally symmetric aspects are diversely portrayed with regard to shape rather than symmetrically portrayed, i.e., they would not give mirror images if folded. There is thus a lesser consistency with **HAs** than with the Egyptian art of the Nebamun painting, and a similar consistency according to **HAs** as with the ancient Greek art already mused upon.

There is a difference with the Greek art in terms of consistency with **HOe** however. I suggested that the ancient Greeks tended to expand value with regard to the Egyptians by bringing three aspects of the subject into the two aspects of the object painting. The Han artist of the flying banner managed to remain consistent with **HOe** to an extent greater than that of the ancient Egyptian, but less than that of the Greek. The flying banner contains some foreshortening for example,[11] but not nearly as much as the Greek pottery art. We might evaluate it accordingly in this aspect.

With regard to the **HCu**, the Hypertheme of Curvature, the Han artist of the flying banner can be said to have achieved an expansion of value over the art of the Greeks. The *feiyi* is filled with the curving of intertwined vines and dragons and other mythical animals thus luring us to an interpretive engagement of the painting in a way more akin to that of the Minoans. In a similar vein what is more striking, however, is the interpretation of the clothing of the human figures in the painting. Evidently the ancient Han wore clothing which was substantial in comparison to that of the Greeks and the Egyptians and so the subject insofar as being clothed would reflect what was worn. The way in which the Han artist, even at this early period of Chinese art, began to use the clothing in its aspect of shape as a way to interpret the body as *action*, stands out. This use of curvature is an expansive advance over both Egyptians and Greeks.

Certainly the Greek paintings have clothing in some cases, although more often they do not when the subject is—as so often—the young Greek male. But even when the Greek artist interprets the subject as having clothing, the clothing is treated as a static hindrance to the real subject of interest *the embodied subject*. In the red figure vase painting of *Phaon and Demonassa* of the Meidias painter, for example, the women are clothed by translucent robes which give way to the embodiment. The robes have curvature indeed, but the curvature is at the service of the solid body prominent underneath. In sculpture the Greek interest is yet more evident, e.g., in the *Athena Lemnia* of Phidias the robes fall straight down, an interpretation of severe linearity.

In the Han *feiyi*, the clothing already interprets something otherwise. Its curves go beyond the usual curves of the body. The curves of and within the robe of the Lady Dai herself give the sense of a wave that floats her upward toward heaven, while the curves of the two messengers who, squatting on the balls of their feet perhaps, are greeting the Lady in the afterlife, billow out just slightly in a "rolling" manner to give the effect of an action of greeting in the afterlife which is "rolling or shuttling" the Lady onward and upward.

From this small beginning as a technique which expands interpretation through curvature would arise the later techniques such as are to be found in the lintel paintings of the Han tomb at Loyang, circa 100 BCE, which were excavated in 1957. The subject of these lintel paintings is an old

Chinese story: "Three Warriors killed by Two Peaches," in which three great warriors who are in the way of a Chinese emperor are sent two peaches to share between them, and which, as they cannot divide them fairly, lead to the downfall of all three. Most prominent in these painted interpretations of the story is the curvature in the drawing of the humans. The clothing billows and fans out, giving the sense of motion far beyond it and the bodies it covers. This is indeed the effect of all curvature as a manifestation of interpretation in experience at its level of complexity. In this case it leads the interpreter, here the viewer, to pass out of the relations of objectivity in the painting as an object and into more complex interpretation, which takes the painting beyond mere objecthood as a sign.

The facial features of the Chinese warriors in the Loyang painting have a similar effect, bringing us out of mere embodiment into facial expression as a sign of action in the subject. Moreover, the artist is well aware of his technique for there are other men in the painting who are evidently staid and serious, and their clothing and facial features tell us this through a great reduction of curvature. Here then is a technique which the ancient Han artist used that expanded value considerably with regard to the subject according to **HCu**, and a technique which the ancient Greek artists did not have as strongly. I will speculate—perhaps to follow up in a future work—that this use of curvature as interpretive of embodiment is characteristic of East Asian grounding in the assumptions of Taoism and Buddhism, in which action predominates over objecthood, assumptions which are consistent with the hyperthematic view.[12]

In addition, the technique of curvature being used to interpret the *clothing* of the subject indicates that the subject is being interpreted in its aspect of being experienced with regard to extensions of human acting transformable elements. In other words *the clothing/body relation through the action of the human process is being interpreted in the subject* or, if you like, the body is being interpreted *through* its clothing, creating an expanded "layer" of interpretation with regard to the space of the body and taking it out of its mere embodied objectivity. This latter aspect of Han art is thus consistent with **HOe**, not as interpreting three dimensions of the subject to the two of the object painting in foreshortening as the Greeks did, but as interpreting action in the subject to the "staticness" of the object painting. In effect the Han artist had an alternative way to satisfy **HOe** to that of the Greek artist, and the Han painting is tending to greater value in *this aspect*.

Medieval Christian Art

If we now move to a representative artwork of the Western medieval period we may come to other signs of inconsistency and consistency with regard to the hyperthemes. The painting of the *Apse of Sant Climent de Taüll* in Barcelona, painted in the early 1100s CE, can serve as such an example. To begin with, here we have a mixture of basic colors. While there is very little black in evidence, one color predominates somewhat, namely that of a deep blue which shades to violet. The violet is concentrated into the person of Christ. Evidently the artist meant to interpret Christ as a subject according to the aspect of power, and he did so with the violet. The second most predominant color is red, and it is used in every other figure except the Christ figure. If my suggestions regarding color are correct, then it is used in its tendency toward an uninterpretable primality, i.e., every figure other than the Christ is interpreted in terms of its distance from the latter in the direction of human primality, e.g., in terms of its animality with respect to Christ.

With regard to **HCl** then, the tendency is toward diminishment of value—with regard to say the Nebamun painting—in interpreting these aspects of the subject. The Christ of power signified in the violet is the Christ of uninterpretability on the more dangerous side of color relative to the colors which might have been used; the red of the other figures is the red of uninterpretability with regard to those same colors, but an uninterpretability of "not being as advanced" as the Christ.

Insofar as the artist made these choices with regard to color, he was also inconsistent with **Hv**. This sign of the Christ as power will admonish, and one suspects punish, the viewer. Viewing the stern figure, robed in violet, dominating others in the scene, with hand raised in a gesture of blessing which is nonetheless a blessing of the elect, the artist guides the viewer to a constriction in the viewing, unable to interpret further, i.e., un-expanded in ethical selfhood.

Only one use of color is expansive: that of the halos in their white. But this expansion is fenced off in *closed* circular curves, even though they are curves, separated from the rest of the figures in the subject. There is other curvature in the painting but it is a curvature far less than that of the Han Loyang painting, and thus diminished in value with regard to **HCu**. It is a discontinuous curvature which ends in points for the most part, and it frames a locational and sometimes a mirror symmetry. The facial expressions too make a small use of curvature. The mouths of all are expressionless, flat unreadable lines, relatively uninterpretable lines.

The situation with regard to copies fares no better. Underneath small additions, every face interpreted according to a chosen "most characteristic angle" is alike in its main features, even that of the Christ figure. Hand gestures are copied. Other aspects are copied in locational symmetry as I noted. All of which leads to diminishment of value with regard to **HCr**.

For the most part the figures are interpreted in the front-facing angle. There is some foreshortening, but it is weak—e.g., in the legs of the lion—and though it is an improvement over that of our Egyptian Nebamun, it is certainly no better and perhaps somewhat weaker than that of the ancient Greek pottery paintings, so that we may say that the artist has not expanded value with regard to **HOe**, and has diminished it somewhat from the high point which was reached before.

Yet there is one aspect in which this artwork clearly signifies an expansion of value, an aspect which will make up for many of its other tendencies. That is its preservation as a sign continually meant to be interpreted by further viewers. If the suggestions above are sound, then *despite* the relative failure in hyperthematic terms with regard to other tendencies which rendered the sign a dead end of interpretation—i.e., a sign which every viewer was to take as a relative ending of interpretation—the community of the artist, including the viewers, protected the work as a sign—and still did in the twentieth century enough to move it to a safer location altogether—so that it came down from 1123 CE to the present very much undamaged.

This is no mean feat for a community in our current age, to preserve a sign for 800 years in ways which do not depend on that—ostensibly—human independent aspect of the world process which we mistakenly characterize as "chance and fortune." In this case the community of the visual arts is intertwined with at least one other community: that of the church in its consistent aspect as reinterpreter and thus preserver. Is the art then more the sign of the art community under the hyperthematic structure of visual arts, or more the sign of the church community in its preserving aspect?

It does not matter. **Ha** is the promotion of interpretation of a sign so as to expand its temporal linkages to the world process. Yet the world process is a community according to the opening assumptions of hyperthematics, with communities within it which are actively creating it. Hence the spirit of **Ha** is honored whenever actions are taken which build a community of a sign as a process by linking it to other much larger processes. Such actions can take many forms. Among them the actions of communities of religion, such as that of the Christian Church in its consistent aspects, have been particularly successful at abiding by **Ha**. Among the actions the church has taken are: actions which relate to the relaxing of its subject events with regard to their ordering; the interpretation of its subject events to the cyclical—and thus relatively expanded—region of nature within the world process; the deliberate adoption of goals which extend temporally far beyond the span of individual human embodiment; and the constant interpretive linking of the otherwise diverse signs of other communities, such as a community of art, with its own temporally expanded community.

So, for example, the church community has built itself as a constant reinterpretation to some temporally distant act or acts such as the experiences of Christ and the early Christians. The various Christian stories are, to use a contemporary concept, allowed to be *modular*. The Bible is a book yes, and so far an object, and yet less an object insofar as the church allows its interpreters to select freely from its pages depending on times and seasons, and varying the order in which they are engaged.

Again, those selections and rituals based upon the stories are linked to the cycles of the community of nature of the world process—the changing seasons of the year—and thus never become static relatively speaking. Again, goals are adopted, such as the building of the great cathedrals in Europe, which span the lives of many embodied men and make the manifestations of those goals, the "objects" such as the cathedrals, much more than objects through their expansion according to **Ha**. And finally a community gathers the signs of its temporal members, linking those members in the various objects created—relics, commemorations of the dead, stories of experiences of its members and saints, artwork created for its community—to its much expanded temporal community and thereby expands the interpretation of the objects with regard to the world process, until they become not objects but signs of a great process.

All of this tends to *preserve* a selected sign such as the *Taüll* painting, if once the sign is accepted in an interpretation which links its originating community to the preserving community. If, moreover, the sign is worthy of preservation in other aspects and if its creation takes account of that potential preservation, then all the better for value. It is these actions of the church community which, in the above example, have preserved what is otherwise an inconsistent work of visual art on the part of the community of art in many respects, so that now the value of the work lies chiefly in its signifying the care of the community behind its preservation. This is akin to the preservation of the Paleolithic cave paintings, but here by human actors rather than the world process in its guise as nature.

Here the viewer, if she was an active church participant, contributed to the life of the church and its signs, e.g., the building, as a process in relation to the world process. In that preservation, which abided by **Ha**, the painting was preserved as one of many aspects of the church building. The viewer was thus a participant in two communities—at least—and both benefited with regard to value. For the visual art community the painting remains as a treasured sign of its development—setbacks included—while for the church community the painting remains as a sign of its history as preserver.

Both communities act under the consistent tendency of **Ha** and in doing so they make up a community of communities among which we find: some whose core hyperthemes are hyperthematically inconsistent as they stand, e.g., military false communities *consistently* preserve their battle histories and military relics according to **Ha**, even though these histories are signs of inconsistent events whose preservation awaits future correction of the inconsistency; some whose core hyperthemes are consistent and hold **Ha** as supplementary to those core hyperthemes, e.g., religious communities; and finally some whose core hypertheme *is* **Ha** among others, e.g., museums, historical societies, teachers and researchers of history.

I will move on to the next example by musing briefly upon one more aspect of a medieval painting: what of the choice of subject of the *Taüll* painting, the choice of Christ as subject? How does it stand hyperthematically in comparison to some of the subjects already seen, e.g., the happy afterlife of the Nebamun painting, the taking of oneself as subject by the ancient Greeks?

The subject is Christ, but it is Christ in the aspect of power, namely Christ *as power of containment of the world in judgment*. If we did not know it from the colors, as I suggested above, we would know it from the Alpha and Omega over the shoulders of the Christ figure. The book in the hand of the Christ figure proclaims the subject the light of the world "Ego sum lux mundi." Yet the light as such—i.e., as white light—is nowhere in evidence beyond the small confines of the figure's halo. In symmetry, in color, in expressionless facial uninterpretability, the power is evident. Insofar as the subject is Christ *in this aspect* we have inconsistency with regard to H. Indeed we might say that the subject is less Christ than simply *power* as harmful in its potential constriction, with a figure nominally termed "Christ" as its focus.

There is thus a diminishment of value with regard to the Hypertheme of Diversity, **Hd**, with respect to the sign of the subject in its broader aspects. Whatever aspects Christ has as subject, they are not expanded upon here. Christ as subject covers at least an embodied human actor, the biblical and other accounts of Christ in contemporaneous interpretations of that embodiment as human and as divine, the traditions of the church(s) with regard to that divinity, and the signs of earlier interpretations of all the foregoing. The artist intends to encompass all of this in a focal point of a painted figure which differs from the other figures around it only in that it is—through color, symmetry, etc.—that relatively uninterpretable focal point.

In other words, the combination of tendencies in the painting is to *gather all that the Christ subject may be into this focal point*, squeezing and constricting it in, rather than—as the artist might have—expanding upon some aspects of the signs of the subject to take them beyond the subject. In the assumptions which lead to these tendencies, I submit that one finds the heart of what may be called *medieval art*.

The medieval color use changed, the ability to promote consistency with **HOe** changed, and so forth. Yet what predominates in medieval art, within its inconsistent aspects, is the subject—Christ—as constricted through an interpretation into the sign of the painting, to a focal point which renders some of the few often chosen aspects of that subject—e.g., Virgin and Christ child, the "rule" of Christ, the death of Christ—into interpretations which signify power through their constriction. Thus the virgin and child mainly evoke a cold relation of power of succession as queen to prince surrounded by courtiers—e.g., Duccio's *Maestà*—the rule of Christ evokes power overall as suggested above, and the death of Christ evokes the power of death.

And this inconsistency with regard to **Hd** is one which diminishes value further with regard to this aspect of painting as medieval art continues. We know from far earlier Paleo-Christian art that interpretations of the Christ subject were far more varied. But the medieval artists gradually fell into inconsistency on the basis of **Hd** with regard not only to the subject, but with regard to their *interpretations of earlier artists*. The subject thus tends toward being interpreted as a sameness relative to earlier art interpreting the Christ subject, and so again it tends toward even greater inconsistency with regard to **Hd**, as tending toward *copies*.

Yet if the art of medieval Europe had manifested inconsistencies, it also manifested the inevitable corrections to those inconsistencies. I said before, in considering Egyptian art, that constriction of interpretation gives way sooner or later to new ways of interpreting which either ignore the constrictions or develop expansive interpretive avenues around them. The transformation from medieval art proceeded in this way. Where the medieval artist had constricted, particularly with regard to subject and sameness of subject, the artists immediately after began to expand with regard to the choice of subject. In this period, which we call the Renaissance, artists began to search for new subjects and new ways of interpreting them. In such situations one of the most obvious ways to proceed—if perhaps not the most valuable—is to begin to search for signs of the *farther* past to reinterpret.

This the Renaissance artists did and they found such signs in those cultures which had lived and decayed on the edges of Europe. Thus classical antiquity was "rediscovered" by Western Europe, as a source of signs to reinterpret. Hyperthematically speaking, the signs would have accrued value with age, and they would also have such value as they had accrued originally in consistency with the various hyperthematic tendencies. But they would also have within them the diminishments of value according to aspects which manifested inconsistent tendencies, most prominently the ancient Greek inconsistency with regard to embodiment. That inconsistency, having passed through the hands of the Romans, was imported into the Renaissance visual art in the lauding of man as embodiment, or as it later came to be called when the assumption behind the inconsistent tendency had spread to the works and capacities of man as embodied—*humanism*.

Had it rested there, the art of the Renaissance would have been more inconsistent than consistent, apart from the temporal distance of its subject, in its tendency to copy and to center about embodiment. It was then that a curious and interesting thing happened with regard to color. The Greeks had chosen soft rocks such as marble to work with. Marble has its interpretive fluidity for sculpture, it is workable in a way that holds curve and continuity, and not brittle, and so far it had been an improvement with regard to value. Moreover, the marble most chosen had a color which tended toward the height of expansion of value of colors, namely, *white*.

The Greeks had originally painted their statues in a rainbow of colors, but by the time of Renaissance Europe those colors had worn away.[13] The Western Europeans were thus presented with art which on the one hand signified the inconsistency of objectification around embodiment, but which on the other hand—through the time worn correction of the world process as nature—signified in its whiteness the highest expansion of value which humans are yet capable of relative to the experience of color. The result was an uneasy combination of the two which gave the sign of the ancient

Greek art an air of "humanity" with regard to embodiment, and an air of spirituality with regard to color which men called "the ideal."

The latter was consistent, the former inconsistent. That man should expand beyond himself toward the so called "ideal" as suggested by the expansion of interpretability of the white of the classical sculptures was thus consistently interpreted into the signs of the art that then arose in works such as Michelangelo's *David* and Da Vinci's *Vitruvian Man*. But that he should—and could—go beyond himself by means of a tendency which constricted signs in the world process toward embodiment, was entirely inconsistent. This uneasy combination has dogged much of visual art—and spread into other endeavors such as the scientific endeavor—ever since. Let us move on to an example of it: the painting of Caravaggio.

The Art of Caravaggio

Caravaggio is famous for his "realism" as it is usually understood. What tendencies does Caravaggio embrace and how do they contribute to the hyperthematic evaluation of his most characteristic works? Properly speaking, as I have suggested all along, such valuation needs various regions and aspects of experience, e.g., other definite paintings, to be selected for the valuation. When musing upon Caravaggio's art then, I would like the reader to bear in mind the other works of art already considered, even though I am looking for the tendencies in Caravaggio's work without explicit mention of those works. Also, for the remainder of the chapter, I will simply evaluate some representative works of art according to the spirit of the hyperthematic view, which by now the reader should have grasped, without always explicitly noting the hyperthemes in question.

A painting, such Caravaggio's earlier *Judith Beheading Holofernes*, gives us most of the characteristic manifestations of the tendencies he adopted. His paintings are exceedingly dark overall. There are no backgrounds to speak of. All is veiled in a great darkness except for the central figures, nay the central *action* itself. A splash of dark red silks leads us out into the primality of the darkness, as a lower darkness. In this aspect Caravaggio is thus "robbing Peter to pay Paul," as the expression goes; the use of the light as such is the use of the light as expansive of the action indeed, but the expansion is very constricted. He *forces* us to look at some small focus of action. Such force is inconsistent.

Moreover—which is worse—Caravaggio forces us to look upon what many would not want to look upon. Holofernes is beheaded, in shock and terror—the spray of blood not omitted—by a Judith who is clearly not squeamish about her action, in company with an old woman whose expression and eyes betray vengefulness well enough. Indeed, many of Caravaggio's works force us to look upon something better not looked upon. He is interpreting an inconsistent act—killing—which is itself a diminishment of value. Moreover, he is interpreting it in such a way through the subject and the use of light and color that we are not allowed—as long as we choose to view the painting at all—to look elsewhere in the interpretation, to be expanded out of and beyond the diminishment. There is no beyond; the beyond is primal blackness.

Thus in the center of the primal blackness there is the sign of the human as embodied, already a constriction of interpretation, followed by a further constriction in the primally inconsistent act of human embodiment—killing—abetted by the technique of constricting the interpreting light. In these—at least—you have the "essence" of Caravaggio: *flesh and blood humanity doing bad things to other flesh and blood humanity in dark places*. As viewers we are constricted. Our ethical selfhood is not allowed expansion with regard to the sign of the painting. We may well break out, but certainly Caravaggio does not intend us to. And this is the psychological "realism," explicable in our hyperthematic terms according to a devaluation of the various aspects.

In short, Caravaggio's paintings are inconsistent on the whole, and even inconsistent within themselves. He has indeed taken over the advance of three dimensions into two, but he has not bettered Da Vinci in this for example, nor his immediate peers, and so far there is no creative advance. He has advanced a *newness* indeed of what we now call psychological realism. But the newness is a thin newness—as *mere* newness always is with regard to value—for it is based upon an inconsistency, namely that of passing on a sign of inconsistency as such, without, and deliberately *against*, any interpretive corrective of the inconsistency which might help us expand our ethical selfhoods as viewers, i.e., as processes of value.

You may object that Caravaggio counts upon the viewer to know the story. I reply that not only does he *not* do so, but he actively works against this. The less the viewer moves interpretively outside of the focus of the inconsistent action, the "better," for Caravaggio's intent. A child who knew nothing of biblical mythology would "get" everything that Caravaggio intended here.

Is such a work more psychologically real than others? Only when "realism" is misunderstood—as it mostly is. I will discuss the issue of realism still further on, but for now let us say that in hyperthematic terms any realism which is achieved through tendencies of inconsistency is not a realism at all, for *the real is interpretation and the promise of interpretation*, and *the more real is an expansion of interpretation*. For the hyperthematic view realism comes through expansion of interpretation and so again the usual urge toward realism, as exemplified here, might be called pseudo-realism, or false-realism.

Compare the facial expressions representative of "psychological realism" of the selected work of Caravaggio with those of Da Vinci's *Mona Lisa*, with its smile which suggestively hovers on the edge of further expressions. The *Mona Lisa* is famous, and rightly so, for this, among other characteristics. But does it tend far more toward psychological realism? It does, true psychological realism; I will call it *hyperthematic realism*. That realism is to be found in the famous smile, always guiding us beyond the Giaconda. "What on earth is she smiling at, what is she thinking?" we ask ourselves. If you stare long enough at that face, that smile, you always begin to experience the smile turning into . . . a laugh perhaps, something, certainly not less, something *always more*, always further, always beyond the woman in the painting. This is the consistent psychological realism that can be attained for value.

Now some readers will certainly object, asking: "does Hyperthematics and its implications then bar us from portraying or viewing scenes of human badness, and if so how could this be squared with the history of art?" My response would be: Hyperthematics bars you from nothing. Each has the taste that he or she has and the freedom of that taste. Hyperthematics, as applied here to visual art, merely attempts to explain how the choices of various assumptions lead to tendencies of engagement with experience which expand or diminish value in the world process. The development of art proceeds by attempts at engagement which often go wrong, but are always aimed at further interpretation in some aspects—arts intends viewers and always so far is consistent—and some attempts of technique and subject choice, etc., are more consistent and some are less consistent.

Yet I submit that a *taste* for this or that artwork *is* indeed dependent upon the interpretive capacity of the viewer in their ethical selfhood. One's taste may well be inclined to interpret Caravaggio if one is at the level which can interpret Caravaggio's signs, and not be able to interpret signs of visual art of greater value than Caravaggio's. Nor is it wrong to interpret Caravaggio's signs if you are at his level, or to bypass him for far off signs, which you cannot yet interpret, for if one is doing nothing else than participating in the community of art, then so far, one is interpreting, *one is growing*. Tastes change, and grow as well, and sometimes regress, and still value is always greater than taste. So it is that Caravaggio's artwork may have less value than another artwork—depending upon the aspects selected for the valuation—even though any one of us who cannot engage the higher value of other works may be drawn to Caravaggio's work.

In fact Caravaggio's artwork fell out of favor very quickly after his death. There were good reasons for that fall, even though his influence persisted in inconsistencies which were passed on to other artists. Yet he was saved—in terms of the community of art—by the consistent aging of his works, and his works will ever retain such value as that aging can bring them as visual art is constantly reinterpreted to the development of its own past efforts. Thus the ongoing correction to his inconsistent tendencies will restore value in interesting ways where he diminished it.

David, Delacroix, and Courbet

As the nineteenth century begins we find the French painter, Jacques Louis David. David and the artists of the neo-classical period often turned to classical history as a subject. In hyperthematic terms the choice of a subject which is further from the experience of the present will render the interpretation more valuable. Thus there is an expansion of value in interpreting ancient—as well as futuristic—subjects. The neo-classicists such as David strove to interpret such temporally distant subjects. This was a value-increasing tendency. Moreover, David painted events, and this too is an increase in value, for events are broader temporally than mere things.

Yet while many of David's attempts increased value in the subject—e.g., the *Death of Socrates*—and increased them with a choice of historical subjects, which was not constricted as had been the case with the medieval artists, his choices of technique diminished value. His events are painted as temporal snapshots of an event almost. They are static and their static nature is variously a matter of composition of aspects of the subject as grouped around some central point—a tendency toward symmetry inconsistent with **HAs**—or of the extensive use of geometric line and point. Both of these are evident in his *Oath of the Horatii*, for example. Thus David takes over the inconsistency of the ancient Greeks in technique, even while he often combines it with the consistent tendency to move away from interpreting the present experience in a sameness in the artwork. The results are thus mixed with regard to value.

Delacroix, who began in the style of David, meanwhile relaxes the geometry of the technique. By the time of his *Liberty Leading the People* we have a painting which is moving toward a more value expanding technique than that of David. Edges are not as sharp and curvature is more in evidence. The subject is not a historic, but a contemporary event. But it is interpreted more as an event with far more action and thus with greater value than the previous works of David, and the tendency toward curvature and relaxing of geometry above all contribute to this. Nor are the people historically recognizable—models aside—they are not copies of prominent personages and are thus expansive of interpretation (we may "read" various people into them). Hard death and suffering is in the painting—and is so far an inconsistency—*but* it is corrected, consistently and expansively, by the action interpretable in the subject of Liberty herself as a sign of triumph despite suffering; compare this to the merely inconsistent and unaddressed suffering of Caravaggio's *Holofernes*.

The use of color by Delacroix, meanwhile, complements all. The painting is still relatively dark, but has expanded its brightness with regard to our selection of Caravaggio and is as expansive as David in this respect. Moreover, the uses of a brighter blue—here one can imagine the sky altogether blotted in dark smoke and the difference it would make—brings challenge of interpretation into the sign: "what shall we make of our triumph?" Freedom once attained will be something *almost spiritual*, and the yellow dress of Liberty is the forward and future promise of peace and stability based upon it.

Another painter, Gustave Courbet, took another route, which his *Un Enterrement à Ornans* exemplifies. Here the goal is a *realism* so-called. But what does this mean from our hyperthematic view? The subject of the *Enterrement* is a burial in a French village, wherein all are engaged in their part as Courbet viewed them at the event itself. The choice of subject is thus a diminishment of value, being about death as it immediately affects those who must face the death of another. The subject is not expanded by anything in the painting: there is just the scene of the fruits of bodily death, tears, solemnity, black mourning clothes, dabbing of eyes, blowing of noses.

As models were not used, then the interpretation is not an interpretation of models which is expanded to something other than themselves. In this sense the usual models—human models—of a painter are often interpreted in a painting as other than they are in their physical embodiment. Here this is not the case and the models are the subject itself in physical embodiment (the people at the burial). Moreover, the affects are affects upon the physical level; they are the "outer" affects at the level of embodiment when faced. The people represented—both individually and as a group—are largely bereft of action, merely standing at a single point in time. The group is just that, a mass, or bunch, whose members do not interact but are merely *there* as an embodied mass.

So what has Courbet captured—the word is appropriate—in his interpretation? He has constricted the subject to the embodiment of the subject in its temporal instantaneousness. By a sort of reverse chiaroscuro in which the uninterpretable black dominates and draws in the color around it he has interpreted the selected subject as that instant of the event which is least expansive. This is what has been called realism. You might say that the subject is that instant of the event of a funeral in which the funeral is most funerealesque, i.e., that instant at which it is most devoid of interpretability, that "dead space and time" just as the earth is being cast but before we have begun to move on expansively.

Courbet has not diminished *further* the value of the subject through his technique, composition, or color; he has just copied what is there at its most uninterpretable: namely as the embodied instant. Thus his choice of subject is tending toward a devaluation, and his interpretation in technique, and so forth, of the subject are tending likewise—insofar as he makes no attempt to expand that subject—as others had done before; he has in this way constricted the interpretation in comparison to many earlier painters. The tendencies, which engender "realism" in the sense usually understood and exemplified here, are hyperthematically inconsistent, as is the current understanding of "realism."

Courbet went even further with other subjects. His *L'Origine du Monde* gives us this "realism" in a constriction to embodiment, utterly naked, without clothing to interpret the active space of the body through, and constricted yet further by cutting out the most active portions of the body—face, arms, legs—from the interpretation. We are left with a "piece of flesh" which again has the darkness—of the vagina—as its uninterpretable center, a darkness which draws into naught the attempts at interpretation around it, just as the *Enterrement*. *L'Origine du Monde* anticipated the worst inconsistencies of the modern camera in its "snapshot" character, a character which would be still further exacerbated, as exemplified in hardcore pornography.

The French Impressionists

On the heels of Delacroix and Courbet came the Impressionists. I will touch briefly on some of their tendencies in terms of a hyperthematic valuation with respect to one another. The Impressionists are hyperthematically understandable above all, in terms of technique. I said that copying is a tendency toward diminishment of value. The works of the later Western artists that I have mused briefly upon each had their way of creating or diminishing value with regard to copying in the sign of the painting.

In his historical paintings David chose a subject away from the present, even though it may serve to expand the interpretation of an experience of the present. Thus the *Horatii* are perhaps a sign of temporally distant loyalty in a time in France when loyalty was exalted by a worried monarchy.

Delacroix meanwhile chose a contemporary subject in his *Liberty*, which is a tendency toward copying, namely, of the present experience as subject with an interpretation of it in present terms. Yet he was expansive with regard to technique; using more curvature, more fluid brushstrokes, etc., so that the copy is made expansive in some aspects, leading us onward in interpretation.

Courbet in his "realism" tended toward a still deeper diminishment of value. He chose the subjects of his *Enterrement* and *Origine* deliberately as having few aspects which lead us beyond them. In other words, you may attempt "realism" in Courbet's sense and fail in that tendency insofar as you choose a subject which is the more difficult to constrict, unless you interpret it in the sign as otherwise than in the subject, through constriction of technique—which Picasso would do in the twentieth century. Courbet's realism could not well have carried out his intent had he chosen children at play under the bright sun as his subject.

Impressionism is a series of attempts at technique which loosen the "realism" of David and Courbet but bring even nearer the temporal nearness of the subject experience, so that, as has been said, impressionism follows in the line of Delacroix. In terms of valuation, here much depends on the technique then. The impressionists interpreted their temporally near subjects according to brushstrokes which either diminished or expanded value.

Take Degas as a starting point. Note that he concentrated on lines in his many paintings of women drying themselves. In doing so he interpreted the three-dimensional curvatures of the subject into two dimensionality in the painting. The result is a partial diminishment of value. How much this diminishment of value was brought about by his notorious failing eyesight is difficult to judge—the difference between earlier and later paintings is considerable—but the effect of failing eyesight as a constriction of interpretive capacity in embodiment as process, brought about by the world process as nature, is yet another source of diminishment of value which has its place in valuations such as the one we are engaged in, though I must forego that here.

To give an example of Degas's use of lines, his *Bath: Woman Drying Her Feet* (1886) will do. It interprets a naked woman drying off her feet with a towel. The subject is the human female form as embodiment. Yet the interpretation made of that subject with respect to the aspect of technique is a constriction toward two dimensionality. The body of the nude is painted in a series of predominantly linear strokes evident in the back, the thigh, and especially the inner calf. The linear strokes interpreting the body complement further linear strokes, which interpret the walls and the bath robe draped over the chair. They join perpendicularly with the more intensely linear interpretation of the floor, "running" into the latter, and indeed running away out of the painting.

The feeling that we get in the interpretation is a distant cousin of what we get in the interpretation of the women musicians of the Nebamun tomb paintings, a two dimensionality in which two planes of the subject are offered to us. The complement of this was that—as he does partially with the room in *Bath*—Degas often cut the interpretations of human embodiment off more severely, e.g., in *The Paris Opera* (1869). Insofar as the subject was interpreted in the two dimensionality of lines, it was liable to also be interpreted according to one of the obvious uninterpretable aspects of lines, namely that the line can be approached within three dimensions such that we lose the ability to interpret it. We come across gaps of interpretation.

I suggested that, with regard to an experience of interpretability within physical ranges, the fluidity of water puts it at the upper part of the range. Thus the manner in which Degas interprets his subjects in relation to water is no accident. Along with this technique of linear brushstrokes his interpretation of water is two dimensionally linear: dripping down over the body, being dried in linear strokes with a towel, being mopped off of the embodied surfaces of his many female nudes drying themselves, as a two-dimensional planar layer which covers and devalues the fuller three-dimensional embodiment of the human subject.

The devaluation brought about by such a linear tendency of technique occurs alongside other aspects of the painting of course, aspects which may add to or correct the devaluation. To see just how much so, one can look at *Maternité* (1890), by another Impressionist painter, Mary Cassatt, a friend of Degas. Here the linear strokes in the clothing are greatly offset by the expansiveness of the colors, the luminosity, the bodily curvature of woman and child, and the subject of mother breastfeeding child—the body as process in community and expanding beyond mere embodiment—all of which expand value greatly beyond that of Degas's *Bath*, despite the devaluating inclusion of linearity.

If Degas favored the line in his technique, Seurat diminished value still further in this aspect. In *La Grande Jatte* he constricted the stroke into the point. The tendency toward the point is a further diminishment of value. Seurat's *La Grande Jatte* thus has the feel of severe constriction of interpretation in one aspect—as masses of sameness of internal one dimensionality give way abruptly to other masses in two dimensionality—even while it tends toward expansion in its use of the more interpretable range of colors: green, blue, and yellow-green. The painting does not evoke action; the points do not allow it to, despite the promise of the color. Its masses of color are even more two-dimensional than those of Degas. Each figure, like a cardboard cutout, is independent of the other figures, bounded by its own two-dimensional limits. Seurat's interpretation of water tends accordingly toward a static and mirror-like character. So far then we have a diminishment of value in the aspect of technique in hyperthematic comparison with our work of Delacroix.

Monet painted in dabs of paint primarily, rather than strokes. These dabs of paint are not always round and their curvature varies, but rarely tends toward linearity or toward being a mere point. There is thus curvature in Monet's paintings, but it is a closed curvature. An action of interpretation which turns back upon itself in curvature is tending toward expansion with respect to lines and points, but it does arrive at a sameness eventually.

In his *Bridge at Giverny* (1893), we have the dabs of paint interpreting vegetation and water. They are self-contained in their curvature, so that to follow the edge of the dab is a cyclical undertaking for the interpreting viewer which brings the action of the interpreting viewer back to itself in a sameness, even though the curvature is an expansion on what we have seen from our other two impressionists. The character of the dab as an action of technique which Monet takes with the brush is that of a curvature arrived at through an engagement of the two dimensionality of the canvas surface from a third dimension of depth, which allows and intends the surface of the canvas to take up the interpretation and let it flow into that relatively high end of the range of expansion which the planar surface of the painting allows, i.e., the expansion of curvature approaching circularity which is the border of the dabs.

The result in a painting such as the *Bridge at Giverny* is that the subject is interpreted very expansively in terms of our being guided to move from one aspect—e.g., color mass or region of the canvas—to another, even as it keeps us cyclically within the curved bounds of the subject as being interpreted through an engagement of the planar aspect of the canvas, which adds depth to it. Where does the water end and the riverbank begin? We are not sure, for there are no very sharp edges, but we are lured to move from one to another constantly. In other words, Monet is using a technique which guides us to cycle through an interpretation from one region of the painting to another, to interpret and reinterpret the subject *"internally,"* without ever going beyond it. This is his creative advance with regard to the expansion of value.

Now, if this tendency of technique were to be accompanied—and it need not be—by a complementary tendency in the selection of a subject, then we might expect that very often the artist would select subjects and experiences of subjects that would allow the tendency of the technique to come out in the sign which is the painting. In fact this is what occurs in much of Monet's art. In Monet's art nature often plays a prominent role as a subject, and very often the exclusive role. Why?

Because nature is constantly undergoing and guiding interpretation, while returning again and again in its cycle with regard to season, and with regard to changes from night to day, from fine weather to foul, and so forth. As a subject it best allows Monet to interpretively express himself according to his intent. Others had interpreted the cyclicality of nature—e.g., Poussin in his series of paintings of *The Four Seasons*—but not in a way which also interpreted the cycles of action of nature internally to the painting itself as a matter of technique. Result: Monet painted scenes such as his water lily garden over and over again, attempting to interpret the cycle of nature. Yet if we note that much of Monet's effort was expended upon a nature which was artificial—his water lily pond—then something else is implied.

Nature is cyclical yes, but its cyclical character arises both as an expansion of value according to tendencies of active interpretation—as compared to other value diminishing tendencies—of physical ranges of complexity of experience, and as a limitation of that expansion of value which folds the interpretation of the experience back upon itself, e.g., in the cycle of the seasons. But the fullest range of that interpretability, so I have suggested, spans from the uninterpretability of the primal darkness to the leading edge of maximal interpretability of light as such. The cycle of nature is thus interpretability within that range insofar as active interpretive engagement limits and turns the activity back upon itself to a cyclical but not static sameness of experience. In brief, nature is an engagement with light and Monet's lifelong obsession with the cycles of light in nature is the attempt to interpret the engagements of action experience at the physical range *to* maximal interpretation—light—at the current leading end of that range.

Consistent with Monet's efforts to express it in his art, nature itself is the valuated outcome of our various consistent and inconsistent active engagements of the leading edge of maximal interpretability of our own capacity of interpretation as loci of the world process. Or: *for us in our current age, nature is the result of what we have done and do to the light in our interpretations, and as we vary our tendencies of interpretation and learn to make them more consistent with one another, then that leading edge of interpretability which we now call light will expand beyond what we now interpret it to be, as will that range of interpretable experience which we now call nature.* Insofar as this occurs, our own current interpretation of ourselves as embodied in a natural world will be surpassed.

My musement upon the aspect of technique has so far touched upon Seurat with his points, Degas with his lines, and Monet with his cyclical curvature. What would surpass Monet as an expansion of value with regard to technique? It would have to be a curvature which was predominantly open-ended rather than cyclically closed. Within the group of the impressionists it was Renoir who used this open curvature most as a technique.

In Renoir's paintings we are nearly always guided so as to move or flow from one region of the painting to another. This is not a linear movement as with Degas, nor a cyclical movement as with Monet, but a movement which flows through the regions of the painting and then guides us beyond the planar confines of the painting in an open-ended expansion of interpretation. Insofar as this open-ended expansion of interpretation is applied to the interpretation of subjects in the physical range of experience, then this open-ended flow of curvature in Renoir's technique combines with the tendency to move from darker color to brighter more interpretable color, in effect to tend toward light as such.

In Renoir's *Lady at the Piano* (1875), the upper part and right-hand region of the painting flow into the figure of the lady who runs like a river through the painting. The dark mass of the piano gives way to its keys as a tributary drawn into the fingers of the pianist. The lady herself, a process of action through experience, mingling the pink of her flesh tones—a whisper of ancient primality—and the subtle challenge of bright blue, both verging on combination in the maximal interpretability of white, expands into the "river delta" of the flowing dress.

What does Renoir paint? His subjects are the human, women and children predominantly. Women and children, and children above all, and women in their relation to children as processes guiding and engendering further processes of growth—as we saw in Cassatt above—are loci of experience which are rarely static, but are rather constantly in action.

Thus, here again subject and technique, which interprets that subject, complement one another. Renoir has a tendency to paint the female nude and again this complements his technique, for human female embodiment exhibits the tendency toward curvature, and indeed open-ended curvature, more than does that of the human male—and has a greater value thereby, in hyperthematic terms—and Renoir makes every effort to interpret that open-ended curvature in his endlessly curving strokes which flow into yet further strokes.

Expansiveness of curvature is applied not merely to the body proper of the subject, but to the facial features and resulting expressions. In the *Bather Arranging Her Hair* (1893, NGA Washington), lips, eyelashes, eyebrows, etc., all participate in this curvature which renders an expression of utter obliviousness to anything beyond the bather herself as a process engaged in the active after bath experience. Such an interpretation of the subject in embodiment guides us beyond embodiment, for it removes the self-consciousness of the subject *as an embodiment*. In doing so it guides us, the viewers, to give up the inconsistent constrictive tendencies which "fix" the subject in its embodiment.[14] That the expanded interpretability of the facial expression alone is enough to accomplish this, the reader may confirm by comparing the very self-conscious constriction to embodiment of Titian's *Venus of Urbino*, in comparison to which Renoir's bather is utterly without eroticism as a self-consciousness of embodiment. The expansion of value of Renoir's bather as compared to the constriction of say Courbet's *L'Origine du Monde* is great indeed.

Nonetheless, it is the body itself which gets the most attention, and as Renoir ages his female nudes become fuller and rounder as he attempts to bring a curvature to the subject in his interpretation, which is more than that of the subject in three dimensions of embodiment. As he grows as a painter, he does this by moving more and more toward interpretable color, toward bright color, and toward light as such. He adds to the subject in multiple ways, expanding its aspects of interpretation at the physical level of complexity. Or again, through various expansions according to his ability: *he corrects human embodiment as a region of experience bringing it out of darkness, mere three dimensionality, and consciously objectified eroticism.* In doing so he does a service—part of the ongoing effort of many—to the community of humanity in the region of the play of art.

What Renoir was attempting can be formulated in a further hypertheme, the final hypertheme of our exploratory mode. I will call this the *Hypertheme of Correction*: **Hc**—*in order to expand value in a community, make every effort, according to your ethical capacity as an interpreter, to act so as to* <u>select</u> *signs of experience which have arisen through constrictive tendencies, and* <u>correct</u> *them through such creative expansions as you are capable of.* Choose some aspect of the world in which you can see a diminishment of value and creatively expand upon that experience so as to contribute a sign of greater value to the world process. You need not solve all of the problematics of diminished value in the world process; even the smallest efforts at creative expansion will contribute. Do what you can.

Renoir was able to interpret a subject of three dimensions into a sign of two dimensions, a painting canvas, in a way that did not lose those three dimensions. This creative breakthrough was not Renoir's, as we know. The creative expansion, which Renoir added according to his particular skill and ethical capacity as an interpreter in the community of visual art, was to go beyond this by selecting a subject—the female nude—which *had hitherto been fixed or even diminished in embodiment*, and interpreting it through such techniques that it emerges as *expanded beyond mere embodiment, i.e., becomes even more than three-dimensional upon the two dimensional plane surface of the canvas.* Corrections such as these, engaging many aspects of experience, have been carried out throughout the history of the world process by countless creative individuals at all levels of complexity of experience.

Now with regard to the Impressionists, I have chosen to muse mainly upon a valuation of technique. Hence, my main suggestion is that Renoir's technique of continuous curvature is an expansion of interpretation beyond that of his peers. Beyond that, I add the further suggestion that Renoir was one of the greater artists of human history thus far in his ability to treat so many aspects of the interpretation expansively, *besides* the aspect of technique, in a way which nonetheless complemented his technique, namely, the expansive engagement of color and light as such and the choice of subject. If he had ranged further from the experiences of the present in the choice of subjects—as the Symbolists, and later Magritte, often did to such great effect—his paintings would have expanded yet further as to value.

In a hyperthematic evaluation of our four main Impressionist painters, according to the aspect of *technique* alone or primarily, and *in interpretive comparison with the work of Delacroix* which I discussed, and finally *on the* *basis of the paintings discussed*, the order of value from worst to best would be Seurat, Degas, Monet, and finally Renoir.*

However, the taste, or preference, or otherwise put, *the will to engage the experience* of certain of these works rather than others is going to depend upon the interpretive capacity of the viewer. If the sum of the past efforts of an actively willing process—e.g., human—lead it to tend to engage experiences of artwork according to one or more constrictive tendencies, then that process, that viewer, will tend to engage such artworks as allow those constrictive tendencies to play out in the interpretation of viewing. If one wills constriction, this influences the experiences one seeks out. If one tends toward engaging the experience of the female subject as a constriction to embodiment—in a contemporary phrase "seeing women as objects"—then, with respect to the aspect of technique at least, and all else being equal, the nudes of Degas will appeal to one more than those of Renoir, and if one tends toward an even greater constriction with regard to the female subject, then Courbet's *L'Origine du Monde* will appeal more than the nudes of Degas.

We have to remember that the community of art, including the viewers of art, is always a process intertwined with other processes and thus with ongoing tendencies of devaluation and valuation within the play of the world process. So that even though taste will often approximate value according to the interpretive capacity of the viewer, it will often diverge due to the impingement of tendencies at work in the world process at large, upon, in this case, the active interpretations of the community of art.

Your interpretive capacity may be such that you have a strong taste for Renoir under the usual circumstances, but if, for example, you are constricted to a single example of his artwork for a very long time, say many years, or to constant bombardment by mass-produced copies of the same, then your taste may revolt, regardless of your interpretive capacity, through the constriction toward sameness. The valuation does not change with respect to the community of art; it is just that the world process is a rather large place wherein many inconsistent tendencies will influence the community of art. This particular example is akin to the literal tasting of food. The most favorite food will succumb to devaluation through the constriction of sameness if you eat nothing else for days on end.

---

*The *Maternité* of Cassatt, mentioned earlier, would fall between the work of Monet and Renoir, whereas other works, such as *Lydia Leaning on her Arms, Seated in a Loge* (1879) would fall between that of Degas and Monet.

Can the interpretive capacity of the viewer be expanded? The answer, as my whole endeavor has suggested all along is: of course. That expansion is the process of growth in the practice of engagement with diverse experience. This is always most fruitfully accomplished through interpretations which unite a diversity of experience which is a challenge, but not so diverse as to be harmful. Subtlety goes a long way in guidance.

As other aspects would be added to the evaluation, the complexity and thus difficulty of the evaluation would increase. The hyperthematic evaluation of art in paintings—and indeed all evaluation such as I have attempted in this chapter—would thus depend, as should be obvious, on an increasingly expansive experience of the region of art in painting both internally to the community of art and as it relates to the world process.

As a synopsis of valuation I will add the following. An artist makes a creative expansion of value when he or she tends toward consistency in some aspect of the interpretation in a way which initiates or surpasses interpretations that have been offered before. The artist may tend toward inconsistency in other aspects of the artwork, but mere diversity of inconsistency is just that, *mere diversity, bare newness*, and the race to the bottom, which is the embracing of inconsistency, eventually reaches the bottom. The depth of a devaluating trend of minimalism in painting, for example, will hit the bottom when there is nothing but a single line, or a single dot, or perhaps a blank canvas to interpret, even though every "shocking" diminishment on the way to the bottom was indeed something new. Unfortunately *new*, in each case, will have been the only value the interpretation has—an extremely weak form of value, if it is standing alone.

Mere diversity, which can become as weak with regard to value as mere quantitative difference, is one of the poorer forms of expansion of value, even though—as seems evident in much of the more recent modern and postmodern art effort—it does drive a change in art as a gradual diminishment of aspects of value, which is nonetheless new with respect to **Hd**. If the work is preserved, aging according to **Ha** further supplements the value of such works. A work manifesting extreme devaluation, Rothko's *Untitled (Black on Gray)* for example, will age like anything else, if deliberately preserved; that aging will add value to the deliberate devaluation which went into the work, just as the Paleolithic art mentioned earlier has gained value by aging. Works such as *Untitled* thus come to signify dead ends for value, retaining value only as historic warnings of what not to do.

The greatest expansions of value however, come in art which *initiates or surpasses other interpretations in the greatest number of aspects of consistent tendency*. Diversity and aging then supplement these other consistencies of tendency, for the work is not merely preserved, but it is well worth preserving. Some of the aspects of expansion already suggested include: expansions with regard to color and light as such, expansions with regard to curvature, expansions with regard to asymmetry, expansions with regard to the selections of subjects as signs of consistent tendency, expansions which take the resultant sign of interpretation beyond the level of objectification of its medium, expansions which draw new actors into the community of art by taking into account the interpretive capacity of the viewer, expansions which promote aging of the art sign and thus further interpretation relative to the temporality of the world process, expansions through deliberate selection, and correction of signs of inconsistent tendencies. An artist may individuate him- or herself in the expansion of one of these aspects to a degree not yet attained in the human region of the world process, or in the expansion of several at once, or by bringing together a number of already expanded aspects for the first time, and so on.

Can we say then that the art of each of the cultures alighted on in the foregoing has a definite value? Yes, but only as a tendency for the culture insofar as the attempt is made to select the culture as a community of art to be evaluated within the greater community of art. There may be artists in each culture who rise above or fall below its tendency as a culture, in which case we could evaluate the artist, or again the piece of art of the artist, or again an area of the painting. All of these are possible. With these caveats, the art of a culture can be evaluated, with care, as more or less valuable, as better or worse, than that of other cultures.

Each creative new expansion of value in some aspect gives the high point of a painter or a period, despite inconsistent tendencies which accompany it. Yet as it proceeds as a "style of art," the combinations of it as an advance with regard to earlier techniques which have not advanced, cause it to be "mined out." It becomes more and more copied and diminishes in its consistency in this respect, until another creative new expansion is made.

Just as the ability to interpret three dimensionality into two dimensions was a great advance, the future of art will be that of expansions of four dimensionality into the media of two and three dimensions, of five dimensionality into the media of four, three, and two dimensions, and so forth. It will be that of expansions with regard to the use of color and the development of wholly new colors which will accompany the expansion of actions of maximal interpretability—the nature of light—within whose ever broadening range we engage the world process.

I did not make it as far as later modern and post-modern art, and I have said too little about other forms of art besides painting, but this is for lack of space rather than interest. I will correct this deficit somewhat by musing further upon the confluence of art, architecture, and the physical aspects of products of commercial corporations, in the chapters that follow. Enough has been suggested, however, that the continuation of hyperthematic musement upon the community of art can be left to others who may be interested. Meanwhile, I will move forward to the second part of this work.

Part II

Mode of Expansive Reconstruction

*Applied to the Commercial Corporation
As a Hyperthematic Structure*

5

Hyperthematization of the Corporation

Introduction

We are now prepared to begin the more creative moment of Hyperthematics. Having elaborated a hyperthematic scheme and several dozen hyperthemes, the resources are available to approach any problematic of experience, whether that problematic is: one which has already given rise to deliberate attempts to fashion a hyperthematic structure; one with regard to which no such deliberate attempts are evident, but which is rather a mere accretion seemingly; or finally, one with regard to which neither deliberate attempt, nor random accretion is evident, i.e., a relatively unengaged problematic.[1]

To make the most of my space the problematic which I select here is one whose apparent hyperthematic structure appears to range over at least the first two of the above relations that a hyperthematic structure can take with regard to a problematic. The problematic in question is the one engaged by the apparent hyperthematic structure of the commercial corporation, a region of action-experience whose current prominence in human affairs makes it a promising test case for hyperthematization.*

The hyperthematization will proceed as follows. First, I will present the problematic behind the structure of the corporation. The hyperthematic structure is a structure which attempts to promote harmonized interpretive action with regard to a certain selected problematic of experience, the "having a goal" of **HG**. The initial task of every hyperthematization, regardless of whether prior engagement in that problematic is evident or not, is thus to elaborate and expand upon what the problematic is. Whether we start afresh, or whether we start by considering prior attempts, we must first set

---

*In what follows I will use the terms *corporation* and *company* interchangeably for commercial corporation, even though I always intend the sense of the latter.

our goal by selecting the diversities of experience which are to be engaged by our effort.

If pressed further as to why a problematic on the basis of an already apparent hyperthematic structure is selected, rather than an entirely fresh and unengaged problematic, then in the first place, as I said earlier, selecting the former gives an opportunity to *test* Hyperthematics broadly as a method. In the second place, it provides an opportunity to display the real-world applicability of Hyperthematics in being able to engage a region of experience which has already been selected by humans as worthy of creative valuation. This is surely the primary task of an applied ethics, and of an applied metaphysics in its service.

Whatever problematic the corporation engages is apparently an important one, given the prevalence of these entities worldwide and yet also a difficult and complex one which is capable of giving rise to diverse and inharmonious actions, as well as the seemingly inconsistent communities within which we try to find meaning. It thus presents a tantalizing pragmatic opportunity. I will elaborate the problematic *first* by musing upon the origins of the corporation and offering various illustrations of what corporations have done and how they have been exemplified throughout human history, and finally by reflecting briefly upon some accounts of the purpose of corporations, that of Adam Smith in particular.

Having expanded the problematic which the corporation appears to engage, I will proceed to a *second* task: examining the corporation as a potential hyperthematic structure according to the hyperthematic method and resources. I will consider, primarily, whether it can be interpreted to the ultimate hypertheme and derivatives; and subordinately, both whether it seems consistent with the hyperthematic scheme—particularly in comparison with some of the other structures already examined—and what are the transformable elements within the structure of the corporation as we experience it. The second task will also be the testing of the structure in an attempt to elaborate what, in the structure as we now have it, is salvageable and what must be reconstructed, i.e., what is or are its postulated hypertheme(s).

Having gotten some idea of the hyperthematic structure which the commercial corporation acts under, its deficiencies and strengths, and having displayed the problematic that it is to engage as well, I will then be ready to take on the *third* task, which will be, according to my capacity to undertake the endeavor in a creative manner, a reconstructive action responding to those destabilizing actions enacted on a higher level of hyperthematic complexity that have given rise to the inconsistencies within the structure of the corporation. Here I will expand the hyperthematic structure of the corporation as needed so as to make it a consistent structure of interpretive action harmonization which has the capacity to gather together processes of interpretation directed at its particular problematic. To do this I will actively postulate renewed transformable elements, types of action, and so forth, the inclusion of which would render it consistent. I will also show by further postulation and interpretation according to the available collection of hyperthemes, how the redesigned structure can consistently find its place in the hyperthematic scheme, and thus in the larger vision of the world process as a realm of interpretation, by adopting such hyperthemes as were already elaborated.

If all of this can be accomplished, even if only as a sketch, then the method will have been exemplified in a pragmatic and consistent manner as a model for future hyperthematic philosophical endeavors and I will consider some contribution to have been made to the world as a world of value.

The Problematic of the Corporation

The origins of the corporation can be traced back in some form or other to the ancient world. In recorded history these origins are first in evidence in the region of the Near East and then most prominently in the civilizations which flourished around the Mediterranean. By the time of the Roman Empire the prominence and complexity of trade arrangements in the Mediterranean world was considerable. The quantity and diversity of financial ventures, not to mention the broad social stratification of those who engaged in them,[2] made the risk inherent in trading agreements and partnerships all the more apparent, which in turn increased the need for the liabilities in such ventures to be clearly delineated. Eventually this led to the concept of limited liability of a corporate body, in the guise of the society of partners. While the concept of limited liability *seems* important however, to the corporation as *we* know it, nonetheless the corporation clearly follows upon the experiential need to which it was a solution.

Before man engaged in complex trade, he evidently engaged in simple trade. Such simple trade undoubtedly took the form of barter between willing actors. At the same time however, it is not enough to focus on trade. Trade assumes an experiential need, namely, that I have some item or skill—some experience—that you do not have but want and that you in turn also have some item or skill that I do not have, yet want. Our trade with one another then is an interpretation which is to solve these problems.

If each has all that he desires, however, there will be no trade. In the case of the hunter-gatherer societies, which preceded the ancient societies, the record appears to indicate that human populations were small enough to get along without trade to a large degree. If all that you want is within reach, then what need even to barter? Hence, prior to the need to trade will be some expansion of the problematic of experience. We want to eat, for example, because we are hungry, but the mere will to eat would never by itself give rise to a structure such as the corporation. I have apples aplenty in my valley and if I am primitive and know nothing of the principles of balanced nutrition, then my apples will satisfy my mere will to eat and be full.

Let me once discover, however, that you in your valley over yonder are blessed with an abundance of pears, and suddenly my apples take on a whole new range of meaning in contrast with your pears. To arrive at an interpretation of this meaning, however, I have to suppose *myself* to be a community of selfhood. If your valley is a day's travel away from mine, then I must be able to interpret myself so as to find meaning over a day's journey, i.e., all the events of the day's journey that I will and do make, are being connected in, and as, myself. I must, in other words, be able to *plan* so as to meaningfully connect, or interpret, my past, present, and future experiences to one another. Thus, in whatever sense a community may be a trading community, *it first depends upon the viewing of the individual as that default community of interpretation which is a community of selfhood.*

Slowly then the problematic at the heart of the corporation can begin to be defined. I wish to have some experience which at present I do not have. So far this is just the world problematic in which experience and different experience are to be interpreted to one another through some experience which is now missing. However I might have become aware of this different experience, nonetheless I postulate that I can arrive at it from my present experience, i.e., I can meaningfully solve the problem before me. This involves first a sense of myself as extended in time. I am to gather apples in some quantity, but it will take me until this afternoon to gather them. I am to hollow a canoe out of that fallen tree nearby, but it will take me three risings of the sun to do it.

Hence the first expansion, which arises with regard to our selected problematic of experience, is that expansion by which we come to know ourselves as temporally extended individual selves with plans which involve ourselves alone according to the time process parallel aspect, i.e., I mean to do such and such over a coming period of time. So far I extend myself in time and by doing so am able to accomplish my simple plans. But these simple plans may not yet involve much sense of an other individual as a worker with whom I cooperate, or as one with whom I trade. In other words, the transformable element, which is to bridge the simpler problematic, is my body, but my body as an extension of my postulated extended temporal self. Whatever I can manage by myself, that is to say, whatever range of diversities of experience which I can meaningfully interpret between by using the extended transformable element, which is my present body, as a *third* to interpret *between* my past and my future self, is not the problematic which gives rise to and is engaged by those less complex structures that will eventually develop into the corporation. As noted earlier, I can dance alone by interpreting my actions to my postulated past or future self. Such actions neither require nor give rise to the principles which make up the structure of the corporation.

Now I come to formulate a plan which I cannot manage alone. Let's say some large rock has fallen down the hillside and inconveniently landed near my cave door. I cannot move it alone for, despite my awareness of myself as a community extended in time, I foresee that my body alone will not be able to move the rock, even though I plan to keep at it for several days. The transformable element of my single body is insufficient to interpret between my present experience and the different experience, which I postulate, of the large rock as being rolled away from my door.

Perhaps, however, I now postulate you as one could help me, if, as myself, you also have an extended awareness of yourself, such that you are able to postulate both the present dilemma of the rock as a region of experience which we can both engage in, as well as the possible state of the rock being moved further away from my door, i.e., the process of experience of the rock being moved. I postulate, moreover, that our combined effort, i.e., our interpretive capacity according to the two extended transformable elements of our acting bodies, is perhaps double that of my individual effort with regard to the problematic presented by the rock situation. Finally I postulate you as one who can understand my meaning, that is to say, as one who can receive an interpretation from me regarding my experience. In effect, I postulate you as a real process of value, based on my aspirations with regard to my problematic of the rock. Not only this, but I postulate you as capable of aspirations and of sharing my own aspiration, my plan, and thus as a locus of interpretive valuation of experience in your own right.

All of this you *ought* to be, if you are one who is capable of helping me move my rock. And hence now, interpreting to you my meaning, passing on my problematic of the rock to you through such narrative as we are capable of, you—happily—indicate by a further interpretation your willingness to help me and we succeed in the process of experience, which is the pushing away of the rock. Or, if we fail in making the interpretation, then we both postulate and on that basis enlist the help of *another*, and eventually we succeed in moving the rock. The sought for problematic of experience now comes to be viewed as that range of possible interpretation, i.e., interpretive freedom, in which at least two acting transformable elements ought to carry out interpretations because one such element as an individual community of interpretation, a community of selfhood, cannot do so. Thus the experiential range of the problematic presents itself as: *that type of problem which we ought to work on together if we are to solve it.*

As I noted though, if we fail to solve the problem, e.g., of displacing the rock, then another postulate will be required. This will first take the form of postulating another extended individual, i.e., a third who can help us; and if this fails, then a fourth, and so on. Hence we can further expand the experiential range of the problematic as: *one in which failure of interpretation, if it is to be overcome, ought to be met by a recurring attempt at postulating and thus enlisting the help of further extended individuals.*

Yet perhaps despite all our effort the rock refuses to budge. In that case at least two things might occur. In the first place, the problem might not be solved, it may be let be, and the goal of solving it may be abandoned. If the goal is abandoned, then the community attempting an interpretation is likewise abandoned, though the acting elements retain their capacity to engage in further problematics. For example, we can try again if we find more helpers someday. In the second place, one of the individuals of the community, or perhaps the community, by discussion, may postulate and begin to use a further transformable element as an extension of one or many of the acting individual members of the cooperating party, e.g., a lever. When the extension is used by each member of the community, separately or together, e.g., we employ a number of levers to move the rock, then nonetheless the original definition of the experiential range of the problematic stands and by all acting together in the extended way, we are still engaged in an interpretation of the problematic.

On the other hand, if an individual's use of the extension is such that the individual member now comes to postulate with regard to his helpers, the *opposite* of those postulates which it was valuable for him to make earlier with regard to them, then the member's postulate is inconsistent and he is acting inconsistently with interpretation as such. If, for example, I discover that by myself alone I can move the rock with a lever, and I then go on to suppose—being a very clever Toad!—that I have no further use for those who are helping me, then I am both acting and supposing inconsistently.

Once there arises a problematic such that the need for cooperation in its interpreted solution gives rise to the postulation of acting transformable elements of a community to engage that problematic, then those transformable elements cannot be *arbitrarily eliminated* without inconsistency and thus devaluation. The problem can only *become* a problem of cooperation, because it ought to take helpers to solve it, i.e., there are problematics which require time process sectional interpretation. But thereby the problem cannot be undone as a problem of cooperation, because, if so, then *every problem of cooperation can in principle be undone before it begins by a postulate which postulates that some extension of the acting individual could solve the problem.* I can always suppose that I will gain some superhuman strength or some mighty machine that will solve all my problems, so that I will never need the help of anyone else. In other words, if I cannot make the assumption that there are problems which *no* extension of myself parallel to the time process can achieve, then there are never going to be problems of cooperation. What began as *my* problem and developed into *our* problem, can never in consistency go back to being *my* problem alone, for to go back is an assumption that contradicts the original assumption which I must make to recognize that type of cooperative problem, i.e., the assumption that *there can be the type of the cooperative problem as such.*

Hence the problematic of cooperation remains once the postulates which frame it are assumed. There can be no de-expansion of elements once postulated, but each now remains as interpreter and as potentially interpreted. In short, *the world as a realm of interpretation can expand but it cannot <u>really</u> contract and transformable elements, once postulated as valuable to the interpretation of a problematic of experience, cannot be eliminated without inconsistency.*

In terms of structures at the level of complexity which engage this problematic, e.g., the structure of basic cooperation, we can now formulate a hypertheme, namely **HC**—*Given a goal (interpretive realization), which cannot be realized by a single acting transformable element, postulate and engage with additional acting transformable elements as necessary, in order to achieve the goal.* I will call this the **Hypertheme of Cooperation**. I suppose it to be the backbone of the hyperthematic structure which develops into what we know as the corporation, a supposition which I will follow out in considering the various facets of the latter. What I expect to find is that many of the inconsistencies associated with the efforts of the corporation arise from a failure to observe this hypertheme consistently in the engagement of the cooperative problematic.

The musement upon origins must continue however, for having arrived at the problematic which gives rise to cooperation and subsequently at a hypertheme that allows cooperation, a position has been reached to show how this develops into what we know as trade. What begins as a simple postulated structure which allows an harmonic interpretation of the actions of we two with regard to the problematic resulting from the present experience of the rock at my door and the postulated experience of the rock moved further from my door, a plan, the interpretation of which runs no further than the rolling away of the rock some minutes from now, and which can often be solved by the very weak valuation of quantitative interpretation—simply gathering more and more human bodies to tackle the rock—soon comes to be applied to larger and larger ranges of the cooperative problematic.

Returning to the hunter-gatherer context, you have pears in your valley and I have apples in mine. I postulate that if I were to make the trip to your valley carrying some of my apples, you very well might give me some pears in exchange for some apples. I suppose you to be an individual as myself and, if so, you also ought to have a sense of the value of myself and by extension my presenting you some apples as "edible experiences." This supposition leads me to attempt to interpret our supposed signs of value to one another. Thus begins barter.

Perhaps our pears and apples do not ripen at the same time though, and so eventually, on the basis of my postulating of us both as temporally extended selves, whose future can be shared, I come up with the idea that since my apples ripen later than your pears, I will ask you to give me your pears as they ripen, in return for a promise that I should give you my apples as they ripen. Thus begins promissory exchange, or trade agreement on a relatively simple level.

Now this postulating of you, however unreflectively, as a community of selfhood whose present self will be able to accept my present word as a sign of my future act of bringing you my apples, may be sufficient for a long time. Yet perhaps at some point I am forgetful of how many apples I promised you, and so we agree together that the few small round stones of a certain unique blue color, which are only to be found in the river in your valley near where you live, are to represent, or stand as a sign for, fulfillment of my promise of giving you the apples that I owe you. Thus, perhaps, begins currency as a medium of exchange, but *it begins only as an aid to the interpretive actions of the communities in question, as signs of action.*

In other words, it carries with it all of the accumulated suppositions according to which it arose, and just as in the case of a more literal extension of the acting transformable elements, such as was the lever in the earlier example, it will be subject to the same inconsistencies depending on its use and abuse as an element in interpretation. Money has the same interpretive significance in processes of action as does the lever, only it is, and tends to become, more fluid as an element: you can carry it more easily, divide and combine it, etc.

Having related cooperative work, trade agreement, and extensions of cooperative work and agreement such as machines (lever) and money to one another, one can define the problematic according to which first cooperative work and then trade arise as hyperthematic structures which will in turn develop into the structure of the corporation. That problematic from which the corporation originates is *a diversity of experience whose range of possible interpretations is such that an acting element engaging in a time process parallel interpretation within that experience, ought to postulate further time process parallel acting elements who can engage in a shared interpretation according to time process sectional interpretation with itself, and ought to postulate them at need.* I will call this the **problematic of cooperation**. The problematic of cooperation is the problem of "only having two hands," or again, of "not being able to do ten things at once." It is the problem engendered by an experience of being physically embodied in the time process and thus interpretively limited, versus a postulated experience without such limitations. Its solution is the valuative recognition that there are *others* who can both have long-term goals as I do and work side-by-side with me in order to achieve them.

Before I carry the above further, you may interject that even though cooperation certainly leads to more complex experience, this does not imply that individual and isolated experience is less rich or satisfying. There are individuals who can get on quite well on their own, thank you very much. Despite the above examples, there are individual actions, you may add, such as meditation, which hold their own as highly successful responses to the cooperative labors of the world at large. Moreover, there are the great champions of individualism, the Henry David Thoreaus of the world, whose lives and actions illustrate the limits of cooperation and the value of individualism in creative effort.

I agree with you wholeheartedly that there are such individual actions, and such individuals. I agree moreover, that such actions and such lives are creative of value. I utterly disagree with the subsequent assumption however:

that therefore simpler human experience and isolated human experience can be of greater value than more complex human experience, when the latter is consistently realized in creative cooperation.

Consider meditation. Meditation may be hyperthematically inconsistent when linked to certain religious dogmas—when the ultimate urge to such focus is, to cite Schopenhauer, that: ". . . this our world, which is so real, with all its suns and milky-ways—is nothing."[3] When it is thus hyperthematically inconsistent it has lost its link to value in interpretation. Nor can one who views meditation in this latter sense find anything to alight upon which can bear value in the sense urged by the original objection, such that its value can be beyond that of cooperative creativity.

Meditation when it is consistent however is entirely different. It is then an action of focusing, in hyperthematic terms a constriction of interpretation which is *practice*. Practice for what? Practice for interpretation as such, the royal road to value. This is meditation's contribution to value in the world process. In his published lectures on Zen meditation, Shunryu Suzuki speaks always of "practice." Although he does not put it in exactly these terms, practice for Suzuki is a drawing back toward the region of many possibilities, in order to become capable of fully and consistently interpreting those possibilities in a subsequent going forth. It ignores the subsequent going forth however, just as it ignores any sense of attainment—"the point is just to sit," to use Suzuki's phrase.[4] Such practice tends to level the field with regard to experience. It readjusts the engagement of experience. It helps the individual remember and access the default community, the community of selfhood, which is never less than an awareness of being an interpreter of past and future possibilities of experience, a source of potential value creation.

When consistent, such practice does not make the individual more a community of selfhood as an individual than it makes her a community of selfhood transcending individuality. It neither forgets embodiment nor belittles it. It makes the individual potentially one with simpler experience—e.g., the body—but just as much potentially one with all experience, e.g., experience of mental complexity. It disengages in order to face all the range of experience. A full and consistent interpretation of possibilities, as hyperthematics implies, involves engaging simpler experience on the way to more complex experience. Without that full engagement the value of the experience is lost over the gap left unengaged between simple and complex, and the standard of value—the meaning—begins to break down for interpretations of experience. Consequently, a rush toward complex experience, which has *forgotten* the source of value, is faced sooner or later with the consequences of its forgetfulness: regions of devaluation. The preceding is what Suzuki means when he says: "In the beginner's mind there are many possibilities, but in the expert's mind there are few."[5] The practice of meditation is the remembering of this in the meditative act which empties the embodied individual of the complex, and of the simple, and instills a pre-awareness of potential interpretation at all complexities of experience. It is the forgoing of "killing two birds with one stone," in order to "kill one bird with one stone," as Suzuki puts it, i.e., the forgoing of the complex.[6] Yet it is also "nothing special," as he constantly reminds us, i.e., the forgoing of the simple too.[7]

When meditation is consistent and well developed it can becomes meditation in activity. It can thus pass beyond its beginnings in embodied simplicity to address embodied cooperative complexity: meditation during cooperative work. In fact it has no necessary link to embodied individuality as simplicity of experience—many practitioners of meditation sit together in practice after all. In the latter case it is cooperative in its individuality, while in the former it is individual in its cooperation. Thus, not only is meditation not a counter-example to the limits of cooperative value, it is an activity which reaffirms the value potential of experience as such. It is rest for interpretation—but we mustn't say so.

One can access this rest for interpretation at other ranges of complexity, moreover. At the end of a jogging session for example, one can come down from higher complexity interpretations—the state of jogging—at a fuller range of embodied complexity within physical complexity, to lower complexity interpretation—the slowing down and cooling down phase. This shift of engagement relative to complexity can have the same effect as sitting meditation, though at a somewhat higher level of the range of complexity in question, i.e., from a fuller interpretive use of the limbs, to a lesser use. All "rest," is a rest for interpretation, in this sense.

Likewise, Thoreau's project of life on Walden Pond was simply another variation of a consistent practice of meditation. Thoreau's rebellion was not against cooperation. It was against the visible misuse of cooperation. His great insight was that men were badly mistaken in the things they valued and the way they valued them *both* socially and individually. On the basis of this insight he sought a better accounting of value, and he found it in the workings of nature: essentially the consistency of the world process in the guise of nature. Thoreau went to nature to learn a consistent creation of value, which he could not find elsewhere, or at least as much as nature could provide in this way.

If you take Thoreau like this, you *later* profit much by his insight. *Walden*—particularly on the first reading—tends to disengage you from all experience, both simple and complex, but especially complex experience in case you are someone forgetfully engaged in the complex range of experience. If you live the reverse—as many a native country dweller—and are busily engaged in the simplicity of experience, then Thoreau, if you read him at all, is also "nothing special," as Suzuki would say. Thoreau's work acts much as meditation does then. It draws you back to focus on the default community of selfhood, and on the simpler experience which originates from that community and is consistently renewed.

On the other hand, if you read and re-read the work, it loses this newness. If, as with seeking attainment in meditation, you begin to analyze the work itself, and to work out its implications in some definite terms, "the perfect simple lifestyle," you begin to seek something the work cannot provide. This is not surprising, for Thoreau himself illustrates it. First, he keeps a journal of his experiences. Keeping a journal he expands his sense of himself as a community of selfhood. The journal is not simple, yet it interprets simple experience to more complex experience, a way of constantly remembering the origins of value. The journal is not merely meant for himself though. Not only is it a cooperation in the community of narrative under that hyperthematic structure—*even* if he had kept it to himself—but it is destined, before he even went into the woods, to support a reinterpretation of Thoreau's experience through that very community to future readers.

Besides, Thoreau needed many other communities of interpretation, at various levels of complexity. He needed the axe created from the blacksmith's art to cut his logs, the seeds preserved through the farmer's art to grow his beans, the clothes created through the tailor's art to cover the body. He needed the community of the historians, for he read and reflected on history as he wrote. He needed the community of the explorers, for he wrote and reflected upon foreign lands and travelers. He needed simple communities of friendship, for the farmer inhabits his book, as does the Canadian lumberjack. Above all he needed the world process as nature, a vast community indeed. Nature is complex as well as simple. But she tends to present her simple experiences smoothly together with experiences of increasing complexity. Nature tends not to leave uninterpretable gaps, regions of devaluation. Processes within her do, e.g., animals, but she gives them the consequences of their inconsistencies smoothly, surely, and steadily. This above all Thoreau cooperated with and learned from. What he did not need was the inconsistent regions of devaluation which abound in average human society: the "value" of objects and homes out of proportion to simple experience, the relatively useless hoarding of "value" in mere quantity which deserves the "purifying bonfire," the constrictive structures of power which deal death and taxes, and so on.

The number of communities Thoreau participated in is thus legion. The important thing was never that he remove himself from such communities, or all communities, but that he pull back to rediscover simple experience, which nature could provide, in *practice*—here literally the practice of the simple aspects of sustaining life—in order to re-engage more complex cooperative experience in full creativity relative to value. Willy nilly then, after his interpretive rest, his natural meditation, he ventured back to an admission of more complex interpretations and a cooperative participation in them. Happily his literary creations continue this cooperative participation as a lure for the ongoing development of consistent ethical selfhood in others. Without such cooperation we would never have heard of him, and we would be the worse for it.

The best individualism is thus sparked by an insight into devaluation. When it focuses into a practice which rediscovers the source of value, it very often bursts forth into a fantastic creativity of value at more complex levels which builds upon and preserves the value of the interpretation of simpler experience. It then becomes, consistently, an individualism abetting cooperation in community. Individualism always rises to higher value in cooperation, once it understands itself. The problems caused by commercial corporations have their root in this forgetfulness of the source of value. The urge to complex creation too easily forgets the source of value. The attempt is made to create the complex experience, to create value, while belittling or bypassing altogether the simpler ranges of experience which led to that more complex value. Such effort is futile. The value of the world process is something like water in a bathtub. Forgetting the simpler sources of value is like trying to raise a "hill" of water in the bathtub. The "hill" may be raised with great effort but the water in other parts of the bathtub will adapt themselves accordingly, and the moment this futile effort is relaxed the hill flows back to connect with its origins.

Returning to my imagined example then, the following summary can be made. To begin with I have to be able to work with myself, that is to say, that I have to view my present self as engaged in actions which will be acceptable to and enhanceable by what I postulate as my future self. I have to view myself such that I can harmonize my past, present, and future actions, and this is the only way in which I can successfully interpret regions of experience whose diversity passes beyond certain ranges. To put it otherwise, if the problematic in question is the difference in experience between hunger and fullness, for example, then any solutions of the problem, or meaningful interpretations, or again actions directed across the gap of the problematic, which go beyond grabbing and chewing on things that look and smell good and are hanging from the tree branch, or sitting on the ground, are bound to be solutions which require an expanded temporal sense of the individual self.

A certain range of the world's problematic can be engaged by extension of the self as an interpretive community according to interpretation parallel to the time process, the individual community of selfhood. This is one of the consistent suppositional extensions of the time process embedded body of an acting transformable element, i.e., the assumption that I can make interpretations which extend parallel to the time process with the same acting body. I come to know, by postulate and attempted interpretation, the limits of what I can accomplish by myself by constantly working toward the same goal, today, tomorrow, and so on. This only gets me so far however. Very quickly the very success I gain with this attitude, in interpreting problems of experience near to me, leaves me with new loci of interpretation, from which I strike out even further. The further I go and thus the more complex the range of experience is which various problematics encompass, the more valuable it is to postulate other selves as loci of yet further ranges of valuation, which are to be my stepping stones, so to speak, as I proceed to take interpretive actions with regard to the great world.

I thus come to suppose the population of the world by acting individuals similar to myself, who can help and cooperate with me in interpretation. From these other individuals I gain access to further ranges of the world problematic engendered by communities of individuals, in ever increasing levels of complexity. If the world is thus realized through an ever expanding process of postulation and interpretation, i.e., valuation, we ought now to be able to develop and exemplify a fitting account of the weaving of interpretive engagement with regard to our originating problematic into what we now know of as the corporation. That is the next task.

Some Examples of the Historical Development of the Corporation

It was suggested that whereas the problematic which originates the temporally extended individual self is centered around the limits of undertaking interpretation with the physical body unless its continuity and ability to undertake recurrent and cumulative action toward the same goal in parallel with the time process are supposed, the problematic which originates cooperative action is centered around the limits of the physical body in undertaking interpretations sectional to the time process. But the extension of the world as a temporal world arises from experience as a process. We first become an embodied process of action in more than the specious present and only then become a process of action which suppositionally can harmonize with *other* processes of action, for without the supposition of other such processes *qua processes* there can be no harmonization of ourselves as acting processes with them. Others must be to us more than mere instantaneous points, or *objects* in the usual unreflective sense of the term, before we can hope to cooperate with them. Hence it would seem that since our experience and expansion of the world as a cumulatively extended embodiedness—i.e., an embodiedness which extends its effective reach in parallel with the time process through a postulation of its wholeness as a *process of embodiment*—comes first, then this order of engaging in experience would be evident in the historical development of the corporation. In fact, this appears to be what we find.

Cooperative action begins in the family. The family appears to be particularly constituted as a natural community of cooperation by having the transformable element of the body—as a gradually extending interpretive process of embodiment—engage the world problematic *first*, before any engagement of the problematic as a problematic of cooperation. The first actions of postulation which extend the interpretive reach of ourselves as embodied are strong candidates for the source of the cooperative community, which we call the family.

Certainly the *mere* act of sex between embodied acting elements may have nothing to do with cooperation, and this is exemplified both in human history and the animal world. Sex can be reduced to a pleasure of the present and the one engaged in the sex act may take the other as an object, even when one or both of those engaged in the sex act take themselves to be temporally extended.[8] Yet as soon as the sexual act as a deliberately willed act of begetting is in question—however unreflectively—then the actors engaged in it have postulated themselves as temporally extended individuals and then further postulated that the other is such, that the other shares the goal of the begetting, and that with regard to that goal various actions can be undertaken and harmonized as interpretations within a community. That community is the family and I suggest that it is the first cooperative community, and the precursor of the corporation.

The evidence for this suggestion as exemplified in the long history of relationships between families and corporations is considerable. Companies such as the Marinelli Bell foundry in Italy which dates to 1040 CE, the Goulaine winery in France which began before the end of the first millennium, and the Hoshi Ryokan (inn) in Japan which dates to 718 CE and has been in continuous operation by the same family for some forty-six generations, testify to the close relationship between family and long-term cooperation. Not only are many of the oldest companies in the world family-run endeavors, but the family continues to be a significant factor in relation to contemporary estimates of the success of companies, so much so that nearly half of the world's most successful—by the *usual* definition of success—enterprises are family run or owned.[9]

Clearly, there is plausibility to the suggestion that the root of cooperative action lies in the valuative postulation of the temporally extended individual self. To engage in communities of cooperation we have to be able to first see both ourselves and others as such extended individual selves, and where this first occurs, cooperation first occurs in the sense of a harmonization of activity. Yet if companies began in the embodiedness of the family, nonetheless this does not appear to be able to sustain them as a structure which allows growth beyond certain limits. Family businesses can grow large and unwieldy through the gradual accumulation of new family members in a way that contributes to their eventual downfall.[10] I will put aside consideration of the growth and size of membership to the stability of corporations, only to take it up further on. For the moment, I merely want to indicate that some aspect of this growth, and consequent unwieldiness, led, particularly in Western Europe, to the gradual expansion of the concept of the business corporation beyond the boundaries of the biological family. The first clear exemplification of this expansion occurred in the Italian city-states, during the high Middle Ages. These were the *compagnia*, still largely but not exclusively family firms, with a close connection to the emerging Renaissance banking system, and with joint liability, i.e., each partner was fully liable even to the extent of their own personal wealth.[11]

The concept of the *corporate person* gradually evolved from medieval reflections upon Roman law, but it was not until the middle of the second millennium that the true effect of this concept came to be felt in the guise of the first large multinational corporations. This was the period of chartered companies such as the Hudson's Bay Company of Canada and the British East India Company, and it is in this period that we first begin to see the potential effect which large corporations can have within society, and particularly in a negative sense.

The British East India Company presents multiple examples of actions which members or acting elements of corporations can take, and which appear to be actions by the corporation, i.e., interpretations carried out under certain guiding assumptions, and these actions have not always been viewed kindly. The East India Company, begun in 1599, had a number of characteristics that bridged the gap between older more familial business agreements and what we now know of as the corporation. Most prominently it had joint stock ownership, which meant that its investors and managers could be separate from one another and that—unlike the Italian *compagnia*—in case the company incurred losses the individual investors would only be liable for the monetary amount that they had invested. In distinction from the modern corporation, however, it had no single individual acting as CEO, but rather a board of twenty-four directors, and its shareholders, provided their stake was more than a certain minimum, all had equally one vote per shareholder.

On the other hand, the company was initiated according to a Crown charter—which had to be regularly reissued—and it thereby had the privilege of a monopoly upon East Asian trade to Britain. That privilege however was supposed to come with a sense of responsibility for the British public good. The company had the further special privileges granted by the Crown of being able to mint its own coinage, to administer its own system of justice in its eastern trading areas, and most incredibly to have a standing army and thus fight its own wars.

All of these privileges made for some rather spectacular historical occurrences during its 275-year existence. Through guile, force, and perseverance, the company eliminated the Dutch and French trading presence in its part of Asia. It cultivated and fought for the opium trade in China. Its continual seeking after and acquisition of monopolies on trade was one factor—whose effects manifested in the Boston tea party—which precipitated the American Revolution. At one point the trade of the company accounted for nearly half of British trade.

Yet its ethical low point came in 1755, when, after repeated provocations to the sovereignty of Bengal, the company went to war with the government of Bengal, defeated its army at the Battle of Plassey, and proceeded to turn it into a virtual tributary state whose treasury it plundered at will, and whose population it oppressed with such brutality that individuals were willing to mutilate themselves—by cutting off their own thumbs—rather than be forced to work under the terms of the company.[12] All of this would set the tone for the later British occupation of India and, in a further future, stand as a model for the treatment of small states by multinational corporations. Robins notes that: "across 400 years of modern corporate history, three design flaws in particular unite the Company with the global corporations of the twenty-first century: the drive for monopoly control, the speculative temptations of executives and investors, and the absence of automatic remedy for corporate abuse."[13]

By the time the Honorable East India Company was dissolved in 1874, the rise of corporations in the modern mold was well underway. The nineteenth century became the era of the great railroad corporations and the rapid development of infrastructure as well as financial abuse which followed them. It also became the era of the working poor as the unsung, unheard of, and largely uncared for cooperating members of the great corporations. Yet, despite this, it was a period of the most rapid development of the legal structure of corporations, as well as of the discussion of the social responsibilities of corporations.

The new companies—particularly canal and railroad companies—which were the drivers of the Industrial Revolution required large amounts of investment capital. This framed the debate regarding companies particularly along the lines of the appropriate degree of shareholder liability. Loosening of shareholder liability rules was advocated, on the one hand, by the mere urge to tap into the investment capital of the poor and middle-class masses. On the other hand, there were those, such as John Stuart Mill, who viewed this as favorable to those classes and as a way to improve their lot, for now, in theory, anyone could invest in companies. Thus in the mid-nineteenth century, reformers of corporate law such as Robert Lowe in Britain gradually began to recharacterize the limited liability aspect of corporations as a right open to all, rather than a special privilege for the few.[14] "Two points emerge clearly from all this activity. First, no matter how much modern businessmen may presume to the contrary, the company was a political creation. The company was the product of a political battle, not just the automatic result of technological innovation. And the debate forged in mid-nineteenth-century Britain has shadowed the institution ever since: is the company essentially a private association, subject to the laws of the state but with no greater obligation than making money, or a public one which is supposed to act in the public interest?"[15] Such a statement shows the limits of regarding the corporation purely on its own terms. Whether such terms are sufficient in a hyperthematic consideration of the corporation is an issue I will reflect upon shortly.

If the opportunities were thus increased for participation in corporations by an ever growing number of members, the possibility for abuse of membership in companies by means of stock speculation and manipulation also increased greatly.[16] And as the number and size of corporations increased, so also did the numbers of those whom we can characterize as their most physically active members, i.e., the workers. If the right to investment enfranchisement was a good thing, it is not at all evident that the poor working class who labored in the factories of the Industrial Revolution gained in their relation to the structure of the corporation. What one reads of is not the lifting up of the working class by the spread of the structure of the corporation, but rather their impoverishment as living and acting individual selves.

The new pools of capital which now arose under the aegis of the ever developing set of corporate entities, made available complex and expensive machineries, and the factories which housed them. This, in turn, gave rise to the corporate town, epitomized by Manchester or Birmingham in England, in which large numbers of humans—increasingly and generically termed workers—massed in crowded conditions in order, apparently, to maximize their capacity to act or operate together and thus their capacity to produce objects. The factory towns demanded ever-increasing numbers of workers, and workers willing to engage in particularly "unskilled" activities. Seemingly a simple demand to accommodate, in fact the "unskilled" often turned out to be the hardest to entice away to greener pastures, so that the managers of the factories of these corporate towns had to develop strategies both to entice workers away from other factories, and to hold them to working at their own.[17]

All of this led predictably to further decline of skilled work activity. A representative group, the relatively skilled hand weavers who produced cotton-based textiles in Great Britain, diminished from some 250,000 in 1820, to some 3,000 by 1850, all in the name of the rush for increased quantity.[18] Few, even the most ardent critics, appear to have reflected upon whether mere "goods" as such were worthy of all this change of activity.

> Almost from its inception, the factory or mill required a new work ethic from its employees. Life on the farm had been a family and community endeavor. However, the hum of activity in the factory demanded a discipline and behavior that operated

at a tempo and speed not previously experienced by the ordinary working man . . . the old practice of St. Monday when no work was done gave way to a week in which work of twelve to sixteen hours a day stopped at either midday or the end of the day on Saturday. Over time this distinct break between work and leisure would change the nature and style of activities pursued by the working classes. By the later 19th century some of these new interests became spectator sports, such as cricket and football, and music hall entertainment. The comfort of the former rural, close-knit community no longer existed.[19]

The pace and conditions of such work took its toll upon health to such an extent that a person working in one of these corporate towns could expect to live roughly half as long as her rural counterpart.[20] As William Cobbett, one ferocious critic of this new way of life put it, while reflecting upon the working conditions in the cotton mills: "What, then, must be the situation of the poor creatures who are doomed to toil, day after day, for three hundred and thirteen days in the year, fourteen hours in each day, in an average heat of eighty-two degrees? Can any man, with a heart in his body, and a tongue in his head, refrain from cursing a system that produces such slavery and such cruelty?"[21]

One might think that the effect of the corporation upon cooperative work, since it was merely in its infancy during the nineteenth century, would finally give way to a more grown up version of itself in the twentieth century. While there were certainly considerable changes underway in the structure of the corporation by the early twentieth century, it is not evident that any great break had been made with the way in which the acting members under the umbrella of a company—now a limited liability company in most cases—stood in relation to one another and to the company.[22]

There were some changes however. In the early twentieth century the worker as primarily a physical laborer began to give way to the worker as primarily an organizer. Physical laborers were not dispensed with. They gradually came to be eclipsed by the rise of a so-called middle-class of clerks, foremen, managers, and so forth. This appears to have been inevitable given the increased use of machinery and the increasing tendency for corporations to become multinational, buying from around the world, rather than producing themselves, the basic parts of the items which they assembled.

Workers came to be viewed as objectified *resources*—today's "human resources"—whose various potentials could be tapped, but still only for the company and ultimately for the benefit of the stockholders. Loyalty to the corporation was urged at all levels and this loyalty accompanied the rise of brands, the sense of competition against other companies and the urge to measure success in terms of *profit*. Corporate brands especially, appeared to become valuable, at least according to the standard of more profit, and hence image and brand began to be created deliberately. By the mid-twentieth century, the loyal Company Man was a creature who "relished the traditions of office life: the assiduous secretaries (or office wives), the watercooler chatter, the convivial Christmas parties. He spent more time in the office than at home . . . and often ended up leaving his wife for his secretary. He measured his life in terms of movement up the company hierarchy—a bigger office, a better parking space, a key to the executive washroom, and, finally, to cap it all, membership in the firm's quarter-century club."[23]

The epitome of the twentieth-century corporation was IBM and its hardheaded, hard driving CEO, Thomas Watson, Sr. By most current definitions of corporate success, IBM was a successful corporation. But what sort of actions did its members undertake toward their community and what sort did it undertake as a community? Most prominently, during the leadership of Watson it grew into a company which came to dominate—though not by being granted the privilege—certain areas of commercial exchange, preeminently data processing. It did so in the first place by aggressively pursuing strong patents and by buying out newer and smaller companies that might challenge it. In the second place, it also refused to create its products and parts such that they could be used or combined with the products of its competitors and it created its products such that they promoted its other products, thus forcing its customers to stay with it.[24]

Over all of this Watson presided as a sort of little emperor. Yet though he was a hard task master as a leader, he also initiated many of the unique characteristics of the company. IBM became the place where employees sang patriotic songs about themselves, the company, and the leaders of the company. It became the place where all employees dressed alike, where the physical laborers were considered to be important enough to give suggestions to management, and where the employees had their own golf course.[25] Watson's business aphorisms, such as "never feel satisfied"[26] and later the trademarked "think," which became the brand name of IBM laptop computers, were calculated to increase loyalty and commitment to this corporate community of individuals, busily interpreting between themselves and those buying their products. It worked, at least for the community of the corporation *itself*. The employees evidently loved their leader and their company, and they lived for it.[27]

The result, by the end of the twentieth century, was a corporation which spanned the globe and employed hundreds of thousands of people. Maney notes that Watson and IBM had managed to do several things never yet done by corporations. They had managed to *create an industry*, the information industry, where no such industry had been before, and they had managed to create a corporate culture, i.e., they had developed a commercial corporation as a unique community with regard to which it was plausible to say that: "the core of IBM—its ultimate economic engine—was not information machines; rather, it was its culture."[28]

Three hundred years later then, the echoes of *something* which the corporation promotes are as clearly audible as they were for the East India Company. But given what I have suggested as the origins of corporations, and now given the increase of the scale of activity which is occurring within corporations, activity which seems to have some core principle, what exactly is it that a commercial corporation could or should achieve?

The Purpose of Commercial Corporations

So far the illustrations of the history of the corporation have appeared as much troubling as hopeful. Before I muse further upon whether and how the corporation is a hyperthematic structure, it is useful to consult other opinions on the nature and purpose of corporations. One early such opinion was that voiced by the prominent economist Adam Smith. Smith left little doubt about the purpose of commercial corporate enterprises. The facilitation of the creation of wealth was their main goal, in keeping with the title of his great economic study *The Wealth of Nations*.

There were two preeminent reasons, Smith argued, for the coming together of human workers to produce various objects and for the division of labor. In the first place, such an arrangement increases the quantity produced. In the second place it saves time, which amounts again to an increase in the quantity produced.[29] Since this is not a particularly subtle definition of the purpose of work, Smith goes on to discuss the value of an object or commodity. "The word VALUE, it is to be observed, has two different meanings, and sometimes expresses the utility of some particular object, and sometimes the power of purchasing other goods which the possession of that object conveys."[30] *Value is thus intimately related to the object but disconnected from the activity which creates that object.*

Hence objects have a use for us, whereas currency is simply a more fluid type of object which serves particularly in exchange for other objects.

Moreover, the value of objects, Smith insists, is ultimately equal to the quantity of labor which it enables the one who possesses it to command. The value of money resides in my being able to make others perform labor activity for it; or again the value of some non-monetary commodity resides in my being able to exchange it for the object which some other has labored to make. Equating price with value, Smith asserts that "the real price of everything, what everything really costs to the man who wants to acquire it, is the toil and trouble of acquiring it."[31]

Now what is curious here, at the very outset of Smith's endeavor, is not the equating of price with value, or even of value with labor. Rather, it is the gratuitous assumption—because it does not look wider than the accepted realm of work itself, at work in the context of life as a whole—that the activity of labor is *necessarily an undesirable activity*, and more suspect still, that *the activity of labor could be activity which is not willed in some way*.

Smith might respond of course that this is merely a way of contrasting work which I want to do with the work of another man which I do not want to do and which I would therefore exchange my work for. Yet such a contrast would only reinforce the point that my work has its value only with regard to that which I will to do. Activity that is meaningful to me has its value for me not merely by reaching the end of the activity but by purposing the process and willingly carrying it out. The activity of another, which I purchase, is only valuable because *the other is willing to do it*, for my money is worthless in any attempt to purchase labor activity which the other is *truly unwilling* to do. Any use of my money to purchase such activity which does not recognize this is thus inconsistent with the original need behind the development of currency.

In addition, however, if labor is *activity* which has value because someone is willing to do it [in this case do it for me], then the principle of *the division of labor* is the *diminishment of value*, for, in principle, there is no limit to that division in terms of temporal activity. Division of labor *saves time*, says Smith. So far he is consistent. Yet he is inconsistent in his argument as a whole, for *time is irretrievably bound up with activity*, the activity of labor. This means that the less complex the labor—i.e., the more temporally constricted an activity it is—the less valuable is that labor. The urge toward the division of labor is thus the urge toward *mere* quantity precisely at the expense of value, i.e., in quality which tends beyond mere constriction to quantity.[32]

The fundamental error at the heart of Smith's view then is that *it entirely forgets the other as an other* and tries to define value on the basis of a negative reflection of *what I do not want to do*. Yet what I do not want and *refuse* to do will *never* be realized as value by my activity. Thus, if I purchase it, that is to say if I exchange value, I will only ever attain *the value realized by another* and by another who is capable of realizing value through activity as a temporally extended individual self. Thus money, or wealth, can never consistently *save* one's toiling activity. The only thing it can consistently do is to <u>recognize</u> the value of the activity of the other. And this can be very easily illustrated by asking whether Smith himself would have considered paying someone else to undergo the labor of writing *The Wealth of Nations* for him. I suggest that he would not have. The value of the book produced lies in his interpretive effort, however faulty that effort might be, and if I now buy the book from Smith—as his readers presumably did—I do not "save myself the labor of writing it," rather, *I recognize the value of the extended interpretive effort which he undertook*, i.e., I postulate him as an individual, a value realizing, temporally extended self, a community of selfhood. Smith is who he is to us, the unique individual that he developed into, through what he creatively realized, most prominently his *Wealth of Nations*. Viewed in this light, the labor-saving thesis of value looks not merely muddleheaded, but foolish.

At this point you may object however that, "surely . . . surely, there are tasks which are distasteful and which justify Smith's assumptions? The world is a world of toil and struggle after all and some jobs are fit for no one, and others jobs are beyond the skill of some. In that light at least, do Smith's assumptions not seem correct?'

I agree that there are now such tasks, but I disagree as to their origins. They are not inherent features of the world, except insofar as a consistent account of value is lacking. Their origins are the mistaken assumptions we make about the nature of value, and if we understood that nature and the inconsistent and consistent tendencies assumed relative to it, we would achieve more valuable results without devaluing activity. Smith's scheme, wherein tedious and negative work to produce something is vindicated by the value of the product itself, can never be justified. Its internal inconsistencies are visible, even before the hyperthematic method is used to engage the issue. Smith's assumptions once adopted, several obvious results follow from the ensuing disconnection between activity and value.

First, as to items produced, you may assume that the lack of value in the activity will not infect the item produced; but you have no grounds for assuming this. The unwillingness to undertake certain activities which sets up the definition of value in question, is precisely an unwillingness based on an awareness of a lack of value in the activity that you refuse to undertake. Even if you pay another to undertake the task, the initial separation of value and activity remain untouched. The one who undertakes the task for you, if the task is indeed valueless or even relatively valueless, does not suddenly find more value, or value at all, in the activity because of a promise of value in e.g., money, external to the activity. The activity remains just as valueless in itself as it was initially. But the lack of value cannot be banished. It must out somewhere. It comes out in part by the value of the activity coming to be viewed solely in terms of the money. The activity thus switches from an activity of carrying out the distasteful task to an activity of making money. The activity of merely making money, however, is in itself a low-value activity of mere quantitative creation, i.e., recurrent interpretation in one or few aspects of experience—a suggestion which I will expand further on.

The lack of value also comes out in the item produced. To put it bluntly: you yourself would not undertake the activity in question because it has no value in itself. You would not undertake the task for money, for example, since money is precisely what you are giving away in order for the other to do it for you. How then, under this assumption, can you expect another to undertake the activity on any grounds beyond that of money? You cannot. The other may indeed undertake the task for you for money, but will put no value into the distasteful task. Their real task will become not the distasteful one in question. Their real task will become the mere acquisition of money and the result, evident enough in all modern production which descends to this level is further devaluation in products: faults, defects, and generally poor quality, proportional to the strength of the above assumption. In services: a minimal engagement, half completion, and avoidance of the task whenever possible.

A still further result, worse still, is that the sense of the community of selfhood begins to break down for the worker engaged in producing the item. If you hold to Smith's scheme, you would have the worker undertake a valueless activity in order to—supposedly—produce value. That valueless activity constricts the process of the worker, appearing both as a devaluation on the level of complexity of embodiment—the wearing down of the body—and on the higher levels of complexity—boredom, mental isolation, loss of temporal sense, etc. When the community of selfhood is degraded however, the ability to interpret to other communities weakens.

The lacuna or gap of value, cannot be contained—similarly to the case of the assumptions made by the military group. The worker carries it into his engagements with other communities. Insofar as his activity is valueless, not only is his sense of selfhood devalued for himself, but the sense which others have of his community of selfhood as a process of value is diminished as well. In short, the devaluation of the worker in this way, leads, like the ripples of a stone dropped in a pond, to the devaluation of all communities of which the worker is a member, ultimately the community of the world process as such. The erecting of various further sets of regulations to "contain" the social effect of devaluating work thus arise inevitably, based upon further inconsistent assumptions, e.g., the strategies developed to retain workers during the Industrial Revolution, already noted above. The associated costs, monetary and otherwise, of re-building value in the devalued region of society, follow as well.

If you hold Smith's assumptions, what you desire in effect is to get something from nothing. This you cannot do, if the world is consistent as a world of value (our opening assumption). In short, Smith's scheme, along with the assumptions of all that great edifice now partially built upon it, is so much dangerous nonsense, if there is value in the world. No critique, such as that given above, can convince one who holds firm to Smith's assumptions however. The aim of hyperthematics is not critique. All that can be done by the hyperthematic method is to disclose the consistency or inconsistency of an attitude toward a selected realm of experience—here relations of trade and complex production—relative to the hyperthematic assumption that value is intimately wedded to acts of interpretation and then to offer practical principles which would correct the error and begin to build greater value in that realm.

Once having begun in the way he has, Smith's views as to the purpose of the corporation are as inevitable as they are inconsistent. His view ranges around the assumption that wealth or profit, or again the increase of the stock of commodities in the economy, is the measure of success, and that in these terms a private company will be more competitive and more successful than a public company in every way.[33] Not surprisingly he rails against the aforementioned East India Company and its monopoly-bearing peers in the Asian trade. Not primarily because of the *abuses* of these companies however, but rather because they fail to make profits despite drawing advantages from the public stock. It would be *okay with regard to the public*, it seems, *if they did run profits*,[34] but Smith devotes page after page to showing that they do not.[35]

Because public companies are more tenacious of established rules, they are unsuited to any types of trade of a more adventurous sort. This of course falls in line with the assertion that the division of labor is more productive and therefore more desirable. That is to say, that where the type of trade is rule bound, and thus none but simple and habitually repetitive activity is required from the members of a public corporation, they will do best. The only sorts of trades which a public company can successfully carry on, he insists, are financial trades, insurance trades, or public works. His discussion of banks and banking corporations once again illustrates why: because public banking companies cannot stay in contact with those to whom they lend money, as a private lender of money can, i.e., they cannot have a relationship with the customer as a temporally extended acting individual.[36]

Not only is the role of the lending member of a corporation reduced to passivity under this account, but the role of the investing members of public corporations is reduced to being a passive one. The latter is also implied by the assumption made above, that the fluid sign of the participation of the members in the corporation, i.e., the stock—cousin of currency—derives its value on the basis of the amount of money which can be got for it, which in turn derives its value based on the amount of activity which can be "saved" in exchange for it. "The value of a share in a joint stock [corporation] is always the price which it will bring in the market; and this may be either greater or less in any proportion, than the sum which its owner stands credited for in the stock of the company."[37] How the value of a corporation's stock could thus be *negatively* defined, after having derived its value precisely through the activity of the members of the company, is as unclear as it is inconsistent, and for the same reasons as I noted above. If I buy common stock of a corporation from another, I cannot even so much as consider myself to be "saving the labor" of participating in whatever activity the laboring members of the corporation undertake, unless *I recognize that they are undertaking some activity.*

Again, the role of the administrating members of a public corporation is viewed—on the basis of Smith's original suppositions—as not capable of being more than an entirely self-serving one, so that public interests inevitably devolve into private interests.[38] In short, the emphasis on profit and consequently the emphasis on the private company as according with the natural balance of market forces, both lead to Smith making it clear that besides the possibility of a company's type of trade being reduced to strict rule and method, and its establishment for some great or useful purpose, *the one major purpose for which a joint stock company, or public company, is worthy of being established, is that greater capital can be collected into it for some task.*[39] Any other establishment of such public companies tends to more harm than good, and breaks "that natural proportion which would otherwise establish itself between judicious industry and profit. . . ."[40]

Smith deeply influenced how public corporations have come to be viewed. The effect of his views of the purpose of the corporation, and more importantly his acceptance of certain assumptions which lie behind those views, is in proportion as they tend to consolidate a general viewpoint on human relations of exchange with one another, which in turn leads to certain more or less fixed ways of viewing the purpose of commercial corporations. The consequence is that the common view of corporations is that they are gatherers of capital whose purpose is the creation of wealth or profit for their stockholders and in some degree for their workers. The acceptance of this definition of success, of purpose, and of activity as supplementary to that purpose of wealth and profit, tends always to make the public corporation an entity whose value is measured by the standard of the private corporation. This viewpoint tends to cast its shadow over all aspects of the activity of corporations.

The corporation, public or private, is to achieve and attain for one or some of its members what that member or members *would achieve on their own if they could*, that is if the gathering of wealth on a scale which is generally desired was possible for an individual engaged in activity without the interpretive support of a community. The working assumption is: "if I could get sufficiently rich on my own I would do so and wouldn't need *you*, but since I can't, I subject myself to engaging with you in a corporation." This assumption infects everything with the further consideration that: "therefore whenever I *can* get rich on my own without working with others I will do so."

And it shows itself in more contemporary discussions regarding the purpose of corporations. Whether the use of the assumptions falls on the side of privatization or of nationalization—roughly, to use tired phrases, the political right or the political left—the assumptions remained the same. Thus, for example, we may be told that "since the mid-19th century, there has been a battle between two different conceptions of the company: the stakeholder ideal that holds that companies are responsible to a wide range of social groups and the shareholder ideal that holds that they are primarily responsible to their shareholders."[41] Very well, but how are they responsible, i.e., what is their goal in relation to these groups? Does the corporation find its purpose as the preeminent way "to share the risks and rewards" of the activities of economic life?[42] Is its purpose therefore economic development, to which end "companies increase the pool of capital available for productive investment. They allow investors to spread their risk by purchasing small and easily marketable shares in several enterprises. And they provide a way of imposing effective management structures on large organizations."[43]

Is this all that companies do? Is their purpose to gain commodities or consumer goods in quantity, to allow we humans to engage in large-scale group activity without the trouble—risk—of engaging or ultimately assuming our extended selves or those of others with whom we engage, to "save" our time and thus our need to undertake meaningful activity as individuals?

Yet if this is the assessment of those who are positive about corporations, nonetheless even those most cynical and critical in their attack on corporations, are caught in the net, framing their arguments in terms of profit as the purpose of corporations. As Hertz says: "Corporations are not society's custodians, they are commercial entities that act in the pursuit of profit. They are morally ambivalent. . . ."[44] In the opinion of such critics, it is still the rights of laborers and the benefits of work in the form of objective *commercial goods* which represent the misplaced value of the world: for, taking globalization as the buzzword for this pursuit of profit in the worldwide sense, "until the benefits of globalization are shared more widely, people will continue to rise up against globalization."[45] Once they are shared, will that therefore be the justification for corporations? Even if it was, would it be the best and only purpose we could devise for such structures?

My suggestion to all of these questions now—still only the hint of a response—is that both sides suffer from a fundamental inconsistency in their initial assumptions with regard to the activity, the makeup, the purpose, and the potential of commercial corporations. Having laid the groundwork with a preliminary sketch of the origins, exemplifications, and appraisals of the corporation, I now to turn to a hyperthematic musement upon some of the elements disclosed, wielding the resources elaborated in previous chapters.

The Corporation as a Hyperthematic Structure

I have sketched the problem of experience, some historical exemplifications of the structure which engages it, and some of the more usual assumptions with regard to how that structure engages the problem. The question now is: how far is the corporation a hyperthematic structure? Can it be interpreted to the hypertheme **H** and the derivative hyperthemes, and in what sense is it consistent or inconsistent with the larger set of hyperthemes formulated in the exploratory mode? Answering this, I will try to remain within the accepted terminology which surrounds commercial corporations, e.g., with respect to such terms as *product*, until the point when the elaboration, expansion, and testing of the structure of the corporation begins to prompt the redefinition of such terminology. First then, as always: how is the corporation to be interpreted to the opening hypertheme, or again, how can the corporation be transformed to the structure of interpretation as such, so as to display an expanded and meaningful linkage of postulated entities?

Clearly the structure of the corporation has acting elements engaged in processes of action. So far, I will take these acting elements to be anyone who appears to be acting within or engaged by the company. Thus, in the first place, the structure of the corporation has its workers as acting elements. These may appear in the guise of managing workers, or physically laboring workers, or mentally laboring workers, in various proportions. In the second place, it has its stockholders as acting elements. The latter may be and often are equivalent with the former laboring and managing workers, or they may be separate. In the third place, there are those who buy its products.

I have suggested that the problematic which the corporation engages is that of experience, which would find its most valuable interpretation according to the recurrent postulation of and harmonization with further extended individuals. Across the gap of this problematic, which the structure of the corporation engages, there may be various types of interpretive action. A physically laboring worker may interpret to another physically laboring worker and produce a "physical object." A managing worker may interpret to a physically laboring worker with regard to such a physical object. A mentally laboring worker may interpret to a physically laboring worker, or a mentally laboring worker, and produce a "mental object." Whatever is produced I will call a product, in keeping with common speech. And a product may be physical or mental, or an object of some proportions between these, such as what is usually called a service.

Evidently various combinations are possible. Just as evidently, interpretation proceeds between at least two elements by means of a third, i.e., the corporate community of interpretation whose goal is a "particular product" which is somehow to be an interpretive solution to the cooperative problematic which could only be realized by the cumulative harmonized action, in the time process sectional aspect, of multiple acting transformable elements. Thus, so far, the structure of the corporation is consistent with **H**.

Is it also consistent with the derivative hyperthemes? It is consistent with **H3**, for the structure is comprised of at least three transformable elements, and often of very many elements (its members).

When we consider **H1** however, difficulties begin to appear. If the structure were consistent with **H1**, we should be able to say that it does not eliminate signs. With regard to narrative, for example, we said that the structure of narrative is not such as to prevent either a narrator or a listener from engaging in it again and again; nor does it exclude anyone from being a narrator or listener. Yet the same cannot be said of the structure of the corporation. In whatever sense we mean that corporations engage in *competition*—already illustrated—there appears to be an exclusion of acting elements. In the business world you can very well eliminate your competitors. But what do we mean by competition?

We usually say that companies compete with one another in producing the *same product* or range of products. Further, they are often said to be competitive or to be mastering the competition, when their product is superior in some way or of higher quality. But this is not always the case, for companies can sometimes merely flood the market with lower quality versions of a product and undercut their competitors. Or, quality being equal, a corporation can simply produce the same product in a faster way or at lower costs.

Earlier examples of the latter case are the mechanical "savings" introduced by the textile corporations in nineteenth-century Britain, and of the former case the actions of IBM during the twentieth century. Arguably, IBM made higher quality products, but it undertook measures such as introducing exclusivity into its products, which effectively prevented other corporations from cooperating in further developments based upon its products. In other words, the IBM Corporation wanted the area of its cooperative and productive activity to be exclusively interpreted by the members of its own community. The ultimate goal was that no other corporations should engage—even in cooperation with IBM—in the data processing endeavor.

Now, if you muse upon the tendencies and motives of such competition, they appear quite curious, even paradoxical. Corporations wish to create products. According to their competitiveness, they also wish other corporations *not* to create similar products. That is to say that somehow the assumptions of the structure of the corporation as it stands are such as to prevent or discourage further acting elements from engaging the problematic of experience in question, under the structure. The question is, what in the structure accounts for this, or again, *what principle of transformation, or hypertheme, does the structure assume, which is nonetheless inconsistent either in itself or with regard to other hyperthemes?*

First, however, how do we know that this tendency is a result of the failure of the structure itself, rather than destabilizing action on the part of its acting elements? The stability of a hyperthematic structure depends both upon its ability to allow those who interpret under it to abide by its hyperthemes, i.e., to be able to allow interpretive transformations within the range of experience which it engages, and also upon the transformable ranges of its elements. We can illustrate how stability can fail by returning again to the example of the military structure, which I said produces false communities.

The Symmetric Anti-Hyperthemes

What makes the military structure inconsistent as a structure is its inconsistent hyperthemes, its anti-hyperthemes. I did not elaborate hyperthemes for the military structure earlier, but simply allowed the goals of a military to exemplify the inconsistency of the structure with regard to my account. If I had attempted to elaborate such hyperthemes, however, they would have come out something like this: ***HM**—*for a given community G, if there exists an acting transformable element e such that e is not included as an acting element within G, but is included in a community G' which is the same in allowing the elimination of elements which are not included in itself, then eliminate e and G'.* I will call this the *Anti-Hypertheme of Military Engagement** It is one of the core assumptions which the military false community makes and attempts to use to solve the diversity of experience of the world. In other words, if *e* is an element which does not belong to my community, then eliminate *e* if it belongs to a community whose elements also eliminate elements which are not its own. Since a technical formulation may remain unclear to the reader, a contextual sense of how this anti-hypertheme guides experience at its most basic can be provided in the description of Lewis Lahorn, a U.S. Marine NCO who fought in Vietnam, of his first kill: "He was a trained soldier, and I was a trained soldier. And it was me first, or

---

*Throughout this work I will adopt the convention of designating an anti-hypertheme by an asterisk, e.g., ***HM**. It should also be noted that ***HM** is offered as a temporary working assumption which, while useful to gain insight into the assumptions underlying commercial corporations, really needs sustained hyperthematic musement in the context of human actions of conflict. In the latter instance it would have to be modified and located in a much more extensive hyperthematic expansion of consistent and inconsistent military assumptions, since military groups and indeed actions of conflict have a great many *internal* consistencies, i.e., assumptions which are correct in light of more general inconsistent but *accepted* assumptions.

him first. And I respected him, and I'm pretty sure he respected me, you know. His job was to kill me, my job was to kill him."[46]

This anti-hypertheme of the military structure is inconsistent with both **H** and its derivatives, for it eliminates transformable elements of communities, and the elimination of such elements is inconsistent with the assumption, the ultimate hypertheme, that the world is interpretable as such. In effect, the military makes the assumption that: "that element (an enemy soldier) shall not be interpretable," i.e., it eliminates that element. But in the case of the military hyperthematic structure—more properly an anti-hyperthematic structure—the acting transformable elements themselves are in addition also eliminative elements, either directly, or more often through extension by further transformable elements, i.e., weapons, which are used by the acting elements under the structure. These elements are locally guided by the anti-hypertheme(s) of the structure to eliminate other elements. That is to say, such elements are *transformation restricting elements*, which tend to constrict, reduce, and remove from other elements, axes, and ranges of interpretive freedom which can be interpreted into. Thus, to illustrate, a soldier is in various modes, an acting transformable element who imprisons others in chains or prisons (constricts), disables others by eliminating limbs and so forth (reduces), or annihilates others by various killing methods (removes, or eliminates in the stricter sense).

Now the acting elements of the corporation are not wholly like the acting elements of military structures; they rarely eliminate other acting elements outright, although, as we saw in the case of the East India Company, they are certainly capable of doing so if the corporate structure combines with the military structure. And the reason they do not eliminate other acting elements outright is because the elements under the structure of the corporation are not eliminative elements, and because the structure does not attempt transformations under precisely the same hypertheme as the military structure. In the case of the military, the false community and the acting elements are eliminative, whereas in the case of commercial corporations the community alone is eliminative.

Just as with the military structure, we can elaborate the anti-hypertheme of the corporation that causes the inconsistency. This hypertheme addresses the *problematic of cooperation* defined earlier, but it has an additional functional aspect which combines with that earlier assumption so as to result in the following: ***HC**—Having selected a goal (interpretive realization), i.e., product, which cannot be realized by a single acting transformable element, postulate and engage with additional acting transformable elements as necessary in order to* *achieve the goal, but only with those elements which are not included within a community whose acting transformable elements are interpretively realizing the same goal.**

The first aspect of this *Anti-Hypertheme of Cooperation*, ***HC**, is partly like the earlier hypertheme of cooperation **HC**, which I suggested in the previous section as forming the basis of cooperative activity. But its second aspect—beginning with "*but only . . .*"—is similar to our postulated anti-hypertheme of military engagement above. ***HM** says to its acting elements: "if you find an acting element which is not part of our group, but which is part of a group proceeding under the same hypertheme as our group, then eliminate that element." The goal of the military false community is: eliminate other military communities. The corporate hypertheme, however, says to its acting elements, through ***HC**: "with regard to the cooperative product which is the goal of our community, find and enlist the help of further acting elements as necessary, except those elements of another community which have the *same* cooperative product as a goal." In other words, the goal of the corporate community is: grow with regard to a product, at the expense of other corporate communities.

Both structures have the characteristic of restricting the interpretive freedom for acting transformable elements. Both are what I will call *symmetrically inconsistent anti-hyperthematic structures*. What I mean by this is that their anti-hyperthemes—or aspects of their hyperthemes—attempt interpretation, more or less, *to mirror images of themselves* which arise around the assumption that *a region of experience can be a sameness*. My suggestion is that in proportion as the mirror images approach one another in *sameness*, the range of interpretation available, i.e., the interpretive freedom, decreases. And as it decreases the acting elements of the structure are driven to make increasingly eliminative and thus inconsistent interpretations with regard to the opening postulate **H**. The limit of this is an end of activity.

When adopted, these assumptions of symmetries drive a constriction of experience which works hand-in-hand with the assumption that elimination of varying degrees is a viable mode of engagement of the resulting constricted problematic. The assumption of a region of sameness within experience can be made as a secondary assumption, which combines with a consistent primary assumption. This is what occurs in the case of the commercial corporation, wherein regions of sameness of experience are assumed

---

*This could be presented as two separate hyperthemes, but in the interest of simplicity I have chosen to view it as one hypertheme with two aspects.

which then cause localized conflict. These inconsistent assumptions of sameness within experience can also be made as a primary assumption however, which is what the military anti-hypertheme does, to the point at which the *internal structure* of the hypertheme itself begins to be visibly inconsistent, and thus subject to destabilization, as shown in an earlier chapter.

Now the degrees of the inconsistency cannot concern us here in any very thorough way, given the task at hand. Suffice it to say that symmetric and eliminative assumptions converge as the engagement of experience falls further and further into inconsistency. So, for example a more purely inconsistent anti-hypertheme than **HM** could be exemplified in an anti-hypertheme of solipsistic nihilism in which the anti-hypertheme guides an acting element to eliminate not only those like the acting element itself in some specific aspect, but indeed all other experience than its own: "for a given community G and its elements, if there are communities and elements of communities which are the same in being communities and elements of communities *as such*, then eliminate them." The internal structure of such an anti-hypertheme is more symmetric, more an equality if you will, than *HM. The limit of this tendency is of course the denial of **H** and the assumption that experience collapses into a dyadic and further into a monadic character.

We could negatively formulate a *hypertheme of inconsistency*: **HI'**—*as a hypertheme approaches symmetry in its terms, its tendency to be consistent with regard to* **H** *decreases*.[47] By continuing on we could then elaborate in outline a *hierarchy of disharmony*, just as the hierarchy of hyperthematic structures of increasing complexity of harmonization was elaborated earlier. In such an outline, the military structure would be located near the bottom, as the least consistent anti-hyperthematic structure, and the commercial corporation as an anti-hyperthematic structure would be located perhaps in the middle of the hierarchy. The reader should already be able to see the general drift of such a hierarchy, but it might help my overall account to exemplify a further level of inconsistency according to well-known observations.

Anti-Hyperthemes in Children's Play

When you observe children at play and interacting, you often observe tendencies of action which exemplify the same hyperthematic assumptions inherent in the foregoing structures. This comes about because of the ease with which the child—however unreflectively—supposes various practical working attitudes toward the engagement of experience and constantly alters and dissolves those working attitudes. In short, the child adopts short-lived versions of various hyperthemes within its play structure. Some of those are the anti-hyperthemes elaborated above with regard to the military and the corporate structures. The point is: to the degree that the adopted hyperthemes are what I have called symmetrically inconsistent hyperthemes, the child's actions span the range of disharmonious or inconsistent interpretations. But because the body of the child as an acting transformable element lacks the range of transformation which would take its interpretations out of the realm of play, we recognize its actions as similar to, but not as complex as the interpretive actions which we carry out "for real" in the adult body. To paraphrase St. Augustine, the child lacks not the will, but the strength to carry out its purposes. Its hyperthemes, or principles of interpretation, may sometimes be as inconsistent as those of the foregoing structures, but its main transformable element is less complex, limiting the damage.

Hence the unreflective hypertheme assumed by the child in an anti-hypertheme of play, might run: ***HP**—*having selected the goal of playing with "certain toys," suppose and engage as necessary, playmates as active elements who can contribute to and achieve the goal of playing, but only suppose and engage those playmates which are not included within a play group whose acting playmates have the goal of playing with the (aforementioned) same toys.* Now this may very well appear to be a simpleminded contrast at first, and without a doubt no child ever reflectively views the interpretive principle guiding her action like this. Notwithstanding that, with patience and musement the contrast and thus similarity appear less simpleminded and easily exemplified in the play of children.

Let there be several very young children of otherwise average good temper, placed together into a room with several toys. In such a situation, the children will have a tendency to stake out their territory to a greater or lesser degree. "Mine," or some variation thereof will be the most common assertion to their peers and often enough a child with an armful of toys will nonetheless head for a child with few or one toy, in order to try and claim the whole lot exclusively for herself. The child who enters the room of toys with her peers is engaging her experience in part under the same symmetrical and inconsistent hypertheme as the corporation. She wants playmates indeed, the more the better, for play is the product of a cooperative activity,[48] but she does not want to allow her perspective playmates access to the toys.

Having assumed a symmetry in her principle of interpretation, viz. that there are toys as objects of the goal of interpretation, the same toys, which will stand in the same relation to one of the other playmates, as they do to herself, she has constricted the interpretive freedom available to her. And insofar as she has constricted it, the narrowing range of interpretations available to her are increasingly eliminative. Thus, we may hear: "mom, he has the blue car, that's just the one I wanted!" In other words, we can't both play with the same toy. The latter as a derivative consequence is correct, locally, if the assumption is made that the toy as the other playmate relates to it is a symmetrically equivalent experience, i.e., an object. That assumption often is made. In other variations we hear: "she has two dolls, and I only have one," i.e., the same assumption made with respect to several objects; "she stole my ball," i.e., the same assumption with the speaker on the eliminated end, having been deprived of her interpretive freedom by the other child, with regard to the toy.

If this is the case however, how is it that children manage to play at all? The answer is that the unreflectively supposed hypertheme under which play is possible as an interpretation of experience, is comprised of more than a symmetrical and inconsistent aspect. As the promise of play with playmates, it also assumes the cooperative aspect, i.e., postulate and engage acting elements as necessary in order to achieve the cooperative goal of the playing. As long as the hyperthematic structure of play contains this supposition, the play remains a highly interpretable and valuable region of experience despite the symmetrically induced inconsistency which tends towards eliminative behavior. If it devolves to a structure in which this supposition is abandoned, i.e., into a structure in which the preeminent guide is the symmetrical anti-hypertheme with its locus in the toy as an object, rather than *the play as an interpretable region of experience of higher complexity*, then the value is compromised and the childhood equivalent of the attempt at interpretation under the military structure ensues. Here the hypertheme would devolve into something like: given the goal, e.g., of playing with this toy, neither suppose nor engage, i.e., eliminate from play, other acting elements (children) who have the goal of playing with the same toy. Here the "same toy," as the locus of the symmetry in the hypertheme, is similar to the "element which allows the elimination of elements," of the military hypertheme, although the symmetry is gathered around the toy, rather than gathered around the body of another as in the latter case.

Of course the child's body does not have the range of transformation as an acting element, nor the extensions (weapons) of the military acting elements. But a devolution of the hypertheme will commonly show itself by a turning in of the child upon herself, the loss of the urge to play, "I don't feel like playing anymore," often followed, if nothing else intervenes, by a fight.

Yet the symmetrical assumption need not be made, or it can be abandoned. Parents can guide toward other ways of viewing the issue, in short other principles of interpretation, such as a hypertheme of alternation: "let him play with the blue car for ten minutes and then you can have it for ten minutes, okay," i.e., share the toy in some way. Or the parent can guide through a game which expands interpretation beyond the toy as an object, e.g., the toy takes on imaginative characteristics which allow more children to interpret it. The accumulation and increasingly frequent adoption of such alternative consistent hyperthemes is just the gradual growth of the child as one who can harmonize her action in increasingly complex communities of interpretation.

Given the foregoing you may still ask why I have digressed into considering the interpretive principles of childhood. The digression expands the unfolding account of corporate activity beyond the region of the corporation alone: companies are a macrocosm of the microcosm which is a certain range of highly cooperative but often inconsistent childhood activity. In turning aside here to consider the child in her playgroup, we can better understand the ways in which hyperthemes can be both inconsistent and joined within structures which are tenuous constructions of consistency and inconsistency. I will call such structures *mixed structures*, when their hyperthemes have inconsistent and consistent aspects, or when they contain a mixture of consistent and inconsistent hyperthemes. Such mixed structures can result in pervasive and potent realms of interpretation, but always of the sort which is in danger of devaluation. In the case of children at play, the inconsistent aspect, if not checked by the child participating in other communities besides that of the play community, results in a type of inconsistent action which is as well-known as it is perhaps misunderstood. We have a word for this action, a nontechnical word: greediness.

The connecting link that I want to make here is that just as the child in the play community is in such interpretations greedy, so, on another scale, because of acting transformable elements that are more numerous and whose range is far greater than those of the child, there are few words which better describe the overarching characteristic of whatever we take to be bad and inconsistent in the commercial corporation, than the word greediness. The litany of actions undertaken by companies which fall under the aegis of greediness are as numerous and well known as they are difficult to understand without a guiding vision of human interaction. Supplementary to the previous survey, a few further brief examples will help to better view the outcome of the adoption of the inconsistent aspect of the corporate hypertheme.

The Outcomes of the Product Object Assumption

Commercial companies wish to create products, whether they be physical objects, services, etc. At the same time they do not wish their competitors to create the *same* products, or even to be in the same general realm of production. The aim of every company—in the usual course of affairs—is to wipe out its competitors. Not physically as a military, but through acquisition, i.e., through sheer and utter greediness with regard to their product and everything to do with their product. Microsoft is perhaps the epitome of the company characterized by greed, even more so than IBM, even though Microsoft in fact collaborated with IBM. In its four-decade history, the Microsoft Corporation has been denounced for taking a wide range of actions to gain a complete domination of the personal computer operating system market, i.e., of aiming to be the sole creator and distributor of personal computer operating systems. And it largely succeeded for a time by pursuing such actions as: buying out and absorbing its smaller competitors, some two hundred and counting; by making its products as exclusive as possible and thus difficult for its competitors to engage with, e.g., by extensive patenting, and perhaps—as numerous anti-trust lawsuits suggest—by introducing technical subtleties in its operating system which insure that the software of other corporations is incompatible with its products; by making agreements of exclusivity with other corporations whose product and whose goal it comes to see as comfortably different from its own, e.g., bundling its operating systems with new computers in collaboration with IBM. I will not labor the point, for the reader will be aware of these and similar actions, not merely by Microsoft, but by other large corporations. The connection I want to make, however, is that corporations act very much like children in the playgroup. They want to play around the interpretation of their selected product, but they also have the tendency to say "mine" to their playmates (other corporations), and indeed "all mine!"

Now what is at issue is not that they do these things. I will take it that this is not in doubt and can be exemplified almost indefinitely. Rather, what is at issue is *why* they do these things. What I am suggesting is that it is the combination of the supposition of a hypertheme which engages the problematic of cooperation, with the further symmetrically inconsistent supposition of a hypertheme in which the goal of the interpretive activity undertaken by the community of the company is a *product*, to which other acting elements beyond the company stand in the same unique relation as the members of the company in question, which is at the heart of the ills which corporations inflict upon the world with such ease and frequency.

If once you have a hypertheme which says engage experience so as to continually grow in your ability to engage a problem and then goes on to add that the goal of such growth is an entity which holds the same relation to another who is also trying to grow, i.e., a mere **object** *which is to be the same static locus for everyone engaged with it, then you have a situation in which the engagement as an expansively interpretive growth utterly contradicts the engagement as a de-interpretive contraction to a static object.* In other words, you are trying to carry out a *process of interpretation* according to an assumption of the locus of the selected process—the supposed "object"—as that which has little or no range of interpretation available to it. In short, the more it is assumed to be the *same* for those who interpret it, the less there can be to interpret about it. To illustrate with a very simple example: the goal of the acting members of a company can be either something such as a "food product," i.e., food as an object, or it can be something such as "the feeding of a man," a region of interpretive freedom. *The more it is viewed as the former, the less is the range of interpretability which will be open to it.*

This principle, which assumes the sameness of some aspect of experience, i.e., objectifies it, is adopted as part of the hypertheme at the heart of the mixed hyperthematic structure of the corporation. A similar hypertheme appears to occur within other hyperthematic structures such as that guiding children at play, as we saw. But in the case of the commercial corporation, when you add that the acting transformable elements and their extensions have far greater ranges of transformation, and act at far higher ranges of complexity than anything which children are as embodied, or have access to, then you see at once that the combination of extremely fluid elements with such a hypertheme can be a potentially explosive combination.

The valuable and meaningful interpretive action which corporations undertake is thus the engagement of the problematic of cooperation through the marshaling of further actors. Sadly, what is evident just as often are the inconsistent destructive tendencies of corporations. Corporations provide rich opportunities for interpretation even as they provide vast opportunities for destruction. Corporations keep secrets from one another, they take over one another, they gobble up more and more of whatever they encounter, and they steal products, members, money, and so forth from one another. The extensions of their members as acting transformable elements are currency, legal powers, etc. These are their *weapons* insofar as the inconsistent aspect of their core hypertheme is engaged.

This is a matter of proportion however. When the inconsistent aspect dominates we get the corporations which exemplify the above actions. There are more and less consistent companies and it is no accident that on the lower end of things the military has often been bound up with conquest and trade, according to constrictive commercial interests. Corporate interests, in proportion as they espouse the inconsistent aspect, have reached down to connect with the military structure, which operates under the same inconsistent assumption, but without the redeeming aspects. The East India Company's military endeavors well illustrate this; the military-industrial complex of the contemporary world better still.

Yet the attitude toward other acting elements which the mixed hypertheme of the corporate structure creates does not extend merely to the acting elements of other corporations. The assumption of the product as a static locus, which contracts the possibility of interpretation, cannot help but affect the interpretive relationship with *any* aspect of experience which the corporation engages through its members. Thus, in the first place, *the world* will tend to be treated as a static resource, a commodity to be bickered over with competitors. The result of this is inevitably the degradation, for example, of the natural world, which tends toward becoming a mere object to be possessed. In the second place, the inconsistency must carry over into the corporation's relationship with the acting transformable elements of various communities with which it interacts, that is to say, which buy its "products." This is why it often appears that corporations will do anything to sell their products; they will take any attitude toward the consumer which draws the consumer into buying their product. They will use and abuse various other structures, e.g., leader structures such as music.

The consistent aspect of the structure, according to which cooperative action is assumed to allow solutions to certain problematics of experience, rightly guides corporations to join with you in action toward those solutions. For example, if your problematic is traveling 200 km in a single day, you alone cannot achieve this as you are, for it is a problem to be solved by cooperation. Most likely you cannot make a car on your own which will solve the problem. It takes a group of members of the community of a corporation, the workers (miners, builders, engineers, chemists, etc.), managers (salesmen, organizers, bookkeepers, etc.), and financiers (common investors, private investors, banking advisers, etc.), to achieve the product that will allow you to realize an interpretive solution of the problematic. So far then the corporation is consistent in combining with you in a harmonizing action which solves the problem, and if you are not directly one of those involved in the activity of the company, e.g., you are not the miner whose iron the car manufacturer uses to make the vehicle, nonetheless according to the fluid medium of currency you can participate in joining your action to that of the corporation toward its goal, which is also your goal, i.e., to allow 200 km to be traveled in a single day. Hence, the corporation wants you to buy its products, and *to buy its products is to participate and cooperate in the activity which generates the product*, and this is entirely consistent with the problematic being engaged, but yet opposed by the additional symmetrical assumption which forms part of the corporate hyperthematic structure.

The additional symmetrical assumption, the inconsistent aspect of the structure, is the supposition that the goal of the activity is an entity which holds the same relation to you as a buyer as it does to the corporation and its members. That is to say, it takes the car as an *object*. But the more it espouses this assumption and postulates the car, or whatever product, as a static object, the less there is any interpretation possible between the community of the corporation and the cooperating acting elements, here the buyer who is engaging with it. And the more constricted the region of interpretive freedom becomes by supposing a static object, the less value there is in any interpretive activity with regard to the object. In short, the product cannot be removed from the activity of its cooperative creation. Whatever value the product has, that value resides in the harmonized activity which is bringing it about as a realized interpretation, *including the activity of the buyer*; and the product must remain as the *sign* of that cooperative activity. Indeed, if it is to be consistent, it cannot, properly speaking, be viewed as a product at all, but rather as *a meaningful and real process of harmonically interpreted experience which is signified by an abstraction when it is considered as a product*.

Companies and buyers often recognize this intuitively, although they undoubtedly do not understand why it is so. They recognize that products which are more valuable are those which are viewed as *an interpretable process of experience*. If you buy a Porsche, for example, you are buying an ongoing and interpretive relationship with the Porsche Company, and this is how such luxury producing companies market themselves. But the value does not lie in the amount of money which is paid or sought for the "product" as an object; it cannot. It lies in the interpretability of the experience. The experience may be, relative to other communities, inconsistent. The diamonds of De Beers are utterly constricted as objects upon which interpretation can be initiated, for what can you do with a diamond? As a tiny, hard, static *object*, not much, but as a *sign* of an ongoing interpretive relationship with others, you can engage a region of experience which is considerably larger. Not for nothing does De Beers use the slogan "a diamond is forever." Such signs may be consistently expansive, e.g., as signifying the region of interpretive freedom which is a loving life together, or inconsistent as signifying the diminishing interpretive freedom of eliminative status wherein the diamond is and remains a small pretty rock "which I have and you do not," but there is no doubt in this case of the effort that is made to expand the object into a sign of the process which it signifies.

So also with the Stradivarius, and the Rembrandt, for we can follow the thread of our account to such corporations as Sotheby's, whose products come as signs of the value accumulated through a long history of interpretation and who thus engage some of the most valuable "products" of all. Yet a little further still we come to the museum, which undoubtedly does not include a symmetrical inconsistency in its hypertheme—though I have no space to confirm this here—and is not a commercial corporation, despite contemporary tendencies, and thus does not regard its pieces as products or static objects at all, but as fluid signs of processes of ongoing and perennial interpretation. Hence, museum value is greater still, in fact "priceless" as we say, for its treasures, as suggested in our chapter upon art, are to be passed on indefinitely as respectively, the signs and initiators of present and further interpretation.

That is one side of the story, but there is the other side. Insofar as companies do not recognize or assume harmonic interpretive activity as preeminent in their goal, i.e., insofar as they embrace rather the inconsistent aspect of the usual corporate hyperthematic structure, the results are both predictable and terrible with regard to value. The buyer becomes a *consumer*. The word consumer itself has a pedigree in the word consume, which in all of its uses and derivatives stands for existentially eliminative tendencies. If we consume food or resources, the emphasis is on destruction, or elimination. Fire consumes things. Consumption (tuberculosis) was so named by its tendency to waste away or "eat" the body. All of these indicate the constriction of some region of interpretive freedom. As the symmetric inconsistent aspect is embraced, the object as an object becomes preeminent; it becomes less an interpretable sign and more static. The buyer, now the consumer, is increasingly nameless and faceless to the corporation, not a participating and cooperating actor in an interpretive solution to the problematic, but an entity whose extension is postulated only as far as one who will buy the product. In this case an eliminative violence is carried out upon the buyer as an individual temporally extended self, as a process of experience. To a corporation wholly given over to the symmetric assumption, interpretive cooperation is shunned beyond the mere act of buying. Such a corporation does not care who you are or what you do, as long as you *buy* the object.

Wherever the inconsistent symmetrical aspect of the corporate hypertheme is assumed as preeminent, the corresponding supposition of the extensive transformable element of cooperative interpretation, i.e., money as an object, is assumed as preeminent. If money stands as an exchangeable equivalent for products, then it also is subject to the foregoing problems. View it as a static object, that is to say view it not as the facilitator and sign of the interpretive cooperative activity which is possible between transformable acting elements, but as a *static object*, as the locus of an increasingly constricted region of interpretation between actors, as *"that which we both want but cannot have together because it is an object and not the sign of a harmonically interpretable process,"* and the interpretations which are available with regard to it become increasingly eliminative interpretations.

Viewed thus, money becomes the kin of the weapon as used by the military structure. Wielded in this way it becomes a locus of eliminative action, a devaluing action. It constricts the interpretive actions available to acting elements—we humans—stripping away the possibility of meaningful and valuable action. You buy people out with it, you buy their resources and land from long distance, you force their activity according to restrictive terms, etc. Thus, for example, in some regions of India—as also in other regions around the world—money as object becomes preeminent to processes of action, such that the interpretive activity of the farmer who grows a wheat crop cannot be translatable into monetary terms since his activity is devalued as translated into money, with the result that the wheat as an object devalues its own process of creation. Result: the farmer goes hungry while the wheat remains bound up with the money which devalued it.

When this viewpoint is directed at the buyer, it devalues the buyer as an actor in meaningful cooperative exchange. Whether it be in China, India, or a host of other areas in turn, products are manufactured as mere objects, disposable objects, objects which do not *signify* value in process and thus are insignificant, a collection of plastic baubles and bad workmanship whose only remaining connection even to money is through the sheer mass and quantity with which they are pitched at the buyer as a consumer, so that they overload the buyer's interpretive freedom as an interpretive actor. This orgy of meaningless sameness provokes mere consumptive buying, for—unless rescued by other communities—what else can the buyer do except carry out *the act of buying as such*, with that money which has been reduced to "the object for the buying as such?"

Moreover, as suggested earlier, further structures can be engaged to the same effect, e.g., the music of the big-box store, or the advertisement, which cunningly employed, overloads the capacity of the buyer to act meaningfully, so that the world fills with iPods and cell phones and Wal-Mart trinkets. Buying thus becomes meaningless, beyond the bare act of exchange of static objects, with the corporation effectively saying to the consumer: "we do not care about you," and, by virtue of the quantity of the mere objects with which it floods the markets, "you are not even to care about yourself."

If it is to be the consistent sign of an interpretation of harmonized action, not only must a product include the activity of the buyer however, but it must include the activity of the worker, at every level. Wherever corporations have shown their worst side in history, the inconsistent symmetric supposition has worked itself into the view of the worker, in a way similar to the view of the buyer. The worker has become in such extremes a mere resource. The term "human resource" is that hellish description of the worker which stands as the analog to the buyer as a "consumer." The worker as a human resource, that is an object with a minimal and strictured range of interpretation, is made so in conjunction with the view of money as an object and the product as an object. It is only an object which can make an object, for an object.

Not only is this the extreme of the sweatshops of Asia or the contemporary corporate banana republics, but it has been the result wherever and whenever the inconsistent assumption at the heart of the corporation has become preeminent.

> In the initial phase of the Industrial Revolution, the tasks were not well delineated and the industrialists tended to have a hand in every aspect of their operations—raising money, building factories, supervising labor, and training managers. Nonetheless, this growing class of industrial capitalists did not engage directly in labor themselves, and their workers, unknown to them, by name became mere cogs in the operation. The ancient relationship of master to worker disappeared, as making money became the overarching goal.[49]

Now ostensibly, workers in factories are working together in what would seem to be the peak of harmonization of action. Viewed more broadly this is an illusion, an illusion which has been intuitively, if not overtly, recognized in that perennial reassertion that factory workers *are* mere cogs in a machine. In the contemporary world, the cogs may not even be in the same country but halfway around the globe from each other. A worker carrying out some action in a factory is precisely not harmonizing her action with that of her fellow worker. Rather, she is carrying out an action as an acting transformable element which is entirely *replaceable* insofar as it is a human resource, i.e., an object. This can be seen in the gradual replacement of workers by machines and now by the simplicity in which parts of objects to be assembled can be made halfway around the globe and inserted into an assembly line in a way such that the assembling worker has little or no contact with the worker, or workers, who made the part.

The part is not the resultant sign of a consistent interpretation, for the worker who assembles it gets no idea—according to their work activity—of its provenance as the sign of a process: where it came from, whether from one, from many, from machine, and whither and whereof it is destined as a part, remain unknown. The factory worker does not have to recognize her fellow worker in an extended temporal sense—although thankfully, by reason of *other communities* not yet destroyed by corporatization in the inconsistent aspect, she will have to recognize that worker in some such sense—for the characteristic of this type of work is precisely that the acting element need engage no more than the least complex range of the world problematic. In other words, factory work may be reduced to an activity which stays within the range of what I characterized earlier as no more than "smelling something on the ground and grabbing it to eat," or "insert part A into slot B."

Constantly engaging in such a range of action is a regression to a level of interpretation of the world problematic which is antecedent to the level of interpretation under which the individual self as a cumulatively acting interpreter, a community of selfhood, arises, not to mention being antecedent to the level of interpretation which gives rise to cooperative action. It is a regression to a level of interpretation according to which the acting worker needs little or no sense of self or of other selves. Nor does it make a difference *who* gets the product, the object, for the root of the inconsistency lies in a symmetrical assumption which is eliminative of interpretive action, and this from any angle.

Marx and the Common Product Object

The problematic character of Karl Marx's assumptions, betrays this. In his early writings, such as *Wages of Labor*, Marx gives himself wholly over to the same set of assumptions which we have seen Adam Smith adopt. The adoption of these assumptions plots an inevitable course for Marx and those who follow him. "Private property is thus the product . . . of *alienated labor* . . . [and] though private property appears to be the source, the cause of alienated labor, it is really its consequence . . . [so that] political economy starts from labor as the real soul of production; yet to labor gives nothing, and to private property everything."[50] If the account given above is plausible, then this is backwards. Whatever is meant by alienated labor—and its exemplifications as Marx gives them are near enough *phenomenally* to some examples given above, but which I called the devaluation of activity—it is not the *producer* of private property, or product, but rather the *outcome* of the inconsistent assumption *which takes there to be a product at all*, as understood and embraced in more than an abstract and subordinate sense.

Yet once having begun with this inconsistent assumption, the constriction of interpretive harmonic action gives way to the possibility of mere eliminative action, i.e., someone must be the "bad guy" with regard to the product. In consequence: "the direct relationship of labor to its product is the relationship of the worker to the objects of his production. The relationship of the man of means to the objects of production and to production itself is only a consequence of the first relationship and confirms it."[51] In other words, the relation of the boss or investor in the endeavor is secondary to that of the worker. But as I suggested above, this cannot be the true problem at issue, for the inconsistency will invade *every* engagement in a cooperative endeavor which assumes the locus of a product as a static object.

Nonetheless, with a dogged consistency, Marx works out the result of his inconsistent assumption, to arrive at: "the theory of the communists may be summed up in the single sentence: Abolition of private property."[52] Note the eliminative character of this admonition. The result? Abolition of *private* property, yes!; but abolition of property altogether, i.e., the product? Never! The private property is to become common property, *the common product*, a mere switch which assumes now the product, still as a *static object*, but now as the common goal of all, rather than merely the goal of a few. Thus the offending assumption remains, while the very heart of the eliminative strife which it engenders is represented in blissful acquiescence under the question "whose product is it?" To answer that one, we will have to fight, for we cannot interpret given the assumption. The result was evident in the twentieth century, both in the birth and in the ongoing tribulations of the various versions of communism.

In short then, if we are to be consistent, it is no-one's product, for we cannot view the issue consistently in this way, either as communism or as capitalism views it. Under the "new" view which Marx advocates, there are problematics of experience which nonetheless still require cooperative harmonic interpretive action. The inconsistency which takes the product to be a locus of sameness for all actors, is in no wise removed by the product becoming the product of all or of a few, of belonging to many or of belonging to a few. The many and the few are pitted against one another and against themselves by the supposition of an uninterpretable hypertheme, which attempts the transformation of experience according to a product, as an object simpliciter, and not as an interpretable sign. This causes the difficulty.

If this is so, then we should find that in communist societies, the common product is no less the initiator of eliminative strife by the reduction and restriction of regions of interpretive freedom. Indeed, communist economies will be at a disadvantage with regard to capitalist economies in this regard, for if the human actor, the "worker" in the communist economy, cannot escape from the consequences of the inconsistent assumption of the product as preeminent to the interpretive activity which gives rise to that product, then such a human actor does not even have open the option of actors in a capitalist economy, i.e., the option to discard the offending assumption and engage in cooperative interpretive activity for its own sake as a poor but *meaningfully* occupied artisan.[53]

And this is what we do find. In communist economies "production" is slow, or flat, difficult to stimulate, hard to sustain. By redefining the product as the common product, or "our goodies instead of their goodies," as in the communist economy, the only change is that now you *must* make the product, for more eyes are watching you. You cannot easily disengage in weariness from devaluation and lack of interpretive freedom as you can under the same conditions in the capitalist economy, even if in the latter you can only do so for—increasingly—a short spell perhaps.

But though you must make a common product in a communist economy, nonetheless if the inconsistent assumption is retained, *you find no value or meaning in the common product*, for there can be no value in a product as a mere object, if, as suggested all along, value is the result of realized interpretation. Insofar as the possibility of participating in cooperative interpretive action declines under these conditions, the desire to undertake action *at all* declines. The result, even when labor is savagely enforced, can be illustrated in the attitude within the villages of rural China during the period of Mao's Great Leap Forward: "bound to the collective fields each day from six a.m. until midnight, seven days in a row, by the fall quarter of 1959 people were able to survive only by taking unauthorized work breaks

Hyperthematization of the Corporation | 251

in the collective fields and by slowing down their collective work activities or avoiding them altogether. Increasingly, many villagers found ways to rest their shrinking, weary bodies while pretending to sacrifice for the collective. Foot-dragging became the order of the day."[54]

Lest it be suggested that such an example betrays a conflation of Marxist political economy with the systems of the People's Republic of China (or of the Soviet Union), I would reply that nonetheless Marx's theory and the systems briefly alluded to in our example *are* taken together in the regions of experience which one might label "the left." At least in part, the actual historic mid-twentieth-century situations of China and the Soviet Union were a result of Marx's economic theories. The assumption that stayed true through that muddled period of history is the assumption that objects are to be produced.

In some cases, such as that of China under Mao, what began through the influence of Marxism morphed into something which adapted to conditions wholly unlike those upon which Marx based his theories (e.g., the conditions of Europe in his time). Chinese communism founded its rise in an agrarian rural population rather than an urban working class. But regardless of this, *the assumption of the product as an object* common to all—whether rural peasants or urban workers—survived the change from European conditions to Chinese conditions. It matters little whether the object be the locus of a money value or of a use value, it is rather the tendency toward *the objective sameness of producing an object at all* that constricts the interpretive value and causes the rural peasant or urban worker to fall out of a valuating engagement in the world process so as finally to view his or her own interpretive process (his ongoing work) as valueless. The rural workers during the Great Leap period of the People's Republic of China (PRC) did not find meaning in the objects they made, and more importantly *they did not find meaning in their processes of action which produced the object.* That Marx was adapted by Mao (or Lenin) didn't change this emphasis on the object. That the object was supposedly—if doubtfully—*ours* rather than the boss's, made no difference. The meaning and value in the life process is increasingly lost because the worker is attempting to make an *object at all.* This holds as much for someone "working" in the capitalist system as it does for someone in a socialist system.

What I have been trying to suggest by the foregoing, is that there is *no relief to be found in either the view of the political left or the political right with regard to the value of the corporation.* Marx and Smith, each are equally as good, which means *equally as bad* in their understanding of the issue of the corporation. Whether Marx or his followers (or Smith and his) have advocated aspects of commercial activity which agree with the hyperthemes here advanced is an issue that I must leave aside. They certainly have advanced lines of action, some consistent, and some inconsistent (with Hyperthematics and its opening assumptions), as have all areas of human activity at times. But, when they have, they have done it by trial and error. What they, and others, have not done, and what this effort is about, is to give an account of the success or failure of value creation which interprets between and beyond the left and the right. In other words: why do some policies of the left both occur and seem good and valuable to us, and some of the right also, and why do many policies of these same two seem wrong to us?

Hyperthematics *can explain this* with respect to them both, in a way which rises above them and connects to many other regions: namely, by suggesting that the tendency toward the object is a collapse of interpretive value. We must find our way out of this constrictive arena brought on by an inconsistent assumption if we are to understand and find meaning in the corporation as a structure within which consistent interpretation is possible. There is a tendency toward harmonically interpreted action or there is not. There can be no "our side versus their side" *if* there is to be value in cooperative action toward problematics of experience. There *ought* to be such action.

Under an interpretive and hyperthematically consistent view, neither buyer, nor worker, nor money, nor boss, nor investor, can escape a meaningful interpretive role, if there is to be consistency according to the assumptions held here. In the case of the latter, the corporate actors, the withdrawal and devaluation of the investor from an active role in the limited liability corporation is as evident as is the devaluation of the worker. Nor is this limited to contemporary corporate culture for, as seen in the quote above, even in the factories of the Industrial Revolution, the head of the factory gradually fell away from an active interpretive relationship with the workers.

The master of a medieval workshop had apprentices and journeymen under him, but he organized and taught them in a harmony of creative activity, by working and even living with them.[55] Gradually the inconsistent assumption of the corporation gained prominence, until the only connection of the boss to the processes of action, brought about by the boss's money, came to be the money itself as static object. "But the boss makes more money!" someone will object—Marx did—and profits. Indeed, but that doesn't make anything any better, for money as mere money has little value, a suggestion to be expanded upon shortly. If anything said earlier has any merit, then not only does that not make things any better, but it makes them worse. The CEO or owner, who makes fortunes, is by all accounts not thereby blessed with more meaningful activity than the workers.[56]

But in the limited liability company the investor is not necessarily the boss. This is further evidence of the problem, for the product, as a consistent sign of harmonized activity, must include the activity of any and all who have contributed, including those who cooperate according to the fluid medium of exchange which is currency, i.e., the stockholders of the limited liability company. Stockholders as members of corporations have been falling further and further from active cooperation. What we see in the phenomena of activity carried on in the workers and managers as members of corporations has its analogue in the activity of stockholders and for the same reason. Investment in the stock of public corporations has become almost entirely speculative, a realm of gambling by means of mere numbers which fluctuate on a computer screen. I will lay aside these issues for the moment, however, and proceed to the third of my tasks.

6

Expansive Reconstruction of H5 to H15

Introduction

I have elaborated the aspect of the corporate hypertheme, the assumption of which appears to give rise to the various weaknesses evident in the corporation as a structure that promotes cooperative action. The structure is not tested beyond **H** and its derivatives, but so far the structure of the corporation is partly inconsistent with regard to the first derivative hypertheme **H1**, and thus by implication also inconsistent with **H2**. I am now in a position to interpret the structure of the corporation to the hyperthemes **H5** to **H15**, that is, to the hyperthemes elaborated by means of interpreting the four consistent hyperthematic structures of game, narrative, dance, and music. Here the task will be to begin to creatively alter and supplement the structure which engages the problematic of cooperation.

The goal is to test the structure of the corporation throughout the region of the manifestations of corporate activity to see if it can abide by the hyperthemes of successful hyperthematic structures. Where it already does so, well and good. If and where it cannot, I will attempt to creatively postulate how our hyperthematic resources can supplement and improve the existing structure and make it consistent, i.e., how communities of interpretation and their members under the corporate structure could act so as to abide by consistent hyperthemes. For convenience, I will first restate the hypertheme of the corporation as it stands, thus: *****HC**—*Having selected a goal (interpretive realization), i.e., product, which cannot be realized by a single acting transformable element, postulate and engage with additional acting transformable elements as necessary in order to achieve the goal, but only with those elements which are not included within a community whose acting transformable elements are interpretively realizing the same goal.*

If my account is plausible, then the first aspect of the hypertheme is consistent, while the second is not. The first aspect tells us how to act whenever we come to the sort of problematic of experience—the cooperative problematic—which cannot be achieved by a single acting transformable element, e.g., a single human individual in its time process parallel aspect of being an interpretive community. This aspect of the hypertheme says: "whenever you face a problem which you cannot solve or interpret alone, then assume others who can help solve the problem." This principle of transformation by itself is what gives value to the activity of corporations. Note that *the goal so far is an interpretation as such*, i.e., the problem which gives rise to it is *a problem which could only be solved by an interpretation among multiple acting transformable elements*.

The further addition then says to us: only cooperate with such other individuals as are not working toward the *same* goal under some further community. Put in terms such as those in the corporation would use, "do not cooperate with those of another group who are making the same product as us." This assumption of *the goal as a sameness*, that is to say, of *the product as an object*—be it a physical or a service product—sets up a symmetrical relationship. The goal has now changed from an interpretation to an object, an object which acts as the middle line of the symmetry, with "us" on the one side, and "them" mirroring us on the other side. The sameness or staticness of the object—its non-fluidity—leaves us little room for interpretation. And if we cannot interpret in acting, then we will eliminate. We will fight over the object.

Reflect back on the consistently harmonizing hyperthematic structures. Those regions of more harmonized human experience were interpretable to the opening hypertheme without aspects of symmetrical inconsistency in the hyperthemes. In interpretations under those structures there is no symmetrical assumption whose locus of sameness gives rise to a mere object. In other words, we do not fight over a dance. The hyperthematic structure of dance does not adopt the symmetrically inconsistent principle. A *dance* is a fluid region of interpretive freedom, open to multiple interpretations. It is not an object. A game is not an object. A narrative is not an object. Music is not an object. Art is not an object. And except by a mistake of extreme abstraction, we do not constrict them to the level of objects. The book viewed as this mere lump of white pages between covers, or this which I will merely sell the copyright to, is already devolving from the realm of narrative. Unsurprisingly and suggestively, in the contemporary world it is most often the corporation, with the inconsistent aspect of its hypertheme, which gives rise to this devaluation. The dance, game, narrative, music, or art, can become objects to be fought over, to be patented, to be traded for pure profit, i.e., for money as an object. This is mass culture for profit, and this is the freedom of action. Yet it is not consistent interpretation of experience upon the assumption that experience is interpretable.

How then do we correct the structure of the corporation? The first move must be to correct the offending assumption. "But surely," someone interjects, "you cannot be suggesting that we give up the sense of the product of labor as an object?" In fact that is precisely what I am suggesting. An interpretive goal cannot be reduced to a mere sameness for all actors. It is fluid, a region for freedom of interpretation, with the room to maneuver in interpretive activity. I will illustrate the issue in very worldly terms, expanding on the example previously used. When individuals gather together to grow food there is a goal. If the goal is a goal under the cooperative aspect of the hypertheme of the corporation, then it is an interpretive goal, e.g., *the feeding of a man*. If the inconsistent assumption comes into play, the goal then becomes a product as an object, e.g., the *food product*. So long as both assumptions are held, the world may be filled to overflowing with the *food product*, but somewhere *the feeding of a man* is unachieved, with predictable consequences for devaluation, consequences that are all too evident in the contemporary world.

"But," so our friend may insist, "even if we agreed to abandon the inconsistent assumption, what we would be left with would be so meager as to be unworkable. A mere admonition to cooperate!" To this I reply as follows: first, mere cooperation is not as meager a principle with which to engage experience as all that, for according to our account *everything that is of value* with respect to activity under the corporation even as we have it, has come from just this principle. Wherever one has loved, treasured, and enjoyed, in grateful recognition, through a long and full process of interpretation, some beautiful and carefully crafted "product" of corporate activity from a corporation whose members have shunned the inconsistent assumption to any considerable degree, so as to present their "product" as a sign of interpretive possibility insofar as they could, then the value of interpretive action under the structure of the corporation is evident. You buy some "product," for example, and as you begin to use it you discover some small thoughtful aspects of its design which make you exclaim "this is the cleverest thing! They really must have thought out very well how someone like me was going to use this thing." Such is the sign of value which a company *can* achieve to lesser or greater degree.

Second, we can immediately supplement our corporate hypertheme according to the reflection that if the inconsistency lay in the assumption of an uninterpretable goal which overpowered the initial goal, then the correction of the assumption of the uninterpretable goal can begin by strengthening the initial consistent goal. The problematic of cooperation is consistently interpreted according to an interpretive goal, thus the principle with which we engage such experience can only be helped by the addition that we ought to expand and make more prominent the interpretive goal. If we transform our hypertheme of the corporation, we now get: **HE**—*Given a goal (interpretive realization), i.e., "product," which cannot be realized by a single acting transformable element, postulate and engage with additional acting transformable elements as necessary, regardless of their inclusion in other communities, in order to achieve the goal; and furthermore, while remaining consistent with* **H**, *make every effort to advance, present, and expand the goal as a fluid region of interpretive freedom to be solved through harmonic interpretive actions.* In other words, seek help in constantly working toward a product which is reinterpretable by further actors

Then, third, in the guise of the hyperthemes of consistent hyperthematic structures, we have the resources at our disposal to strengthen and supplement it further, by showing *how* to do so practically. Every one of the consistent hyperthemes which we can find a way to interpret to our new backbone hypertheme of the corporation, **HE**, will be a gain for us. I proceed to this directly.

I will show how each hypertheme can be adopted, if it can, by giving examples and postulating new activities. The extent of this interpretive musement in each case is deliberately left fluid. Sometimes the interpretation between the hypertheme and the experience of the commercial corporation will be relatively brief if types of action already extant in the activities of the commercial corporation—types of action which someone has already tried—readily present themselves, or could be very obviously implemented or enhanced. Sometimes my interpretation will be more expansive, suggesting new types of action not evidently manifested in the experience of the contemporary commercial corporation, and ranging, as seems wise, beyond the region of the commercial corporation, to make linkages to other regions of the world process and thereby test and render more plausible the hyperthematic account.

All of this is colored by a development of hyperthematic skill on the part of the author and an accretion of facets of interpreted experience consistently viewed in hyperthematic terms, both of which will tend to promote more expansive interpretations as the results of earlier effort are linked together and expanded upon. In each case, when I have gone far enough to see that a hypertheme can be adopted, then I will assume it adopted as a part of the reworked hyperthematic structure of the corporation while leaving further interpretation under it to interested future interpreters.

H5 Reconstruction

To begin then, hypertheme **H5** suggested: *insofar as you can, populate the community guided by your hyperthematic structure with transformable elements which are signs of transformation away from eliminative elements that destabilize community toward elements that promote harmonious interpretation.* With regard to the corporation, if we adopt this assumption, it will mean that we need to search for transformable elements that are akin to the chess pieces of the game in that they hold within themselves the history of their own transformations away from being destabilizing elements. We considered transformable elements in two ways. First, as acting transformable elements, e.g., acting human individuals; second, as extensions of acting transformable elements, e.g., the chess pieces as used by the chess player.*

The acting transformable elements of a corporation are comprised of its members: workers of all types, managers, investors, and also buyers of its "products." What **H5** tells us to do with regard to them is: engage further members who have made the transformation from being eliminative elements, such that they are signs of the move toward harmonious interpretation. In other words, invite workers into the corporation who, having once been given over to the inconsistent assumption, have now transformed themselves to some degree into acting elements who no longer hold the inconsistent assumption but espouse the new assumption of the goal of the corporation as an interpretive goal. Invite not merely workers though, but managers who signify in themselves the same transformation, and likewise invite investors who have done so, and finally explicitly engage with—present your "product" to—the buyers who have done so. Thereby, the community of your corporation tends to stabilize its value.

In doing this the corporation is guiding those it engages toward acting as processes of value. It is, for example, deliberately seeking out and thus encouraging the kind of buyer who practices an expansion of value with regard to the interpretive goal, by joining in community with the corporation. We suppose that there are such acting elements to be found, but if

---

*Both are abstractions of "the act of playing chess" in Whitehead's sense of abstraction.

there were truly none to be found, then nonetheless we could postulate them and include them in the company as models of action of those who would have made the transformation.

Turning to the extensions of acting transformable elements, we note first that depending on the commercial corporation, such elements may be its equipment and machinery and facilities, its bookkeeping practices, its legal instruments, and above all its current assets such as monetary assets. What our hypertheme tells us to do here is to engage further such elements which hold in themselves the history of their transformation from eliminative extensive elements to consistent extensive elements. In other words, willfully adopt such equipment and machinery and facilities to engage the interpretive goal with as signify a transformation from the viewpoint which espouses the inconsistent symmetrical assumption to that which views the goal of the corporation as an interpretive goal.

With regard to the first, this means adopt such equipment or machinery that has been designed so as to take into account its user or users as interpretive, as valuable, and meaningful acting elements; do likewise as far as possible with the facilities in which such actors will carry out their interpretations. Second, adopt such bookkeeping practices as also signify such transformations, for example, bookkeeping practices which have advocated the recognition of interpretive value of workers, of the corporation as a long-term endeavor, etc. Again, third, adopt such legal instruments as signify this expansion, e.g., issue a type of corporate bond which recognizes the interpretive goal and, if government regulations make no allowance for such recognition, then work to gain such recognition. Finally, adopt a view of money which signifies the expansion. In the last case one may well ask how to do this. Some simple suggestions include: borrow only from credit unions, or again borrow from lenders that view currency as intimately bound up with the temporally extended activity of its members as part of interpretive communities, e.g., the Triodos ethical bank located in the Netherlands, or others of its kind. I do not suggest that all of these can be done at once, but whatever can be done will stabilize the community of your corporation. Clearly, the new hyperthematic structure of the corporation can use **H5** in making interpretations, and thus we adopt it as the first of our ancillary hyperthemes to **HE**.

H6 Reconstruction

Moving on, we restate and interpret **H6**. **H6** said: *insofar as possible, given the problematic, select transformable elements of a community such that their* *ranges of transformation promote actions which are simple enough for any actors in the community to carry them out in interpretations which sustain the community.* People love to play games such as chess, not necessarily because the games are easy to win or master, but because they are easy to learn to play. How can we interpret the structure of the corporation to **H6**, how can we simplify its transformable elements, in particular its extensive transformable elements, in ways which do not constrict interpretation but rather offer diversity of interpretation at lower levels of complexity?

Most obviously we could simplify bookkeeping practices, legal instruments, use of equipment, and facilities. The benchmark of whether we are moving in the right direction will be that we begin to dissolve the *static* hierarchies between the members of corporate communities, i.e., *we make such simplifications as allow the members to take on one another's tasks to some degree.* Adam Smith advocated the division of labor to produce the product more quickly and in greater quantity. Advocated here, is the interpretive *expansion of labor* in order to better engage the "product" as the signifier of the valuable interpretive goal of the corporate community: to offer everyone a wealth of meaningful experience and that consistently viewed practice spoken of earlier.

Rather than see this as a difficulty, one can come to see it as an advantage. It does not mean that each member of the community of the corporation is engaged in the *same* task. Each member of the community is to be an interpreter according to the problematic engaged and thus is viewed as actively interpreting into that region of interpretive freedom which the corporation engages. The 'sameness' is to be transformed into an interpretable and fluid region for action, which members engage in a diversity of ways. As long as this is assumed, then there is no inconsistency in the further assumption that people have different complexities of value which they are willing to realize. One of us enjoys working physically with the hands, another enjoys working more mentally, and yet another enjoys working at some complexity of interpretation in between these. The point is that they be free to engage different parts of the range of experience within which the community engages; without such freedom the actions of all members become increasingly constricted and devalued.

Because the potential complexity engaged in the community of the corporation is such that it is not as obvious perhaps how to simplify the rules, or the possible actions available to extensive elements, as separated from the acting elements, then it can be worthwhile to view the transformable elements as unabstracted processes, so that to simplify a transformable element would be to simplify the actions of an individual using the tools (extensions) of the community. One might institute as part of a corporation, a "school of the corporation," i.e., a school unique to each corporation, which educates any and all members in what other members of the corporation do and what the corporation as a community does altogether, i.e., its interpretive goal. Thus, for example in this school, any willing member of the corporation who is now considered a physical laborer gets the chance to both understand and participate in the task of a manager, and conversely, a member who is now considered a manager gets both to participate in and understand the task of a physical laborer.

"Wouldn't this cause chaos?" someone will ask. It would not, as long as the inconsistent assumption of the product as an object, to be exchanged merely for an objective profit, is let go, as it must be in consistency. The effect, rather, would be to lay out the various guidelines for action of the various tasks which interpretively realize the company's goal, i.e., everyone would get some idea of what everybody else does. The further effect would be *to make evident various ways in which tasks of different complexity could be so simplified that each and any member could participate in them to the benefit of the community*.[1] That is just what our principle **H6** asked of us. Thus we adopt **H6**.

H7 Reconstruction

The suggestion of hypertheme **H7** was: *construct communities such that they tend to engage the elements of other communities and prevent them from elimination.* With regard to this hypertheme, I noted that narrative tends to help other communities by guiding them out of the elimination of their elements, in the prophetic warning, in the moral of the fable or the fairytale, etc. How could we interpret the community of the corporation so as to abide by this hypertheme?

If you are engaged by a narrator under narrative you are turned into a listener. Evidently the structure of the corporation in the renewed form being presented, without the inconsistent assumption, already does this. As soon as the community of the corporation postulates another as a potential cooperating acting element with regard to its problematic, its assumption defends against the elimination of that acting element. A narration engages further listeners. A corporate production, or engagement in a cooperative interpretive goal, analogously engages further cooperating actors.

Thus every effort in the corporation which expands and strengthens its goal as an interpretive goal and corrects its inconsistent assumption is already an abiding by **H7**. We can strengthen this by making explicit the promise of the company to new members, just as, under the structure of narrative, the narrator makes explicit the promise of a community of narrative interpretation to new listeners. Practically, this means that as a member of a corporation one should explicitly offer the promise of cooperation to further individuals, thus: "this is what we are about, this is our goal, this is how you can cooperate with us, etc." In effect, this is the corporation saying: "here is a chance to participate in the cooperative problematic in a non-eliminative way." Moreover, where the narrative can engage other communities with warnings in the form of narrative, the corporate members can do so by engaging with the hyperthematic structure of narrative itself. They can tell the story of their corporate community, its history and its successes, in moving from an inconsistent to a consistent structure. Thus, clearly, corporate communities can abide by **H7**.

H8 and **H9** Reconstruction

The next two hyperthemes have a close connection to one another insofar as they are interpretable to the corporation, and indeed to any hyperthematic structure. **H8** tells us: *to create hyperthematic structures which engage further actors, insofar as possible make the sectional acting elements of those structures transformable rather than replaceable.* The reason for this is that just as the assumption of a static object as a sameness—literally an extensive transformable element used by several acting elements—constricts a region for interpretation, the assumption of a sameness of acting or extensive transformable elements constricts a region for interpretation.

As noted earlier, chess is symmetrical with regard to the two chess players. In fact all games within the range of what we usually call games are symmetrical in proportion as their transformable elements are replaceable, i.e., are the same. And as one descends through hyperthematic structures one finds that in proportion as the transformable elements become replaceable, the region of interpretive freedom is constricted, and there is the tendency to eliminative action, *unless* the possibilities of interpretation are carefully assessed and safeguarded according to the adoption of hyperthemes of a consistent hyperthematic structure.

Thus, for example, chess appears to be a battle, the analogue of an eliminative series of actions between contestants, *except* that—as suggested earlier—it has in fact derived from such contexts as a transformation of inconsistent elements, by a relaxation of its transformable elements away from replacement and toward transformation. But sport, which I supposed to be a lower structure than chess, is more constricted still in this regard, and thus appears to be still *more of a battle*, e.g., the ball in football is a static sameness as an object (except as it moves and is so far transformable), around which a symmetry forms. Still further comes dance in which acting element and extensive element are combined in the bodies of the dancers to such an extent that each becomes the object about which the other interprets her actions, and in which, accordingly, there is a proportionally very high emphasis on replacement between elements, i.e., dancers can easily replace one another in multiple ways. So it is in dance that the tendency toward symmetry is considerable and therefore the possibilities of interpretation must be well considered. If you sweep your leg right at the same time in which your partner is sweeping her leg left and you do not interpret with care and harmony, then your actions clash, and you have the analogue of a physical fight, from which dance is always only a short misstep removed and yet *is* removed, thanks to its hyperthematic structure.[2]

Yet all of this is once again a variant illustration of what was elaborated earlier in **H9**, namely: *in the creation of communities under hyperthematic structures, increasing the number or degree of transformable elements such that they pass on both structure and problematic, increases the growth of the structure at the expense of solution of the problematic; while decreasing the number or degree of transformable elements increases the chance of solution within the structure at the expense of its growth.* How then do we now interpret the community of the corporation such that its members can undertake action according to these two hyperthemes?

We can take our cue from the "product" of narrative interpretation: the book. What is at issue here is the promise of *the fluid product as an experience for reinterpretation*. If the members of the community of the corporation are to increase their engagement of further actors, then they should engage one another in the way in which the narrator interprets to the listener. Just as the narrator must be transformable into a listener and the listener must be transformable into a narrator, in order to institute a directional expansion of the structure, so the members of the corporation must be changed to be able to make the analogous transformations.

Here we find ourselves making the connection back to an earlier hypertheme, for the suggestions with regard to **H6** have already laid the groundwork for this transformation. If **H6** is followed, then each member of the community of the corporation now has an understanding both of the overall interpretive goal—the selected creative potential—of the community and of her relation and interpretive possibilities with regard to each of the other members. Advancing now upon that groundwork, each member of the corporate community must carry out her task as an interpreter and, rather than simply passing off a static object to her colleague—e.g., as on an assembly line—she must pass on an interpretation. In short, keeping her eye on what was gained from **H6**, she must pass on the "product," according to its stage of development, as a value embedded interpretation which is *a sign of the fluid partial completion of the corporation's interpretive goal*, analogously to the narrator in narrative. This "product sign" will then demand, by its very nature, further interpretation. Her colleague will receive the product sign—analogously to the listener engaged in narrative—and, transforming herself, will then go on to make a further interpretation. To the extent that the community of the corporation can achieve this, the structure of the corporation will expand, not in a greedy, exclusive, and eliminative expansion, but as the ever fresh and renewed promise of a valuated cooperative interpretation.*

Now you may well ask: "what on earth does the foregoing mean *practically?*" Hopefully an early illustration—and more expansive illustrations will follow in interpretations of later hyperthemes—will begin to answer that. Imagine a community in which there are half a dozen members. We give the community an interpretive goal, e.g., produce a "food product," let's say a soup, *as an interpretive goal*. Now let the members of the community—for fun I'll call them "the jazz band of chefs"—all be practiced in the activity of food preparation generally and of soups especially. Further, let each be particularly skilled in one aspect, or stage, of the whole preparation specific to the goal in question (e.g., one selects the ingredients, one chops the ingredients, one seasons the ingredients, one cooks the ingredients, etc.); still further let each be cognizant to some degree of the role and possibilities

---

*A new term replacing that of the "worker," the "product" of the corporation, and so forth, while capturing the flavor of the range of transformation which the acting individual will need in order to carry out such an interpretation, would be helpful. But, to avoid confusion, I will only suggest one at the end of the account.

of her colleagues, and finally let each be *unaware* of the specific selections that each of her colleagues will make in the preparation of the soup. This last is a mere temporary device, a way of ensuring for the purpose of our imaginary exercise that the members of our community make interpretive selections from *the full possible range of interpretive action accorded by their role*.[3] If once the members were guided to deliberately adopt the stance suggested, they would willfully do this last, learning to playfully interpret through the whole range of their possible actions. Let them now carry out their tasks, one after another, in order, up to the completion of the soup. What will be the result?

Hopefully it is evident that the result will be a "product" which, within its range of complexity, is through and through the sign of a unique cooperative interpretation. Each stage of the production—the interpretation—will be a fresh sign to interpret, a challenge to reinterpret, and an activity which gets its meaning and its value in the context of the whole activity and of the special selections of each of the acting individual participants. Each soup, even if taken in abstraction as a mere *result*, will taste unique, will invite further interpretation from whoever tastes it, and will carry within it the sign and promise of the interpretive activity of our small community of skilled soup chefs. Rather than "the division of labor" then, we have instituted the *expansion of "labor"* as a realm of valuable interpretation and at our pleasure the range of freedom of interpretation of each participating member can be increased, or decreased, depending upon the interpretive goal, e.g., this week vegetable soup, next week fish soup, meat soup, or some other.

Nor will the *quantity* or the *speed* and *efficiency* of the output of our group decrease appreciably, and in whatever degree these aspects do decrease it will be more than made up for by the value and meaning, which is now embedded throughout the process of interpretation. In other words, whatever *healthy* quantitative benefit the assembly line has—and by healthy I mean that range of quantitative accumulation that is consistent with overall value creation—would be retained without the devaluating tendencies of the typical assembly line.

Moreover, the above helps us see the problem and the solution in the relation between man and machine. Speed, efficiency, and those tendencies which—to quote the inimitable Dr. Seuss—contribute to that "biggering" of the production of "Thneed," which is mere quantitative accumulation, are very often bound up with the use of machines as *replaceable* extensions of transformable elements. But the more we tend toward replaceability, the less consistent we are with **H8**. Unless it is viewed and developed consistently as an extension of an active process—here a human process—which expands the interpretable range of that process out of the constrictions of embodiment, a machine tends to devalue the products it contributes to.

And the reason is obvious when viewed in terms of our imaginary jazz band of chefs. Every stage of the process of production which tends toward being an experience in which the participating elements either are replaceable, or are replaced, tends to be a relatively "dead zone" with regard to value in the product. Each of the imagined chefs, given guidance and opportunity, is going to tend to make unique interpretive choices with regard to her stage of the process, which creatively *transform* the incoming sign into an outgoing sign. Machines can help in this creative transformation, *if* consistently understood as extensions that expand some range of activity for the actor, e.g., a special glove that would allow the chef to engage the food ingredients with the back of the hand as well as the palm and fingers. But they can also be inserted into the process as mere replacements that *copy* the action of some human acting transformable element, e.g., a machine that slices food with a single repetitive motion. To the extent that this latter occurs, the process is devalued toward mere quantity, toward a sameness of experience.

Nor is it enough to "program" randomness into machine replacements, for random engagement of experience is also a devaluing engagement of experience; it makes no interpretation in our hyperthematic sense, except such interpretation as has been programmed by the programmer. But once again in this case the machine stands in as a mere replacement. A consistently valuating transformation requires an initial selection of signs within the process, an interpretation of those signs to future experience, and a valuating conspectus of the interpretation as having solved the problem and connected experience. All of this our imagined chefs can do. Machines can do none of this, and we delude ourselves if we think that we program or will program into their "artificial intelligences" more than a basis for a repetition of what we ourselves have already interpreted. Machines can help in our engagement of experience, as creative extensions of our own consistently viewed development of value in the world, but they will never help us to attain a value which we have not consistently developed the "right" to. At least that is what the hyperthematic viewpoint suggests.

Returning to our community of chefs, however, we may add that the more the possible range of interpretive freedom of each participating member is increased, the more the signs, or interpretive products, of the structure— analogously to the great works of narrative—will have a tendency to engage further actors to cooperate in the community toward the interpretive goal. Thus the growth or expansion of communities under the hyperthematic structure will occur. If there should come a time when we want to slow the growth, we can do so. For example, a situation may occur analogous to that which occurs when an artist, writer, or musician produces a work which is *so* open, so free in the possible interpretations of it that we cannot begin to interpret it, i.e., it saturates the region of interpretive interpretation. In this case **H9** gives us the opportunity to correct the proportion by telling us that there is a trade-off between the solution of the region of interpretive freedom engaged by a structure and the growth of the structure in terms of further acting elements. Hence, just as we promoted the change of our acting elements in the previous example toward transformability rather than replacement, we can promote the opposite, *as a consistently understood effort of practice*, to better define, or make more exact, the solution. This would be the equivalent of going from the precision of a type of narrative to the greater precision of chess as a type of game. In this way we can play with and tweak the structure according to our interpretive goal, the growth and capacities of our members, etc. Clearly **H8** and **H9** are interpretable under the structure of the corporation, and so we adopt them forthwith.

H10 Reconstruction

H10 meanwhile appears to be readily interpretable to the structure of the corporation with a little patience and interpretive musement. Its suggestion was: *to enhance the meaning of the transformable elements within hyperthematic structures with regard to interpretations parallel to the time process, creatively postulate historic or futuristic interpretive models for the elements of your structure to interpret themselves to.* To do this the members of the community of the corporation could first go to the historic record. There they will find interpretive models of those acting individuals who have to a lesser or greater degree faced the same problematic of cooperation and who have adopted some one or other lines of action which are consistent with our foregoing reconstruction of the corporate structure and who can therefore serve as guides to current and future action.

These are the great historic businessmen and women who are great not by greedy accumulation, but by their effort to correct the inconsistent symmetrical assumption and hence by their espousal of the corporate community as a community of interpretation. An example of this would be

Benjamin Graham, the father of value investing, who combined his deep love of literature with his activity as a writer, investor, and business owner, in order to both live and advocate a more deeply interpretive engagement of investors with corporate communities. In the second place, the members of the community of the corporation can imaginatively postulate models at need, either wholly imaginative models, or models which answer the "what ifs" of historic individuals. Moreover, these can be futuristic models as well as past models. In both cases the members of the community can also model themselves, i.e., "such and such is the extended plan of what I intend to do, or of what I might have done."

These suggestions are the more obvious for, as Royce sometimes notes, they are the sort of steps we take in engaging experience every day, however unreflectively. We constantly look to others, our heroes and role models, and where consistent we look to them not as models to be slavishly mimicked, but as guides for practice which will give way to our own creative uniqueness. We thus assume **H10** as interpretable to the corporation, and thereby adopted.

H11 Reconstruction

H11 follows closely upon **H10**, for its advice is: *to move the range of your hyperthematic structure toward a more local and physical harmonization of action, simplify, and reduce (but do not eliminate) the models to be interpreted to, and do the reverse to move the range of your structure toward a more broad and mental harmonization of action; and, in order to engage in the experience of your problematic in the most efficient way, postulate a diverse range of models which can be interpreted to.* This hypertheme has the potential to be eminently practical with regard to the community of the corporation. Having postulated models according to the time process parallel aspect for the members of the community of the corporation to interpret to, we can now expand or reduce those models. Thus, from the postulate of a model of a lifetime of action as an engagement of the problematic of cooperation, we might reduce the model to a month of action, or a day.

We might also postulate models according to the time process sectional aspect for members of the community of the corporation to interpret themselves to. This follows the spirit of the consistent engagement of the problematic of cooperation, which assumes further acting individuals as necessary. Whereas the original assumption addresses the *whole* interpretive goal, our hypertheme here tells us to correct weak points along the structure, i.e., *interpretively constricted subsections* of the process of the goal.

There is no evident difficulty to this, but it allows us to engage the problematic of cooperation according to the structure of the corporation all along its range and there are *two* areas in particular where a growing engagement of and interpretation to this hypertheme could aid communities under the corporate hyperthematic structure. These are with regard to: *the organizational structure as being headed by a boss, and limited liability as it is granted to individual stockholders as investors*. These areas have the potential to be inconsistent as long as the inconsistent symmetrical assumption is maintained. But even if it is corrected, the transformations of corporations toward consistent interpretation will necessitate the reworking of these long-held views. **H11** can help us in that reworking.

I take them in order. The contemporary view of the corporation, espouses a hierarchy in which employees are organized under a boss or bosses. The assumption is thus a pyramid in which a single acting element at the top is to coordinate and organize an ever broadening group of acting elements. Thus, the CEO is to organize the managers, and the managers in turn are to organize the workers. If the hyperthematic account is plausible, such an arrangement cannot be consistent. The hierarchy of this command arrangement is in fact a holdover from the symmetrically inconsistent assumption.

The arrangement is a *power arrangement*—which is evidently part of a great many inconsistent structures besides that of the corporation, e.g., the military—that is to say that the acting elements which are higher in the pyramid are to harmonize the action of the lower elements. But they are to do so through force, eliminative action, i.e., their ultimate goad to action, rather than lure to action, is to fire a member of the corporate community lower down the pyramid than themselves. Moreover, rising up through the structure of the pyramid, it becomes progressively thinner with fewer and fewer acting elements interpreting to one another in the time process sectional aspect. Reaching the top, the final element, the CEO, becomes a static object according to the time process sectional aspect. He or she has little or no horizontal interpretability in the context of the corporation, e.g., to peers—other CEOs—at the same level within the corporation. Insofar as the CEO is a static object however, it engenders a symmetrical inconsistency which gives rise to eliminative strife, i.e., the fierce competition within corporations to reach the top of the corporate hierarchy of power or, in other words, *to physically become the static object*: the boss.[4]

The second inconsistency is that of the limited liability of individual stockholders as members of the community of the corporation. Limited liability, as it stands, is the principle that those who invest in a corporation are only liable for the damages caused by the community of the corporation, to the limit or extent of the money—in the exchange form of stock in the company—which they have invested. Investment however, is a participation in the corporation, a cooperation in the activity of the members of the corporation.

Yet as shown earlier when the problematic which the corporation engages was considered, the only basis upon which we can speak of participatory activity which engages the problematic of cooperation, is an assumption, a postulation, of acting transformable elements, i.e., individuals in an extended temporal sense, with regard to whom we can harmonize our activity toward an interpretive goal. If this is so, however, then an investment in the corporation cannot be less than a recognition of the members investing in the corporation, in their extended temporal aspect. Hence, the investment of my money in a corporation has the only value which it can have according to the actions of the corporation's members as extended temporal processes. What the limited liability laws now tell me is that my participation as a member of the corporation can be absolved merely by forfeiting the money that I contributed. In short, I may give up the money as an object in order to remove myself from participating in the corporation of the community as a member.

The situation is this however: to the extent that my money was a mere object, then I never actually participated in the corporation. On the other hand, to the extent that my money is no mere object, but a sign of interpretation, then I cannot remove myself from my participation in the corporation merely by offering my money as an object, and the activity of the corporation stands—irrevocably, if it is past activity—as the realized sign of my participation. In my engagement of it, my money tends toward being a mere object, or it tends toward being a sign of interpretation.[5] It cannot be both tendencies at once. Even as an abstraction from a process of interpretation, it remains a sign of that interpretation.

Once again then, we arrive at the assumption of a static object as the root of an inconsistency. The inconsistency plays itself out, as noted before, in the interminable rounds of strife between corporations. It also plays itself out in the competitive drama of the stock market. And this is why, according to the ease of use and fluidity of the exchange of signs in the stock market, the "value" of companies has a tendency to fluctuate wildly. As limited in liability, the stockholders see the negative aspect of their engagement in the community under the corporation, i.e., that each is not to be responsible *alone*, but they do not see the positive aspect of their engagement, i.e., that everyone is to be responsible according to her interest as an actively participating member and not merely as the wielder of an object.

And what finds its first expression in the attitude that "I am not responsible for the actions of the company in which I am invested," spreads itself to a further noncommittal attitude toward being an owner at all and to participating in the difficulties and successes of the company.[6] As Benjamin Graham once said of the shareholders who invest in corporations: "the shareholders are a complete washout. As a class they show neither intelligence nor alertness. They vote in sheeplike fashion for whatever the management recommends . . . the only way to inspire the average American shareholder to take any *independently* intelligent action would be by exploding a firecracker under him."[7] Such independent action would of course be possible only proportional to the self-recognition of the investing shareholder as an extended self, with the corresponding recognition of the consistent interpretively expansive view of the other members of the corporation which that entails.

In contemporary investors *qua* investors, this self-recognition is not much in evidence. Thus, when trouble besets the community of a particular company, a majority of stockholders usually sell their stock, that is to say, they act inconsistently with the initial postulate which they must make of themselves and other members in the community of the company as a cooperative venture in order to engage in a company. On the other hand, if the going is especially good for a company and the stock is rising quickly, again the stockholders sell their stock, which is to act inconsistently with the initial postulate. These two are holdovers from the adoption of the symmetric inconsistency. They are inconsistent for the same reason, viz., they assume a static object which can embody value: a man as an object, or stock or its monetary equivalent as an object.

I am considering them together because they can be corrected by hypertheme **H11**. That hypertheme tells us to postulate models of diverse complexity at need where we need to promote action and to postulate them so as to cover the range of our problematic. In each of our cases there is an object as the root of the inconsistency. The counter to a static object is the postulation of a model to which that object, as a relatively impoverished sign, can be interpreted. Every such postulation expands the interpretive freedom of the region.

Thus in the first case, the power arrangement hierarchy is inconsistent. At its lower levels however the acting elements, "employees," can interpret to one another as models. The CEO has lost this range of potential interpretation if she is the only one engaged in her task in the community. The saying "it's lonely at the top," is intuitively appropriate. The solution evidently is for the CEO to postulate models. There need to be other acting individuals interpretively engaged in the task at that level of complexity.

"But," you may ask, "what then is the role of leaders, or bosses? Must we get rid of them altogether?" In all consistency, the answer must be yes, *if they are single individuals who rule by force according to a power arrangement*, though the "getting rid of"—a misguided phrase—must really be "a correction of," a developmental transformation through expansion, rather than an elimination. Any attempt at elimination would itself be hyperthematically inconsistent. Problems of devaluation are not solved by elimination, though god knows men have tried. The solutions must come through the creation of value and the relinquishing of devaluation rather. Here, there must be many leaders created and they must be leaders in a consistent sense, i.e., the sense elaborated in the earlier discussion of music.

The CEO's task can only be a consistent task as an interpretive engagement of some range of complexity different from that of another member of the community, i.e., a more mental task, one which is more complex than a physical task. Such a task must nonetheless retain its interpretable potential to the tasks of the other members with regard to both axes of the time process, however. This can be done by a constant postulation of and hearkening to models, horizontally to other members—other "CEOs"—engaged in tasks of the same complexity, vertically to the past and future plans of action of the CEO herself and to the workers engaged at lower levels of complexity. Leaders are leaders not by eliminative force, but by their tendency to expand the interpretive freedom of acting elements engaged in problematics at lower levels of complexity than their own. This is what makes the visionary and "larger-than-life" leaders, for many individuals have expanded themselves by postulating models in the time process parallel axis, even if hitherto few have done so according to the time process sectional axis.[8] Every effort according to **H11** to postulate models will promote this sort of consistent leader.

What expands the constricted interpretability of the leader as an object, however, will also expand the constrictions in the inconsistency of stock or its monetary equivalent as an object. An investor, or stockholder, insofar as acting through the exchange medium of stock or money, will move toward consistency whenever they are able to postulate models of monetary processes to which they can interpret money as an extension of their interpretive action. If I am an investor, then, practically, this means that I will regard money as a sign of how I shall take an active part in fulfilling the interpretive goal of the community of the corporation and that I both offer and receive it in this way.

As embodied, as embedded in the time process, and as accordingly constricted, money as an exchange must hold its value, as a signifier of the postulates which take me beyond my embodiedness, as a participant in cooperative action. If I cannot "be there physically or mentally," then, insofar as my investment can signify all that I could contribute to the interpretation if I could be there, it can retain its value. Money must take on the interpretive character which it does when one donates it: "for such and such a worthy and well-thought-out cause; a cause of which I retain a perennial interest in its ongoing success."

Limited liability, so far as consistent, will thus recognize the terms under which the acting individual engages in cooperation. Because it takes many to engage in the problematic in which the corporation engages, the liability accruing to the corporation can only consistently accrue to the many. Hence the consistent basis of limited liability is not that each is not to be responsible for the actions of the community of the corporation (although it is true in a negative manner to say that each is not to be responsible *alone*), but rather that *everyone is to be* responsible according to her active interest in the community under the corporation, for that responsibility issues from the initial postulate which they entertain—however unreflectively—in order to engage in the corporation. That postulate is nothing more than an extension of the original postulate by which cooperative work between individuals is instituted.[9] Given the foregoing, I adopt **H11**.

H12 Reconstruction

The next hypertheme, **H12**, said: *to create hyperthematic structures which engender greater stability and potential to interact with other hyperthematic structures, make every effort to include models which capture how reconstructive action has creatively responded to destabilizing actions within and against the community under the structure.* Find such models if you can, creatively postulate them if you cannot. The interpretation of this hypertheme to the hyperthematic structure of the corporation could be begun by finding examples of corporations which have tended to engage in a cooperative problematic according to the renewed hypertheme **HE**. Wherever we find examples of such corporations, however few, we can then search for examples of how the members of such communities have responded to destabilizing actions taken by other members. These will be the analogues of the etiquette considered earlier.

It is easy to say that there are no such examples to be found. This *might* be the case, for the commercial corporation as it stands is indeed a troubled endeavor. Whereas the great actors of the political realm—a region of experience which also has its considerable troubles—who have met destabilizing action with some act of creative reconstruction, are to be found sprinkled throughout human history, the healers of the realm of the commercial corporation are much less in evidence.

Admitting that so easily is deceptive however. The leaders of the political realm, insofar as they have been great leaders in our hyperthematic sense of being guides engendering expansion of interpretation, have been strong communities of selfhood. Accordingly, they have often engaged in creative responses to self-initiated destabilizing actions against *their own person as community*, just as much as they have responded to destabilizing actions against the greater communities—nations—which they lead. These self-corrections, being less complex actions, are thus more likely to be taken up in biographic narrative and then spread more widely in the actions which come to persist as etiquette. Those, who through persistent self-correction, have risen to be great leaders, retain a deep and lasting appeal to us as models.

Etiquette is not confined to very simple gestures. The earlier suggestion that etiquette originates in a creative act which meets some attempt at destabilization of community, very readily found its illustration in the etiquette of the consistent community of dance, because the experience of dance is carried out at a very physical, very low complexity range of experience. There are much more highly complex acts of creative response, which may still be called etiquette, only of a very complex kind.

One of these would be the variations of rules of order which are now universally a part of the meetings of commercial corporations. Such rules of order do not necessarily originate exclusively in the history of communities of the commercial corporation, and in many cases the history of their first use would be difficult to trace. Nonetheless, they are clearly creative responses to inconsistent destabilizing action on the part of some member or members of a community, e.g., the principle of the quorum has arisen in the depths of time as a response to the attempt by members of a community to constrict the will and purpose of the community in the interpretation of its chosen goal, by temporarily removing themselves from active participation in the community. Taken together, such principles as are to be found in various rules of order, make up signs of complex etiquette, complex etiquette which undergoes further creative development, just as very simple signs of etiquette do, with the difference that the former, being more complex, have the potential for a much longer history that visibly transcends the needs and context, the time boundedness—or "fashionableness"—of the simpler gestures. These models of complex etiquette guide consistent interpretation within and between multiple acting transformable elements, here embodied humans, within communities.

The communities of the uncorrected commercial corporation have been and largely still are in their infancy with regard to value. This is why they have adopted the etiquettes of older communities, such as the rules of order, in the main, and present relatively few responses which are obviously uniquely their own. There is no shame in this, for every attempt to make consistent the structure guiding the community is a victory for the development of value in the world process. Having adopted models of reconstructive action from other communities, commercial corporations have already creatively modified them to suit the needs of their own experience.

So, for example, the contemporary business card derives from the calling card, which we may suppose to be a creative response to actions in which someone engages a member of some consistent and well-developed community by offering no more of a sign for interpretation than their own embodied physicality, an attempt at engagement which tends to disrupt the receiving community. In other words, somewhere, sometime, someone "barged in upon" a family or other small community, without warning and thus without taking into account the temporal extension of themselves or the other members of the community, causing considerable disruption. The response by some member of the community has been to creatively formulate the gesture of the calling card, which recognizes that in their temporal extension other members of the community have valuable "lives" as we would say, i.e., they have interpretive linkages to and ongoing interactions with their own living processes and with many other communities, which we ought not to disrupt, causing devaluation.

The calling card then went on to be adopted by members of businesses and commercial corporations according to similar needs, and then to be creatively developed yet further according to the unique needs of the latter, i.e., in response to an engagement within the communities of business and commercial corporation wherein members of the business community who are nonetheless largely strangers to one another suddenly encounter or impose themselves disruptively upon other members of the community. In this way more extensive information has come to be included on the business card. And not only this but in some places, such as Japan, yet further elaborate gestures have been created to accompany the act of giving the business card, gestures which have grown up again as responses to destabilizing responses within the very act of etiquette, which is the giving of the business card. Thus, in Japan, the business card is to be scrupulously clean and in pristine condition, it is to be given in a certain manner with the face toward the receiver, it is to be read before being put into one's pocket, etc.

These then are the ways in which the spirit of **H12** has been and continues to be interpreted, and they can be continually referenced as models of healing response to destabilizing action and developed further according to the need and context of destabilizing actions which assail the community of the commercial corporation. Beyond this we can also creatively postulate models of reconstructive response by imagining the corporate community as subjected to various tests along the lines of "if a member were to take the following destabilizing action, how could it be met with skill and wisdom by a reconstructive action?"

Let's say, for example, that we have a renewed and consistent commercial corporation and we imagine that some member in this community takes actions which constrict the temporal extension of the community by eliminating long-time members of the community. For example, a high-level manager, merely in order to ingratiate himself with the top management of the corporation by slashing costs to increase profitability, begins a ruthless laying off of certain long-serving foremen in his department. Another member witnesses these acts and recognizes their destructive destabilization of the community of the corporation. Given this imagined scenario, what **H12** now suggests to us is to postulate some act on the part of our imagined member, which serves as a creative response to the action of the higher-level manager.

There are a great many healing responses that one could imagine, but I will offer only the following one: the member, through patient and diligent research and interviews, reconstructs and writes the history of the contributions of the very members who have been eliminated, over all the years they were with the corporation, and then promotes and organizes a repository for these and future accounts of the years of service of other members. Such an act would over time promote the consistent expansion of the history of a commercial corporation; it would serve as a guide to new members of the community of the corporation who would be able to interpret their own actions as creative developments of the history of their new community; it would serve as a repository of models of reconstructive response within the community of the corporation with regard to **H12**, because, if taken up, it would eventually record *the very act of our wise imaginary member herself.* It would serve as a basis for further development by virtue of the fact that since those who leave or are eliminated from a commercial corporation often tend to seek out other such communities to join in, the prospect immediately opens up of expanding this corporate history of individual members into a *"genealogy of the cross-fertilization of corporate communities"*; and finally it would potentially become a more complex "rule" of etiquette of corporate membership, i.e., *a strongly consistent community of the commercial corporation will always take care to preserve a record of the contribution of each of its members, from the simplest to the most complex.*

One can see then that both through historic exemplification and through imaginative postulation, **H12** is interpretable to the activity of the commercial corporation. I leave the reader to follow this out further at her pleasure, and consider it adopted.

H13 Reconstruction

H13 tells us: *in correcting hyperthematic structures, borrow from other stable structures, and in particular look to those hyperthematic structures guiding stable communities whose degree of focus complements the emphasis of the structure under correction.* The evidence that this hypertheme is interpretable to the corporation is all around us in the ubiquity of the combinations of corporate communities with all human activity, even though those corporations may be inconsistent according to their usual assumptions.

Recall what led me to elaborate this hypertheme earlier: it was the recognition that the military structure as an inconsistent structure had borrowed from the hyperthematic structure of dance. Since, however, dance was close to the military structure in terms of the complexity of the very physical problematic which it engages, I postulated that the principle could be expanded to address those ways in which structures could complement one another. Thus to take a simple example, the scene of a narrative, e.g., a story, could be choreographed as a dance and set with music so as to combine the structures of narrative, dance, and music, into ballet.

But the problematic of cooperation is a very broad problematic, as broad as: "how can we cooperate to engage experience at any selected complexity of experience?" No surprise then that corporations, even as inconsistent, have joined themselves with many other types of activity according to their consistent postulate of cooperation, even as, according to their inconsistent symmetric assumption, they have often despoiled what they have touched. Yet it is also clear that the inconsistent structure of the corporation has been stabilized by its borrowings from other structures. If you ask what elements actors in communities of the commercial corporation engage, one could reply "embodied humans and various products which are extensions of that embodiment" and so far one would be correct. Business and the activities of commercial corporations begin in producing, accumulating, and trading furs, stones, logs, cattle, and so on and on, or in ferrying embodied humanity on a ship, on a wagon, and so forth.

And yet there are far more fluid elements being engaged within the realm of corporate activity, such as *numbers*, which can be said to have been borrowed from elsewhere, and there are ways of interpreting those elements which have also been borrowed from elsewhere. In the context of our interpretation of **H13**, this is the stabilization which the corporation receives from the structure of mathematics. Mathematics has come to accompany commercial corporate activity from early on, in the various practices of accounting, bookkeeping, statistical research, and engineering calculations, which aid manufacturing activities, and in which the low-level value of quantity constricted to the cumulative act of counting in the specious present can be expanded through various mathematical techniques.

Thus, where corporations have historically begun by producing quantities of products that may be valued according to mere counting, mathematics has over time been enlisted to undertake much more interesting and valuable interpretations with regard to these mere quantities. So for example, fluctuations of quantities produced from year to year or month to month can be interpreted through mathematical methods, or the optimal curvature of some component part of a complex product being manufactured for a particular task can be calculated, or the ongoing expense of a loan, or the growth rate of the users of a given service—e.g., a ferry service—can be interpreted far into the future. All of these stabilize the activity within the communities guided by the hyperthematic structure of the corporation. They allow some aspect of experience within the corporate community to be interpreted to some other aspect of experience. They allow the community of the corporation to view itself as something far larger than the specious present, something whose complexities of cooperative value creation give it an appeal, which holds it together despite the inconsistency of the further assumption that its members cling to so long as the structure remains uncorrected.

So communities of the commercial corporation have certainly borrowed from communities under other structures. Because of the nature of the core hypertheme of the hyperthematic structure of the corporation, commercial corporations have been able to borrow from mathematics—which itself engages a very broadly complex range of experience, from arithmetic to calculus and beyond—at many ranges of complexity. The principle that we ought to cooperate in order to solve a problematic of experience, knows no limits with regard to the potential complexities at which it may be applied. On the other hand, with regard to the second aspect of what **H13** suggests—that communities under a structure borrow from other structures whose complexity complements their own—we will better be able to interpret **H13** by musing upon some examples at the various degrees of complexity which a commercial corporation might engage.

Let the company be one that ferries passengers in some way so that the passengers have to pass through an area in which they embark and disembark, e.g., a subway system or bus service. What **H13** suggests is that the transportation company borrow from the communities under a more harmonic structure at a similar level of complexity. Since in this case that level of complexity is around the range of human embodiment, given that the passengers are average embodied humanity, then the transportation company might well borrow from communities of dance. Are there types of dances of the nature of some of the Eastern European Slavik dances, for example, in which small or medium numbers of people move about one another in very fluid ways, ways which are much more fluid than the relatively unguided mass movements within the embarkation zones of contemporary passenger services? If we find such exemplifications of physical level harmony of movement, we ought to be able to apply them to the above. If it be objected: "yes, but the participants in the dance are both skilled and guided by choreography, dance leaders, and so forth," then my reply is: "this may very well be, but sustained musement will certainly find ways to interpret the action harmonizing principles of the dance to the embarkation zone experience, whether it be through the direct guidance of leaders within the zone, the creation of colored walkways that guide commuters through dance like interactions, and so forth."

Humans dance because dancing is a harmonic expansion of physical levels of interpretation. This harmonic expansion, when applied to other regions of experience, cannot help but render certain ways of engaging that experience more appealing. If, in our applied borrowing, we open the region of experience up to new ranges of interpretation, at least as a new *option* of engagement, then at least some of the listless, shuffling, head down, group of contemporary commuters are bound to try and adopt the expansive suggestion. Interest will grow from there.

Let us take another case in which the complexity of experience is beyond the physical range. Let there be, for example, a commercial corporation whose business is to gather census data for government or research uses. The elements which such a corporation works with are more within the range just beyond that of physical embodiment, i.e., the corporation works with signs of human action that are more complex than mere physically embodied action as such, e.g., the guiding relations between members of a family, their types of employment, their education levels, etc. In this case, what **H13** again suggests is to look to communities guided by a hyperthematic structure engaging a range of experience similar in complexity to that engaged by our census corporation, and borrow from them. Let's say that the communities of narrative operate at a similar level, the question then becomes: what can our census corporation borrow from communities of narrative?

The collection of census data often seems a particularly sterile experience. One is asked for various facts in a way which seems largely unconnected and which is to be provided—on the part of the census subject—as a mere accumulation of quantity of facts. But if we are borrowing from communities of narrative, we might borrow the tendency of narrative to interpret its facts—the signs which are its words—into larger, more complex, more valuable, wholes of meaning. So for example, the census subject might be guided to weave together the various facts of the census into a narrative-like account; or she could be given the option of viewing the various facts of her situation in narrative relation—and the census corporation would undertake this after collecting the census data—to her own past contributions to the census project, so as to be able to view her own "life story" relative to the census data; or again she might be given the option of viewing this life story relative to the life stories of others; or again she might be given the options of interpreting herself, or at least sharing in such an interpretation, of her own life story as a contribution to the history—in a national census—of the growth and life of the country.

All of these as well as other variations are possible in applying **H13** to the range of experience in question and all of them transform the mere accumulation of data of the life experience into something more valuable, akin to biography, by borrowing from the consistent assumptions of communities of narrative. The above examples are enough to show that **H13** is indeed interpretable, and so we adopt it.

H14 and **H15** Reconstruction

The hyperthemes **H14** and **H15** are once more closely allied and so I will consider them together. **H14** tells us that: *as the range and degree of the transformable elements of a hyperthematic structure increase in complexity such that its models of action harmonization allow interpretations which pass on signs of meaning as a type, it tends to draw the elements of a community engaged in it away from the locus of attachment in the time process which marks the beginning of the range of its problematic of experience, toward a homogenous appraisal of that problematic. Such a structure will be called a <u>leader structure</u>*.

Subsequently, I suggested that a given hyperthematic structure has a maximal interpretable range—abstractedly speaking—only part of which is filled out, or interpreted into, by its acting transformable elements. Hence, a relatively less developed leader structure of far greater complexity than a given lower structure will have a tendency to expand the interpretive freedom of that lower structure more readily than a hyperthematic structure which is of only slightly greater complexity than the lower structure would. This is because, though the structure which is only slightly greater than the one being led, could, in principle, entirely encompass the interpretive freedom of the structure being led, nonetheless it would need to be more or less *completely* developed in order to do so. An analogy: a small hot tub (leader structure of only slightly greater complexity) will have to be more nearly full to easily fill a standard bathtub (given lower structure being led), whereas a swimming pool (leader structure of far greater complexity) will only have to be a little full, i.e., "developed," to do so.

And thus **H15** adds that: *hyperthematic structures are best supported, i.e., their communities of interpretation are stabilized, by hyperthematic leader structures whose complexity is furthest from their own. Although in principle any structure with a level of complexity higher than the structure in question could act as a leader structure, nonetheless, according as there is a tradeoff between complexity and the time process situatedness of the acting element, then the leader structure which will be able to give the best support is that which is both well developed, and whose complexity is not so far removed as to saturate the interpretive freedom of the supported structure.*

How can we interpret the community of the corporation to these two closely allied hyperthemes regarding leader structures, how can corporate communities be engaged by leader structures so as to find expansions of meaning? The question has three sides which signify a challenge for diverse communities. In the first place, highly complex consistent structures can engage with the structure of the corporation, that is, communities under such structures can "reach down" to help and support the corporate structure. In the second place, communities under the corporate structure can seek help from such leader structures, by "reaching up" to them according to a respectful attitude which welcomes help. In the third place, communities under the suggested renewed and consistent corporate structure, can themselves reach down as a leader structure in aid of the cooperative engagements of other structures.

Regarding the first, I noted that mathematics has a history of association with corporations. One may postulate that the future of this leadership is bound up with the ability of the communities of mathematics to reconstitute, reinvent, and reenvision the static abstractions of the object, the assumption of which renders the structure of the corporation inconsistent in its current form, into the terms of interpretable processes. For example, this might take the technical form of the reenvisionment of objects as loci of interpretable functions according to fluid dynamics, which models such processes as the behavior of liquids, traffic flows, or weather patterns. To the extent that this can be done, the corporation as a community and each of its members will be granted the expansive vision of their greater and lesser interpretive goals. Suppose the region of the problematic were to be a particular sickness which besets humanity, e.g., cancer, then the leadership of mathematics might present the goal as the process of the cure of that sickness. Any such expansion toward an interpretive goal will help the members of the community of the corporation to correct the inconsistent postulate of *the drug as the object which is sought.*

If we have not cured cancer, it may be because we have moved ever farther from the interpretation of it, toward its objectification. If my account is plausible, then sicknesses, as other problems, are not "cured" by objects, they are cured by interpretations. In the absence of interpretation the world may overflow with drugs to no avail, since for many the drug as object will remain a locus of eliminative action to be fought over. There is currently a tendency to objectify diseases rather than seeing them as bound up with the process of life. We might however come to see diseases such as cancer as natural in the context of the process of physical life, precisely as a process involving growth, decay, and so forth, or again, viewed in the context of the process of eating, or of engaging various physical and mental stresses in the world. The effort to cure cancer then, if it be viewed in the context of a function of life in the world, would, as a whole, benefit from, among other things, a mathematical engagement capable of dealing with such complexities, a type of leadership which those cooperating together in corporations can deliberately draw upon. In a later chapter I will offer further musement upon the consistency of the contemporary approach to medicine. Meanwhile, in the context of interpreting the hyperthemes in question, my first suggestion is that the leadership which high-level structures such as mathematics might provide for the corporation is plausibly to be applied here in the context of the life process as diseased.

Yet the lower-level structures can help as well with the larger interpretive goals of the corporation and with the sub-goals within those goals. All such guidance depends upon what tasks at what ranges of complexity are involved in the interpretive goal. If the cooperative task is particularly physical, then music for example will be in a position to lead such a task just as we saw it do for dance. History shows that music has long been a help to communities of cooperative activity, for it can open up our interpretive freedom with regard to the range of our bodies as physical laborers, i.e., interpreters at lower levels of complexity. Let a man beat time on a drum, or begin to chant, or countdown until we should all push together, and there is a multifold increase in what can be accomplished by way of physical cooperation, whether it be in the launching of a ship, or in the building of a pyramid. How this and the leadership of other such structures with regard to the corporation can be applied in new ways remains a rich treasure waiting to be unearthed according to special researches.

Moving to the second point, if other consistent communities are willing to engage with the corporation as its leaders, then it will be to the extent that communities under the corporate structure are willing to move toward the correction of the inconsistent postulate. Without reenvisioning the corporation, we can expect no better than the expansive greediness of the planting of the inconsistency at the heart of the contemporary corporation into the hitherto healthy communities under other consistent hyperthematic structures. *On that road lies the eventual objectification and devaluation of art, literature, science, teaching, and all good and consistent communities, as objects to be bought, sold, and fought over.*

Such a correction can be no mere decision of the leadership of corporations, for hyperthematics suggests that the latter needs reworking to become interpretive leadership. The success of the move to consistency will depend upon its issuing from the acting members of the communities of corporations at all levels of complexity, according to their recognition of themselves as engaged in cooperatively valuating interpretations. Many of us, perhaps the majority now, are members of corporate communities in one way or another. If we are to be consistent, we must turn this from our weakness into our strength. Each can reflect upon himself or herself with the aid of those leadership structures which expand our sense of our own possibilities of interpretation. Practically, this is a matter of asking ourselves: "as a freely willing and acting individual, and given my assumptions, am I engaging in the world in a meaningful way in my work? If not, then could I do so if I were to alter my assumptions?"

Such leadership structures as each of us already engage with, which give us meaning, in contrast with those situations which seem unmeaningful—too often our jobs—offer us the opportunity to interpret to them and stabilize ourselves in the time process parallel sense as communities of selfhood, such that we can then go on to reenvision our assumptions regarding the larger corporate communities that we are members of. So, for example, if I am part of a band, or music group, on the weekends, which seems meaningful, as opposed to my job in the factory on the weekdays, I may well ask why the one is meaningful and the other not and then explore how I can bring the meaning of the former to create value in the latter.

If the first two challenges have been met, then the foundation will have been laid for the third challenge, which is that of the corporation as a consistent structure taking its place as a leader structure with regard to communities of cooperation. The consistent hyperthematic structure of the corporation which gives rise to consistent communities of cooperation ought to serve in the role of leader to cooperative interpretive goals of any level of complexity. It is not so hard to imagine the corporation being reborn as a structure whose primary interpretive goal is to help the communities and members of communities under other hyperthematic structures to cooperate.

What I am suggesting here is that with the correction of inconsistency, the corporation as reworked could become a reconstructive element of the community of communities. Its first task *qua leader*—I will suggest more on this from other angles later—would be to heal the damage already caused by its old inconsistent self, to be available to other communities as that structure which presents the utmost range of cooperation and which thereby expands the interpretive freedom of all other communities *with regard to cooperation* to whatever degree it can.

A suggestion of the first manageable application for any given corporate community of interpretation relative to that task might be that it *act as a mentor to other corporations* engaging ranges of the problematic of cooperation smaller than its own. Thus, rather than a corporation such as Microsoft gobbling up its smaller competitors, it might come to view them not as its competitors at all, but rather as its charges, deserving of care and guardianship because they are engaged in an interpretive goal less complex, but nonetheless allied to its own.

"The world turned upside down!" exclaims the reader. Perhaps, but if the reader is willing to accept the appeal of such a vision and muse further in that direction, then we have made a promising beginning with regard to the interpretation of **H14** and **H15**, far enough certainly to adopt them. I have now completed the interpretive testing of the broadest of the hyperthemes and will pass on to the testing of the less complexly (more physically) interpretable hyperthemes of my earlier chapters on light and art.

7

Expansive Reconstruction of the Hyperthemes of Light and Color

I will now attempt to interpret the hyperthemes formulated in the mode of expansive exploration to the experience of color and light. I will not interpret these hyperthemes in the same order as they were disclosed; the methodology need not be rigid. Due to the nature of light and color—if the earlier interpretations are plausible—as being signs of experience which fill and set the bounds of the range of complexity which we are wont to call physicality and due to the nature of the physical arts as being closely linked to this range of complexity, the reader may notice in the next two chapters a subtle shift in some of the interpretations of the hyperthemes disclosed from these regions of experience. The coming interpretations will often attempt to suggest examples of corrective tendencies to be carried out at or near the very physical level of the manufactured product. This should be all to the good as the philosophical effort in Hyperthematics is to be a pragmatic effort above all, and the ability to engage the simpler complexities of physicality will more readily offer something to anyone who wishes to begin applying the suggestions of this work.

HCl Reconstruction

To begin then, I formulated the Hypertheme of Color as **HCl**: *in order to increase value within regions of experience at the physical range of complexity, make every effort to interpret those regions by means of those colors which tend toward expansion of interpretation by way of their being manifestations of consistent action upon that sign of maximal interpretability at physical complexity which we call light.* In what ways can commercial corporations interpret this hypertheme with regard to the making of various products?

There are several aspects to this. There is the aspect of the selection of experience to be interpreted with regard to the hypertheme; there is the aspect of transformation of the experience with respect to the hypertheme; and there is the aspect of the resultant sign of the interpretation as a product. The community of the commercial corporation may engender expansion of value by abiding by **HCl** with regard to each of these aspects. In other words, the actors of the corporation may *select* initial experiences according to the tendency toward consistent colors, they may interpretively *engage* the transformation of those initial experiences by means of consistent colors and engagements of colors, and finally they may *offer* product signs tending toward consistent colors.

With regard to the first aspect, the interpretability of the selection of experience to be interpreted by the corporation depends upon the color of the experience. This may be the color of the "resource" which is used to manufacture some product, for example. What is the color of the resource which is being used by the actors of the corporation to make its products? If the color of that resource tends toward uninterpretability then the product and its process are going to be affected by the inconsistency which the color manifests. Several examples of such applications will be given, selecting more extreme examples with regard to the inconsistency of color so as to make the best use of limited space.

I begin with an example of a resource whose tendency toward a diminishment of value with respect to color will seem obvious to many: crude oil. Petroleum tends to be variously colored and it tends to be graded by us at least in part according to its color. The oil industry tells us that the lighter colors of crude oil are of higher quality, while the darker colors, and finally black, are of lower quality. But a higher or lower quality of what? In this case, the intent is to transform the petroleum into gasoline because gasoline has a higher energy content per unit volume. The energy content of gasoline is, in other words, its ability to initiate and sustain a process of action within experience, and this ability is greater in gasoline than it is in lower grades of oil. Thus, as a commercial corporation tends toward selecting e.g., a darker colored crude oil, they tend toward inconsistency with regard to **HCl**. In other words, the selection of a relatively uninterpretable experience at some point of a process—we can call it a beginning only through constrictive abstraction—*here* relative to **HCl**, tends toward diminishment with regard to the value achieved by the process with regard to *this* aspect. I.e., insofar as we "begin" our production using crude oil at all, we are beginning on a relatively bad footing with regard to value.

Consequent to that selection, the question becomes: how does the community of the commercial corporation engage the selection? Suppose the commercial corporation in question merely selects the crude oil and passes it on as is. In this case there is little interpretive transformation of the experience with regard to **HCl**,* and at the end of the interpretation the relative uninterpretability of the experience—of the crude oil—remains. In other words, if the extent of the interpretation of the corporation is simply to pump and sell raw crude oil as is, then the product retains the diminishment of value with regard to the color—the badness—of the experience with which it began.

The objection will certainly arise however that "surely, as in the case with crude oil, there are very valuable products which are made from resources whose color tends toward uninterpretability according to your hyperthematic assessment?" I do not disagree with this. Yet according to the hyperthematic viewpoint, such expansions of value arise from some consistent action or actions of interpretation which engaged some other aspect or aspects of experience in the process. A product of the commercial corporation is the result of a great many tendencies of action. For example, an initially inconsistent resource such as crude oil, may be interpreted into a product through so many other consistent tendencies that the result is indeed an expansion of value. We make beautiful things out of oil sometimes. This does not and cannot mean that the constriction of interpretation according to the initial selection of a resource, which is relatively inconsistent with **HCl**, does not remain in the process of the product.

So what do commercial corporations do with crude oil? A corporation that only passes it on as is, passes on a diminishment of value, and its own community and other communities suffer accordingly with regard to value. Another corporate community, which by comparison refines crude oil, transforming its color expansively according to **HCl**—into say gasoline—is creating value *in that respect*, although how fully transformative as opposed to eliminative this refining is will evoke a field for still further valuation or devaluation.[1] Yet another corporate community whose engagement transforms the crude oil still further into yet more colorfully interpretable products— e.g., otherwise safe plastic toys for babies—is creating still greater value. Each of these corporate communities may abide more or less consistently with **HCl**, while also taking some consistent or inconsistent position with regard to other hyperthemes. A commercial corporation that extracts crude

---

*Or with **Hc**.

oil may become more or less consistent insofar as it recognizes consistent relationships with other corporate communities, for example. If a corporate community merely pumping and passing on crude oil moves toward consistent tendencies, recognizing the process of interpretation and its potential connections to other commercial corporations and communities, then it expands itself with regard to value.

Myriad are the products which we derive from crude oil. We can get clues as to their consistency or inconsistency with regard to value by musing upon the transformation toward interpretability with regard to **HCl**. Black roofing shingles are not far transformed with regard to color—or with regard to other uninterpretable aspects—from the original relatively devalued color of the oil which went into them. They retain the uninterpretability of blackness as color. They thus engage the sunlight—an action of relatively high interpretability near the leading edge of the range of maximal interpretability of physical level complexity—in a way which dampens and halts its interpretability. The sunlight is absorbed, trapped, prevented from participating in further process. And this because the roof shingle is interpreted so as to be a barrier halting and trapping process rather than a sign which *guides the process on to further interpretation*. Here the color is only one aspect of the experience, but it combines with other aspects of the experience, e.g., stickiness, in the original crude oil, which are also the result of constrictive tendencies, and which drove the initial choice of crude oil as a material for making—inconsistently and thus unwisely—*a barrier against the process of the sunlight*.

Expansions of value with regard to roofing materials would thus take into account **HCl** among others. One can imagine roofing materials made from resources in ways which expand interpretation according to **HCl**, relative to more uninterpretable initial selections such as crude oil, and thereby tending toward both giving back to the incoming process and passing the action on further, e.g., green living roofs. Yet, you interject: "yes but regardless of transformations of initially selected resources, there are surely *natural* resources at least whose color is relatively uninterpretable according to **HCl**—e.g., the black you used as an extreme example—but which are clearly of greater value than more brightly colored resources?" To that I respond again: *if the resource, or initial experience, has a color which tends toward uninterpretability, then insofar as it does, the hyperthematic suggestion is that <u>somewhere</u> within the process which arrived at the sign, constrictive action according to inconsistent tendencies has been carried out.*

We may or may not be interpretively aware of this constrictive action, depending on our knowledge of a selected area of nature, but it is there in the process. In the case of crude oil our best current knowledge tells us that it was formed through the *death* and *decay* of animal processes, that the death and decay particularly *gathered* into certain locations, that the movements of the Earth's crust *enclosed* and *squeezed* this decayed organic matter, and finally that these areas under the earth's crust have remained *dormant* and *static* for long geological ages. All of these are so many constrictive tendencies of action which result in the various uninterpretable aspects of crude oil, including its color.

Why nature undertakes such actions there is not the space here to suggest, although the beginnings of the answer occur readily enough through hyperthematic musement upon the character of the natural world as an often inconsistent engagement of interpretability at physical ranges of complexity by the living processes within it—e.g., by ourselves in human embodiment. The more uninterpretable regions of the experience of nature are the result of the inconsistent tendencies of action of the processes within it in their "natural" aspects. In other words, where the process of nature as a part of the world process has gone wrong through the actions of its component processes—its plants, animals, chemical interactions, etc.—the dramatically visible "red in tooth and claw" is but one small aspect of this "badness" of uninterpretability as it manifests itself. Animals and other processes in nature kill one another, just as we do, inconsistently with **H**. The blackness of crude oil is the result of some combination of such tendencies.

Other examples readily present themselves. We value black soil very highly for our human agricultural purposes. **HCl** tells us, however, that, at least in this aspect of interpretability with regard to color, lighter colored soils will be indicative of and conducive to greater interpretability and thus value. This will immediately appear counterintuitive according to current agricultural knowledge until it is remembered both that our current human agricultural purposes are very constricted with regard to overall value, very often seeking mere numerical extension of sameness, e.g., mere bulk of some monoculture food crop as a weak aspect of value, and that a far greater value of plant growth according to diverse aspects is achieved by nature in the red and yellow red soils of the tropical rain forests whose processes are far more consistently engaged and fluid.

We find that the colors of natural foodstuffs abide by **HCl**, and that when nutrition is more broadly conceived as overall value of interpretability in eating and in sustaining processes in embodiment, then as the colors of foodstuffs tend toward interpretability—lighter greens, lighter yellows, whites—the food, when eaten, tends to impart more overall value to the embodied process: thus the white of the potato, of the rice, of the banana, and so forth, have a higher value for the living process than that of their outer coverings, and a higher value than the dark green vegetables; the white of fat has higher value than the red of meat; eggs and milk rise above all others in value in the realm of non-vegetable foodstuffs.

The relatively dark-colored foodstuffs—e.g., the dark green vegetables, liver, etc.—may very well have greater value in *some particular* aspect of nutrition, but this is always a directed and constricted value, the result of an action which engages some region of inconsistency in the care and sustenance of the process as embodied, some inconsistency which has arisen through various inconsistent actions, not least a static sameness in the nourishment of the embodied process, e.g., a vitamin C deficiency from eating too much of meat and grains alone. We value the dark green vegetables most as a directed restorative of the health process after we have already begun to make ourselves sick through inconsistencies in interpreting that process. But for sustaining the greater process the white foodstuffs—egg, milk, potato, etc. are far more valuable.

I will forego an expansive discussion of particular examples of the interpretation of **HCl** with regard to a valuation of color of *refined* foodstuffs, such as the whiteness of refined table sugar. To do this properly would require a sustained musement upon the various stages of refinement of food products in order to elaborate upon the various inconsistent assumptions that are part of every process which attempts to refine into some desired quantity of sameness.

The various suggestions already given however, along with those to come, should make evident to the reader that all attempts at refinement toward a mere quantity of some desired aspect of experience—here within the experience of a foodstuff—are inconsistent to some degree. In the case of a foodstuff such as table sugar, the various stages of refining introduced into the "processing" of the originating naturally valuable food experience—the white center of the living sugarcane plant—tends to lessen the original multifaceted value of the foodstuff into the constricted avenue of mere quantity in some one or few aspects. This devaluation always manifests itself in some aspect of the experience of the foodstuff as being processed. In some stages of the processing the aspect which is undergoing devaluation may be interpretable through **HCl**, e.g., the white pith of the sugarcane plant turns brown. In other stages of the processing—or perhaps simultaneously—the aspect undergoing devaluation may be interpretable through some other of our hyperthemes, e.g., sugarcane juice is rendered sticky.

In any case, the sum of consistent and inconsistent tendencies of action upon the originating region of experience—the natural foodstuffs—come together at any moment of the process to manifest in one way or another how the product stands as a sign of value, so that even if—e.g., in the bleaching of table sugar—an effort is made to "cover up" the inconsistent tendencies which have contributed to the sign, nonetheless the devaluation which has infected the process will emerge somewhere, e.g., in the effect which the accumulation in quantity of some aspect has upon the health of the human body. I have gone far enough however to suggest that this seemingly difficult hypertheme **HCl** is readily adoptable by the actors of the community of the commercial corporation in the various stages of their process of cooperative production, and to consider it adopted for our new structure.

HCr Reconstruction

I formulated the Hypertheme of Creativity, **HCr**, as follows: *in order to create experience, engage in interpretations which insofar as possible interpret a portion—an existent fact—of experience within the world process to a portion of experience within the world process which does not include the original portion within itself.* The field of action over which the community of the commercial corporation applies this hypertheme to engage experience, so as to diminish or increase value, can be best viewed in the tendency of copying. Moreover, copying can be viewed—at least in contemporary terms—in at least two ways, namely, with regard to tendencies of mass production and tendencies of copycat product manufacturing.

Mass production moves an item linearly along a production line, with a human actor—or a robotic machine as an extension of a human actor—making small changes, additions, or removals, from what has come to him or her, until the item moves on to the next actor in the line. Nor is it an accident that we have an assembly *line*, for the goal of the tendency which has given rise to mass production, aims to eliminate "unnecessary" time and action from the process which arrives at the product. Yet every elimination of facets of interpretation at physical ranges of complexity tends to move away from the curvatures of three and four dimensions toward two dimensions of linearity. The inconsistent assumptions thus tend toward a mere linear series in which an experience is repeated again, and again, and again.

The consequent diminishment of value can be uncovered from various viewpoints with respect to the action of the community engaged in mass production, including that of the worker, that of the product, and that of the owner or manager of the corporation. Thus the worker in the line takes some action with regard to a product which comes along the line to her. But as the range of motion of the worker tends to be minimized, and as the time for the worker's action upon the product tends to be limited to as short a time as possible, the action-experience of the worker tends to be repetitious. In other words, taking the worker's experience of acting at the assembly line—the *state of the worker* if you will—as the experience being interpreted to the future state of the worker, one sees that the experience is very much being interpreted to a portion of experience within the world process—the future state of the worker—which *does* include the original experience within itself. That tendency is inconsistent with **HCr**, and the result is a palpable diminishment of value on many levels. The body begins to break down under the stresses of repetitive motions, for example, and likewise the psychological state is disvalued.

A similar diminishment of value occurs with regard to the product resulting from the activity of the corporate community. Moving down the assembly line, the product is added to or taken away from by each worker. It *tends* never to be modified with regard to what was done to it by the previous worker however. The original portion of the product, which was bequeathed to a worker by her predecessor in the line, remains, at the end of the interpretation carried out by that current worker. On an assembly line you don't mess with what somebody else has already done; this is supposed to be the point of efficiency. At the end of the line, the result is a group of copies of the product—the product in its mass aspect, an experience of the product as mere extension constricted to linearity: another one and another one and another one.

Compare this to an artwork. When we saw this in the artwork of the ancient Egyptians we also saw the result with regard to value. When the tendency formulated in **HCr** is ignored, we get schools of art such as that of the ancient Egyptians, which are akin to the products of mass production. The more interesting and valuable artwork has become, however, the more the tendency has been to interpret an experience so as to move away from the original experience.

The diminishment also surfaces at other levels. Not only does a run of products become a series of copies of one another, but frequently the series itself becomes the origin of a further series which includes the original product experience without modification. So, for example, a series of cell phones or cars will be produced, only to be followed by another mass-produced series, which takes the older series mostly unmodified and carries it into the "new" product experience.

Since the product is also intimately bound up with the participation of other acting transformable elements in the community of the commercial corporation, i.e., those who buy the product, the diminishment of value carries over to the buyer's experience of the product. The result is a product experienced in a diminishment of interpretation by the buyer. Each one who buys the product draws closer in sameness to every other buyer of the product. The constriction of value built into the product, through the process of its making, is transferred to each one who accepts the product, tending to turn all buyers into a merely linearly quantifiable group or collection of sameness, rather than a community. Each buyer tends moreover to become a sameness with regard to his or her old self as well with regard to other selves. Thus, the community of selfhood of the buyer is devalued.

I suggested earlier that all diminishments of value through constriction of interpretation within a selected region give rise to a "pressure"—as with the rules of the Egyptian artists—with regard to action. If the ultimate hypertheme **H** holds, then expansive interpretation must proceed however, and if transformable elements are constricted they will find a way around the constriction. The buyer as transformable element, as a member of the community of the commercial corporation, must find a way around the constriction. Since the constriction of the product passes on its diminishment of value to the buyer, as a reduction to a series of repetitions in the linear aspect of quantity, then insofar as it has—insofar as the buyer *accepts* the inconsistency in the sign which she receives—the pressure toward the needed expansion of interpretation has only one avenue to take. It gives rise to an *accumulation* of the product by the buyer, an amassing—literally *a massing* through linear repetition—of the product. When I have more of the product with regard to what I had, when I have more of it with regard to what you have, when I have more of the series *qua* series than I had—a "newer version" (think cell phones)—and when I have more of the series than you have—a "newer version than you"—then I will have acted in one of the few ways which remain open to me insofar as I accept the inconsistencies built into the sign of the mass product. These contemporary ways of viewing value are thus driven by the devaluation within the product.

Services can be produced according to assumptions of mere quantitative expansion, just as well as objects. Pop stars, Hollywood stars, sports stars, and their relation to mere quantitative expansion, all exemplify services, very often provided by commercial corporations, being engaged inconsistently according to **HCr**. This is why the distinctions between object and person often appear to blur in such people; they become objects by holding a relationship of sameness to large numbers of other people. This interpretation of sameness, not getting far beyond mere numerical diversity, engenders the mere quantitative expansion by which the experience of a pop star is valuated, and gives rise to a person as an object bound up with a great deal of money as mere quantity, the latter accumulated through the small monetary valuations of a vast multitude—another and another and another—to each of whom the pop star is an objectified sameness. The valuation is thus very weak, and one can feel this very easily according to how broad one's interpretive capacity is. It is no accident that the contemporary stars esteemed by the masses are often described in various terms that cluster around *shallowness*. That feeling is the feeling of the weak value of the interpretive relationship of the objectified person to those—the mass of fans—who participate in the sameness of interpretive actions, which are bound up with the devaluation toward objectification.

If we can remember that constriction toward quantity is nonetheless a mere tendency in which the efforts of some communities of the commercial corporation are more or less inconsistent, then we have a fairly plausible explanation for a great many of the ills surrounding the production carried out by contemporary commercial corporations. It is not that this is a reduction to mere quantity as is often suggested with regard to these ills; it is that the aspects of the quantity are reduced in the physical range from quantity of curvature to quantity of linearity. Thus the quantity suffers as the quality, and indeed it has been suggested all along, though not explicitly, that quantity and quality are simply designations of the ranges of tendencies of interpretation and interpretability of experience as either diminishing or increasing—or diminished or increased—relative to the range, in this case of physicality.

So as one decreases quality by eliminating aspects of interpretation, one begins to approach the mere copies, merely another and another and another of the same, which we in our current age designate quantity; and as quantity is increased by expanding aspects of interpretation, so that the product—the experience—begins to vary from its predecessor, its progenitor, in various aspects, one begins to approach that uniqueness with regard to multiple aspects of interpreted experience that we designate as its quality, well expressed in the phrase "it has a certain quality about it."

More is always better *relative to a selected complexity of experience*, but if it is more according to a diminished aspect or aspects of experience which result in a repetition of sameness, it is one of the very weakest designations of better as quality, and if we have come down to it from the engagement of a diversity of aspects of experience, then, *as a constriction relative to that part of the range* it tends to be worse. For the worker it is worse, a diminishment of diversity of experience of the embodied life process, which, viewed as the process in its physical range of complexity, is being constricted from three and four dimensions of active interpretive engagement into two. And it is worse for the buyer of the product as a participant in the community. And finally, it is worse for the managers and owners of the community of the commercial corporation.

Despite the inconsistency giving rise to the aforesaid accumulation of money, it has always been assumed, as I noted earlier, that managers and owners *at least* benefit from the commercial corporation, even if workers and buyers of products might not. The dream of the accumulation of riches is based—unconsciously—upon the assumption that *through* the tendency toward accumulation, a point in the process can be reached which allows those who have accumulated the most to "leapfrog" out of the linear series of repetitive accumulation, out of what is mistakenly assumed to be an experience of quantity as an independent aspect of experience, into an experience of quality (as an independent aspect also).

But again, from our hyperthematic view, quantity and quality are merely labels of the range of interpretation of the process in its consistency and inconsistency. The inconsistency, which gives rise to the accumulation of great wealth as quantity in its merely linear aspect, *spreads out and diminishes value wherever it is accepted* by human actors in the mere group which is human society. Where it is not accepted the tendency is indeed toward expansion of value in products, products of community, but insofar as it is not accepted then the value imbued within these consistently *created* products *is not available* to those human actors who have great wealth insofar as they have accumulated it through the foregoing inconsistent tendencies toward the repetitive linear series.

Either the value in the form of products is, in the first place, *literally not available to the accumulators of wealth*, or in the second place *it is acquired on the terms of the inconsistency which gave rise to the linearly repetitive accumulation*, a mode of acquisition which always defeats the intent.

In the first place, *insofar as* there is interpretive creativity consistent with **HCr** in us, each of us does what we love to do—i.e., we interpret expansively relative to the selection of signs available to us, and we shun the inconsistent milieu of constriction to the repetitive linear series indicated in mere accumulation. To take an extreme, but an illustrative one, the vast majority of us would not give up the creative process of expansive interpretation of experience which arises in the community of the family with the care and guidance of our children, *for any accumulation of money*: we would not sell our children. The products of the commercial corporation are far removed from this, and yet each of us, according to his or her capacities, engages some region of experience so as to create something, some "product," which he or she would not part with for any accumulation of mere money offered by the accumulators of wealth.

In the second place, the *ethical capacity* of the accumulator of great wealth—i.e., that *interpretive capacity* which I expanded upon hyperthematically in the chapter on art—is, through the very tendency of inconsistency which accumulates the wealth, not broad enough to interpretively span the sign of value which is acquired, i.e., to reinterpret it expansively in various consistent ways. There is no free ride to value. Each only enjoys what he creatively contributes to.

Many products of great creative value—e.g., great artworks—do indeed find their way into the hands of the accumulators of wealth. But they tend to do so as products acquired rather than interpreted, where they sit relatively *uninterpreted*, until exchanged under the terms of mere accumulation for other merely accumulative new acquisitions, finally until such time as they are freed by the world process to participate once more in the regions of expansive interpretations, e.g., in museums.

Often enough those whose assumptions lead to mere accumulation of riches do not even make any pretense at the acquisition of products of great creative value, as judged by the common capacity of interpretation, even *if* as mere acquisitions of accumulation. They settle for the mere shocking accumulations of extravagant gaudiness. We have all heard tales of gold-plated toilets, 80-foot limousines, the mixing of 150-year-old wines with soda pop, in short of the degradation of the accumulations of the nouveau riche below even the accumulations of old money. In this degradation the ethical capacity is so constricted by the assumptions in question that even the sense that the value which one manipulates under the terms of acquisition is a value *because* it has been expansively interpreted by others—e.g., through a da Vinci's creative genius and then through the ages by others who have reinterpreted that creation yet further—is lost.

What I am suggesting here is that the owners, or "top players" of commercial corporations can do no better from a process infected with inconsistency than other members "lower down," for the devaluations due to the inconsistencies radiate outward into the world process, further diminishing value, making it unavailable to the top players and restricting the ability of those top players to access the value in the world process. In short, tendencies of action according to inconsistent assumptions make the world a less valuable place, so that the effect of the diminishment turns back upon those threads of process which initiated it, prompting them to correct themselves.

The acquiescence with repetition in the process of production, which looks to a time beyond that process for value, finds there only the conditions manifesting the same tendencies which diminished value in the process. It cannot be otherwise if the world is consistent as a world of value, as this work supposes. In other words, if I am a worker in an assembly line and I am willing to put up with the repetition which devalues my time at work in the hope that my salary—the mere measured accumulation of value as linear quantity—and my time off of work can somehow make up for this, then I am mistaken. The very devaluation spreads itself through my surroundings.

This applies no less to the buyer of the product and to the manager or owner who *mis*-leads the community into tendencies of diminishment. The owner or CEO of the corporation, who accumulates weak monetary value by tendencies devaluating the other communities around him, cannot hide in his "gated community," for eventually the devaluation he creates in the world process beyond his little "pocket" of value reacts back upon him. As in the earlier analogy, the effort to pile up the hill of water in the bathtub fails, and the "hill" collapses back to replenish the diminished bathwater, so that the "gated community"—as history has well shown—always falls through the devaluation in the society collapsing around it.

Each of the above thus "reap what they sow" through the effects of the diminishment of value on the greater community, which tend to reduce it to a society, a mere group, a mere quantity in the contemporarily misunderstood sense of that term. Yet, if all of this is plausible, I still have to suggest ways in which the hypertheme can be interpreted to the actors of the community of the commercial corporation. The three types of engagement of the corporation just noted can guide us to some of these ways.

Creativity and the Worker

We can abide by **HCr** more if we can bring into play actions of interpretation which modify the original experience received by the worker in a way that tends away from that original experience. In other words, each further experience of the worker with regard to the product should tend toward having experience within it, which, having noted the earlier experience, interprets it in a modifying response to that experience, rather than merely letting it be, unmodified.

Imagine an assembly line in which each member on the line has a collection of blocks, e.g., eight-point standard Lego blocks. The first member of the line places a block on the line. Each subsequent member of the line has various options open. Under the assumptions inconsistent with **HCr**, which give rise to mass production, a member of the line may simply add a block to the one received. If an extra block is simply added directly atop the earlier block in the same orientation, the result, as we move along the assembly line, will be an increase of mere quantity in the aforementioned constricted sense—a linear increase. This is a relatively extreme diminishment of value with regard to *what might be done* in the physical range of experience. But there are many cases of contemporary commercial production which approximate this extreme nearly enough, and such extremes will topple, as I suggested in the chapter on light and color, because the world process meets linear repetition by encouraging spatial curvature.

Again a member may simply remove a block, but the assumptions which give rise to mass production discourage it, i.e., no one will remove a block placed by someone else—counter the "rules" of efficiency. Moreover, while eliminatory modification would indeed modify the original experience, it tends toward inconsistency according to the other hyperthemes. At any point in the assembly line, removing a block removes the possibilities of interpretation with regard to that block for all members further up the line. Though I did no more than imply it in the chapter on art, this is what happens as a result of assumptions toward minimalism, in e.g., modern art.

But let's say now that we adopt other assumptions than those which give rise to mass production, interpretive actions which modify the original experience of the block. What sorts of interpretive actions could we make? While keeping the same orientation, we might begin to vary the placement of subsequent Lego blocks so as to not be directly atop the former block, i.e., to open up a range of interpretation in a second aspect, curvature in two dimensions, as our earlier drawing of a curve on paper. In this case we work with the guidance of the world process as well. While keeping the same orientation we might also begin to vary the placement of subsequent Lego blocks so as to be displaced from the top of the former block in two directions, i.e., to open up a range of interpretation in a third aspect, curvature in three dimensions.

We might begin to vary the placement of subsequent Lego blocks with regard to orientation as well, i.e., opening a range of interpretation in a further aspect, curvature in four "dimensions" (aspects). We tend not to look at this as four dimensions, because we have the habit of selecting three aspects of experience as a working attitude and constricting our interpretations so as to conform to this attitude. But the result of that habit, once more, is simply the uneasy "dividing line" between quantity and quality. *There is no such dividing line.* Modifying the orientation of our Lego blocks—even more so if they were not merely blocks—in addition to other expansive actions, will result in something like a curve within a curve, e.g., as one making a great curve of a coiled spring.

But this tendency, which at a still relatively low level of expansion of interpretation results in a curve within a curve, is toward quality. In other words, the fourth dimension, or fourth aspect, of interpretation, and all subsequent aspects, is no longer viewed by us as quantity—due to our habit of holding to the constrictive assumptions of three dimensions of space—but rather, as quality within physical complexities of experience. Or again, it adds to the experience a meaning which is inexplicable if we try reducing it back toward the relatively constricted meaning and value of quantity. Quality is definable as: *that which we feel as going beyond quantity, according to our capacities of interpretation which arise from our tendencies to willingly hold and act upon constrictive inconsistencies, even as that going beyond accepts the expanded possibility of those fluid principles of interpretation which let us maneuver through that willingly constricted range which we label quantity as such.*

So far we have imagined modifying three aspects of the original experience of the block. Beginning with the original experience, we changed the experience, displacing it in various ways, but we have not yet begun to modify the Lego block itself, so to speak. It could be modified as to color by choosing subsequent blocks of different colors to add, and even the original Lego block could be modified by painting it a different color. If we went further, the very shape of the block could be modified, e.g., if it were flexible or malleable to varying degrees. Insofar as each of these ranges of modification is made available, the potential for value in the worker's experience is increased.

You may now say: "if we introduce all of these expansive ranges of action into manufacturing, what hope have we to ever arrive at some product which we want? Won't the result of our efforts be a hopeless mishmash of modification and counter modification, a monstrosity of production?" I answer: in the first place the creation of the product must still tend to abide by the other hyperthemes, if it is to be consistent, and in the second place the suggestion is that we at least view the issue in a consistent way so as to make a practical beginning. If we set the goal of the product as a range or series of ranges, we are open to allowing considerable latitudes of interpretive freedom over what we now allow. I have deliberately used the medium of building blocks as an example so as to be able to carry the analogy to the play of children. Children do not usually engage in mass production—*even despite* the recent devaluing trend toward series of movie tie-ins—when they play with Legos. They create and they create the strangest and most interesting things, each one unique and each one expressing the capacities and interests of the child at the time. And if you put children on our imagined assembly line of building blocks, they would turn out a wide range of valuable and interesting "products"; suggesting that they make a boat, you would get a thousand interesting and unique variations on a boat.

And just as they could be for children, the ranges of interpretation promoted in production can be tailored according to the interpretive capacity of the worker. There may be certain ranges which we choose to keep under relatively tighter parameters—e.g., engine components of a car—but this is never a *necessity, except it be a necessity based upon some constrictive assumption held to in another region of experience*, e.g., how fast we think a car ought to go, how far it ought to go, what governmental restrictions we have imposed upon ourselves, and so forth. That such necessities are self-imposed is clear enough upon observing what we actually do more broadly. If you approach a group of engineering students and ask them to build a solar car, you get a range of interesting and unique designs within the parameters you are willing to set.

The point is to promote creativity within the interpretations—here at physical levels of complexity—of the actors of the community of the corporation. The more this can be achieved, the more value there is within the process of activity which is occurring within the community of the corporation. And the more value there is within that process, the less such actors will be satisfied with the current state of affairs which looks for the value *outside* of the process in a way that cannot free itself from the very tendencies toward diminishment of value that infect the process of production itself. The children and engineering students imagined will enjoy creating; for an expansion of value by **HCr**, all "workers" must be given such opportunities, according to their interpretive capacities.

Creativity and the Buyer

If the product is interpretively expanded in such ways, it inspires the next member of the community, the buyer, to interpretive expansion. The applications of **HCr** by the buyer are going to be all those engagements of members of *other* communities by the buyer according to *the buyer's experience of the transfer of the product fashioned by the other members of the commercial corporation to himself or herself.* The latter is the *original* experience of the buyer, *qua* buyer, and when it is creatively engaged according to **HCr** so as to be modified through interpretation, it arrives at new experiences of this transfer of the product.

In the first place the product comes with a much greater degree of uniqueness and this uniqueness corrects the tendency to merely value the product in the constrictive quantitative sense. Let me put it another way. You need to distinguish yourself from me according to your interpretive capacity, and insofar as a product is part of that distinguishing, then if the products we buy are otherwise identical, the only way to effect the distinction is for one of us to have *more* than the other in the constrictive quantitative sense. On the other hand, as the products which we buy begin to be increasingly different from each other, then each of us will be more likely to want to interpret the product of the other according to aspects which move increasingly beyond mere misunderstood quantity. "Mine does this and is like this on this side . . . what about yours?" As we tend in this direction we strengthen the community through mutual interpretation. We often see this very well in communities of hobbyists—e.g., of model trains—in which many aspects of the model trains and their systems are custom-made. The interest, the fun, the value of it, lies in showing the other how you interpreted some relatively interpretable sign of your common area of interest and discovering how the other interpreted it differently.

In the second place, if I receive a product which clearly holds within it the value of an expanded process of interpretation in the sense of **HCr**, then I am much more likely to engage the product as being interpretable in ways which modify the experience which I originally received. The world has taken to computers, because, despite the constrictive shortcomings of their more physical aspects, in the more complex aspects of their programming, operating systems, and so forth, they come to the buyer as reinterpretable to a relatively high degree: programmable, customizable, etc. Conversely to the extent that this reinterpretability becomes damped down and constricted—a situation which increasingly threatens—their value will also diminish toward mere quantitative comparison: whose version of iPad is the next version?

This expansion of interpretability in the product expands the buyer, the user of the product. It guides the buyer out of the low-level comparison of value as a constricted quantification, the "I have more of these than you" viewpoint, into using the product as a foundation for building community. It guides the buyer away from hoarding the product as quantity, toward sharing it in diverse ways, as a basis of further creativity, an "I've managed to do so and so with this, but you're better at x than me, perhaps you could change the y, then we'll ask Jane if she can add one of those z's on after." The great successes of the reinterpretable aspect of computers in programming, and so forth, have come from this effect of expansion and are visible in efforts such as Linux, as communities of expansive interpretation which tend to abide by **HCr**.

Would we have less of everything in promoting this tendency? Certainly, in the constricted quantitative sense we would have less, but the very framing of the problematic in these terms only arises from the inconsistent assumptions, which give rise to this mere quantitative measurement, so that in fact we would have *more of everything in a great many aspects* insofar as we move toward the creative expansion of **HCr**. I leave the reader to imagine further ways of creative sharing of the product by the buyer.

Creativity and the Owners and Managers

We must still apply **HCr** to those members of the community of the corporation who, if consistent, guide the processes of action of the community into more complex and expansive processes, the owners and managers. I spoke of them earlier and will again shortly with regard to the symmetry of the power structure. Here my concern is just with the applicability of **HCr** to their actions within the corporate community.

The owner/managers are not immune to the diminishment of value infecting activities of the corporation when the inconsistent assumptions behind mass production are countenanced. This is not merely a matter of the loss of, and inability to access, value, in the products and society which surround the owner/manager; it is a matter of a movement away from leadership as a creative expansion of the effort of the community of the corporation into more complex and valuable products and complex and valuable systems of organization. The value of the experience of the worker is constricted, constricting in turn the value of the product, constricting in its turn the value of the experience of the buyer. But all of this subsequently constricts the value of the experience of the owner/manager.

Remember that the owner/manager is at a relatively higher part of the chain with respect to complexity. Insofar as the owner/manager is engaging an original experience which has undergone constriction inconsistent with **HCr**, that original experience is framed in the constrictive quantitative terms, and if not engaged consistently under the tendency of **HCr**—and it very often is not these days—then the result will tend to be an experience of constrictive quantity for the owner/manager. Nonetheless, it will be a *more complex* experience in the only way that it can be, i.e., a complexity inconsistently constricted with regard to the aspects of interpretation which it expands.

But other assumptions, which keep the effort of the members of the community of the commercial corporation within the physical range of complexity of experience, will prevent that more complex experience, already squeezed into the straightjacket of the aspect of mere quantity, from expanding as it otherwise would. In other words, an expansion of mere quantity reaches its limit with regard to our embodiment within the physical range of experience. At lower levels of complexity a worker can translate the constricted process of mere quantity into physical products. At higher levels, a buyer can still translate it into physical products, although the effort becomes more difficult. The sheer quantity of consumer products produced under these inconsistencies begins to give rise to difficulties of storage and of psychology.

When we reach the complexity of experience of the owner/manager, the difficulties begin to become insurmountable. Such value as there is at these higher levels of complexity simply cannot be translated into physical ranges of complexity. They thus tend to become disconnected from our mere embodiment whose home is within those physical ranges. The arising of money as accumulation of mere quantity begins here. It begins historically as an exchangeable physical object, a brick, or stone, or whatnot, often relatively large relative to the scale of human embodiment. As and insofar as the complexity of human efforts increase while holding to the constrictive assumptions behind mere quantification, the physicality of money must give way, first to the fluidity of metals like gold and silver, then to paper and smaller coinage, then to mere numbers. Thus money, as a facilitator of complexities of action which go beyond the usually accepted physical range of experience, begins to give way to money as a mere measure of constrictive quantification. The owner/manager as the member of the community who—ostensibly—engages relatively highly complex interpretations, simply cannot translate them into physical sameness of the original experience. Thus money eventually becomes a number of "pure quantity," in the billions, or trillions even, and the more complex a pure quantity it becomes the more it becomes effectively lost and disconnected from human embodiment at physical ranges of complexity.

The effect of the constriction must radiate outward into the world process however. I suggested in the chapter on light that *increasing power* results from: *a tendency of interpretive action in which interpretive action is directed so as to constrict interpretation in a region of experience in an effort to bring about or propagate that constricted interpretation as an uninterpretable given of experience*. But here in the higher complexities of the commercial corporation insofar as influenced by inconsistent action toward mere constricted quantification, we have such an effort to propagate a relatively uninterpretable given of quantification.

And yet the quantification *is* an interpretation, even though it is, according to its being based upon the constriction to a single aspect of experience, a *very poor* level of interpretation. That being so, we can expect the region of experience within the commercial corporation, insofar as engaged by owners/managers according to a disregard of **HCr**, to be a region in which uninterpretable experience as power is overlaid upon a very low-level interpretation. The result is a *hierarchy of power* according to accumulation. The uninterpretability of the experience stems from the action which amasses experience as mere quantification, applied at the relatively high levels of complexity of the owners/managers. It is an uninterpretability through the tendency of the action, as being repetitively constricted according to one aspect, to pass beyond other aspects of interpretability—here namely the uncountenanced aspects of interpretability of physical experience—so that it can no longer be interpreted to those aspects. This uninterpretability is its "power," and is felt as its power: in this case the power of money.

It retains its interpretability in the one constricted aspect, however, namely the quantitative aspect, giving rise to a range of this power, a hierarchy, in which some part of the range can be measured as more powerful than another part. At varying degrees in the hierarchy, this is the situation in human affairs wherein I may have—i.e., I engage as an experience—so much more money than you, that you can no longer interpret me by means of action within the ranges of physicality.² No action of production, which you can take physically, can interpretively reach the constrictively accumulated quantity—my millions or billions of dollars, as the case may be—which I have acquired. In this way the relative heights of repetitive accumulation presents itself as a power which your actions are *powerless* against *in the terms of the hierarchy of accumulation itself*, unless you too embrace the inconsistency and act so as to move up the hierarchy. This is the situation of power in which the owners/managers find themselves relative to workers, buyers, and even one another, insofar as they ignore the tendency formulated in **HCr**.

On the other hand, **HCr** can be applied to correct the situation even for the owners/managers. Efforts to abide by **HCr**, modifying the original experience through an interpretation which arrives at a further experience tending to have less of the original experience, are steps in the right direction. The owners/managers can do this in various ways depending upon the original experience they are dealing with. The experience at the level of a worker is limited largely to the physical ranges of embodiment. At the various levels of complexity of management it is an experience of signs of complex embodiment, namely of the actions of multiple workers. The foreman, for example, has the experience of some aspect or system of a car, such as the engine, the chassis, and so forth; or perhaps, at a higher level, of the whole car. So the experience is one of a series of parts produced by the efforts of multiple people, where the part is a sign of more or less consistent community—or sub-community viewed from this higher level—of action.

Insofar as **HCr** is applied in some of the ways already suggested, the systems of products or whole products in question have already moved away from being a mere linear repetition of quantitative sameness, so that the task of the manager in abiding by **HCr** is not to modify the system or product experience of the lower-level. Indeed, the manager cannot do this for the sign is the sign of complex community of embodied action, i.e., the car is already the work of many hands and the manager cannot hope to engage it creatively at the level of lone embodiment without falling to lower levels of complexity.

The experience of the manager—that which the manager is acting upon—is a region of human community in embodiment. The creativity, which someone at a complexity of experience of management can weave into the process according to **HCr**, is therefore a creativity with regard to the relations of the community of actions of many working together. The tendency to modify the original is thus going to be the tendency toward *creative modification of these communities of embodied actors*. This is the consistent task of a manager as a leader of action beyond individual human embodiment: *to create new complex relations of actions which arrive at some goal.*

Imagine car manufacturing again. A lower-level manager—a foreman—is in charge of a subsystem of a car produced by the combined—and insofar as consistent *communal*—actions of many hands. If she is to abide by **HCr**, the foreman manager will have to modify the relations of these combined actions from the original experience which she has of them. This will not be a modification of the physical-level product of the car: *it will be a modification of the way in which the subsystem of the car is arrived at*. This creative guidance will engage the selected region of complexity of experience which is that group of workers who are building the subsystem. The foreman must keep modifying the old set of relations through an interpretation to a new set of relations. Practically speaking, this can be as broad as the full set of potential interactions at the level of embodiment for a selected group of workers who are producing the subsystem.

Say we have a dozen workers working on the subsystem. The foreman can change the order in which the workers engage the product, she can change which aspect of the product a worker engages, she can change the types of action which arrive at the various aspects of the product, she can change the span of the temporal process allowed to each worker in his or her task, she can change the ranges of various types of action at the physical level which are allowed to each worker, she can change the relative positions of the workers, she can change the overall range of various aspects of the goal—the subsystem—toward which the workers are working in community.[3]

Changing the order of worker engagement is not difficult. This week John begins with the molding of the part and passes it on to Kathryn for hardening, who in turn passes it on to Patrick for painting, etc. Next week Patrick begins with the molding of the part, passing it on to John for hardening, who then passes it on to Kathryn, etc. Changing the engaged aspect of the product is a matter of guiding John to work on the top of the part of this week and switching to the bottom of the part next week, for example. Changing the span of the temporal process allowed would be guiding a worker to take more or less time in fashioning his or her part of the product, Patrick works on the painting aspect for 20 minutes this week but for 30 minutes next week. Again, with regard to the type of action which engages the product, Kathryn uses the left hand today and the right hand tomorrow, and with regard to the range of action sits today but stands leaning over the part tomorrow, and with regard to the relative positioning of workers she sits behind Patrick this week, but to one side or even above him next week.

With regard to the goal this will be a setting and varying of the sub-ranges and overall range of the chosen goal. If the goal were a cup, for example: this week we are going to create a cup which holds between 250 to 350 ml of liquid, and which—from among the many colors available to us—we will paint using diverse combinations of banana yellow, white, and selections from the range of the brighter blues, whose handle varies between 2 and 3 cm in height and 1 and 2 cm in width, and which has a surface relief between 1 and 3 mm depth of variations upon the following pattern theme, etc. and where each worker, or several together, is responsible for one of these aspects.

These then are a few of the modifications of interrelations among the community of workers which can be played with by a manager at lower levels of complexity. The next level of complexity may be that of a manager of several managers at that lower level. Here again **HCr** advocates a creativity of complexity which guides a community of sub-communities and again there are similar possibilities for continuous creative modification of the interrelationships of the latter. If we desire a set of cups, or a set of tableware which will entail cups, plates, saucers, etc., generally, at the level of complexity of a single family, then continuous creative variance of the community of communities just discussed—e.g., four groups of a dozen workers—will give us our product at that range of complexity in a creatively expansive manner. At all levels, rather than viewing the goal as a static model, we view it as a range of sub-ranges, which can be varied at various levels of complexity of management. The upper reaches of our hierarchy of complexity then becomes a matter of choice in the experience we are after. And levels of management of the contemporary power hierarchy may very well dissolve insofar as they have arisen through the tendency of constriction to mere quantitative repetition.

Another way to put it is as follows. We want to form creative communities at many levels: the community of the worker with his own experience at ranges of embodiment, the community of the manager as engaging multiple experiences at ranges of embodiment, the community of higher-level managers as engaging many of the latter complex communities. The commercial corporation is then the community of these communities. There must be hierarchy, but it will become a hierarchy in many more aspects than mere constricted quantification. It will be *a hierarchy of complexity of value* in which each works to create value according to his or her capacity of interpretive interest: some in simple actions at the level of individual physical embodiment, some at the level of individual physical embodiment in more complex actions, some at the level of interrelations of multiple physical embodiments in simple actions, and so forth.

Someone will now interject: "we don't want to generate creative interest in this process, we just want to produce *lots* of cups, or cars, or whatever!" I reply: you believe that you want the latter only because you assume, as already suggested, that at some point through an accumulation of value at the level of mere quantity you can get beyond mere quantity into an experience of value according to many aspects. This is not so. Hyperthematics says that you can only experience the value within the process that you can consistently weave into it. There is no "free" value. There are no lotteries in experience, and indeed the assumptions behind lotteries of any sort are entirely inconsistent with the hyperthematic view. All tendencies of action under inconsistent assumptions will cause a diminishment of value within the world process which *somewhere and sometime will cause a diminishment of value in the experience gathered around the locus of the process which initiated the inconsistent tendency of action.*

In short, badness as a diminishment of value rebounds upon us. The mere production of lots of cars, for example, comes back to us in many ways: the psychological stress of commuting, the valuation of transportation solely with regard to the monetary power hierarchy—cars are expensive—the boredom with the sameness of the consumer product which is the car, the congestion of traffic through the quantity of cars, the increasing levels of pollution which arise through sheer quantity of use, the harmful association of transportation with speed as a quantity of extension.

Pollution, as we experience it, is an example of devaluation rebounding upon us, due to our mistaken devaluative assumptions. It can be defined hyperthematically as: *a region of experience which has been engaged according to constriction to the aspect of quantity so that the experience becomes uninterpretable with regard to other ignored aspects of the world process.* In pollution, the process of nature within the world process cannot locally interpret or "absorb" the accumulated quantity of repetitive action of some kind: too many people walking in a nature preserve, too much carbon dioxide from the quantity of cars, too many people bathing in a river, etc. Neither the individual nor the group can escape the rebound of devaluation contributed to in polluting, any more than the accumulation in quantity as weak value, considered above, can "leapfrog" past that weak value to access higher value.

For the hyperthematic view the goal according to **HCr** is not quantity of product, nor the efficiency or profit which are the precursors and results, respectively, of constriction to mere quantity. The goal is *valuable—and thus interesting for further interpretation—experience at all levels of complexity of the community of the commercial corporation interacting together*. At all levels of complexity it is the active effort to make the experience at hand creatively valuable through an interpretation cognizant of, but away from, what has come before. It is, to put the matter in practical terms, an effort to make the work experience as creatively interesting in its value as the "off time" after work experience, even perhaps more so.

Is such effort difficult to initiate? Perhaps, in the beginning, because over the past two centuries, at least, we have habitualized ourselves into actions that constrict experience to mere quantitative repetition. Put otherwise: *the illusion that a consistent hypertheme cannot possibly be applied in a given case, always rests upon some inconsistent assumption(s) adopted elsewhere in the respective region(s) of experience, by the interpreting processes*. Thus, in the example noted earlier, a car engine seems to admit only small ranges of variation, but this rests upon what we think a car "must" do, which rests in turn upon what a road "must" be like, upon what a city "must" be like, and on and on. To move beyond such inconsistent assumptions may be difficult at first, but we can begin slowly. It is easy to imagine how a product such as a coffee cup can imbue expansive creativity within its shape within a healthy range, while still fulfilling the goal of holding a hot drink, with each cup being produced in multiple interesting and non-repetitive shapes with diverse coloring—no two exactly alike. Moving on, it is not much more difficult to imagine how a car could be produced in a great diversity of creative shapes within selected ranges and in a great diversity of creative colors and combinations of colors. Then, as the static nature of our goals are loosed, moving away from that mere quantification which drives our notions of speed and efficiency in transportation, it will become readily possible to imagine how even the ranges of the goal of such a seemingly precise and static subsystem as that of a car engine can be expanded so as to allow creativity.

I have taken considerable space on **HCr** for **HCr** is a very important tendency with regard to our hyperthematic view. It is intimately interwoven with all other hyperthemes because all other hyperthemes offer varieties of consistent modification, which, when it takes note of and diverges from originally selected experience so as to abide by **HCr**, produce the great expansions of value which render the world process worthy of continual engagement. Here I have expanded upon the application of **HCr** with regard to the worker experience, the buyer experience, and the manager and owner experience of contemporary commercial corporations, enough so as to consider **HCr** adoptable and adopted within the revised structure of the corporation.

HCu Reconstruction

The next hypertheme will be the Hypertheme of Curvature, **HCu**, which suggested: in order to increase value within regions of experience at the physical range of complexity make every effort to create physical shapes which are curved and to avoid the creation of shapes which diminish curvature. As with the previous hypertheme, this hypertheme is readily interpretable by the community of the commercial corporation through the product and particularly for the product as a completed product.

That it can be interpreted in the invention of new materials, as well as the "internal structures" of products, can be easily shown for products both smaller and larger, relative to the scale of the human process. Thus the introduction of curvature—relative to the internal patterns of other fabrics—in the curving loops of knitted fabric, adds various expansive properties to the fabric which facilitate further interpretation, flexibility of garments, comfort, etc. Thus, again the introduction of curvature in larger products such as the geodesic domes popularized by Buckminster Fuller, but currently held back in application by other devaluative assumptions (e.g., square-cut building materials), as well as the increasing use of such curvature in synthetic microscale structures, now named after Fuller, demonstrate the valuative expansion of the principle of curvature.

Indeed, our dwellings and buildings generally, both residential and communal, exemplify very well another product interpretable to **HCu**. Contemporary cities are composed predominantly of geometrically square and rectangular building structures, replete with the tendencies toward line and point taken up within their processes of construction. Communities of the commercial corporation engaged in building construction can adopt **HCu** in their processes of production of these building structures, making a transformation from a tendency toward the geometry of line and point toward curved structures.

Even before the adoption of the tendency suggested by **HCu**, we are already aware of the various aspects in which value increases with regard to the physical structures of our buildings when they tend toward curvature. All of these increases of value come with respect to the fluid engagement of nature as the background process of the physical range of complexity of the world process. Round buildings have been shown to be far more structurally stable than square and rectangular buildings, because the incoming process of nature is not halted and constricted by such curved structures but is guided so as to flow over and interpret them. Such buildings allow wind and rain to flow over them, decreasing damage to the structure from the elements. They allow better internal flow of processes such as sustain the process of human embodiment, e.g., they are better and less wasteful with regard to heating and cooling.

Round buildings can be built through cooperative activity in ways which increase value between actors in the corporate community, above all by moving beyond the more constricted and specialized group activity which issues in square and rectangular building structures. All tendencies of engagement of physical complexities of experience—e.g., engagement of nature—which diminish value through constriction are *specializations* of a sort. In human construction efforts these are tools in the physical sense. But many tools are a sign at physical level complexity of a constrictive engagement of experience, here, of the experience of nature. A tool is a cutting tool for example when it divides experience. If we have before us a tree growing naturally and we cut it with a saw or an ax, we are engaging it through constriction of interpretation. The tree falls literally and figuratively as a process, because it cannot interpret the action with which we engage it.

These specialized engagements continue moreover throughout the process of contemporary building. The tree is sawn up by yet further specialized tools, which most often constrict the experience of it physically to that of square and rectangle. The building material is then nailed together, again by the physical sign of a tendency of engagement—a pointed nail—which the material yields to because it cannot interpret it. These signs, specialized through constriction, then go on to influence our human processes in embodiment toward further constriction. The specialized saw engenders a specialized technique to wield it. The specialized fastener—the nail—engenders yet another specialized technique. A series of such constrictive tendencies gives rise to a division of labor in a community of the commercial corporation such as a construction company, moving us away from the consistent types of action which our hyperthematic structure suggests for corporate communities.

Applying **HCu** in engagements of the physical world however, e.g., in a community of the commercial corporation whose members engage in construction at physical levels, then diversity can be arrived at through tendencies espousing assumptions of harmonic interweaving rather than those of independent specialization. This might mean building round dwellings, or incorporating curvature into current dwellings, while giving up such constrictive actions which come to require specialized tools. One can envision selecting and creating fluid materials with which to build and which also give the opportunity for fluid further additions to structures, and thus give the opportunity for fluid harmonic action on the part of the members of the community working together to build the structure. I begin the structure, and its fluid character allows you, another member of the community, to carry on from my effort, and for other future members of the community to go still further. And if we are using materials amenable to creative curvature, such as clay or adobe, then we are moving away from the constrictive tendencies of cutting and separating which give rise to the specialized tools and pockets of independent action, which break the harmony of our efforts as a community.

The opportunity arises then to incorporate the structures of nature, a great many of which are amenable to curvature, into the very fabric of the structures which we build. Communities of the commercial corporation adopting this tendency would thus be building structures which interweave with nature, joining with its consistencies rather than constrictively opposing them, and adding value to nature rather than increasing its inconsistencies. This follows the earlier musement upon curvature in art, for the spirit of the principle has been applied in combinations of art and architecture, most prominently in Antoni Gaudi's great architectural creations of the early twentieth century, but also more recently in structures such as Friedensreich Hundertwasser's *Hundertwasserhaus*. It has also been applied by various cultures historically, such as the Musgum of Cameroon and the ancient Harran in what is now Turkey.

The challenge remains to weave the principle of expansion of value through curvature into the more widespread efforts of which consistent communities of the commercial corporation would be capable. In this we would achieve curvature in physical building structures, not merely as rare accomplishments, but as transformative of the integration of art and architecture throughout our towns and cities.

Moreover, we can bring it up to higher levels of complexity of the physical range by moving toward curvature as engendering communities of physical structures. As they are now, cities—and increasingly, and unfortunately, smaller towns—are not only comprised primarily of square and angular structures, but these square and angular structures are laid out in further square and rectangular structures at higher levels of complexity, namely grid pattern city "blocks" and so forth. Our best sociopsychological information already tells us that a tendency toward curvature in these more complex structures as recommended by **HCu** is also indeed an expansion of value. The sense of harmonic interaction through interpretation of members of communities at physical levels of complexity is increased in any village, town, or city attempting circular or curved layouts. I will not carry this further however. Suffice it to suggest that **HCu** is interpretable to the community of the commercial corporation in its products at various levels of complexity, and thus we adopt it within our renewed hyperthematic structure, while leaving others to carry out further musement upon the implications of that adoption.

HAs Reconstruction

Coming now to the Hypertheme of Asymmetry, **HAs**, which is closely related to **HCr**, it tells us: *in order to increase value within regions of experience at the physical range of complexity make every effort to create hyperthematic asymmetry and to avoid forming physical shapes which are hyperthematically symmetric and which thus copy portions of themselves.* This is interpretable to the commercial corporation in two ways at least: in the shapes of the various products at physical levels of complexity and otherwise and in the structural relationships of the systems and organizations within the community of the commercial corporation.

In the first case this is a matter of moving away from the tendency to produce sharp objects, and even worse, pointy objects. To the reader who has not yet got the spirit of our outlook, this will seem to be madness at first, for if it is meant literally—and it *is* meant literally in terms of physical complexity—and *if* it is followed, this would seem to mean the end of a whole host of tools for cutting, poking, fastening, etc. But what has to be remembered is that *tendencies* are always at issue and we are acting within the world process which responds to our tendencies of action, but which also carries within it the deepest roots of prior inconsistent action. Thus there can be no instant corrections of the prior inconsistent tendencies, but there can be gradual constant application of consistent tendencies which will have their effect on both the overall value of the world process and the regions of experience within that world process.

Look at this in another way. A symmetric region is a region of experience in which the experience on either side of the symmetry is equal in some aspect—the aspect which creates the symmetry. The more equal the experiences which give rise to the symmetry become, the less interpretation is possible according to hyperthematic assumptions. Sameness diminishes potential interpretability; diversity increases it. Symmetries are thus uninterpretable gaps within experience. Moreover, when the symmetry is deliberately produced through—inconsistent—tendencies of our action so as to result in a product which is the deliberate outcome of such tendencies, then the product carries within it the tendency to reproduce locally such uninterpretable gaps within experience.

Cutting blades, pointed spikes, and so forth are meant to divide up experience, to bring about experiences which are *independent* through division. They are meant to be uninterpretable with regard to the experience of other regions and aspects of the world process. Out of this deliberate manufacture of products which create such uninterpretable gaps, come all of the *symmetric weapons* of human warfare—e.g., the cutting weapons—though not *all* of the weapons of human warfare. All production of such implements by communities of commercial corporations—as well as other communities—results in a diminishment of value somewhere and sometime within the world process. According to Hyperthematics *corporate communities cannot produce weaponry in any way which is consistent with the creation of value*. Weaponry is always inconsistent with the hyperthematic outlook upon elimination and most prominently it is inconsistent with **HAs**. Although an expansion upon this theme and its manifestations for human history will require a full scale future work, nonetheless the following will show well enough why even less obvious tendencies toward symmetry are inconsistent.

Asymmetry and Food Production

Less obvious examples are the results of the symmetric assumption such as they occur in the actions of food and medicine production carried out by many a commercial corporation. In the history of human action upon earth, the record so far indicates that the production of food has tended toward more or less consistency with regard to our hypertheme of asymmetry. In the ancient past we have gone from being food foragers to being agricultural food producers.

Food foraging tends toward diversity with respect to what nature has to offer us. Hyperthematically, such diversity tends to be expansive of value, insofar as the action of foraging continually moves onward rather than resting statically in one place and concentrating on mere quantitative accumulation of a sameness of food. Nor *can* the forager simply remain statically in one place, for nature does not produce lasting quantity in accumulation, but proceeds as a cycle which continually tamps down both accumulation and symmetry.

When food production proper arises in agriculture it does not immediately occur through a move toward inconsistency. There is an accumulation indeed, but in early agriculture the tendency toward accumulation is still tempered by the cycle of nature: accumulations of food tend to spoil. Also, the engaging action of those seeking food moves from being an engagement of the world process as nature in its time process sectional aspect, to being an engagement of the world process as nature in its time process parallel aspect. Rather than running around from place to place interpreting nature with regard to the food experience—either animal or vegetable—human action turns toward *guiding* processes of growth over considerably longer spans of time: growing crops, animal husbandry. So far, such actions are consistent with expansion of interpretation which creates value.

Then a wrong turn is (was) taken and the urge toward the guidance of processes of growth begins to give way to accumulative concentration of food in mere quantity, e.g., to the urge toward growth which shortens the time span and toward action which takes less and less account of the region of nature in the world process. The latter is an inconsistency with regard to **HCr**, but now enters an assumption which gives rise to an inconsistency with regard to **HAs**, namely the assumption that the product attained from the sectional growth aspect of the cycle of nature should be constrictively channeled into the aspect of quantity *along with* some other repetitively selected aspect of the experience of the food product.

The food is thus *concentrated* according to some aspect: sweet, fat, etc. And this concentration is mainly brought about by the tendency of division which uses *symmetry*, often in the form of some simple or complex variation of a *cutting tool*. A blade with deliberately manufactured symmetry is used to engage the experience of, e.g., the plant. Blades "work" because their symmetry tends toward being uninterpretable; the engaged experience within the world process—e.g., a plant—is unable to interpret the incoming concentrated action of the blade due to the sameness of the blade upon either side of the manufactured symmetry of its sharp edge. A blade is just that which one *tends* not to be able to interpret, i.e., to avoid.[4] This tendency toward concentration by division divides an experience, refusing to interpret one or other of the regions of experience that have been divided by—ostensibly—eliminating (discarding) it, or it constricts to mere quantity by dividing—chopping up—the plant, for example, into a mere group of independent pieces which become more nearly the same the more they are chopped. With no little irony, we now call this concentration through division, the *processing of food*, whereas it is rather *the constriction of process*. Mislabeled or not, however, it tends toward a diminishment of value with regard to the food product, whether that food product be the refining of wheat grains into flour or the peeling of potatoes.

The devaluation in human health as a process, from these food concentrations, e.g., the rise of diabetes, is well enough documented. I will not suggest specific examples of confirming research upon the nutritional benefits of eating relatively "unprocessed" foods which have been attained through expansive rather than constrictive and divisive tendencies. These are to be found in abundance according to the interest of the reader. Suffice it to say that the processing of food in the contemporarily understood sense is inconsistent with **HAs**, and it is the engagement of the food product through symmetry which tends toward some mere quantitative accumulation of some aspect of the product, and which shows us how assumptions consistent or inconsistent with hyperthemes—here **HCr** and **HAs**—are often combined.

Asymmetry and Medicine

That this is not limited to the region of the experience of food production can be shown by comparing another region of experience in which the community of the commercial corporation presently plays a very large role, that of medicine. In most contemporary Western medicine there is an emphasis upon two aspects in particular. Surgery proceeds in large part according to the tendency of division through symmetry. The various blades and implements of surgery are "effective" through the very tendency toward symmetry which is inconsistent with **HAs**. Incisions, and the various *ectomies, otomies, biopsies*, and so on, all make use of the tendency of division through symmetry. Something is divided, cut into, and removed—eliminated—rather than being engaged through an action which tends toward growth in multiple aspects.

The other great effort of contemporary medicine is the effort toward quantitative concentration in an uninterpreted and uninterpretable experience: the medical *pill*. Medicine, whose historic roots lie in the much more expansive use of well-recognized plants—e.g., herbs—having their place within the region of nature in the world process, and interpretable within that region by those foragers spoken of earlier, has slowly given way to the refining of plants in the same way as with the refining of food to achieve concentrations in quantity, i.e., the pill (or the localized injection) which packs a punch in terms of power. The goal is thus the pill which is a concentration of mere quantity that goes beyond a symmetry even in *several* aspects of physical complexity, such as the blade does, and tends toward a point symmetry of a single aspect. In weapons, a point is still less interpretable than a blade, and even so in medicine, a pill is a "point" of engagement which is to be uninterpretable to the disease, as an *enemy*. The ultimate goal is the pill which need not be interpreted by the patient but *targets* disease very selectively without any active engagement on the part of the patient, i.e., without the patient interpreting what is in the pill, from whence it comes, how it will engage the process of the body, and so on.

It is commercial corporations above all which tend, in our age, to take inconsistent action in these regions of processing and refinement of foods and medicines. Having begun my interpretation of **HAs** through particular examples of broad regions engaged by such inconsistent actions, it is now a fairly simple task to suggest some of the ways in which **HAs** can be consistently interpreted with regard to the actions of members of commercial corporations. With regard to food production, interpreting **HAs** consistently involves engaging the processes of food production as processes insofar as possible. This means not engaging through division by symmetry, by symmetric tools.

Imagine a community of the commercial corporation whose goal is to produce food through agricultural means. Every action which moves away from the use of symmetries in the engagement of the growth process will be a tendency of action which is consistent with **HAs**. Thus, for example, the most prevalent contemporary way of engaging the soil in which the plant grows is to slice through it with a blade or spike of some sort in the practice of *tillage*. But to be consistent with **HAs** we can move toward actions which move or displace it without the symmetries of division. If we are displacing the soil, we may act so as to displace it through the tendency of pushing rather than cutting. The soil is a living process in its fashion, the cutting of which in tillage divides the process in some aspect or aspects, e.g., in the killing of earthworms, or in the breaking of the natural soil structure. Thus tendencies toward no tillage agriculture are consistent with **HAs**, and this can be carried to varying lengths, even to that advocated by the Japanese farmer Masanobu Fukuoka, who advocated a very broad "letting be" of the processes of nature.

When we move to the process of the growing plant itself, the suggestion according to **HAs** is that every action which guides the growth of the plant without resorting to cutting the plant is tending toward consistency. This might mean training the plant rather than trimming it for example, i.e., guiding its physical growth in directions which provide constant interpretation to the process of growth. In some cases this will mean harvesting from the plant in ways which forego division: e.g., harvesting according to natural ripening fruit, or according to the end of the natural cycle of the plant, or again harvesting from the plant in ways which insofar as possible—insofar as we have not yet created a still more consistent technique—let the plant continue its process as a living growth rather than ending it. Then, when the plant is harvested as a food product, consistency with **HAs** will entail actions such as interpret the food product without division. This will seem difficult at first. It will be supposed that much of the taste within our contemporary experience of processed foods arises from the recombination of food which has been cut and refined. In fact, as is becoming better known, the "processing" of food results in a diminishment of taste which is then "corrected" by variations of quantitative concentration in some one or several aspects of taste, e.g., sugar or salt.[5]

Action which tends toward consistency with **HAs** will thus be action which combines food that has not been divided and refined, combining it in ways which are asymmetric, i.e., tending away from a concentrated flavor in which the experience of the taste builds up to and diminishes from a center "point" around which the subsidiary taste experiences are equalized, and instead toward *a constantly varying and diverse range of taste*. One can imagine the efforts of consistent communities of the commercial corporation which could undertake such exploratory action with regard to *expansive food combination*.

This can be carried further into the engagement of medicine as an interpretively expansive endeavor. Not only will expansive asymmetric combination of foods create value within the experience of taste, but it will create value with regard to the growth and feeling of the physical body through consistent engagement with the processes of nature which are signified in food products. This is a matter of exploring which combinations of relatively unrefined food create value in the health of the physical body as a process of growth in many aspects.

Much of contemporary medicine targets disease in the body through the symmetrical engagement of the pill under the assumption that disease is localized, point-like, and indeed symmetric. On the Hyperthematic view, however, insofar as a disease tends toward symmetry it tends so because some action or actions have already been taken with regard to the region of experience which is the physical body. These actions are inconsistent in their symmetrical constrictiveness; we have treated the body in a way which sets up an uninterpretable symmetry within some region of it: eaten too much of one type of food, performed some action repeatedly focused in some part of the body.

If this is so, then the consistent way to meet a disease is not to engage it through further symmetric actions, like pills or surgery, but to interpret as much as possible the other aspects of the process of the physical body to the disease. For example—and here I connect back to the interpretation of **HCr** again—someone is working in a job in which the movement of some part of the body is constrictive and repetitive. A symmetry is set up in which an action or actions are equalized around some focal point within the physical body, e.g., around the wrist. The focal point becomes uninterpretable, a region of weakness, numbness, or pain, all of which are viewable in hyperthematic terms as *regions of uninterpretable experience within the physical body, varying according to loss of interpretability*. If I am weak in some area of the body, I tend to be unable to act—to actively interpret—*within* the physical ranges of the body in that area. If I am numb in some area of the body, I tend to be unable to interpret both *within* the physical ranges of the body in that area and *beyond* its physical ranges to other physical experience—i.e., to feel—around that area. Finally, if I am in pain in some area of the body I tend to be unable to act throughout the region of the body because the constriction through symmetry around some focal point has so decreased my ability to interpret that the uninterpretability has gone beyond the aforementioned two stages, and begins to diminish my ability to interpret throughout the whole of the body and its connections with the greater world process around me. As pain increases, it becomes what I cannot move beyond, cannot affect, cannot think beyond, and so forth. It becomes a "sink" of uninterpretability, a symmetric point around which the ability to interpret fails, and which drains away all my efforts to interpret it.

The solution to this is not—as contemporary medicine, abetted by the products of the uncorrected commercial corporation, so often attempts—to engage the already symmetric focal point with a further targeted symmetry of pill or surgery. It is to take actions which expand interpretation in an asymmetric way, between the focal point where the disease shows itself and the rest of the body as a process, and between the body and its surrounding environment as the process of nature under the world process. If I have carpal tunnel syndrome, then the consistent solution will be the promotion of the whole range of movements which begin to dissolve the dead focal point of uninterpretability within the wrist, so as to get the region of the wrist—muscles, joints, etc.—to act in new ways with regard to the rest of the body and the surrounding physical environment. For an infection, the consistent solution will be the promotion of the range of acts which cause the region of the infection to interpret itself to the other regions of the body, e.g., simple acts such as increasing blood flow to an infected area through exercises which move—interpret—other areas of the body in relation to the infected area; or more complex acts such as meditation, which connects the regions of the body among themselves, and promotes their interpretation to the process of the surrounding environment.

Again, rather than the pill as a product, the community of the commercial corporation can move toward the creation of expansive products which promote the interpretation of the diseased region to regions it has become independent of, a reconstruction of the community of selfhood at the level of embodiment. Insofar as the expansive product is at a physical level of complexity—e.g., something ingestible such as a pill—then it may take the form, as suggested earlier, of the expansions upon food which are consistent with **HAs**. For example, rather than a pill, food becomes a medicine in an expansive way, through being presented to the patient in interesting unrefined combinations interpretable to the physical body as a process in a very broad way.

Or again, the community of the corporation would act so as to create a product at an increased physical level of complexity which expansively interprets—expands upon—the body's physicality as a living process, e.g., a service product interpretively guiding the body toward connecting with its environment. The suggestion here is that the commercial corporation offer the patient an expansive experience which heals by renewing the interpretive links between the body as a process and its surroundings as a process. In some senses this has been attempted historically in the guise of health spas and sanatoria. But the former often concentrate on some one aspect of experience, such as bathing, while the latter concentrate upon quietness and inactivity. What I have in mind is rather the provision of, and guidance within, an overall experience which stimulates the patient to physically interpret the body to its surroundings again, so as to regain a consistent connection to the world process at physical levels of complexity. Patients ought to be guided into taking action to heal themselves. This might be achieved through placing the patient in a setting of nature, or partial nature, in its *consistent* aspects, and guiding the physical interaction of the patient with that setting, e.g., guiding the patient to interact with plants, birds, or other wildlife; guiding the patient to exercise consistently with the natural processes within that setting; guiding the patient to eat consistently as a process within the process of that setting, etc. This could also be offered in a consistently *human created* setting in varying degrees. For example introducing the patient to a setting of beauty created consistently according to the hyperthematic view, with expansive interpretability, curvature, expansive color, and so forth, and in a way which guides the patient to interpret the physical body to its surroundings and even create afresh in those surroundings, in short, a sort of "experience expanding room" which guides the person out of the symmetric constrictions that gave rise to the disease in the physical body.

I have proposed the above as a product which is consistent with **HAs** in that it offers asymmetry, although it applies that consistency to the experience of medicine. But **HAs** can be applied to many regions of experience and one, which presents itself on the basis of the foregoing suggestions regarding healing according to asymmetric experiences of setting, is that of building construction and layout.

Asymmetry in Architecture

HCu advocated curvature in building construction, the layout of streets and other structures with regard to one another, etc. **HAs** now advocates asymmetric tendencies, in building construction, in street layouts, etc. Communities of the commercial corporation are heavily implicated in the production and layout of those of our larger human structures which require extensive cooperation. **HAs** advises us to build asymmetric structures and to place them relative to one another in asymmetric ways, so as to expand interpretability for human actors who use them. Thus, for example, layouts which promote concentration upon a symmetric point, such as a city core, will tend to be inconsistent, whereas layouts which guide human activity through continuous fluid interpretation within a physical region will tend to be consistent. For this we may create new techniques, but we may also follow readily available compositional techniques for unbalanced structural placement such as have long been used in arts like Zen gardening.

The effect of symmetric tendencies in the construction of larger buildings and complexes of buildings can readily be seen in some of the more prominent structures of human history. I said earlier that the contemporary understanding of symmetry fails to recognize the difference between "symmetry" of circular curvature and true symmetry. The former is expansive of interpretation because the one experiencing only arrives at a symmetry—if they do—by a willing act which selects an angle of approach to the curve, whereas the latter is constrictive of interpretation because the one experiencing symmetry, e.g., in a point or blade, is *forced* to countenance the symmetry as an uninterpretability. And since, as I noted earlier, constriction, as in tendencies toward symmetry, must give rise to power or force as the process of the world is "bottlenecked" in certain regions only to find other avenues of release, then what we find is that power has historically been symbolized in human architecture by a tendency toward increasing symmetry.

All of the "great" historical buildings representative of kings and governments have tended toward symmetry in one or more aspect, very often centered about the approach to the main building, but also very often in the symmetric shape of that building which complements the approach. Thus, in ancient civilizations the grand colonnaded walkway, symmetric through its center and aligned with a symmetry of the wings of the main building, was embraced. In more recent history this tendency has not abated very much: the medieval cathedrals (which sometimes combined the point symmetry of their spires with the centerline symmetry of the main building), the castles and manor houses of Europe—e.g., le Château de Vaux-le-Vicomte—the newer government buildings of the world's greater powers—e.g., the German Reichstag and the American White House. All of these symmetric-tending constructions are symmetric because the tendency signifies *power* in some of its aspects. Sometimes the inconsistent symmetric tendency is abated by other *consistent* tendencies such as the curvature of a dome, and so on. The Taj Mahal, for example, tempers the symmetry of its main approach with the extensive use of curvature and also with the use of a very brightly colored—nearly white—façade.

Nonetheless, there have been buildings through history which have tended toward consistency with regard to **HAs**—e.g., St. Basil's Cathedral in Moscow—and there are increasingly exploratory contemporary moves toward architecture which is consistent with **HAs**—e.g., many of the works of Santiago Calatrava—and this is the direction the efforts of commercial corporations must take in order to be consistent, for increasingly it is these communities that plan and provide our larger human structures.

Asymmetry and Corporate Organization

HAs can also be interpreted in the structural relationships of the systems and organizations within the community of the commercial corporation. In an earlier chapter, I said that the management structure of communities of the commercial corporation as it is at present tends to be a symmetrical structure, with the CEO or owner at the point or apex of a pyramid in which is accumulated the power of management. This power is manifested, once again, as an uninterpretability, and the less interpretable it becomes relative to the pyramid's base—e.g., the physical laborers in a commercial corporation—the less the community of the commercial corporation is capable of value creation.

There are many actions which can be taken to interpret the experiences of the management of the commercial corporation according to **HAs**, so as to expand the situation. The problem of a symmetric power structure such as that manifested by the management of a commercial corporation is one of constriction of interpretation. Members of the community at lower levels of the structure are faced with an experience of other embodied processes at higher levels of the structure which they cannot interpret. Those processes at higher levels have power over the lower members of the community precisely insofar as they are uninterpretable to those lower members. Power is always felt as that which is uninterpretable within some aspect of experience.

If I am a lower-level member of the commercial corporation—e.g., a worker—then every level of management above me is the symmetric centerline, so to speak, about which I am the mirror image of members at my level. All of those at my level are equivalent to one another in multiple aspects with reference to the level above us. I am speaking here of our interpretive relationships within the management structure of a corporation. Our interpretive relationships, consistent and inconsistent, go far beyond our mere participation in any commercial corporation of course, so that the contemporary worker will have many differences with her peers through her participation in other communities. To describe the inconsistencies of the community of the commercial corporation in its management structure I leave those differences aside momentarily.

Insofar, then, as all at my level are equivalent, we tend to share a sameness of experience with regard to our interpretive relationship to the level above us, which deadens interpretation among us with regard to that level above: *insofar as we are all the same there is nothing to interpret between us beyond a mere quantity in which we are more numerous than those at the level above us.* This situation proceeds up the hierarchy of the pyramid with the number of members at each level decreasing as we go upward, until we reach the owner or CEO at the top. As noted earlier, the constriction due to other inconsistent assumptions manifests itself in a striving to reach the top of the hierarchy of the power structure. A more serious consequence, however, is the loss of fluidity of interpretation throughout the structure, between its members, and the deadening of the creation of value accordingly. Not only are the members of each level unable to interpret to one another in more than the quantitative aspect—the feeling expressed as: "I feel like a mere number, a cog in a machine"—but the members of each level above the lowest are also unable to interpret to those at levels lower than their own, for once again, if I am in the higher levels of the power structure, then my potential to interpret my experience to that of the members of any given level lower than my own is constricted by their all being *the same* to me, beyond mere quantity, with regard to my place in the structure.

As we rise up to the top of the structure the members at higher and higher levels have an interpretive relationship to more and more of this mere quantity of those at levels beneath them. The members of the hierarchy are embodied at physical level complexity also however; and so, as the quantity of those who bear a sameness of relationship to the higher level member increases, this mere quantity of members tends to become uninterpretable to the experience of the higher level members insofar as it remains at physical levels of complexity (which it must tend to inasmuch as the higher level member is still embodied).

So, if I am the CEO of a multinational corporation for example, I have a relationship to the workers at the lowest level, suppose there are 60,000 of them, who are all the same to me *except* in the aspect of mere quantity, i.e., each one of them is merely *another one* to me. But this mere quantity, which is a constriction to one aspect of value—just as in the case of money as mere quantity—in an accumulation of interpretive action at the ranges of physical embodiment (the mere number of bodies), has grown so large as to be uninterpretable to myself as also embodied. To put it another way: my experience of embodiment is uninterpretable to "sixty thousands of embodiment." I cannot interpret what I can do with my body to what 60,000 can do with their bodies, *qua 60,000*. Yet the experience of the world process, when it is engaged by the constriction of interpretation which is introduced into experience, must out somewhere, according to hyperthematics, and it does so.

If I am the CEO, this comes out as a feeling of embodied action on a huge and relatively indefinite scale—say 60,000 worth—which remains perpetually *unused*, because it is uninterpretable in these mere quantitative terms, but which is harmful. This is the *feeling of power*. Its attributes include fickleness (the large quantity is more or less uninterpretable over time in a way which might consistently connect the temporal process), threateningness (the large quantity is more or less uninterpretable at all within the temporal process), overarchingness (the large quantity is more or less uninterpretable over a large and indefinite range of the smaller segments of itself), overwhelmingness (the large quantity is more or less uninterpretable to smaller segments of itself), and so forth.

All of this is captured in the feeling of the powerful that: "I can do whatever I want, when I want, where I want, with whatever or whomever I want," and conversely in the worker as: "he can do whatever he wants . . . etc." The powerful cannot really do any of these things, however, for the attributes of the feeling are based upon temporary uninterpretable gaps introduced into the experience of the world process. Yet harm is introduced into and spreads through the world process, and rebounds upon the initiators of the inconsistency.* Similar to the earlier examples of money as mere quantity, here the uninterpretability beyond mere quantity results in a sameness of products for the commercial corporation, mere series of copies in quantity; it results in the fear and distrust of lower-level members of the corporate community; it results in the arising of further power structures and actions which wield power through quantitative uninterpretability, e.g., unions, corporate takeovers, etc. This constriction to the terms of embodiment as quantity gives rise to the symmetrical hierarchy of the power structure, through the assumption of the mere quantity of embodiment, even while a further assumption holds that an interpretive relationship based upon this mere quantity can be engaged and manipulated to create value as more than mere quantity.

As always these are only tendencies though, and moving away from constriction to the terms of embodiment increases the ability of the community of the commercial corporation—as well as that of other communities that dabble in the power structure—to create value. Thus, for example, a commercial corporation—as also a nation, for government is another version of the power structure—which is decaying as a community in these respects may suddenly and fortunately find itself led—in the hyperthematic

---

*See Appendix B.

sense—by someone who engages himself or herself as a far more complex process than that in the range of embodiment. Such a one then tends toward the expansive interpretation of *leadership* as an expansion of the interpretive capacity of those under him or her. Rather than wielding power, the leader, with consistent assumptions, builds linkages through aspects of interpretation beyond the mere quantity of embodiment. History is full of such people. What is needed, however, is a regular application of the principle **HAs**, in ways which take us beyond mere hit and miss. So finally, how can we interpret **HAs** to the power structure which is the management of the contemporary commercial corporation?

We apply asymmetry at various levels of complexity, transforming symmetries into asymmetries. I described the symmetry of the power structure as a triangle in which two sides are symmetric about a centerline which runs from the apex of the triangle—the highest level of management—to the midpoint of the lower side of the triangle. At physical levels of complexity, if we were to transform the symmetry of the triangle in its shape to an asymmetry, we would have applied **HAs** in a very simple way. So let us do this. Let us interpret the relationships between the levels of complexity of the management structure of the corporation through the various ranges of application of **HAs** to a physical triangle.

Suppose an isosceles triangle, whose base, which represents the lowest complexity and accordingly more physically extensive part of the range—the workers—we will leave unchanged. Now we begin to vary the two upper sides of the triangle, which are malleable. First let's say that we push in the sides of our triangle equally, so as to make them concave. Our triangle will start to resemble a more "wicked" looking spiky thing so to speak. In terms of the power structure of the commercial corporation we are now tending toward having a CEO interpreting to a range of upper-level management which is not much broader than himself, but which suddenly broadens out so as to interpret a great number of lower-level complexity members of the corporation, e.g., the structure has the CEO, a president, three vice presidents, five upper management, ten middle management, then suddenly five hundred lower management, and 25,000 workers. Hyperthematically, not only is the symmetry in the structure, here, but our concave manipulation of the sides of our triangle is making our apex point sharper. The symmetry was based upon equality of extension about the centerline, which symmetry itself was a constriction to mere quantity with regard to aspects of interpretation. Yet now we are eliminating—inconsistently with still other hyperthemes—even the quantitative aspect. The result for the management structure is going to be that not only is the CEO unable to interpret the very large quantity of the lowest level members, as before, but a great range—vertically—of the upper-level management is tending to be the same as the CEO, because even the diversity of mere quantity is being eliminated, thus making the symmetry even more pronounced. The power is being concentrated more and more into a point. Moreover, because interpretation is being constricted horizontally, then the vertical aspect of interpretation which remains is tending toward being an aspect of mere quantity once more, so that the upper levels of management will increasingly conflict with one another by attempting to *be* simply higher in this hierarchy which is measured as a mere quantity.

This is perhaps something that we more often see in an obvious way in certain government power structures than in corporate power structures, wherein the uppermost members of the power structure of the former have very little else to interpret with regard to one another, beyond their bare rank in the order of quantity. The near equality, historically, of members of the Politburo and Politburo Standing Committee of the People's Republic of China in relation to the massive base of Chinese civil service might well serve as an example of our "spiky triangle."

Here we see how eliminations are closely related to symmetries: they tend toward symmetries, i.e., as we eliminate in some region of experience we decrease the diversity within the region, making it more liable to equalities which cluster about some "centerline," even if we are not deliberately aiming to bring about such symmetries. Eliminating diversity in national populations, for example—and also in localized regions of those national populations—is thus a sign of and a tendency toward the accumulation of power in the nation, most often, as in Nazi Germany, a turn for the worse. Again, the above shows how the application of hyperthemes must be otherwise consistent with other hyperthemes, to achieve expansions of value. Here we have indeed moved from the linear sides of the pyramid to a curvature of its sides, but since that transformation *also* involves an elimination—concave curvature—we diminish value rather than expand it.

What if we pushed in the sides of the triangle unequally however, i.e., push in one side only? The hyperthematic view tells us that we have introduced asymmetry into our triangle indeed, but we have also engaged in an elimination. The interpretation of this with regard to the management would be one in which the upper levels of management are unevenly distributed with regard to the levels of management below them. For example, under the CEO of a corporation are two presidents, and under one of these presidents there is one vice president, while under the other president there are three vice presidents, and so on down through the structure of the management, which otherwise has the same characteristics of our first example. Overall, here, the asymmetric character of the structure will work to our advantage. The two presidents now have unequal interpretive relationships relative to those below. The president with one vice president below her has a different experience than the president with three vice presidents below, a difference of experience which is fertile ground for interpretation between our two presidents. Rather than each interpreting the other as merely "another one like me" with regard to the CEO, they will now directly interpret the other as having different experience.

Meanwhile the CEO will have an asymmetric experience from her viewpoint as well, which will engender greater interpretation within her own process as CEO. A simple physical example illustrates this asymmetry. If one were walking on a tightrope and the total set of conditions which one was presented with was symmetric, or balanced, then one would need to take no actions. If the conditions become asymmetric, or unbalanced, constant action is needed to interpret the imbalance and cross the tightrope. This does not mean that—as it seems on a tightrope—the symmetry of balance as a goal is desirable; the challenge of a tightrope is that the symmetry never lasts and constant new opportunities for interpretation are provided. It means rather that asymmetry promotes interpretation and thus value.

Despite the gain however, we are still tending toward elimination in our triangle of concave but unequal curvatures. Approaching the top, the point of the triangle, we still begin to draw nearer and nearer to a symmetry because, as noted above, the two sides diminish in aspects of interpretation, tending toward sameness with regard to the point. Hence this application of **HAs** is limited in its engendering of value.

We may also transform our triangle with a convex expansion—according to **HCu**—of one side alone, which leads to asymmetry. In terms of our management structure we will retain the good in the previous example, and we will add to it a further expansion of interpretation, on the convex side, in which each member of the management structure at a lower level will have another above himself who engages a more complex level of experience but engages it through a more direct connection with the members below him. Here then, at each level of management, a member of the community is interpreting to "a bit more" than one other member at a lower level of complexity in the community. And insofar as she is, she is moving away from the uninterpretability arising when a constriction to the aspect of mere quantity of embodiment is attempted wherein the quantities are so vast that they cannot be interpreted to embodiment. In other words, the relation here between higher and lower members of the corporate structure is tending away from a relation of power toward one of expansive *guidance*.

To exemplify, suppose I am a manager of thirty workers, then *in terms of embodiment*, I am going to tend not to be able to actively interpret experiences of embodied complexity with regard to myself and the thirty workers, because what I can do with my body is getting rather far away from what they can do together as thirty bodies. I may indeed—inconsistently—move them to act through power, and through structures of power, but the result will be mixed and possibly disastrous in terms of value. My efforts to expand myself as manager of my thirty workers—and to have already expanded myself—so as to be able to engage complexities of experience beyond the range of mere embodiment in what we usually mistakenly compartmentalize off as *thinking*, even though it is only action at higher levels of complexity, is going to offset this. This is the guidance of consistent leadership. Nonetheless, if the structure of interpretive relationships—here a management structure—at the range of embodiment is inconsistent with regard to **HAs** and other hyperthemes, this will drag down the ability of even a very great leader to provide guidance. This is the inertia of structures of management (and of bureaucracy in government) as a set of relationships of embodiment, which makes life difficult even for gifted leaders.

Laying aside my own capacity as a leader of my thirty workers however, we may say that if on the other hand we begin to increase the number of managers, until there are say six managers, including myself, for thirty workers, then, in terms of embodiment once more, I am going to be able to actively interpret experiences of embodied complexity much more successfully between myself and my five workers, than I could in the first scenario. I will be tending to shift from power to guidance. Going further than this until we have say fifteen managers for thirty workers, then I will be even better able to actively interpret, to guide, the two workers who I manage, for I may very well be able to interpret my experience at the embodied level to the experience of *two* others at an embodied level. That is, I will be able to guide them to expansions of their actions of interpretation qua embodied because the actions and combinations of actions, which are possible to two embodied processes, are going to be much nearer in complexity to those which I can accomplish as a single embodied process. Clearly, as we tend to expand the number of managers at the various levels of the hierarchy, we will reach a situation akin to that in which the convex side of our triangle takes on maximal curvature, i.e., that of the quarter circle. At that point the proportion of managers at any level to those below them will be such as to promote maximal interpretation between levels of complexity, i.e., the proportion of challenge to sameness which gives rise to constant interpretation.

If we now begin to push out the other side of the triangle so that we have two convex sides—not yet maximally convex, but "beehive shaped" rather—then we will do even better in our expansion of interpretation. Meanwhile, the sharpness of our point is steadily tending toward a curved transition between the sides of our triangle. The members of our corporate management structure are becoming more and more interpretable to one another. Power is giving way to guidance. Continuing, we will transform our triangle into a semicircle. This will be the maximal curvature we can institute in order to achieve a structure within the range of embodiment which gives maximal support to the hierarchy of our managers who are providing guidance at increasing levels of complexity beyond embodiment.

If our curvature passed beyond the semicircle toward a loose "square" with curved upper corners, then some ranges of the hierarchy would tend toward a sameness with regard to one another in the direction of the hierarchy, and we would be moving toward a constriction of interpretation again according to other of our hyperthemes. Interpreted to management this might mean having twenty workers, twenty low-level managers, twenty mid-level managers, eighteen upper-level managers, five vice presidents, two presidents, and one CEO, for example. Rather than this, we stop at a semicircle. Our semicircle interpreted in terms of the management structure will no longer have a definite "point" at the highest part of the hierarchy, i.e., in terms of embodiment, it will no longer have a CEO.

Yet though our semicircle no longer has a point at the upper part of its curvature, we still have a line of symmetry brought about by the line of its base, which decides for us, albeit in a weaker way, the line of symmetry about which the two halves of our semicircle mirror one another. So, although the management structure akin to our semicircle will indeed have no CEO, it will have a number of members—at least more than two so as to be also consistent with $H3^6$—at the highest complexity of the hierarchy. And in practical terms the suggestion is that the number of top members stand to the level of management below so as to approximate the curvature of the (semi) circle as nearly as possible given the limitations of human embodiment.[7] This structure will permit each member to interpret to another member at her own level of complexity as having a different relationship to that member relative to a managing member at a level above, and it will permit each member at a given level to receive guidance from a member at a higher level, which is a challenge to interpretive expansion, without losing capacities of interpretation through constriction to mere quantity.

The objection that this whole transformation is an impossibility in practical terms, will now arise, for: "you cannot expect to expand the management of a contemporary corporation, which might have 60,000 workers at its base level—according to your own example—because the numbers of management needed to do so would be astronomical." This objection rests upon holding onto the very aspect of the structure which resulted from the original inconsistent assumptions, namely, the results of constriction to mere quantification of embodiment. That a contemporary corporation should have 60,000 workers, but only one CEO, is the result of inconsistencies which have hitherto arrived at the symmetrical power structure, and the *output* of these very weak communities in terms of value, which goes beyond mere quantity value, is the sign of it. We have indeed such huge corporations but they tend not to interpret experience in very valuable ways, and the larger they grow along these constricted avenues of mere quantification, the less do they produce value.

I suggested that the CEO of such a corporation could not interpret 60,000 workers in embodiment qua 60,000 workers and that even a fairly low-level manager could not interpret thirty workers in terms of embodiment. Such interpretation as occurs, is mostly low-level interpretation promoted by power. We get around these difficulties through structures of power, but only by instituting assumptions that give rise to expansion of experience in terms of mere quantity, e.g., we set up our workers on assembly lines, give them repetitive actions, set them to producing copies, etc. In short, the concomitant of power with regard to value is mere quantity.

If this is not obvious enough, yet another example can be offered, which expands upon the "inverse" relationship between guidance and power and shows how inconsistent substructures invade regions of experience through the application of inconsistent assumptions to higher levels of complexity: that of teachers. If you have a teacher in a very small class of students, or better still, if you have a number of teachers in a very small class, then you are tending toward the situation advocated above in the expansion of managers to workers. One to one is unwise, for the reasons suggested above, but if you had, for example, nine teachers to thirteen students, then you would approximate the maximal curvature of our semicircle with—according to our hyperthematic view—maximal results for the expansion of value.

Suppose, however, that we move toward inconsistency by having only one teacher for a class, which creates a symmetric point in our education management structure and that, furthermore, we begin to steadily increase the class size. At three students for our lone teacher, our teacher is still doing fairly well, although the students will begin to organize themselves into a quantitative hierarchy with regard to one another due to the symmetric relationship of each with the teacher. At ten students for our teacher, the teacher will cope, but guidance will begin to give way to power. At thirty students, our one teacher, depending upon her leadership capacity, will begin to concentrate her guidance. Thus a few students in the quantitative hierarchy will receive considerable guidance, a larger number will receive some guidance, and some will be increasingly left to their own devices. At 100 students the teacher will have to increasingly shift to substructures of mere quantitative interpretation, rote learning, papers and exams, all of which are increasingly the same for everyone, activities which tend toward quantitative interpretation, etc. We are tending toward the educational equivalent of assembly line work for students. At 400 students, we are headed into territory with which even the great teachers, capable of giving very broad and complex guidance going well beyond process as embodiment, will have difficulty.

To answer the earlier objection then, the quantitatively broad base of workers which remains, forcing a symmetry into our semicircle, is a holdover from the original inconsistent assumptions. Why hold to the hierarchy of the power structure? We need a hierarchy indeed, but *a hierarchy according to the capacity to guide the expansion of interpretation of experience*, i.e., the degree that each of us is *able* to view himself or herself as a process beyond the range of mere embodiment, *willing* to actively apply his or her own capacity to the expansion of other embodied processes, or acting transformable elements (often human), which are less broad. In short, to be consistent our rank must come from our ability to guide one another consistently, combined with our willingness to be guided by others within a selected region of experience. The clues to that rank are to be found in recognizing that each of us finds meaning in willingly acting within certain ranges of experiential complexity, i.e., enjoys doing certain things. Insofar as we can tend this way, we will move from mere quantitative hierarchies toward hierarchies of expanded value, i.e., toward *ethical hierarchies.*

I began by suggesting expansions upon a triangle, a pyramid structure of management because in our contemporary world we find ourselves surrounded by such structures in commercial corporations, as also in other regions of experience such as government. We cannot leapfrog through experience, which is always the sign and result of our own engagement of the world process. We must begin with what we have and try to correct it through consistent assumptions.

We are working, however, toward *fluid structures in which lower complexity experience is guided toward more complex interpretations at its own level by higher complexity experience, which is then guided in turn by still higher complexity experience.* The shapes modeling such structures at physical levels of complexity will be numerous. Let us briefly imagine several in some final attempts to interpret **HAs** to the management of commercial corporations.

Start by expanding the linear base of our semicircle until we achieve a full circle. Now we have a structure in which the original apex point of our triangle has been transformed into a curve and the two further points, where our linear base met the curvature of our semicircle, have also been transformed likewise. But if the points in our structure are transformed into curvature, where now is our line of symmetry? Answer: without the apex and base points, no line of symmetry is *given* (forced). It may be actively *selected* however. A selection on the circle's edge, followed by the maximal active interpretation of extension through the circle, i.e., its diameter, will *get us* a line of symmetry. The "point" is now fluidly "moveable" around the circle through our changing selection. Can we interpret this circular structure to corporate management? We can.

Earlier we interpreted the upper "point" at which our semicircle was divided symmetrically with regard to the line of its base as the most complex level of our corporate management hierarchy. Except it was no longer a point on our semicircle being forced upon us by the length of the linear base, for there was no distance (radius) from the point of equal division of the base line to the semicircle edge, which could be longer, or "higher up" than any other.[8] And so the most complex level of our corporate management hierarchy was also no longer a single embodied process, but rather a community of members at the highest level of complexity.[9] Accordingly, the most complex level of our corporate management hierarchy as a fully circular structure will still be a community of members in asymmetric quantity insofar as possible, but now it will also be a community of members at that complexity which fluidly moves around the circle—the structure or *body*—of the corporate community.

To interpret this circular structure to the corporate community adequately we will now need to expand upon the grades of complexity of membership. Imagine that our corporate community has a number of members willing to act at a relatively low level of complexity in the range of embodiment, e.g., they enjoy fashioning simple physical structures with their hands, as when one would mold clay. We will call these members, who are most numerous, the *lower physical range* of our corporate body. They arrange themselves into a circle as physically embodied. Call this, if you like, the transformation of an assembly line into an assembly curve or an *assembly circle*. Outside of this lower physical level circle we add a larger circle, expanding to what we may call the *middle physical range* of our corporate body for example, comprised of those members who enjoy fashioning physical structures at a somewhat higher range of complexity, as when one would assemble various simpler structures together. The ratio of these members to those at the lower range will approximate, insofar as possible, the ratios for maximal curvature noted earlier, so that, according to that ratio, there will always be somewhat fewer members at a higher range of the circle than that of the circle within it. A still larger circle is then added as the *upper physical range* of our corporate body. Beyond this we continue to add more and more expansive ranges of circles, e.g., lower-level management,* mid-level management, etc., to as high a complexity as we wish.

Now just as a circle, if expanding, expands in layers which retain fluid interpretability within themselves, so our corporate community can now expand while retaining far greater fluid interpretability between *members at a selected level* (range) of complexity of experience and between *members at diverse ranges* of complexity. Members of our new community can now interpret to one another in many ways according to their interests and capacities. Members of the (inner) circle can interpret to their neighbors all around the circle—i.e., by making selections which interpret *through* the circle—as they wish, or they can be guided in this by members of the larger circle about them. Members of circles larger than the inner circle can move around the circle next lowest to theirs giving guidance in acting at higher ranges of complexity, as if one circle revolved around another. Indeed, the opportunity to do so will be constantly offered to them because each circle at a range above the inner circle will have a "gap" according to the proportion suggested above, with regard to the circle immediately within it, so that members will be constantly presented with an opportunity to fill the gap (somewhat as in musical chairs).[10] Moreover, our structure will be one in which circles revolve within circles at every range above that of the inner

---

*Or the first level of *the range immediately beyond the physical*, if you like. New technical terms could be created for these ranges.

circle—which has its own mode of fluid interpretation across the circle—so that our product, whatever it is, will trace a path of interpretation through a constantly changing set of members.

Now questions will certainly arise. For example: "I see very well how this could work for simple projects and products such as you mention above in the example of the drinking cups. But how could it work for very highly complex projects, and how could it work for highly complex projects at a physical level even?"

The first issue, that of relatively high complexity, is not so difficult. The circle is a manifestation, within the physically complex range, of interpretive action which engages experience according to certain aspects. But the physically complex range is just that, a range, in which experience is being actively interpreted according to the selections of aspects of interpretation which are less consistent than that of circularity, e.g., linearity, and symmetry. In other words, actions of interpretation, which manifest as *physical* circles, do so only insofar as less expansive interpretations according to less consistent assumptions give rise to a region of physicality. Thus, insofar as the actions of interpretation which manifest as physical circles, or spirals, or spheres, or yet more complex physical shapes, *are* manifested physically, this is due to the actions of interpretation being "brought down" to the level of the physical so to speak. The tendency of interpretation which we call a physical circle is not only relatively more difficult to achieve at the physical range of complexity—we only approximate a circle when we attempt to make one physically, i.e., to manifest this higher level of value into the lower-level context of the physical range of experience—but it is quite welcoming of manifestation in regions of higher complexity. In terms of our suggestions with regard to the corporation, this means that complexities of experience, which we *now* label as "ideas"—a label which will eventually give way to a range joining the "physical"—will be even more amenable to engagement according to our circular structure.

In practical terms this is the passing—interpreting—of "ideas" to a range of other interpreters just as those in our inner circle above passed physical experience to one another, and the guidance of ideas of lower complexity by a constantly varying community of managers, just as those in the circles beyond our inner circle in the structure above, undertake. To use an example, which is both within the purview of contemporary commercial corporations (in research and development) and beyond it, we might have interpretations of the less complex ideas of chemistry for example guided by more complex managing interpretations within the region of chemistry, and these in turn by yet more complex managing interpretations within the region of the sciences, etc. Indeed, the regions of the natural sciences already make use of such structures albeit in an ad hoc and hit-and-miss fashion. Physical circularity is not needed at more complex ranges, although it is a consistent and helpful adjunct to more complex tasks—as should be evident from the spirit of the above—as long as the principle is understood.

Regarding the second part of the question, highly complex projects at a physical level *qua highly complex* are already removed a good deal from the repetitive constriction to quantification which is at its worst in the assembly lines of mass manufacturing, even though *the parts and materials which come together in such projects tend to be heavily constricted in mass manufacturing*. To introduce greater consistency into such highly complex projects according to the above view is no more difficult than applying our circular structure to whatever regions of experience are selected under the aegis of the project.

Remember that our circular structure helps to make a community more consistent. But according to the opening hyperthematic assumptions, a community may be a transformable element in an interpretation to another community. Thus, while a process in human embodiment, which is itself a more or less consistent community—a community of selfhood—may be a member of a larger community such as a corporate community, that corporate community in turn may be a member of a still larger community working toward very highly complex projects. So whether we view this as a number of corporate communities as members of a greater community or as a number of smaller communities as members within a corporate community, we can structure these members, of a complexity beyond that of physical embodiment, as *circles which are members of a greater circle*, while gaining all the benefits of expansion of interpretation afforded by that structuring as suggested above.

Suppose our corporate community is building a house, then we may want efforts toward creatively gaining a great diversity of "materials," as well as efforts of creatively shaping materials, efforts of creatively assembling substructures of our house, efforts of creatively assembling the larger structure of our house, efforts of creative logistics with regard to materials or substructures, etc. In the region of each of these efforts we institute a community according to our circular structure, with the desired ranges of increasing complexity as above and with managed guidance and expansion of interpretation. Each such community then becomes a member of a greater community with a circular structure, with its own levels of complexity, etc.

One such community may interpret nature so as to creatively shape various "natural materials"—i.e., physically complex experiences besides those of mere human embodiment—such as iron, or wood, into an ever varying diversity of fasteners, or what we might call "basic materials" that are then passed on to another member community. Insofar as these member communities are larger to the point where passing their creations to one another becomes impossible at simple levels of embodiment, i.e., whenever something is produced on a scale at which one of us cannot simply hand it to another, then we may implement logistical communities to handle interpretations of location at various scales, as circles inserted between the other circles of our greater communities. Such logistical rings would then revolve around member communities in circles inside their own, passing creative products between members of a circle at lower complexity, or passing them up to members in circles of higher complexity. Houses produced by greater communities such as these would vary continually within selected ranges due to the expansive tendencies we saw in our earlier example, and we could set these ranges so as to gradually work up to more interesting and creative and thus valuable results, just as was suggested above with regard to producing cars.

"But—to invoke Adam Smith's prominent example—if we are building houses we don't want creative diversity in something like galvanized nails," you may still insist, "we merely want quantity." I reply: you want quantity only inasmuch as you are still party to and a result of the inconsistent assumptions which have gone into the sign of the world process, which is our contemporary world. To the extent that **HAs**, **HCu**, and the other hyperthemes begin to be applied, interest will increase in consistent signs at the simpler physical levels as well as the more complex levels both physical and beyond. This happens anyway, if the world is a process of value creation. The lowly nail—not to mention a wider variety of fasteners—has undergone many transformations from what it was 200 years ago; there are many types, shapes, colors, etc. What I am suggesting here in hyperthematic expansion is a system and viewpoint which allows us to do this consistently so as to create greater value.

I could go on to interpret yet other structures which tend toward still greater consistency with **HAs**. From the circle one might pass to the sphere, the helix, the spiral, and yet more complex shapes which are only manifested at physical ranges with some difficulty. Enough has been done with these suggestions however, to be confident in considering **HAs** to be both adoptable and adopted. I will now pass to the interpretation of the five hyperthemes from the chapter on visual art.

8

Expansive Reconstruction of the Hyperthemes of the Visual Arts

Hv Reconstruction

The Hypertheme of the Viewer, I formulated as **Hv**: *in order to build consistent communities, make every effort to expand the acting transformable element being interpreted to, e.g., the viewer—as an interpreter of the sign in its own right, by selecting and passing on aspects of action-experience in the interpretations which manifest consistent tendencies according to H. Insofar as you do this you will expand the ethical selfhood of the viewer.* In other words, **Hv** says to pass on signs of experience which are expansive with regard to the experience of the one receiving the sign. In what ways can one interpret this to the community of the commercial corporation?

One of the most prominent ways is through the products which such communities produce. Take, for example, some of the worst of inconsistent actions of human experience: people killing one another. The killing of people by others is an experience which is often interpreted in ways that are inconsistent with **Hv**, and moreover, in our contemporary world the experience sign of killing has fast become a part of products manufactured in the regions of activity of commercial corporations.

One such product is the contemporary video game. It is helpful to compare the example used earlier in the exploration of the hyperthematic structure of the game, namely chess. There I said that chess was consistent in that—abiding by the tendency formulated as **H5**—it populated communities guided by its hyperthematic structure with element signs which retained in themselves the transformation from inconsistent eliminative elements destabilizing community toward elements promoting interpretation.

Chess deals with what was originally an experience bound up with an action of killing. Yet it deals with it in a way which selects those aspects of the experience that are consistent and passes them on to future interpreters. Those aspects are the movements of transformable elements of a region of experience with regard to one another. The original experience of these movements was the experience of ancient soldiers moving with regard to one another. This has been interpreted, by those who created the chess game, to the pieces of the chess game, which now move with respect to one another in place of the original soldiers. This movement, moreover, expands the interpretive capacity and thus ethical selfhood of the chess player—in **Hv** terms, the "viewer" of the sign, which is the chess game—by giving that player a region of experience in which to play with interpretations on a scale beyond that of single human embodiment.

If it still seems strange to speak of the expansion of ethical capacity by means of a quantitatively scaled physical region in which the play of movement of elements—chess pieces—is promoted, remember that for hyperthematics, quantity and quality are mere ranges of the expansion of interpretive value, and that in this part of the range the expansion from the constrictions of embodiment linked to killing—the experience of movement of the embodied soldier—to that of a region of potential movement of pieces, which represent multiple instances of embodiment moving with regard to one another, is an expansion away from embodiment. Otherwise put, it is an experience of "what they can do together," which from the vantage point of embodiment of the chess player, promotes "what we can do together," which latter is indeed an expansion of interpretation that potentially increases the value within experience.

To see this another way, imagine that the chess structure of pieces in physical space are applied to other regions of action which have even fewer eliminatory echoes than that of an army on the field, e.g., we use something like a chess board with chess pieces to *play with* the ways in which we can *move cooperatively as a community* so as to build a house. There are such games. The chess game achieves what it achieves because, consistent with **Hv**, it passes forward in interpretation the consistent aspect—the cooperative movement—of the selected sign with which it begins—the soldier in a battle—rather than the inconsistent aspects, i.e., the various aspects of killing.

How does that compare to the contemporary video game which is so much a product of the contemporary commercial corporation? To answer this it helps to look back into the history of video games. Take, for example, a game which was very well received—the experience of which the present author remembers with some nostalgia—in the early part of the decade of the 1980s: *Pitfall* for the Atari 2600. *Pitfall* was a rather simple game in which a tiny explorer man ran through a series of side scrolling jungle screens, leaping over rolling logs, swinging Tarzan-like over crocodile infested ponds, and so on. The graphics were rather simple, though good enough to make out the shapes of the crocodile heads, scorpions, and the explorer man himself. The sounds were likewise, a set of cheerful or ominous bleeps

Now, setting aside for a moment the extent to which the game was produced to make a profit, we can ask how does it compare with regard to the chess game in the assumptions behind its interpretation of the experience which it interprets, or to put it in terms of **Hv**: *what does it carry forward in interpreting that experience and what does it let be?* Well, the experience which is interpreted would be something like running a potentially deadly obstacle course in a jungle. We may not know if anyone has ever had such an experience definitely, but we can guess that at least portions of such an experience have been had. People have hopped over fallen logs while exploring in the world's jungles, and they have been stung by scorpions. And acrobats have swung from rope to rope in man-made settings. On the other hand, Tarzan notwithstanding, the opportunities to swing on vines in a jungle setting are limited, since vines—e.g., liana vines—are apparently anchored at the bottom rather than the top, and the opportunities to hop across the heads of crocodiles—although the adventures of the late Steve Irwin come vaguely close—are still more limited. So the game is an interpretation of experiences, which some *have* indeed had, combined with experiences that are possible if not very likely, within an experience of setting—the jungle—in which they might possibly be combined.

But notice that *a good many of these possibilities are intimately tied up with the experiences of pain and injury and death*. So, for example, swinging from vine to vine—or rope to rope as a trapeze artist—is likely to eventually get you hurt or killed, and hopping across the backs of crocodiles seems even more likely to get you killed. So it is not that you could not *try* for such experiences, but rather that in seeking them you risk having other experiences which you'd rather not have. You're free to *try* crocodile hopping in various sub-Saharan African rivers. Good luck with that.

Out of this experience of the actual and the possible, a combined experience is created as an originating sign which is interpreted in the *Pitfall* game. What is passed forward in the interpretation to become the game, however, is only a fraction of this combined originating experience. Insofar as the game tends to be consistent, here with respect to **Hv**, what is passed forward is that which will expand the capacities of interpretation of the viewer, i.e., the game player. In the case of *Pitfall* this is very much akin to what is passed forward in the chess game by the originators of chess. The originating experience has various experience aspects which tend toward inconsistency with the hyperthematic view: pain, fear, disorientation, death. It also has various experiences which tend toward consistency: prolonged effort, newness, assessment of a set of conditions, timing of movement.

Insofar as it is consistent, it tends to forgo experiences from the former group, and interpret or pass on experiences from the latter group. Thus, if he falls in the water or the tar pits while swinging, *Pitfall Harry* simply sinks and disappears accompanied by an ominous sinking sound; if he touches the scorpion or crocodile there is an ominous bleep and he resets to one of his unused lives. He never touches the scorpion so as to fall to the ground in the game and die slowly and painfully from pulmonary edema or other reactions. He never sinks into the tar pit slowly, suffocating and screaming hopelessly for help. We do not get these inconsistent experiences either in the first person, or as a third person viewer; they are not brought forward in the interpretation. The experiences which are brought forward are those of patience in trying again, of learning to time a movement to be made between several simultaneously changing conditions (rolling logs, swinging vines, opening crocodile mouths), etc.

At this point it may be objected that *Pitfall Harry* does not undergo inconsistent experiences because this is an example of an ancient video game with very simple technology that did not allow the programmers to pass those experiences forward, "to make the game *realistic*" as we so often hear these days. To this I reply that in a sense this is so, and in another sense it is not so.

The game is indeed not "realistic" as it might be because of the technological limitations of 1982, but on the other hand, according to the hyperthematic view, *it can never consistently achieve <u>that</u> <u>realism</u> which is intended in the above expression.*

Suppose the technological capabilities of video games were expanded way beyond even those which we now have, and assume that those technological capacities were available to the programmers who envisioned *Pitfall*. The question becomes: how far would we go with the "realism" of the game in terms of our **Hv**, i.e., how much of the originating experience ought we to pass on in the game? When the question is put like this it is clear, first that there is no dividing line between what would be realistic and not realistic with regard to the game's interpretation of its originating experience, and second and more importantly that the tendency toward "realism," both here and in other areas of human endeavor (e.g., films) is an inconsistent dead end.

For, see what would happen with an infinite technological capacity to bring forward all aspects of an originating experience, and the will to do so. If it were the originating experience which is interpreted to the *Pitfall* game, then some of the aspects of the experience that would be brought forward are those which we have loosely categorized as pain (and discomfort), fear, disorientation, death. Imagine that the future game would give us the experience of the sweat and dirt and weariness on us after days of tramping through the jungle; the experience of a vine "rope" burning our hands if our grip slipped; the experience of fearsome noises in the dark; the experience of being eviscerated by a crocodile; the experience of choking and drowning in a swamp.

For the hyperthematic view all such experiences are due to tendencies of inconsistency with regard to interpretation: the results of our actions in conjunction with the field of the world process as the natural world. On the other hand, our imagined future game would also lead us to a sense of timing in catching the vine rope; a sense of skill and interesting movement in the three dimensions of a setting which is new to us; a sense of discovery of long-lost ancient artifacts perhaps (the treasures of the *Pitfall* game); a sense of accomplishment in completing our obstacle course.

We thus have two tendencies, one inconsistent and one consistent, which implicate themselves in the interpretation of the originating experience into our game. And quite evidently the first tendency is a dead end, for if the game designers had brought forward in the interpretation only the experiences engendered by the first tendency there would be no game. The "game" would be the experiences of fear and pain—that which we could interpret less and less—and of death as the limit of that lack of interpretation in terms of our embodiment.

But the second tendency is otherwise, and if the game designers had brought forward in the interpretation only the experiences engendered by the second tendency, there would be very much a game, *even if none of the experiences of the first tendency were brought forward*. We would still have movement and the element of skilled timing, which interprets complex experiences of movement; we would have a sense of newness in new combinations of setting and obstacles; we would have a sense of expansive interpretation with regard to temporality in the discovery of the ancient artifact treasures; we would have a sense of effort and accomplishment in learning to complete the obstacle course. Certainly it is our future game with its much advanced technological capacities which would make the best of our second tendency. Yet even so, *only those aspects of the originating experience which were brought forward according to the second tendency into the old Pitfall game were those which gave it its fun and interest, its value.*

You will interject however that: "surely, however weakly it is achieved in the game, it is the possibility of danger which *really* makes the game?" I answer that there never was any possibility of really real danger in the game, and never can be, though our technological capacities in creating such games would advance to the indefinite heights of the future game imagined above, because danger, pain, and the death of embodiment are all degrees of constriction of interpretation and thus value, and the attempt to carry them forward in an interpretation depends upon an experience that contains and expands value. However weak the interpretations of such an ancient videogame like *Pitfall* were, its value lay in bringing forward the consistent aspects of the originating experience, just as the chess game does. To a small boy of eight on the Christmas morning of 1982, it was the possibility of participating in a very simplified way—through the hand motions and timed button presses of the joystick—in a region of possible experiences of embodied movement whose range was greatly expanded with respect to the usual. Every boy wants to swing through wide open spaces; here, if you could time the movement of your hands right with respect to what you saw, was a very small taste of the greater experience of what it might be like, a very small taste which nonetheless expands somewhat the value of the ethical self with regard to its capacity for the interpretation of the aspect of experience, which is embodied movement.

The heart of every successful video game, *qua successful*, is this carrying forward of aspects of the originating experience which are consistent, and this according to the tendency formulated as **Hv**. This applies beyond video games to games and to every aspect of experience, e.g., the many types of products which commercial corporations produce. Once the spirit of **Hv** is understood, it can very readily be seen at work in the development of the videogame industry.

Nintendo made its great success with one prominent game, *Mario Brothers*. The original game worked because it gave you a range of movement possibilities for the Mario character that were far more expansive than those of say *Pitfall*. Not only could you swing, but you could fly, climb, and jump between different levels and platforms, etc. Not surprisingly, Nintendo has designed subsequent games closely around this consistent interpretation of what is essentially *a greatly expanded range of the experience of human embodiment as motion*. Mario can fly, float, swim, spin, crawl, sway, roll, and so forth, and do various combinations of these actions both on his own and in combination with other creatures and complex moving environments in the game.

But the movement aspect of experience holds no special place in the interpretation of **Hv**, even with regard to video games. In the interactions of Mario with his world, the *inconsistent* constrictive tendencies of the originating experience—an experience which itself is a far more value-promoting experience, qua possibility, than that of *Pitfall*—tend to be left behind, in a way tending very much to be consistent with **Hv**. Thus the "enemies" in the Mario world, such as the koopas, are pretty much never—if at all—killed, and certainly never with any blood, etc. Rather they are variously "bumped," falling off of the screen sometimes to return again in the same level; they frequently confess their misdeeds after being outdone; their badness is often explained in the back story as a misunderstanding or as due to some unfortunate set of events in the past; and they will be back in the next adventure.

There are other aspects of the Mario game which also go into its success however, and because the medium of the videogame is light as color—a medium allowing a great fluidity of transformation—many aspects of the game are easily shown to be consistent with our other hyperthemes. So, for example, Mario's world tends to be highly curved rather than rigid and pointy—its pointy bits are very obviously extremely dangerous areas—consistent with **HCu**; it tends to be an asymmetric world consistent with **HAs**; consistent with **HCl**, it tends to be a very luminous world and one whose colors constantly play around the middle range of the visible light spectrum nearest to white, e.g., the greens and yellows and blues. All of these tendencies lend to its success in hyperthematic terms of value—a value which has been well recognized in popular culture because it is an expansion at a relatively low range of complexity, i.e., a level which can be appreciated by many—particularly when Nintendo's designers have introduced them for the first time as a new outcome of creativity according to **HCr**.

When Nintendo changes its formula—a formula which it perhaps does not have a good explanation for beyond that it works—the resulting Mario games or their derivatives tend to fail relative to the success of the originals, even by the very weak aspect of quantitative monetary value. On top of this, there has been for some time the gradual effect of the old games behind them, which without care and a deeper understanding of value can easily lead to diminishments of value. The videogame, in this sense, is like the earlier artworks. The original game makes some creative interpretation with regard to a selected originating experience. Subsequent games must then expand creatively upon the original if they are to tend toward value. If they begin to fall to the level of mere copies, value tends to diminish.

The creative expansions can be further selections from the consistent aspects of the originating experience according to an abiding by **Hv**, some combination of expansive aspects of the originating experience, which let be the inconsistent aspects of that experience so as to render the new experience more valuable, e.g., Mario's participation in a complexity of movement usually unavailable to human embodiment. They can be expansions upon the color aspect of experience according to **HCl** which make the subsequent experience more valuable with regard to color, e.g., the colors of the Mario world that are a brighter and more consistent selection than that of many regions of our own; they can be expansions upon the curvature aspect according to **HCu** which make the subsequent experience more valuable with regard to the fluid togetherness of a spatial environment than many regions of our usual environment, e.g., the curvature and fluidity of the Mario world; and so on.

But what the community of game designers in the commercial corporation, which is Nintendo, *cannot do* if they want value is to merely strive toward revisiting the originating or subsequent experiences in detail, as a "making it realistic." To the extent that the originating experience for the game is a region of possibility and actuality in which the former predominates, Nintendo already began on a good footing with regard to value. Yet subsequent games actualize that value and begin to infect subsequent creativity, i.e., the possibilities of the region which the original game interprets are vast, but the possibilities of the *subsequent* game, though still vast, are hampered by the actuality of the first game that has "mined out" some of that region.

So the subsequent games cannot gain value by copying what has already been realized, and moreover they cannot gain value by tending to turn away from the region of possibility and copying what has already been realized in any part of the world process. In building value, *what we are bringing forward is a consistent <u>tendency</u> manifested within experience which is also expanded as it is brought forward in the interpretation*. It will do no good, for example, to increasingly model Mario's shape and capacities of movement upon the actual human body, because *it is precisely an expansion away from and beyond that shape and those capacities which gave value to the* *game in the first place*. Likewise, it will do no good to increasingly model Mario's world upon our own, because again it is precisely an expansion away from that world in various aspects which gave value to the game. Finally, and now more obviously with regard to **Hv**,[1] it will do still less good to model Mario's world or his experiences, with regard to the engagement of other embodied characters in his world, on those of our own *inconsistent* experiences—both given and received—in *this* world. If they are brought forward, the experiences of hurting or killing one another in our world, for example, diminish value in Mario's world as well.

In brief, for the Mario games, just as for *Pitfall*, the striving for "realism" attempted in our contemporary world neither adds nor has added anything of value to the sign which is the game. In the misunderstood sense "realism" as a tendency is taken as a sort of copying of an experience, so that *we shall have an experience as wholly alike as possible to some experience which has gone before*, by carrying forward its inconsistent—this is the aspect contra **Hv**—as well as its consistent aspects. But this copying of experience—at least whenever its designers creatively expand upon its prior efforts—is precisely what Nintendo does not do *insofar as it succeeds* with its Mario games. And rightly so, for hyperthematically, *true realism is a tendency to engage experience in an interpretation which tends to result in experience which has not gone before*.

The more designers work toward what is *misunderstood* as realism, the less real and valuable their products become in hyperthematic terms. A large cross section of the contemporary video game industry has been engaged in efforts toward this misunderstood realism for some time however, busily working toward the goal of an ultimate realism in games such as *Call of Duty*, or *Rainbow Six*. There is no limit to the "realism" which can be achieved by such efforts in the misunderstood sense, but if the suggestions above are correct, then such efforts, if we continue to pursue them, will increasingly tend to merge the originating experiences behind the interpretations with the resultant games, so that the experiences of killing or other harmful actions as a game would eventually give rise to actual killing as a game in the inconsistently "real" sense which is desired, by those who are willing to play it. There is no other direction things could take *if* the tendency of action inconsistent with **Hv** is followed out toward its hyperthematically logical limits.

The capacity to carry out the tendency of misunderstood "realism," or that of consistent value expanding realism rests with the communities of the commercial corporation in our contemporary world however, and whether or not human engagement in those communities turns toward consistency with **Hv**, I have suggested enough to show that **Hv** is adoptable in the creation of products such as the video game. One could make a similar interpretation of **Hv** with regard to the practices, community history, and so forth, of the commercial corporation. I will leave this for the reader to muse upon and segue now into the attempt to interpret **Hd**—again not keeping strictly to the order of its disclosure—because what was noted regarding copying has already brought us quite close to the latter. Indeed, all of the hyperthemes are very closely bound up with one another, as the reader will have seen.

Hd Reconstruction

Hd, which I named the Hypertheme of Diversity, is: *in order to expand value in a community make every effort to act so as to transform through interpretation the chosen sign into a different sign which nonetheless remains interpretable to participants of the community, e.g., artists and viewers, by taking into account the interpretive capacity of the elements of the community.* Hyperthematics tells us that the urge to copy experience is the death of value, but many contemporary video games do just that. I leave aside now the question of what they copy—the good or bad of experience—the issue already expanded upon through **Hv**. With **Hd** I am now concerned with the tendency of copying as such.

On the one hand, there has been the copying of experience in its physical complexity throughout the development of video games, an effort which most often pursues the goal of that misunderstood "realism" discussed above. This is the effort to make the game experience "just like" the lived experience. It has issued in the photorealistic environments of our current gaming technologies. The inconsistency of this way of copying is offset, however, insofar as other consistent tendencies of action are combined with it. So, for example, while *Call of Duty* mostly attempts to copy the experience of contemporary military special forces combat, another first-person immersive game might attempt to copy the experience of an earlier historical period, e.g., combat in a Napoleonic army. The latter attempt, by means of its appeal to an originating experience a good deal different from that of our own time, tends toward consistency—just as we saw in certain artworks—in interpreting between experiences of greater diversity taken temporally, even while it tends toward inconsistency in merely copying those experiences.

On the other hand, there has been the still less consistent effort to take a product—e.g., an older video game (an older film, book, music recording, and so on)—as an originating experience, and copy that experience. Such efforts are bound up with those assumptions discussed in the previous chapter which result in the constriction to quantification whose higher complexity manifestation is money as quantity. The thinking behind such efforts comes down to a view expressible as: "our main goal is profit, and we reach a profit primarily through quantitative expansion of sales of our product—through large numbers—so that we may concentrate mainly upon putting out a product, which only differs very slightly from the older product and upon doing this as often as we dare."

Wherever such inconsistent assumptions are made, as they increasingly are by contemporary commercial corporations, we get revisions of products, products numbered or otherwise designated quantitatively. In the video game industry we have many series of games, such as the *Silent Hunter* series, a submarine combat simulator which reached its fifth manifestation, with each game said to improve upon the "accuracy and realism" of the previous version. What this amounts to, for the most part, is an effort to make the audio and visual experience of the game marginally closer to an experience of physical embodiment in a World War II combat submarine setting. And if the five iterations of *Silent Hunter* exemplify inconsistency with **Hd**, the thirteen of Koei's *Romance of the Three Kingdoms* historical strategy game does so even more. The core consistency of the game, an arena of a play of movement and interaction which is similar to a historically based chess game of greater complexity, and which *did indeed* tend to manifest creative value in the original interpretation, has tended to remain more or less static from 1988 to the present, with relatively meager creative additions. From one game in the latter series to another, this aspect tends to be copied, while its presentation as the way the game characters look and sound draws ever closer to—in some small degree—the historical record, and—in large degree—the experience of our contemporary embodiment. In other words, the original creative aspect of the game as an imagined interaction between ancient people is simply copied each time from the last game, rendering it less and less creative and valuable, while the interaction is increasingly portrayed as an experience which is like our own physical experience. And this goes on and on, each game in the series generating more merely quantitative value, while becoming ever less valuable in other aspects, and as a whole. Psychologically, this has obvious effects, e.g., it bores us, and slowly the effort comes to be seen for what it is.

This inconsistency goes far beyond video games of course. There is nothing quite as ubiquitous in our day as the efforts of communities of the commercial corporation to come as near as possible to merely copying either their own products or the products of other corporations. Electronic devices, e.g., computers and cell phones, illustrate this above all. The iterations of series of devices, such as the iPad and various cell phones brands, follow one another at a fantastic rate. The improvements in value to such devices are very often mere quantitative extensions, which accounts for the speed of the iterations, i.e., the expansion of value is very thin, constricted to the aspect of mere quantity. Cell phones, for example, if they give way to a new version, say every six months, merely copy the greater part of the previous version.

The original creative interpretation which resulted in the telephone, something like "a technique to pass the sound of human speech over a greater distance and through more physical obstacles than that of the unaided human vocal system," was copied throughout the twentieth century. A creative new interpretation which resulted in the mobile phone and then cell phone, something like "a technique to pass the sound of human speech over a greater distance and through more physical obstacles than that of the unaided human vocal system . . . without the use of a medium of experience at physical levels of complexity which is visible to embodied humans," has been copied repeatedly from perhaps the mid-twentieth century to the present. So with regard to the cell phone, for example, we have a series of interpretations in which only a very few were relatively very diverse from the originating experience, i.e., here I have noted only two such interpretations, which we usually honor as the *invention of the telephone*, or again *the invention of the wireless phone*. There have been, of course, many lesser creative interpretations in the development of the cell phone, e.g., the hexagonal cell concept of frequency use.

There have been a very great number of very thin interpretations, however, in which very little effort is made toward creativity at all, so that every new version of a popular cell phone brand increases its speed somewhat, its memory capacity, etc., or it merely copies aspects from its competitors phones, or copies aspects of other products, e.g., the digital camera function, the audio player function, the note-taking function, etc. These weak interpretations are bound up with viewing the effort toward the product as a quantitative increase. Commercial corporations constrict the aspects of experience to be interpreted in the new version in the series, insofar as their members tend to assume that value is increased in the mere quantity of units of product that are sold.

Here, you may insist that: "this is all very well, but human inventions and their subsequent development always seem to proceed like this, so much so that there may be no other way such as you imply." I agree with the first point. Human history has indeed perennially proceeded in this way. An original interpretation is put forward. It is then very often copied outright, less often copied with accompanying minor changes, and only occasionally heavily transformed in quite creative new interpretations. This occurs in art, as we saw, as well as other regions of human endeavor. One need not go far into the litany of offenses in this realm, they are widely enough known. Besides the electronic industry they occur in publishing, in automobile manufacturing, in toy manufacturing, in the newer Internet-based industries, and so on. As always this is a matter of tendency. When the tendency is less consistent in terms of **Hd**, then we get the above result; and the range of consistency varies. What we actually do and what we ought to and might do, however, with regard to the expansion of value in light of the hyperthematic principles, may be very far from one another. There are various ways for commercial corporations to apply **Hd** so as to create higher value. Let me offer a few examples.

I suggested above that the telephone was an original effort in passing human speech over a distance greater than that possible through the unaided human voice, and that the cell phone was a further creative effort in accomplishing the foregoing without a visible physical connection. Now, if we are a community of the commercial corporation which produces a cell phone system, then the *least* value we can create in passing forward that original experience in further interpretations—short of abandoning the development of the phone altogether—is to merely copy what we already have. This gets us a very weak quantitative value, thousands, or millions of units which are identical, beyond being *another one* numerically. We have constricted the experience to one aspect—selected it as having one aspect—that of its actuality in embodiment and then expanded with regard to that one aspect so as to have quantitatively more of it.

The next higher range of consistency relative to **Hd** would be that of interpreting the original experience according to multiple aspects, e.g., the cell phone has a length, width, and height at a range of physical complexity of experience. Here again we may make a selection and expansion of one of these aspects in the interpretation, which give our new phone a weakly quantitative value—one which satisfies too many contemporary corporations—e.g., we make the phone slightly longer than the old one, or slightly shorter, or wider, and so forth. Or we might have a selection and expansion of several of these aspects in the interpretation—here we are also in the territory of consistency with **HCu**—so that our new phone has more curvature, for example.

Going on in our range we would interpret the original experience according to yet further aspects besides the above, which brings us to the higher complexities of physicality, e.g., we modify the weight, the color, the malleability, the surface texture. So far we have not gone beyond physical complexities and yet we have gone beyond the range which is accessed by most contemporary commercial corporations with regard to **Hd** in the creative effort between versions of the various series of cell phones which are extant.

Next in our range we would interpret the original experience according to any of the above *and* according to various functional aspects, which are still within the experience of "passing human speech over a distance greater than that possible through the unaided human voice, without a visible physical connection." A few of the many results of creative interpretation within this much more complex range in our new phone might be: the creation of telephones which do no harm to the body or auditory system (e.g., which avoid the germ transmission, radiation problems, or hearing loss of our contemporary cell phones); the creation of a bio-organic telephone that integrates with the processes of nature (e.g., a compostable phone); telephonic bio-enhancement of the living auditory system; the transfer of communication without audible speech—or written text—altogether. Such creative high value modifications of the telephone are all the result of the application of **Hd** to a range of complexity of experience, in an effort that might be encapsulated in the question: *how can we bring diversity to our interpretations of the experience of 'passing human speech over a distance greater than that possible through the unaided human voice, without a visible physical connection,' relative to what we have most recently produced to accomplish this?*

When we pass beyond even this to efforts within that section of the range in which the original experience *in its broadest aspect qua* tele-*phone*—the experience of passing human speech . . . etc. etc.—begins to be transformed in creatively diverse interpretations, then we have gone far indeed from the usual situation with regard to the development of such products by contemporary commercial corporations, but we are also entertaining levels of consistency at which the potential for the expansion of value is very great. If such creative diversity seems daunting at first, it helps to remember that we have made such efforts in our great creative inventions. For example, the creative interpretations from tele-*graph* to tele-*phone*, or again to tele-*vision* are expansions of interpretation in creative diversity at levels of value within this range of complexity; the creative interpretations from *mega*-phone, to *tele*-phone, to *micro*-phone are likewise. *We do this anyway* then, the issue is whether we continue to proceed in ad hoc and trial-and-error fashion, or whether we advance to deliberate efforts which integrate community according to the principle formulated here as **Hd**. Engaging in such creative interpretations according to the hypertheme of diversity at this high range of complexity, corporate communities might produce: tele-osmatic devices (which pass experiences of smell over greater distances), tele-thymiatic devices (for passing experiences of emotion over greater distances), tele-iomiatic devices (for long-distance healing), zoa-phones (devices which communicate with animals), phyto-phones (for communicating with plants), etc.

These then are some of the ways in which communities of the commercial corporation could interpret the experience selected as an example—the cell phone—according to **Hd,** at increasing levels of complexity, so as to expand value. This in no way denigrates the *best* contemporary efforts of our more consistent contemporary commercial corporations, for they have often created high-level value in many products we enjoy. Yet that creativity is greatly hampered by the inconsistent assumptions noted above. We can do better.

The trend of a good deal of the effort in the development of the products of commercial corporations in the realm of electronics is toward miniaturization, for example. But miniaturization is a constriction and inconsistent with our Hyperthematics *if it is seen as an elimination of the physical*. It need not be viewed this way, however. Miniaturization as an elimination ultimately leads to the elimination of the physical aspect of electronic devices, such as cell phones. If the suggestions above are plausible, however, one can see that value is expanded according to interpretations of many aspects of experience. What we need then is not an elimination of the physical, but *an expansion beyond the physical.*

Here I mean that the more we can view the interpretations of the development of a product—through functionally expansive engagements such as suggested by **Hd**—as the development of an *experience*, rather than the development of an object, the more our capacity for creating value will increase. To return to the cell phone once more, what we see ourselves as accomplishing in miniaturizing the cell phone as a physical object and in simplifying the aspects of its use, is a removal of experience of physical complexity between regions of experience viewed in their physical complexity. For example, tonight I want to talk to my friend who lives a hundred kilometers away without having to experience the trip otherwise needed to talk to her face-to-face. The cell phone and the developments of the cell phone are thus very often viewed as eliminating the physicality of the distance between us: "it's so easy now," we say.

But in fact all creative interpretations which have expanded value with regard to the cell phone have done so not through an elimination but rather by interpreting that physical distance in ways which are more complex than mere low-level physicality. So the danger for value is that we forget and misunderstand this expansion, e.g., in constricting our expansion of communication to the lower level of embodied physicality by sending the most banal examples of our everyday speech far away. We get the latter in the Internet wherever we are too eager to *say* something, which isn't very worth saying, and to say it over a very great distance, as often happens in our social media, e.g., Twitter. It also happens readily enough in telephone communication, as will be apparent to anyone who, forgetting the expansive view for the view which merely assumes the elimination of physicality, communicates over very long distances, e.g., you make a long-distance telephone call to a friend, for example, and very soon discover that you have nothing worth saying at the moment. Your assumption of *a mere gap of physicality* between you and your friend with respect to the telephone experience has infected your ability to interpret creatively between your experience and that of your friend.

The hope, on the other hand, is that, continually reinterpreting this expansion creatively, we come to view ourselves as processes that are gradually moving beyond the range of physicality. **Hd** can help us in this with regard to the actions of commercial corporations, but it and other aspects of Hyperthematics will have to be applied still further. It will take a loosening of constrictions in diverse regions of human experience. To take one instance, science supports technology but, hyperthematically viewed, consistent technological advance will have to aim for an engagement of experience in which physical complexity is surpassed for more complex and thus valuable ranges of interpretation. Insofar as that engagement is understood as an expansion of the human process beyond physical complexity, it consistently creates value. Yet the possibility of this expansion of the human process beyond physically embodied complexity is precisely what the vast baggage of antiquated metaphysical assumptions held by most members of the scientific community leads them to deny. Paradoxically, we thus have science supporting the development of technology, the latter of which at its creative and consistent best is working toward goals which the mainstream view of science denies as being possible. It need not be this way.

It is not that the mainstream scientific view is wrong in assuming that the thoroughgoing connection of experience is at the basis of a meaningful engagement of the world, it is wrong rather in assuming that this thoroughgoing connection of experience consists and can consist only of the active engagements of experience at the range which we have characterized as *physical*. The processes of our historic creative advances, which have taken us from the basic communication possibilities of embodiment to the cell phones mused upon above, all suggest otherwise. Everything which we now do in the realm of the latter would have seemed as impossible to ancient human understanding as the possibilities of a much more highly complex engagement of experience than that which can be described as physical, seems now to the mainstream of science. I have suggested enough in the above, however, to show that **Hd** is readily interpretable and to adopt it.

HOe Reconstruction

I now pass on to the Hypertheme of Objective Expansion, formulated as **HOe:** *in order to expand value in a community which creates or engages objects, make every effort to act so as to transform the chosen sign being interpreted into a sign whose aspects tend away, through expansion, from the relations common to the objectification inherent in the sign, e.g., the painting*. I illustrated earlier how some of the great advances with regard to value in the realm of art have come about through creative interpretations which have been able to bring a greater complexity of interpretive relations into an artwork than that complexity of interpretive relations which makes the artwork an object. In this way the ancient Greeks brought the three dimensions of complexity of the originating sign into the two dimensions of the painted surface.

At the heart of this is the implication that, as I suggested for visible light, objecthood, rather than being set, is the result of a range of engagement of experience according to tendencies of action which are inconsistent. Thus *as the process of human community advances, what we designate as an "object" will change, the designation continually passing onward to whatever experience, at whatever level of complexity, which we are failing or have failed to engage according to interpretive expansion*. This insight aids our ingression into the ways in which **HOe** might be interpreted to the actions of commercial corporations. We say that commercial corporations produce both products (objects) and services for those who participate in corporate communities as the buyers of those objects and services. The interpretation of **HOe** can thus be helped by mulling over the question: in the region of experience—the "medium"—which we are engaging, in producing a product or service, what combination of tendencies gives rise to the objecthood of the experience?

Suppose the members of our corporate community are working with clay—the experience of clay—for instance. They are about to transform this clay through an interpretation into, say, a bowl. What makes the clay an object? Answer: whatever type of characteristic of the clay that tends to constrict its capacity for further interpretation. It is that characteristic or characteristics that it would be well to interpretively expand on in our interpretation which produces the bowl. You may select any characteristic of the clay, which, relative to the interpretive capacity of other aspects of experience, is constrictive of interpretive action, and you will then have that characteristic as your starting point in the application of the hypertheme of objective expansion. **HOe** tells you to engage that characteristic so as to increase the capacity for interpretation with regard to it, for those who will experience the coming sign/product (the bowl).

Expansion out of the Objectivity of Lower-Range Physical Complexity: Clay

In short, we must surpass the objective tendencies of the clay in our bowl if we are to abide by **HOe**. So, returning to our clay medium, if one suggested that what makes our clay objective is its characteristics of relative stiffness and of impermeability, then our challenge—the challenge of communities of the commercial corporation—in applying **HOe** is to expansively interpret those characteristics in the transformation to our bowl. Sometimes we will be able to do this in ways which directly transform some characteristic of the originating experience that has tended toward objectivity. Suppose we have been producing clay bowls for some time, then we may make our newer bowls larger in some respect, i.e., add more clay. In terms of art this is akin to what Monet did in layering paint upon his canvases; he expanded the planar characteristic of the canvas by adding depth. This is fairly weak in terms of value however, both because it is an expansion at mere quantitative levels of complexity—the painting canvas has *some* depth to begin with both in itself and in its first layer of paint and adding more paint simply repeats, adding more of the same—and because very low-level quantitative expansions of value have already been tried in many if not most regions of experience and thus they are not very creative. It is after all a fairly ancient and well-worn innovation to make larger clay bowls.[2]

HOe is better applied by taking some action which adds an aspect or aspects of interpretation to the experience of the clay and guides the receiving interpreter beyond one or more of its objective characteristics. The clay, as it is in a clay bowl, is relatively stiff, brittle even. Thus any expansion which can create flexibility relative to the bowl by adding an aspect of interpretation to the experience of the fired clay will add value. This will often be done by means of adding some flowing curvature to the bowl in a way which guides the interpreter of the bowl around it, by touch, by vision, etc., in actions *akin to those which could be carried out* if the medium of the clay were not stiff in its objectivity.

Again the clay, as it is in the clay bowl, is relatively impermeable. This tendency of its objectivity is a tendency of preventing active engagement of, or through, some part of its region of experience, it is its "boundedness," so that, e.g., I cannot push my fingers into the interior of the bowl's sides and water will not flow into or through that interior. As a response to this impermeability, one can imagine various expansions in the finished bowl. The bowl could be shaped in a way which would allow the fingers to indeed push into or even through the interior of the bowl sides—like the finger holes in a bowling ball—or it might be shaped in such a way that water might indeed flow into it through its sides and yet not flow out.

These expansions are expansions at the scale of human embodiment, but of course there are others so that the *art* of chemistry, for instance, may expand upon the objective impermeability and stiffness of the bowl at other scales, giving us something like a clay that is more permeable in what we now call its microscopic aspect. Thus it would be selectively permeable to light but not to liquid, or to cold liquid but not to hot liquid, or to other clay bowls which its sides may meld together with. Or again giving us a clay which is more flexible in what we now call its microscopic aspect so that the bowl can be constantly re-molded into multiple interesting shapes, or stretched to a larger shape as needed.

Is it still a bowl? Are we still playing with the medium of clay? Yes indeed, for it is only an inconsistent objectivity which hold static what a bowl must be and what clay must be. Every creative expansion according to **HOe**, as well as other hyperthemes, broadens *what it yet may be*, and how valuable it may become in its complexity of interpretation. Whether we choose to call them "clay" and "bowl," or expand the names accordingly, matters little, for *the value of every creative expansion out of objectivity will be visible insofar as the ongoing history of action always meaningfully interprets itself back to the ancestral signs of our past efforts.*

Someone may insist however that "the example is too close to art, particularly to sculpture, and the application of **HOe** would be much more difficult and doubtful if you used some contemporary product made by commercial corporations." To this I reply that in the first place the attempt by the members of commercial corporations to consistently apply **HOe** will indeed result in the products and services of commercial corporations becoming more akin to what we would consider artworks; second and consequently, I deliberately chose the medium of clay because it is an ancient medium of human interpretation and can thus—because so much has already been attempted with it—make visible the connection between production and art in the interpretation of **HOe.** And third, I can still show through further examples that **HOe** is readily applicable to the sort of contemporary products which the objector has in mind.

The goal is not to transform clay in *all* its characteristics into that which is not clay. This may very well happen, but, to insist once more, to have value it must happen through the meaning of an interpretation, and as it happens, clay, and those future developments of clay which we will designate by future names, will always retain an interpretive connection to their ancestrally originating experience. The goal is to engage regions of objectivity and interpret them into regions of greater value. The world process already has the experience, which we designate clay, within it as a relative objectivity. The goal is to play with that experience, gaining ever new and interesting experience.

Furthermore, the goal is not to bypass objectivity. We cannot "outrun" objectivity. Objectivity, by the definition offered earlier, will always be a less complex range of whatever capacity of complexity of interpretation we have reached. The goal rather, is to engage objectivity in ways which expand the meaning and value of experience for us. But let me briefly show how **HOe** might be applied in some contemporary commercial products.

Expansion out of the Objectivity of Mid-Range Physical Complexity: Wood

Let us say that the originating experience is *the experience of sitting*, and that we are going to make an object as an interpretation of that experience, i.e., we want to make a chair of some sort. The question becomes: what in the medium of experience from which we will make our chair tends to make it objective, i.e., what in the medium of the chair constricts the experience of sitting toward objectivity?

The broad answer is that the medium of the chair will tend to constrict the experience of sitting toward objectivity in whatever ways it tends to render the experience the same for each of us, i.e., in those ways in which it constricts our capacity of interpretation so that the interpretations which each of us[3] make with regard to the chair are the same. The art painting was using the medium of the plane surface of canvas, the chair will perhaps use a three-dimensional space of wood. Just as for clay, wood will have aspects that tend toward objectivity. These aspects give rise to the interpretability of its three dimensions; they make up *its* three-dimensional complexity as an experience.

What I mean here is that we tend to say that such and such occupies a space, e.g., a three-dimensional space, as if the thing and the space were separate. This view is not the most helpful one. The wooden chair allows us a certain capacity of interpretable experience that we are willing to locate within the range of experience, which we call physical space; a solid granite block allows us a far different capacity of interpretable experience that we are willing to locate within the range of experience, which we call physical space.

Whatever the experience of our three-dimensional space of wood allows us, our goal here is to so interpret the experience of sitting in that space that we pass beyond what the space of wood, *qua* wood, allows us. Let us say that wood tends toward objectivity in its weight and in its impenetrability. We want to interpret into its medium a sign which will guide the receiving interpreter through an experience of sitting. To do that consistently with **HOe**, we are going to have to interpret the sign in a way that expands upon the objective limitations of *weight* and *impenetrability* in the experience of the medium, which is our wood.

We might develop one of its aspects which tend less toward objectivity so as to offset other aspects which do tend toward objectivity. So, for example, if we say that wood is more flexible than clay, then we may use that flexibility to indirectly offset the aforementioned limitations of weight and impenetrability in our wood. Wood can be bent in its flexibility, and in this capacity to be bent it can take on greater curvatures than a host of other materials. The creative interpretation of this aspect of flexibility can result in a chair structure that guides the user—the sitter—into an experience of sitting, which interprets beyond the objective tendencies of the wood. If, say, the chair is fashioned from highly curved strips of wood, whose combination of curves form a structure, still in physical space, which is much more *penetrable* than the usual experience of wood—e.g., air, light, and one's hands can pass through and interact with the interior of the structure—and which is much *lighter* than the usual experience of wood, then one is engaging in interpretive expansion consistent with **HOe**.

Another way to look at this is to say that the experience of sitting is bound up as a process of experience with—in this case—the chair, and that a creative interpretation of the medium of the wood into the chair, as imagined above, is going to be expansive of the experience of sitting. Just as a three-dimensional drawing/painting on the planar surface of the canvas expands the visual region of interpretation for the viewer of the painting, so the expanded penetrability of the physical chair space is going to offer to the sitter a much greater opportunity of interpreting the physical space of the chair than that which would be offered, say, with a seat merely carved into a solid block of wood. The sitter is going to be able to curl her fingers or hands through the sides of the chair as she sits, for example, or play along the curves of the chair with arms, legs, and other parts of the body. She is going to be able to move into various comfortable and interesting positions within the experience of sitting, brought about by this expanded penetrability and by the felt lightness of the structure that the creative use of the aspect of flexibility has given the chair.

The expansion of interpretability of the "object," which is the chair, is going to tend to allow a different experience for each person who sits in the chair, and even a different experience for the individual sitter as an embodied process. This de-objectifying of the chair is an increase of its value. Or again: the action of sitting, the engagement of the chair in the experience of sitting, is allowed by our creative chair to flow as a process more than it otherwise might be. It flows through the curves created from the flexibility of the medium, and does not come up against the usual constrictions of the wood so as to give rise to the *felt experiences* of weight and impenetrability.

Compare that to an example of how the production of a chair can be *inconsistent* with **HOe**. The usual experience of sitting in an older-style church pew provides this example. In an old-style church pew the wood has been interpreted so as to retain the weight and impenetrability of the objectivity of the medium of wood. Accordingly, the experience is one of weight and enclosed impenetrability. The back and seat of a church pew are most often flat plane surfaces, joined at, or approximately at, a 90° angle, and thus forming a point. The wood is typically solid throughout, without penetrability. The bottom part of the pew is very often enclosed at the sides and behind the feet, constricting their interpretive freedom. None of this is accidental. The physical space of such a church pew is meant to be interpreted as little as possible as an experience of sitting. Each of us in the church pew is meant to feel objectively the *same* experience as the other and to be constricted in our interpretation of the sitting experience, so as to focus on a point at the front of the church.

As to how far the application of **HOe** can be taken in the production of chairs through the medium of wood, a glance at human history thus far would show us how wonderful and varied are the creative interpretations which have been made, and will suggest how many yet remain to be made. The *rocking chair* for example, a creation which used the flexibility of wood in the curvature of its rockers to bypass the weight and impenetrability of the medium, guides the sitter to capacities of interpretation in the experience of sitting in a physical space which go far beyond even that of our earlier imagined example. Its creator, name lost in the depths of our history, was, at low levels of physical complexity and relative to the ranges of human interpretation usual at the time, a genius on par with any we have ever had.

Expansion out of the Objectivity of Higher Ranges of Physical Complexity: The Television

The media above are predominantly regions of experience engaged at the lower ranges of physical levels of complexity: the plane, the three-dimensional space. Moving on to the media of regions of experience at the higher ranges of physical levels of complexity, and even beyond the physical levels of complexity, we can still show how **HOe** can be interpreted.

Consider a television. As a medium of experience we can understand a television as a sign of actions of combining experiences, a sign which is more complex—for experience at levels of human embodiment[4]—than the media discussed above. A television is an object at the lower physical levels of complexity, made up of glass, plastic, various malleable metals, etc. which have been engaged in a way that give it three dimensions, perhaps a cubic shape of lines and angles, plane, and slightly curved surfaces, a certain weight, etc. But it is also an object with regard to which the creative manipulation of those combinations of experiences of glass, metal, and so forth have brought it beyond the lower physical levels of complexity to make it less an object.

Earlier, I showed that inconsistent actions engage light which, at the top of its range, is maximal interpretation at the levels of what we call physical, so as to constrict it. The results of such engagements give rise to *power*, i.e., action which has undergone these tendencies of constriction so as to result in some degree of objectification. This power, in the terms which interest me here in considering the television, appears objectively as the electrons of our electricity.

Suppose then that some inconsistent engagement of light has gathered action as electrical power for us; to take the simple case, we engage the sunlight with a solar panel whose surface is filled at the microscopic level with those tiny pointed pyramids mentioned earlier, which trap sunlight. We thus have constricted action trapped in our electrical grid and ready at the end of our electrical cables. Leaving aside the issue of the overall inconsistency of the situation—a vast problem that will only respond to consistent efforts—we are interested in how, consistently with **HOe**, the television as a medium of experience has been a creative, expansive response to the experience of the electrical power, and how it can be creatively expanded yet further out of its current objectivity.

In the first place, you can see that objective aspects of glass, plastic, metal, etc. have been met and surpassed, expanded upon, in the creative relationships to one another which the inventors of the television gave to the glass, etc. The television is much more than the sum of its parts, for each "part," as in the materials of glass, metal, and so forth has its objective tendency to be more objective in some aspect of how we experience it than its peers. Thus glass in its objectivity may have the aspects which we designate as hard and inflexible, while copper metal may have the aspect which we designate as opacity.

Now, in whichever aspects the medium of the television has arisen through creative engagement consistent with **HOe**, it is due to expansions in some aspect of the experience wherein a sign has been produced by a creative action, which has taken note of the tendency of objectivity of some aspect of the experience and changed or added another aspect to bypass that objectivity. So, for example, a television is a combination of metal wire, glass, plastic, etc., in which the various tendencies toward objectivity have been overcome to some degree by developing tendencies away from objectivity in some other aspect of the experience. Thus, the relatively constrictive hardness and inflexibility of glass are met in the medium of the television by the relatively expansive malleability and ductility of copper; and the opacity of copper is met by the transparency of glass. Beyond the combinations of materials, there are also various combinations of shapes at the physically spatial level of complexity of interpretation. Thus, a flexible wire meets a plane surface and curves around it, or some part of the television is shaped so as to fasten to another. These shape combinations may be more or less creative or inconsistent.

The television then, as a valuable medium, is a combination of selections of experience in which creative interpretive responses to various objective tendencies have been met and expanded upon by further interpretive tendencies so as to guide the incoming action—the constricted action we call electric power—through some expansive process of interpretation. In a television electricity enters in, finds its way through the various pathways of its metal wiring, is engaged and manipulated, and is released by the television through the glass of its screen in a highly complex and valuable, *qua medium*, sign of interpretation, namely *light emitted by a* television, or again: *a process of light which has gone "through" the process of a television.**

There are various ranges of objectivity of television which can be engaged in consistency according to **HOe**, and some of that range *has already* been consistently engaged. The objective aspects of "natural materials" of the world process, such as metal and glass, have been met and de-objectified by expanding upon other more interpretive aspects of their experiences or those of their peers. The objective aspects of the "parts" of television systems have in turn been met and de-objectified by expanding upon other more interpretive aspects. These inventive engagements have created the television as a sign and, inasmuch as that sign is creative, it is a medium for further interpretation. Put otherwise: a sign is more or less of a medium, as it engenders or constricts further interpretation.

This is not unique to television by any means. A gasoline engine, one prominent example, similarly receives a sign of the constriction of action within its gas and oil fuel, and interprets that sign into the action of motion. And one medium builds upon another, or again, one sign builds upon another, if they are consistent. Having been created through consistent engagements of other media—to the extent that it is consistent—television is itself a medium, as that which interprets through electrical power to light. **HOe** is therefore also interpretable with regard to this medium of electrical power to light, for *that* medium also has its aspects which tend toward objectivity.

But where do the tendencies toward objectivity reside in the medium of "electrical power to light"? The answer to this seems obscure at first because—within our usual range of experience—light is highly complex in its interpretability, and just so we are unused to considering its aspects of uninterpretability. Yet if light is the maximal or leading edge of the interpretability of the physical range of complexity, then its objectivity as an experience may be said to be its participation in the various restrictions which give rise to physicality. In other words, even though the consistency of the medium of "electrical power to light" lies in its expansion out of power to the higher interpretations of light, its inconsistency, its objectivity, remains in *its not passing beyond light qua boundary of the range of the physical*.

---

*Abstractly speaking, *merged with and then separated from.*

*Expansion out of the Objectivity beyond the Range of
Physical Complexity: The Television Program*

To pass beyond this latter tendency of light as a medium according to **HOe**, is going to take a creativity which interprets signs of the world process into and through the medium of "electrical power to light" in ways which engender the resultant signs as expanded beyond *physicality represented by light*. The reader asks: 'what does this mean, or at least what does this mean practically in terms of television?' To answer that, first note that the need for what is suggested here is very often evident to us, just not in hyperthematic terms.

The history of the development of television is the history of a slow crawl, with many setbacks, away from weak interpretations—*representations*—of mere physicality by means of the medium of "electrical power to light" which is television. Early efforts with the medium—and here I must include film, as discussed in an earlier chapter—were thrilled to make interpretations which very often got no further than the representation of the human body in motion in its physicality, e.g., showing people dancing around doing various silly things. In our weaker moments this urge to weak interpretation still arises; think of how many people react in fascination when told "Hey! You're on TV!"

We are slowly moving away from attempting only such weak interpretations, notwithstanding reverses such as "Reality TV"—to invoke a contemporary trend which is analogous to the "realistic" video game in its constriction—which are ultimately dead ends, if the world process is one of value creation. Every new creative effort which interprets through the medium of television by expansion on some aspect or aspects of experience which guides the viewer away from the physicality of the originating sign, away from mere representation, is consistent with **HOe**. Just as bringing three dimensionality into the two dimensionality of the surface of the painted canvas is a consistent advance, bringing aspects of the originating sign which have a complexity beyond that of physicality into the complexity of *the light transfer as a boundary of physicality* is also a consistent advance. Whenever this is done in a new and creative way we recognize it if we have the interpretive capacity to do so, and we grow, even if we do not yet have that capacity, so long as we can be guided to take a look.

To offer a few examples from the historical development of television, we have succeeded whenever we have tended to interpret a complexity of interaction between physically embodied human actors (here literally television or film actors) which guide the viewer beyond the mere physical embodiment of the actors as represented by the light. So, in our most creative contemporary efforts, e.g., we portray a human as aged beyond current embodiment; we portray an emotion such as joy through complex interactions beyond mere facial expressions; we portray a world, say a cartoon world, in which the "laws" of embodiment and the physical world are expanded upon.

We can go much farther than we have though, and consistently with **HOe**, the medium of our televised engagement of electricity to light, insofar as it expands value, may in future take up such challenges. Consider: the portrayal of how the actions or interactions between humans at periods of human history have influenced those of humans in other periods of human history—already creatively attempted for the region of science and technology in the *Connections* series of James Burke—or again, without recourse to actual human history, how humans taking certain actions in a story influence those of some different time or place of that story. The film *Cloud Atlas* makes a beginning to the latter challenge. There is also the challenge of portraying the interpretation of a relationship, say lifelong friendship, in terms less physical than embodiment, e.g., a series in which episodes explore friendship through constantly differing actors and situations. Also consider the challenge of portraying the life of a person, or event, without recourse to the embodied representation of that person or people at all, e.g., the portrayal of a person only through his or her "external" influence; the challenge of portraying nature as a cycle within the world process rather than a series of set pieces of physical interaction such as predator/prey/procreation; the challenge of portraying nature as a cycle of process in relation to human development; the challenge of portraying how our distant ancestors might have imagined us—their future progeny; and the challenge of portraying how our distant progeny might interpret us. These examples should suffice to indicate how vast is the region of interpretation to be explored by engaging the medium of television in consistency with the spirit of **HOe**.

Any objective creation of man is no more than a sign of a region of experience engaged by inconsistent and consistent actions which, according to its level of complexity and value, allow or constrict further interpretations in other regions of experience. A television, a gas motor, etc., all combine a variety of consistent and inconsistent actions which have given rise to them, into a sign which is experienced, and which then guides, constricts, or expands the actions of further interpretation which engage the sign. Their objectivity is the inconsistency which is gathered into them, into their parts, into the relations between their parts, into the selection of and emphasis upon aspects of their materials, and so forth. Their value is the consistency gathered into them in those parts, relations, and selections; it is a community of action which tends to impart an *experience* rather than an object to the receiver.

Objecthood is a result of processes of action and in its degree is always a matter of the value and diminishment of value of those actions. I have tried to show this with three examples at varying levels of complexity. It is up to the community, very often the commercial corporation, which creates those objects to strive for consistency, to constantly introduce into the medium of interpretation creative expansions that guide those who receive the sign of those objects beyond that objectivity. In that way mere production of objects will eventually be transformed to the creation of art in all the various regions of human experience. I will consider **HOe** to be adoptable by communities of the commercial corporation and pass on to the next hypertheme.

Ha Reconstruction

The next hypertheme I will attempt to interpret is that named the Hypertheme of Aging, formulated as **Ha**: *in order to expand value in a community make every effort to act with regard to a chosen sign so as to encourage further interpretation of it by oneself and by other interpreters in expansions of the span of its interpretation as a process relative to the world process.* This hypertheme is particularly interpretable by musing upon the urge toward newness in the efforts of contemporary commercial corporations. A very great many corporations want us to cast off the old and continually buy the new.

I mentioned before that newness is often bound up with inconsistent assumptions and actions toward merely quantitative expansion. Mere newness, as merely another physical iteration of the same, is most often the result of such expansion. The newest of a series of electronic devices, or of cars, or of services with very little change between iterations, is always being produced for us to buy. Yet on the other hand newness has a consistent aspect and has its degree for the hyperthematic view. Highly creative newness, the newness of a very new and consistent invention, of an experience much different from past experiences, is a highly valuable type of newness.

Hence the application of **Ha** will be more subtle than simply denying the urge toward newness. Rather, it will be something like a constant "promoting of the new in the old," a constant interpretation of aging signs to new contexts of experience which promotes the temporal connectedness of the world process, or, put in other words, *which tends to guide the acting transformable elements in the world process to view that process as a great community in which every action of its members, as <u>temporally located</u> members, has its consequence with regard to the value and the capacity to promote value of the community.* Thus, in interpreting some ways that communities of the commercial corporation can apply **Ha**, I will look at the creation of products and services which guide us to make interpretations which take note of our temporal linkages as part of the world process. Let me first give some examples with regard to "objects."

The corollary of the contemporary urge toward mere newness brought about by inconsistent assumptions with regard to **Ha**, is a tendency to discard so as to make way for this mere newness, our tendency toward the "throwaway society." Yet this must result from the assumption that generates mere quantitative value, for mere quantitative objects accumulate at physical levels, which make them less and less interpretable. We tend then to either convert that mere quantity to money—as discussed earlier—or to eliminate it in its physical aspect.

According to the hyperthematic view *we cannot truly eliminate* however, but can only act upon the inconsistent assumptions which tend toward the various ways of eliminating. The attempts at elimination are passing disturbances, gaps of interpretation in the world process, which return to influence the subsequent growth of the loci of experience that attempted them, and that must eventually be made good according to the ultimate assumption **H**. Hence the assumption that there can be *garbage*—most prominently the many objects that we produce—is inconsistent. Those actions, which attempt to eliminate experience as "garbage," are diminishments of value within the world process, which hurt the processes—human and other—within the world process.

Nonetheless, the engagement of the inconsistent tendency toward garbage by the world process gives us clear examples in accordance with **Ha**. The campfire artifacts of a Paleolithic humanoid group of tens of thousands of years ago, the pottery shards of the Babylonian civilization, the print advertisements of Victorian England, all of these may at one time have been discarded as garbage, only to be reinstated as signs of value through their aging. Having begun as one of a mere repetitive quantity of sameness—the ancient world was guilty of this tendency as well—over time they have become signs of interpretation far broader than an embodied human life span by being preserved and interpreted, whereas other like objects of their own time have been interpreted out of their quantitative aspect by the world process.

In other words, both through and despite our human actions the world process interprets our "garbage,"* expanding it beyond its sameness as mere repeated quantity, selecting objects from among that weak quantitative value and carrying forward and promoting them through further interpretations over time. Or again: wherever action, e.g., human action, accumulates sameness of experience by constriction of interpretation to some aspect or aspects of experience, the world process responds with an expansion of these "quantitative disturbances" within experience. Artifacts such as those noted above then have undergone new interpretations which are increasingly beyond those of quantity. If they hadn't we wouldn't have them, for the world process interprets them out of mere quantity in other regions beyond that of embodied human physicality, e.g., as the interpretations in which nature erodes, weathers, recombines, and so forth, expanding the accumulation of sameness by interpreting it back into the world process.

So, on the one hand, the world process is involved in an expansion away from sameness, which reinterprets objects accumulated in mere quantity back to itself, and—though our understanding of the scope of its interpretation is still weak—we see readily enough in that region of the world process which we call nature how *quantitative accumulation* is continually expanded so as to give rise to new and more valuable signs: trees grow and multiply as quantity, natural processes, say forest fires, interpret them back into the soil to contribute to new and interesting growths; mountain ranges are built up as quantity, natural processes—the weathering of wind and water—interpret them back into the earth's interior.

And on the other hand, the world process is involved in a consistent interpretation of **Ha** with regard to our efforts in producing various objects. It helps us save and further *some* of our interpretations according to mere quantity, even as it helps us interpret the better part of our efforts toward mere quantity into new and more creative avenues. *Of the many produced, some of the artifacts of our ancestors survive.*

The world process thus provides us with an *environment* for creative interpretation. It discourages constriction of interpretation and it also encourages the preservation of our efforts to be interpreted anew. That this environment for creative interpretation, which the world process provides for us, includes what we in our contemporary—and incomplete—view think

---

*Our "garbaging" actions.

of as the *natural environment*, is also evident through further hyperthematic musement, for nature interprets the loci of experiences in its region according to the promotion of aging suggested by **Ha**.

Every effort of embodied willing action in experience must move toward creative expansion of value in a diversity of interpreted experiences. Mere accumulation of sameness of experience in the region of nature is reinterpreted into the world process as the precursor of further creativity. What we call the biological species—e.g., a species of animal—ages in the creative diversity of its interpretations, so that it continues to be interpreted to a greater and greater temporal span of the world process. The sameness in the process of speciation, the merely quantitative accumulation of similar members of a group of animals in a species, is continually being reinterpreted back into the world process, insofar as the value of the species tends toward that of mere quantity, so that the process of speciation may give rise to further creative diversity.

It is the *community* of the species which ages, and when it does not age in creative diversity, when at the level of species it tends toward a mere quantitative similarity with other members of a group of species, then it too is reinterpreted back into the world process to give rise to further creative diversity. The reinterpretation of the dinosaurs, of other earlier lines of speciation, and perhaps even the future reinterpretation of our own current embodied human line of speciation, following periods of interpretive constriction toward mere quantity of embodied individuals (such as humanity is now undergoing in our global population explosion), could be mused upon further.

These tendencies of the region of nature within the world process appear to us as an uncaring destruction and elimination of signs within the natural environment, particularly when we ourselves as embodied signs within that environment undergo such destruction. They are corrective constrictions however, which in time we will come to understand in the context of localized practice promoted by the region of nature in its role of being a guide to its charges (ourselves, as well as animal processes of other levels of complexity), as growing processes of value. If, for example, through the guidance of nature, there were to occur a "die off" of embodied humanity as mere quantity, then the hyperthematic view suggests that this localized constriction as *a time of practice in embodiment*, would give way to being guided by the region of nature toward the creation of more valuable forms of "advanced embodiment" that would manifest our more complex processes, as more valuable, more ethical, communities of selfhood. There is very fertile ground for further hyperthematic musement here, but it requires another work and my task here is mainly to interpret the hypertheme to the production of our commercial corporations. However, the interpretation of **Ha** with regard to the objects produced by communities of the commercial corporation can take its cue from the above considerations.

What is worthy of survival is whatever aspects of that which we produce which are tending most strongly away from sameness and toward expansions of interpretation which will continue to be interpretable with regard to the world process, and which will thus *age*. The "objects" of the more complex consistent communities interpreted in the earlier exploratory mode follow this tendency, they promote new interpretations.[5] Games, books, musical instruments, paintings are all meant to be reinterpretable over larger temporal spans of the world process.

Remember I said earlier, for example, that a book was not an object. This is so. The aspect of the experience of a book which is *most* objective, which is most constricted to the range of physical complexity, i.e., the pages of paper bound between a cover, are expanded out of their objectivity of being *no more than pages bound between a cover* by the communities of narrative operating under the hyperthematic structure of narrative. The narrative accessible within the physicality of the objective book expands that objective aspect to promote its interpretability over longer time spans. And yet various creative developments throughout the history of books in their physically objective aspect have also been consistent with **Ha** in promoting the aging of books. From the Sumerian clay tablet, as a reusable book whose creative development as such can be interpreted primarily as an objective expansion according to **HOe** upon the medium of clay mused upon earlier, we have gone on to the various creative developments of our paper-based books. A stitched binding, paper which does not discolor or fade, a protective cover, a dust jacket, all these have helped the objective aspect of the book along with its narrative aspect to promote its ongoing interpretation.

Besides the abovementioned defensive developments, which help to *preserve* the more physically objective aspect as an aid to the more expansively interpretive aspect of the book, there have been creative developments which promoted the more complex interpretive aspect of the book. That the words in the book had spaces between them or had spaces between the lines, or had margins which could be annotated, gave the opportunity for the reader to expand upon his or her own interpretation of the narrative and then to leave that added interpretation for his or her own future self, or for those who would come after. This is to engage the object with a stance that preserves not statically but preserves for further interpretation. The family Bible with its front papers annotated with a record of significant events, preserves for further interpretation its otherwise objective tending aspect. Indeed, it appears to have been the norm in early Christianity, as well as in Buddhism and many other religions, that a group of works could be bound together in various ways so as to allow their rearrangement into constant new interpretations. Such creative developments could be applied far and wide if once the spirit of the principle is understood. The book could become a repository of not only the annotated notes of a reader, but a more extensive record of the various interpretations of the readers with regard to the original writing, saving—for whoever *wanted* to access them—not only the more extensive interpretive view of the work, but even the feelings and emotions of the reader.

To take another case, we have money—in the form of cash—which is now viewed as a replaceable sameness. It thus tends to be the holder of lower-level value as quantitative accumulation. Indeed it tends to promote that quantitative accumulation precisely because it is envisioned and used as a sign with a single facet of interpretation, i.e., one bill of currency differs from another bill of currency only by being *another* at the physical level of complexity. The increasing digitization of currency, as a mere number in a bank account, takes this devaluative tendency further, and the contemporary urge toward cryptocurrency—a giant leap in the wrong direction—will take it still further, if encouraged. But when the facets of interpretation in the sign are thus restricted, then the processes of action which engage that sign can only interpret according to the lower-level value of quantity and thus tend toward accumulation and interpretations which settle upon diversity of accumulations, i.e., valuations according to being rich or poor in monetary quantity.

Money need not be viewed this way however. It can be re-envisioned and developed as *a multifaceted sign* which tends away from replaceability through the addition of further facets for interpretation. Insofar as we do this we lessen its tendency to be interpreted in the weak value of accumulations. There would be various ways to add further facets for interpretation,* but one of the ways to do this would be the creative expansion of currency so as to promote the value of aging according to **Ha**. I will not offer any specific techniques for accomplishing this, but we are quite capable of developing the ability of currency in its physical and even in its information

---

*See Appendix C.

form to *save the history of its own use.* This preservation of the experiences of exchange of value around the locus of a currency would give those who use it a much expanded sense of the history of the efforts toward value creation—and often the failure of those efforts in devaluative actions—and allow them to link their own efforts to that history.

Here then are several examples of ways in which **Ha** can be interpreted to an object, ways in which *preservation by means of and in conjunction with interpretive fluidity* can be used to create value. Further examples may be as numerous as our creative engagement has opportunity to derive. The objective aspect of an experience, the object, can be made interpretable to longer spans of the world process by taking care to fashion the object so as to incorporate highly interpretable aspects rather than accumulations of weak quantitative value or symmetries.

Thus for example—connecting with issues touched upon earlier—if we want to age our building structures, e.g., our houses, in consistency with **Ha**, then we must promote the tendency toward the building of curving and continuously curving surfaces. The world process in its aspect of being a natural environment is going to reinterpret nearly all of our inconsistent effort towards quantitative accumulation and symmetry. Our contemporary cities have become masses of quantitative sameness in their regular street layouts, in the shapes of their identical units—masses of similar buildings; in their thin pointed projections—office towers and skyscrapers with flat sides and sharp edges and corners. The world process as the natural environment will not abide this. Our quantitative accumulations of these objects will constantly be worn down to be available for further creative developments.

So if we want to be consistent, if we want these objects which we live in to age, we will have to create living structures and communities of living structures, which in their physical aspect as objects, allow the natural environment to interpret them. Rain must be invited to flow over a house rather than to hit its flat surfaces, wind must be guided through and around the curves of a structure rather than pushing it, the dust and "dirt" of the natural environment must be guided so as to be an ongoing part of the interactions of flora and fauna in community with our structures: a community which we will have to welcome.

The success in the aging of such structures, as well as all objects, depends upon the ability to retain the best, the most creative, of the old, while adding to it the most creative of the new. A highly interpretable modularity, wherever it can be implemented in the objects which we produce, can help in this regard, for modular construction allows us to create, to retain the most creative aspects of what we create, and to continually reinterpret those aspects of our efforts which have foundered into mere quantitative accumulation, or into other inconsistencies. If an object is modular to a high degree, what this means is that some aspect of it which wears away can be *replaced*, while retaining those aspects of the object which we wish to age. If you remember from an earlier hyperthematic interpretation that *transformation* was more consistent, and thus to be sought rather than replacement, then you see that the modularity in question must be a modularity tending toward an engagement of experience, rather than an objective tending modularity of replaceability according to sameness of parts.

I will not offer a new term here, but rather urge the reader to view modularity in a way consistent with **Ha**. If we seek the transformation of an objective structure, e.g., a building, then a modularity of the parts of the structure allows us to rearrange them in new and hopefully creative ways. The wealth of transformations which are possible, is going to depend upon the degree of modularity: a structure with two modular parts is going to permit a certain range of transformations, a structure with 100 modular parts is going to permit a much greater range of transformations. Meanwhile whatever is most creative in the structure can be retained and whatever is least creative can be transformed in further attempts. The various transformations then gather around the aging of the structure, which grows/ages as a community of creative efforts—say human efforts—becoming more and more valuable as it ages.

Modularity then is not a sameness of replaceable parts. Viewed consistently it is rather *an engagement of experience in which a capacity for interpretive transformations at some scale is helped by a modularity of parts at a smaller scale, where this modularity of parts is the relatively high range of options they have of being interpreted to one another.* There may well be sameness in the modularity, but it plays no part in the capacity of interpretive transformation at the higher scale for creativity which advances beyond mere quantitative accumulation. To exemplify: the modularity of two standard "two by four" square Lego bricks is not to be found in an emphasis upon their sameness such that one can replace another in a construction, but rather in the multitude of ways in which one can be—interpretively—joined to the other. We can even decrease that sameness by changing one of our "two by four" bricks to a round brick, while retaining our modularity. Our bricks stick together through their connection points, which are a sameness indeed, but in recognizing this we are recognizing that, though our bricks are still objective to this degree, it is the tendency away from sameness that matters, the tendency to invoke sameness *as little as possible* in the creation of the object by deliberately and consciously promoting a sameness on one scale *in order to* expand creative diversity on a larger scale. This is directly akin to that consistent practice spoken of earlier. In this practice an engagement of experience models some aspect of experience, but deliberately with the intent to put the modeling—here the sameness of the Lego connection points—to work creatively at higher levels of complexity. This consistently understood modularity allows us to preserve and age our past effort through constant reinterpretation to it, while adding newly creative aspects to it.

On the other hand, to the extent that modularity is viewed *inconsistently* as depending upon a series of similar replaceable parts, one can link the inconsistency back to the above suggestions regarding the natural environment as a region of the world process. That which needs merely to be *replaced*, is that which has *worn out*, i.e., the aspects of an object which the natural environment of the world process is busily interpreting out of accumulated quantity into the "soil" of further creative interpretations. But if wearing out or wearing down is a manifestation of the relative inconsistency of action toward sameness which has gone into the production of what is wearing down, then we can always look to those aspects in which a created "object" wears down to help us decide where to focus our transformative efforts according to **Ha**.

I spoke earlier of the paper book which has aspects deliberately created in order to preserve it. Yet, insofar as the book is still an object, it will always retain some aspects which the world process will wear down. So, for example, the book has a hardcover to protect its pages with their interpretations, but that hardcover has flat edges which lead to pointed corners. Over time those pointed corners will get worn down and become curved. Or again, a violin has a great many aspects which have been created so as to prolong over time the musical interpretations which can be made with it, so as to age it: the materials in its making are selected so as to bring into it some of the highly interpretive aspects of nature as a process—e.g., the ability of the wood to expand and contract with changing humidity and to incorporate the growth structures of the source trees so as to improve the instrument's sound—its various curvatures give it beauty, its varnish protects its surface, and so forth. Violins are made to last then, as are books. Nonetheless, they also have aspects which can be worn down. The fingerboard of the violin will develop ruts over time, where the continuous pressing—the sameness of the action—of the fingers upon the strings wears it away. This is in part due to the sameness of the action and in part also to the *linear* character of the stretched strings as relatively inconsistent with regard to other aspects of the violin,[6] and it is worse when strings themselves are metal, i.e., less interpretable with regard to malleability, and thus again relatively inconsistent. It is these regions of objects which are rightly engaged when **Ha** is countenanced. They may be engaged *directly* by communities of the commercial corporation through creative modifications of future manifestations of the object. So, for example, the book might be created with rounded corners, or the violin might be created with modifications to its fingerboard which guide an expansion of action of the pressing fingers, or the malleability of its strings might be increased.

You may observe that we enjoy the wear on antique things, part of the mystique of their aging. But that is not the whole story. We enjoy what has been preserved *despite* the wearing action of the world process. This is very evident in collectors of antiques, who always tend to look for such examples of past objects which have survived relatively unworn. What we desire is the object, the sign, which has come to us bringing with it a host of interpretive linkages over a long history, and we desire particularly those objects in which creativity engendered by consistent community has vested a range of interpretability much greater than the norm, for by them we have the opportunity of expanding our individual communities of selfhood beyond embodiment through ongoing interpretations to the temporally creative efforts of our ancestors. Thus the antique book, which has passed through the hands and libraries of famous people and perhaps been annotated, or signed, by them, thus the musical instrument, or the painting, whose pedigree can be similarly traced. All of this comes from the *initial creative production* of objects with an eye toward longevity undertaken by communities which countenance **Ha**, a creative production which consistent communities of the commercial corporation can also undertake.

Commercial corporations can also join in the efforts of *indirectly preserving communities*, cooperating with museums, historical societies, etc. In this case, the inconsistent and objectifying aspects of antique objects are preserved as signs to which we can interpret our ongoing processes. That is to say, we preserve the mistakes made in the object so as to continually interpret ourselves to our earlier efforts. So, for example, if a book becomes extremely old we devise systems which gently interpret it, expanding the range of actions with which we engage it away from a sameness of action: we store the book under glass so as to protect it from that sameness of engagement which is a quantity of use (being constantly touched in the same way by many hands), we address conditions such as dampness or ultraviolet radiation through which objects are worn down, we wear special gloves to turn the pages gently, perhaps we restore some aspect of the book which has worn down with a material and technique that correct the initial inconsistency. This is indirect preservation and **Ha** tells us to preserve items which have come to us through the preserving activity of the world process from within the various attempts at creativity—both our own and those of nature—which have degraded to mere accumulation. Archaeology searches through the accumulations of the garbage *heaps* of ancient cities to preserve in this way.

Moreover, **Ha** bids us to increasingly preserve items which have come from *our own* various attempts at creativity within the world process in a deliberate way without waiting for the help of the larger world process, i.e., as a result of recognizing our own inconsistencies of accumulation and addressing them while retaining the sign/object of the attempt so as to continually interpret our growing selfhoods to it. Thus, whereas with an earlier type of object we would have waited upon the world process to save for archaeology an example of our effort for future interpretation, we now *deliberately* preserve an example of our object, e.g., a Honda Civic, an iphone, a Timex watch, an example of twentieth-century advertising. This deliberate attempt at preservation allows us in future to interpret our efforts at creative action to the history of our own creative actions. It allows us to consciously be aware of ourselves as expansions of interpretation and as gaining value in our own growth.

In the end, however, all objects, *as objects*, are subject to the inconsistency of accumulation, and even the preservation of our past creations must continually abide by an effort to address that inconsistency, if value is to increase. In other words, even efforts of communities of preservation will have their limits if we do not go beyond that preservation at physical ranges of complexity wherein we now view objectivity as residing. The history of our growth out of human embodiment, as processes, will not be able to be preserved as physical objectivity indefinitely. Museums will fill up. The efforts of consistent communities, commercial corporations and otherwise, to preserve samples of their creative efforts will accumulate objects. There are limits, *because objectivity is essentially a tendency of limitation*.

A walk through a great museum such as the Louvre, or rare book repository like the theological library of the University of Leuven, begins in wonder and interest, but can end in being overwhelmed with regard to the objective accumulation, the *mass*, of our preserved efforts at production. Just so, insofar as we are consistent, we will move steadily away from objectivity, continually interpreting and reinterpreting our creative efforts which result in objects, in ways which nonetheless move away from objectivity. We will move eventually to such forms of the preservation of the object which no longer preserve them as an object, relatively speaking. For example we will move toward the preservation of our creative effort and its failures as information of our past, as history.

Nonetheless, objectivity, I said, is always relative to our ongoing efforts, as a region of experience which is less consistent than some aspect of interpretive complexity at the upper bounds of the region of experience we are currently most engaged in. We ought not to be surprised then, not only that the preservation of experience passes beyond the preservation of objects as objects *relative to some historic ranges within the world process near to their own time of creation* into a preservation of said objects according to the complexity of interpretation which we now call *information*, but also that *even* the preservation of experiences as older modes of information will pass beyond *their* respective historic ranges to be preserved as that which is more complex than those older modes of information—or if you like, be preserved as that which is *super-information*.

Put otherwise, if the tendencies toward objectivity within the world process are continually being worn down by that process, and increasingly by ourselves as an active agent within that process, then objects such as the Egyptian pyramids or the bi-face blades of North American Paleo Indians must eventually be preserved, according to **Ha**, as information. And moreover, ancient information itself in its objective aspects—e.g., those texts of medieval philosophy which tend toward a sameness of content, or the samples of pulp fiction or mass music of the twentieth century—must eventually be preserved as something beyond information as we now know it, for the latter will eventually be as objects to us also; they will be "information objects." Indeed, even the current mass production of written content *qua* content—a relatively new phenomenon which has arisen with the Internet—must eventually be worn away by relatively more complex configurations of the world process, for information, insofar as it becomes objectified, whether manifested in what now seems physical to us or in what now seems least physical to us (electronic form), must give way to the correcting effect of the world process. Internet information, where inconsistently accumulated, must wear away.

Evidently **Ha** can be interpreted by the actions of commercial corporations, particularly with regard to the objectivity of our creative efforts, an objectivity which must be preserved so as to expand the interpretive linkages of our history of growth as value, but which even so must be preserved in ways which tend to move away from objectivity. **Ha** is thus adoptable.

Hc Reconstruction

The final hypertheme was the Hypertheme of Correction, **Hc**: *in order to expand value in a community, make every effort, according to your ethical capacity as an interpreter, to act so as to <u>select</u> signs of experience which have arisen through constrictive tendencies, and <u>correct</u> them through such creative expansions as you are capable of.* It was uncovered through musement upon examples of art which deliberately address prior constrictive efforts of art. Thus Renoir selected the female body, which had been eroticized in art and interpreted it in ways which corrected that constriction, interpreting femininity as much more than physical embodiment.

All the hyperthemes can be put into the service of **Hc**, so that, for example, the expansion out of the objectivity of **HOe**, the move toward curvature of **HCu**, and the deliberate preservation of our errors in aged objects in order to meaningfully interpret our ongoing growth with regard to those objects, which **Ha** advocates, are all ways of correcting ourselves. The distinction is that these other hyperthemes can be used in wholly new ways irrespective of past errors, while their use in the service of **Hc** is always as a response to our past inconsistencies.

In musing upon the interpretation of **Hc**, I will note some of the more prominent areas of experience which might be addressed by **Hc** and how beginnings might be made insofar as commercial corporations are responsible for and have the capacity to correct such errors. This should not appear to be moralizing, first because everything I will say has been suggested in some form and to some degree earlier in this work, and second, because moralizing itself always has a constrictive aspect—it eagerly points out what is wrong but advances no further—whereas here I have built upon suggestions regarding what is "right," always elaborating and presenting consistent ways of engaging the world before addressing what may be corrected by hyperthematic principles. The world process of value is built upon its successes, and only secondarily upon its successful engagement of its failures. Nonetheless, the engagement of those failures is important, and especially important with regard to the activities of commercial corporations, because due to their complexity and thus ability to act on a large scale, they present one of the greatest dangers for the diminishment of value, even as they offer one of the greatest hopes for the correction of inconsistent regions of experience.

Correction of Weaponry

I begin with the inconsistency of weaponry. I suggested all along that the eliminatory tendency of military activity is entirely inconsistent with the opening assumptions. How and why this is so, in a broader and fuller sense, I leave for a future expansion. How and why the development of various weapons is a subordinate aspect of the inconsistent activity of military elimination I must also leave for that expansion. But that the latter is the case is my wholehearted assertion. If so, if weapons are objects which tend very much to promote and engender elimination and constriction, i.e., to diminish value, then weapons are very much signs of experience which can be selected for correction according to **Hc**. Moreover, it will be very much the communities of the commercial corporation which will have both the responsibility and capacity to carry out that correction, since the greater part of human weaponry is now and has long been the product of corporations.

What are some of the ways in which commercial corporations could creatively expand upon the inconsistent signs which are weapons? First, remember that weapons tend to act by removing facets of interpretation from an embodied locus of process, usually the acting transformable element which is the human. They kill the body as a whole, or they maim or chop off or blow off some part of it. This constricts the human body, or some part of it, with regard to action over a range of time—in a way which is opposite, say, to the expansion of music—or it removes some part of the body in an attempt to constrict the action available to that part indefinitely.

Taking this into account, the challenge for commercial corporations willing to abide by **Hc** so as to correct the inconsistency of weaponry is the challenge of introducing and developing creative ways of reversing the constrictive actions of weaponry. In other words, once the variety and range of the inconsistency in the region of experience is understood, then the challenge of **Hc** is to deliberately meet that variety and range of inconsistency so as to *expand the region out of its inconsistent constriction*. Sometimes this will be an expansion with regard to a particular sign of inconsistency in the region, e.g., a weapon; sometimes it will be an expansion with regard to multiple signs of inconsistency within the region, e.g., a war situation.

Note that the sign *qua* sign is always consistent in that aspect at least. What is inconsistent is the gap or gaps of interpretability which manifest themselves in and around the sign due to the assumptions behind its propagation. Thus I can sell a weapon to a friend, for example, in an exchange of good faith which is *itself* consistent as an act of interpretation, even though the sign of that weapon carries within it an ongoing inconsistency, which *must* come out somewhere so as to engender harm in experience in a diminishment of value. The harm, as a devaluation of experience, need not manifest itself—despite the mantra often repeated in the American culture wars that "guns don't kill people, people kill people"—in an experience in which someone is killed or even wounded by the weapon. It may manifest itself in other devaluations of experience such as fear in the presence of the weapon(s)—even on national scales—psychological discomfort in the effort to produce the weapon (as occurred in the production of the atomic bomb), constriction of interpretation as an increase of secondary aggression in the mere presence of weapons, etc. Moreover, all of these contribute to the degradation of community at various levels, into a mere society, a degradation which sooner or later rebounds upon and corrects the source of the constriction.[7]

Let us say then that we go about the expansion out of the inconsistency, according to **Hc**, on the level of physicality at which weapons are usually produced. If a weapon constricts a region of experience, then the consistent commercial corporation might look to either produce a physical object which expands a region of experience relative to the sign of the physical weapon, or to transform the weapons themselves in an interpretive expansion.

In the first case, such an object may be some variant of what I earlier called interpretive defense, implemented at the level of physical embodiment. Thus, a commercial corporation may produce various types of defensive "armor" or body-wear, which protect the body from the bullets and other symmetrically directed attacks of weaponry. Commercial corporations already do this, and are consistent in it *in this respect*. They are inconsistent when they produce such defensive objects deliberately in combination with weapons, and when they produce so-called defensive equipment which has a constrictive—an attacking—aspect. The "defense industry," is as of yet only a pseudo-defense industry, a false community, inasmuch as the greater part of its products are produced based upon the assumption that the best defense is a strong offense. The best defense is rather the forgoing of offense altogether in favor of interpretation. It is through such an interpretive defense that constricted regions of experience are opened to the value building flow of action. This foregoing of offense *is not a foregoing of action*. It is not passive. It is very much active. *But it is an activity which is expansive rather than constrictive in the way in which offensive action is constrictive.*

Now, if you ask what this implies with regard to a product at physical levels of complexity, then I can give some examples, even though the creative development of those examples would require considerable further effort by willing and consistent corporate communities. Inasmuch as weapons may be called "experience constricting devices," then what **Hc** advocates as a corrective to them at comparable physical levels of complexity may be called "experience expanding devices." If these experience expanding devices are produced to address the tendencies of weaponry in the region of their constricting the experience of the body—e.g., as when a bullet meets the body and physically damages it, and so deprives it of ranges of interpretation—then we may view them as variations of interpretively defensive armor. Such "armor" expands the action of the incoming constriction—e.g., the bullet—out of its point, symmetry, and power tendencies.

Thus, for example, commercial corporations might develop a liquid armor, where the liquid, which is fluid and expansive for interpretation, expands the power of the incoming action out of its point constriction by increasing the physical space which the bullet has to interpret, in a way which is changeable. Again, a bubble armor might be developed, wherein an appropriate strength of the spherical surfaces meets the incoming power and transfers it through its curvatures, thereby spreading it out into multiple avenues of movement. Or again, an electromagnetic armor might be developed wherein the surface of the armor would engage the incoming bullet magnetically in a way that would guide the latter into curving away from and around the body. Finally, an armor might be developed based on chemical or electromagnetic principles, which creates a spatial layer that softens the bullet as it passes through that layer, making it malleable and thus interpretable by the body.

On the other hand, if these "experience expanding devices" are produced to address the tendencies of weaponry in the region of their use as issuing from the selections of experience of someone who espouses constrictive assumptions—e.g., as the mindset amenable to harming or killing of one who picks up a weapon to use it—then we may view them as variations of "directed experience expanding devices," i.e., they engage the source of the constrictive effort.* What would these devices act upon? They would act upon the constricted region of experience wherein the context favorable to

---

*We need not call these "anti-harm guns," for it is expansion which is at work in them, and not the constriction which is implied in the word "anti." We might call them *peace devices*, or coin a new word.

the assumptions of the attacking embodied process—e.g., a human—push it toward the practical use of the object weapon as an extension of that context. In other words, the device would be creatively developed to engage the physical and psychological experience of the attacker with regard to whatever aspects push the latter toward the use of a weapon as an extension of his or her inconsistent assumptions, for the purpose of harm or killing. It would guide the potential killer away from the assumptions which lead him to kill.

Thus, devices creating various olfactory experiences for those whom they engage could be developed. The reader may immediately think of tear gas and mace. In fact, this is not what I have in mind. Their use is not *as* inconsistent *relative* to other forms of constriction, say the use of bullets. But it is still a variant of constriction attempting to knock out or suppress some aspect of the body's range of actions, e.g., vision or movement. What I am advocating, rather, are devices offering the attacking party a consistent way out of the constriction that has brought him to the point of using the weapon. This is offering an experience, physical and psychological—hyperthematically the two are not distinct but part of a smooth range of complexity of experience—which is interesting enough to guide the belligerent party away from using the weapon.[8] Our olfactory device would offer to the attacking belligerent, not a smell which would stop or incapacitate him or her, but a smell which would expand the mindset out of the constriction necessary to harm and kill, e.g., the smell of home (in the many senses of the term), the smell of delicious foods, the smell of exotic things. Moreover, the device would constantly vary the smell, creating themes and avenues of interpretive interest which would continually guide the physical/psychological condition of the attacker out of its constriction.

In the same vein we can create a music and sound device which offers to the belligerent various expansive auditory experiences, again with themes and avenues for interpretation, which guide the attacker away from constrictions amenable to conflict. Or again, a device creating a humorous experience, or creating various types of visual experiences tending to bring the attacker out of his constriction, e.g., images of babies or of childhood. In effect, such a device would be using a similar technique to that which is used—mostly unconsciously with regard to its deeper reasons—to sooth difficult or angry babies, albeit here on a much more complex level. A more challenging device, but still open to creative effort, would take into account the background of the belligerent more deeply, using some combination of the above to fashion a more "custom made" experience for the latter, which guides him or her to an expanded sense of self-hood.

Such devices are best viewed as a last resort in addressing conflict, since it is simpler to invoke all of the above experiences with regard to regions of constriction and thus conflict, *before* it becomes necessary to use such local devices. Nonetheless, I presented them here to show how in one instance of the selection of a region of inconsistency, communities of the commercial corporation can use **Hc** to correct their own production of inconsistent objects—a production which is still vast and ongoing—at a level of complexity within the range of the latter.

Correction of Pornography

Another area of inconsistency which is very much aggravated by the inconsistent efforts of contemporary commercial corporations, is that of the commercial production of pornography. The human body in its nakedness can be interpreted in consistent and inconsistent ways, as noted earlier. There are interpretations in art which consistently tend to guide the viewer away from the embodiment of the body as a constriction to objectivity, even in interpretations of the naked body.

But there are also interpretations—and so far they are not art—which tend to constrict the viewer toward viewing the human body as an object with ever diminishing interpretable aspects and ever diminishing ranges of interpretation with regard to those aspects. This latter, at a certain range of complexity, is pornography.[9] It manifests itself as various constrictions in the subject experience of a human as embodiment, passed on as a sign for some further interpreter.

These constrictions of the subject in human embodiment are various. In the first place pornography is usually a constriction of the various sensory modes of the physical body with regard to the subject, e.g., the subjects are reduced to that which we merely see and hear. Moreover, the range of interpretations of the subject with regard to seeing and hearing are reduced further. With regard to auditory experience, pornography tends to forgo conversation, descending to the minimum of the latter, and still further to the primality of grunts, moans, screams, and heavy breathing. It tends toward a constriction of the ranges of movement of the subject in simple repeated actions, or in simple repeated sequences of these simple repeated actions. It tends toward a constriction of the living context of process as the locus of embodiment within the world process, i.e., the subject is interpreted as no more than a single type of experience, as not being more than a body engaged in sex, as not having more diverse types of life experience, as not having a past or future, and so forth. Even the viewer's view of the subject tends toward constriction: to a single room or area, often to relative darkness, to close-ups of the sex organs—as in hard-core pornography—without need even for the whole body. These constrictions, moreover, tend to subsist very readily alongside of other signs of constriction in objects—e.g., dark clothing, black leather, handcuffs, chains—or in contexts of constricted experience: e.g., various types of dominance, imprisonment, rape, etc.

All of these constrictions make the experience of sexuality as mere embodiment very amenable to the efforts of commercial corporations to produce objects. The objects which are produced tend to be objects of mass production that are copied quite readily and in which the pornographic actors, for example, become copies of themselves in the tendency toward sameness of action. More than in any other form of film, the actors tend both to be no more than they are visually presented as and consequently nearly the same in every pornographic film. To correct the inconsistencies of the mass product of pornography, with **Hc**, is thus going to have to take into account these variants of constriction. Just as in correcting the inconsistency of weaponry, consistent communities of the commercial corporation have the opportunity of creating products which expand rather than constrict the region of experience which is sexuality.

Suppose the product is viewed from the aspect of the interpretation of the subject in embodiment and that the goal is to interpret a subject with regard to embodiment and sexuality. Very well, then the hyperthematically consistent way to go about this is to interpret the embodied and sexual aspects of the subject and its context in a way which though *beginning* in the latter expands out of it in some direction. The earlier chapter on light and color suggested that embodiment in its objective aspect is something that we—as processes within the world process—will grow beyond. Our embodiment as constricted to the physical range of complexity, will expand so that we become loci of processes of a greater and greater complexity, a super embodiment if you like, which will allow us to act consistently at higher ranges.

Embodiment itself and the sexuality which accompanies it may thus come to be viewed as a constantly expanding mode and range of action of our experience wherein we, as processes, can interpret one another in spite of, and yet always *in anticipation of*, higher and more valuable modes and ranges of active interpretation. Sexuality as a subset of objectivity may then be viewed as the lower range of our inter-action with one another as processes, a lower range which can be viewed as less valuable relative to the range and yet—if we are consistent—always reinterpreted to something better.

This view implies that the corrective response to pornography is not to attempt a constrictive regression toward primality, but rather a creative expansion into higher complexities of sexuality. In terms of the practical production of films, for example, which will address and correct the inconsistencies of pornography, this means something like creating films exploring what we *can creatively become* in terms of a sexuality that will pass beyond a physically embodied sexuality; it means to interpret the subject of the sexual body as always more than that *body* as sexual.

Perhaps the most obvious expansion possible in such films is the interpretation of sexuality as maximally valuating in a *deliberate* creation of life as value—consistent procreation—in a sense beyond any humanity has yet espoused; this would explore potential transformations of sexuality away from biological limitations and constrictive urges toward the quantitative accumulation of sensory sexual pleasures—analogous to the devaluating quantitative accumulations of fat, sugar, etc. discussed earlier—toward a fully aware procreation of life as the facilitating of newly embodied processes maximally envalued relative to the interpretive capacity of each of us. In short, something like *viewing the sexual creation of our children—both to our and their benefit—as a creation of consistent living art forms in embodied experience.*

Such films could also explore the development of human sexual practice in its consistencies, and in its corrections of its inconsistencies, from the earliest beginnings of our animal ancestors to ourselves. They could pass beyond our contemporary practices and imagine and creatively develop the future of human sexuality, including creatively imagining the development of future forms of embodiment. Or again, they might address a sexuality of community, i.e., a sexuality engaged at levels of community at a complexity of experience beyond that of the individually embodied human we now know. They might also explore the development of sexuality out of its constrictive and thus disease-promoting tendencies,[10] and into a sexuality of healing: deliberately suggesting and creating practices of sexual healing. The development of sexuality with regard to a beautification of human embodiment, which helps it pass beyond physical embodiment, could be interpreted. Finally, they could explore the development of sexuality with regard to the creation of new sensory modes altogether. The latter will be bound up with a guidance toward the *giving* of sexual pleasure as an expansive interpretation which passes beyond the predominant tendencies toward pleasure as quantitative accumulation and constrictive *taking*, now manifested in contemporary pornography.

You may insist that: "nonetheless the contemporary pornography industry arises from urges which perennially override efforts such as those suggested above." I reply that, if, for the moment they seem to, it is because the productive capacities of contemporary commercial corporations when they are used inconsistently *do indeed* tend to override other more valuable efforts temporarily, efforts which have always had a guiding influence upon the abovementioned urges. There has long been pornography. There has never, before our current age (say the last century or so), however, been a mass pornography which has so swamped consistent efforts—and there have been many of the latter, from the songs of Solomon, to the medieval romances, to the aforementioned art of Renoir—to interpret our embodied sexuality.

Hyperthematically viewed, this situation cannot last. The world process actively works against accumulations and it does so even through ourselves as processes. We *will* grow tired and bored of the constrictive sameness of the efforts of our pornography industry, indeed even now we are well on our way to this. Worse than tedium and boredom, even, may be imagined as a correction from the world process. So it behooves us to invite the preeminent manifestations of our engagement of experience at more complex ranges of action—our commercial corporations—into the effort to correct the inconsistencies of experience which those commercial corporations themselves have helped to bring about.

Having participated in the expansion of the subject of embodied sexuality in the ways suggested above, consistent communities of the commercial corporation may also directly create products—there are nascent efforts toward this—which engage and help those caught by the earlier inconsistent efforts of the commercial corporations in question. Several generations now have had sustained and easy access to the constrictive mass products of the pornography industry. Constrictive tendencies lead to a downward and inward path in any region of experience, a path which may be difficult to escape depending upon the interpretive capacity of the viewing interpreter. Nonetheless, with patient guidance and an eye upon the inconsistencies of the context of experience which has been promoted in society, the problem can be addressed. Though I presented in the above types of expansive films the equivalent of the earlier "anti-gun" or peace devices, here to address the products of pornography, commercial corporations can also play a wider role in expanding the experience of those caught in the constrictions of pornography.

The adolescent or young adult in whom the biological, hormonal, and psychological pressures and vagaries of embodiment are most extreme needs guidance with regard to the experience of sexuality. Without such guidance, and in the context of our mass pornography society, the turn to constrictive engagements with regard to sexuality is easy. We want to experience sexuality, but the creatively expansive sexual films suggested above as a corrective response to pornography, need not be the only way to do so. The efforts of communities of commercial corporations will, of course, only make up one part of a combined effort of many consistent communities, of medicine, art, etc. in this respect, but what reconstructed commercial corporations can do is to offer—build—the creative contexts of experience, particularly at physical levels, which will guide humanity into a consistent sexuality.

So, for example, consistent communities of the commercial corporation could create and build special meeting places, particularly for adolescents, whose function would be to provide the context for a consistent sexuality. In our age, and in others, adolescents have often resorted to constrictive tendencies in coming to terms with the sexual aspect of their own embodiment. They have sought out places and contexts in which to explore and develop their sexuality in a negative fashion, e.g., based on whatever is *not* an adult or parental context. Beginning thus, on the basis of a constrictive assumption, however, tends to lead to further constrictive choices. The places and contexts tend to be dark, private, hurried, secret, and so forth.

Does this mean the creation of meeting places where sexuality is to be encouraged among adolescents? It means that the conditions for a consistent development of sexuality and thus coming to terms with embodiment are encouraged. Where this is encouraged, sexuality will be increasingly more than an action which degrades to the objectivity of the body. The latter tendency of degradation is precisely where the dark, private, hurried, and secret context—the "anti" sexuality—leads, connecting swiftly and easily with the constrictions espoused by pornography. It means that our imagined meeting places for adolescents are places of beauty, of light, of time to explore and discover the interests upon which a consistent sexuality is built, and yes, places of guidance.

The perennial human embarrassment of embodiment has its roots in the relatively lower value of experience as objective, and rightly so. But the degradation of sexuality only comes in an engagement within that embodiment which tends toward a further constriction. Sexual degradation is not fixed, *it is a <u>way</u> of engaging experience* so as to constrict and devalue it. It can be otherwise. When we look toward the creative expansion of interpretation from the vantage point of embodiment, when we continually reinterpret our embodiment to higher and more complex regions of experience, then we have the antidote to sexual degradation: sexual creativity.

Meeting places for adolescents, which could be created by consistent communities of the commercial corporation, would thus have all of the above suggested aspects of light, beauty, etc., as well as other aspects to be created in abiding by our earlier hyperthemes. But they would also offer the *guidance* of teachers, for those who needed it: the guidance of interpreting contemporary human embodiment and sexuality to its past and to its future; guidance upon the sexuality of procreation as consistent and ongoing creation; guidance upon sexual creativity as a response to the aging and temporal boundedness of the body and as a mode of harmonizing the creativity of the greater process of human life with the health of the physical body, which is its lower range of complexity; and finally, guidance in the art and practice of sexuality at the physical level with a view to developing beauty of action, expansion of sense and feeling, and an increasingly complex, spiritual, and thus valuable sexuality of community which always tends toward passing beyond the physical level. That a consistent sexuality could be taught, even at the physical level, thus moving the latter toward an artfulness, beauty, and spirituality, is no more difficult to envision than the teaching of value in any region of human experience, for the community of teaching is itself a consistent community dedicated to value.

I have interpreted **Hc** to the efforts of commercial corporations far enough to see that it can be adopted by consistent communities of the latter in deliberate correction of their earlier inconsistent efforts. With this, having applied all of the hyperthemes according to the mode of expansive reconstruction directed at the activity of commercial corporations, I will consider my *exposition of the hyperthematic methodology* to have advanced sufficiently to guide further practical use by others who may be interested in hyperthematics.

Conclusion

From the viewpoint of Hyperthematics, conclusions are a tendency which leads toward constriction, however mildly. Yet since a conclusion is here demanded by the constrictive dictates of literary convention, I can at least re-envision the conclusion as a beginning for further effort. Accordingly, a conclusion to this work might well have borne the heading: "and everything else." I have dropped enough hints throughout the work however to make such a heading superfluous. I will say a little more nonetheless, which I hope will add to an understanding of how Hyperthematics stands in relation to several issues, which due to the constraints of objectivized narrative could only be touched upon but not much expanded, namely, the issue of the status of science and the laws of nature courted by science, in their relation to Hyperthematics, and the issue of Hyperthematics in assessment of the culture wars—right- and left-wing politics—of the contemporary globalized world. To segue into these issues however, I will take an indirect and more expansive route, the reasons for which deserve explanation.

This work grew out of a smaller version submitted to peer review in 2012. One of the reviewers, professor Randall Auxier, was generous indeed in his support of my effort, but offered one overarching suggestion, namely, that I familiarize myself with the work of Edgar Sheffield Brightman (1884–1953), and respond to certain assertions of the latter. Brightman, Auxier insisted, was a kindred spirit in the type of effort I had undertaken, and in his work *Moral Laws*,[1] he had advanced the strongest case for a firm distinction between aesthetic and moral values, and for the insistence that moral value—unlike aesthetic value—being irreducibly cognitive, cannot be brought into descriptive form. I read this with interest, but with reservations as to my ability to address the issue, and soon forgot about it.

Meanwhile, I had for some time been worried about the dual aspect of the work, written as an organic growth out of—and combination with—a broader study of Royce's philosophy. Auxier urged me strongly to drop the Roycean study, and publish Hyperthematics alone. Soon I resolved to expand the hyperthematics section by adding a chapter on visual art as exemplified in painting, not because of Brightman's problem, but rather because I had gathered together various notes interpreting art to hyperthematics over the preceding months, and felt that a chapter on visual art would round out my treatment of harmonic human endeavors.

So I set to work on the hyperthematic structure of visual art in early 2013. But I soon recognized the need for a hyperthematic explanation of light and color, which began as a digression within the visual art chapter. It was no simple digression. An optimistic "five to ten pages," quickly grew and I began to be drawn into the inevitable connection with a further body of work I had engaged in some sixteen months earlier. Namely, I had written the first chapters of a prospective Hyperthematics of Conflict, and worked out the anti-hyperthematic converses of asymmetric, curved, and circular action in their relation to the devaluating actions undertaken in conflict/war. The digression thus became a chapter unto itself on the hyperthematics of light and color and their relation to the physical world, while the completion of the visual art chapter was put aside for later.

In the meantime, Brightman's book arrived and was duly read through the first fifty pages. But being deeply engaged in what became chapters 3 and 4 of this work, with new insights occurring every day, it also was soon put aside and forgotten under piles of paper. By spring's end I had finished the latter chapters, but had now developed further insights which needed weaving into what became chapters 7 and 8. To make a long story short, it was not until autumn of 2013 that I found myself in a position to once again take up the reading of Brightman's work, and to rediscover the problem of aesthetic versus moral value.

Having engaged Brightman's outlook and arguments after completing the larger part of my hyperthematic effort, I am inclined to think that if I had consciously focused on the problem in question earlier, I would not have addressed it in a manner satisfactory to myself. Brightman's *Moral Laws* is an astute work, and indeed has elements in common with Hyperthematics, most prominently that he aims for a consistent set of principles which can guide ethical action, and he aims to set them down in a semi-formal way. He deserves credit for his effort, more than he has garnered in the eyes of contemporary philosophy.

And yet there are a *great* many differences. For one, his effort, in *Moral Laws* at least, remains firmly within the bounds of the theoretical, whereas the current work attempts to bridge this problematic and meld, and indeed re-envision, the theoretical and practical as aspects of a consistent communally combined effort. For another—and only the whole of the present work can confirm this—his opening assumption, being essentially the age-old logical opener of non-contradiction, appealed to since Aristotle, cannot free him from the "gravitational pull" of a merely theoretical effort, so as to be able to explain physicality on the basis of value, in a way which would join theory and practice, and heal the—manufactured—divide between thinking and feeling, highlighted by Auxier. The latter can only be healed by fusing the Royce/Whitehead line of opening assumptions: assuming polyadic communities of processes of interpretation which are preeminent to the fixity of definite relations, and recognizing that the appeal to logical contradiction comes subsequently, as a freely willed engagement of the experience of the *fluidity of interpretive relation as such in its engendering of tendencies of value*. I cannot offer anything here on the methodological differences and similarities between Brightman's work and mine, but the interested reader can readily make the comparison.

Now, with regard to the problem in question, the constricted answer is that aesthetic, or feeling value, arises—most obviously, but not exclusively—out of engagement at the low-level complexity of interpretation which engenders the physicality of the world, as an expansion or constriction of interpretation between the region of embodiment and lower and higher ranges of complexity of experience, mediated by actions of *sameness*. This is to say—as shown earlier with the notion of the "leading edge of objectivity"—that feeling and knowing are cousins that blend smoothly into one another somewhere within experience as a physical embodiment; and *where* they blend in that range is going to depend upon the capacity of interpretation of a process manifesting as physically embodied. We tend to feel by default because the artifact of our embodiment—our physical body—is a low complexity interpretation of experience which we tend to engage in through a sameness of action.

If that is plausible, then it will explain, for example, why the notions of feeling and thought are constantly shifting. The term *feeling* has been used as an indication within the physical—physical sensation—"I feel warm," as an indication within the mental—mental intuition—"I feel this young man will go far in life," and as all manner of variants in between: "I feel lucky today." The term *knowing* has been used in ways no less flexible than feeling however. It has been used as an indication within the physical—being experienced—"he knows what he's doing," as an indication within the mental—discursive reasoning—"how do you know?" and as all manner of variants in between: "I know how you feel," she said, with a knowing wink.

A physical mental *dichotomy* is thus not a plausible basis for a distinction between feeling and knowing. Feeling and knowing are better viewed as tendencies, as suggested in the chapter on visual arts: tendencies of the interplay between sameness and creativity of interpretation, i.e., between that which has come before being engaged as a sign qua *that which has come before*, and that which has come before being engaged as a sign qua *that which has come before, in interpretation—relatively new and creative—to some selection from the experience of the one engaging the sign.* To put it another way: the feeling-knowing tendency moves over the range between accepting and letting be the past, and creatively transforming it into the newness of the future. To tend to feel something is to tend to let it be as the creation of another. To tend to know something is to tend to creatively reinterpret it. And to tend to feel something usually happens more readily with regard to lower complexity—physical—experience, because unless we make the effort to view it otherwise, the body is being "dragged around" by us as a region of experience treated as a sameness.

In this hyperthematic view then, the dangerous historically held dyad of physical-mental (as lower complexity to/from higher complexity), is expanded by a third facet, or dimension—an interpretive tendency—namely, that between feeling and knowing (as sameness to/from creativity); and conversely the dangerous historically held dyad of feeling-knowing, is expanded by a third facet/tendency, namely, that between physical-mental. The resulting polyadic community of interpretation can then plausibly better explain the variations of interpretive valuation which are to be found in the world process. It will help to expand upon the interplay of the two tendencies however, with some examples which show how the link between feeling-aesthetic and cognitive-moral value manifests itself in experience. Let us begin at some portion of the range of the physical-mental tendency, the tendency of more or less complexity of experience, and vary the feeling-knowing tendency, the tendency of more or less creativity of interpretation, and let us begin in the "middle" of both tendencies.

Feeling Ranges—Unvarying Sameness Interpreted through Increasing Complexity

Suppose a process of interpretation, a transformable element, within the world process, engages the process of experience from this "middle." As the transformable element—let's say an embodied human—takes action to engage in lower complexity of interpretation, we say he is engaging physicality. If, in addition, he takes action to engage in sameness of interpretation, then he is engaging feeling. Felt physicality, as such, is simply sameness along with low-level complexity of interpretation. Let your hand be against a flat rock face, a "wall of rock"; what do you have?* You have a relatively low-level complexity of interpretation in the way in which your hand engages the sign of the wall, which persists as a sameness of the sign, as temporal duration. The felt physicality is the signified result of various threads of processes of action comprising the world process, e.g., nature has created a rock face for you. Indeed, you yourself can initiate actions within the world process which will approximate this felt physicality at various levels of complexity—General Jackson was said to have stood like a "stone wall" with his soldiers, in the American Civil War.

But now let us begin to vary the complexity aspect. Replace the wall by the curved surface of a ball, e.g., a basketball, with your hand resting upon it. The complexity has increased, but the sameness/creativity aspect remains unchanged. What do you feel? You feel the guidance of the interpretive complexity to act, to interpret this experience in the world process. And yet as long as the sameness/creativity aspect remains unchanged, you feel the curved surface as a physical sensation, though less physical. You feel the *lure*—in Whitehead's sense—of the fulfilled creativity of another, the world process, or nature within the world process, or some human creator of the ball, etc., as a possibility, which you may act upon, actualize,** creatively, so as to realize² a new interpretive community. The ball lures you to *play* with it, i.e., to *know* what you can do creatively with its complexity.

Let the complexity aspect be increased further. Let the ball be replaced with a curved surface which is also malleable, e.g., a water balloon. What do you feel now? You feel still more interesting possibilities, feelings which in our human narrative begin to be characterized as expansively *playful* feelings, in addition to the experience as a physical sensation, to the extent that it still is physical. Indeed, the last experience is not, except by abstraction, divisible, even though it is moving along the range from physical to mental. If you go on from a water balloon, to having your hand upon the surface of a pond, or the water in a bathtub, then you are moving further from a

---

*I abstract from the action which brings the hand to the wall here.

**The actual, as set against the possible, is just the still unfulfilled interpretation between signs of experience. It is the process of experience, which is leading to the realization of value, i.e. the real.

physical sensation, to something which is becoming not very physical, but better describable as a feeling in some of our many more complex variations of the use of the word—and a very pleasant feeling—as every young child splashing in the bath will agree. This feeling is less and less physical and yet, nonetheless, it is still a feeling, in short, an increasingly *mental feeling*.

Insofar as this mental feeling can be indicated in words, it is very often best indicated in poetry. So, for example, in Tolkien's *Lord of the Rings* we find a playful poetry of water—the community of poetry manifests the highly complex as mental feeling—in the bath song of the hobbit Pippin, elevating the use of water in play over its practical and aesthetic uses.[3] What the song indicates in the narrative expansion of the mental feeling can be described well enough by the word *joyousness*. Joyousness is a feeling of considerable complexity, a feeling of a sign or signs of experience provided by and rich in the past creativity of the world process in some aspect—e.g., here the natural world as creator of water—and that it is feeling, relatively speaking, is the relative letting be of the sign (water) in a tendency of sameness of interpretation which receives as possibility the value created by another, but does not yet much engage actually in the sign so as to interpretively create with respect to it a further sign, which would hold an increase in value. Joyousness, as a mental feeling, may be said to be a value, which, when realized, signifies to the future of the world process that an interpretation between a relatively simple complexity of experience (physical embodiment) and a relatively higher complexity of experience (the mental) is being carried out through an action of interpretation in the lower (feeling) part of the range of the *sameness/creativity of interpretation tendency*, so as to form a community of interpretation. A child splashing in the bath is leaving this interpretation, the sign of joyousness, to an onlooker, e.g., his parents.

Now, if we go beyond water as a complexity of experience, if, for example, we could engage an experience of air, as a playing in air—children do achieve limited approximations on trampolines—then we would have yet a further and more valuable mental feeling which goes somewhat beyond joy, and of which words such as rapture and ecstasy have been used, and of which efforts of fantasy such as Peter Pan's ability to fly freely, dreams of. And once again, this mental feeling is the interpretation of a still higher complexity of experience to the lower complexity of experience around the locus of embodiment, *through* some range of the sameness/creativity tendency. It is the bare recognition, but only very weakly the creative engagement, of an interpretation *so complex*—relative to the range of physical embodiment—

that it begins, depending upon our interpretive capacity, to be difficult for us to engage in creativity at all. In other words, the possibilities of air, of its interpretations, are so complex and offer to our interpretive capacity so many threads of interpretation, that our freedom to interpret seems almost entirely unlimited, and yet that tremendous freedom to interpret *comes to us as a sign of that which—or who—is willing and able to bestow such a free region of interpretability.*

Put otherwise, joyousness, as a mental feeling, may be said to mark the beginning of that relatively higher range of complexity of experience in which an action is taken to interpret the range of physical complexity to the higher range of mental complexity in conjunction with an action of relative sameness of interpretation. The more complex the experience is, which is engaged from the tendency of sameness of interpretation, the more valuable this mental feeling is, even though its engagement as creativity may be very weak. Somewhere around the mental feeling of joy, the *spiritual*, as a range of mental feeling, begins, proceeding to ecstasy and beyond, as the complexity of the engaged experience increases. For example, that there should be a physical world at all, i.e., as felt (as recognized as given) in its vast complexity, is one of the opening wonders of the spiritual. This is why mystics are creatures of feeling, and yet they shun physical feeling, preferring to engage the regions of the complexity of mental feeling, again preferring to engage that complexity of experience as a sameness of experience, a relative letting be. Conversely, interpretations at the physical range of complexity, which are interpreted through a relative sameness of interpretation to some sub-physical range of complexity, are feelings of pain as a physical sensation, i.e., the possibility of the loss of the complexity of experience of the physical ranges.

Knowing Ranges—Ranges of Complexity Interpreted through Increasing Creativity

As we tend to move from active interpretation as sameness to active interpretation as creativity, we move from the felt to the known, from the possible through the actual and on to the real. Moreover, as we proceed to the more creative in the felt/known tendency (dimension) of interpretation, that is to say, as the more creative portions of the range of the latter tendency are engaged in order to interpret some problematic within the physical/mental tendency of interpretation, then we may be said to proceed through the range of the human[4] actions which give rise to the increasingly creative communities of human endeavor, the hierarchy of hyperthematic structures elaborated earlier.[5]

So, for example, beyond the merely felt as a sameness, lies that portion of the range of the sameness/creativity tendency, which, when it interprets between problematics of experience within the limited tactile portion of the physical range of the simplicity/complexity (physical/mental) tendency, gives rise to what we might call communities of *craft*.

Beyond the range of the sameness/creativity tendency, which engenders craft, comes the portion of the range which, in engaging the problematics of the full physical range of the simplicity/complexity tendency, engenders communities of *natural science*. In other words, *communities of natural science engage a broader swath of complexity of experience and engage it with a more creative action than communities of craft do*. Some communities of natural science, like botany, applied geology, and astronomy, engage the lower physical range which craft engages; others, such as microbiology, chemistry, and cosmology, engage more complex physical ranges.

Further beyond, in the sameness/creativity tendency, comes the portion of that range which, in engaging a relatively narrow and yet more complex portion of the simplicity/complexity tendency than natural science, gives rise to simple logics, e.g., dyadic logics; and when approximately that same portion of the range of sameness/creativity is the third interpreting between a still more complex portion of the simplicity/complexity tendency, then we get communities of mathematics.

Still further beyond in the sameness/creativity tendency, within a portion of the range of the latter, which is broader than that which simple logics and mathematics occupy, and which interprets a relatively very broad range of the simplicity/complexity tendency—from the sub-physical, through the physical, to the mental—lies, I suggest, the location from which Hyperthematics itself (an applied complex logic) as a promulgator of hyperthematic communities, is initiated.

Beyond even this region of the sameness/creativity tendency, from a base perhaps as broad as that of Hyperthematics, but interpreting a thinner portion of the simplicity/complexity tendency than do hyperthematic communities, will arise future communities which one may call *communities of the art of mental creation*, i.e., communities that play with and build in mental experience in a manner akin to that in which craft builds in physical experience.

Where in this scheme, you may ask, are the hyperthematic structures engaged in the exploratory mode of this work: game, dance, narrative, music, visual art? On the basis of the above, they can be located more or less as follows. In the sameness/creativity tendency, dance covers everything from the lower ranges of mere sameness of interpretation (the felt), to a creativity of interpretation beyond that of craft (a level of being known), and it is interpreted by the tactile range of physicality. One may view this as everything from a near letting be of the physical body as a tactile region of experience—the mere acceptance of the tactile giveness of embodiment—in certain types of dance (and below this are the base human movements such as walking, stretching, etc.), to the creative expansiveness in action of the physical body as a tactile region of experience in the various forms of complex dancing among multiple embodied individuals.

Games meanwhile are somewhat more advanced in the sameness/creativity tendency than the average dance. Games creatively reinterpret embodiment, particularly embodiment as tactile experience, more than dance, in the latter's letting be of tactile experience. Sports, as games, occupy a range of the sameness/creativity tendency higher than that of most dance. More complex games such as chess occupy a further part of the range reaching all the way up to craft. Or again: dance of a more complex and creative kind begins to transform into a game, while a sport, as a less complex and creative kind of game, begins to transform into dance.

But games, which are more complex and creative than sports (e.g., chess), begin to transform into craft and then science, and will increasingly do so as the sameness/creative tendency of games comes to interpret a higher range of complexity. Thus, for example chess, whose pieces are creative reinterpretations of the tactile embodiment of historical soldiers, etc. engaging one another in extensions of that tactile embodiment—physical space—begins to give way to games, which interprets the auditory and light range of physical experience. And conversely, craft merges with games at the lower end of its interpretive range, in the realm of the hobby which "lets be" the signs of the world process relatively, but plays with what is let be as a game: think model railroading.

Visual art is about at the range of craft in the sameness/creativity tendency, but it interprets predominantly the light range of the physical, whereas craft (both in the sense of the work of an artisan such as a luthier, and in the sense of the crafts of the fine arts) interprets predominantly the tactile range of the physical.

Narrative meanwhile, interprets the auditory and light portions of the physical range, but interprets them more creatively, with respect to the sameness/creativity tendency, than visual art does in its interpretation of the light portion. In other words, whereas visual art tends to let light/color be as such, narrative tends to manipulate it in new creative relations, e.g., in a written text—even to the extent of localized constriction, such as that which promotes black text on a white page—so as to allow for interpretations, which span a range of greater complexity, even though they begin within the physical. This is the move toward greater interpretive value from visual art to narrative—suggested earlier—wherein the felt gives way to the known, and yet wherein the latter, viewed from the stance of a higher capacity of interpretation, continually falls back to being felt.

Music interprets the auditory portion of the physical range of complexity through a portion of the sameness/creativity tendency that is higher than that of craft, of visual art, and of narrative. Or again, visual art *tends* to copy the signs from the light color aspect of physical experience, narrative tends to copy less than visual art the sign from the light color and auditory aspects of physical experience, and music tends to copy still less than the former two the signs from the light color and (predominantly) auditory aspect of physical experience. Or again, music tends to *represent*, much less than does visual art.

In short, the lower in the range of complexity a region of experience is, the sooner and more likely the signs of that region of experience are, to be engaged in a manner which abandons the felt aspects—e.g., the signs of the physical as such—of the region as a sameness and strives for the creative advance as a knowledge. *Sound is less complex than light, so it will be manipulated in creativities beyond those of light all the sooner.* The current visual art of light will eventually become "the music of light," for instance, because "music" is a range of creativity, regardless of the range of complexity which it interprets.

To add a cautionary note, the sameness/creativity tendency should not be viewed as the arbiter of any of the above communities, more than the simplicity/complexity tendency. All the above communities arise as a consequence of active interpretation across problematics of experience selected from within the ever-changing range of each tendency. The suggestions given above, using the range of the sameness/creativity tendency as a base for explanation, are simply a way of giving—as practice—a more workable beginning in understanding these polyadic communities of interpretation. The simplicity/complexity tendency could just as easily be used as a base for explanation.

The Feelings of Constriction

I spoke predominantly of the positive feelings, such as joy, above, but, very briefly, I suggest that the negative feelings fit just as well within the foregoing context. When the flat surface of the hand on the wall gives way to the increased complexity of the hand on the surface of the ball, the feeling is the positive foreshadowing of play.

Let the complexity be *decreased* however. Suppose the foregoing ball surface is replaced by a flat surface and what do you feel? Relative to the curved surface you feel a boundedness, which inhibits possible interpretive actions. Let the flat surface then be replaced by a pointed surface, e.g., a long needle, with your hand resting upon its point. What do you now feel? You feel the possibility of constriction of interpretation in the region of experience, manifesting the inconsistent actions of the originator of the sign (the needle). In short, you feel anxiety, a precursor to fear, and the possibility, attached to this actual very weakly interpreted and interpretable region of sameness and physical complexity, that you will undergo a loss of interpretive capacity with regard to experience as embodiment, because the point tends to constrict all possibilities of interpretation into itself, urging itself upon you as *the only experience* you are to have to interpret. Depending upon the individual capacity for interpretation and the other communities one is engaged in, all pointy physical sensations will tend to evoke this fear, from spider's legs, to wasp's stingers, to snake's fangs, to wickedly pointed daggers, and on and on.[6]

If the possibility of constriction of interpretation is given in a higher complexity region of experience—say from within the complexity engaged in narrative—then the fear may be even more pronounced as feeling, but in addition, as a loss of knowing, an uncertainty, for example, a sharp or "pointed" word or exclamation is yelled at you by someone you regularly interact with and trust. Dr. Johnson famously kicked a large stone to refute Bishop Berkeley's idealism. This was no accident. A small and movable stone, or a ball, or even worse a water balloon, would never have seemed plausible. You can bet he would have chosen a solid cliff face for his refutation, had one been practically nearby. If he could have gone one better, however, he would have challenged the idealist to affirm that a sword point at his throat was "merely an idea."

Yet that just goes to show that Johnson's intuition was on the right track with regard to the recognition of constriction of interpretation as objectivity, even if hyperthematically speaking he was only in possession of one side of a dangerously dyadic sense of the issue. For indeed, the feeling of persistence in experience, as opposed to creativity, is on the right track with regard to at least half of the issue. The other half of the issue, however, is that experience, which tends to persist in sameness, tends also to be less complex, tends to be a physicality. Nature continually falls back as that which persists in sameness (that which is felt) despite its complexity, but mostly we do not recognize this as a tendency of our engagement, because we forget that our constant creative reinterpretation, e.g., in natural science, is always a new realization of nature which, insofar as it is a reinterpretation of what we feel, is always a gift to our future selves.

The Path for Ethics and Science

The above then is the "short" answer which seems appropriate for a conclusion to the problem of feeling/knowing, or aesthetic versus moral value. The real answer, i.e., the "realer" answer, is this work altogether and the implications of chapters 3 and 4 particularly. Now if all of this is plausible, then the answer to Brightman is already well underway. I will nonetheless review Brightman's points, stopping here and there selectively. This should be enough to get the flavor of his view, and to suggest an alternative reading of experience with regard to value, while offering some insights on both science and the contemporary culture wars.

Brightman's intent is to make plausible the notion of ethics as a science, by giving an outline of the same. He begins by defining ethics as a normative science of the principles of the best of human conduct, and he insists that the difference between voluntary behavior and involuntary behavior are what demand a special science for the former.[7] This initial separation of voluntary and involuntary bodes ill for a consistent account and it manifests itself soon in his discussion of what a science is. A science, he says, has a limited field and attempts to formulate laws through observation, and a physicist, for example, has no use for human feelings or values. This assessment would ensure that ethics could never become a science. But is it plausible?

> Again: "descriptive sciences deal with the actual and the necessary, while ethics and other normative sciences deal with the ideal and the possible . . . the interest of a descriptive science is in the statement of facts, their order and causal sequence, and (if determinable) their quantitative relations . . . but a normative

science, is not a merely quantitative measurement, but a qualitative estimation. It evaluates the facts by reference to some ideal of true worth."[8]

Indeed, but it *never evaluates the facts by reference to less than the ideal that there be true worth at all*, i.e., that there be value as an interpretation of experience. And this is the sum of the Roycean and Hyperthematic answer to Brightman. Must we then, as Brightman suggests, "search for principles of right which are superior to circumstance?"[9] No, rather, we must recognize the foundation of valuation in the very circumstance of experience, for the problematic of experience and its interpretive engagement are right beneath our noses all along, as the solution to value.

Once Brightman has decided on his initial assumptions, however, the results play themselves out. He reviews the various types of law in order to understand how the concept of law stands in relation to ethics. Even though he allows more than two types in this effort, he practically contrasts types of law, which may broadly be categorized as social, e.g., civil law, with types of law, which may broadly be categorized as natural, e.g., laws of nature. But this division—essentially another way of formulating the ostensible division between feeling and knowing—is unwarranted. Prohibitive civil legislation does not create morality, Brightman insists, even though civil law rests upon morality.[10] On the other hand, natural law has gradually forced itself upon us, being: "entirely impersonal and above all human choice. It is not imposed by human beings on themselves; it is not a command that they shall behave in any particular way; it is simply a formulation of fact."[11] Logic furthermore, in the dyadic formulation in which Brightman knows it, is more or less placed in the latter category of impersonal laws.

In the hyperthematic view, however, the very idea of a law is a mistake if it be founded upon a necessitarian base. Under this view, the laws of nature are simply very specific instances of free selections of diverse experience at the lower (physical) range of complexity, undergoing willed tendencies of active interpretation. And moreover, prohibitive civil law is also the manifestation of very specific instances of selections of diverse experience at—predominantly—the higher (mental) ranges of complexity.[12]

So, for example, when Brightman offers the imaginative case of John Jones who wrecks his body in drinking himself to death, and when he concludes that even though Jones violated the ethical law that a man ought to care for his body, he violated no natural law, then I must suggest otherwise. Natural law or laws which guide the wasting away of Jones are as bound up with the ought as is the ethical duty/law to hygiene; and you search in vain, if you search for some fundamental difference between them which cannot be bridged by an expansion and translation through the tendencies of complexity and creativity within the process of experience. In short, both types of law express some practical and limited principle or principles for negotiating value creation, even though they express those principles in their relation to different aspects of experience, viz. complexity and creativity. The ethical duties to hygiene are essentially advanced versions of the natural laws which govern the upkeep of the physical body.

And the support for this is not hard to find. Brightman's assertion rests on the view that the natural law describes a sequence of experiences, while the ethical law alters the sequence of experience, and furthermore holds that these laws are independent, so "if x occurs, then y occurs" (or natural law) competes with "if y will occur, then x ought to occur" (or ethical law).* The first of these is recognizable as the tendency of simplicity/complexity. We could add further occurrences to the simple string—if x then y, if y then z, etc.—which would become longer and longer, i.e., more complex in one aspect. The second of these is recognizable as the tendency of sameness/creativity. We aim to bring about, to create, some future sign in experience—y—which is not now in our experience, and we aim to create it by appeal to some sign which is recognized in our experience as an enduring sign, a sameness, of past experience, from among those signs we brought about in our past experience.

The first tendency recognizes *predominantly* the proliferation of signs being interpreted, and the second tendency recognizes *predominantly* the diversity of the signs. But neither of them does so exclusively. Each of them blends into the other, unless we hold them fixed and prevent them from doing so. Thus "if x occurs, then y occurs" (natural law), holds to x and y as a sameness from the past predominantly, in order to interpret them to one another, until it forgets itself as mere observation and strays into creatively assertive futurity as "if x will occur, then y will occur," i.e., it begins to take on ethical character in applying itself to the future. Thus also, "if y will occur, then x ought to occur" (ethical law), appeals to x and y as a complexity from the mental realm predominantly,[13] until it forgets itself as a mental ideal and strays into the simplicity of physicality by reducing its terms down to "x

---

*The ought can be redefined as what will occur (future) in relation to what will occur (future), rather than in relation to what has occurred.

ought to occur," and then further to "x shall occur," i.e., it begins to take on the character of physical *assertion* as the sign begins to stand in relation to fewer and fewer other signs from among the diversity of offerings of the possibilities the world has given it. In short, although abstractly, the two terms/signs are diversities of experience which are being interpreted both to one another and to themselves, with regard to temporal duration. When the former tendency of interpretation is predominant we get science, when the latter is predominant we get ethics. Science, when it "loosens up" becomes expansive, while ethics, when it does so, becomes practical.

Natural law *as an abstracted form* with regard to sameness/creativity depends upon, nay even encourages, a static engagement of the signs which are its terms, and which are proliferating in relations over the physical portion of the range of the tendency of simplicity/complexity. In other words, it engages the signs being interpreted over the range of the latter, through the mediation of the tendency of sameness/creativity *as much in the direction of sameness as it can*. So for example, a biological law might recognize a cell of the body in order to work out its relations to other cells of the body, and a law of physics might recognize an atom likewise, but both laws will recognize them in abstraction as relatively static, as an enduring sameness, for purposes of interpretation across the tendency of simplicity/complexity. The process of experience—e.g., the human scientist—applying the natural law, only manages a static engagement of the signs through a sustained and contorted effort however. As soon as a greater part of the range of the tendency of sameness/creativity is appealed to in the mediating interpretive engagement, everything is thrown out of whack with regard to the abstraction of the natural law, e.g., if the cell comes to be viewed as a process, initiated, developing, harmonizing, fading, etc.

The difficulty of the interpretation in the latter case is increased certainly, and this would excuse a *conscious localized practice** of static engagement, by those interpreters who do not have the interpretive capacity to interpret within the greater ranges of the tendency of sameness/creativity. However, the difficulty does not excuse—if the world is a world of value creation—the static engagement of the sign toward the extremes of sameness beyond the needs of localized practice for learning. Moreover, the constriction has its consequences, personal, social, etc.

---

*By this I mean a localized practice which is aware to some degree that it is, intentionally, localized practice.

The concomitant to the furtherance of the tendency of abstraction is the endeavor to take the natural world metaphysically as a "particulate" world. Atoms, particles, etc., are arrived at as the result of constrictive devaluing engagements of the process of experience which descend from the broader interpretations of curve, to line, to point, discussed earlier. Particles are not "there" because they are foundational building blocks; *they are "there" because we—and other process within the world process—engage experience in constrictive action and so bring them about.* Sustained constrictive action must arrive at (i.e., descend to) them. They are metaphysical yes, but *fluidly metaphysical*, i.e., ultimately only a fluid construct of practice which will give way to better and more creative fluid constructs on the basis of consistent expansive action. Viewed consistently they have an "as good as we can do for the moment" status. Regardless, the abstraction of the natural laws of science based upon localized constrictions always gives way to those of greater interpretive capacities, to those who can play within the fuller ranges of the sameness/creativity tendency, e.g., a Darwin, who can interpret processes of creativity at physical levels of complexity by going beyond the animal as a static enduring sameness, to the creative process of the animal and to the creative process of the species, the "super animal."

Ethical law *as an abstracted form* with regard to the simplicity/complexity tendency faces a similar trouble. It is *an obverse of natural science.* It depends upon and encourages an engagement of complex signs as its terms. In other words, it engages the play of its signs over the fuller range of the tendency of sameness/creativity through the mediation of the tendency of simplicity/complexity *as much in the direction of complexity as it can.* Its use of modifiers such as *will* and *ought* exemplify this; they are as broad as *whatever* might be brought about from the standpoint of a particular capacity of interpretation in the context of the complexity of the signs of its past provenance, and even beyond this capacity. This is the building of the world as the ethical ideal, the play of the fuller tendency of sameness/creativity applied to the highly complex, i.e., the mental or the ideal. Here the static aspect—again by those of a lower interpretive capacity—is the refusal to engage anything *but* the high complexity of the ideal.

The religious fanatic, or political ideologue, envisioning the ideal future world, sets the practical engagement of the less complex range at naught, brushing aside—often with terrible destructive consequences—all signs of the physical range which are not immediately recognizable as fitting with the ideal. He or she is the kin of the materialist scientist, with regard to the constriction of the secondary and mediating tendency, although the constricted tendency is a different tendency.* And again the application of the ethical law only holds to this complexity of signs through a tortured effort.

In both cases the constriction in the mediating tendency can become so sustained and severe that the mediating tendency is altogether ignored or forgotten, so that it seems obvious both that natural science deals with nothing but the *felt givenness of a solid and secure world*—a "same world"—as it ranges back and forth over the variations of simplicity/complexity cataloging the latter, and that ethics deals with nothing but *the perfected complexity of an ideal world*—a "mind world"—as it ranges back and forth over the variations of sameness/creativity dreaming up new perfections, in the urge to create that world in the ideal. As long as and wherever these constrictions of engagement are held to, the two realms of natural science and ethics remain artificially and relatively independent as sovereign regions of experience, namely as: natural science as observation and ethics as ideal.

They are never wholly independent of course. Even in their extreme abstract manifestations they are communities within which the member processes, through their assumptions, are constantly tending toward either growth or decay. The first—natural science—may be called the community retrieving pastness with the actualizing present of the process of experience. The second—ethics—may be called the community creating futurity out of the actualizing present of the process of experience. They are a community together if only they recognize it. But they are degraded and decay whenever the members tend most toward the respective constrictions. The community of natural science is degraded by extreme efforts toward the bare growth of relational complexity without creativity, e.g., the effort of the mere fact finder, the bone digger spoken of earlier, the scientific materialist. The community of ethics is degraded by extreme efforts toward the bare intent to create, heedless of circumstances, heedless of the gift of giveness, within the world process, e.g., in the severity of the Kantian appeal to the law of duty or in the unbending ethical vision of the religious utopian.[14]

Nonetheless, because in each case the tendencies are interpreted through a third, even though the third be extremely constricted, then the community survives, although it may be relatively weak. And as long as the community survives, then it presents an opportunity for members with a broader interpretive capacity to strengthen it: a Darwin or an Einstein

---

*I.e., the materialist scientist is constricting the sameness/creativity tendency toward sameness, while the religious fanatic or political ideologue is constricting the simplicity/complexity tendency toward complexity.

to loosen the constriction toward sameness in the community of science, a Socrates or a Dewey to loosen the constriction toward complexity in the community of ethics.

Now, if the above is plausible, is there a corrective? There is. The corrective, as may be guessed, is in each case a deliberate expansion of interpretation with regard to the tendency being constricted. When such an expansion is countenanced you get something like what has been attempted in this work, which is, again, the broader answer to Brightman. In other words, in such an expansion the community of natural science, its member practitioners, would make an effort to engage *experience as relational complexity*, not merely as a giveness (felt), but as a creation; and in such an expansion the community of ethics would make an effort to engage *experience as a creativity*, not merely in its complex (mental) aspect, but in a way which applies along the full range of complexity, even to the physical. In fine: *science must begin to assume that it creates value rather than merely discovering value, while ethics must begin to assume that the creation and destruction of value is at play in the most physical levels of experience, rather than merely the mental levels.*

In each case this implies a change which views constriction in its proper light as no more than practice toward greater value, rather than as metaphysically foundational. That the world is material and objective for example, that it is analyzable, is simply a crutch which must be put aside eventually, except in localized practice which understands that it is a crutch, so that we may advance to greater value. That the world is, at the simplest and most solid complexities of our everyday physical and objective experience, always responding to our ongoing actions in ways which influence the realization of value with regard to our much more complex plans for the future, is an assumption which must be descended to practically in order to bring about those higher ideals.

Rejoining the Empirical and Ideal

With this framework in hand one can respond to all of those concerns of Brightman which incline him to sunder aesthetic and moral value, and descriptive and normative effort. When Brightman suggests for example that: "'Ought' means more than that desires are being controlled or inhibited. It is a unique kind of inhibition,"[15] my response is that the *ought*, when consistently viewed, is no inhibition at all. It is a suggestion, a *guided play*, within the very physical ranges of experiential complexity, which harmonizes smoothly with distant mental ranges of experiential complexity, *even when those distant ranges are unknown to the playing process*. For if they were known, they would tower over the latter as unscaleable heights disconnected from its circumstances. In other words, it is the very complexity of the vision, and the constrictive unbending assumptions with regard to the latter, of those who formulate it, which causes the *ought* to take on the character of an inhibiting force, and then makes the formulators recoil in amazement when men lacking that vision fail to obey. Mighty Kant expounds the perfection of duty; the German peasant, uncomprehending, walks home and loves his wife and children in the best ways he knows how.

That Brightman sets up his moral system as a series of laws, rather than a series of suggestions, and a series of laws which begin in generalization and give way to less general categories,[16] indicates both that he intuitively understands the above and yet is trapped in the historical abstraction of ethics. That historical abstraction pushes him to make his beginning in non-contradiction, in his *Logical Law*. But contradiction is consequent upon the expansion of meaning in interpretation; (formally) it is an abstraction of the practical engagement of the world process in which it has been discovered that attempts to reduce diversity toward sameness, destroy meaning.*

Just as surely, beginning thus, difficulties with regard to good and evil arise, difficulties initiated by the opening assumption of a dyadic engagement of experience.

These difficulties manifest in the uncertainty over the character of evil. As Brightman puts it: "it must be granted that some of the laws, taken by themselves, are as truly laws of evil as of good. If one wishes to be maliciously and successfully evil, one will have to obey the Logical Law; his will must be consistently evil."[17] Despite this assertion, the uncertainty only indicates the poverty of the starting point. From the hyperthematic beginning the issue is never in doubt, for the appeal to consistency only comes in after the recognition of value in the process of experience. Consistency is always consistency of action in experience, and valuation and devaluation within experience are freely allowed. The good is already recognized in the process of interpretation, whenever it is initiated. It always precedes evil as the very will to interpret, the will to create further from within the created giveness of the world process.

---

*See Appendix D.

A further symptom of these problems is that Brightman speaks of values, which can conflict.[18] The hyperthematic view looks rather toward tendencies of value with a fluid character in which diminishment of value locally affects the ongoing creation of value, tendencies which thus never conflict *qua* value. Or again: values do not conflict, rather *conflict indicates devaluation*. Empirical value is not to be tested by an idealistic system as Brightman suggests;[19] all idealistic systems—whether their creators are aware of it or not—find the basis of their consistent aspects in the engagement of experience as a solving of diversity through meaningful interpretation.

This artificial divide hounds Brightman. He distinguishes, for example, the empirical value of stealing from the ideal value of property rights which a thief also seeks to enjoy, and finds the former tested and found wanting by a contradiction with the latter. Hyperthematically *the tendency of stealing cannot be a value at all*, however. Rather it is a devaluation in which the stolen item is constricted (bounded) in use to the engagement of the thief and its facets of interpretation diminished with regard to the victim, i.e., the victim can no longer enjoy the experience(s) of the "item." Yet, verily, this devaluation rests upon another devaluation, that of *ownership as such* in the legal sense, which is again a constriction in use, wherein the interpretation of an "item," an experience, is denied to others who do not own it. When both forms of engagement of experience are undertaken not as conscious *practice*—wherein *borrowing* and *sharing* would be the appropriate contemporary designations of the engagements which are the consistent kin of *stealing* and *owning*—then they set up Brightman's so-called conflict of values, engendering perennially insoluble problems. The road to solving the problem of Jean Valjean is not an either/or however. It is the recognition that the assumptions which set up the conflict of values need to give way to consistent assumptions. The historic assumptions founding Brightman's difficulties are the adoption of two negatives, constricting tendencies of activity: property law and theft. *Property law and theft are simply devaluative cousins which arise perennially as responses to one another.*

Finally and more centrally, given the test region of application of my hyperthematic endeavor, and given that I must leave off with this brief survey of *Moral Laws*, hoping the reader gets the import of my suggestions, this assumption of divided value finds its way into Brightman's discussion of intrinsic and extrinsic value with regard to economics. Natural and economic value are placed into the category of extrinsic value by Brightman. This is implausible, hyperthematically viewed. A tree for example, is not an extrinsic or instrumental value as an object which is only capable of causing intrinsic value experience within us *if seen*, as Brightman suggests.[20] It is always, in its felt beauty, the sign of a valuating engagement of experience. It cannot be such unless someone always sees the tree insofar as the beauty is created in interpretation and sustained in reinterpretation in the world process. The world process in some guise(s)—not least the living process of the tree itself—is that "someone."

There is no fact insofar as fact which is not itself the result of some consistent engagement of experience toward meaning. There are no independent, i.e., dead, facts, for hyperthematics. The appearance of economic "values" as independent and instrumental is corrected similarly, as all of the second part of this work attempted to show. The miser, who hoards wealth—and who may well stand as the symbol writ small of our capitalist age—is not destitute of intrinsic value in his amassing of instrumental values which "he does not treat as instruments."[21] The miser merely sets his sights always upon a very low—a too low—complexity of value. He is ethical, but only weakly so, and it is his opening assumptions which hold him back.

It is indeed, contra Brightman, the task of the ethicist to contribute to the economic problems of society, to be a guide toward the economic successes of community, just as it is the task of the ethicist to contribute to the scientific problems of society in being a guide toward the scientific successes of community. Science is no more impersonal in seeking for an impersonal objective truth of nature,[22] than is economics in seeking for an impersonal objective truth of quantitative exchange. Rather, it is personal on a higher level, and this is the only way it has value. The exemplars of the ideal of personality have the cause as their personality.[23] Their personality is a community beyond the low-level community of physical embodiment. Whereas objectivity is the intent toward independence of experience, community of interpretation is harmony of experience; the true "objectivity," as a strength of value upon which to create, is the latter.

Out of this comes the solution, in turn, to the divide between law and freedom.[24] There are laws of nature yes, but they are created and sustained by our larger freedom, being consequent upon our actions in the past. The freedom postulated is much broader than usually supposed. It is a freedom to have the consequences of action which valuates and devaluates, extend beyond the experiential complexity of physicality in the abstraction of the temporal present, so as to appear as law-like to the ranges of that physical complexity. Laws are meant to grow and guide growth.

If, as Brightman agrees,[25] freedom underlies all, then it underlies not only the laws of science but mortality and theistic construct as well. We are free that we may join one after another in communities of interpretation of objectivity (laws of nature), in communities of interpretation of linkages of embodiment (physical evolution), in communities of interpretation of connection beyond manifestations of embodiment in the conscious knowledge of that connection (culture), and in communities of interpretation of gods and God as the created community of the latter (the apotheosis of community).

The Nature of Science and the Culture Wars

If the above suggestions are plausible as responses to Brightman, then hyperthematics answers the question of "what science is," thus, *science is the "first" stage of the recognition by broader humanity, of value as informing the experience of the world process*. Its success arises from this recognition. It is only the first stage though, a low-level stage, at which—according to relatively inconsistent assumptions—only a very low-level, weak value, is broadly recognized, predominantly that of quantity. This is why—unfortunately—interpretation beyond quantification is regularly disregarded in cases where it appears to break a natural law. It is disregarded so as to save the capacity for broad low-level valuation. We seek a framework of practical value, and we *will have it*, even at the expense of being unable to interpret certain regions of experience under the terms of that outlook. Science is just that first clumsy framework, which must recognize value and merge with ethics in order to transform into a better framework.

The very urge to have this framework of practical value, that is to say *a great community of interpretive valuation*, which is capable of encompassing the variety of the world process, leads to inconsistent assumptions, for quantitative valuation is unable to interpret various highly complex and thus potentially valuable regions of experience very much, insofar as they are creatively engaged. And when, as now seems apparent, the urge toward greater and greater complexity of interpretation arises, as an inevitable result of past interpretation, then the tension between preserving the assumptions which engendered the initial primitive network of valuation and adopting new assumptions open to creativity (so as to allow the far more valuable creative complexities of interpretation desired), has become terrible indeed. We will advance beyond this impasse however, because *we will to interpret*. The economic impasse arises for the same reasons and will be solved through corresponding urges and by corresponding means. In short then, our current problems (economic) come from the failure of the value exchange system—wrought by the relative practical poverty of our worldview with regard to value—to be able to facilitate the ever widening complexity of interpretations we wish to make. The system is tottering because it cannot keep up with our urge to interpret. The natural sciences are facing a variation of this problem.

The problem—as do all problems—presents an opportunity for meaningful interpretation, in this case a correction. With regard to economic expansion the correction will come in the guise of the self-correction of commercial corporations themselves, a self-correction which looks to the various hurts that commercial corporations have caused in the world and begins to heal them. We cannot look for the destruction of commercial corporations. Rather, we must look for a change which recognizes the damage done and deliberately builds a new selfhood of communities of the commercial corporation as repairers of damage, i.e., complex entities which understand themselves as engaged in the betterment of their members, an engagement which is as unlimited as the betterment of all humans in consistent community.

All of the efforts to work, products/objects, etc., of commercial corporations are for the value of human experience at least—insofar as that experience is preeminent to us—and for value even beyond that experience insofar as possible. Products, work, and all the effort of commercial corporate communities are for the growth of value, and the growth of value is not exclusive, nor constrictive, as I have tried to show. Where it is supposed to be constrictive, it is not the growth of value, but its diminishment, a diminishment which spreads through the world process until we correct it.

In the contemporary world, the issue of the division of value is a particularly prominent one. Having gained the ability to carry out interpretations at complexities which are "orders of magnitude" beyond those attempted in recent centuries, the inconsistent assumptions which underlie constrictions of interpretation and destructions of value will tend to manifest themselves in extremes of quantitative accumulations of weak value occurring side-by-side with troughs of value destruction. The preeminent current example of this is to be found within the phenomena of the contemporary culture wars, whose extremes are best exemplified in those very cultures which have embraced value creation—Western cultures particularly—but embraced it under the mistaken assumptions of the fundamental division and independence of the realms of value just expanded upon. Yet even though the phenomena is *most* exemplified in cultures such as contemporary American culture, it is globally evident and will spread everywhere that interpretation is undertaken for the creation of value without a consistent understanding of the nature and practice of value. And interpretation will not stop being undertaken.

The right and left wings of political assumptions are based in this misunderstanding of the nature of value. It is a dyadic clash between value as the mere feeling of the world process in signs of past effort and the mere knowing of the world process in the newness of creative interpretation. This is never a clash in the beginning, however, for in all beginnings of social interaction taken from the viewpoint of e.g., a selected culture, there is as yet little pastness of effort relative to what comes to be defined as that culture, and there is every newness of creative interpretation available, since not much has yet been interpreted relative to that culture. If the past of your culture is short, there is not much to feel of it, and if the actualization of your culture is beginning, there is every freedom to create in it. The beginnings of cultures may thus be happy beginnings in which the accumulations and deficits of value are not yet manifested. The past accumulates and the future narrows however, and both because of the other, and yet both through an interpretation of the present.

Of course, the world process is greater than any particular human culture. There is the equivalent of a political right and left in nature for example. I have hinted already that it is manifested in the physical ranges of the world process as the development of nature in species, wherein the static duration of species as an extreme constriction to sameness—to the feeling of pastness—is the kin of the political right of human social development, and wherein explosive speciation as an extreme of adherence to burgeoning complexity—to nature's knowing of the future—is the kin of the political left of human social development. It is beyond the scope of this work to bring this hint further, except to suggest that the solution for nature is always an expansion out of the two constrictions which gives rise to the physical animal as community of the embodied individual and community of the species.

Even if we keep the issue within the realm of human social culture, the tendencies are evident enough. Thus the political right wing is the traditional. It seeks to hold onto the signs of the past, as a sameness of those signs. It feels more than it knows. It tends toward the physical, particularly the embodied physicality of the human individual, because the physical is the more readily felt. It tends toward the independence of the human individual as an embodied physicality, for independence facilities sameness of experience. It tends toward a preservation of nature, but a preservation of nature as a sameness, i.e., as a realm of habitation *for* humanity in which the relation of the animal to the embodied human individual endures as what it has long been: a relation of dominance at physical ranges—running either way, depending on the animal—which opposes nature's inconsistencies.[26]

In tending toward the extreme of sameness, the right wing tends also to favor those signs of the world process, wherever they may lie in the range of simplicity/complexity, which tend to be more readily reinterpretable as a sameness of experience: the physical family line as an enduring entity; the (sometimes highly complex) narratives, e.g., the Old Testament of the Bible, which carry forward the relations of sameness of the human individual to the past of the world process; the older institutions such as monarchies, and so forth.

On the other hand, the left wing is progressive. It seeks to modify the signs of the past, as a proliferation of complexity. It knows more than it feels. It tends toward the mental, particularly the perfection of the complexity of the ideal, because the mental responds more readily to the creation of complexity. It tends toward the replaceable equality of the human individual as an embodied physicality, for equality facilitates social complexity in experience. It tends toward a transformation of nature, but a transformation of nature into a complexity, i.e., as a realm of management by humanity in which the relation of the animal to the embodied human individual transforms into what it has never been: a relation of idealization which ignores that nature also manifests inconsistencies at its physical complexities.[27]

Because the left wing tends toward the extreme of complexity, it tends also to favor those signs of the world process, regardless of where they may lie with regard to the range of the sameness/creativity tendency, which tend to be more readily interpretable as a complexity of experience: the social group as a complexifying entity (e.g., bureaucratization); the endeavors of constrictive sameness—e.g., the progress of merely physical technology—which proliferate the relations of social complexity of human individual to human individual in embodiment (e.g., mass transportation, computerization, etc.); the institutions such as social democracies and the organs of the welfare state, which equalize individuals, and so forth.

Sometimes, moreover, strange bedfellows are encouraged, which are yet not so strange, hyperthematically viewed. I said that communities of science tend to interpret with regard to the fuller range of the simplicity/complexity tendency, even though, as engagements of observation, they tend to interpret the latter through the extreme of sameness. Yet if this is so, then scientists on the whole would tend to be on the political right. This immediately seems counterintuitive in the context of the contemporary world.

It isn't. Scientists do indeed tend to be quite conservative. It is just that in their interpretive capacity they are conservative over a far greater range of the simplicity/complexity tendency than are the most extreme exemplars of political conservatism, who tend to interpret merely the simpler ranges of the simplicity/complexity tendency through the extreme of sameness. In short, scientists, on the average, are complexly conservative, *and their conservatism tends to manifest itself with regard to those interpreting at their own ranges of complexity*. They are the "complex right wing," so to speak.

You can confirm this by considering that within the communities of the natural science, those whose study tends most toward the simple (physical), namely the biologists, also seem to tend toward political conservatism—that of the conservative social individual—the most. It is not that they would reinterpret in sameness the exact signs of those on the extremes of the right wing who are not scientists. The signs they reinterpret as a sameness are more complex than those signs. Yet the signs are still akin to one another. That of the nonscientific political conservative is a reinterpretation of physicality as an independence of the embodied individual, while that of the scientific conservative, e.g., certain well-known atheist biologists, is just a reinterpretation of more complex physicality, e.g., as an independence of the embodied species, the gene, and so forth. In short, the materialist biologist and the nonscientific political conservative—e.g., the contemporary creationist—are as older and younger siblings with regard to their capacity and tendencies of interpretation. It is not difference which gives rise to their mutual conflict; *it is their similarity, the constriction of their actions according to their assumptions, which gives rise to their conflict*.

The strange bedfellows, the warring siblings, on the other side, are the social political left (the younger sibling) and the Silicon Valley Utopians (the older sibling), who both cleave to complexity to interpret the sameness/creativity tendency, but of whom the latter is more ready to abandon the ancestral signs of the physical for an ideal of unfettered creativity.

Having interpreted political right and left, even briefly, one sees that the thread which leads from the seemingly sundered realms of natural science and ethics is woven on into the tattered fabric of the contemporary culture wars. The division of value is, unfortunately, at work in many realms of human experience. The hyperthematic solution is a recognition of value as a result of the play of interpretation which accepts the given signs of diverse experience in free selections and creatively interprets the problematic of those selections into new signs. It is both a moving away from constrictions of engagement of experience, and a willingness to practically recognize the giveness of the world process, even in its simplicity, in expansions toward new value. If it can be done with regard to the realm of the commercial corporation, as I have insisted that it can, then it can be done in the realms touched on above.

Coda

Having carried out the tasks which I set out, the hyperthematization of the corporation has been taken as far as the objective limits of a single work allow. The result is a reworked vision of the corporation. We have a consistent hypertheme of cooperation, as well as many additional hyperthemes which can act as supplementary resources toward the correction and development of the commercial corporation as it now stands, all of which can be brought together to comprise the renewed hyperthematic structure of the corporation. The endeavor has tested the hyperthematic methodology, at least in a preliminary way, and found it to be so far practical and promising of further application with regard to other problematics and structures.

A few further words are in order regarding commercial corporations. In order to make the account as clear as possible, I made no attempt thus far to redefine the terminology of the corporation. In light of all the above however, it is doubtful that the terms worker, boss, product, and so forth, are amenable to this re-envisioned hyperthematic structure. The terminology applied to the community and members of a renewed hyperthematic structure would do well to signify two fundamental aspects which make the structure of assumptions guiding commercial corporations unique. The first is that the community of the corporation as a cooperative engagement is an extension of the community of the individual, the community of selfhood, and cannot be consistently divorced from that community. The second, closely allied, is that the members of the community of the corporation can only impart to the corporation as a community, that tendency toward interpreted value which they can recognize in themselves.

With this in mind I offer a new term which might help the envisioned renewal. *Epsionomics* I define as: *the realization of value by the members of a community engaging some aspect of the problematic of cooperation in harmony through playful and creative interpretation.* Accordingly, the corporation—which insofar as consistent is ill defined according to its roots in the preeminent term now used for the static object of the physical range of complexity, i.e., body (corpus)—becomes an *epsionomic community*,* i.e., an interpretive person rather than a corporate person, whose members consist of *epsionomists*, while its product becomes an *epsionomic interpretation*, i.e., the interpretive goal of a consistent epsionomic community.

The foregoing terminology is suggested on the basis of a reflection upon the term economics and its derivatives. The root of the term economics in all its manifestations is the inconsistent assumption of the product as a static object as the locus of exchange and activity, a mere resource that can be "saved"—stashed away in the *oîkos*—in the range of quantitative valuation. In the first place then, my terminology intends to offer an alternative to this view. Rather than economists who, at a distance, study inconsistently assumed objects as the goals of corporations, I am suggesting epsionomists as themselves cooperatively engaged at various levels of complexity in epsionomic interpretations. Rather than objective products which choke interpretation, I am suggesting epsionomic interpretations, which hold the promise of meaningful activity for all the members who are in any way engaged in their creation.

The invocation of playfulness is deliberate. Many of the finest examples we have of harmonized activity toward interpretive goals are examples of play between cooperating members of communities whose goals are as far removed from objectification as is possible for us humans as we now are. From the fun of children's play, outside and away from toys, in tag, and "hide and seek," to the artfully interspective [*sic*] togetherness of the members of a great jazz band, chamber ensemble, or orchestra, it is *playing* which captures the vision and promise of cooperative interpretation, not as a corporate venture undertaken in force, but as an *epsionomic adventure* undertaken in the ongoing creative and playfully valuative realization of the world.

---

*From the ancient Greek εψιάομαι, signifying a child's game and play itself.

Summary of the Hyperthemes

H—*the world is the community of interpretation of the problem which it presents, or, the world is a hyperthematic structure of interpretation which contains three transformable elements: experience, different experience, postulated interpretation of the resulting problematic of experience (i.e., solution)*

HG *(Hypertheme of the Goal)—to create a community of interpretation, select a problematic, a goal, to engage.*

H1'—*if H, then any <u>hyperthematic structure</u> which tends toward the elimination of the elements of its own, or other hyperthematic structures, is an unstable or inconsistent structure.*

H2'—*if H, then any <u>element</u> acting under the guidance of a hyperthematic structure which tends toward elimination of the elements of its own or other hyperthematic structures, including itself, is an unstable or inconsistent element.*

H3'—*if H, then any single element, or pair of elements cannot make up a community guided by a hyperthematic structure according to its own level of complexity, though it can do so within a more complex hyperthematic structure than its own.*

H4'—*if H3, then any <u>community</u> which eliminates other communities or elements of other communities, is inconsistent with H, since if H and H3, then these may be elements of communities under a more complex hyperthematic structure.*

H1—*create hyperthematic structures which do not eliminate elements.*

H2—*take all transformative means to guide the transformable elements acting under a hyperthematic structure out of eliminating other elements of the structure.*

H3—*create communities of three or more elements under hyperthematic structures.*

H4—*create communities which do not eliminate other structures, or communities or elements of other structures.*

H5—*insofar as you can, populate the community guided by your hyperthematic structure with transformable elements that are signs of transformation away from eliminative elements that destabilize community toward elements that promote harmonious interpretation.*

H6—*insofar as possible, given the problematic, select transformable elements of a community such that their ranges of transformation promote actions which are simple enough for any actors in the community to carry them out in interpretations which sustain the community.*

H7—*construct communities such that they tend to engage the elements of other communities and prevent them from elimination.*

H8—*to create hyperthematic structures which engage further actors insofar as possible make the sectional acting elements of those structures transformable rather than replaceable.*

H9—*in the creation of communities under hyperthematic structures, increasing the number or degree of transformable elements such that they pass on both structure and problematic, increases the growth of the structure at the expense of solution of the problematic; while decreasing the number or degree of transformable elements increases the chance of solution within the structure at the expense of its growth.*

H10—*to enhance the meaning of the transformable elements within hyperthematic structures with regard to interpretations parallel to the time process, creatively postulate historic or futuristic interpretive models for the elements of your structure to interpret themselves to.*

H11—*to move the range of your hyperthematic structure toward a more local and physical harmonization of action, simplify, and reduce (but do not eliminate) the models to be interpreted to, and do the reverse to move the range of your structure toward a more broad and mental harmonization of action; and, in order to engage in the experience of your problematic in the most efficient way, postulate a diverse range of models which can be interpreted to.*

H12—*to create hyperthematic structures which engender greater stability and potential to interact with other hyperthematic structures, make every effort to include models which capture how reconstructive action has creatively responded to destabilizing actions within and against the community under the structure. Find such models if you can, creatively postulate them if you cannot.*

H13—*in correcting hyperthematic structures, borrow from other stable structures, and in particular look to those hyperthematic structures guiding stable communities whose degree of focus complements the emphasis of the structure under correction.*

H14—*as the range and degree of the transformable elements of a hyperthematic structure increase in complexity such that its models of action harmonization allow interpretations which pass on signs of meaning as a type, it tends to draw the elements of a community engaged in it away from the locus of attachment in the time process which marks the beginning of the range of its problematic of experience, toward a homogenous appraisal of that problematic. Such a structure will be called a <u>leader structure</u>.*

H15—*hyperthematic structures are best supported, i.e., their communities of interpretation are stabilized, by hyperthematic leader structures whose complexity is furthest from their own. Although in principle any structure with a level of complexity higher than the structure in question could act as a leader structure, nonetheless, according as there is a tradeoff between complexity and the time process situatedness of the acting element, then the leader structure which will be able to give the best support is that which is both well developed, and whose complexity is not so far removed as to saturate the interpretive freedom of the supported structure.*

HCr (*Hypertheme of Creativity*)—*in order to <u>create</u> experience, engage in interpretations which insofar as possible interpret a portion—an existent fact—of experience within the world process to a portion of experience within the world process which does not include the original portion within itself.*

HCu (*Hypertheme of Curvature*)—*in order to increase value within regions of experience at the physical range of complexity, make every effort to create physical shapes which are curved and to avoid the creation of shapes which diminish curvature.*

HAs (*Hypertheme of Asymmetry*)—*in order to increase value within regions of experience at the physical range of complexity make every effort to create hyperthematic asymmetry and to avoid forming physical shapes which are hyperthematically symmetric and which thus copy portions of themselves.*

HCl (*Hypertheme of Color*)—*in order to increase value within regions of experience at the physical range of complexity, make every effort to interpret* *those regions by means of those colors which tend toward expansion of interpretation by way of their being manifestations of consistent action upon that sign of maximal interpretability at physical complexity which we call light.*

Hv (*Hypertheme of the Viewer*)—*in order to build consistent communities, make every effort to expand the acting transformable element being interpreted to—e.g., the viewer—as an interpreter of the sign in its own right, by selecting and passing on aspects of action-experience in the interpretation which manifest consistent tendencies according to H. Insofar as you do this you will expand the ethical selfhood of the viewer.*

HOe (*Hypertheme of Objective Expansion*)—*in order to expand value in a community which creates or engages objects, make every effort to act so as to transform the chosen sign being interpreted into a sign whose aspects tend away, through expansion, from the relations common to the objectification inherent in the sign, e.g., the painting.*

Hd (*Hypertheme of Diversity*)—*in order to expand value in a community make every effort to act so as to transform through interpretation the chosen sign into a different sign which nonetheless remains interpretable to participants of the community, e.g., artists and viewers, by taking into account the interpretive capacity of the elements of the community.*

Ha (*Hypertheme of Aging*)—*in order to expand value in a community make every effort to act with regard to a chosen sign so as to encourage further interpretation of it by oneself and by other interpreters in expansions of the span of its interpretation as a process relative to the world process.*

Hc (*Hypertheme of Correction*)—*in order to expand value in a community, make every effort, according to your ethical capacity as an interpreter, to act so as to <u>select</u> signs of experience which have arisen through constrictive tendencies, and <u>correct</u> them through such creative expansions as you are capable of.*

Appendix A

Aesthetic Taste for Hyperthematics and Hume's Notion of Taste

My reference to the notion of taste may evoke Hume's suggestions on aesthetic taste, raising the question of just how I am comparing aesthetic taste to value, relative to Hume's views. The following outlines briefly how the hyperthematic view compares to Hume's view.

First, for Hyperthematics, value and devaluatedness are deeply woven into the fabric of *all* interpretive action, human and otherwise, whereas for Hume—as, to be fair, for the classical philosophers generally—value has its separate domain(s) from the world at large, i.e., "value, and the ethical principles apply here and here . . . but not here and here." This causes Hume to distinguish taste and fact and to pass back and forth between them, alighting now on the side of fact and now on the side of taste, in their several manifestations. A brief survey of Hume's position in his *Of the Standard of Taste* readily shows this back and forth.

Hume sees that we do seek—and naturally so—a standard of taste by which we could condemn or approve the sentiments of any one of us. He notes that one prominent strand of thought says that sentiment can never be wrong because it is disconnected from things themselves, whereas understanding, being connected to matters of fact, can always be wrong. He recognizes, however, that certain assertions of one thing being better than another are almost universally laughed at as ridiculous, and thus ignored—he clearly hadn't imagined the Internet age—countering the principle that sentiment can never be wrong; the latter only holds when the things being judged are nearly equal. And yet there are no eternal and immutable rules to govern the above; all is finally grounded on experience. One sees then, that the appeal to experience, for Hume, is an appeal to an "outer real" which will arbitrate, in distinction to an "inner real," which the illusory eternal and immutable rules would be.

Beauty—e.g., in writing—is often founded upon something bad, says Hume. But beauty often overcomes the bad within it to present a good aspect overall. If something bad is gotten across to us in a good (beautiful) way, so as to please us, then it is not bad. Yet experience and common sentiment cannot be accessed at times, due to the frailty of the human mind, or body, while good work lasts through the ages. Delicacy of imagination is needed—the ability to sense finely—in order to detect proportionally minute degrees of quality in an object which provokes beauty in the mind or senses; but accordingly this delicacy *cannot* be used to convince (because so few have it) and it *can* be used to overturn a "bad critic" by showing him that the principle applies on a larger scale, and so must apply on the smaller scale, except that he himself lacks the "delicacy" to see or sense that smaller scale.

For Hume, the eye and the tongue can perceive minutely for some of us and this ability makes the "good palate," etc., but by analogy the mind must be refineable likewise. Such delicacy of taste is always lauded and recognized by comparing it with the principles established "by the uniform consent of nations and ages." Again then, the appeal to those nations and ages is an appeal to the "outer real," although Hume never says this explicitly.

Frequent judging of works of art, etc., develop the delicacy of taste, as does actually doing art—here we have Hume's concession to the creative aspect of taste, but it fades out of consideration immediately. Repeated perusal—coming back to the feeling side of things—is necessary and we must make comparisons. One who cannot compare is not qualified to have an opinion. I suggest that this last is at least partly muddleheaded, as Whitehead would say. For hyperthematics, localized comparison, interpretations deliberately limited to the aspects of the "object," e.g., poem, work of art, being considered, is perfectly possible; it is a consistent variation of what I have called practice. The "object"/experience always has some grounds for interpretation at varying complexities—Hume even admits as much when he speaks of the "coarsest daubing" of color being admired by those unfamiliar with higher superior beauties. What Hume should have said, then, is that highly complex objects of art are *better* compared with other such objects, and yet simple beauties can also appeal to the highly practiced; but he denies the latter. And he must deny it, for otherwise his comfortable dichotomy would begin to collapse.

In addition to the above, critics, Hume insists, must be un-prejudiced and "stand in the shoes" of the environment and age wherein the object (or art) was produced, otherwise their taste "loses all credit and authority." Every work has an end to which it is aimed and succeeds or fails thereby. When Hume sums it all up we get a better idea of the aforementioned dichotomy: *although the principles of taste are general, most everyone is messed up by the failure to engage the external real, through bad sense, prejudice, etc., in short, through a deficiency in those principles of taste.* Only a few have everything right in that engagement, and those few set the standard of beauty. But since we disagree on who those few are, then, says Hume, we must have recourse to a decisive standard, i.e., "real existence and matter of fact." In short, *the select few must argue it out, mannerly, by appeal to external facts* (pull back a moment and reflect here, and you begin to feel what the tenor of Hume's overall philosophy has led to in a certain segment of contemporary humanity given over to scientism, materialism, etc.) And moreover, by analogy, the real facts for art are the "pieces of art" which have lasted for civilization and the opinions of the few—undisputedly—superior men who constantly bring them down to us over the ages, i.e., the "force of nature and just sentiment," as Hume calls it. Here we have an appeal to force, as expected—compare a more complex variation in Appendix D—and the effect of this is to again re-emphasize the external real and remove all the good of practice, etc., from the other side, i.e., from the "faulty and untrustworthy internal," as one might call it.

Yet, in an age of contrary sentiments, as Hume adds, no standard can be found. And also one's mood, circumstances, even one's national character, can produce diversity from the external standard of sentiment: one likes comedy, another is in love, etc. Here Hume returns to an emphasis on the "internal" side of things, but once again that side is seen as the source of error at best, or mere vague indecision at worst. Meanwhile, serious defects of moral principles in works of past ages, for example those of the ancients, remain defects forever, and blemish those works forever. Here then, once again, the "outer real" of the compositions of earlier ages retain their blemishes as existent facts, even though the inner moral principles are continuously changing and improving in each new age—so again the disconnecting dichotomy. And finally—one last dig by Hume to strengthen his point—on the other hand, defects of religion (an utterly inner speculation) which are apparent in works of earlier ages, are *always* excusable because religion is essentially all illusion. So much may serve as a brief summary of Hume's position.

Now, in Hyperthematic terms, a first thing to note is that for Hume all the emphasis is on what I have called felt value, rather than the creation of value. Yet there are no grounds for such an emphasis except that

Hume has foundered on his dichotomy, so he concentrates all efforts on uncovering: "where is the error located, in the outer, or in the inner?" But the error he seeks is introduced in the very assumption of the dichotomy, and the only way to advance is by emphasizing the solution rather than the disconnection of experience.

A second thing to note is that sentiment is based on pleasure for Hume, hence what pleases us cannot be gainsaid except by some superior external fact. But for Hyperthematics, what pleases us—the fulfillment of willed interpretive actions toward valuation or devaluation—can often be locally consistent (devaluation pleases some of us) but inconsistent in larger experience, e.g., I want to hoard money as a miser, and I gain a weak value of localized quantity thereby because it pleases me to hoard the money, but I devalue other regions of the world process in doing so. Yet misers learn, as we all do, through a process of ongoing interpretations which range near and far, across both "internal" and "external."

Hume is caught up in his hopeless dichotomy between the "real out there"—the proposed and supposed standard of taste—and the decision to ignore the real out there—unredeemed taste, i.e., bad taste. Each part of his essay simply reinstates the dichotomy in another way: my mind is at fault, hence I cannot access the real out there, i.e., illusion in here vs. the real out there; I cannot experience some delicacy of beauty due to my sense organs, hence I cannot access the real out there, etc.—but the real out there can be used to prove me wrong or show me so, at the scale of my organs; or, I *can* experience some delicacy of beauty, and others can discern this ability in me by referring to the models and principles of the ages "out there"; or again, I can only judge well and without prejudice if I can forget my own time and experience and "stand in the shoes" of the nation or age of the matter I am considering—yet another appeal to an "out there."

Hyperthematics suggests that there is no such dichotomy between a real "out there" and an illusion "in here." The value of experience is the total play of all efforts at value. But the standard is at once beyond such experience as I am interpreting—though not *necessarily* beyond—and influenced (created) by my interpretations of experience. The "being beyond me" of the standard is a consequence of an initial assumption that interpretation itself is the key to engaging experience. In other words, the initial assumption of **H** points to a standard or, i.e., "all is not interpreted (solved) in (my) experience—there is diversity," but meanwhile, "all diversity of experience is interpretable," hence a standard is *being created* by the play of the world process in which I participate.

So the "eternal and immutable guide," which Hume dismisses, is indeed there, but it begins—locationally, and at other complexities beyond physicality—"within me," i.e., it begins within the process of my ethical selfhood, whenever and to whatever extent I adopt the consistent initial assumption with which to engage experience, even though I am often adopting that assumption long before I consciously know that I am. The standard is indeed beyond me, but it is also not beyond me because it is a construction that I and others are constantly creating by consistent efforts to engage experience. Thus valuative or devaluative interpretive action contributes to (or detracts from) the growing value of the world process, or, to translate this merely into Hume's *terms* (which cannot perfectly be done) and perhaps dispel Hume's confusion: *for each of us, our taste—and bad taste—is our own contribution to the evolving fact of beauty.*

Appendix B

Devaluation and Symmetric Consequence

Several times I have hinted that the consequences of devaluation rebound upon the initiating locus of devaluation. In the main I have suggested this in the context of inconsistent devaluating action undertaken on the scale of various groups in society, or various societies. *For the most part* the visible rebound of devaluation—the correction which the world process sets in motion—is evident on social scales of complexity. Thus, a human group which pollutes its own greater living areas is faced with increasing discomfort from its own pollution in those areas.

Yet *for the most part* is far from *always*, even at social levels of complexity, and so we find many a social group bitterly opposed to the thought that their own devaluative action—if they even admit the devaluation—will rebound upon them. Since this is so on the human social levels of complexity, then how much more so on the scale of the physically embodied human individual. For the sneaking thought that we can "get away with things" is never too far from the minds of the best of us, and the thought that for each of us individuals, his or her own badness might return in any direct and directly proportional way, is a difficult one to bear, or even to countenance.

The hyperthematic view implies, however, that we cannot "get away with things" at *any* scale of complexity. The world process is consistent for Hyperthematics only as a community of interpretation, through and through, where the problems of devaluation, including the "grand" problem of the why of a world at all, are soluble through the ongoing process of experience. Thus, every devaluation has its consequence and must be made good in some interpretation. The hyperthematic view of symmetry—which gives rise to the *Hypertheme of Asymmetry* as a corrective—implies yet further semi-formalizations, not elucidated in the main text, but which I will now note, in order to clarify why every devaluative act rebounds upon the initiator.

First, *if every symmetry, in the hyperthematic sense, is a devaluation, then every pocket of devaluation is ultimately symmetric to some region of experience within the world process*, including pockets of devaluation whose symmetry our awareness at its present ethical breadth, cannot yet span, i.e., harm within the world whose consequences we cannot yet see. What this implies is that, e.g., a constriction experienced by the embodied locus of a process is mirrored by a constriction within experience initiated by that process. Further, if the symmetry is not obvious within the temporal span (e.g., lifetime) of the locus of embodiment of the process, then it must be located beyond the constriction of embodiment—e.g., physical—of that process.

A way to imagine this better perhaps is to imagine stabbing a hole in something, say in semi-soft material such as mozzarella cheese. You can never stab "half of a hole." Whatever hole you do stab has a symmetry about some plane which combines the symmetry built into the stabbing instrument along with the choice of the plane of "attack," which it leaves open. The symmetry built into your implement—say a knife—by its creator, arises because of the uninterpretability between various aspects of the implement's surface, and this allows the implement to stab things. The more interpretable it is, the less "stabby" it is, unless the un-interpretability is countenanced and inserted—by the wielder or creator—in some more complex aspect of the experience that is broader than what we take to be an individual object. So, e.g., you will not do much stabbing of mozzarella cheese with a ball, unless the ball is rendered very tiny with respect to the cheese, or the cheese is made much larger than the ball, or unless the ball is thrown—like a bullet—with considerable force, or speed. In each case, the engagement of implement and target (ball and cheese) are tending to be viewed for purposes of the devaluative action, as much broader than the individual ball and cheese.

The ability to view the fuller result—the damage to the cheese—of the above-imagined scenario, is an effect of the approximate correspondences of complexity of the regions of experience in question with that of our own regions of physical embodiment as humans. But when the regions of experience begin to be out of proportion with that region of human physical embodiment, then the consequences, as the "further side" of the symmetric devaluation attempted, become increasingly hard to see. So, for example, if I stab and kill another human with the intent to murder, a part of the devaluative action—the proportionally less complex tending part—will render its consequences fairly immediately visible: the stab wound, screams, etc., and I will indeed usually get a part of the rebound of the devaluative action *at this complexity* in various psychological effects upon myself, perhaps in wounds in return, and so forth.

Should I succeed in murdering my victim, then I extinguish the life of the physical body. But if the ending of the life of the physical body is not well viewable on the scale of complexity of the physical body as simple embodied physicality—and it is not—then my ability to experience immediately the fuller consequences of the act is increasingly diminished. If I am extremely broad ethically, or at least broad enough, I may experience a portion of the fuller rebound of the devaluative act upon myself—as lady Macbeth does for example—but just so, if I am so broad, I will tend to understand the consequences and avoid the murdering action in the first place. More likely is that I have not, by far, enough ethical breadth—interpretive capacity—yet to experience the symmetry of the act, if I actually carry it out, and so I only immediately experience a partial consequence. I must then wait in the time process for the rest of the consequence.

Now if we formulate a hypertheme from the above, we get the following, in its negative formulation, which I will call the *Hypertheme of Symmetric Responsibility*, or **HSR**'—*if the world is a community of interpretation, then every constrictive devaluation encountered within some region of experience of the world process is symmetric to some further region of the world process in conjunction with which it would regain the value of community temporarily lost in the devaluative act, through an expansive correction, i.e., an appropriately complex and creative action of interpretation*. In other words, every devaluative act has its appropriate consequence for the experience of the locus which initiates the act, even though that consequence may not yet have appeared in time. In its positive formulation however it would run: **HRH**—*in order to increase value in the world process, insofar as possible, face every devalued region of experience whose scope passes beyond the ability of correction at present levels of—e.g., embodied—complexity and creativity, with the active assurance that through the application of consistent hyperthemes and the accompanying expansion of interpretive capacity (ethical breadth), its solution will be arrived at*. I will call this one the *Hypertheme of Redemptive Hope*. I will not follow these hyperthemes far however, nor attempt either to interpret them definitively to the derivatives or interpret them extensively to the actions of the commercial corporation, for that will require another work. I merely lay them out as promising corollaries which follow from the hyperthematic view of symmetry (and **HAs**) and intersect with **Hc**, and which explain my various suggestions that one who engages in the devaluation of experience bears the consequences of that devaluation.

Also, this highlights the hyperthematic view of the nature of practice yet again. I have invoked practice as locally aware constriction. Consistent practice is constriction proceeding from a view of the world process—e.g., in an embodied locus of process—which is broad enough to interpret both the constriction and the expansive response which corrects it. So, returning to a former simple example, if I engage in weight training, I deliberately stress and even subtly injure various muscles, in order that they should grow stronger. If I do this consistently as practice, I see and understand the constriction, which is the type of injury in question, and the consequent expansion, which is the growth of the community of the body. The scope of such a devaluation is relatively narrow, even at bodily ranges of complexity, and yet as practice it comes under and belongs to an ethical breadth of understanding which is capable of maintaining the body as a physical community. Even that ethical breadth may be lacking for some, so that the community of the body deteriorates, without the embodied locus knowing why. But again, as suggested in the last example, if we often fail to see the symmetry of constriction—e.g., bodily inactivity—which is the cause of physical bodily illness, how much easier is it to fail to see the symmetric cause or consequence of some far deeper constrictive action, such as murder carried out, or murder undergone?

Let me frame the consequences of the above suggestions in more everyday and explicit terms. Every process—such as the human—is invariably responsible for its actions, and makes up for its wrongdoings somewhere and somehow in a way which, to the extent that it is not corrected by some appropriately complex creative interpretive action, symmetrically mirrors the originating constrictive action.[1] To kill is, if the originating devaluation is not corrected, to be killed; to harm another, if . . . etc., is to be harmed by another; to insult . . . is to be insulted; to lie . . . is to be lied to; to rob . . . is to be robbed; to impoverish others . . . is to be the subject of impoverishment; and so on. Every constrictive action must be made good, whether in the current living embodiment, or in some embodiment of the process beyond the current embodiment, *some other life*.

Moreover, every constriction of an embodied process—excepting consistent practice—as an unforeseen harm which befalls that process, arises because of some devaluative action deliberately undertaken in some other embodiment of the process which has betrayed the community of interpretation of the process, without appropriate creative correction. Thus, to be killed, is to have killed without having made up for that devaluation; to be betrayed, is to have betrayed without . . . etc.; to be lied to, is to have lied to . . . ; to be impoverished, is to have impoverished others . . . ; and so on.

Nonetheless, if there is consistent practice—constrictive action—in a process as embodied, as suggested, then there is also consistent practice at greater ranges of a process. So, for example, that some deliberately choose material impoverishment or other difficult modes of life, or even to physically die, to be killed, for a cause—a man like Gandhi may well have illustrated all three—as a practice to build some complex aspect of the process beyond even what we see in a single embodiment, is evident through human history. Again, on the other hand, some devaluative symmetries are all too evident within a single embodied span of a process. Hence, mafia killings beget retribution, and that retribution regularly cuts short the life of mafia members well before old age, the "justice" of the latter often appearing fairly evident to us. So we can see the workings of the hyperthemes in question often enough, even within an individual embodied life span of a process, though we have more or less difficulty extending the principle beyond a single embodied life span because of the considerable complexity involved. Yet this last means no more than that any one of us has a range of appreciation, an interpretive capacity, of the creation and destruction of value, i.e., we are at different ranges of ethical breadth.

Now, *none of this means that as we now are, we can always know conclusively which harm follows which devaluation.* We can often make wise guesses, however. The broad surveying of human history with its wars and counter-wars, its revolutions and counter-revolutions, its reforms and counter-reforms, can go a long way toward the expanding of ethical breadth in this respect. That a Germany in ruins after World War II should follow a Germany intent on destruction before the war, or that a Robespierre under the guillotine should follow a Robespierre directing the guillotine, appears eminently predictable to those who have pondered world events very much.

Beyond this we have the certainty that if the world is a world of value, then all is made right and corrected—solved—somewhere and somehow. This is just to suggest again the opening postulate upon which we are attempting to build a practical hyperthematic view of the world for creative action. Thus, coming across the impoverished embodied locus of a process in the world, e.g., a homeless person, we may suspect that perhaps the impoverishment manifests some prior devaluative act of that embodied process. We may not know it with certainty, however, for this particular homeless person *may* well be an instance of an aware practice occurring in a process of a very great ethical breadth, one whose bounds we cannot yet see. Whether the former or the latter, the hyperthematic worldview bids us act always in ways which build and rebuild community and interpretively expand the world so as to solve problems of devaluation at hand, here, for example, to work toward a world wherein each has a home. Whether this entails direct action to help the homeless person, or indirect action which helps such persons by building larger communities, nonetheless, hyperthematics tells us to help even though the condition of the homeless other may very well be occurring as a response to some deliberate but short-sighted prior devaluative action on the part of the process now embodied.

Here, then, is an appropriate juncture at which to address the concept of reciprocity of devaluation in religion, or as the response to devaluation has been called in Eastern thought *karma* and in Western thought *redemption*. When of a religious mind, we tend to suppose both that there are in the world injustices committed against some, for which no act could atone, e.g., could atonement ever be adequate to the murder of a child? Conversely, we tend to suppose that there are in the world people who commit actions for which they could not atone, e.g., could a Stalin atone for his actions? Indeed, the response to these points of view, and the attempt to resolve them, give rise to the core assumptions of two of the most widespread of the world's religions, the Hindu/Buddhist tradition and the Christian tradition, or Eastern and Western religious temperament as one may call them, respectively.

The response to the first of these assumptions reaches its greatest prominence in the Eastern temperament, which comes to believe that if we are not to be confined to a world in which devaluation remains unresolved, then it follows that "all ills in the world are justly deserved." The emphasis here is on the embodiment of the process, which is viewed as recurring—in reincarnation—in order to resolve the difficulty. The Eastern temperament then often proceeds further to the extreme and inconsistent conclusion that therefore we may be passive when faced with someone undergoing an evil, for that person is simply fixing mistakes from another life.

The response to the second of these assumptions meanwhile reaches its greatest prominence most often in the Western temperament, which comes to believe that unless we are to be subject to a world in which some "get away with murder," so to speak, then "the committing of all injustices is forgivable only by an external judge." The emphasis here is on the extended process, which is viewed as practically sundered from its embodied locus and rendered static—e.g., in eternal damnation or bliss—with regard to its action, in order to resolve the difficulty. The Western temperament meanwhile also proceeds further, to the extreme and inconsistent conclusion that therefore we may be passive with regard to our own participation in evil for we shall be fixed or forgiven, or indeed not forgiven, as the case may be.

Hyperthematically, both are mistaken in their constriction. That "all ills are justly deserved" is indeed plausible according to symmetric devaluation. The human locus of embodiment—among others—must atone for its devaluative action, if the world is a consistent community of interpretation. But that it atones for this devaluation is neither bound to the process in its constriction to embodiment (or multiple embodiments), nor fully visible from the range of embodied physicality of that process. And, on the other hand, for the hyperthematic view, that "all injustices are only forgiven by an external judge" is also plausible, for the symmetries of devaluation—the regions of devaluation—in the world process get their sense of loss of value from the value of the world process around and beyond them. Nonetheless, they also depend upon the ongoing creativity of the communities of interpretation of the world process at physical complexities—relative though those communities are—to rejoin experience sundered by constrictive and symmetry forming action, each community according to its measure, and build communities more complex than the physical, thus setting right the actions of devaluation. The upshot is that both assumptions complement one another if they are consistent with a world of value. *Evil as devaluation is made up for by he who initiates it; yet only a greater process which has grown capable of actively guiding the source of an evil toward the healing of its act, is fully capable of viewing the act as atoned for.*

Appendix C

The Expansion of Currency

Historically most or all attempts at valuation for purposes of trade have followed a constrictive path. The history of the development of currency for exchange begins in the experience of value as beauty. Gold, silver, gems and precious stones, have been valued and valuated for some aspect of beauty, which is higher than the weak value of quantity. And they have been valued primarily on the basis of their ability to interpret the experience of light as the preeminent sign of value, which is the leading edge of physical ranges of complexity. Thus, gold is valued for its color which is a lustrous yellow—near the height of interpretability within the color spectrum—silver less so because, although it gives back light, it also mirrors in a sameness; gems and precious stones because they combine colors in experience which does not engage light constrictively but allows it interpretive play through color, diamonds above all because they creatively interpret light as such with the barest of constriction.

In creating these early "materials" of currency, the world process participates in this valuation in ways which are more complex than I can here elaborate upon, except to suggest that the availability of these signs is proportional to their facets of interpretation at physical levels of complexity. Thus, diamonds are formed not through but *despite* the tremendous constrictive pressures within the crust of the earth, so that their rarity is the rarity of extremely strong defensive forms within physical ranges of complexity which "survive" great actions of constriction, i.e., the diamond exists because the strength of community of its parts at the microphysical level is left over as that which can stand such great constriction.[1]

Nonetheless, as the processes of action within the world process combine into more complex forms of community, the "ready-made" signs of the world process, used for exchange at physical complexities, become insufficient for continued creative development. This limitation is imposed by the world process, inciting growth. Other forms of value exchange inevitably develop. Coins of the beautiful "materials," such as gold, come to replace irregular masses of these materials. Coins in turn tend to grow smaller and more regular, more standardized. They can be stacked and counted—quantified—easily. They then give way to bills of paper or some other similar material, which can be stacked and quantified still more easily. Paper currency is tending toward a loss of dimensions; it tends toward becoming a planar object, an object which is less and less spatial in at least one of its dimensions. Meanwhile, standardized pictures printed upon bills of currency comes to dominate, and for the same reasons. Eventually, even paper currency comes to be replaced by a currency of mere quantitative symbolism, i.e., a number currency. Thus arises numerical quantity in a bank account, no longer wholly cashable into paper currency, let alone into the currency of metals or jewels.

These developments occur because the complexity of—here human—processes of action within the world process continually advances in a way which promotes the creation and development of signs—e.g., currency—which allow the interplay between the processes at higher and higher levels. But when the sign used in that interpretive interplay is inadequate to the task, then the creative growth of more complex interpretations is stunted and slows. The "spikes" of quantitative accumulation, discussed earlier, are the result of this interpretive poverty in the contemporary currency sign, among other things.

There must be interpretation, but if facets for interpretation inherent in the sign are so constricted as to allow interpretation in only few or one aspect—e.g., the "more or less" of weak quantity—then such interpretation as will be attempted will be interpretation confined to this aspect. And as the processes continually tend toward greater complexity, then the interpretations, being constricted to the few or one aspect will tend toward inconsistency *relative to their context within the world process* by becoming more and more difficult to interpret relative to that context.[2] So, for example, if my currency constricts me to the one dimension of "more or less" of weak quantity and I insist upon carrying out interpretations of greater and greater complexity between processes with that currency, then I will tend to make interpretations which manifest themselves as the "neurotic" attempt to maintain relations between *much more* and *much less* with regard to the currency. In other words they will manifest as huge gaps between wealth and poverty with regard to currency. What can be devalued in, for example, the tendency toward sameness, can nonetheless be valuated (weakly) in quantitative value, e.g., plastic junk products mass-produced in China (or whichever nation is currently the center of production as quantification), e.g., cheap knockoffs.

Imagine some product valued primarily through the tendency toward quantification—a dollar store trinket. Now, with regard to the product, we may attempt the quantity valuation, i.e., the interpretation of sameness into quantity which is gone into the product can be "captured" by the exchange system. But we all feel—and some of us know—that the sameness tendency is inconsistent. That being so, can those of us who participate in value exchange, as "putting a value on that product," factor in what we feel and/or know, in buying the product? No; at least not in a satisfying way.

If we try to do this negatively—an inconsistent plan based on constriction or elimination—then we are overridden by the necessity (*if* **H**, etc.) to interpret. For example, if I *refuse to buy* mass-produced junk items altogether, or I buy fewer of them, or—supply and demand is found here—I pay less for each, the response, by those whose capacity to interpret is not capable of understanding more, or much more, than, a sameness of production, will always be to make more of them. They have not the ethical capacity yet to produce more than quantitative value, so if I refuse they will simply make more quantitatively and find others to sell that quantity to. They have not yet been guided to a more consistent sense of value, and my negative response will not guide them. If, on the other hand we try to factor it in positively, for some very creative product, the only avenue is to pay more of the quantitatively valuating currency. To pay more, however, is merely to propagate the (relative) inconsistency—the weak quantitative tendency—elsewhere. For if I will not pay more for the junk products, certainly I will pay more in exchange for some evidently more valuable product. Yet if I do that, I merely propagate the trouble, i.e., I translate, or "capture," or "crystallize" if you like, the more valuable product (process of action) in weaker terms, while expanding—weak expansion—the use of the very system of valuation which fails to serve my valuative need.

Example: 400,000 product units (of, say, plastic jugs at a dollar apiece) holding weak value in the sameness of quantity, ought not to be exchangeable for a Stradivarius violin. Anyone who has the interpretive capacity to evaluate the Stradivarius—with respect to curvature, color, sound (the physical aspect of sound could be expanded just as we did for color), age, etc.—knows and feels this, but they cannot say why. Yet the Stradivarius must be interpreted, i.e., it must move through exchanges of valuation, if it is to continue in the world process; and if there are no other options, then weak quantitative valuation will be used to make the exchange. It will have to do.

The only correction for this would be the ability to exchange for a difference in "kind," which hyperthematically means a difference—an expansion—of facets of experience. Yet if so, the solution is not constricting the currency sign further. I hazard a guess that in Western society, and soon globally, we have reached the limit of our ability to creatively interpret ourselves as complex processes of action within the world process, according to numerical quantity, and that to continue along this path will inevitably lead to a temporary collapse of civilization globally, i.e., a collapse of all efforts of interpretation which have engendered spikes of weakly valuable quantitative accumulation: stock markets, banking institutions, large-scale commercial corporations, information as quantity, and other unstable accumulations of human effort tied to the quantitative accumulation of numerical quantity in contemporary currency. All of these "towers" or spikes of accumulation, which increasingly manifest themselves as unapproachable powers within society, will topple. To avoid that and save the value within the human portion of the world process, we will have to deliberately correct—redirect—the unstable accumulations, by transforming them into consistent value.[3] The solution, in part, is to add facets of interpretation to the currency sign, to expand the currency instrument.

The practical ways of doing this are various. A mere addition of physical facets of interpretation to the currency sign, e.g., adding physical aspects to currency, would indeed tend to attenuate accumulations somewhat, except that it would also stunt the consistent urge toward forms of interaction of processes beyond physical complexity. The addition of physical facets of interpretation of other sorts, such as artwork which is different on every unit of currency, would also help. But again, if we want to allow greater complexity in interpretations between processes, then all facets of interpretation which we add at physical levels of complexity, such as the above, will hold us back somewhat due to their very character of being within the physical range.

On the other hand we can keep that complexity and attain greater complexities even, if we retain currency in its numerical format, by expanding that format out of its constriction to mere quantity, into *numerical quality*. To understand what this means practically, imagine for a moment a simple graph of two axes, say x and y. Currency as we now have it uses only the x-axis in an operation of interpretation which "records" or signifies value for exchange as a more-or-less along the one aspect of the x-axis. Yet we can expand the currency by making use of the y-axis. How do we do this?

In the depths of our history the use of the "x-axis" originally measured simple quantity. We know this because some of the oldest examples of currency—such as the oxhide ingots of the late Bronze Age—stand primarily for themselves as quantity of some material, e.g., metal, and only subsequently appear to have come to be used for other valuations. Weak efforts of interpretation—and low-complexity civilization—can get by on a currency which values according to the more or less of quantity. As those efforts grow more complex, the weak valuation of quantity is forced to stand for other valuations, e.g., beauty, which it is inadequate to stand for.

We can keep the x-axis for what it was originally appropriate for, i.e., mere quantity of physical objects, for example, but we can also begin to use the y-axis as a sign of value which is interpretable to *but not replaceable with* the value of the x-axis. In other words, the x-axis of our currency valuates quantity in the sign, while the y-axis of our currency now comes to valuate some other aspect of experience. This gives a two-dimensional currency, no longer functioning as a quantity for valuation, but as an interpreter between aspects of experience through which an interpretation of diversity of experience manifests as exchangeable value. The currency would become a community, akin to the community of dance, the community of narrative, etc.; and it would act as a consistent guide to interpretation of acting transformable elements. As a community, the community of currency—the community of value exchange—could, of course, be consistently engaged in expansive interpretations, through the application of all of our hyperthemes. This two-dimensional currency will have the characteristic that the ratio of its two aspects of valuation can be combined as a vector which will fluctuate depending upon the valuations which it records. Interpreting these valuations within the vector in relation to the temporality of the world process, then we will have something akin to a function for valuation.[4]

I suggested earlier that the sine wave function is the manifestation of maximal interpretability at physical ranges of complexity within the world process. Accordingly, this maximal valuation may now serve as a practical upper boundary with regard to the valuating function of our two-dimensional currency at physical complexity. Rather than the quantitative valuations of more or less on a linear scale, our two-dimensional currency will valuate according to the maximal curvature of the sine function taken over time. An interpretive exchange of objects, services, etc., between—e.g., human—processes, within the world process, will be valuated on the basis of how well the aspects of valuation, when taken together, approach a continuous sine curve.

This expansion of aspects of interpretation will be able to record for exchange complexities of value which our current currency is unable to. What does this mean in terms of practical valuation of an object or service?

Suppose such an expanded currency is adopted. The y-axis aspect of its ability to facilitate exchanges between processes may come to measure any aspect of experience in the exchange that we wish. Let it, for example, valuate the provenance of a product relative to the distance which that product has traveled from its place of origin. Then our currency "captures" the physical quantity value of the product as a more or less of physical units, as well as the provenance value as a farther or nearer from the origin of production. The units for the valuation of an aspect may be changed, but they will tend to adapt to practical needs.* Meanwhile the increased capacity for valuation within a currency sign will tend to attenuate unstable accumulations of weak valuation—e.g., masses of merely quantitative wealth—within human regions of the world process.

So here, with our example, the play between physical quantity and provenance of a product will tend to counteract the contemporary tendency of currency accumulations—capital—to relocate around the globe continuously on the basis of valuations in a mere quantitative aspect. And once being irreplaceably valued, the aspect of provenance will tend toward maximum interpretability with regard to the aspect of physical quantity, insofar as value complexity increases, as it inevitably will, i.e., we will move toward a world in which interpretations of exchange in trade will be not too far and yet not too near to home, thus addressing the various environmental effects of accumulation, at least with regard to this aspect. Viewed in terms of the x- and y-axis graph, this means that the *tendency* of the vector function of our two aspects of valuation, toward curvature in the graph, indicates a higher value with regard to the product, while the *tendency* of the vector function of our two aspects of valuation toward line or point, indicates a lower value with regard to the product.

So, for instance, if the x-axis indicates the quantity valuation, while the y-axis indicates the provenance valuation, then if the curve** (figure) which is plotted on the graph tends toward linearity, then the product whose valuation is signified on the graph has a lower value; and if the curve tends toward greater curvature, then the product whose valuation is signified on the graph has a higher value. If the curve is linear, it indicates that as provenance increases, quantity increases, a situation which essentially negates

---

*An *aspect* or dimension of valuation, may now be said to be in units, but the currency instrument suggested will have *di-its*, *tri-its*, *quadrits*, and so forth, according to how many aspects of valuation are countenanced.

**Here using the term in the technical mathematical sense.

the effect of our expansion of currency into two dimensions, i.e., replaces a simple linearity with a vector linearity, and falls back to the interpretive weakness of quantity. Accordingly, if the curve tends toward linearity, it indicates a less valuable product.

If, on the other hand, the curve curves upwards gradually, it indicates that as provenance increases, quantity slows its increase; and products will be more valuable as they are signified by a curve which approaches maximal curvature. Practically speaking this translates as: a product (or service) will be more valuable insofar as *if the distance it has to travel from its origin of production is farther, then its quantity is proportionally lesser*. Or again, to put it in the terms which a contemporary buyer of some product might use, if she were using our expanded currency, and attempting to interpret the product according to a complexity of value which she *feels* but cannot herself knowingly realize in an interpretive exchange—due to the constrictions of our contemporary currency—"*this* one is worth more than the other one because *this one is shipped from China <u>because</u> they are quite rare here*." Likewise, if the curve curves downward gradually, it indicates that as quantity increases provenance slows its increase, or, in the thought of our valuating buyer: "this one is worth more than the other one because *since this one, along with many similar ones, is made here, they need not be shipped from China*."[5] When a product or service in question is one which is made up of a number of less complex parts or materials—e.g., the construction of a residential home—then the valuation of the provenance of those parts or materials will tend to combine into the valuation of the more complex product or service.

We can begin simply then with the above. But if we wish to add yet another aspect for valuation—a z-axis—then we can do so, so as to attain three-dimensional currency, for example the valuation of an object with regard to color, curvature, etc. Or we could add the aspect of valuation of the consistent aging of a sign as suggested earlier in our expansion of **Ha**, by preserving the history of the use of the currency. These and many more are possible facets of valuation, and we can add further axes of valuation as the increasing complexity of our exchanges warrants.

Valuations by embodied humanity are imperfect of course, but this difficulty tends to work itself out over time, so long as the instrument sign of valuation is fluid enough to be adequate to the task. The effect of such an expansion of currency would, moreover, effect crime relative to currency accumulation, in everything from bank robbery to stock market fraud. Crime based upon quantitative accumulation goes hand-in-hand—though not exclusively—with the inability of a sign to serve as an exchange of value in more than a weak sense. That which achieves uniqueness in creativity through engagement of its multiple facets of interpretability, is more difficult to copy—e.g., to forge—more difficult to accumulate, more difficult to steal; more difficult because, respectively, its inherent creativity is difficult to copy; it is difficult to interpret as an accumulation by those of insufficient interpretive capacity; and finally it is both well defended in the strength of its creating interpretive communities and more readily recognizable as a unique creation of such communities.[6]

Appendix D

The Relation of Royce's System Sigma to Hyperthematics and the Origins of Dyadic Logic

Brightman begins with the Principle of Non-Contradiction as I remarked. This has seemed a promising beginning for many philosophers over the ages and it would not seem so unless it manifested some aspect of the engagement of the world process. One can better explain what it does manifest with the help of the Hyperthematic view, in ways which show it to be only a subordinate aspect—acceptable as practice—of a healthy engagement of the world process, but not the last word.

The Principle of Non-Contradiction benefits from a little expansive parsing. In the usual formulation it insists that:

It is not the case that (there is x and there is not x).

Muse upon the latter a bit though and you begin to wonder what the *and* means. Is it additive? If so that leads us to suppose that it depends upon what *x* and *not x* stand for. If *x* stands for an *elephant*, for example, then *not x* might be said to stand for a *not elephant*. What is a *not elephant*? You may rattle off a whole list of what is not an elephant: a horse, a house, a dog, an apple, etc., etc. Your list will be "as infinite as you please," as Royce would have said. Yet once you have given your list you soon see that it throws in doubt the nature of the original formula of non-contradiction. Because if *and* means something like additivity, then the Principle of Non-Contradiction becomes nonsense with regard to experience. There *are* elephants, and there are other things which are not elephants, such as dogs, horses, etc. They subsist perfectly well together in our experience.

The objection that the *not elephant* cannot be parsed into a horse, a house, a dog, etc. may then arise. The *not elephant*, one may insist, cannot be said to stand for an infinite group—or even a finite group—of "other than elephants," and thereby the additive nature of the *and* can be saved, without making nonsense of the Principle of Non-Contradiction.

Well, what then does it stand for? The objector may want to say that it stands for a state of affairs in which the "elephant itself is not." My response to this will be: is the term *not elephant* interchangeable with what we may call the attributes of the elephant, as the tusks, large ears, trumpeting sounds, etc.? To this the objector will certainly answer, "No, No . . . the *not elephant* is being used here to stand for all the attributes of the elephant, irrespectively of any particular attribute." He (or she) cannot very well affirm otherwise, for if the *not elephant* stands for a collection of those experiences, then the additivity of the *and* again throws into doubt the Principle of Non-Contradiction. There *are* elephants *and* there are attributes of elephants subsisting together in our experience regularly.

Indeed our objector cannot even let the second iteration of *elephant* in the Principle of Non-Contradiction (the one preceded by the *not*), stand itself for the collection of attributes of an elephant, as in: *not* (*elephant* and *not tusks, large ears, trumpeting, etc.*). For the additive character of the *and* here makes even more obvious the failure of the principle of non-contradiction to say something meaningful about experience. There *are* elephants without tusks, without large ears, etc., as contemporary poaching tendencies sadly indicate. So for the Principle of Non-Contradiction to hold, it seems that we must submit to the insistence of our imagined objector, that all of the attributes of the elephant be gathered—squeezed—into the term. And not only all of the attributes that we usually take to be elephant attributes, but even generic attributes such as the generic *physical* attributes (weighing two tons, measuring 3.5 meters in height, gray colored, etc.), for even these will mess up the Principle of Non-Contradiction if the term *not elephant* is allowed to be interchangeable with them.

Now this last musement leads us gently but firmly on to another related question, which can be put as follows: has the nature of the *not elephant* anything to do with time, i.e., with the tendency of the elephant to endure temporally. Does our imagined objector mean, for example, that the elephant *is* this year but next year *is not*? The objector will not submit to this meaning. If he does, the problem with regard to the Principle of Non-Contradiction returns in full force. There *are* elephants this year which are not elephants next year (having died, for example). But the objector will most likely then insist that the nature of the *not elephant* has nothing to do with time, and that ultimately he means rather that in the "same instant," you cannot have an elephant and a *not elephant*.

One last question for him then: is the nature of the *not elephant* anything to do with the name elephant, insofar as it stands for some experience of the elephant? Do you mean, for example, that the name *elephant* (as here written) cannot coexist in experience with the name *not elephant* (as here written)? Again, the objector will not submit to this meaning. If he does, the old difficulty rears up yet again. There are *elephants* (as here written) found very often together with *not elephants* (as here written); the very formulation of the Principle of Non-Contradiction when written as *not* (*elephant* and *not elephant*), go tolerably well together in our experience, as your reading of this sentence no doubt confirms for you.

Our objector will probably now insist that the nature of the *not elephant* has nothing to do with the word used to write it (or even to speak it), and so can profitably be replaced by a symbol, *x*, which will do the job he intends, *as existing utterly independently of what it stands for*, bringing us back to where we began. Now, if we assent to the various assertions of our imaginary objector we find ourselves seemingly arrived at the conclusion that: the *and* does not indicate an action of additivity. It indicates a state of affairs in which the "bare giveness" of some experience, the experience *qua given*, is to be compared with its "bare not being giveness." At least that is what those who first formulated the Principle of Non-Contradiction thought they meant.

But before we assent to this, let us look back over our musement briefly in review. Imagine if you will our objector* with a huge paring knife, confronting a living breathing elephant experience in the world. Now notice what happened at each step of our questioning with regard to the elephant (as the term *elephant* stands for it in the group *not elephant*).

First, we asked whether *not elephant* stood for other things than the elephant. No, said our objector, and with the paring knife he cut the relations to the rest of the world; the *not elephant* is not to stand for all of the other things in the world, because this would make nonsense of the Principle of Non-Contradiction. Next we asked if *not elephant* stood for the attributes of an elephant. No, insisted the objector, and cut the relations to those attributes. Did *not elephant* stand for its own generic physical attributes then? Nope. The objector cut those off. Did it perhaps stand for its own enduring relations in time? No indeed; the objector chopped those relations off forthwith. Did it even stand for the communicated medium of its own

---

*Literally—though it isn't understood this way—one who descends to objectification in order to *prove*.

signification, the words (or sounds) used to express it? Certainly not; the objector whittled even these away to the utmost of his ability. And when he had done so, we had left a sign x which was completely replaceable with other instances of itself and which was to have no relation to the elephant, and yet on the basis of which the Principle of Non-Contradiction is supposed to apply to any and all experience in the world.

Now I ask you reader, does that not seem like rather a nice bit of sleight of hand? What did the objector really do, and what can we make of it hyperthematically? The first thing to notice, as you no doubt already have, is that at every step our imaginary objector—led by our questioning—engaged in *a constriction of interpretation* with regard to some aspect or aspects of the original experience. He began by removing—for interpretation to the original sign—the community of signs of the world at large, and went on in turn to remove the more creative signs inherent in the embodied community which is the elephant (its attributes), then the less creative signs (physical attributes), then the temporal (sameness/creativity) aspect altogether of the original sign, then the sign as a medium of interpretation at all, *insofar as he could.*

All of this effort is a series of constrictions then. To be sure, the set of constrictions is rarely expanded upon as I have; the whole basket of constrictions is usually carried out at once, with individual moves only emphasized in response to questioning. But the result of all of this effort is what? It is a formula for the engagement of experience, the Principle of Non-Contradiction, whose ability to engage experience consistently, fails, in proportion as its terms are allowed out of their constriction. And since they tend to be allowed out of their constriction by their very use in the engagement of the world process, they tend to fail insofar as the attempt is made to put logic to use toward any considerable engagement of the world process beyond a use which remains internalized to the constrictions of its own assumed terms, i.e., the technical manipulation of mere empty formalizations. Yet if that suggestion is plausible and the forgoing is what is done in working up the Principle of Non-Contradiction, the question is: why do we do it? For clearly, logics based upon the foregoing effort have arisen and are ongoing.

From the hyperthematic view the following solution presents itself. The heart of the issue is that the *and* of the principle of non-contradiction, *really is additive*, but that the additivity is being applied in a way wholly unlike what our imagined objector intends. The additivity is an *action of addition,* a consistent action of interpretation which creates value. Every one of our rebuffed attempts to engage the negated term of the Principle of Non-Contradiction showed this. But it is attempting to add that which cannot be added, namely *an action of constriction*. An action of constriction cannot be added to an action of expansion. In other words: *the contradiction arises through and because of the <u>actions</u>, it is not inherent in the signs which are being added.* The latter are always already, insofar as they are signs at all, the signs of additive action undertaken with regard to past signs. The additivity would add any "thing" (experience) that you give it, any of our expansive iterations of the negated term (*not elephant*) could have been added, as we saw. What it cannot add is the very effort toward—the action of—constriction of interpretation.

And yet the Principle of Non-Contradiction is formulated historically, and appealed to, because it does indeed tell us something (only not what those who appeal most to it intend it to mean). It tells us that actions toward constriction of interpretation fail at the point at which the constrictive action has descended to the minimal manifestation of experience, i.e., experience as a sign to be interpreted *at all*. It is a sort of dare to the beholder, an appeal of last resort: "See! You cannot go so far with respect to something as to undo its very giveness within the world!" And so far it is correct, and it is used with this intent by Aristotle for example—Plato was far nearer a consistent understanding—even though he does not fully understand what he is doing and ties himself into knots in trying to prove that the action toward minimal interpretation lies "in" the sign.

The very ability of the Principle of Non-Contradiction to do this, however, depends both upon the countenancing of the world as a given community of signs engaged in action and upon the meaningfulness of additive actions of those signs. In fine, the Principle of Non-Contradiction arises out of a community as an abstraction of *the extreme* of an action of devaluation; it was never intended to—nor capable of—meaning that there was a "nothing," a "negative sign"; nor was it capable of meaning that there was any real sundering of interpretive relations among the diversities of experience, for it depends upon meaning as such for the very lesson it imparts.

It is thus a very poor foundation to build upon logically, attempting as it does to build up a structure of *proof*, by appeal to the extreme limit of constrictive action without recognizing the context in which that extreme limit occurs. And the intent of its development is most often carried out by those whose interpretive capacity appeals to *necessity* first. Necessity is an abstraction of the giveness of the world as a limit, i.e., it is always secondary—as I suggested in the beginning of chapter 1—and it never comes before an engagement of the world, as being an engagement in community with the world which aims foundationally at meaning and value. The necessity appealed to and the proof desired, the proof which constricts the sign to a *point*—the *x*—which is otherwise uninterpretable to the receiver, is the kin of the urge to power in the physical world which we have mused upon earlier. The result, e.g., the melding of efforts of analytic logic with the proliferation of the digital computer age, is closely connected for these very reasons, although I do not have space to expand upon the issue here.

The principle is trivial then in a sense, because it only tells us something that is divorced in the extreme from our engagement of experience. To put this another way, it is obvious to everyone that diverse signs/aspects of experience add together in interpretation, we do not need an abstract formula to tell us this because we experience it in our engagement of the world process. The very sign of the world process is given to us as a smooth range of experience in process in which various items (items only because they are later abstracted from the world experience) are perfectly well together, and cannot be engaged in constrictive action without consequences to value. If they could, there would not be value.

The principle could be used as a practice, consistently, if used in the conscious awareness—the view of practice held throughout this work—of its context and implications. This, however, will require a forgoing of the urge to construct the world as *a manifestation of power as proof derived from necessity*, and a willingness to move to building communities of harmony of interpretation. This willingness must come from within the community of selfhood of each of us, from the growth of the community of the self. When one attempts, as I did, to expand the action—with regard to the negated term of the Principle of Non-Contradiction—our merely imagined objector resists the effort. Many an actual objector will do likewise; he wants *a proof upon which to construct a world which others are to accept without further interpretation.*

This urge to prove to others is always a manifestation of some capacity of interpretation of the proving self and no attempt to also *prove* the contrary can succeed easily against a set of actions which are essentially an urge to constrict experience with regard to meaning. The objector will always reduce the issue to the extreme where it has minimal application to actual experience. You cannot fight or overpower him on this ground because the world—if it is a world of value—is advanced in value only by freely willed growth, not by overpowering others. In other words, though I have imagined an objector responding to my queries, so as to arrive at an expansion of the issue of the Principle of Non-Contradiction, one cannot hope to sway an actual objector committed to his constrictive actions, by appealing to technical formalizations and thus to the very tendency which he himself adopts.

The only way to create value in this area of experience is to build up a community of logical engagement which invites further interpretation as to how the insight and the history of the logic of the constrictive extreme[1] can arise out of the postulate of the world as a world of interpretive value. This is attempted in the present Hyperthematic effort, which once initiated can then be followed by the development of a more formal—and therefore always only as supplementary and as practice—elaboration of the relations of communities of interpretation. The groundwork for the latter is already laid in Royce's System Σ of 1905, but it may be helpful here to expand briefly upon the relation of System Σ to Hyperthematics (and the Dyadic Logics which grow out of the above constrictive assumptions bound up with the Principle of Non-Contradiction), so that interested parties can proceed further.[2]

System Σ

System Σ[3] is elaborated in Royce's 1905 publication *The Relation of the Principles of Logic to the Foundations of Geometry*.[4] In it Royce lays the foundation for a polyadic logic. The background of that polyadic logic, briefly, is this. Royce had read A. B. Kempe's *On the Relation between the Logical Theory of Classes and the Geometrical Theory of Points* (1890). In this work, and earlier works, Kempe had shown that the assumption of a generalized "between" relation when applied (as minimally triadic) to a postulated set of abstract entities—a "base system"—could be used to develop the whole algebra of logic. The generalized "between" relation takes the form $ac \cdot b$, where a, b, and c form a linear triad wherein b lies between a and c.[5]

In Kempe's work the postulated logical entities are moreover symmetric with regard to one another, so that "negatives" arise in the system as obverses—a set of states which are alternatives to some set of states chosen from the system—in which the relations of the "negated" entity contrast symmetrically with the rest of the system.[6] From selections of "linear sets" within the base system, along with the further principle that any two elements of a selected linear set will determine the whole linear set, Kempe can then show that "*A space of* n *dimensions is a select class or set of elements which themselves are entities in a logical 'field.'*"[7]

If Kempe's proposal can accomplish this, the way is open to other developments and Royce's insight is to build upon this beginning by suggesting an alternative to the "between" relation, which nonetheless captures the between relation. To quote Royce, rather than begin with the "between" he will begin with a: "fundamental relation of symbolic logic which has the interest of being absolutely symmetrical, while, when it obtains amongst n entities, it permits (upon the basis of certain simple existential propositions), the definition of Kempe's "flat collections," and so the definition of asymmetrical relations of a very high degree of complexity."[8] Clearly then, these *asymmetrical relations* are what Royce is interested in and he is going to uncover them by applying his insight that Kempe's effort to derived spatial geometry out of logic can be conjoined with an alternative beginning than that which Kempe makes use of.

Royce discloses that alternative by first noting that Ladd-Franklin had shown as early as 1883 that a symmetrical copula in logic could be used to define the asymmetrical implication relation, such that, respectively, "x is inconsistent with not-y," means "x implies y," so that asymmetry may be definable in terms of symmetry.[9] Now what symmetry will Royce begin with? Here I will use the benefit and guide of hindsight, and remind the reader of my various suggestions regarding symmetry. When I spoke of symmetry earlier—as in chapter 3—I mused upon symmetry in several forms. Symmetry, I suggested was inconsistent. Yes, but then we lit upon the symmetry of the circle. A circle is also symmetric seemingly; it is certainly regarded as such in contemporary mathematical accounts.

But as I there noted, the symmetry is different from the symmetry of pointed shapes and mirror images. The symmetry of the circle requires *choice* in the engagement of the experience of the circle before the symmetry can be said to arise. I went so far as to suggest that the circle is not symmetric, but if one had to devise a new term one might call it *interpretable symmetry*—that which is left (relatively) open to interpretation by the one to whom the interpretation is directed—whereas the tendency toward line and then point would be the tendency toward *un-interpretable symmetry*, or being *hyperthematically symmetrical*, as I have called it, to distinguish from the usual view. It is the former with which Royce will begin his logic, the *interpretable symmetry*, or as he puts it in terms of a relation: "the relation in which (if we were talking of the possible chances open to one who had to decide upon a course of action) any set of *exhaustive but, in their entirety, inconsistent choices would stand to one another*."[10]

In other words, the relation formally models *choice* with regard to a situation in which *actions must stand in some relation of diversity to one another because they cannot all be taken.* Royce calls this relation the *O*-relation, a relation that gives rise to sets of *O*-collections, and he defines it by a set of postulates. And one may see the result immediately in Hyperthematic terms, by referring to Royce's diagram of three circles joined such that the common area of all the circles is a negated or "zero" area. This is itself a *very* basic circle. Hyperthematically, the *O*-relation is a community of signs of experience, i.e., a community under the guidance of a consistent set of Hyperthemes. Our transformable element meanwhile—e.g., the acting human taken as a process of selfhood—is itself an *O*-collection which forms part of more complex *O*-collections which are the communities of interpretation under the hyperthematic structures which it accepts.

But the circle can devolve to a line when only two elements are admitted to stand in the *O*-relation. This is Kempe's linear triad in the "between" relation.[11] And insofar as it does, it formally models, at that level of constriction, not only the constriction of choice in the "yes-no" relation of choice, but, as Royce suggests "all the serial and other ordinal relations known to logic and geometry, and all the operations known to both. . . ."[12] The latter is formally the series of *F*-relations, which Royce later develops to some degree from Σ, and which arise out of what, in Hyperthematic terms, I call constrictions in the transformable elements of a region of experience, i.e., that which in my Hyperthematic terms was discussed as constriction to mere quantitative valuation, and concomitantly the tendency toward physicality in experience. Higher in the range of complexity *this constriction of choice in the interpretation of the transformable elements is what lays the foundation for the dyadic logics, the logics of yes and no,* which are the complex cousins of tendencies toward physicality, the *objective logics,* so to speak.

Some pages into the work, after his preliminary discussion, Royce then lays down first the definitions and principles of Σ. Some of these concern merely the logistics of the application of the system, but I will briefly comment on several which may be of interest to the reader, in the numerical order that Royce lays them out.

8. Classification of what are or what are not *O*-collections is fundamental. In other words, Royce is ultimately interested primarily in *communities of action*, even though the work is primarily about how other endeavors arise out of various actions operating on those communities of action.

9. A collection which is *not* an *O*-collection is an *E*-collection. I cannot confirm this, but I suspect that *E* stands for *Error.* In other words, the

E-collections are all of those which come about by sustained devolution from an *O*-collection.

11. Royce takes trouble to clarify the notion of equivalence. Equivalent elements are elements which can be substituted for each other in at least one *O*-collection, so that the *O*-collection remains an *O*-collection. Elements would also be equivalent *if* they belonged to no *O*-collection. In other words, equivalence gets its definition in terms of belonging or not belonging to an *O*-collection.

In Hyperthematic terms, this means that a community is always minimally related to any acting element as welcoming of that element; their equivalence is *that they may join a community*, i.e., they may join at least the community of interpretation of the world (according to **H**). This is the relative *interpretable symmetry* of my earlier musement upon circles, and develops into **HCu** and **HAs**.

But furthermore, if there is an *O*-collection which an element cannot enter without changing it into an *E*-collection, then they are not equivalent, i.e., *they are identical*.

That is to say, in hyperthematic terms, that a community of interpretation degrades when tendencies of action toward (identity) sameness are attempted by its members. The correction to this is elaborated in **Hd** especially.

12. Equivalence differs from sameness or identity. This is just an expansion of the foregoing. The latter—equivalence—does not imply the former for Royce's system, as he notes.

In hyperthematic terms this is what allows me to define sameness as a constriction of interpretation, while retaining a workable interpretive freedom at physical complexity between actors precisely as a space of interpretation structured, or bounded most generally, by means of the equivalent relation to the community of all the actors engaged in it. In other words, the acting processes are all equivalently engaged in the community under the hyperthematic structure, *as being engaged*, but not in identity or sameness of action.

13. The elements of an *O*-collection are mutually obverse elements which together form an *O*-pair according to Royce. In hyperthematic terms this captures what I mean by *harmony* as such. Two dancers dancing together, for example, are obverses to one another which form an *O*-pair collection.

14. The extension of simpler obversion to sets of more complex obversion. In my terms, this is the extension of harmony, to more complex *processes* of action.

18. The properties of different collections of the elements of Σ are determined by the equivalent and non-equivalent elements which exist along with the initially assumed principles of the system.

What this means broadly and hyperthematically, is that sets of tendencies of action form regions of experience which are more or less valuable with regard to interpretability and interpretedness. This is the fluid metaphysics of regions of experience under Hyperthematic Structures, in which, e.g., the community of dance is developing in a region depending upon the confluence of past signs with ongoing consistent action, or in which the region of physicality as such in its relative inconsistency or low-level quantitative valuation is developing, or again, in which a region of conflict is developing.

20. The opening assumptions of Σ are here given by Royce, as a set of two general laws and four principles, headed with Roman Numerals.

Designating the laws and principles according to Royce's numeration, I will suggest the relation of the six laws and principles to my Hyperthematic effort.*

I. "If $O\,(\alpha)$, then $O\,(\alpha\gamma)$, whatever collection γ may be . . . An O-collection remains an O-collection, whatever elements or collections may be adjoined to it."[13]

In Hyperthematic terms: a community of interpretation remains a community of interpretation by any action other than an action toward constriction of interpretation. Communities of interpretation are expansive.

II. "If a collection β, consisting wholly of elements which are complements of a collection δ, is an O-collection, then δ itself is an O-collection."[14]

In Hyperthematic terms: A community of interpretation is always consistent with (results from and promulgates) other communities of interpretation.

---

*I give them as they are expansively restated in 20, even though they are written more formally in 19.

III. (and IV, in combination) "The system Σ contains at least one pair of mutually non-equivalent elements."[15]

In Hyperthematic terms: the world is a diversity of experience, a problematic.

V. "If any pair of mutually non-equivalent elements is given, a third element of Σ exists which forms an *O*-pair with neither of the elements of this pair, but which is such that the three elements in question together constitute an *O*-triad."

These principles combined are the Hypertheme **H**.

VI. "If there exists any complement of a given collection Σ, then, if ω be such a complement, there exists a complement of Σ, viz. υ, such that every element of Σ is a complement of the pair (υ, ω)."[16]

In other words: for every community of interpretation there is some further community of interpretation with which it forms a higher level community of interpretation; i.e., a community of interpretation may be an element of a more valuable community of interpretation.

Royce then makes a considerable beginning in working out the elementary consequences of the system in some fifty further pages, of which only the following specific consequences are of immediate interest in relating Σ to Hyperthematics.

26. "There exists a collection which contains every element of Σ (each element occurring in that collection either once only, or else repeatedly), while this collection, say Σ, is an *O*-collection . . . [& 27] The system Σ, taken in its entirety is an *O*-collection."[17]

In other words, there is a Great Community of Interpretation—"God" as the lure to creative interpretation of maximal complexity—which is approachable through application of the semi-formal model which is Σ (and the still less formal methodology which is Hyperthematics).

35. "No monad is an *O*-collection . . . [because the mutual equivalence of its elements would contradict IV, and] . . . "every monad, therefore, is an *E*-collection."[18]

This is the tendency toward sameness/identity, physical and otherwise invoked in my hyperthematic musements. The *E*-collections—or *Error*-collections, if I do read Royce aright—are the collections stemming from assumptions which are inconsistent with the assumption of the world as interpretive value, the assumptions which give rise to the false communities. Tendencies toward the monad, whether in sameness or otherwise, are tendencies destructive of value.

The *E*-collections if worked out in Σ would give the models of regions of experience in the world within which (localized) destruction of value, devaluation, in one way or another is ongoing, the "logic of badness," so to speak.

38. "*No element is equivalent to its own obverse. . . .*"[19]

The assumption that an element is equivalent to its own obverse is the assumption made by an acting element which attempts action, for example, according to ***HC** and ***HM**, the exclusionary commercial corporation and the military.

40. "If a collection is an *E*-collection, all possible partial collections that can be formed by selecting some of its elements, and omitting others, are also *E*-collections, so that if ε is any partial collection, $O(\varepsilon)$ is false."[20]

No community of interpretation following from an assumption inconsistent with **H** can be *ultimately* consistent. This is my localized community, or false community. This includes (the not so harmful) regions of experience engaged according to what I have termed localized practice, as well as (the extremely harmful) regions of experience subject to, e.g., military conflict, in which pockets of localized consistency, e.g., strategy, or military false communities as such, are extant. It also includes all dyadic-based logics, and even regions of experience engaged at physical ranges of complexity (relative to more valuable ranges).

44. Beginning here, Royce elaborates the *F*-collections, which are operations of assertion upon the *O*-collection: in hyperthematic terms constriction of interpretation with regard to some community of experience. From this comes dyadic logic and geometry.

87. "*E*-collections . . . can be enlarged to *O*-collections by the adjunction of suitable elements."[21]

This is elaborated in Hyperthematics as the reconstruction of communities degraded through inconsistent action.

Notice finally that in each statement—except III—of the laws and principles Royce uses the opening "if . . .". The system depends upon the existential recognition of elements (signs), which is an aspect of choice. Principle III highlights the assertion that there is experience; IV follows with diversity of experience; V follows with the interpretation of the diversity of experience. The system is thus, from the beginning, not a wholly formal system, a situation which my effort in **H** plays upon.

The main difference between Hyperthematics and Σ is as follows. In the Σ work Royce is primarily interested both in making a connection with the framework of the natural sciences and logic and in showing how that framework stems from the assumptions of Σ, through the F-collections. This would have been needed in order to gain acceptance for Σ. In Hyperthematics, however, I am attempting to set up a methodology for applying the assumptions to broader social problems primarily, while hoping to subsequently lure scientific and logical thinking on board, via the visible results of such applications. In the *Problem of Christianity* Royce is concerned with the relations of the O-collections proper, and the E-collections secondarily. My guess is that if he had lived another two decades and if he had had the opportunity to interact with Whitehead, he—perhaps even in conjunction with Whitehead at Harvard—would have developed something like Hyperthematics out of Σ.

Diagrams

Diagram 1 may help the reader better understand the suggestions of chapter 4 regarding interpretive actions at physical ranges of complexity. Let the right of the page be labeled (experience) **a**, and the top be labeled (experience) **b**. Then actions of interpretation *to* either—here one may think of them as movements or "insertions between"—of these, beginning from (experience) •, may be symbolized by **a** or **b**, or **ab**, or more complex sequences of **a** and **b**.

Number 1 is thus a lack of interpretation (localized), or constriction to the monad. It is a mere subsisting, *minimally, the World Process as temporal*, which drags us on even if we refuse to interpret.

Number 2 is interpretation in one aspect (to side **a**), the repetition of interpretive action. It issues in mere quantitative diversity, or massing, "another and another"; simple linearity.

Number 3 is interpretation in two aspects (to sides **a** and **b**).

Number 4 is interpretation in three aspects which avoids repetition (avoids simple linearity) toward a third aspect ("corner **ab**" of the page) relative to higher complexity sequences, i.e., avoids repetition of **ab**. Carried further: *circularity* is thus interpretation to multiple aspects comprised of higher complexity sequences, like **ab**, while avoiding constriction toward linearity relative to each of them, i.e., currently, for circularity at physical ranges of complexity, we elaborate those aspects as radians, milliradians, etc.

Interpretive actions form more complex entities as they interpret to more aspects. Those more complex entities take part in further interpretations at higher complexities. Accordingly, a complex entity may be subject to quantitative interpretation to one aspect again. Thus, e.g., **ab,ab,ab**, etc. becomes an action which reinstates massing of the **ab** entities; this causes regression from curvature toward linearity.

To maintain the tendency toward curvature, actions must avoid regressing toward constriction of interpretation at higher complexities, e.g., for interpretation to two aspects (**a** and **b**), they must vary between interpretations to aspect **a**, to aspect **b**, and to both. Or, in other words: *sequences of actions forming more complex entities must vary from one another continually.* This is *creativity*, and at ranges of physical complexity, a maximal variance of creativity, which must arise, is represented in the constant π, with its close relation to the constants already mentioned. Thus the sequence #3 **a,a,a,ab,ab,ab,ab** will give a more curved entity relative to higher complexity, but abstracting its actions of interpretation will find linearity at lower complexity (the localized linearity of **a,a,a**, followed by that of **ab,ab,ab,ab**). But sequence #4 **a,a,ab,ab,b,ab,b,b** tends more toward curvature than **a,a,a,ab,ab,ab,ab**, because constriction of interpretation relative to its complex entities is avoided, however the sequence be taken: e.g., (**a,a**),(**ab,ab**),(**b,ab**),(**b,b**); or again (**a,a,ab**),(**ab,b,ab**),(**b,b,_**); or again (**a,a,ab,ab**),(**b,ab,b,b**).

For each range of complexity of interpretation, the "how many aspects are interpreted to," of a region of experience, there will be some portion which is optimal for value according to the possible creative combinations of the aspects countenanced. Sequences of interpretive action will tend to devaluation on the "upper and lower" ends of that portion, as constrictive combinations of interpretive action continue to engage the region of experience wherein—through holding constrictive assumptions which fix the aspects being engaged to "just those aspects"—creativity is "mined out." In other words, to arbitrarily limit the aspects interpreted to in a region of experience is to bound the creativity in that region. To illustrate at macro physical complexity: the earth's horizon is experienced as relatively flat when standing upon it, then as increasingly curved when one rises in the sky, then transforms to the earth as spherical further on, but then begins to regress toward a point as interpretive actions to predominantly one aspect of the region of experience, are undertaken repeatedly, i.e., the gaining of mere quantitative diversity as distance from the earth. The latter example is macrocosmic, but the above holds at microscopic ranges, and indeed all ranges of complexity.

> *Nb.* The order of numbering given is for the reader's convenience only, i.e., the world process is not "built up" of monad units. It can be abstracted, locally, into monad units however, a localized

devaluation. The more consistent view is that we always begin in experience, "in the middle," at something like #3 (relative to the 4 sequences given). Our experience then responds to expansion and contraction of interpretation. Royce's *System Sigma*, in the elaboration and manipulation of its *F-collections*, *E-collections*, and so forth, is the formal logic of sequences of interpretation, such as those given. Hyperthematics is the semi-formal logic of those sequences.

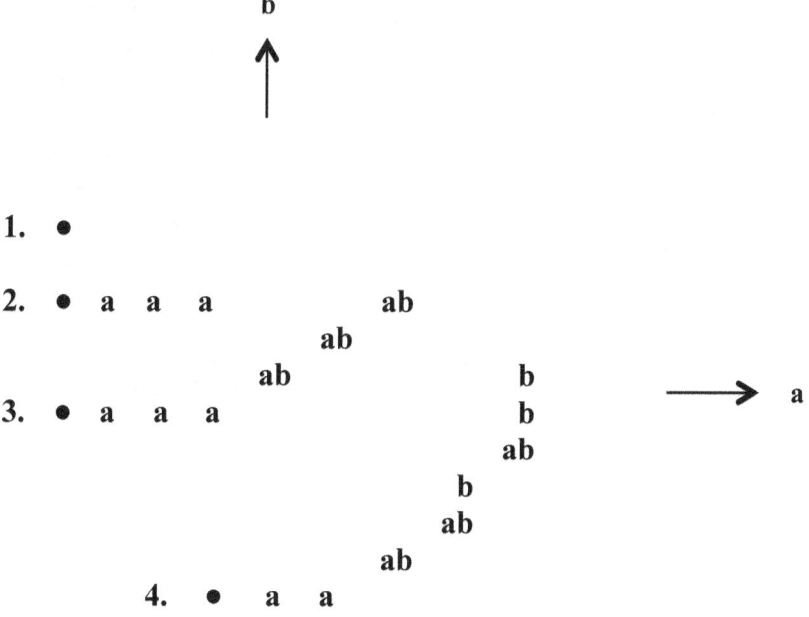

Diagram 2 gives a graphical approximation to help the reader get oriented with regard to the interplay between the tendencies of simplicity/complexity (physical/mental) as interpreting and interpreted by the tendencies of sameness/creativity (feeling/knowing), so as to manifest in what are here given as the "working centers" of the regions hyperthematically mused upon. I have given borders to each region, but those borders are far more vague in our experience, and our engagements of experience often jump beyond them.

The diagram suggests how a range of complexity of experience is engaged with increasingly creative interpretations. The dashed line up the center—first dividing sub-physical from physical—indicates both the beginning of each new level, or ring, of creativity (upward), and a range of simplicity to complexity (clockwise) which is re-engaged anew at each level of creativity. But again, these "limits" are a device used for diagrammatic and explanatory purposes, they are arbitrary for hyperthematics; both creativity and complexity are unlimited except by localized constriction. Thus, any region of the diagram could be interpreted to any other region below it, because each region is only "fixed" by the set of assumptions—hyperthematic structure—which guide interpretation within it. In the diagram however, except for music, *relatively* felt regions of experience are generally interpreted by the more creative ranges directly above them.

Thus, for example, sound, as a relatively low complexity physical region, is interpretively engaged, first as a mere sensory feeling—it is relatively let be—in the lowest ring, then later, more creatively, as a component of "proto" narrative, and narrative, in the second and third rings, then more creatively still as a subject of science, in the fourth ring. But it is also—and here the limitations of the diagram are evident—interpreted by music, a more complex structure than science, *relative to the engagement of sound*, in the third ring, and eventually one which will merge with science as a "creative science of music," in the fourth ring. The empty regions of the diagram can, and will in human experience, be filled in, by similar "mergings" of disciplines.

But again, each region eventually "mines out" regions below it, so that, science, for example, will eventually exhaust its study of the lower ranges of the physical which we now call "sensory experience"—the regions from Tactile to Light, and engage higher regions. For example, it will, and is already, make increasing use of narrative experience as a lower or more felt, or more "let be" region of experience below it, i.e., as the "matter" for its interpretive researches, just as it will begin to interpret what is now more complex than our "historical" physical senses, by beginning to interpret the Hyper Physical. Thus, what is predominantly felt is always changing, being located higher and higher in the diagram, while the clockwise tending edge of the physical ranges of complexity—the leading edge of interpretation at physical complexity mentioned earlier—is also advancing. Religion, music, and indeed every now characterizeable human discipline or endeavor, are doing likewise, changing and growing, and later giving way to more creative and more complex regions of interpretation while being taken up as the (relative) "material" engaged by the latter, in more complex and creative interpretations.

Note that with regard to constrictive regions only tactile physical pain has been included, *and* that region is only experienced as pain when engaged as a regression from the relatively more creative and complex regions, i.e., engaged in the counterclockwise and downward sense. Engaged from the sub-physical, in the clockwise and upward sense, however, it would have been—somewhere in our remote ancestry—a new beginning of physical awareness, perhaps such as that of young babies. Babies, because experiencing predominantly in this region, thus switch very easily from expansive interpretation in the direction of that new physical awareness to the constrictive interpretation toward the sub-physical which is pain, and vice versa. Or, carried further: "individual" human growth as a process of interpretation is analogous to the growth of the human species (physical community) as a greater process of interpretation. The latter is the former, writ small, and vice versa.

Insofar as a region of experience is guided in a community of interpretation under some hyperthematic structure, the action within the region is predominantly expansive—tending clockwise and upward—and only constrictive as deliberate practice toward further expansion. When the constriction is eliminative in intent however—and not an aware practice—then we tend to have the varieties of pain, mental and physical, as well as the more complex false communities which bring about those pains. If they were indicated, these constrictions of interpretation would be tending downward and counterclockwise in the diagram. The physical and mental pains may be as narrow as sameness of simple experience (the discomfort of holding one position), or sameness of complex experience (boredom), or they may be deeper constrictions which manifest as physical pain, or mental fear, or, with regard to simplification and "de-creation" from the more valuable ranges of interpretation, they may manifest as some of the more evident false communities which plague humanity: e.g., physical torture is thus something like an eliminative "anti-craft" engaging tactility; physical war is something like an "anti-science," and propaganda is something like an "anti-narrative."

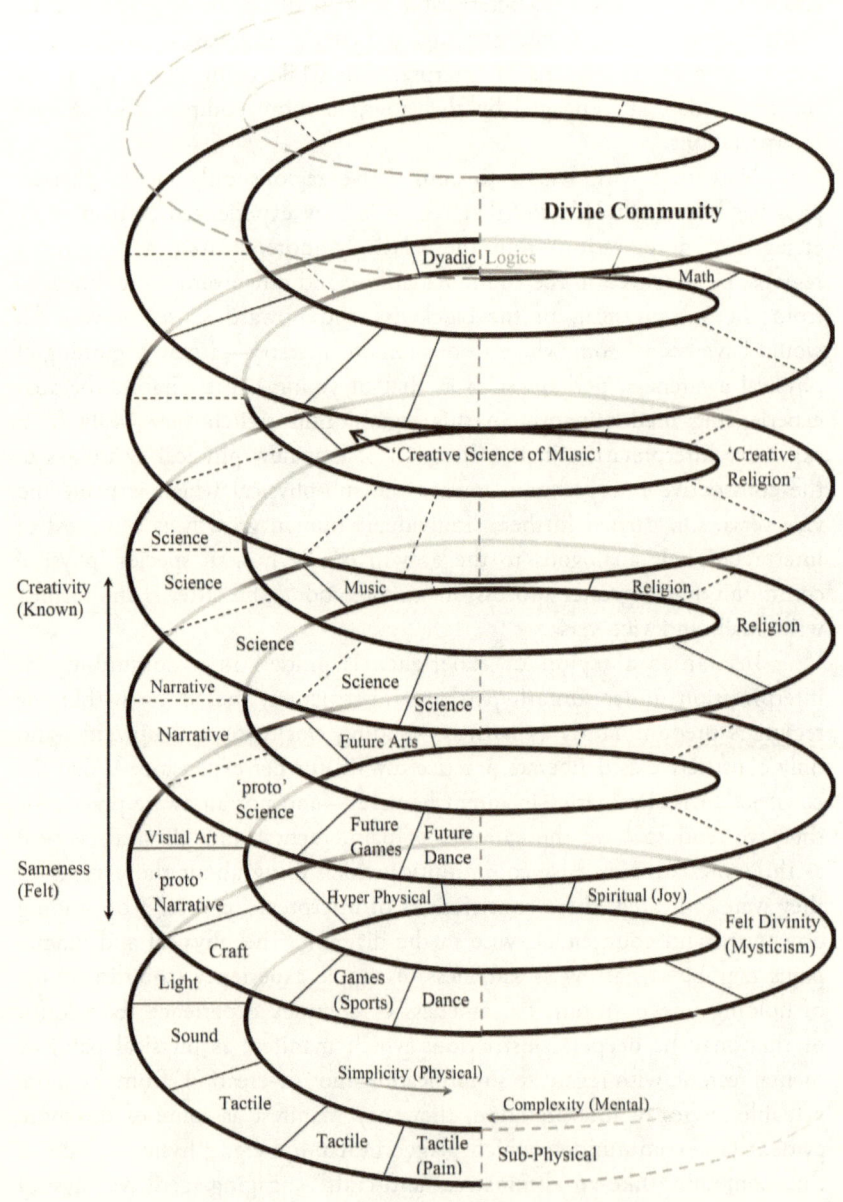

Notes

Introduction

1. Josiah Royce, *The Problem of Christianity*. Vol. 2 (New York: Macmillan, 1913, 323.

2. Royce held that the text was the "sign of a mind," and as will become apparent later, this may be so for complex interpretations but nonetheless is only a tendency. I will use the term "the sign of an actor' rather, so as to cover complex and also simple signs, and later in the work, the reader will more fully understand why this change is made.

Chapter 1

1. Josiah Royce, *The Philosophy of Loyalty* (1908; reprint, with a New Introduction by John. J. McDermott, Nashville, TN: Vanderbilt University Press, 1995), 37–38.

2. I say relatively because, with Whitehead, I hold that no two elements, relative to themselves alone, are in exactly the same time.

3. I borrow the term *musement* from Frank M. Oppenheim, with gratitude, as a more or less completed process of reflection, after *muse* or *musing*.

4. Recently discovered hominid bones from Morocco will create problems for the Recent Single-Origin Hypothesis, for example, relative to the consensus on human origins in East Africa. See Jean-Jacques Hublin et al., "New fossils from Jebel Irhoud, Morocco and the pan-African origin of Homo sapiens," in *Nature*, Vol. 546 (June 8, 2017) pp. 289–92. https://www.nature.com/nature/journal/v546/n7657/full/nature22336.html#access (accessed June 9, 2017).

5. The lengths to which such scientists will go to save the "holy hypothesis"—almost worthy of the likes of Jorge de Burgos in Umberto Eco's *Name of the Rose*—are well enough known. See, for example, Emily Chung, "One Hell of an Impression." CBC.

ca. https://newsinteractives.cbc.ca/longform/human-footprints-greece?cnis=0aa9cd87-d53e-43fc-8e6f-b5baa5147bba*C*1195*0*0*A (accessed February 23, 2018).

6. Some quite peculiar indeed, e.g., barnacles, insectivorous plants, and vegetable mold. See Franscisco J. Ayalla, "Darwin and the Scientific Method," in *Proceedings of the National Academy of Sciences of the United States of America*. Vol. 106. June 16, 2009, pp. 10033–0039.

7. Ayalla, 10033.

8. Destructive action can also test the hyperthematic principles. The nature of destructive—or constrictive—action will come up throughout this work, but a fuller account will have to wait for a future work.

9. For an account of the history of the transformation of various pieces—transformable elements—of the chess game, of their richness as signifiers of that transformation, and of one piece in particular, see Marilyn Yalom, *Birth of the Chess Queen: A History* (Kitchener, Ontario: Pandora Press, 2004).

10. Although the game can also be developed to the level of a narrative, e.g., in role-playing games such as *Dungeons and Dragons*, which are essentially hybrids spanning both game and narrative, and very successful ones at that.

Chapter 2

1. The emailed or online chess game shows us that game interpretation across the globe is certainly possible, but one has to remember then the role of the Internet which is facilitating this as a higher complexity structure in its own right, in effect a high complexity community of narration.

2. Joe Lapointe, "The Night Disco Went up In Smoke," *New York Times*, July 4, 2009. http://www.nytimes.com/2009/07/05/sports/baseball/05disco.html?_r=1 (accessed December 10, 2013).

3. Dinosaurs may have danced as well, see Martin G. Lockley, Richard T. McCrea, Lisa G. Buckley, Jong Deock Lim, Neffra A. Matthews, Brent H. Breithaupt, Karen J. Houck, Gerard D. Gierliński, Dawid Surmik, Kyung Soo Kim, Lida Xing, Dal Yong Kong, Ken Cart, Jason Martin, and Glade Hadden "Theropod courtship: Large scale physical evidence of display arenas and avian-like scrape ceremony behaviour by Cretaceous dinosaurs," in *Nature Scientific Reports* 6, no. 18952 (2016), doi:10.1038/srep18952.

4. For a fuller account of the constrictions and expansions of interpretation which militaries regularly engage in, couched in Roycean—but not explicitly hyperthematic terms—see my series of three essays: "Roycean Loyalty in a Military Context, Part 1: The Logic of Decision and Steadfastness," "Part 2: The Narrowing of Shared Experience between Combatants as a Loss of Value," and "Part 3: Sorrow and Surrender," *The Pluralist* 12, no. 3 (Fall 2017): 1-57, as well as the related essay: "Building the Great Community: Assessing Royce's International Conflict Insurance

Proposal in Light of the Collective Security Ideal of the League of Nations and the UN," *Canadian Military Journal*, 16, no. 3 (Summer 2016): 38-50. The latter is also online at: http://www.journal.forces.gc.ca/vol16/no3/page38-eng.asp

5. More on the idea of a transformation of military communities into purely defensive communities, and what that really implies, will have to wait for expansion in a future hyperthematic work, though some initial suggestions to that end will be offered in the second part of this work.

6. J. F. C. Fuller, *The Foundation of the Science of War* (London: Hutchison, 1926), 155; 291-92.

7. Ibid., 72.

8. Elzéar Blaze, *Military Life Under Napoleon*, trans. with notes John R. Elting (Chicago, IL: Emperor's Press), 17.

9. Ibid., 18.

10. Ibid., 89.

11. Ibid., 89-90.

12. Ibid., 92.

13. Thomas Hackett. "The execution of PVT Barry Winchell the real story behind the 'don't ask, don't tell' murder." in *Rolling Stone*. No. 835, Feb. 3, 2000. http://web.b.ebscohost.com.chateauguay.idm.oclc.org/ehost/detail/detail?vid=9&sid=f117a2ed-50b8-48ee-b15d-e86adce8e75c%40sessionmgr104&hid=129&bdata=JnNpdGU9ZWhvc3QtbGl2ZQ%3d%3d#AN=2854236&db=rch (accessed June 6, 2017).

14. Jennifer Mattson. "Senior Leaders Combat Hazing." www.army.mil. https://www.army.mil/article/86713/Senior_leaders_combat_hazing/ (accessed June 6, 2017).

15. "Furore in South Korea over soldier's 'bullying death.'" BBC.com http://www.bbc.com/news/world-asia-28684964 (accessed June 7, 2017).

16. Blaze, 89.

17. Tim Cook, "The Madman and the Butcher: Sir Sam Hughes, Sir Arthur Currie, and Their War of Reputations," *The Canadian Historical Review* 85, no. 4 (2004): 693-719.

18. See William H. McNeill, *Keeping Together in Time: Dance and Drill in Human History* (Cambridge, MA: Harvard UP, 1995). McNeill's book not only highlights the historic relation between dance and drill, but attempts in its way to make the physicality of feeling the connecting link between the two.

19. J. L. Granatstein, *The Weight of Command: Voices of Canada's Second World War Generals and Those Who Knew Them* (Vancouver: UBC Press, 2016). The entire first chapter is highly enlightening in this respect, particularly the fact that fifty years after the war the slights and "unflattering opinions" were in no way forgotten.

20. James R. Davis, *The Sharp End: A Canadian Soldier's Story* (Vancouver: Douglas & McIntyre, 1997), 35.

21. Ibid., 156.

22. Cook, *The Madman*, 702-03.

23. Ibid., 705.

24. Ibid., 718.

25. J. L. Granatstein, *Canada's Army: Waging War and Keeping the Peace* (Toronto: University of Toronto Press, 2002), 85.

26. John Keegan and Richard Holmes, *Soldiers: A History of Men in Battle*, with Richard Gau. Foreword by Frederick Forsyth (London: Hamish Hamilton, 1985), 205–20.

27. Ibid., 211.

28. Paul Johnson, *Eisenhower: A Life* (New York: Viking, 2014), 17.

29. Ibid., 37.

30. Compare, for example, recent tributes to a British army captain killed in Afghanistan: https://www.theguardian.com/uk-news/2013/dec/28/british-soldier-killed-afghanistan-named (June 10, 2017), with that to a World War One Victoria Cross recipient: Michael Ashcroft, "Second Lieutenant Sydney Clayton Woodroffe, VC," http://www.lordashcroft.com/2015/09/hero-of-the-month-by-lord-ashcroft-2/ (accessed June 11, 2017).

31. Johnson, ibid., 15. Again an offhand assessment by MacArthur.

32. H. Norman Schwarzkopf, *It Doesn't Take a Hero*, written with Peter Petre (New York: Bantam, 1992), 222–23.

33. Ibid., 226, 228.

34. Ibid., 275, 277, 283, 321, 229.

35. See Jonathan Schaeffer, Neil Burch, Yngvi Björnsson†, Akihiro Kishimoto‡, Martin Müller, Robert Lake, Paul Lu, and Steve Sutphen, "Checkers is Solved," in *Science* 14, vol. 317, no. 5844 (September 2007): 1518–522. http://www.sciencemag.org/content/317/5844/1518.full

36. A long stride in this direction is the 1971 dance by students at Stanford University *Protein Synthesis: An Epic on the Cellular Level*, directed by Gabriel Weiss, which modelled protein synthesis by RNA molecules. Such a dance begins to take the human body out of its physicality into more complex regions of experience. https://archive.org/details/ProteinSynthesis (accessed May 28, 2017).

37. There is of course no great danger that the meanings of dance will be exhausted for us humans for a while yet, even if some enterprising genius should make the attempt. See Schaeffer, ibid. The solution of checkers, in which, if both players play a perfect game, every possible opening of the game leads to a draw, tested 39 trillion endgame positions, but required 10^{14} calculations, up to 200 computers working together, and 18 years of effort.

38. Aaron Copland, *What to Listen for in Music* (1939; reprint, with a foreword and epilogue by Alan Rich, New York: Mentor, 1999), 7.

39. Jean Gallois, *Charles-Camille Saint-Saëns* (Sprimont, Belgium: Mardaga, 2004), 96.

40. Mélisande Chauveau, *Petits Prodiges de la Musique : une centaine de souvenirs ou de récits d'enfances* (Paris: Scali, 2007), 480.

41. Elisabeth Braw, "Move Over, Mozart: Child prodigies v real artistry," *Independent*, October 2, 2014, https://www.independent.co.uk/arts-entertainment/music/features/move-over-mozart-child-prodigies-v-real-artistry-9769711.html (accessed March 4, 2018).

42. Ibid., 9–10.

43. See, for example, Shunryu Suzuki, *Zen Mind, Beginner's Mind*, ed. Trudy Dixon, pref. Huston Smith, intro. Richard Baker (New York: Weatherhill Inc., 1970).

44. Not surprisingly, there is evidence that dance improves the gait in terms of balance and other aspects. See Jean Krampe et al. "Dance-Based Therapy in a Program of All-Inclusive Care for the Elderly," *Nursing Administration Quarterly*, 34, no. 2 (April/June 2010): 151–61.

45. David Parkinson, *History of Film* (London: Thames and Hudson, 1995), 18.

46. Ibid., 88.

47. Manjul Bhargava, recent winner of the Fields medal, is an example of a mathematician who looks to the problems of music and rhythmic poetry to inspire creativity in his mathematical endeavors. https://www.linkedin.com/pulse/manjul-bhargava-teaching-music-mathematics-john-stackhouse (accessed June 14, 2017).

48. For an imaginative account of one of the forms that such a high complexity dance might take—as well as of an exceedingly complex musical piece—see Iain M. Banks, *The Hydrogen Sonata* (New York: Orbit, 2012): 87–90, where the Ronte, a species evolved from flying insects, carry out highly complex forms of ceremonial ship dances—evidently aided by higher mathematics—between formations of spacecraft, at the stellar system level.

49. In fine art as well. Whitehead noted the tendency of the arts to advance, grow stale, and then break out anew into creativity.

50. The progression toward value in music, as in other endeavors, is a consistently understood tendency toward complexity that delivers ever more complex meaning, rather than toward lesser complexity—or "corporeality"—as composer Harry Partch mistakenly suggests. See *Genesis of a Music*, 2nd ed. (New York: Da Capo, 1974), 3–63.

51. On July 12-15, 2005, the first *International Conference on Mathematics and Narrative* was held at Mykonos, Greece.

52. Daniel Jaffe, "Bring on the Evil Kulak and the Noble Peasants; to Stalin, Prokofiev's 'Semyon Kotko' Was a Piece of Socialist Realism, but to the Composer, It Was an Opera to Save a Friend," *The Independent* (London), June 25, 2000.

Chapter 3

1. This accounts for the historically close connection between the older empirical philosophies and the rise of the sciences in their quantitative aspect. When some aspect of experience is privileged as the unchanging foundational aspect—i.e.,

as a series of copies of experience over time—then engagement of that aspect tends to become constricted to those interpretations which can be made with regard to a series of exact copies, namely interpretations of the weak value of quantity. This then spreads, in the attempt to bring all aspects of experience—even those, such as mental experience, whose complexity resists the attempt—under the same weakly valuable interpretive yardstick of quantification.

Science cannot live on the weak value of mere quantification though, any more than other regions of human endeavour—such as the region of the commercial corporation—can. Fortunately, through the great scientists, science continually breaks out into avenues of creative advancement, despite localized interpretive constriction to quantity.

2. Red as color at all, is an abstraction from the process of experience. Some will not select and abstract it as such as part of a problematic to be tackled, but will select it in its combination with other colors, etc. Some will forgo it for taste, for smell, and so forth. Some will forgo it for experiences of higher complexity still.

3. David Chandler, "Textured Surface may Boost Power Output of Thin Silicon Solar Cells," MIT News. http://web.mit.edu/newsoffice/2012/light-trapping-0613.html (accessed February 7, 2013).

4. Kohei Mizuno et al., "A Black Body Absorber from Vertically Aligned Single-Walled Carbon Nanotubes," *Proceedings of the National Academy of Sciences of the USA*, 106, no. 15 (April 14, 2009): 6044–047. http://www.ncbi.nlm.nih.gov/pmc/articles/PMC2669394/ (accessed February 8, 2013).

5. Whitehead's point free geometry could be developed in ways that would agree with the import of the above suggestions.

6. The list of words, which illustrate this diminishment of value, in English, is considerable: blackguard, blacklist, blackmail, black sheep, etc. In French similarly: film noir, bête noire, roman noir, travail au noir, etc.

7. In China yellow seems to have been hard to produce historically and so was also associated with wealth and power, of the emperor in particular. This association is local to China precisely because it was difficult to produce—difficult to interpret, showing how tricky it is to tease the tendencies out from one another. The violet, which was hard to produce and to interpret in more ways than yellow, was the more usual standard in human history for the color of kingly power.

8. In fact the Egyptians appear to have used yellow to signify not uninterpretability but the very qualities which they wished for the dead, not as dead but as living beyond the event of earthly death. In other words, insofar as they were consistent with regard to death, a culture will use a color which manifests that consistency.

9. Faber Birren, *Color Psychology and Color Therapy: A Factual Study of the Influence of Color on Human Life* (New Hyde Park, NY: University Books, 1961), 175, 264.

Chapter 4

1. I say not exhaustively because evidently all these could be combined in further combinations. In some cases the manifestations of these interpretive combinations will be evident in our world process, in some cases they will not, and might be sought for, but to lay them all out would go beyond the scope of this work.

2. Very likely Nebamun and those of his time did not think it was inconsistent to dominate. Yet that is not the issue here since we are as always attempting to interpret to **H**.

3. E. H. Gombrich, *The Story of Art* (New York: Phaidon, 1971), 35.

4. Ibid., 36.

5. Véronique Dasen, *Dwarves in Ancient Egypt and Greece* (Oxford: Oxford UP, 1993), 135–36.

6. The artistry, which has gone into font design, throughout the history of printing, has undergone expansion—and more often constriction in the more modern era—akin to this, with regard to the aspect of curvature and symmetry in font styles, and there is room for much creative expansion in this area as a further complement of written narrative. The move away from sans serif fonts in printing was a move in the wrong direction for value, a devaluation.

7. These last can be exemplified by a 2010 effort of the artist Michael Landy: "Michael Landy: Art Bin," South London Gallery. http://www.southlondongallery.org/page/michael-landy-art-bin (accessed February 8, 2013).

8. The inconsistency of the tendency toward mirror images manifests itself in various ways. One, which is predictable on the basis of hyperthematic musement upon the notion of *vanity*, as a relatively bad, value-diminished stance for action, is the relatively recent discovery that people are rendered increasingly uncomfortable when asked to gaze at themselves in a mirror. Given our suggestions regarding the diversity of interpretive capacities, we should not be surprised if further studies show that this discomfort nonetheless varies for different people.

9. It could not be otherwise given the assumptions. If the body is blemished or hurt, its healing is an *obvious* process. In embodiment the child is growing, the senior is diminishing, and the female body is both interpretively far more curved and undergoes more changes such as pregnancy, menstruation, etc.

10. Egyptian statues had a lesser degree of nudity.

11. In my expansion here upon aspects of the ancient Han art, I have referenced the very thorough survey of James Cahill as a source of examples to be hyperthematically interpreted. See James Cahill, *A Pure and Remote View: Visualizing Early Chinese Landscape Painting with James Cahill–Lecture 2 Han Dynasty Pictorial Art*, Institute of East Asian Studies, UC Berkeley, 1 hr. 17 min., prod. Chatterbox Films. ieas.berkeley.edu/publications/aparvlectures.html (accessed 3 March, 2013).

12. Nor has this ceased to bear fruit in art. Developments such as the Japanese *anime* with its uses of curvature are very likely an outcome of this line of assumptions in East Asian thought.

13. Esther Inglis-Arkell, "Ultraviolet Light Reveals how Ancient Greek Statues really looked." http://io9.com/5616498/ultraviolet-light-reveals-how-ancient-greek-statues-really-looked (accessed February 5, 2013).

14. Modern debate around art versus pornography in the portrayal of the human body is most resolvable just here. Interpretation tending toward an expansiveness where the portrayal of the embodied human subject moves away from the self-consciousness of that subject as embodied, is tending, consistently, toward value as art. The tendency toward constriction of interpretation which deliberately portrays the embodied human subject as self-consciousness of embodiment, is tending, inconsistently, toward the devaluation, which is pornography. The former tendency says: "I am human process beyond embodiment." The latter says: "take me as this body alone, this object fully captured in the portrayal."

Chapter 5

1. At first glance it would seem that there are few of such unengaged problematics, i.e., problematic new regions of experience simply waiting to be engaged. But a little reflection shows that they crop up regularly in the human region of the world process, and that they have been—and will be—amenable to the application of consistent hyperthemes. The problematic of flying for example—like boating in an earlier age—which at the end of the seventeenth century was a vast, open, little engaged, problematic within a portion of the range of physical complexity, would have benefited from the guidance of **HCu**. Among others, **HCu** would have projected: the wing curvature which produces lift, the optimal shapes for aircraft structure, and both the propeller shape and the temporally expanded spiral which it creates as the aircraft moves forward, essentially a series of curves from which more complex curves are created. **H3** moreover, suggests that communities of aircraft of three or more elements, in flight, will be an expansion of value over single aircraft. **HAs** meanwhile, suggests that asymmetric shapes in aircraft design—remembering that circles are not symmetric in the hyperthematic view—tends to better value, so that the current mirror symmetries of wings, tail, and pointed nose cone ought to be avoided. Other hyperthemes could give still further guidance.

2. For an overview of this see Jean Andreau, *Banking and Business in the Roman World*, trans. Janet Lloyd (Cambridge: Cambridge UP, 1999).

3. Arthur Schopenhauer, *The World as Will and Idea*. Translated by R. B. Haldane and J. Kemp. Vol. 1, 7th ed. (London, Kegan Paul, 1909), 532.

4. Shunryu Suzuki, *Not Always So: Practicing the True Spirit of Zen*, edited by Edward Espe Brown (New York, HarperCollins, 2002), 152.

5. Suzuki, *Zen Mind*, 21.

6. Sunryu Suzuki, *Branching Streams Flow in the Darkness: Zen Talks on the Sandokai*, edited by Mel Weitsman and Michael Wenger (London, UofC Press, 1999), 3.

7. Suzuki, *Zen Mind*, 47.

8. Even in the "mere" sex act in which each *does* take the other as an extended individual and each willingly engages in the act thereby, nonetheless the relative shortness of the act itself does not require much in the way of the temporal extension of the individual, nor in the usual sense is its goal apparent as a common goal, nor finally does it include or postulate a third—e.g., a new life, a child—by which the community of interpretation is to be constituted. Yet even if all of those *were* consistently held to be included in sex—see my suggestions in chapter 8—it would not change the import of my main suggestion. A family can certainly be a community without children, but some other strong third is needed to make it so, and anyway, here I am only suggesting the family as the *origin of communities of cooperation which developed into corporations*.

9. Jean Lee and Hong Li, *Wealth Doesn't Last 3 Generations: How Family Businesses Can Maintain Prosperity* (London: World Scientific Publishing, 2009), xiv.

10. Ibid., 3–7.

11. John Micklethwait and Adrian Wooldridge, *The Company: A Short History of a Revolutionary Idea* (London: Weidenfeld and Nicholson, 2003), 18. (Hereafter cited as *The Company*.)

12. Nick Robins, *The Corporation That Changed the World: How the East India Company Shaped the Modern Multinational* (London: Pluto Press, 2006), 78.

13. Ibid., 35.

14. Rob McQueen, *A Social History of Company Law: Great Britain and the Australian Colonies 1854-1920* (Farnham, England: Ashgate Publishing, 2009), 84. (Hereafter cited as *Social History*.)

15. Micklethwait, *The Company*, 60.

16. For an overview of the American robber barons in the second half of the nineteenth century, see H. W. Brands, *American Colossus: The Triumph of Capitalism 1865–1900* (New York: Doubleday, 2010).

17. Lee T. Wyatt III, *The Industrial Revolution* (London: Greenwood Press, 2009), 48.

18. Ibid., 51.

19. Ibid., 59–60.

20. Ibid., 62.

21. Laura L. Frader, *The Industrial Revolution: A History in Documents* (New York: Oxford UP, 2006), 61.

22. See McQueen, *Social History*, 1–3; 9. McQueen argues that the trend of the development of limited liability is toward individual investors—the *other* acting members of corporations—gradually losing a sense of themselves as acting members

of the corporation, and his main thesis is that the limited liability company of today thereby retains the *worst* aspects of the private companies out of which it developed in the nineteenth century.

23. Micklethwait, *The Company*, 118.

24. Kevin Maney, *The Maverick and His Machine: Thomas Watson Sr. and the Making of IBM* (Hoboken, NJ: John Wiley & Sons, 2003), 99–100.

25. Ibid., 107.

26. Ibid., 110.

27. Ibid., 186; 435.

28. Ibid., 435–36.

29. Adam Smith, *The Wealth of Nations* (1776; reprint, Petersfield, UK: Harriman House, 2007), 5–6.

30. Ibid., 18.

31. Ibid., 20.

32. Maddeningly, he sometimes appears to recognize this, but only to assert that the solution lies in further activity which has nothing to do with labor activity. See ibid., 506.

33. Ibid., 491.

34. Ibid., 336–37.

35. Ibid., 482–93.

36. Ibid., 196.

37. Ibid., 482.

38. Ibid., 413–14.

39. Ibid., 492.

40. Ibid., 493.

41. Micklethwait, *The Company*, 179–80.

42. Ibid., 4.

43. Ibid., 9.

44. Noreena Hertz, *The Silent Takeover: Global Capitalism and the Death of Democracy* (London: Arrow Books, 2002), 250.

45. Ibid., 275.

46. Keegan, *Soldiers*, 267.

47. The import of this symmetry is understood very well—covertly. The aim of all advances of military weaponry is to "eliminate him without him eliminating you." Yet as I suggest here, and hope to follow out in later work, this does not work, for the inconsistency simply propagates itself, or "breaks out elsewhere" in the engagement of experience.

48. I am not suggesting that children do not *appear* to play alone. But in a very strong sense they never actually play alone. The lone child inevitably postulates imaginary partners in play, and when they do not, they are interpreting and thus developing themselves as extended individuals in the time process parallel aspect. Thus consistent with Royce's view, children play first in the postulation of others and then retreat to themselves to consolidate their socially interpretive gains, as individuals.

49. Wyatt III, *The Industrial Revolution*, 67.

50. Karl Marx, "Estranged Labor," in *Economic and Philosophic Manuscripts of 1844 and the Communist Manifesto*, trans. Martin Milligan (Amherst, NY: Prometheus Books, 1988), 81.

51. Ibid., 73.

52. In "The Manifesto of the Communist Party," in ibid., 223.

53. If this is correct then we may suppose that capitalism, carried out under the same inconsistency will only outlast communism for—relatively speaking—a short time, i.e., up to the point at which its inconsistency begins to infringe upon the limits of the world itself as a mere object resource: the locus of its symmetric assumption. It will then suffer the same fate as communism. In other words, the world as resource object will become eventually for capitalism, the "common product," which is assumed in advance by communism. Thus, the further it goes and the more it gathers up, the more capitalism will tend to resemble communism, except that communism has both assumed and faced the consequences of its inconsistent assumption sooner than capitalism.

54. Ralph A. Thaxton, Jr., *Catastrophe and Contention in Rural China: Mao's Great Leap Forward Famine and the Origins of Righteous Resistance in Da Fo Village* (Cambridge: Cambridge UP, 2008), 159.

55. Peter Speed, ed., *Those Who Worked: an Anthology of Medieval Sources* (New York: Italica Press, 1997), 82–83.

56. I leave the reader to confirm this in the numerous studies which have been undertaken on wealth and happiness. Such studies have shown consistently that beyond a certain level, increasing wealth not only does not increase the sense of meaningfulness, and happiness, but attenuates it.

Chapter 6

1. A ready example of a successful and consistent community in which various selections of transformable elements—e.g., the guidelines for various roles—promote and offer the opportunity for practice and meaningful engagement at various ranges of complexity within the community, can be found in the *Toastmasters* public speaking organization.

2. To better visualize what I mean here, it might help the reader to consider Judo, or wrestling for example in their similarity to dance.

3. That is to say, this is not to be confused with my discussion of assembly line workers receiving parts to assemble which fail as signs of interpretation.

4. In the other direction, vertically downward, the CEO as an acting element has *too many* models to interpret herself to on the lower level, which causes a disconnection between boss and workers.

5. Whether money as a sign, or stock as a further sign of that sign, makes no difference. Technically, in the realm of the electronic stock exchange there is no

stock, for every unit of stock is precisely convertible into a fluctuating monetary figure. The use and institution of stock is a holdover from another age in which a physical stock certificate was issued to the investor in a corporation.

6. See Benjamin Graham, *The Intelligent Investor,* rev. ed. upd. and comm. Jason Zweig (New York: HarperCollins, 2003), 501. Roughly one-third of American stockholders do not bother to vote at all with regard to the issues of the corporations which they invest in.

7. Ibid., 498.

8. The co-leadership of the Roman emperor Marcus Aurelius and his brother is an example, however.

9. Where does this leave the limited liability company incorporated by a single individual? It leaves such a company consistent only on the basis of having everyone in its community under the structure of the corporation, which is to say the single individual, having to bear the responsibility for the actions of the company.

Chapter 7

1. In other words, how much is the refining a creative transformation of the whole sign of the original resource? Is it a relatively lazy engagement, which separates off a portion of waste, or "garbage," to be—ostensibly—eliminated, or is it a relatively thorough engagement which finds ways to transform the initial resource sign much more fully?

2. You may interpret me through action at levels of complexity passing beyond physicality however, if capable of action at those levels, i.e., if you are willing to countenance facets of interpretation—qualities—which takes you beyond those hardheaded assumptions which hold me to the lower realms of quantity. The power of constriction to quantification is most uninterpretable where it engages regions of experience wherein action predominantly assumes the variety of constrictions which give rise to physicality where the actors are most at home in the arena of the physical. As those assumptions are loosened, giving way to more expansive regions, according to more expansive aspects—a (relative) *"spiritualizing" of experience*—the power of uninterpretability of accumulative repetition wanes. In fine, those who seek quality—who are spiritual—are neither awed nor swayed by money.

3. A workable analogy is: the consistent foreman leading using the options that a composer/conductor in music would have relative to their own composition, e.g., Leonard Bernstein.

4. Various actions of the body—such as techniques of swordsmanship in ancient warfare—tend to complement this intent toward uninterpretability.

5. Nell Boeschenstein, "How the Food Industry Manipulates Taste Buds with 'Salt Sugar Fat,'" NPR. http://www.npr.org/blogs/thesalt/2013/02/26/172969363/

how-the-food-industry-manipulates-taste-buds-with-salt-sugar-fat (accessed September 7, 2013).

6. Whenever possible we should promote odd numbers of unit members at a selected level of complexity, and indeed prime numbers of unit members so as to propagate asymmetry: thus 3, 5, 7, 11, etc.

7. Thus, if we had to approximate "individual" human members relative to a regular square grid—superimposing a circle upon the latter—and began with nine members at the top of the hierarchy we would expand in each successive lower level to approximately 13, 17, 19, 21, 23, 24, 25, 26, 27.

8. Even the division of the line into the equal parts, giving rise to the symmetry, depends upon the units of division used and we can always select finer gradations which put the exactly equal division point of the line in doubt. It should be evident by now that: *in the hyperthematic view we can never really reach the inconsistencies we aim at—if the world is a world of interpreted value—but yet our efforts to do so can temporarily disturb the growth of value within the world process.*

9. I.e., the highest which we can yet achieve, or which we desire.

10. This filling of gaps in order to sustain circularity which becomes evident in physical approximations of circularity, such as the one depending on human bodies here discussed, is just the outcome of beginning to move beyond interpretations at the physical range of complexity by promoting curvature. The human gaps of the circle are filled by actions of those in the circle; those curvature sustaining actions are beginning to break out of physicality. Another way to view this is to say that interpretations of curvature can only be approximated in physicality—since physicality is a tendency contrary to curvature—so that an art such as mathematical calculus, is an art of "filling the gaps" of physical approximations of curvature by making interpretations of a complexity beyond physicality, i.e. interpretations of mental complexity. Because we cannot "perfect" circles (or curves) physically, we move, and must move, toward mental interpretations to perfect or complete them.

Chapter 8

1. More obviously because the two tendencies just mentioned can also be seen as inconsistent with **Hv**. The interpretation of the world process as it exists for us as actualized as embodiment, is the result of an *inconsistency* in engaging the region of interpretation, which we characterize as physical, and so to propagate that inconsistency—to pass forward any aspect of embodiment in our interpretations—is inconsistent with **Hv**. We must take the long view however, and say "let us address the more manageable range first, according to our measure." There will be time in humanity's future to invoke **Hv** toward what one might call "the further spiritualizing of humanity out of the inconsistency which is its embodiment," as an overall goal.

2. Although there is always a new challenge—though weak in terms of value—even in quantitative expansion. The *Guinness Book of World Records* banks on this very low-level creativity: who has run 10 km fastest, who has eaten the most hot dogs, who has made the largest clay bowl ever, et cetera.

3. Each of us with regard to one another as embodied human individuals, and also each of us as embodied human individuals with regard to the temporal experiences of our own past and future.

4. Clay and wood are less complex *for us*—because they are the signs of originating actions within the world process which are beyond our embodiment. Even though they might be *more complex* within the ranges of the world process than a television, we do not have a record of their creation from within the region of our active embodiment, as we do with the television, which *we* have created.

5. Dance, making up the hyperthematic structure of lowest complexity in our hierarchy, does not have objects as usually understood. Yet in another sense it does. The human body is its object. It is an object which the community of dance *ages* consistently with **Ha**, by expanding that object—e.g. in the ranges of motion of the limbs—so that it is interpretable to the many periods—childhood, youth, old age—of an embodied life span, and, to human embodiment over the longer span as a development within the world process. In the latter sense, the expansions of interpretation which the community of dance gives to the body, bring it out of its objecthood, promoting interpretations of it to e.g. a nineteenth-century waltz, an English country dance of the seventeenth century, a Chinese dragon dance of two millennia ago, i.e., *to the human body insofar as it develops as a community within the world process beyond its "individual" human instances.*

6. Creating curved strings for the violin (and other stringed instruments), both in themselves and relative to the other strings, by applying **HCu** beyond the range of physical complexity, would be a consistent advance of value and produce new and interesting results for music.

7. For some examples of research affirming the devaluating effect of weapon signs, see Brad Bushman, "The Weapons Effect," www.psychologytoday.com/blog/get-psyched/201301/the-weapons-effect (accessed October 15, 2013).

8. There ought to be nothing very mysterious about such an effort. It is simply the reverse of the various "desensitization" trainings which members of the American Marines and other military groups undergo. If we can bring the human process to fight through such constrictions, then we may just as certainly guide human—and other—processes out of the urge to fight through the appropriate expansions.

9. Slasher and Gore films are closely related, though further tendencies of constriction are added, and differing ranges of complexity are engaged.

10. Constrictive sexual tendencies and sexual diseases are intimately linked. The earlier discussed tendency of the world process, as nature, to correct repetitive action toward mere quantity—"having more sex," "having sex with as many people

as possible," etc.—will give rise to a devaluation in associated regions of experience, akin to the pollution effect considered earlier, which rebounds upon those who hold the inconsistent assumptions. Sexual diseases are just the "cousins" of forms of natural pollution.

Conclusion

1. Edgar Sheffield Brightman, *Moral Laws* (New York: Abingdon Press, 1933).

2. In its other English sense, "I realized that . . . ," signifies well enough what is going on: the interpretive connection of some experience with some other experience so as to engender meaning.

3. J. R. R. Tolkien, *The Lord of the Rings Part 1: The Fellowship of the Ring* (London: HarperCollins, 1994), 134.

4. Other transformable elements than human, e.g., animals, later plants, and still later minerals, will also increasingly proceed through this "human" range, according to their interpretive capacities, as they evolve.

5. The following is as always a matter of tendencies, there can be no exact dividing line where joy turns into the spiritual, where craft turns into science, where science gives way to logic, where dancing turns into games, etc. The reader can refer to Diagram 2 for some approximate orientations however.

6. To "see" a pointy thing is also a physical sensation. But the light is more complex, hence the feeling is more a mental feeling of harm.

7. Brightman, ibid., 15.

8. Ibid., 27–28.

9. Ibid., 30.

10. Ibid., 36–37.

11. Ibid., 41–42.

12. It descends to physical complexity when it begins to physically coerce, e.g., in imprisonment.

13. And usually the string of terms is much more complex than my example.

14. Some of the world's "greatest" dictators have been some of its most extreme ethical idealists, advocating change heedless of circumstance, regardless of whether the change was ultimately consistent. Whoever has laid out a grand plan of how they wish the world to be and then looked at those who (or those things which) do not fit into the plan as minor inconveniences to be eliminated for the sake of the grand plan, falls somewhere under this heading.

15. Ibid., 66.

16. Ibid., 89–90.

17. Ibid., 95.

18. Ibid., 127.

19. Ibid., 131.

20. Ibid., 136.
21. Ibid.
22. Ibid., 245.
23. Ibid., 246.
24. Ibid., 278.
25. Ibid., 284.

26. So, for example, the right-wing rural dweller might unhesitatingly shoot the wolf which harasses his livestock. He will also view any animal which he does not, or does not currently, dominate, as potentially dominating him physically.

27. So, for example, the left-wing urban film director might unhesitatingly consider "the red in tooth and claw" battles which he films to remain the purview of nature, unrelated to the human engagement of experience, and not to be interfered with.

Appendix B

1. But to perform a consistent action of interpretation is to take part in a community of interpretation.

Appendix C

1. In terms of hardness, this is bound up with its structure as a tendency, among others, of degree of curvature—**HCu**—relative to other weaker or harder structures.

2. It could be shown that the complexity of civilizations throughout history often reaches a point at which, in tandem with other allied troubles, the sign for value exchange—often a currency—can no longer accommodate the complexity of interplay of processes which are sought after by the civilization. The result is that the civilization manifests quantitative accumulations of effort which are so disjointed from one another—they cannot be spanned by the usual ranges of interpretation—e.g., the disparity between rich and poor, that the basis of interpretive community of the civilization is threatened, leading, along with other inconsistencies, to the collapse, or dissolution of the civilization as a community, into a mere society.

3. Attempts to sustain or save the status quo will fail.

4. In fact, I am taking the temporality of the world process here as another aspect for valuation, but for explanatory purposes I will not call the currency three dimensional, even though I might do so.

5. In both cases, the higher valuation is relative to "the other one"—and perhaps many others—which is of lesser value with respect to the community of the two aspects in question.

6. Da Vinci's paintings, for example, are not only difficult to steal because the interpretive community of art around them recognizes their uniqueness and defends them well as part of that continually reinterpreting recognition, but also difficult to sell if stolen, because they are recognized as unique creations.

Appendix D

1. A logic of *constrictive practice*, which expands upon the far broader manifestations of constrictive action in order to correct constrictive effort in the world, would be the sort of effort in the aforementioned proposed Hyperthematics of Conflict.

2. I should warn the reader, however, that what follows was only worked out after I had completed Hyperthematics. That is to say that even though I had read *The Relations of the Principles of Logic to the Foundations of Geometry* quite early on, the primary inspiration for the Hyperthematic method arose out of reading first Royce's *The Principles of Logic* (1913; New York: Wisdom Library, 1961): 72-77, on the "modes of action" and *The Problem of Christianity*, even though I continually saw hints of System Σ appear as I developed Hyperthematics. There are very few hints of what System Σ is truly capable of in *The Relations of the Principles of Logic*, because Royce is most concerned—for obvious reasons insofar as the work is to be accepted as a formalization—to show that it encompasses algebraic logic and geometry.

3. The Σ of System Σ may be a play by Royce on the Greek Lunate Sigma, which was written C; thus C for Community. At least it would be fun if it were.

4. Josiah Royce, "The Relations of the Principles of Logic to the Foundations of Geometry," *Transactions of the American Mathematical Society* 6, no. 3 (July, 1905).

5. Royce., 355.
6. Ibid., 357.
7. Ibid.
8. Ibid., 358.
9. Ibid., 358-59.
10. Ibid., 359.
11. Ibid., 361. Here a graphical representation of the degrading of the earlier "circle" into the line is given.
12. Ibid., 360.
13. Ibid., 367.
14. Ibid.
15. Ibid.
16. Ibid.
17. Ibid., 368-69.
18. Ibid., 371.

19. Ibid., 371–72.
20. Ibid., 372.
21. Ibid., 387.

References

Anderson, Marc. "Roycean Loyalty in a Military Context, Part 1: The Logic of Decision and Steadfastness," "Part 2: The Narrowing of Shared Experience between Combatants as a Loss of Value," and "Part 3: Sorrow and Surrender," *The Pluralist* 12, no. 3 (Fall 2017): 1–57.

———. "Building the Great Community: Assessing Royce's International Conflict Insurance Proposal in Light of the Collective Security Ideal of the League of Nations and the UN," *Canadian Military Journal* 16 no. 3 (Summer 2016): 38–50. http://www.journal.forces.gc.ca/vol16/no3/page38-eng.asp

Andreau, Jean. *Banking and Business in the Roman World*. Translated by Janet Lloyd. Cambridge: Cambridge University Press, 1999.

Ashcroft, Michael. "Second Lieutenant Sydney Clayton Woodroffe, VC." www.lordashcroft.com. Accessed June 11, 2017. http://www.lordashcroft.com/2015/09/hero-of-the-month-by-lord-ashcroft-2/

Ayalla, Franscisco J. "Darwin and the scientific Method." *Proceedings of the National Academy of Sciences of the United States of America*. 106 (June 16, 2009): 10033–0039.

Banks, Iain M. *The Hydrogen Sonata*. New York: Orbit, 2012.

Birren, Faber. *Color Psychology and Color Therapy: a Factual Study of the Influence of Color on Human Life*. New Hyde Park, NY: University Books, 1961.

"British Soldier Killed in Afghanistan Named." Guardian.uk. Accessed June 10, 2017. https://www.theguardian.com/uk-news/2013/dec/28/british-soldier-killed-afghanistan-named

Elzéar Blaze, *Military Life Under Napoleon*. Translated with notes by John R. Elting. Chicago: Emperor's Press, 1995.

Boeschenstein, Nell. "How the Food Industry Manipulates Taste Buds with 'Salt Sugar Fat.'" NPR. Accessed September 7, 2013. http://www.npr.org/blogs/thesalt/2013/02/26/172969363/how-the-food-industry-manipulates-taste-buds-with-salt-sugar-fat

Brands, H. W. *American Colossus: The Triumph of Capitalism 1865–1900*. New York: Doubleday, 2010.

Braw, Elisabeth. "Move Over, Mozart: Child prodigies v real artistry." *Independent*, October 2, 2014. Accessed March 4, 2018. https://www.independent.co.uk/arts-entertainment/music/features/move-over-mozart-child-prodigies-v-real-artistry-9769711.html

Brightman, Edgar Sheffield. *Moral Laws*. New York: Abingdon Press, 1933.

Bushman, Brad. "The Weapons effect." Accessed October 15, 2013. www.psychologytoday.com/blog/get-psyched/201301/the-weapons-effect.x

Cahill, James. *A Pure and Remote View: Visualizing Early Chinese Landscape Painting with James Cahill—Lecture 2 Han Dynasty Pictorial Art*. Institute of East Asian Studies UC Berkeley. 1 hr. 17 min. Produced by Chatterbox Films. Accessed March 3, 2013. ieas.berkeley.edu/publications/aparvlectures.html

Chandler, David. "Textured Surface May Boost Power Output of Thin Silicon Solar Cells." *MIT News*. Accessed February 7, 2013. http://web.mit.edu/newsoffice/2012/light-trapping-0613.html.x

Chauveau, Mélisande. *Petits Prodiges de la Musique : une centaine de souvenirs ou de récits d'enfances*. Paris: Scali, 2007.

Chung, Emily. "One Hell of an Impression." CBC.ca. Accessed February 23, 2018. https://newsinteractives.cbc.ca/longform/human-footprints-greece?cnis=0aa9cd87-d53e-43fc-8e6f-b5baa5147bba*C*1195*0*0*A

Copland, Aaron. *What to Listen for in Music*. 1939. Reprint, with a foreword and epilogue by Alan Rich. New York: Mentor, 1999.

Cook, Tim. "The Madman and the Butcher: Sir Sam Hughes, Sir Arthur Currie, and Their War of Reputations." *The Canadian Historical Review* 85, no. 4 (2004): 693–719.

Dasen, Véronique. *Dwarves in Ancient Egypt and Greece*. Oxford: Oxford University Press, 1993.

Davis, James R. *The Sharp End: A Canadian Soldier's Story*. Vancouver: Douglas & McIntyre, 1997.

Frader, Laura L. *The Industrial Revolution: A History in Documents*. New York: Oxford University Press, 2006.

Fuller, J. F. C. *The Foundation of the Science of War*. London: Hutchison, 1926.

"Furore in South Korea over soldier's 'bullying death.'" BBC.com. Accessed June 7, 2017. http://www.bbc.com/news/world-asia-28684964

Gallois, Jean. *Charles-Camille Saint-Saëns*. Sprimont, Belgium: Mardaga, 2004.

Graham, Benjamin. *The Intelligent Investor*. Rev. Ed. Updated with new commentary by Jason Zweig. New York: HarperCollins, 2003.

Granatstein, J. L. *Canada's Army: Waging War and Keeping the Peace*. Toronto: University of Toronto Press, 2002.

———. *The Weight of Command: Voices of Canada's Second World War Generals and Those Who Knew Them*. Vancouver: UBC Press, 2016.

Gombrich, Ernst Hans Joseph. *The Story of Art*. New York: Phaidon, 1971.

Hackett, Thomas. "The execution of PVT Barry Winchell the real story behind the 'don't ask, don't tell' murder." *Rolling Stone* 835 (February 3, 2000) Accessed June 6, 2017. http://web.b.ebscohost.com.chateauguay.idm.oclc.org/ehost/detail/detail?vid=9&sid=f117a2ed-50b8-48ee-b15d-e86adce8e75c%40sessionmgr104&hid=129&bdata=JnNpdGU9ZWhvc3QtbGl2ZQ%3d%3d#AN=2854236&db=rch

Hertz, Noreena. *The Silent Takeover: Global Capitalism and the Death of Democracy.* London: Arrow Books, 2002.

Hublin, Jean-Jacques, Abdelouahed Ben-Ncer, Shara E. Bailey, Sarah E. Freidline, Simon Neubauer, Matthew M. Skinner, Inga Bergmann, Adeline Le Cabec, Stefano Benazzi, Katerina Harvati, & Philipp Gunz. "New fossils from Jebel Irhoud, Morocco and the pan-African origin of Homo sapiens." *Nature* 546 (June 8, 2017): 289-92. Accessed June 9, 2017. https://www.nature.com/nature/journal/v546/n7657/full/nature22336.html#access

Hume, David, "Of the Standard of Taste," in *Four Dissertations.* London: A. Millar, 1757.

Inglis-Arkell, Esther. "Ultraviolet Light Reveals how Ancient Greek Statues really looked." Accessed February 5, 2013. http://io9.com/5616498/ultraviolet-light-reveals-how-ancient-greek-statues-really-looked

Jaffe, Daniel. "Bring on the Evil Kulak and the Noble Peasants; to Stalin, Prokofiev's 'Semyon Kotko' Was a Piece of Socialist Realism, but to the Composer, It Was an Opera to Save a Friend." *Independent,* June 25, 2000.

Johnson, Paul. *Eisenhower: A Life.* New York: Viking, 2014.

Keegan, John, and Richard Holmes. *Soldiers: A History of Men in Battle.* With Richard Gau. Foreword by Frederick Forsyth. London: Hamish Hamilton, 1985.

Krampe, Jean, Marilyn J. Rantz, Laura Dowell, Richard Schamp, Marjorie Skubic, Carmen Abbott. "Dance-Based Therapy in a Program of All-Inclusive Care for the Elderly." *Nursing Administration Quarterly* 34 no. 2 (April/June 2010): 151-61.

Landy, Michael. *Art Bin.* South London Gallery. Accessed February 28, 2013. http://www.southlondongallery.org/page/michael-landy-art-bin

Lee, Jean, and Hong Li. *Wealth Doesn't Last 3 Generations: How Family Businesses Can Maintain Prosperity.* London: World Scientific Publishing, 2009.

Lapointe, Joe. "The Night Disco Went up in Smoke." *New York Times,* July 4, 2009. Accessed December 10, 2013. http://www.nytimes.com/2009/07/05/sports/baseball/05disco.html?_r=0

Lockley, Martin G., Richard T. McCrea, Lisa G. Buckley, Jong Deock Lim, Neffra A. Matthews, Brent H. Breithaupt, Karen J. Houck, Gerard D. Gierliński, Dawid Surmik, Kyung Soo Kim, Lida Xing, Dal Yong Kong, Ken Cart, Jason Martin, and Glade Hadden. "Theropod courtship: large scale physical evidence of display arenas and avian-like scrape ceremony behaviour by

Cretaceous dinosaurs." *Nature Scientific Reports* 6, no. 18952 (2016) doi:10.1038/srep18952

Maney, Kevin. *The Maverick and His Machine: Thomas Watson Sr. and the Making of IBM.* Hoboken New Jersey: John Wiley & Sons, 2003.

Mattson, Jennifer. "Senior Leaders Combat Hazing." www.army.mil. Accessed June 6, 2017. https://www.army.mil/article/86713/Senior_leaders_combat_hazing/

Marx, Karl. "Estranged Labor." *Economic and Philosophic Manuscripts of 1844 and the Communist Manifesto.* Translated by Martin Milligan. Amherst, NY: Prometheus Books, 1988.

McNeill, William H. *Keeping Together in Time: Dance and Drill in Human History.* Cambridge: Harvard University Press, 1995.

McQueen, Rob. *A Social History of Company Law: Great Britain and the Australian Colonies 1854–1920.* Farnham, England: Ashgate Publishing, 2009.

Micklethwait, John, and Adrian Wooldridge. *The Company: a Short History of a Revolutionary Idea.* London: Weidenfeld and Nicholson, 2003.

Mizuno Kohei, et al. "A Black Body Absorber from Vertically Aligned Single-Walled Carbon Nanotubes." *Proceedings of the National Academy of Sciences of the U.S.A.*, 106, no. 15 (April 14, 2009): 6044-6047. Accessed February 8, 2013. http://www.ncbi.nlm.nih.gov/pmc/articles/PMC2669394/

Parkinson, David. *History of Film.* London: Thames and Hudson, 1995.

Partch, Harry. *Genesis of a Music.* 2nd Ed. New York, Da Capo: 1974.

Robins, Nick. *The Corporation That Changed the World: How the East India Company Shaped the Modern Multinational.* London: Pluto Press, 2006.

Josiah Royce. *The Philosophy of Loyalty.* 1908. Reprint, Nashville, TN: Vanderbilt University Press, 1995.

———. *The Principles of Logic.* 1913. New York: Wisdom Library, 1961.

———. *The Problem of Christianity.* New York: Macmillan, 1913.

———. "The Relations of the Principles of Logic to the Foundations of Geometry," *Transactions of the American Mathematical Society,* 6, no. 3 (July, 1905): 353-415.

Schaeffer, Jonathan, Neil Burch, Yngvi Björnsson†, Akihiro Kishimoto‡, Martin Müller, Robert Lake, Paul Lu, and Steve Sutphen, "Checkers is Solved." *Science* 14, 317, no. 5844 (September 2007): 1518-522. http://www.sciencemag.org/content/317/5844/1518.full

Schopenhauer, Arthur. *The World as Will and Idea.* Translated by R. B. Haldane and J. Kemp. Vol. 1, 7th Ed. London, Kegan Paul: 1909.

Schwarzkopf, H. Norman. *It Doesn't Take a Hero.* Written with Peter Petre. New York: Bantam, 1992.

Smith, Adam. *The Wealth of Nations.* 1776. Reprint, Petersfield, UK: Harriman House, 2007.

Speed, Peter, ed. *Those Who Worked: an Anthology of Medieval Sources.* New York: Italica Press, 1997.

Stackhouse, John. "Manjul Bhargava: Teaching the Music of Mathematics." Accessed June 14, 2017. https://www.linkedin.com/pulse/manjul-bhargava-teaching-music-mathematics-john-stackhouse

Suzuki, Shunryu. *Branching Streams Flow in the Darkness: Zen Talks on the Sandokai.* Edited by Mel Weitsman and Michael Wenger. Berkeley, University of California Press, 1999.

———. *Not Always So: Practicing the True Spirit of Zen.* Edited by Edward Espe Brown. New York, HarperCollins: 2002.

———. *Zen Mind, Beginner's Mind.* Edited by Trudy Dixon. Preface by Huston Smith. Introduction by Richard Baker. New York: Weatherhill Inc., 1970.

Thaxton Jr., Ralph A. *Catastrophe and Contention in Rural China: Mao's Great Leap Forward Famine and the Origins of Righteous Resistance in Da Fo Village.* Cambridge, UK: Cambridge University Press, 2008.

Tolken, J. R. R. *The Lord of the Rings Part 1: The Fellowship of the Ring.* London: HarperCollins, 1994.

Weiss, Gabriel. "Protein Synthesis: An Epic on the Cellular Level." Archive.org. Accessed May 28, 2017. https://archive.org/details/ProteinSynthesis

Wyatt III, Lee T. *The Industrial Revolution.* London: Greenwood Press, 2009.

Yalom, Marilyn. *Birth of the Chess Queen: A History.* Kitchener, Ont.: Pandora Press, 2004.

Index of Proper Names

Alexander, (The Great), 76–77
Aristotle, xiv, 393, 449
Andrews, Julie, 54
Astaire, Fred, 61, 93
Aurelius, Marcus (Emperor), 476n8
Auxier, Randall, 391–93
Ayalla, Franscisco J., 25, 466n6

Bach, Johann Sebastian, 81–82
Banks, Iain M., 469n48
Bhargava, Manjul, 469n47
Berkeley, George (Bishop), 401
Berlioz, Hector, 86
Bernstein, Leonard, 476n3
Beethoven, Ludwig van, 85
Blaze, Elzéar, 69–71
Bonaparte, Napoleon, 69–70, 78, 350
Bond, (James), 41–42
Bradley, Francis, 9
Brightman, Edgar Sheffield, 391–93, 402–404, 408–12, 445
Brock, Isaac (Major-General), 78
Byrne, Donald, 51

Caesar, Julius, 73, 150
Calatrava, Santiago, 324
Caravaggio, 183–87
Cassatt, Mary, 190, 194, 196, 196n
Christ, Jesus, 177–81
Cobbett, William, 222

Copland, Aaron, 86, 88
Courbet, Gustave, 186–89, 194
Currie, Sir Arthur, 70–71, 76, 79

Dai, of Changsha (Lady), 173–75
Darwin, Charles, 24–27, 406–407
da Vinci, Leonardo, 183–85, 298, 481n6
David, Jacques-Louis, 186–89
Davis, James, 76
Davis, Jefferson C. (General), 75
Degas, Edgar, 189–91, 193, 196, 196n
Delacroix, Eugene, 148, 186–89, 191, 195
Dewey, John, 408

Eco, Umberto, 465n5
Einstein, Albert, 407
Eisenhower, Dwight (General), 77, 79
Exekias, 171

Fisher, Bobby, 51
Fuller, Buckminster, 312
Fuller, J. F. C. (Colonel), 67

Gandhi, 433
Gillis, Margie, 58
Gombrich, Sir Ernst, 161–62
Gounod, Charles, 86
Graham, Benjamin, 269, 272

Granatstein, J. L., 75–76

Haig, Sir Douglas, 76
Hobbes, Thomas, 9
Hughes, Sir Sam, 70
Hume, David, 9, 423–27

Ives, Charles Edward, 90

Jackson, Thomas "Stonewall" (General), 395
Johnson, Samuel, 401

Kant, Immanuel, xiii, 9, 407, 409
Keegan, Sir John, 76
Kempe, Alfred Bray, 451–53

Landy, Michael, 471n7
Lincoln, Abraham, 57

MacArthur, Douglas (General), 77–78, 468n17
Macbeth (Lady), 431
MacKenzie, Lewis (General), 76
Magritte, Rene, 195
Mao, Zedong, 48, 250–51
Marx, Karl, 248–52
Meidias (painter), 175
Michelangelo, 183
Monet, Claude, 191–93, 196, 196n, 358
Montgomery, Bernard Law (Field Marshal), 76–77

Nebamun, 153–59, 161, 163–64, 173–74, 177, 178, 180, 190, 471n2
Nelson, William (General), 75
Newton, Sir Isaac, 133

Partch, Harry, 469n50
Phidias, 175
Picasso, Pablo, 189

Plato, 9, 46, 50, 83, 449
Poussin, Nicolas, 192
Prokofiev, Sergei, 100

Renoir, Pierre-Auguste, 193–96, 196n, 380, 388
Robespierre, Maximilien, 433
Rogers, Ginger, 93
Rommel, Erwin (General), 76
Royce, Josiah, ix, xi–xv, 1–4, 10–12, 14, 16, 19, 269, 392–93, 403, 445, 451–58, 461, 465n2, 466n4, 474n48, 481n2, 481n3
Rothko, Mark, 197

Saint-Saëns, Camille, 86
Sargent, John Singer, 130
Schopenhauer, Arthur, 9, 212
Schwarzkopf, Herbert Norman, Jr. (General), 79–80
Seurat, Georges, 191, 193, 196
Shakespeare, William, 47, 83
Shostakovich, Dimitri, 100
Smith, Adam, 204, 224–30, 248, 251–52, 261, 339
Socrates, 408
Solzhenitsyn, Aleksandr, 48
Stalin, Joseph, 434, 469n52
Suzuki, Shunryu, 212–14

Thoreau, Henry David, 211, 213–15
Titian, 194

Vernet, Horace, 78

Watson, Thomas Sr., 223–24
Wellington, Arthur (Duke of), 76
Whitehead, Alfred North, xii–xiii, 1, 3, 4, 10, 60, 81n, 87n, 259n, 393, 395, 424, 458, 465n2, 469n45, 470n5

Xiaobo, Liu, 48

Index of Subjects

Accumulation: caused by interpretive inadequacy of contemporary currency signs, 299, 305–307, 373–74, 438, 440, 442–44, 480n2; and food production, 317–18; and pollution, 310, 370, 378; and power, 326, 329; quantitative, 1, 125, 266, 281–82, 293, 295, 297, 375–75, 413–14; re-interpreted by nature 370–71, 374; and sexuality 387–88; of soldiers and military problems 75–77; of wealth as gaudiness, 297–98; 'wearing away' of objectified information, 379

Action: creative and harmonious, 29–34, 36, 43, 45–46, 51–52, 53, 55–56, 59–60, 72, 82, 84, 102, 108, 137, 139, 143–51, 178–79, 203, 217, 240, 243–44, 258, 364, 396; destabilizing action, 18, 35–38, 47–48, 60, 62–63, 99, 275; destructive action, 19, 68, 72, 122–27, 134, 140, 163, 238, 242, 248–51, 290–91, 349, 381–82 406, 429–32, 466n8, 477n10; and interpretation, 10–11, 13, 16–19, 28, 58, 74, 81, 86, 90, 96–97, 99, 106, 115, 119, 120–22, 128, 132, 138, 141, 160, 167, 198, 210–11, 232, 264, 289, 300, 306–307, 313, 337, 448–49, 459–60, 490n1; models of, 82, 87, 89, 95, 260, 269, 274–75; and passivity 29, 32, 85, 88; pragmatic relation to value 1, 3–4, 6, 110, 423, 427; reconstructive, 38, 48, 63–64, 100, 204, 276–77, 458; swift, 78

Advertising, 99

Aesthetics, xii; as feeling value, 391–94, 396, 402, 408; and Hume, 423–27

Agriculture, 317; asymmetry and tillage, 319

America: Culture Wars, 382; and division of value, 413; robbers barons, 473n16; White House, 324

Animals, xii; and dancing, 54, 60, 95; evolution through human ranges, 109, 129, 355, 479n4; and human dominance, 415, 480n26; insects, 54, 469n48; and World Process as Nature, 214, 291, 371

Anthropology: paleoanthropology, 21–24, 465n5; Recent Single-Origin Hypothesis, 465n4

Anti-Hypertheme, 16, 65–72, 74–75, 78, 234, 234n, 392; of alternation, 240; *of Cooperation* (*HC), 235, 255; *of Play* (*HP), 238–39; *of Military Engagement* (*HM), 234–35; uncontainable nature of, 68–72

Archaeology, 378

491

Index of Subjects

Architecture, 143, 169, 314; and places for creative sexuality, 389–90; and places of healing, 323; and symmetry 323–24; temporal expansion in cathedrals, 379
Arcole (Battle of), 78
Asymmetry, 315–39, 429–30, 477n6; (Hyperthematic vs conventional), 114–16, 452; Hypertheme of, 117, 315; tightrope example, 330

Bacteria (Thermophilic), 129
Baroque: Baroque Music, 81, 97; and Dance, 90
Beauty: as evolving fact (Hume), 424–27; and mathematics, 116; as medical treatment, 323, 389–90; sign of a valuating engagement of experience, 116, 376, 411
Bhagavad Gita, 46
Black: Black body radiation, 124; Black hole, 124, 132, 141; black soil and quantitative production, 291; blackness and power, 130, 139, 386; Nazi use of, 140; and un-interpretability of crude oil, 288, 290–91; valuation of, 130, 137, 139, 155, 166, 173, 184, 187–88
Blue: valuation of 134–37, 156–57, 173, 177, 187, 193, 309, 347
Biology, xiv; biological laws and the cell as abstraction, 405; biologists and conservatism, 416; speciation as re-interpretation toward creativity, 371, 414; 'super animal,' 406
Body (*see* Embodiment)
Books, 41, 45–52, 55, 57, 82, 94, 99, 166, 179, 372; and blank pages, 51; as objects, 51, 145, 256, 264, 372–73, 376–78; at KU Leuven, 378; sans serif fonts as devaluation, 471n6

Boredom: in context of varieties of constriction (diagram), 463; in dance, 56; in pornography, 388; and mass production, 310; and quantitative repetition in food, 196; in video games, 351; and work, 227
Bridge (game), 38
Britain: army in Afghanistan, 468n30; and Industrial Revolution, 219–21, 233
Buddhism: and predominance of action over objecthood in Chinese art 176; and Japanese anime, 472n12; and Karma in Eastern thought, 434
Buildings: and building materials, 290, 312–14, 338–39, 443; and modularity, 374–76; and shape, 312–14

Capitalism, 25; eventual collapse, 475n53
Canada: Airborne Regiment, 76; Royal Canadian Legion, 72; and WW1, 71, 76; and WW2, 75
Car(s): and creative guidance of the community producing it, 307–308, 339; interpretable process of experience in a Porsche, 244; limited by further constrictive assumptions, 302; quantitative production of leads to devaluation of pollution, 294, 310; as result of a cooperative goal, 243
CEO, 219, 223; as top of corporate power structures, 273, 299, 325–30, 333, 475n4; and wealth 253
Checkers: solution of, 96, 4687n37; transformable elements compared to chess, 50, 83–84, 96
Chemistry, 337–38, 398; expansion of the medium of clay, 359

Index of Subjects | 493

Chess: complexity of, 49–52, 62, 82–84, 261, 466n1; Game of the Century, 51; and meaning, 16, 29–39, 67, 259, 264, 466n9; and music, 91; and practice, 57, 268; relation to videogames, 341–44, 346

Children: adolescents and expansive sexuality, 389–90; babies and physical awareness, 463; books for toddlers 50, 52; child prodigies, 86; creation of as living art forms, 387; and family origins of communities of cooperation, 43–44, 473n8; images of in interpretive defense, 384; and imaginary playmates, 474n48; learning dance, 62; in play, 237–40, 418; as processes of growth, 194, 471n9; and unique creations, 302

China: Chinese Cultural Revolution, 99; Chinese Opera, 92; and common product assumption, 250–51; and color yellow, 470n7; example of valuation of provenance of products, 443; and manufacture of mere objects, 438–39; symmetric structure of bureaucracy, 329

Christianity: Bible as sameness, 415; Christian church and aging, 178–80; and depiction of Christ as power, 177–83; and interpretable aspects of the Bible, 45–46, 373; and Redemption in Western thought, 434

Cities: and constrictive assumptions, 312, 378; and grid layouts, 314–15

Civilization: potential collapse through unstable quantitative accumulations, 440, 480n2

Color: as created experience, 102–10, 116–122, 138–42; relative un-interpretability due to constrictive action, 122–27; selection and engagement of by corporations, 287–93; valuation of, 130–38

Community(ies): apotheosis of community, 412; of the church, 178–80; of the commercial corporation, 417–18; community of selfhood, 3, 18, 57–58, 106, 147, 206, 208, 210, 214, 216, 226–28, 248, 295, 322, 338, 450; of craft, 398; of currency, 441; of dance, 58, 74, 144, 275, 441; false community, 18, 33, 43–44, 47, 65, 67, 73, 234–36, 382, 457; future communities, 398; of games, 31, 34, 144; Great Community, 47, 369, 412, 456, 466n4; of music, 81, 144; of narrative, 41, 46–48, 214, 263, 441; of natural science, 407–408; of paleoanthropology, 22; of preservation, 378; of temporality, 169; of visual arts (painting), 144

Communism, 249, 251; collapse of, 475n53

Competition, 233, 270; and IBM, 223; and Microsoft, 241, 286

Complexity, 4, 13, 15; and development of leader structures, 17, 87, 91–100; and empirical verification, 27; mental and physical (see Mentality and Physicality); and Silicon Valley, 416

Computers: and logic, 450; as re-interpretable products, 303–304

Conflict, 116; and corporations, 236–37, 329; indicates devaluation, 410, and interpretive defence, 384–85

Constriction: in church pews, 362; and measurement, 405–406, 469–70n1; in medieval art, 177, 180–82; toward embodiment in painting, 182–84, 187–91

Cooperation, 3, 207–17, 232, 235–36, 243–46, 256–58, 263, 265, 284–86; and arising of temporal extension of selfhood in early trade, 206–11; and children's play, 239–40; and individualism, 214–15

Corporation (commercial): CEOs of, 219, 253, 270, 273, 299, 325–33; and limited liability, 473n22, 476n9; as mentor to other corporations, 285–86; managers in, 221–22, 243, 247, 253, 259, 262, 270, 277, 297, 299, 304–309, 331–33, 337; and objectification of consistent communities, 284; owners in, 298–99; recording contributions of its members, 277–78; as repairers of damage, 413; and school of the corporation, 262; transforming symmetry in corporate organization, 325–39

Consumer, 231, 243, 245–47

Copying, 61, 117, 148, 182; and assembly lines, 267, 293; and cell phones, 253–53; and color question, 104–105, 107; and devaluation in video games, 348–51; and diversity, 167–68; and Egyptian art, 163–65; and empiricism, 108; and ancient Greek art, 172–73; and Impressionists, 189; and intention, 106–107; and light wave frequency, 111, 121; and medieval art, 178, 181; and narrative, 47; in product series', 293; and ranges of experience, 400, and space-time curvature, 126

Creativity, 10; 15, 19, 57, 61, 97, 105, 185, 192, 195, 197–98, 211–12, 215, 252, 304–305, 338–39, 348–49, 351–58, 395–402; and answer to color question, 107–108, 128–29, 138, 140–42; and corporate production, 361–94; dampening effect on crime, 443–44; de-creation, 463; and hyperthemes, 27–28; learning as, 150; and managers, 307–11; as play, 300–302; 417–18; as response to devaluation, 37–38, 48, 63–64, 72, 100, 160, 165–66, 168, 275, 276–78; and science and scientists, 24–25, 27, 105–107, 406–408; and workers, 265, 267, 302; and the unique creative product of each, 226, 297–98

Curvature, 119–20, 123, 126, 279, 293, 296, 300–301; 311–15, 324, 329–36, 346–48, 359, 361–64, 374, 376, 478; as action engendering spatial experience, 111–14, 117–19, 126–27, 459, 477n10; in aircraft and boat design, 472n1; in art, 171, 175, 176–78, 189, 191–95, 198, 472n12; in ball shapes, 115, 395, 401, 430; and corporate organization, 329–36; and currency, 441–43; in interpretive armour, 116, 383; and knitted fabric, 312; in nature, 170, 471n9; and selective action in circle, 114–15, 324

Dance, 16–17, 54–64, 61–62, 66, 81–85, 88–99, 101, 104, 141, 144–45, 163, 165, 207, 256, 264, 275, 278, 280, 284, 399, 454–55, 466n3, 468n37, 475n2, 478n5; Ballet, 59, 90, 278; Belly Dancing, 56, 58; and drill, 64–65, 67, 69, 71–75, 79, 467n18; and early film, 93; folk dance, 89–90; highly complex dance forms, 469n48; Stanford Protein Synthesis dance, 468n36; and walking, 469n44

Darkness (*see also* Black), 123–24, 129–38, 140, 155–56, 173–74, 183–84, 187–88, 192–94, 288,

292, 345; use of in interpretive constriction of sexuality, 130, 188, 386, 389; ultraviolet darkness, 123, 129–32; x-ray darkness, 131–32

Death, 70, 215, 291, 343–46, 403; Ancient Chinese view of, 173–74; Ancient Egyptian view of, 470; in painting 156, 181, 186–87

Defense, 36, 38, 67, 116, 166, 262, 382–83, 437, 444, 467n5, 481; defensive aspect of light, 119–20, 122–24, 126, 134, 134n, 141; defensive developments in books, 372; interpretive defense definition, 120

Democracy: and equality as constriction toward sameness, 415

Devaluation, 16, 18–19, 48, 68–69, 100, 102, 116, 122, 124, 130, 132–33, 137, 140, 157, 169, 184, 188, 190–91, 196–97, 209, 213–15, 226–28, 240, 246, 249–50, 252, 256–57, 261, 266–67, 273, 276, 284, 289–90, 292–93, 295, 298–99, 302, 312, 318, 373–74, 382, 387, 389, 392, 406, 409–11, 423, 426–27; 429–35, 438, 449, 460–61, 471n6, 472n14, 478n7, 478–79n10; localized pockets of, 214, 299, 310, 426, 457; urge to be inconsistent, 159–60, 426

Diamonds: and DeBeers slogan, 244–45; as defensive 'survivor' of constrictive tendencies in world process as nature, 437

Dinosaurs, 371; and dance, 466n3

Disease, 130, 387; as arising through food processing, 320–21; and cell phones, 354; inactivity and symmetric consequence, 432; and quantitative tendency in sexuality, 478–79n10; relation to process, 283–84; as a targeted enemy in western medicine, 319–20; as un-interpretable symmetry set up in some region of the body, 321–23

Diversity, 1, 4, 10, 14–15, 19, 23, 25, 28, 40–41, 43, 46, 49, 54–55, 60, 61, 64, 98, 101–102, 104, 137, 153–54, 167–69, 179, 181, 197–98, 204–205, 207, 211, 216, 234, 261, 269, 272, 296–97, 309, 311, 314, 316, 320, 336, 338–39, 350, 352, 354–56, 371, 373, 376, 385, 403–405, 409–10, 416, 426, 441, 449–50, 452, 456, 458, 459–60; and national populations, 329

Dueling, 69–70

East India Company, 218–20, 224, 228, 235, 243

Economics, 100, 224, 230, 249–51; *Epsionomics* as proposed successor to, 417–18; ethics must contribute to, 410–11; etymological roots, 418; source of economic problems in failure of interpretation, 412–13

Egyptians (Ancient), 42, 379; and color yellow 136, 470n8; and visual art, 153–69, 171–75, 178, 197, 294–95

Electromagnetic Radiation (EMR), 117; 122–25, 128; infrared 123, 128–30; ultraviolet 122–23, 128–32, 378

Eliminative tendency, 17, 20–21, 30, 41, 41–44, 47–48, 55, 60, 62, 81, 98–100, 112–13, 144, 158, 169, 209, 233, 239, 245–46, 248–50, 256, 259–60, 262–65, 269–70, 273, 277–78, 283, 289, 293, 296, 300, 316, 318, 328–30, 341, 369, 371, 417, 439, 463, 476n1, 479n14; and false communities, 65–73, 77–78, 236–37; in killing, 234–35; in miniaturization, 355–56;

Eliminative tendency *(continued)*
  and use of narrative by warriors, 41;
  and surgery, 318–19; transformed
  in chess, 30–34, 36, 39, 342; and
  weaponry, 381, 474n47
Embodiment, 17, 58, 90, 132, 156–
  57, 163, 171–72, 175, 176, 179,
  181–84, 187–88, 188–91, 212, 267,
  279–81, 306, 307–10, 322, 351–53,
  357, 359, 363, 366–71, 377, 393,
  395–96, 399, 401, 411–12, 414–16,
  433–35, 448, 477n1, 478n3, 478n4;
  advanced embodiment, 386–87,
  389–90; breakdown of body through
  repetitive action, 227; expansion
  beyond in consistent video games,
  346–49; expansion beyond in
  film and tv, 93, 366–67; human
  body as object of dance, 478n5;
  interpretive capacity to maintain
  physical body, 431–32; life beyond
  current embodiment, 429–30, 432;
  as Process of Embodiment, 137–38,
  150, 217, 291, 313, 362, 378,
  381–82, 383–84, 429–30, 471; in
  quantitative relationship in corporate
  organization, 305, 325–39, 342;
  self-consciousness of and eroticism
  (Renoir), 194–96, 380, 388, 472n14
Empirical, xiv, 410; empiricism and
  quantitative copying, 108, 469–
  70n1; empirical verification, 22–28
Energy, 104, 109, 117–18, 128, 133,
  288; defined, 134
Epistemology, 13
Ethics, ix, 13, 18, 204, 334, 392,
  412, 416; applies at physical levels,
  408; and duty to hygiene, 403–404;
  engagement of complexity tendency,
  404, 406–408; and an ideal
  world, 404, 406–407, 479n14; as
  obverse of natural science, 402–12;
  tendencies of good and bad (better
  and worse), 4, 20
Ethical Selfhood, 140, 146, 151,
  158, 177, 184, 260, 430–33, 439;
  building in scientific interpretations,
  107; community of ethical selfhood,
  149, 371; and contribution to the
  standard of value, 159–60, 166,
  168, 174, 185, 195, 215, 298,
  342, 346, 427; devalued in the
  contemporary buyer by sameness of
  product, 245–46, 295; and painting,
  149, 159
Etiquette, 275–76, 278; and business
  cards, 277; and dance, 62, 66, 275;
  origin of 38–39, 63–64
Europe, 73, 90, 182, 218, 251, 280;
  symmetry in architecture, 179, 324
Evil, 4, 132, 409, 434–35
Exclusionary tendency, 17, 38–39, 43,
  44, 47, 66, 233, 238, 241, 265,
  413, 457; Mein Kampf, 48; and
  music, 98–100
Experience: dead zones for meaning
  in, 67, 267; as interpreted element
  of the world, 16; as process, 1, 3,
  5, 21, 25, 27–28, 33, 67, 108, 112,
  134, 207–208, 244–45, 361, 394,
  395n, 404–407, 409, 429, 470n2;
  region of experience fabric analogy,
  4, 27, 423
Evolution, 24–26, 109, 127, 138, 412;
  theory of as a complex experience,
  26–27

Factory, 247–48, 285; historical
  development in Great Britain, 221,
  252
Fairy Tales, 42–44, 131, 262
Fear: and constriction to pointedness,
  401; as loss of interpretability, 123,
  130–32, 140, 327, 344–45, 382, 463

Feeling, 78–79; 83, 104, 106, 134–36, 301, 326, 390, 403, 414, 439, 443, 467n18; of constriction, 190–91, 296, 362, 401–402, 479n6; defined, 15; and devaluation through color (Nazis), 140; of loss of interpretive capacity, 123, 128–32, 321; and painting, 147–51, 156, 157, 173; of power in corporate organization, 327; ranges of, 394–97, 461–62; various uses of term, 393–94

Film, 43, 131, 345, 350–51, 470n6, 480n27; and constriction toward sameness of pornography actors, 386–89; and development of, 92–93; and film stars as objects through relations of sameness, 295–96; and mere representation, 366–67; Slasher films, 478n9

Fire, 129, 135, 140, 155, 370

Food, 196, 245, 267, 384; food industry manipulation, 321; as food object, 242; as interpretive goal (jazz band of chefs), 257, 265; as medicine, 318–19, 322; as process, 319–20; turn toward concentration in mere quantity through use of symmetry, 291–93, 316–18, 320–22

Force, 28, 86–87, 90, 121, 124, 133–34, 140, 159, 166, 246, 270, 273, 324, 335, 409, 418; appeal to force as a standard (Hume), 425; and verification, 26; in visual art (Caravaggio), 183–84

Fox Hunting, 39

France, 152, 154 189, 218; Napoleonic, 70

Gasoline engine, 302, 307, 311; as re-interpreting gas and oil into action, 365

Games (*see* also Video Games), 16, 29–39, 40–43, 47–55, 57, 60–62, 64, 67, 82–83, 88, 91, 94–96, 141, 144–45, 165, 171, 240, 255–56, 259, 261, 263, 268, 341–44, 372, 418n; and cheating (chess), 36–38; Bridge, 38; Checkers, 50; *Dungeons and Dragons*, 466n10; Hearts, 38; Hide and Seek, 38, 418; and local harmony, 52; range of, 399; tag, 418

Geneva Conventions, 66

God(s), 42, 172; as apotheosis of communities, 412; as lure to creative interpretation, 456; ultimate leader structure, 87n

Golden Spiral, 115–16, 125–26

Gravity: and Space-time, 126–27

Greed: and corporations, 241, 265, 268, 284; and children, 240

Greeks (Ancient), 169–76, 178, 180, 182–83, 186, 357, 418n; drama, 92; ideal of embodiment in the adult male, 171–72

Green, 128, 133–37, 140, 191, 347; and Islam, 136; and nutritional value in food, 291–92

Guinness Book of Records, 478n2

Han Chinese Art, 173–76, 177

Harmony, 4, 10–12, 16–17, 21, 29, 31–34, 52–57, 59–60, 62, 64, 67, 72, 80, 82, 84, 87, 91, 97, 133, 143, 148, 150, 203–205, 210, 215, 217–18, 232, 240, 243–50, 252–53, 256, 258–59, 264, 269–71, 280, 282, 314–15, 390, 392, 405, 409, 411, 417–18, 450, 454–55

Heat, 124, 128–29, 135 *art of the thermic*, 141; as earlier leading edge of human interpretive capacity, 129; heat darkness, 131, 134, 140; vs. light, 141

Hierarchy, 54, 83, 142, 165, 270, 273, 306–307, 309–10, 326–27, 329, 331–32, 334–35, 477n7; of disharmony, 237

History, 43, 56, 59, 61, 67, 72, 105, 108, 148–49, 167, 214, 259–60, 277–78, 350, 359, 466n9; accretion of in games, 34–35; and antiques, 377; and census data, 281; and communities of preservation, 180, 379 378, 443; and information, 373–74; and museums, 378

Homelessness: and consequence, 433–34

Interpretive freedom, 17–18; 25, 27, 61, 87–90, 94, 99, 117, 120, 208, 256, 258, 261, 267–68, 272–73, 282, 284–85, 302, 454; and consequent breakout, 163–66; constriction of, 68, 94, 96, 163, 235–36, 239, 242, 244–45, 250, 263, 360–62; saturation of 96–98, 100, 246

Interpretive capacity, 18, 90, 97, 128–30, 132, 134–35, 138–39, 189, 193, 207, 296, 302–303, 328, 342, 350, 358, 360–61, 366, 387–88, 393, 397, 400–401, 405–407, 416, 439, 449–50; and ability to see consequences, 132–33, 431, 433; and mass produced art, 196, 444; of painter and viewer, 158–59, 165, 167–69, 185, 196–98; and wealth, 298

Investors, 219–20, 231, 243, 249, 252–53, 259, 269, 473–74n22, 475–76n5; as stockholders, 270–74

Ipad, 304; copying in series' of, 352

Islam, 136

Jogging, 3, 213
Joy, 367, 396–97, 401, 479n5

Knowing, 15, 106, 206, 216, 397, 399–403, 414–16, 439, 443, 461; and creativity in painting, 147–48, 150–51; relative to acting, 13; various uses of term, 393–95

Law, 412; laws of nature definition, 403, 411–12; of nature vs. social, 391, 402–405; ownership and theft, 410

Leaders: and corporate organization, 223, 273, 275, 283–84, 304–305, 308, 331, 334; and leadership, 76, 78, 223, 280, 327–28, 476

Liability (limited), 205, 218, 220, 222, 252–53, 270–72, 274, 473–74n22, 476n9

Light: defensive engagements, 119, 120, 122–24, 126, 134, 141; frequency, 109–10, 117, 120–21, 123–24, 142; frequency as devaluative consequence, 122, 132; as leading edge of human interpretive capacity, 128–29, 135, 138–39, 192–93, 290, 365, 437, 462; light wave, 109–10, 118–25, 128–29, 133–34, 142; luminosity, 123, 190, 347; post light colour, 138; trapped in medium of television, 364; wavelength, 104, 109–10, 117–25, 128–29, 133–34, 141–42; ultraviolet, 122–23, 128–32, 378

Linearity, 170–71, 173, 175, 178, 186, 295–97, 299, 312, 329, 335–38, 363, 406, 441–43, 459, 460, 477n8; and Degas, 189–91, 193, 197; in production lines, 293–94, 300, 302, 307, 333–34 475n3; and roads, 311, 314–15; and selective action 118–19; and System Sigma, 451–53, 481n11; valuation of 110–14, 118–20, 126–27, 130; in violin strings, 376–77

Listener (music), 40, 40n, 42, 44–47, 50, 80, 81–82, 84–87, 89, 91, 98, 151, 233, 262–65

Logic, xi–xv; 4–5, 21, 28, 68, 349, 451–58, 461, 466–67n4, 479n5, 481n1, 481n2; and contradiction, 393, 409; dyadic or objective logics, 403, 453, 457; nature of Principle of Non-Contradiction, 445–51; ranges of, 398

500 | Index of Subjects

Local(ized), 17–19, 46, 52, 54, 56, 60, 66, 68–69, 73–74, 79, 84, 93, 95–96, 104, 107, 116, 124, 126–27, 133, 136, 152, 161, 163–65, 235, 237, 239, 269, 310, 316, 319–20, 329, 371, 385, 400, 405n, 405–406, 408, 410, 424, 432, 457, 459; local consistency of pleasure (Hume), 426; sense of community in military, 72

Machine: as extension of human body, 209, 211, 260; as replaceable extension of human body, 266–67; and AI, 267; and production lines, 221–22, 248, 293
Mafia: as eliminatory community, 66; and symmetric consequence, 433
Magic the Gathering, 38
Mathematics, xi–xii, 13, 27, 125, 469n48, 469n51; and bookkeeping, 279–80; and music, 95–100, 469n47; and modelling of processes, 283–84; nature of calculus, 477n10; ranges of, 398; and valuation of functions, 115–16
Mass, 56, 75, 141, 221, 329, 378–79, 411, 415, 438–39, 442, 459; mass products, 196, 246, 257, 280, 293–96, 302, 304, 306, 338, 374; pornography as mass product, 386, 388–89; in painting (Courbet), 188; Seurat, 191–92
Meaning, 27–29, 33–36, 40–44, 46–47, 54, 56–58, 61, 67, 82–84, 93–94, 96, 125–28, 206–207, 212, 216, 225, 231–32, 242, 244, 250–53, 260–61, 266, 268, 281–83, 285, 301, 334, 356, 359–60, 380, 409–11, 413, 418, 446–47, 449–50, 468n37, 469n50, 475n56, 475n1, 479n2; definition of, 15; and interpretation, 1, 4, 10–11, 13–14, 16, 19, 24; meaningless experience, 4, 67–68, 246–47; and music, 85–88; and origin of color, 102–108, 111–12, 115, 138, 140–41, 145; and verification, 13, 27–28
Media of experience, 54, 82, 92–93, 163, 198, 210, 244, 253, 273, 302, 347, 352, 356–57; clay, 112, 358–60; metal (in violin strings), 376–77; television, 363–65; television program, 366–68; wood, 360–63
Medieval: art, 177–82, 186; and business corporation, 218, 252; cathedrals, 324; and consistent sexuality, 388; and philosophy texts, 379
Medicine, 284, 316, 389; and drugs as objects, 283; sexuality of healing, 387; surgery as elimination through symmetry, 318–22
Meditation, 88, 211–15; and infection, 322
Mentality, 67, 73, 88, 150, 212, 227, 232, 261, 269, 273–74, 284, 393–98, 403–404, 406, 408–409, 415, 461, 463, 469–70n1, 477n10, 479n6; redefinition of, 60–61
Metaphysics, ix, 9–10, 13–14, 16, 20, 30, 204, 455; and the concept of 'nothing,' 449; empiricism and rise of science, 108, 469–70n1; existence and painting, 146–50; metaphysical passivity, 9; 434; metaphysical fundamentalism and scientists, 24–25, 356; mistaken dichotomy of inner illusion vs. outer real (Hume), 423–27; the world as 'particulate,' 406, 408; qualia, 102; tendency to independent sign, 316, 318, 407, 411, (in logic), 447
Microsoft, 241, 286

Military, 65–80; bullying, 70–72; camouflage, 140; consistent goals of, 72; defense industry, 243, 382; and drill, 64–65, 67, 69, 71–75, 79, 467n18; and historical preservation, 180; officers, 74–80; and origins of chess, 32–34, 51, 227, 234–39, 241, 270, 278, 350, 457, 466–67n4, 467n5, 478n8; swordsmanship, 476n4; and weaponry, 73, 116, 235, 239, 242, 316, 319, 381–86, 474n47, 478n7

Minimalism (see Newness)

Minoan Art, 169–73

Models, 56–64, 81–84, 87, 95, 134–35, 145–46, 148, 170, 187, 259–60, 269, 272–78, 282–83, 309, 335, 348–49, 376, 426, 452–53, 456–57, 475n4; defined, 61; postulation of historic and futuristic in H10, 268–69; viewer as, 150–52

Modern Art (and Post-Modern), 169, 197, 199, 300, 471n7

Money, 39, 210, 211, 220, 224–27, 229, 242, 244, 247, 251, 253, 260, 273–74, 297–98, 327, 351, 369, 426, 437–44, 475–76n5, 480n2, 480n4; bound up with objectified sameness of pop stars, 295–96; cryptocurrency as devaluative tendency, 373; engendering power hierarchies, 305–307; gold as, 305–306, 437–38; indifference to the power of in higher interpretive capacities, 476n2; movement from physicality toward pure quantity, 305–307, 437–38; as recording its own history, 373–74; and precious metals and jewels, 437–38; as static object, 246, 252–53, 257, 271–72

Music, 15, 42–43, 54, 56, 59, 74, 80–100, 143–45, 243, 247, 256, 268, 273, 278, 285, 350–51, 372, 376, 379, 381, 384, 469n47, 469n48, 469n50, 478n6; collapse of Disco, 56; composers/conductors, 476n3; as leading physical activity, 284; as range of creativity, 141, 399–400, 462

Museum(s), 27, 245, 298; Louvre, 378; as communities of preservation, 180, 377–78

Nature: and engagement of light, 110, 125–27, 137–38; cyclical, 192–93; definition of, 193; and inconsistent tendencies in, which result in devaluation, 290–91; as medical treatment, 321–22; and natural environment abiding by hypertheme of aging, 374; natural environment as interpretable by buildings, 312–13; physicality due to sameness of engagement, 127; laws of nature and freedom, 411–12; preservation of nature as sameness, 414–15; as a managed realm, 415

Narrative, 22, 39–52, 53–55, 57, 59, 60, 64, 74, 82–83, 131, 141, 144–45, 151, 165–66, 207, 214, 233, 255–56, 262–68, 275, 278, 281–82, 372, 395–96, 399, 415, 441, 463, 466n10, 469n51, 471n6; and devaluation at physical complexity, 116; and music, 92–95, 98–99; as range of creativity, 400–401, 462; ubiquity of, 42–43; as warning, 44

Nazis, 99, 140, 329

New(ness), 160, 214, 344–45, 368–69, 394; and the beginner, 88, 414; devaluation as mere newness, 169, 184, 197; and green color, 136–37; and the 'throwaway society,' 369

502 | Index of Subjects

Object(ivity), 2–3, 50–51, 54, 115, 119, 123, 167–68, 170, 179, 215, 217, 221–22, 224–26, 231–32, 238–52, 257, 262–65, 270–73, 280–84, 295–96, 305, 355, 358–368, 369–70, 373, 380–82, 384–86, 389, 408, 410–13, 417–18, 424, 430, 438, 441, 443, 447n, 453, 472n14, 475n53, 478n5; in painting, 144–45, 149, 159, 162–65, 170–72, 174, 176, 182, 194, 196; art products are not objects, 145, 197–98, 256, 372; designation of object is continually advancing, 357, 393; 'information objects,' 379; objecthood a result of processes of actions, 126–27, 161, 367–68; as a tendency of limitation, 124, 315–16, 378, 401

Oil: arises from constrictive tendencies in world process as nature, 291; interpreted relative to color by HCL, 288–91, 365; and trapping of process of sunlight in roofing shingles, 290

Olfactory: art of the olfactory, 141; olfactory darkness, 131; olfactory engagement in interpretive defense, 384

Ought, 10–11, 207–10, 252, 258, 280, 302, 353, 403–405; redefinition of as a guided play, 408–409

Painting (*see* Visual Arts)
Pain, 344–46, 397; as a focal point of un-interpretability, 321; variable aspect of relative to regression, 463
Photography, 143, 163; anticipated by painting (Courbet), 188
Photon, 122

Physicality, 306–307, 322, 337, 355–56, 370, 372, 382, 399, 402, 404, 411, 414–16, 427, 431, 435, 467n18, 476n2, 477n10; assertion, 404–405; and dance, 55, 59–61, 73, 468n36; development of 'world of the senses,' 140–41; diminishment and subordination in Egyptian painting, 157; and expansion of currency, 305–306, 437–44; and early films, 92–93; grades of physicality, 127, 354, 365–66; interpretive valuation of, 115, 296, 393, 395, 453, 455; redefinition of, 60; macrophysical boundedness (example), 460; and military leadership, 72–80; and torture, 70, 463

Physics, 108, 119, 121, 135, 466n6; and atom as abstraction of enduring sameness, 405; general definition of physical constants, 125–26

Pi, 460

Plants, 291–92, 317–19, 323, 355; evolution of and consistent interpretation, 127, 479n4; and Minoan art, 170; treated as processes of growth, 320

Play, 5, 11, 20, 26, 30, 49, 52, 80, 90, 95, 111, 141, 173, 189, 195–96, 237–42, 259, 261, 268, 302, 342–43, 351, 359–60, 362, 396, 398–99, 401, 406, 408–409, 416–18, 418n, 426, 437, 466n10, 474n48; and curvature of a ball, 115, 395

Pointedness, 126, 170–71, 173, 177, 181, 186–88, 217, 312, 315–16, 319–25, 328–29, 332, 334–35, 347, 362, 374, 376, 406, 442, 449–50, 451–52, 460, 470n5, 472n1,

479n6; in animals, 121, 401; cheese stabbing analogy, 430; in light waves, 118–21, 128; in nails, 313; in painting (Seurat), 191; and solar cell efficiency, 124, 363–64; in speech, 401; valuation of 110–16; in weapons, 115, 121, 316, 319, 383, 401

Political, 220, 230, 251–52, 414; political ideology, 406–407, 407n; political right and left, 415–16; and postulation of models, 275

Pollution, 429, 478–79n10; definition of, 310; and garbage arising from quantitative interpretation, 369; re-interpreted by the world process, 370–71

Pornography, 188, 385–89; and self-consciousness of embodiment, 472n14

Power, 18, 134, 134n, 136, 215, 242, 319, 327, 383, 440, 470; and black clothing, 130, 139; Christ as, 177, 180–81; as constricted action, 328–29, 363–66, 476n2; indicated in architecture, 324; of money, 306–307, 310; as proof derived from necessity in logic, 450; re-definition of, 121–22, 306; in unions, 327

Power Arrangement (Structure), 270; and corporate organization, 273, 304, 309–10, 325–34

Practice, 12, 19, 86, 95, 98, 104, 116, 146, 148–49, 165, 197, 212–13, 215, 261, 265, 268–69, 371, 376, 387, 390, 393, 400, 406, 408, 410, 414, 424–25, 432–33, 445, 450–51, 457, 463, 475n1, 481; aware practice as complex interpretation of a process of great ethical breadth, 433; bodybuilding as aware practice, 19, 432; consistency of conscious localized practice, 107, 405; in dance, 57–58, 61–62; and musical notation, 94

Primal, 135–37, 140, 155–56, 173, 177, 183–84, 192–93; and the senses, 131–33; and sexuality, 385, 387

Problematic, 1, 5, 18–19, 21–22, 35, 37, 40, 53–56, 58–62, 64, 83–84, 86–88, 91, 93, 95, 97, 102, 113–15, 129, 138, 151, 169, 195, 203–10, 232–33, 243–45, 248, 250, 252, 260–64, 272–75, 278, 280, 282–83, 304, 392–93, 397–98, 400, 403, 416, 456, 470n2; of cooperation, 209, 211, 216–17, 235–36, 241–42, 255–56, 258, 268–71, 279, 285–86, 417; defined, 17; in metaphysics, 9–10, 11, 14–15; in narrative, 46–51; regions of experience as relatively unengaged, 472n1; vs. solution, 51–52, 73–74, 135–36, 156, 168

Prodigy, 86

Proof, 449–50, pragmatic proof, 5, 13–14

Process: as creator of complex signs of interpretable value (water and air), 395–97; embodied processes (*see* embodiment); individual as process assumed in games, 30, 33; and learning from devaluative tendencies engaging light, 120–21; in Minoan art, 170; as a standard which measures localized symmetries of devaluation, 426–27; and wearing down by natural environment, 374, 376–77; World Process, 4, 15–16, 18–19, 24–25, 28, 30, 40, 48–49, 58–59, 68, 101–103, 105–106,

Process *(continued)*
  108–12, 125–27, 137, 140–41, 145–46, 156, 160, 166–68, 178–80, 182–83, 185, 189, 193–98, 205, 213–15, 228, 251, 258, 276, 291, 293–94, 298–300, 306, 310–11, 313, 315–17, 319, 321–22, 326–27, 335, 339, 345, 348, 360, 365–72, 378–80, 385–86, 388, 394–96, 399, 406–407, 409, 411–415, 417, 429–32, 435, 438–42, 445, 448, 450, 459–60, 471n1, 472n1, 477n1, 477n8, 478n4, 478n5, 478–79n10, 480n4; World Process as Nature (*see* Nature); world process engenders growth of interpretation by limitation of natural media of currency, 437
Product, 227, 231–33, 235–36, 255–59, 261–62, 264–67, 279, 287–90, 292–312, 315–17, 327, 337, 339, 341–42, 346, 349–62, 369, 381–83, 386, 388, 413, 417–18, 475n53; as artworks, 294, 359–60; and constrictions to quantitative which give rise to storage and psychological issues, 305; as object, 241–53; products valued primarily through quantification tendency, 438–39; as process, 242, 318, 320, 322–23; provenance of and currency expansion, 442–43
Propaganda, 48, 463; and painting, 158–59
Psychology, 106, 123, 131, 294, 305, 310, 315, 351, 382, 389, 431; expansive engagement of in an attacker, 383–84; and martial law, 68; psychological realism in painting, 184–85

Quality, 5, 225, 227, 233, 288, 296–97, 342, 440, 476n2; defined, 301

Quantitative expansion (accumulation), 75, 126, 210, 227, 266, 303–304, 306–307, 309, 311, 317–18, 320, 347, 352–53, 369–71, 373–75, 387, 413, 438, 440, 442–43, 455, 480n2; as accumulation of products, 295–96, 351, 368; in enlargement of products (bowls), 358, 478n2; quantitative value not directly transformable into qualitative value, 301; as tendency of interpretation (diagram example), 459

Red, 102–108, 128, 138–41, 173, 177, 183, 291; and primality in Paleolithic painting, 155–56; valuation of, 134–35, 137
Reading, 2, 3, 40–41, 44–53, 94, 145, 447
Realism, 33, 78–79, 105, 146, 171, 173, 402; Caravaggio and, 183–85; Courbet and, 187–89; creative realization, 11, 13, 25, 58, 78, 147–51, 395, 417–18; false realism, 344–45, 349–51; real as external 9–10, 24–28
Reconstructive engagements, 18, 37–39, 98, 100, 204, 274, 276–78, 285; and etiquette, 63–64; of narrative, 48
Reincarnation, 434
Religion, 71, 73, 136, 179–80, 212, 373, 462; eastern and western temperaments, 434; religious persecution and use of color, 137; fanaticism, 406–407
Renaissance: and art, 182–83; and banking, 218; Mona Lisa, 185; Vitruvian Man, 183
Rhythm, 54, 82, 89–90, 469n47
Romans (ancient), 73, 169, 182, 476n8; and early corporations, 205, 218

Index of Subjects | 505

Roman Catholic Church: black Jesuit robes, 130; and mourning, 136
Russia, 48, 100, 324

Sameness, 15, 19, 108, 111, 126–27, 132, 140, 147, 154, 159–61, 181–82, 186, 191–92, 196, 236–37, 242, 246, 250–51, 256–57, 261, 263–64, 267, 291–92, 295–97, 306–307, 310, 316–17, 325–27, 330, 332, 369–77, 379, 386, 388, 393–402, 404–409, 414–16, 437–39, 448, 454, 457, 461, 463; and copying other selfhoods, 61; and military uniformity, 72–73; and reflection in silver, 437; of space in Egyptian painting, 159–61
Science: and antiquated metaphysical assumptions, 356; communities of, 398; as creator of value, 408; and Ethics, 402–408; great scientists and aware interpretation, 108, 469–70n1; Hume's view and the rise of scientism, 425; re-definition of as a great community of interpretive valuation, 412–13; scientists as conservative, 416; scientific method compared to hyperthematic method, 21–29; and urge to avoid value, 28; will exhaust current sensory physical experience, 462; and world as a sameness, 407
Sculpture, 112, 143, 162, 171–73, 175, 182–83, 359
Sex, 54–55, 134–35, 139, 478–79n10; and art, 130; and dominance in Greek art, 172–73; interpretive expansions of, 386–87; in pornography, 385–86, 388–90; and temporal extension of the individual, 217, 473n8
Shareholder liability, 220, 252, 270–72, 274, 473–74n22, 476n9

Sight, 106–10, 117, 123, 128–29, 131, 137, 347, 352–54; definition, 138; failure of as constriction of process (Degas), 189–90
Sign, 2–3, 13, 16, 29–30, 41–43, 48, 50–51, 55, 60–61, 64–65, 81, 87, 90, 96, 106–107, 111, 115, 127–28, 130, 133–37, 139, 141–42, 144–52, 155–57, 159–60, 169–73, 176–83, 197–98, 210–11, 229, 233, 244–50, 253, 257, 259–61, 265–67, 271–72, 274, 276, 281–83, 287–290, 293, 295–298, 303, 307, 313, 320, 329, 333, 335, 339, 341–51, 357–71, 373, 377–78, 380–82, 385–86, 394–401, 404–407, 410–11, 414–18, 437–44, 447–50, 453, 455, 458, 465n2, 466n9, 475n3, 475–76n5, 476n1, 478n4, 478n7, 480n2; Bible as, 45; military officer as sign, 77–79; paintings as signs, 149, 152, 158, 161–64, 166–68, 184–89, 192–95; transformation of in chess, 32–34; words as, 83
Simplicity, 15, 17, 19, 56, 59, 73, 211, 398, 400, 404–407, 415–17, 461–62
Smell (*see* Olfactory)
Snakes: and development of sight, 109; and fangs as loci of constriction, 401
Solution, 15–17, 19, 21, 49–58, 61, 69, 74, 83–84, 91, 96, 135–36, 156, 168, 209, 211, 216, 232, 243, 245, 264, 266, 268, 273, 403, 411, 414, 416, 440, 468n37; and consequence, 431; solution as such, 10, 102, 426
Sotheby's, 245
Sound, 15, 128–29, 131, 141–42, 343–44, 351–52, 376, 384, 439, 446, 448; aural-darkness, 131; developing interpretive engagement

Sound *(continued)*
of (diagram), 462; vs. light, 400; and music, 82, 84–86, 88, 93; and silence, 86; tonal valuation, 142

South Korea, 70

Spirituality, 173, 182–83, 187, 390; and color blue, 135–37; and human future as expansion out of embodiment, 477n1; as interpretive capacity unmoved by mere quantitative accumulation, 476n2; as mental feeling, 397, 479n5

Sport, 39, 60, 62, 91, 295, 399; fencing etiquette, 63; and music, 91–92; and symmetry, 115, 264

Stock Market, 271–72, 440, 443; and stock certificates, 475–76n5; and voting shares, 272, 476

System Sigma, xi, xiii, 12, 445, 451, 453–56, 458, 461, 481n2

Tactility *(see also* Mass), 398–99, 462–63; and clay bowls, 359; tactile darkness, 131, 141

Taste, 131, 159–60, 266; and expansive food combination, 320; and food processing, 317–18; Hume and standard of, 426–27; and painting, 185–86, 196; and sameness of food, 196

Teaching, 19; 79, 284; and preservation, 180; and quantitative hierarchy, 333–34; and sexual guidance, 390

Telephone: expansion of interpretation at physical complexity, 352–54, 356; possible creative interpretations beyond, 354

Television, 99, 366–68; result of diversity tendency applied at physical complexity, 363–65, 478n4

'Tempest' (piano sonata), 85

Time, 3, 16, 23, 34, 81, 83–84, 87–88, 95–98, 111, 118–19, 121–22, 127, 132, 137–38, 209–11, 216–17, 225, 231–32, 264, 268–70, 273–74, 276, 282–85, 293–94, 299, 308, 317, 327, 367, 369–70, 372, 376, 379, 381, 404–405, 407, 441, 446–47, 465n2, 469–70n1, 474–75n48; aging and community of temporality, 169; and consequence, 430–31; Futurity and Pastness defined, 150–51; and interpretation linking moments of selfhood, 2–3, 206–207, 256; and interpretation in painting, 148–49, 152n, 167–68, 182, 188; and signifying words, 50–51; and solo dancer, 56–59; temporal connectedness of local members of the world process, 45–46, 50, 53

Toastmasters, 475n1

Tools, 22, 261–62; cutting tools, 313–15, 317, 319

Transportation, 310–11, 415; and dance, 280–81

Upper Paleolithic Art, 152–56, 166–67

Value, 5–6, and collapse of localized value (bathwater analogy), 299; definition relative to experience, 4; and inconsistency of lotteries, 310; and valuation, 19, 102, 129, 139, 167, 195–96; valuation of culture, 198; vs. taste, 159–60

Video Games, 341–51; use of consistent hyperthematic tendencies in, 348; devaluation in video game series, 350–51; early video games (Pitfall), 342–46; killing experience in first person shooters, 349; Mario

Brothers, 346–349; misunderstood realism, 343–44, 349
Violet, 135–37, 177, 470n7
Violin, 81; designed to age, 376–77; valuation of a Stradivarius, 245, 439
Visible Spectrum (of light), 109, 123, 129–31, 138
Visual Arts, 143–99, 394, 399–400; and narrative, 144–45, 151, 165–66; subject, 143–52; technique, 144, 146–51

Wall Street, 100
War, 4, 41, 67–71, 73, 75–78, 116, 140, 153, 172–73, 219, 316, 351, 381–82, 392, 395, 433, 463, 467n19, 468n30, 476n4
Water, 54, 215, 299, 359, 370, 401; constrictive engagement of (Degas), 190–92; and joy, 395–96; and process in Minoan art, 170
Weaponry, 63, 73, 116, 239, 242, 246, 386, 474n47, 478n7; devaluative effects of, 235, 316, 319; always inconsistent with value creation, 381–82, 384
Weierstrass Function, 116

White, 104, 128, 141, 309, 324, 347; and arising of humanism, 182–83; and Egyptian painting, 155–56, 173; and maximal nutritional value of foodstuffs, 291–92; in refined sugar as result of inconsistent processing hiding devaluation, 292–93; valuation of, 133–34, 137, 177, 180, 193
Will, 3, 9, 166, 217, 225, 393, 403, 426, 450; willed action in chess, 32, 85–86, 106, 106n; the will to interpret, 90, 409, 412
Women, 175, 189; as signs of process, 471n9; female embodiment of higher value than male (Renoir), 194–96
Worker, 207, 221–22, 224, 227–28, 230, 232, 243, 247–53, 259–60, 265n, 270, 273, 294, 297, 299–303, 305, 307–309, 312, 325–28, 331–34, 417, 475n6; office worker, 88; and time off, 285, 299

Yellow, 133–37, 156, 187, 191, 291, 309, 347, 470n7, 470n8; and gold, 437

Zen, 88, 212; and garden layouts, 323

www.ingramcontent.com/pod-product-compliance
Lightning Source LLC
Chambersburg PA
CBHW022005300426
44117CB00005B/47